The Oxford Anthology of Canadian Literature

Edited by
Robert Weaver
and
William Toye

Toronto Oxford University Press 1973

Drawings by DOUG PANTON

© Oxford University Press (Canadian Branch) 1973

1 2 3 4 5 6 – 8 7 6 5 4 3

Printed in Canada by
John Deyell Company

Contents

Contents | v

Chronological List of Authors

GROUPED ACCORDING TO THE PERIOD OF THEIR FIRST IMPORTANT PUBLICATIONS

Acknowledgements

MILTON ACORN. All poems reprinted from *I've Tasted My Blood* by Milton Acorn, The Ryerson Press, by permission of Mr Acorn. MARGARET ATWOOD. Reprinted by permission of Miss Atwood and The House of Anansi: 'This is a Photograph of Me' from *The Circle Game* by Margaret Atwood; 'They Travel by Air' from *Power Politics* by Margaret Atwood. Reprinted by permission of the Oxford University Press (Canadian Branch): 'The Animals in That Country' from *The Animals in That Country* by Margaret Atwood; 'Death of a Young Son by Drowning', 'Dream 1: The Bush Garden', and 'Dream 2: Brian the Still-Hunter' from *The Journals of Susanna Moodie* by Margaret Atwood; 'Three Desk Objects' from *Procedures for Underground* by Margaret Atwood. MARGARET AVISON. 'Snow' reprinted from *Winter Sun* by Margaret Avison by permission of Miss Avison. 'Twilight' and 'In a Season of Unemployment' reprinted from *The Dumbfounding*, poems by Margaret Avison, by permission of W.W. Norton & Company Inc. Copyright © 1966 by Margaret Avison. EARLE BIRNEY. All poems reprinted from *Selected Poems 1940-1966* by Earle Birney by permission of The Canadian Publishers, McClelland and Stewart Limited, Toronto. MARIE-CLAIRE BLAIS. 'Her Beautiful Beast' reprinted from *Mad Shadows* by Marie-Claire Blais by permission of The Canadian Publishers, McClelland and Stewart Limited, Toronto. GEORGE BOWERING. Both poems reprinted from *Touch: Selected Poems 1960-1970* by George Bowering by permission of The Canadian Publishers, McClelland and Stewart Limited, Toronto. MORLEY CALLAGHAN. Reprinted by permission of Mr Callaghan and The Macmillan Company of Canada Limited: 'The Boxing Match' from *That Summer in Paris* by Morley Callaghan; 'Two Fishermen' from *Morley Callaghan's Stories* by Morley Callaghan. BLISS CARMAN. 'Low Tide on Grand Pré' reprinted from *Bliss Carman's Poems* by Bliss Carman by permission of The Canadian Publishers, McClelland and Stewart Limited, Toronto. EMILY CARR. 'Sophie' from *Klee Wyck* by Emily Carr. © 1941, by Clarke, Irwin & Company Limited. Used by permission. ROCH CARRIER. 'The Woman Who Changed His Life' reprinted from *Is It the Sun, Philibert?* by Roch Carrier by permission of the House of Anansi Press Limited. EUGÈNE CLOUTIER. 'In the Land of Evangeline' reprinted from *No Passport: A Discovery of Canada* by Eugène Cloutier by permission of the

Oxford University Press (Canadian Branch). LEONARD COHEN. All poems reprinted from *Selected Poems, 1956-1968* by Leonard Cohen by permission of The Canadian Publishers, McClelland and Stewart Limited, Toronto. 'God is Alive' reprinted from *Beautiful Losers* by Leonard Cohen by permission of The Canadian Publishers, McClelland and Stewart Limited, Toronto. JOHN ROBERT COLOMBO. Reprinted by permission of Mr Colombo: 'Immigrants' from *The Mackenzie Poems* (1966) by John Robert Colombo; 'Last Letter', from *Made in Canada* (1970) by John Robert Colombo. RALPH CONNOR. 'Glengarry' reprinted from *Postscript to Adventure* by Ralph Connor by permission of Professor J. King Gordon. ROBERTSON DAVIES. 'It Does No Good to be Afraid' reprinted from *Fifth Business* by Robertson Davies by permission of The Macmillan Company of Canada Limited. KILDARE DOBBS. 'Views of Venice' reprinted from *Running to Paradise* by Kildare Dobbs by permission of the Oxford University Press (Canadian Branch). LOUIS DUDEK. 'The Marine Aquarium', which first appeared in *The Tamarack Review*, is reprinted by permission of Mr Dudek. JACQUES FERRON. 'Ulysses' and 'The Sirens' reprinted from *Tales from the Uncertain Country* by Jacques Ferron by permission of The House of Anansi Press Limited. NORTHROP FRYE. Preface to *The Bush Garden* reprinted from *The Bush Garden* by Northrop Frye by permission of the House of Anansi Press Limited. ROBERT FULFORD. 'The Authentic Voice of Canada' reprinted from *Crisis at the Victory Burlesk* by Robert Fulford by permission of the Oxford University Press (Canadian Branch). MAVIS GALLANT. 'My Wife is a North American . . .' reprinted from *A Fairly Good Time* by Mavis Gallant by permission of Random House, Inc. SAINT-DENYS-GARNEAU. 'Bird Cage' and 'A Dead Man Asks for a Drink' reprinted by permission of F.R. Scott; 'Landscape in Two Colours on a Ground of Sky' reprinted by permission of John Glassco and Les Editions Fides. HUGH GARNER. 'Hunky' reprinted from *Hugh Garner's Best Stories*, copyright Hugh Garner, 1960 and 1972. JOHN GLASSCO. Reprinted by permission of the Oxford University Press (Canadian Branch): 'Memoirs of Montparnasse' from *Memoirs of Montparnasse* by John Glassco; 'Quebec Farmhouse' from *Selected Poems* by John Glassco. PHYLLIS GOTLIEB. Both poems reprinted from *Ordinary, Moving* by Phyllis Gotlieb by permission of the Oxford University Press (Canadian Branch). ALAIN GRANDBOIS. 'Cries' reprinted by permission of M. Grandbois and Eldon Grier. FREDERICK P. GROVE. Reprinted by permission of Mr A.L. Grove, Toronto, Ontario: 'Ellen's Confession' from *Settlers of the Marsh* by Frederick P. Grove; 'The Happiest Year of Her Life' from *In Search of Myself* by Frederick P. Grove. ANNE HÉBERT. 'The Little Towns' reprinted by permission of John Glassco. 'Manor Life' and 'The Tomb of the Kings' reprinted by permission of F.R. Scott, the latter from *Dialogue sur la Traduction à propos de Tombeau des Rois* by Anne Hébert and F.R. Scott. DAVID HELWIG. All poems reprinted from *The Sign of the Gunman* by David Helwig by permission of Oberon Press. HUGH HOOD. 'Recollections of the Works Department' reprinted from *Flying a Red Kite: Stories by Hugh Hood*, The Ryerson Press, by permission of McGraw-Hill Ryerson Limited. GEORGE JOHNSTON. 'O Earth, Turn!' from *Happy Enough: Poems 1935-1972* reprinted by permission; copyright © 1955 The New Yorker Magazine, Inc. All other poems reprinted from *Happy Enough* by George Johnston by permission of the Oxford University Press (Canadian Branch). D.G. JONES. 'Portrait of Anne Hébert' reprinted from *The Sun is Axeman* by D.G. Jones, by permission of the University of Toronto Press. Copyright Canada 1961 by the University of Toronto Press. 'I Thought There Were Limits' and 'Pastoral' reprinted from *Phrases from*

Orpheus by D.G. Jones by permission of the Oxford University Press (Canadian Branch). A.M. KLEIN. All poems reprinted from *The Rocking Chair* by A.M. Klein, The Ryerson Press, by permission of McGraw-Hill Ryerson Limited. MARGARET LAURENCE. 'The Holy Terror' reprinted from *The Stone Angel* by Margaret Laurence by permission of The Canadian Publishers, McClelland and Stewart Limited, Toronto. IRVING LAYTON. All poems reprinted from *The Collected Poems of Irving Layton* by Irving Layton by permission of The Canadian Publishers, McClelland and Stewart Limited, Toronto. STEPHEN LEACOCK. 'Small Town: Mariposa, Ont.' reprinted from *Sunshine Sketches of a Little Town* by Stephen Leacock by permission of The Canadian Publishers, McClelland and Stewart Limited, Toronto. DENNIS LEE. Both poems reprinted from *Civil Elegies and Other Poems* by Dennis Lee by permission of the House of Anansi Press Limited. DOROTHY LIVESAY. Both poems reprinted from *Collected Poems: The Two Seasons* by Dorothy Livesay, The Ryerson Press, by permission of McGraw-Hill Ryerson Limited. GWENDOLYN MacEWEN. Reprinted by permission of The Macmillan Company of Canada Limited: 'This Northern Mouth' and 'The Portage' from *The Shadow-Maker* by Gwendolyn MacEwen; 'The Armies of the Moon' from *Armies of the Moon* by Gwendolyn MacEwen. 'Poems in Braille' reprinted from *Breakfast for Barbarians* by Gwendolyn MacEwen, The Ryerson Press, by permission of McGraw-Hill Ryerson Limited. HUGH MacLENNAN. 'The Martells Find a Son' reprinted from *The Watch That Ends the Night* by permission of Mr MacLennan. MARSHALL McLUHAN. 'The Phonograph' from *Understanding Media: The Extensions of Man* by Marshall McLuhan. Copyright © 1964 by Marshall McLuhan. Used by permission of the McGraw-Hill Book Company. JAY MACPHERSON. All poems reprinted from *The Boatman and Other Poems* by Jay Macpherson by permission of the Oxford University Press (Canadian Branch). ELI MANDEL. Reprinted by permission of Mr Mandel: 'Houdini' from *An Idiot Joy* by Eli Mandel; 'On the 25th Anniversary of the Liberation of Auschwitz', which first appeared in *The Canadian Forum*. GASTON MIRON. 'Héritage de la tristesse' and 'October' reprinted by permission of Fred Cogswell. 'My Sad One and Serene', which first appeared in Issue 5 of *Ellipse*, reprinted by permission of D.J. Jones. ALICE MUNRO. 'Walker Brothers Cowboy' reprinted from *Dance of the Happy Shades* by Alice Munro, The Ryerson Press, by permission of McGraw-Hill Ryerson Limited. ÉMILE NELLIGAN. 'By the Fireside' reprinted from *Selected Poems of Emile Nelligan* translated by P.F. Widdows and M.M. Corbeil, The Ryerson Press, by permission of McGraw-Hill Ryerson Limited and Les Editions Fides; 'The Ship of Gold' reprinted by permission of A.J.M. Smith and Les Editions Fides; 'The Poet's Wine' reprinted by permission of George Johnston and Les Editions Fides. JOHN NEWLOVE. All poems reprinted from *Black Night Window* by John Newlove by permission of The Canadian Publishers, McClelland and Stewart Limited, Toronto. ALDEN NOWLAN. 'A Little-travelled Road', 'Johnnie's Poem', and 'A Matter of Etiquette' from *Between Tears and Laughter* by Alden Nowlan. © 1971 by Clarke, Irwin & Company Limited. Used by permission. 'July 15' from *Bread, Wine and Salt* by Alden Nowlan. © 1967 by Clarke, Irwin & Company Limited. Used by permission. MICHAEL ONDAATJE. 'Letters & Other Worlds', which first appeared in *White Pelican*, reprinted from *Rat Jelly* (Coach House Press, 1973). © Michael Ondaatje. Extracts from *The Collected Works of Billy the Kid* by Michael Ondaatje reprinted by permission of the House of Anansi Press Limited. P.K. PAGE. All poems reprinted from *Cry Ararat* by P.K. Page by permission of The Canadian

Publishers, McClelland and Stewart Limited, Toronto. E.J. PRATT. Reprinted from *Collected Poems* by E.J. Pratt by permission of The Macmillan Company of Canada Limited: 'The End of the *Titanic*' from the poem 'The Titanic' and 'The Death of Brébeuf' from the poem 'Brébeuf and His Brethren'. AL PURDY. All poems reprinted from *Selected Poems* by Al Purdy by permission of The Canadian Publishers, McClelland and Stewart Limited, Toronto. JAMES REANEY. 'To the Avon River Above Stratford, Canada' and 'Town House & Country Mouse' reprinted from *Twelve Letters to a Small Town* by James Reaney by permission of Professor Reaney and his literary agent. The excerpt from *The Easter Egg* reprinted from *Masks of Childhood* by James Reaney by permission of Professor Reaney and New Press, Toronto. MORDECAI RICHLER. 'Benny' reprinted from *The Street* by Mordecai Richler by permission of The Canadian Publishers, McClelland and Stewart Limited, Toronto. RINGUET. 'Giving God His Due' and 'The Expatriate' reprinted from *Thirty Acres* by Philippe Ringuet, translated by Felix Walter, by permission of The Macmillan Company of Canada Limited. CHARLES G.D. ROBERTS. 'The Tantramar Revisited' and 'The Pea-Fields' reprinted from *The Selected Poems of Sir Charles G.D. Roberts* by permission of Lady Roberts. 'The Prisoners of the Pitcher-Plant' reprinted from *The Last Barrier and Other Stories* by Charles G.D. Roberts by permission of The Canadian Publishers, McClelland and Stewart Limited, Toronto. SINCLAIR ROSS. 'The Lamp at Noon' reprinted from *The Lamp at Noon and Other Stories* by Sinclair Ross by permission of The Canadian Publishers, McClelland and Stewart Limited, Toronto. GABRIELLE ROY. 'The School on the Little Water Hen' reprinted from *Where Nests the Water Hen* by Gabrielle Roy by permission of Harcourt Brace Jovanovich, Inc. GEORGE RYGA. 'Indian' reprinted from *The Ecstasy of Rita Joe and Other Plays* (New Press) by George Ryga by permission of Mr Ryga and his agent. DUNCAN CAMPBELL SCOTT. Reprinted by permission of Mrs Duncan Campbell Scott: 'The Forsaken' and 'A Night in June' from *Poems of Duncan Campbell Scott*; 'The Desjardins' from *In the Village of Viger* by Duncan Campbell Scott. F.R. SCOTT. All poems reprinted from *Selected Poems* by F.R. Scott by permission of Professor Scott. A.J.M. SMITH. 'To Frank Scott, Esq.' included by permission of Professor Smith. All other poems reprinted from *Poems New & Collected* by A.J.M. Smith by permission of the Oxford University Press (Canadian Branch). RAYMOND SOUSTER. 'Colonial Saturday Night' and 'Lagoons, Hanlan's Point' reprinted from *The Colour of the Times* by Raymond Souster, The Ryerson Press, by permission of McGraw-Hill Ryerson Limited. 'The Day Before Christmas', 'Milk Chocolate Girl' and 'Unadulterated Poetry' reprinted from *As Is* by Raymond Souster by permission of the Oxford University Press (Canadian Branch). PIERRE VALLIÈRES. 'Memoirs of a Revolutionary' reprinted from *White Niggers of America* by Pierre Vallières by permission of The Canadian Publishers, McClelland and Stewart Limited, Toronto. MIRIAM WADDINGTON. All poems reprinted from *Driving Home: Poems New and Selected* by Miriam Waddington by permission of the Oxford University Press (Canadian Branch). PHYLLIS WEBB. All poems reprinted from *Selected Poems 1954-1965* by Phyllis Webb by permission of Miss Webb. ANNE WILKINSON. All poems reprinted from *Collected Poems of Anne Wilkinson* by Anne Wilkinson by permission of The Macmillan Company of Canada Limited. ETHEL WILSON. 'Fog' reprinted from *Mrs Golightly & Other Stories* by Ethel Wilson by permission of The Macmillan Company of Canada Limited. GEORGE WOODCOCK. 'Encounter with an Archangel' reprinted from *The Rejection of Politics* by George Woodcock by permission of Mr Woodcock and New Press, Toronto.

Photograph Credits

ACORN Howard Anderson Photography Ltd. ATWOOD, GLASSCO, NEWLOVE, PURDY, F.R. SCOTT, SMITH William Toye. AVISON, BIRNEY, BOWERING, JONES, LAYTON, MACEWEN, MANDEL, SOUSTER Sheldon Grimson. BLAIS, PAGE Wheler-Scott Ltd., and McClelland and Stewart Limited. CALLAGHAN Norman Chamberlin. CARMAN, DUNCAN, GROVE, HEARNE, LAMPMAN, LEACOCK, MARIE DE L'INCARNATION, ROBERTS, D.C. SCOTT, The Public Archives of Canada. CARR Vancouver Art Gallery. CARRIER, GARNEAU, HEBERT Canada Wide Feature Service Ltd. CLOUTIER Studio Jac-Guy. COHEN, FERRON, VALLIERES Montreal Star-Canada Wide. COLOMBO Michael Yates. DE MILLE, HALIBURTON Nova Scotia Archives. DOBBS, FULFORD, MACLENNAN Toronto Star Syndicate. DUDEK Edith Owen. FRYE Brigdens Limited. GOTLIEB Toronto Sun Syndicate. GRANDBOIS André Larose. HOOD Sam Tata. JOHNSTON John Garner. LAURENCE, ROY McClelland and Stewart Limited. LEE Graeme Gibson. LIVESAY David Street. MCLUHAN Horst Ehricht. MIRON James Gauthier and Keystone Press Agency. MOODIE Metropolitan Toronto Library Board. NELLIGAN Librairie Beauchemin Limitée. NOWLAN Drawing by M. Donaldson. PRATT Ashley & Crippen. REANEY Lee and The London Free Press. RICHLER Jack Clayton and McClelland and Stewart Limited. ROSS Wm. Notman & Son and McClelland and Stewart Limited. RYGA Mari Berg. WEBB Canadian Broadcasting Corporation. WILKINSON Lutz Dille. WOODCOCK University of British Columbia Department of Extension.

Preface

This anthology attempts to give a general view of our writing from the early days to the present. Within the limitations of its length it answers the questions: Who are our writers? What have they written? What is their writing like? While the selections range from the seventeenth century to the 1970s, two thirds of the book is devoted to many of the writers who created the present self-confident literary climate that had its beginnings in the late 1940s.

The selections represent not only the tastes of two editors whose interest in Canadian literature goes back more than twenty-five years, but what we thought would be an approachable introduction to the work of the eighty writers included. (We know there are omissions—particularly of some younger writers from Québec—but here we must plead the old excuse of space limitations.) Our informal notes about the contributors are intended to give a sense of the personalities and creative activity that have produced our literature. With their biographical and literary information, these notes taken together form something of a capsule history of Canadian writing.

The arrangement of the book has been dictated by the alphabetical sequence of the authors' names and therefore lends itself to browsing among familiar and unfamiliar writers. Some may find as we did that the accidental juxtaposition resulting from this arrangement is refreshing—it is somehow liberating to view our writing apart from categories. But for those who wish to approach it according to theme, subject, region, or period, we have provided lists.

Though the selections have been chosen solely with the aim of providing interesting examples of the contributors' work, a glance at the themes and subjects will show that they contain a good deal of variety. The themes we have assigned to the material—we hope not too arbitrarily—reveal some characteristics of our literature, in both English and French, that have often been noticed. Alienation. The victim. Endurance. A hostile natural environment. These are some of the themes explored by Margaret Atwood in her arresting study of Canadian literature, appropriately called *Survival*. They are not, of course, uniquely Canadian preoccupations. Indeed, alienation is world-wide; the victim can be discovered everywhere. But it seems that in Canadian writing, while there is love and humour, and nature is sometimes benign and celebrated for its benevolence, and there are even small triumphs from time to time, the mood is most often sombre—not unlike that of other literatures in the twentieth century.

There are numerous cross-references in the book. We have three of Margaret Atwood's poems from *The Journals of Susanna Moodie* and Mrs Moodie herself; an extract from Samuel Hearne's *A Journey from Prince of Wales's Fort* and John Newlove's 'Samuel Hearne in Wintertime'; a 'found poem' by John Robert Colombo based on a piece of journalism by William Lyon Mackenzie and Mackenzie himself; a passage from the *Jesuit Relations* that is a kind of epilogue to an extract from Pratt's *Brébeuf and His Brethren*; and a description by Pierre Vallières of Gaston Miron, who is in the book with his poetry. There are poems about writers who are contributors and in the introductions numerous contributors have been quoted as critics. The anthology conveys a real sense of a community of writers.

Our writers have often had to persevere in a society without sympathy for, or even recognition of, their literary activities. Now, in a much more responsive and expanding literary climate, and even though their concern with negative themes like alienation and failure is as pervasive as ever, they have suddenly begun to find a real audience. Readers of imaginative writing in this country are probably more numerous than ever before and we suspect that many have now become curious about the background of their own literature. There are of course many anthologies of Canadian writing—a number are listed at the back of this book —but they tend to focus on a single literary genre. It is our hope that *The Oxford Anthology of Canadian Literature*—which is a miscellany of fiction and other prose, poetry and drama, from the whole body of our writing—will bring together even more Canadian readers and Canadian writers, offering both pleasures and discoveries and tantalizing some of you into making further investigations of your own.

The Oxford Anthology of Canadian Literature

b. 1923

Milton Acorn

MILTON ACORN once described himself as 'a carpenter, a socialist and a poet'. Al Purdy, in his introduction to *I've Tasted My Blood*, wrote that Acorn 'was a carpenter by trade, but had decided to give it up and be a writer, just like that. I went along when he sold his expensive-looking tools at a shop on St Antoine St [in Montreal]. Talk about burning your bridges! But Milton had made up his mind to sell those tools, and couldn't be convinced to wait until he had made some money writing.' This unusual figure among Canadian poets was born in Charlottetown, P.E.I. His formal education was scanty. He has lived at various times in Vancouver, Toronto, and Montreal; in Vancouver he was involved in the founding of the 'underground' newspaper *Georgia Straight*. He has read in coffee houses across the country, working out the final versions of some of his poems in collaboration with his audiences; has been active in the free-speech movement centred in the Allan Gardens in downtown Toronto; and described himself as a Canadian patriot even before he quite realized the importance of that position. His books of poetry are *In Love and Anger* (1956), *Against a League of Liars*

(1960), *The Brain's the Target* (1960), *Jawbreakers* (1963), and *I've Tasted My Blood* (1970). When *I've Tasted My Blood* failed to win a Governor General's Award, Acorn became the first and so far the only recipient of the Canadian Poetry Award, which has been referred to as the anti-Governor General's medal. The presentation was made by some fellow poets at Grossman's Tavern in Toronto, and Acorn was described that evening as the 'People's Poet'.

Al Purdy writes that 'Acorn's poems for me are marked by idealism and compassion for people. In some of them it's possible to discern the shadowy figures of, say, Bertolt Brecht and Mayakovsky. . . . But politics is only one side of Milton Acorn. He also writes lyrics of nature, sensitive love poems, pieces that see inside the human character like a cardiogram of the intellect. As well, some beautiful evocations of his native Prince Edward Island . . . Ideally he lives in the child's dream country . . . and wakes up every morning in the real world that inspires him with such savage discontent.'

There is an article on Acorn's poetry by Dorothy Livesay in Issue 40 of *Canadian Literature* (Spring 1969).

ON SAINT-URBAIN STREET

My room's bigger than a coffin
but not so well made.
The couple on my left drink, and
at two a.m. the old man shouts
of going back to Russia.
About five he or his wrung-out wife
puke up their passage money.

The janitor (pay, five a week
plus a one-bed apartment
with furnace in kitchen) has
one laughing babe at home
and two girls, for lack of room,
in the orphanage.
On holidays they appear
with their soul-smashed faces.

Upstairs the Negro girl
answers the phone, sings my name
in a voice like a bad angel's.
Her boyfriends change
every weekend, like the movies.
But my room's cheap, tho'
when the wind shifts north
I wear my overcoat
to type this bitter little poem.

YOU GROWING

You growing and your thought threading
The delicate strength of your focus
Out of a clamour of voices
Demanding faces and noises
Apart from me but vivid
As when I kissed you and chuckled

Wherever you are be fearless
And wherever I am I hope to know
You're moving vivid beyond me
So I grow by the strength
Of you fighting for your self,
Many selves, your life, many lives, your people.

I'VE TASTED MY BLOOD

If this brain's over-tempered
consider that the fire was want
and the hammers were fists.
I've tasted my blood too much
to love what I was born to.

But my mother's look
was a field of brown oats, soft-bearded;
her voice rain and air rich with lilacs:
and I loved her too much to like
how she dragged her days like a sled over gravel.

Playmates? I remember where their skulls roll!
One died hungry, gnawing grey perch-planks;
one fell, and landed so hard he splashed;
and many and many
come up atom by atom
in the worm-casts of Europe.

My deep prayer a curse.
My deep prayer the promise that this won't be.
My deep prayer my cunning,
my love, my anger,
and often even my forgiveness
that this won't be and be.
I've tasted my blood too much
to abide what I was born to.

THE FIGHTS

What an elusive target
the brain is! Set up
like a coconut on a flexible stem
it has 101 evasions.
A twisted nod slews a punch
a thin gillette's width
past a brain, or
a rude brush-cut to the chin

tucks one brain safe under another.
Two of these targets are
set up to be knocked down
for 25 dollars or a million.

In that TV picture in the parlor
the men, tho linked move to move
in a chancy dance,
are abstractions only.
Come to ringside, with two
experts in there! See
each step or blow pivoted,
balanced and sudden as gunfire.
See muscles wriggle, shine
in sweat like windshield rain.

In stinking dancehalls, in
the forums of small towns,
punches are cheaper but
still pieces of death.
For the brain's the target
with its hungers
and code of honour. See
in those stinking little towns,
with long counts, swindling judges,
how fury ends with the last gong.
No matter who's the cheated one
they hug like a girl and man.

It's craft and
the body rhythmic and terrible,
the game of struggle.
We need something of its nature
but not this;
for the brain's the target
and round by round it's whittled
til nothing's left of a man
but a jerky bum, humming
with a gentleness less than human.

b. 1939

Margaret Atwood

MARGARET ATWOOD is an immensely talented writer who has produced a remarkable body of work and acquired a large following in the six years since her first book was published. She was born in Ottawa and has subsequently lived in northern Québec, Toronto, Vancouver, Cambridge, Mass., Montreal, and Edmonton. She graduated from Victoria College, University of Toronto, and received an A.M. degree from Radcliffe College (Harvard) in 1962. She has taught English at the University of British Columbia, Sir George Williams University, Montreal, and the University of Alberta. At present she is Writer-in-Residence at the University of Toronto.

Her first book of poetry, *The Circle Game* (1966), won the Governor General's Award. This was followed by *The Animals in That Country* (1968), *The Journals of Susanna Moodie* (1970), *Procedures for Underground* (1970), and *Power Politics* (1971). She is also the author of two arresting novels—*The Edible Woman* (1970), for which she has written a screenplay, and *Surfacing* (1972) —and of *Survival: A Thematic Guide to Canadian Literature* (1972), a brilliant study that illuminates the persistent victim theme in our literature.

Margaret Atwood creates in her poems a mysterious, threatening dream universe. She moves within it isolated from all that surrounds her, alienated even from herself, seeing memories, relationships, and the concrete details of everyday life reorder themselves, change, and take on disturbing new perspectives. It is a world of ambiguities and opposites—order and chaos, violence and peace, past and present, life and death, love and indifference—for which reconciliations are sought and never quite achieved. She describes it clinically, in simple, straightforward language, so as to control it, give it order, and reveal its meaning and herself to herself.

Three of the following poems—'The Bush Garden', 'Brian the Still-Hunter', and 'Death of a Young Son by Drowning' —are from *The Journals of Susanna Moodie*, a sequence of poems suggested by the experiences of a pioneer in which the themes of alienation and assimilation are memorably treated. (See the note on Mrs Moodie on page 339.) Mrs Moodie's own account of Brian the Still-Hunter begins on page 340.

THE ANIMALS IN THAT COUNTRY

In that country the animals
have the faces of people:

the ceremonial
cats possessing the streets

the fox run
politely to earth, the huntsmen
standing around him, fixed
in their tapestry of manners

the bull, embroidered
with blood and given
an elegant death, trumpets, his name
stamped on him, heraldic brand
because

(when he rolled
on the sand, sword in his heart, the teeth
in his blue mouth were human)

he is really a man

even the wolves, holding resonant
conversation in their
forests thickened with legend.

     In this country the animals
     have the faces of
     animals.

     Their eyes
     flash once in car headlights
     and are gone.

     Their deaths are not elegant.

     They have the faces of
     no-one.

THIS IS A PHOTOGRAPH OF ME

It was taken some time ago.
At first it seems to be
a smeared
print: blurred lines and grey flecks
blended with the paper;

then, as you scan
it, you see in the left-hand corner
a thing that is like a branch: part of a tree
(balsam or spruce) emerging
and, to the right, halfway up
what ought to be a gentle
slope, a small frame house.

In the background there is a lake,
and beyond that, some low hills.

(The photograph was taken
the day after I drowned.

I am in the lake, in the centre
of the picture, just under the surface.

It is difficult to say where
precisely, or to say
how large or small I am:
the effect of water
on light is a distortion

but if you look long enough,
eventually
you will be able to see me.)

THREE DESK OBJECTS

What suns had to rise and set
what eyes had to blink out
what hands and fingers
had to let go of their heat

before you appeared on my desk
black light
portable and radiant

and you, my electric typewriter
with your cord and hungry plug
drinking a sinister transfusion
from the other side of the wall

what histories of slaughter
have left these scars on your keys

What multiple deaths have set loose this clock
the small wheels that grind
their teeth under the metal scalp

My cool machines
resting there so familiar
so hard and perfect

I am afraid to touch you
I think you will cry out in pain

I think you will be warm, like skin.

DREAM 1: THE BUSH GARDEN

I stood once more in that garden
sold, deserted and
gone to seed

In the dream I could
see down through the earth, could see
the potatoes curled
like pale grubs in the soil
the radishes thrusting down
their fleshy snouts, the beets
pulsing like slow amphibian hearts

Around my feet
the strawberries were surging, huge
and shining

When I bent
to pick, my hands
came away red and wet

In the dream I said
I should have known
anything planted here
would come up blood

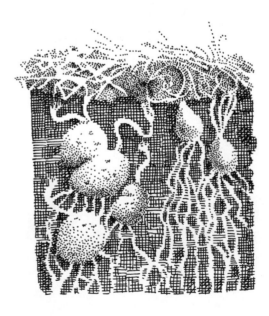

DREAM 2: BRIAN THE STILL-HUNTER

The man I saw in the forest
used to come to our house
every morning, never said anything;
I learned from the neighbours later
he once tried to cut his throat.

I found him at the end of the path
sitting on a fallen tree
cleaning his gun.

There was no wind;
around us the leaves rustled.

He said to me:
I kill because I have to

but every time I aim, I feel
my skin grow fur
my head heavy with antlers
and during the stretched instant
the bullet glides on its thread of speed
my soul runs innocent as hooves.

Is God just to his creatures?

I die more often than many.

He looked up and I saw
the white scar made by the hunting knife
around his neck.

When I woke
I remembered: he has been gone
twenty years and not heard from.

DEATH OF A YOUNG SON BY DROWNING

He, who navigated with success
the dangerous river of his own birth
once more set forth

on a voyage of discovery
into the land I floated on
but could not touch to claim.

His feet slid on the bank,
the currents took him;
he swirled with ice and trees in the swollen water

and plunged into distant regions,
his head a bathysphere;
through his eyes' thin glass bubbles

he looked out, reckless adventurer
on a landscape stranger than Uranus
we have all been to and some remember.

There was an accident; the air locked,
he was hung in the river like a heart.
They retrieved the swamped body,

cairn of my plans and future charts,
with poles and hooks
from among the nudging logs.

It was spring, the sun kept shining, the new grass
lept to solidity;
my hands glistened with details.

After the long trip I was tired of waves.
My foot hit rock. The dreamed sails
collapsed, ragged.

I planted him in this country
like a flag.

THEY TRAVEL BY AIR

A different room, this month
a worse one, where your
body with head
attached and my head with
body attached coincide briefly

I want questions and you want
only answers, but the building
is warming up, there is not much

time and time is not
fast enough for us any
more, the building sweeps
away, we are off course, we
separate, we hurtle towards each other
at the speed of sound, everything roars

we collide sightlessly and
fall, the pieces of us
mixed as disaster
and hit the pavement of this room
in a blur of silver fragments

Margaret Avison

MARGARET AVISON was born in Galt, Ont., and educated at the University of Toronto. She has been a librarian, a lecturer in English at Scarborough College, University of Toronto, and since 1968 has been a social worker at the Presbyterian Church Mission in Toronto.

She is not a prolific poet. Throughout the forties and fifties she published sparingly in magazines. Her first book, *Winter Sun*, did not appear until 1960; it won the Governor General's Award. Her second book, *The Dumbfounding*, was published in 1966. 'Margaret Avison insists on the power and privacy of the poetic imagination,' Ernest Redekop writes in his study of the poet. 'Just beneath the surface of things lies a radically different world, and this world can be recreated by the "optic heart".' A key phrase in the poem 'Snow', the 'optic heart' reveals 'creation's unseen freight' and gives us new insights into the relationship of man and the world he lives in and, in some religious poems, of man and God. Another critic, A.J.M. Smith, has written: 'The peculiar virtue of this poetry arises from the intimacy with which the poet invites us to share her improvisational insights and home-made constructs. She writes to herself—as well as for the reader. She has to discover things and the ubiquitous unexpected connections of things for herself. Only after that can she point them out to the rest of us.' Margaret Avison's minute identification of sensation and thought, her way of making several things happen simultaneously, of making one thing seem to be two things (the stripes on the man's shirt in 'In a Season of Unemployment' are for an instant electronic rays), require a good deal of concentration to be appreciated. But her poems offer a rare imaginative experience and are among the best ever written by a Canadian.

Ernest Redekop's book on Margaret Avison's poetry is in Copp Clark's Studies in Canadian Literature series. Also recommended is A.J.M. Smith's 'Critical Improvisations on Margaret Avison's *Winter Sun*' in Issue 18 of *The Tamarack Review* (Winter 1961).

TWILIGHT

Three minutes ago it was almost dark.
Now all the darkness is in the
leaves (there are no more
low garage roofs, etc.).

But the sky itself has become mauve.
Yet it is raining.
The trees rustle and tap with rain.
... Yet the sun is gone.
It would even be gone from the mountaintops
if there were mountains.

In cities this mauve sky
may be of man.

The taps listen, in the unlighted bathroom.

Perfume of light.

It is gone. It is all over:
until the hills close to behind
the ultimate straggler, it will
never
be so again.

The insect of thought retracts its claws;
it wilts.

SNOW

Nobody stuffs the world in at your eyes.
The optic heart must venture: a jail-break
And re-creation. Sedges and wild rice
Chase rivery pewter. The astonished cinders quake
With rhizomes. All ways through the electric air
Trundle candy-bright disks; they are desolate
Toys if the soul's gates seal, and cannot bear,
Must shudder under, creation's unseen freight.
But soft, there is snow's legend: colour of mourning

Along the yellow Yangtze where the wheel
Spins an indifferent stasis that's death's warning.
Asters of tumbled quietness reveal
Their petals. Suffering this starry blur
The rest may ring your change, sad listener.

IN A SEASON OF UNEMPLOYMENT

These green painted park benches are
all new. The Park Commissioner had them
planted.
Sparrows go on
having dust baths at the edge of
the park maple's shadow, just where
the bench is cemented down, planted
and then cemented.

    Not a breath moves
    this newspaper.
    I'd rather read it by the Lapland sun at midnight. Here we're
    bricked in early by a
    stifling dark.

On that bench a man in a
pencil-striped white shirt
keeps his head up and steady.

    The newspaper-astronaut says
    'I feel excellent under the condition of weightlessness.'
And from his bench a
scatter of black bands in the hollow-air
ray out—too quick for the eye—
and cease.

    'Ground observers watching him on a TV circuit said
    At the time of this report he
    was smiling,' Moscow ra-
    dio reported.
I glance across at him, and mark that
he is feeling
excellent too, I guess, and
weightless and
'smiling.'

b. 1904

Earle Birney

EARLE BIRNEY began publishing relatively late—at least for a poet, since poets generally begin young—but now, as he approaches seventy, critics and other poets remark on the liveliness and youthfulness of his recent work. His slowness to begin publishing is explained partly by his involvement in academic studies, teaching, and as literary editor of *The Canadian Forum* (1936-1940). He was born in Calgary and brought up in Banff and Creston, B.C. After graduating from high school in 1920 he worked for two years as a manual labourer to earn money to attend the University of British Columbia. Upon graduation he continued his education at the University of Toronto, where he studied Old and Middle English, and the University of London, where he did research on Chaucer. He received a Ph.D. from Toronto in 1936 and taught at University College there for six years. He served as an officer overseas during the Second World War, was on the staff of the CBC's International Service immediately after the war, and in 1946 became professor of English at the University of British Columbia, where he eventually established and

headed the Department of Creative Writing. He has been Poet-in-Residence at several universities in Canada and the United States and in recent years has read his own work, and often the work of other Canadian poets, on platforms and radio and television, not only in Canada and the United States but in many faraway places of the world.

Earle Birney's first two books—*David and Other Poems* (1942) and *Now is Time* (1945)—both won Governor General's Awards. *The Strait of Anian: Selected Poems* appeared in 1948 and *Trial of a City and Other Verse* in 1952. In addition to poetry he published in this period two works of fiction: *Turvey* (1949), a picaresque novel about the Second World War that has also had some success in dramatic adaptations, and *Down the Long Table* (1955), which has political and social overtones. Later books of poetry are *Ice Cod Bell or Stone* (1962) and *Near False Creek Mouth* (1964), which contain poems that grew out of visits to Asia, Mexico, and Peru. Of the second of these collections, Birney wrote: 'Most of the poems involve people and places thousands of miles away from False Creek, near whose mouth I live, but they are all close to us now, not only in time-space, but in the sharing of needs and hopes—and premonitions of disaster.' Birney's *Selected Poems* was published in 1966. Of this book the poet wrote that 'my hardcover collection is a handsomely illustrated, if badly proofread, book; but it sells for six dollars.' So in 1969 there appeared *The Poems of Earle Birney*, more modest in size, much more modest in price, and in paperback. His most recent collection is *Rag & Bone Shop* (1971). A series of interesting CBC radio talks by Birney has been published in *The Creative Writer* (1966).

Birney's concern with the efforts of man to come to terms both with hostile nature and with society and its disorders has found expression in a rich and varied body of work—in narrative poems, meditative lyrics, nature poems, comic and satirical poems, and in experiments with form and structure—with typography, orthography, and concrete poetry. His poems often begin with an observation or experience and develop into meditations on its meaning for him. In 'The Road to Nijmégen' the poet's memory of 'the gentle and true' lights up the 'Lazarus tomb' of a war-torn land; and in 'The Bear on the Delhi Road'—which Birney wrote over a year after glimpsing from his passing car two Kashmiri men and a bear on a roadside in northern India—two bear-trainers are seen trying 'to free myth from reality'.

Richard Robillard has written a brief study of Earle Birney's work (including an analysis of the imagery in 'Bushed') for the Canadian Writers series of the New Canadian Library, in which *The Poems of Earle Birney* also appears. There are illuminating articles on Birney by Paul West in Issue 13 of *Canadian Literature* (Spring 1962), by A.J.M. Smith on his *Selected Poems* in Issue 30 (Autumn 1966), and by George Woodcock in *Odysseus Ever Returning* (1970) in the New Canadian Library.

THE ROAD TO NIJMÉGEN

December my dear on the road to Nijmégen
between the stones and the bitten sky was your face

Not yours at first but only the countenance of lank canals
and gathered stares   (too rapt to note my passing)
of graves with frosted billy-tins for epitaphs
and bones of tanks beside the stoven bridges
and old men in the mist who knifed at roots
hacking the last chips from a boulevard of stumps.

These for miles and the fangs of homes
but more the women wheeling into the wind
on the tireless rims of their cycles
like tattered sailboats tossing over the cobbles
and the children groping in gravel for knobs of coal
or clustered like wintered flies at the back of messhuts
their legs standing like dead stems out of their clogs

Numbed on the long road to mangled Nijmégen
I thought that only the living of others assures us
the gentle and true we remember as trees walking
Their arms reach down from the light of kindness
into this Lazarus tomb

So peering through sleet as we neared Nijmégen
I glimpsed the rainbow arch of your eyes
Over the clank of the jeep   your quick grave laughter
outrising at last the rockets
brought me what spells I repeat as I travel this road
that arrives at no future

and what creed I bring to our daily crimes
to this guilt
in the griefs of the old and the tombs of the young

Holland, January 1945

THE BEAR ON THE DELHI ROAD

Unreal   tall as a myth
by the road the Himalayan bear
is beating the brilliant air
with his crooked arms
About him two men   bare
spindly as locusts   leap

One pulls on a ring
in the great soft nose   His mate
flicks   flicks with a stick
up at the rolling eyes

They have not led him here
down from the fabulous hills
to this bald alien plain
and the clamorous world   to kill
but simply to teach him to dance

They are peaceful both   these spare
men of Kashmir   and the bear
alive is their living   too
If   far on the Delhi way
around him galvanic they dance
it is merely to wear   wear
from his shaggy body the tranced
wish forever to stay
only an ambling bear
four-footed in berries

It is no more joyous for them
in this hot dust to prance
out of reach of the praying claws
sharpened to paw for ants
in the shadows of deodars
It is not easy to free
myth from reality
or rear this fellow up
to lurch   lurch with them
in the tranced dancing of men

Srinagar 1958 — Île des Porquerolles 1959

BUSHED

He invented a rainbow but lightning struck it
shattered it into the lake-lap of a mountain
so big his mind slowed when he looked at it

Yet he built a shack on the shore
learned to roast porcupine belly and
wore the quills on his hatband

At first he was out with the dawn
whether it yellowed bright as wood-columbine
or was only a fuzzed moth in a flannel of storm
But he found the mountain was clearly alive
sent messages whizzing down every hot morning
boomed proclamations at noon and spread out
a white guard of goat
before falling asleep on its feet at sundown

When he tried his eyes on the lake   ospreys
would fall like valkyries
choosing the cut-throat
He took then to waiting
till the night smoke rose from the boil of the sunset

But the moon carved unknown totems
out of the lakeshore
owls in the beardusky woods derided him
moosehorned cedars circled his swamps and tossed
their antlers up to the stars
Then he knew   though the mountain slept   the winds
were shaping its peak to an arrowhead
poised

And now he could only
bar himself in and wait
for the great flint to come singing into his heart

1951

Marie-Claire Blais

MARIE-CLAIRE BLAIS is a prodigy whose first novel, *La Belle Bête*, was written when she was eighteen. She published eleven books by the time she was thirty and, with the exception of Gabrielle Roy, has been the only Québec writer whose novels have consistently been published in English Canada and the United States very soon after their first appearance in French. The eldest of four children, she was born in a working-class district in Quebec City. She was educated in a convent school but left without graduating; she then worked for a time in a shoe factory and an office. She read widely from an early age in modern French, German, and American writing, and took some courses in literature and philosophy at Université Laval. There she was encouraged by one of her professors, Jeanne Lapointe, and by the famous head of Laval's School of Social Sciences, the Reverend Georges-Henri Lévesque. In 1962, in Montreal, she met the American critic Edmund Wilson, who was working on a book about Canadian writers and society (*O Canada*), and he sponsored her for a Guggenheim Fellowship. She moved to the United States, where she has lived ever since in an isolated house on Cape Cod, except for occasional periods spent in Paris.

Marie-Claire Blais does not write about the actual world of French Canada. Hers is a dark imaginary landscape filled with grotesque, mysterious, desolate images and monstrous acts. *La Belle Bête* is about Isabelle-Marie, her beautiful idiot brother Patrice, and their mother, the vain Louise, who smothers Patrice with affection while scorning her daughter. Isabelle is consumed with a passionate hatred of her brother—his beauty is an ever-present reminder of her own ugliness and she eventually disfigures him. *La Belle Bête* was published in English as *Mad Shadows* (1960), from which two extracts are given here.

In an interview with Marie-Claire Blais in 1965 (*The Tamarack Review*, Issue 37, Autumn 1965), Barry Callaghan comments on the morbidness of French-Canadian writing at that time. Miss Blais said: 'Oh . . . it is because they are not happy. But it is not French Canada only. It is France too. They also have this sadness about living. . . .' Later she said: '. . . I have been interested in the problems . . . *le problème du mal* . . . good and evil. My first and second novels are about passion, the emotions which are so dangerous to liberate . . . Writing about *Mad Shadows*, the critic and translator Philip Stratford compared her fiction with the work of the French Catholic novelists François Mauriac, Georges Bernanos, and Julien Green. Marie-Claire Blais, he says, 'shares with these novelists a fascination with aberrant, fated evil in human form and is as obsessed as they are with the mystery of damnation. This is to be the staple of all her following works. It will be expressed now in lyric sadness, now in ironic mirth, now with social overtones, but all her characters will live and suffer in the same lonely depraved world, where innocence is always doomed and the forces of night always triumph over the glimmer of day. In *Mad Shadows* we have the baldest, most primitive expression of this haunted vision.'

Marie-Claire Blais's other novels in English translation are: *Tête-Blanche* (1961), *The Day is Dark* and *Three Travelers* (1967), *A Season in the Life of Emmanuel* (1966), and *The Manuscripts of Pauline Archange* (1969).

A study of Marie-Claire Blais by Philip Stratford is included in the series Canadian Writers and Their Works published by Forum House. *Mad Shadows* has been published in the New Canadian Library.

HER BEAUTIFUL BEAST

Louise set off by herself. She would miss her child. Without him she was lost, shorn of both roots and flowers. At forty, Louise was still a frivolous doll, empty and excessively concerned with her slender body. Patrice's beauty was to her but a reflection of her own.

She also needed the false security of luxury. Luxury! She craved it. Her pleasures were those of someone who had grown neither wiser nor stronger through suffering. Though she was not intelligent and had the soul of a mannequin, in her veins ran a streak of foresight and cunning. Her daughter exasperated her. 'Can you expect anything but trouble from someone so ugly?' And yet Isabelle-Marie took after her father, that gallant dreamer and poet who used to speak of his land as though of a virgin consecrated to God. How could such a man have felt passionate about Louise, with her flighty, skin-deep beauty? Because Louise knew how to pounce on vulnerable spirits, taken by her charms. She used her body with the single-minded determination of a prostitute, and had the same obsession with money.

Isabelle-Marie was ten years old when her father died. Since then she had withdrawn into her sorrow, and contempt for Louise had shriveled her soul.

Louise set off by herself. Separated for the first time in her life from Patrice, she felt severed in two.

'I want some bread, give me some bread, Isabelle.'

At noon the table was bright with sunshine but the faces were pale. Isabelle-Marie hid the bread in her apron, standing in front of Patrice who, in his desperation, looked more and more like himself, like an idiot. At last Isabelle-Marie was free not to fear her brother. She could try anything; he knew no way of defending himself.

By depriving him of food she could make him pale and wan, and this creature who had never known the touch of misery would become her puppet, her own spindly puppet. Yes, Isabelle-Marie wanted to make him ugly. For a moment she shied away from this perverse desire, then she gave in to it. Oh, to watch the slow disintegration of his beauty! Was this a crime? But why? . . . Did Patrice deserve his beauty?

The poison burst within her and she was amazed by her own strength. And what about me? . . . Is it my fault that I am ugly?

Patrice held out both hands and looked around as though seeking his mother, needing her shoulder.

'I'm hungry, I'm hungry.'

He went on tormenting his sister, pleading with her in a trembling voice while she, carried away by her new power, shoved him with her elbow and disappeared with the bread, as though she were protecting a child from fire or undeserved punishment.

Patrice did not know how to fight back. He hugged himself and cried.

Mercilessly, Isabelle-Marie resisted his laments. Then, like a feeble, daydreaming child, Patrice fell into a gentle sleep, his stomach empty and hollow, such a gentle sleep that it was barely sleep at all.

The first few nights he woke screaming, hammering his fists against the door until a strange kind of death finally came over him. He collapsed, and 'rested'. At other times, in delirium, he would go out and run around the garden like a madman. He held out his arms and raced toward the lake, where he plunged his feverish face and his whole famished body into the water.

His suffering was great, but he reacted to it like an idiot. He devoured whatever he could find in the fields, rolling in the grass, abandoning himself to his terrible hunger. On the fourth day, Isabelle-Marie found him less dazzling. There were rings under his eyes and his lips were purplish. Having half succeeded in her revenge, she lost interest. On the fifth day she saw her brother lying near the door, his chest swollen outward, very still. He wore a vague smile. She looked at him for a long time, until her soul could stand it no longer.

'After all, Patrice is only a child.'

She lifted him, but his weight was more than she could bear. She laid him over her knees, mournfully, as though he were dying.

Isabelle-Marie began to rock her brother back and forth. His white

body lay in her arms with one limp hand around her neck. He rested his face against her with his eyes closed, instinctively accepting any shoulder as a refuge for his innocent brow. Abandoning himself thus to Isabelle-Marie, he was seeking the warmth of his mother. Isabelle-Marie did not try to raise him to his feet.

The three mountains were reflected in the lake like phantom swimmers. The strange chill which permeates the shore rose beneath Isabelle-Marie's feet and she stared into the distance, without moving, in no way afraid of this living statue that slept on, as if attached to her thigh. Patrice was breathing with difficulty. His was the sickly sleep of an invalid who has reached the end of a desperate crisis. His lower lip curved into a smile, but it was only the half-smile of suffering, all the more distressing on a face that was never troubled. Isabelle-Marie noticed the dust in his luxurious hair and the blotches on his bloodless cheeks. But his forehead kept its youthful pride, an admirable, guiltless forehead which she now held against her shoulder with more compassion. Patrice would probably always be handsome and empty. But some of his strength was gone. Isabelle-Marie ran her hand through her brother's hair and laughed as she shook him.

'Are you asleep, my child?'

She watched for the faint quivers of fear in his thick lashes.

'You know, my child, I feel sorry for you.'

But he was not listening. It would be so easy to claw this innocent face that did not struggle, to unleash her fiendish nails upon him, but she withdrew her hand and bit her lip. Then she laughed as she ruffled his hair in a wild burst of tenderness.

'My Beautiful Beast . . . oh, my Beautiful Beast!'

Patrice shuddered. He was hungry. His body was very warm as it rested against his sister's flesh. She pretended to be casual.

"Why then, get up! I'll give you some bread, my Beautiful Beast, of course I will. Stand up!'

But he could not stand alone. Isabelle took him in her arms and carried him with his head over her shoulder, like a child who has fainted. She thought how simple it would be to walk out into the lake and lower her brother into the water, to drown this near-corpse.

Then coming to her senses, she thought, After all, even an animal has a right to live.

Wandering in the woods, she wept, suddenly sorry for what she had done, or was it rather the poignancy she felt in carrying in her arms a body without a soul? Louise's great hero no longer weighed as much as a man. He was ephemeral and pure, already beyond suffering. Clasping his body to her, Isabelle-Marie ran back to the house, consumed by a passionate instinct to protect her brother.

When she arrived, she was dripping with perspiration, and her ankle was slightly bruised.

And now she did not know how to make Patrice well again. Nor did he try to help himself. Louise had coddled her son so much that he was quite unprepared for Isabelle-Marie's cruelty. So Patrice lingered in fever and delirium, without any desire to eat. He lay dreaming, white between white sheets. In his imagination, all the water left the lake. He found himself looking for his reflection in the disappearing water and cried out, but no mirror reflected his face nor echoed his cry. At night, when he heard his sister's sobbing, he thrashed in his bed.

Frantic at the approaching return of her mother, Isabelle-Marie was even more striken, more heartbroken. The faintest murmur of distress brought her to Patrice's bedside, where she sponged his brow, soothed him, and offered him cool drinks. The boy distrusted his sister deeply, with the blind fear of a slave. Only his own reflection made him feel secure. In the midst of his worst nightmares, Isabelle-Marie would bring him a mirror, and he would smile at his perfect teeth, his pure mouth. An illusion of peace held him spellbound, though it did not cure him.

Patrice wasted away languidly, as though savouring his own misfortune.

'Drink, Patrice, please drink.'

His lips seemed defiant in their laziness. He smoothed the sheets and sank gently against the pillows. A miracle was transfiguring his features, one by one, into a new and disturbing kind of beauty. Isabelle-Marie thought that her victim had been rescued from evil and ugliness, because privation had subjected Patrice to the strange magic of death, in which all faces are beautiful.

Though thin, he was dazzling. Though young, she was withered.

'Mother will come back,' begged Patrice. 'Won't she?'

'Of course, she will, my Beautiful Beast, and you will be happy again.'

Suddenly she began to scrutinize him with her dark eyes, as though she were holding him between her gaze and her mouth, as though she did not want this creature, who even yet did not know suffering, to escape from her clutches.

'Would you like a little wine?'

He did not answer. Hallucinations made him tremble again, and he began to perspire, to cry out, his mouth pressed against Isabelle-Marie's shoulder.

'Come now, be a good boy.'

He drowned the girl's bare neck in burning tears, clutched at her waist, and Isabelle-Marie experienced an excruciating longing to die, to disappear in the shadows.

She then found that part of her desire to hurt her brother was a masochistic fear that she would lose him. But the boy still lingered on in delicious lethargy.

Isabelle-Marie devoted herself to him night and day, at once fearing and enjoying his famished cries. Patrice grew thinner.

* * *

One day when the pain was more excruciating than ever, when Isabelle-Marie began to fear a final night of agony, Louise arrived, tall, rested, a flaming red hat on her dyed hair. The trip had given her skin the inviting glow of a woman who is just mature enough to beautiful.

But she was not alone; with her was an elegantly dressed man of her own age. Standing before them, Isabelle-Marie wore a faint smile. For a number of years now, her mother had been promising the arrival of this friend, whom she described as being of 'well-sculptured and manly build'.

'Oh, Isabelle-Marie, how sad you look!'

Then her voice suddenly changed.

'Where is Patrice? Have you met my son, Lanz? There has never been a child like him. My friends say that only a genius could be so beautiful!'

'Patrice . . . Patrice,' she called, cupping her gloved hands.

Isabelle-Marie stood firmly in front of her.

'He is asleep, Mother.'

Louise rested her head on the shoulder of her exquisite admirer. He seemed unconcerned.

'Asleep. He must have been running too much again. I knew it! By the way, Lanz, you haven't met my daughter Isabelle.'

Isabelle-Marie did not hold out her hand. The look in Lanz's eyes reminded her of how ugly she was.

'Lanz,' Louise continued in a melting voice. 'You must excuse my daughter. She is a savage; no discipline ever had any effect on her.'

She laughed, showing off her deceitful mouth. Isabelle-Marie noticed nervous lines beneath her make-up, and a tiny vein which ran from her eye to her delicate nose, like a tear of blood.

'We must wake him,' said Louise.

'He is very sick.'

Louise faltered, but found renewed strength in the presence of her admirer. She began to pull the gloves from her fingers, with elegant, deliberately slow gestures.

She turned back again, her face suddenly soured and wrinkled by this unexpected sorrow.

'Patrice is sick?'

As she crossed the room, she took off her hat and let her hands fall to her sides. She stopped on the threshold.

'Patrice, Patrice, what is the matter?'

Lying on his back like a marble god, pale, with his mouth half open, Patrice stared at his mother. Louise suddenly felt lacerated and oppressed.

She threw herself upon him. She could feel his feverish body beneath her own.

'Patrice, my dearest, what is the matter? I'll never go away again, not ever. I'll always come back to you. But I am back now. Patrice . . . Patrice . . .'

Patrice cried plaintively into her hair. Louise caressed him as though he were a corpse.

'What happened, Patrice? Please tell me.'

'I can't remember.'

Isabelle-Marie listened. Her brother would not tell. His impoverished mind would protect her. She laughed inside herself and, for a moment, a gleam of perversity shone in her eyes. Lanz was disturbed to see such coarse features and this body as mean as a dented sword. He twirled the little gold cane which he used, with infinite grace, to support his lame leg. This infirmity, which enhanced his proud bearing and broad shoulders, captured the essence of his vanity. Isabelle-Marie found him more virile and impressive in profile. A ray of sunshine gave his dark beard the look of an unfinished mask. Behind this he hid the cruelty of his eyes, the falsely masculine expression of a man who knows no other role to play in life but that of a man of fashion.

Isabelle-Marie was repelled at the thought that this creature was her mother's lover, for she considered Louise too absurd to inspire any kind of desire, even a physical one. Lanz disgusted her. She passed judgement upon him. Hadn't she the privilege of passing judgement upon those who contributed to her suffering?

A cold sweat bathed her brow; she wiped it away with a frantic gesture and leaned her head against the casement of the door. She heard Patrice's squeals, little cries of delight like those of a young animal. She almost fainted, the way she had years before, when Patrice was being admired on the train. Her body became rigid. Then she grew calm again.

Louise was appalled. She bent over her son, begging him not to die. He fell asleep, warmed by her breath, having finally found in his mother the mirror he had been seeking.

'Isabelle,' shrieked Louise, 'I know what was wrong with this child! Me! He needed me . . .'

Isabelle-Marie sneered and disappeared across the fields.

MAD SHADOWS
Translated by Merloyd Lawrence

b. 1935

George Bowering

Though only in his mid-thirties, GEORGE BOWERING has a substantial career behind him as a much-published poet, an editor of small magazines, a critic, and a university teacher. He was born in Penticton, B.C., and educated at the University of British Columbia. There he was one of the editors of *Tish*, a poetry magazine that gathered together a number of young west-coast writers who were influenced by the American poets associated with Black Mountain College in North Carolina (Charles Olson and others). Bowering taught at the University of Alberta in Calgary (now the University of Calgary) and was Writer-in-Residence and later a teacher at Sir George Williams University in Montreal. He has since returned to the west coast to teach at Simon Fraser University in Vancouver. He edits his own poetry magazine, *Imago*, in which he publishes young poets active in the Vancouver area and in Montreal and Ontario. Among Bowering's own poetry collections are *Points on the Grid* (1964); *The Man in Yellow Boots* (1965); *The Silver Wire* (1966); *Baseball* (1967), a sequence of poems in a pennant-shaped format; *Two Police Poems* (1968); two winners of the

Governor General's Award published in 1969, *Rocky Mountain Foot* and *The Gangs of Kosmos*; *Sitting in Mexico* (1970); and *Touch: Selected Poems 1960-1970* (1971). Bowering has also published one novel, *Mirror on the Floor* (1966), and has been a frequent contributor to *Canadian Literature* with critical essays on James Reaney, Margaret Laurence, and Al Purdy among others. In 1970 he published a book on Purdy in Copp Clark's Studies in Canadian Literature series.

While Bowering, like other Canadian poets, has been influenced by developments in modern American poetry—for instance in his plain, often monosyllabic diction and his virtual avoidance of abstraction and metaphor—his best poems have a life of their own. His terse recitals of images and acts can evoke intense feelings and associations. Reviewing *The Silver Wire* in the *University of Toronto Quarterly*, Professor Hugh MacCallum wrote: 'Its gaze is directed outward, not inward, and he has an ebullient sense of participating in what he sees around him. The speaker in these poems achieves at times an almost bardic simplicity of manner that allows him to revel in the ordinary, the commonplace, the self-evident. But there is also a kind of wonder at the fullness and assertiveness of phenomena. Energy is the thing that arouses the poet's imagination—energy in landscape, man, or woman.'

GRANDFATHER

Grandfather
        Jabez Harry Bowering
strode across the Canadian prairie
hacking down trees
            & building churches
delivering personal baptist sermons in them
leading Holy holy holy lord god almighty songs in them
red haired man squared off in the pulpit
reading Saul on the road to Damascus at them

Left home
        big walled Bristol town
at age eight
          to make a living
buried his stubby fingers in root snarled earth
for a suit of clothes & seven hundred gruelly meals a year
taking an anabaptist cane across the back every day
for four years till he was whipt out of England

Twelve years old
          & across the ocean alone
to apocalyptic Canada
            Ontario of bone bending labor
six years on the road to Damascus till his eyes were blinded
with the blast of Christ & he wandered west
to Brandon among wheat kings & heathen Saturday nights
young red haired Bristol boy shoveling coal
in the basement of Brandon college five in the morning

Then built his first wooden church & married
a sick girl who bore two live children & died
leaving several pitiful letters & the Manitoba night

He moved west with another wife & built children & churches
Saskatchewan Alberta British Columbia Holy holy holy
lord god almighty
          struck his labored bones with pain

& left him a postmaster prodding grandchildren with crutches
another dead wife & a glass bowl of photographs
& holy books unopened save the bible by the bed

Till he died the day before his eighty fifth birthday
in a Catholic hospital of sheets white as his hair

MOON SHADOW

Last night the rainbow
round the moon

climbed with how sad steps
as I walkt home

colour surrounding me
cloud around my head.

I am moon!
Arrows fly at me!

I slide cold & pale
over cold earth
of Alberta winter!

I show one face
to the world,
immaculate still,
inscrutable female
male animal ball
of rock
shining with borrowed light

rolling in that light
the other side of
forgetful space!

I am a shining tear
of the sun

full moon, silver,
who but myself knows
where the sun shall set?

I am able to instruct
the whole universe,

instruct the heart,
the weeping eye
of any single man.

Slide over the moon-
lit earth, a shadow
of a chariot.

    Walk homeward
forgetful where I have been

with how sad steps
my shadow before me

on the earth, moon shadow
rainbow round my heart,
wondering where in the universe I am.

b. 1903

Morley Callaghan

MORLEY CALLAGHAN is Canada's most distinguished novelist and short-story writer. His career reaches back to that Golden Age of modern writing that found its main stimulus in Paris and New York in the 1920s, yet he has occupied a curious position in the literary history of his own country, where he has been both honoured and put down, and at times almost ignored. Today he is admired by most younger writers of fiction in Canada as their only true predecessor in this country, and he is being discovered by a new generation of readers through reprints of his early books. He was born in Toronto in a Roman Catholic family of Irish background and educated in the city's schools. He attended St Michael's College, University of Toronto, and later studied law at Osgoode Hall; although he was called to the bar, he never practised. In the summers, while he was at university, he worked as a reporter on the Toronto *Star*—where he met Ernest Hemingway, who was also then a *Star* reporter —and began to write short stories that were often based on incidents he had observed while working for the newspaper. Then for a year or so he and a friend operated a bookstore in downtown

Toronto. His short stories began to appear in such experimental literary magazines as *transition* and *This Quarter*. Later he contributed fiction regularly to *Atlantic Monthly*, *Esquire*, *Harper's Bazaar*, *Scribner's*, and *The New Yorker*. His first novel, *Strange Fugitive*, one of the earliest gangster novels, was published in 1928, and his first collection of stories, *A Native Argosy*, appeared the following year. After his marriage, early in 1929, he and his wife spent most of the remainder of the year in Paris, where English and American expatriate writers formed a kind of literary village. The experiences of that summer, and particularly Callaghan's friendship with Hemingway and F. Scott Fitzgerald, were described in a memoir, *That Summer in Paris* (1963), from which a short extract begins on page 43. Towards the end of 1929 the Callaghans returned to Toronto. Except for brief periods they have lived there ever since.

In the 1930s Callaghan began to publish a work of fiction almost every year: *It's Never Over* (1930); *No Man's Meat* (1931), a novella; *A Broken Journey* (1932); *Such is My Beloved* (1934); *They Shall Inherit the Earth* (1935); *Now That*

April's Here and Other Stories (1936); and *More Joy in Heaven* (1937). In such novels as *It's Never Over* and *More Joy in Heaven* he entered again the world of the criminal he had explored in his first book. Another favourite Callaghan theme is the paradoxical nature of innocence in the complexities of modern society. In the late 1930s Morley Callaghan wrote the first of several stage plays, and during the Second World War he became a public figure and a participant in a CBC public affairs radio series, 'Things to Come', which later became the program 'Citizen's Forum'. This career in radio and later television continued in the postwar years, when Morley Callaghan was a regular member of the panel program 'Now I Ask You' and a frequent guest on Nathan Cohen's series 'Fighting Words'. But the war years were not a good time for his writing, and it was not until 1951 that he published a new novel, *The Loved and The Lost*, which won the Governor General's Award for fiction. A big, retrospective collection of his short stories, *Morley Callaghan's Stories*, appeared in 1959. The novels *The Many Colored Coat* and *A Passion in Rome* were published in 1960 and 1961. The American man of letters Edmund Wilson, in his book *O Canada* (1965), described Morley Callaghan as 'today perhaps the most unjustly neglected novelist in the English-speaking world' and concluded his essay on Callaghan's work by 'wondering whether the primary reason for the current underestimation of Morley Callaghan may not be simply a general incapacity—apparently shared by his compatriots—for believing that a writer whose work may be mentioned without absurdity in association with Chekhov's and Turgenev's can possibly be functioning in Toronto.'

In discussing the short stories, we cannot do better than quote from a review Robert Weaver wrote thirteen years ago of *Morley Callaghan's Stories* (Issue 2, Autumn 1959, of *Canadian Literature*), which refers to 'their odd, wistful, lyric quality . . . they require from the reader a kind of quiet, unhurried sympathy that most of us are too impatient to give.' They reveal a narrow, stifling world of a few small towns in southern Ontario and an old downtown section of Toronto; the characters who inhabit it are lonely, marginal people who feel alien and vulnerable in their environment. 'Two Fishermen', about a hangman who has arrived in a small Ontario town to do his job, is one of Callaghan's best-known stories.

In 1970 Morley Callaghan received two awards, suggesting that Canadians were not indifferent to his presence in their midst. The Canada Council gave him the $15,000 Molson Award, presented each year to three people prominent in the arts in Canada. Then he was the recipient of the $50,000 Royal Bank Award for 1970. Given for 'work that serves humanity', this award had previously gone to Cardinal Léger, to the neuro-surgeon Dr Wilder Penfield, and to the atomic scientist Dr C. J. Mackenzie; with Morley Callaghan, the Royal Bank honoured a Canadian artist for the first time. In his speech on this occasion Callaghan commented on a society obsessed with technology and information, and said: 'Technology may triumphantly take a man to the moon, but the man takes all his despairing questions and his secret loneliness with him . . . I mean the desperate real loneliness we suffer in our relationship with other people . . . The long loneliness of the inner world. The domain left now to the imaginative writer, whispering to the reader about it in this private world. A man must stand for something. I stand for the sanctity of this private world.'

There are two critical studies of Morley Callaghan: one by Brandon Conron in the Twayne World Authors Series (1966, Burns & MacEachern) and the other by Victor Hoar in the Studies in Canadian Literature series (1969, Copp Clark). An essay on Callaghan's work is included in George Woodcock's *Odysseus Ever Returning* (1970) in the New Canadian Library. There is an interview with Morley Callaghan by Robert Weaver in the anthology *The First Five Years: A Selection from 'The Tamarack Review'* (1962) and another by Donald Cameron in *Conversations with Canadian Novelists* (1972).

Seven of Callaghan's books are available in paperback. *Such is My Beloved, More Joy in Heaven,* and *They Shall Inherit the Earth* have been reprinted in the New Canadian Library and *Morley Callaghan's Stories, The Loved and The Lost, The Many Colored Coat,* and *It's Never Over* are in the Laurentian Library.

TWO FISHERMEN

The only reporter on the town paper, the *Examiner*, was Michael Foster, a tall, long-legged, eager young fellow, who wanted to go to the city some day and work on an important newspaper.

The morning he went into Bagley's Hotel, he wasn't at all sure of himself. He went over to the desk and whispered to the proprietor, Ted Bagley, 'Did he come here, Mr Bagley?'

Bagley said slowly, 'Two men came here from this morning's train. They're registered.' He put his spatulate forefinger on the open book and said, 'Two men. One of them's a drummer. This one here, T. Woodley. I know because he was through this way last year and just a minute ago he walked across the road to Molson's hardware store. The other one . . . here's his name, K. Smith.'

'Who's K. Smith?' Michael asked.

'I don't know. A mild, harmless-looking little guy.'

'Did he look like the hangman, Mr Bagley?'

'I couldn't say that, seeing as I never saw one. He was awfully polite and asked where he could get a boat so he could go fishing on the lake this evening, so I said likely down at Smollet's place by the power-house.'

'Well, thanks. I guess if he was the hangman, he'd go over to the jail first,' Michael said.

He went along the street, past the Baptist church to the old jail with the high brick fence around it. Two tall maple trees, with branches drooping low over the sidewalk, shaded one of the walls from the morning sunlight. Last night, behind those walls, three carpenters, working by lamplight, had nailed the timbers for the scaffold. In the morning, young Thomas Delaney, who had grown up in the town, was being hanged: he had killed old Mathew Rhinehart whom he had caught molesting his wife when she had been berry-picking in the hills behind the town. There had been a struggle and Thomas Delaney had taken a bad beating before he had killed Rhinehart. Last night a crowd had gathered on the sidewalk by the lamp-post, and while moths and smaller insects swarmed around the high blue carbon light, the crowd had thrown sticks and bottles and small stones at the out-of-town workmen in the jail yard. Billy Hilton, the town constable, had stood under the light with his head down, pretending not to notice anything. Thomas Delaney was only three years older than Michael Foster.

Michael went straight to the jail office, where Henry Steadman, the sheriff, a squat, heavy man, was sitting on the desk idly wetting his long moustaches with his tongue. 'Hello, Michael, what do you want?' he asked.

'Hello, Mr Steadman, the *Examiner* would like to know if the hangman arrived yet.'

'Why ask me?'

'I thought he'd come here to test the gallows. Won't he?'

'My, you're a smart young fellow, Michael, thinking of that.'

'Is he in there now, Mr Steadman?'

'Don't ask me. I'm saying nothing. Say, Michael, do you think there's going to be trouble? You ought to know. Does anybody seem sore at me? I can't do nothing. You can see that.'

'I don't think anybody blames you, Mr Steadman. Look here, can't I see the hangman? Is his name K. Smith?'

'What does it matter to you, Michael? Be a sport, go on away and don't bother us any more.'

'All right, Mr Steadman,' Michael said very competently, 'just leave it to me.'

Early that evening, when the sun was setting, Michael Foster walked south of the town on the dusty road leading to the power-house and Smollet's fishing pier. He knew that if Mr K. Smith wanted to get a boat he would go down to the pier. Fine powdered road dust whitened Michael's shoes. Ahead of him he saw the power-plant, square and low, and the smooth lake water. Behind him the sun was hanging over the blue hills beyond the town and shining brilliantly on square patches of farm land. The air around the power-house smelt of steam.

Out on the jutting, tumbledown pier of rock and logs, Michael saw a little fellow without a hat, sitting down with his knees hunched up to his chin, a very small man with little grey baby curls on the back of his neck, who stared steadily far out over the water. In his hand he was holding a stick with a heavy fishing-line twined around it and a gleaming copper spoon bait, the hooks brightened with bits of feathers such as they used in the neighbourhood when trolling for lake trout. Apprehensively Michael walked out over the rocks toward the stranger and called, 'Were you thinking of going fishing, mister?' Standing up, the man smiled. He had a large head, tapering down to a small chin, a birdlike neck, and a very wistful smile. Puckering his mouth up, he said shyly to Michael, 'Did you intend to go fishing?'

'That's what I came down here for. I was going to get a boat back at the boat-house there. How would you like if we went together?'

'I'd like it first rate,' the shy little man said eagerly. 'We could take turns rowing. Does that appeal to you?'

'Fine. Fine. You wait here and I'll go back to Smollet's place and ask for a row-boat and I'll row around here and get you.'

'Thanks. Thanks very much,' the mild little man said as he began to untie his line. He seemed very enthusiastic.

When Michael brought the boat around to the end of the old pier and invited the stranger to make himself comfortable so he could handle the line, the stranger protested comically that he ought to be allowed to row.

Pulling strongly at the oars, Michael was soon out in the deep water and the little man was letting his line out slowly. In one furtive glance, he had noticed that the man's hair, grey at the temples, was inclined to curl to his ears. The line was out full length. It was twisted around the little man's forefinger, which he let drag in the water. And then Michael looked full at him and smiled because he thought he seemed so meek and quizzical. 'He's a nice little guy,' Michael assured himself and he said, 'I work on the town paper, the *Examiner*.'

'Is it a good paper? Do you like the work?'

'Yes. But it's nothing like a first-class city paper and I don't expect to be working on it long. I want to get a reporter's job on a city paper. My name's Michael Foster.'

'Mine's Smith. Just call me Smitty.'

'I was wondering if you'd been over to the jail yet.'

Up to this time the little man had been smiling with the charming ease of a small boy who finds himself free, but now he became furtive and disappointed. Hesitating, he said, 'Yes, I was over there first thing this morning.'

'Oh, I just knew you'd go there,' Michael said. They were a bit afraid of each other. By this time they were far out on the water which had a mill-pond smoothness. The town seemed to get smaller, with white houses in rows and streets forming geometric patterns, just as the blue hills behind the town seemed to get larger at sundown.

Finally Michael said, 'Do you know this Thomas Delaney that's dying in the morning?' He knew his voice was slow and resentful.

'No. I don't know anything about him. I never read about them. Aren't there any fish at all in this old lake? I'd like to catch some fish,' he said rapidly. 'I told my wife I'd bring her home some fish.' Glancing at Michael, he was appealing, without speaking, that they should do nothing to spoil an evening's fishing.

The little man began to talk eagerly about fishing as he pulled out a small flask from his hip pocket. 'Scotch,' he said, chuckling with delight. 'Here, take a swig.' Michael drank from the flask and passed it back. Tilting his head back and saying, 'Here's to you, Michael,' the little man took a long pull at the flask. 'The only time I take a drink,' he said still chuckling, 'is when I go on a fishing trip by myself. I usually go by my-self,' he added apologetically as if he wanted the young fellow to see how much he appreciated his company.

They had gone far out on the water but they had caught nothing. It began to get dark. 'No fish tonight, I guess, Smitty,' Michael said.

'It's a crying shame,' Smitty said. 'I looked forward to coming up here when I found out the place was on the lake. I wanted to get some fishing in. I promised my wife I'd bring her back some fish. She'd often like to go fishing with me, but of course, she can't because she can't travel around from place to place like I do. Whenever I get a call to go some place, I al-ways look at the map to see if it's by a lake or on a river, then I take my lines and hooks along.'

'If you took another job, you and your wife could probably go fishing together,' Michael suggested.

'I don't know about that. We sometimes go fishing together anyway.' He looked away, waiting for Michael to be repelled and insist that he ought to give up the job. And he wasn't ashamed as he looked down at the water, but he knew that Michael thought he ought to be ashamed. 'Some-body's got to do my job. There's got to be a hangman,' he said.

'I just meant that if it was such disagreeable work, Smitty.'

The little man did not answer for a long time. Michael rowed steadily with sweeping, tireless strokes. Huddled at the end of the boat, Smitty suddenly looked up with a kind of melancholy hopelessness and said mildly, 'The job hasn't been so disagreeable.'

'Good God, man, you don't mean you like it?'

'Oh no,' he said, to be obliging, as if he knew what Michael expected him to say. 'I mean you get used to it, that's all.' But he looked down again at the water, knowing he ought to be ashamed of himself.

'Have you got any children?'

'I sure have. Five. The oldest boy is fourteen. It's funny, but they're all a lot bigger and taller than I am. Isn't that funny?'

They started a conversation about fishing rivers that ran into the lake farther north. They felt friendly again. The little man, who had an extra-ordinary gift for story-telling, made many quaint faces, puckered up his lips, screwed up his eyes and moved around restlessly as if he wanted to get up in the boat and stride around for the sake of more expression. Again he brought out the whisky flask and Michael stopped rowing. Grinning, they toasted each other and said together, 'Happy days.' The boat remained motionless on the placid water. Far out, the sun's last rays gleamed on the water-line. And then it got dark and they could only see the town lights. It was time to turn around and pull for the shore. The little man tried to take the oars from Michael, who shook his head resolutely and insisted that he would prefer to have his friend catch a fish on the way back to the shore.

'It's too late now, and we may have scared all the fish away,' Smitty laughed happily. 'But we're having a grand time, aren't we?'

When they reached the old pier by the power-house, it was full night and they hadn't caught a single fish. As the boat bumped against the rocks Michael said, 'You can get out here. I'll take the boat around to Smollet's.'

'Won't you be coming my way?'

'Not just now. I'll probably talk with Smollet a while.'

The little man got out of the boat and stood on the pier looking down at Michael. 'I was thinking dawn would be the best time to catch some fish,' he said. 'At about five o'clock. I'll have an hour and a half to spare anyway. How would you like that?' He was speaking with so much eagerness that Michael found himself saying, 'I could try. But if I'm not here at dawn, you go on without me.'

'All right. I'll walk back to the hotel now.'

'Good night, Smitty.'

'Good night, Michael. We had a fine neighbourly time, didn't we?'

As Michael rowed the boat around to the boat-house, he hoped that Smitty wouldn't realize he didn't want to be seen walking back to town with him. And later, when he was going slowly along the dusty road in the dark and hearing all the crickets chirping in the ditches, he couldn't figure out why he felt so ashamed of himself.

At seven o'clock next morning Thomas Delaney was hanged in the town jail yard. There was hardly a breeze on that leaden grey morning and there were no small whitecaps out over the lake. It would have been a fine morning for fishing. Michael went down to the jail, for he thought it his duty as a newspaperman to have all the facts, but he was afraid he might get sick. He hardly spoke to all the men and women who were crowded under the maple trees by the jail wall. Everybody he knew was staring at the wall and muttering angrily. Two of Thomas Delaney's brothers, big, strapping fellows with bearded faces, were there on the sidewalk. Three automobiles were at the front of the jail.

Michael, the town newspaperman, was admitted into the courtyard by old Willie Mathews, one of the guards, who said that two newspapermen from the city were at the gallows on the other side of the building. 'I guess you can go around there, too, if you want to,' Mathews said, as he sat down slowly on the step. White-faced, and afraid, Michael sat down on the step with Mathews and they waited and said nothing.

At last the old fellow said, 'Those people outside there are pretty sore, ain't they?'

'They're pretty sullen, all right. I saw two of Delaney's brothers there.'

'I wish they'd go,' Mathews said. 'I don't want to see anything. I didn't even look at Delaney. I don't want to hear anything. I'm sick.' He put his head back against the wall and closed his eyes.

The old fellow and Michael sat close together till a small procession came around the corner from the other side of the yard. First came Mr Steadman, the sheriff, with his head down as though he were crying, then Dr Parker, the physician, then two hard-looking young newspapermen from the city, walking with their hats on the backs of their heads, and behind them came the little hangman, erect, stepping out with military precision and carrying himself with a strange cocky dignity. He was dressed in a long black cut-away coat with grey striped trousers, a gates-ajar collar, and a narrow red tie, as if he alone felt the formal importance of the occasion. He walked with brusque precision till he saw Michael, who was standing up, staring at him with his mouth open.

The little hangman grinned and as soon as the procession reached the doorstep, he shook hands with Michael. They were all looking at Michael. As though his work were over now, the hangman said eagerly to Michael, 'I thought I'd see you here. You didn't get down to the pier at dawn?'

'No. I couldn't make it.'

'That was tough, Michael. I looked for you,' he said. 'But never mind. I've got something for you.' As they all went into the jail, Dr Parker glanced angrily at Michael, then turned his back on him. In the office, where the doctor prepared to sign a certificate, Smitty was bending down over his fishing basket, which was in the corner. Then he pulled out two good-sized salmon-bellied trout, folded in a newspaper, and said, 'I was saving these for you, Michael. I got four in an hour's fishing.' Then he said, 'I'll talk about that later, if you'll wait. We'll be busy here, and I've got to change my clothes.'

Michael went out to the street with Dr Parker and the two city newspapermen. Under his arm he was carrying the fish, folded in the newspaper. Outside, at the jail door, Michael thought that the doctor and the two newspapermen were standing a little apart from him. Then the small crowd, with their clothes all dust-soiled from the road, surged forward, and the doctor said to them, 'You might as well go home, boys. It's all over.'

'Where's old Steadman?' somebody demanded.

'We'll wait for the hangman,' somebody else shouted.

The doctor walked away by himself. For a while Michael stood beside the two city newspapermen, and tried to look as nonchalant as they were looking, but he lost confidence in them when he smelled whisky. They only talked to each other. Then they mingled with the crowd, and Michael stood alone. At last he could stand there no longer looking at all those people he knew so well, so he too moved out and joined the crowd.

When the sheriff came out with the hangman and two of the guards, they got half-way down to one of the automobiles before someone threw an old boot. Steadman ducked into one of the cars, as the boot hit him on the shoulder, and the two guards followed him. The hangman, dismayed, stood alone on the sidewalk. Those in the car must have thought at first that the hangman was with them for the car suddenly shot forward, leaving him alone on the sidewalk. The crowd threw small rocks and sticks, hooting at him as the automobile backed up slowly towards him. One small stone hit him on the head. Blood trickled from the side of his head as he looked around helplessly at all the angry people. He had the same expression on his face, Michael thought, as he had had last night when he had seemed ashamed and had looked down steadily at the water. Only now, he looked around wildly, looking for someone to help him as the crowd kept pelting him. Farther and farther Michael backed into the crowd and all the time he felt dreadfully ashamed as though he were betraying Smitty, who last night had had such a good neighbourly time with him. 'It's different now, it's different,' he kept thinking, as he held the fish in the newspaper tight under his arm. Smitty started to run toward the automobile, but James Mortimer, a big fisherman, shot out his foot and tripped him and sent him sprawling on his face.

Mortimer, the big fisherman, looking for something to throw, said to Michael, 'Sock him, sock him.'

Michael shook his head and felt sick.

'What's the matter with you, Michael?'

'Nothing. I got nothing against him.'

The big fisherman started pounding his fists up and down in the air. 'He just doesn't mean anything to me at all,' Michael said quickly. The fisherman, bending down, kicked a small rock loose from the road bed and heaved it at the hangman. Then he said, 'What are you holding there, Michael, what's under your arm? Fish. Pitch them at him. Here, give them to me.' Still in a fury, he snatched the fish, and threw them one at a time at the little man just as he was getting up from the road. The fish fell in the thick dust in front of him, sending up a little cloud. Smitty seemed to stare at the fish with his mouth hanging open, then he didn't even look at the crowd. That expression on Smitty's face as he saw the fish on the road made Michael hot with shame and he tried to get out of the crowd.

Smitty had his hands over his head, to shield his face as the crowd pelted him, yelling 'Sock the little rat. Throw the runt in the lake.' The sheriff pulled him into the automobile. The car shot forward in a cloud of dust.

THE BOXING MATCH

During a visit to Paris in the summer of 1929, Morley Callaghan made friends with two other young writers: Ernest Hemingway and Scott Fitzgerald.

A week later, a little after three, I was at home doing some work on a new novel. My wife was puttering around. Later on I was to call for Ernest. A knock came on the door. And there were Scott and Ernest. The two old friends seemed to be in the best of humour. I could hardly conceal my pleasure. When I had come to Paris I had wanted to enjoy the company of these two men. Now they were together and they had come to my place—my friends. They had had lunch, Ernest said, and had decided to pick me up rather than wait for me. And Scott now was having his way. Ernest was carrying the bag that held the gloves. While I was getting ready, Scott talked to Loretto. But Ernest, having spotted a copy of *The New York Times Book Review* on top of our trunk, began to go through it carefully. I can still see him standing by the window, slowly turning the pages. I can see us waiting at the door until he had finished reading a review.

On the way to the American Club in the taxi, it seemed to me that Scott and Ernest were at ease with each other. There was no sense of strain and Scott looked alert and happy. We joked a bit. At the club—I remember the scene so vividly—I remember how Scott, there for the first time, looked around in surprise. The floor had no mat. Through the doorway opening into the next room, he could see two young fellows playing billiards. Scott sat down on the bench by the wall, while Ernest and I stripped. Then Ernest had him take out his watch and gave him his instructions. A round was to be three minutes, then a minute for a rest. As he took these instructions, listening carefully, Scott had none of Miró's air of high professionalism. He was too enchanted at being there with us. Moving off the bench, he squatted down, a little smile on his face. 'Time,' he called.

Our first round was like most of the rounds we had fought that summer, with me shuffling around, and Ernest, familiar with my style, leading and chasing after me. No longer did he rush in with his old brisk confidence. Now he kept an eye on my left and he was harder to hit. As I shuffled around I could hear the sound of clicking billiard balls from the adjoining room.

'Time,' Scott called promptly. When we sat down beside him, he was rather quiet, meditative, and I could tell by the expression on his face that he was mystified. He must have come there with some kind of a picture of Ernest, the fighter, in his head. For Ernest and me it was just like any other day. We chatted and laughed. And it didn't seem to be important to us that Scott was there. He had made no comment that could bother us. He seemed to be content that he was there concentrating on the minute hand of his watch. 'Time,' he called.

Right at the beginning of that round Ernest got careless; he came in too fast, his left down, and he got smacked on the mouth. His lip began to bleed. It had often happened. It should have meant nothing to him. Hadn't he joked with Jimmy, the bartender, about always having me for a friend while I could make his lip bleed? Out of the corner of his eye he may have seen the shocked expression on Scott's face. Or the taste of blood in his mouth may have made him want to fight more savagely. He came lunging in, swinging more recklessly. As I circled around him, I kept jabbing at his bleeding mouth. I had to forget all about Scott, for Ernest had become rougher, his punching a little wilder than usual. His heavy punches, if they had landed, would have stunned me. I had to punch faster and harder myself to keep away from him. It bothered me that he was taking the punches on the face like a man telling himself he only needed to land one big punch himself.

Out of the corner of my eye, as I bobbed and weaved, I could see one of the young fellows who had been playing billiards come to the door and stand there, watching. He was in his shirt-sleeves, but he was wearing a vest. He held his cue in his hand like a staff. I could see Scott on the bench. I was wondering why I was tiring, for I hadn't been hit solidly. Then Ernest, wiping the blood from his mouth with his glove, and probably made careless with exasperation and embarrassment from having Scott there, came leaping in at me. Stepping in, I beat him to the punch. The timing must have been just right. I caught him on the jaw; spinning around he went down, sprawled out on his back.

If Ernest and I had been there alone I would have laughed. I was sure of my boxing friendship with him; in a sense I was sure of him, too. Ridiculous things had happened in that room. Hadn't he spat in my face? And I felt no surprise seeing him flat on his back. Shaking his head a little to clear it, he rested a moment on his back. As he rose slowly, I expected him to curse, then laugh.

'Oh, my God!' Scott cried suddenly. When I looked at him, alarmed, he was shaking his head helplessly. 'I let the round go four minutes,' he said.

'Christ!' Ernest yelled. He got up. He was silent for a few seconds. Scott, staring at his watch, was mute and wondering. I wished I were miles away. 'All right, Scott,' Ernest said savagely, 'If you want to see me getting the shit knocked out of me, just say so. Only don't say you made a mistake,' and he stomped off to the shower room to wipe the blood from his mouth.

As I tried to grasp the meaning behind his fierce words I felt helpless with wonder, and nervous too; I seemed to be on the edge of some dark pit, and I could only stare blankly at Scott, who, as his eyes met mine, looked sick. Ernest had told me he had been avoiding Scott because Scott was a drunk and a nuisance and he didn't want to be bothered with him. It was plain now it wasn't the whole story. Lashing out with those bitter angry words, Ernest had practically shouted that he was aware Scott had some deep hidden animosity toward him. Shaken as I was, it flashed through my mind, Is the animosity in Scott, or is it really in Ernest? And why should it be in Ernest? Did Scott do something for him once? Is it that Scott helped him along and for months and months he's wanted to be free of him? Or does he think he knows something–knows Scott has to resent him? What is it? Not just that Scott's a drunk. I knew there was something else.

Then Scott came over to me, his face ashen, and he whispered, 'Don't you see I got fascinated watching? I forgot all about the watch. My God, he thinks I did it on purpose. Why would I do it on purpose?'

'You wouldn't,' I said, deeply moved, for he looked so stricken. For weeks he had been heaping his admiration of Ernest on me, his hero worship, and I knew of his eagerness for the companionship. Anyone who could say that he was under some secret and malevolent compulsion to let the round go on would have to say, too, that all men are twisted and no man knows what is in his heart. All I knew was that for weeks he had wanted to be here with us, and now that he was here it had brought him this.

'Look, Scott,' I whispered. 'If you did it on purpose you wouldn't have suddenly cried out that you had let the round go on. You didn't need to. You would have kept quiet. Ernest will see it himself.' But Scott didn't answer. He looked as lonely and as desperate as he had looked that night when he had insisted on coming to the Deux Magots with Loretto and me. The anguish in his face was the anguish of a man who felt that everything he had stood for when he had been at his best, had been belittled.

'Come on, Scott,' I whispered. 'Ernest didn't mean it. It's a thing I might have said myself. A guy gets sore and blurts out the first crazy thing that comes into his head.'

'No, you heard him. He believes I did it on purpose,' he whispered bitterly. 'What can I do, Morley?'

'Don't do anything,' I whispered. 'Forget the whole thing. He'll want to forget it himself. You'll see.'

He moved away from me as Ernest returned from the shower room. With his face washed, Ernest looked much calmer. He had probably done a lot of thinking, too. Yet he offered no retraction. For my part, I tried to ignore the whole incident. Since we had had a good two or three minutes' rest to make up for the long round, why couldn't we go on now? I asked. It gave us something to do. Ernest and I squared off.

Scott, appearing alert and efficient, and hiding his terrible sense of insult and bitterness, called 'Time.' As I look back now I wonder why it didn't occur to me, as we began the round, that Ernest might try to kill me. But between us there was no hostility. The fact that I had been popping him, and then had clipped him and knocked him down, was part of our boxing. We went a good brisk round, both keeping out of trouble. When we clinched, my eye would wander to Scott, sitting there so white-faced. Poor Scott. Then suddenly he made it worse. The corner of a wrestling mat stuck out from under the parallel bars, and when I half tripped on it and went down on one knee, Scott, to mollify Ernest, called out foolishly, but eagerly, 'One knockdown to Ernest, one to Morley,' and if I had been Ernest, I think I would have snarled at him, no matter how good his intentions were.

But it was to continue to be a terrible and ridiculous afternoon for Ernest. It is a wonder he didn't go a little mad.

As soon as we had finished the round, that slender young fellow who had been playing billiards, the one wearing the vest, who had been standing watching, his cue in his hand, came over to us. He might have been an inch taller than me, but he was very slender; he couldn't have weighed more than a hundred and thirty-five pounds. A student probably. 'Excuse me,' he said to Ernest in an English accent. 'I've been watching. Do you mind me saying something? Well, in boxing it isn't enough to be aggressive and always punching. If you don't mind me saying so, the real science of boxing is in defence, in not getting hit.'

It was incredible. The student was prepared to tell Ernest how to box. I was shocked and fearful. Both Scott and I, gaping at the student, must have been sharing the same sense of dread. What would Ernest do? A man can stand only so many mortifications in a single afternoon. If Ernest had grabbed the presumptuous fellow's billiard cue and broken it over his head, I wouldn't have been surprised.

Yet Ernest, after waiting a moment, the moment of astonishment, asked quietly, 'Do you think you could show me?'

'Well, I could try,' the young fellow said modestly.

'Good,' said Ernest. 'No, wait. Don't show me. Show him,' and he pointed at me. 'I'll watch.'

Now I, in my turn, felt a twinge of resentment against Ernest. The student didn't want to show me how to box; he wanted to show Ernest, didn't he? I was to be used as a tuning fork. And who could tell whether or not this slender fellow was an English lightweight champion? Scott hadn't said a word. Nor did he speak as he removed Ernest's gloves and laced them on the intruder. Squaring off with him, I was ready to cover up like a turtle. As we circled around each other, I tried warily to make him lead at me. A feeble left did come at me, but it seemed to be only a feint. This boy was obviously a counterpuncher. Sooner or later I would have to lead at him. He had probably worked with pros. He was probably a hooker; I had always been rattled by a good hooker. I would lead now, then he would blow my head off. But gradually I was forcing him into a corner. Suddenly I caught a familiar expression in his eyes. I could see he was more scared of me than I was of him. As I began to flail away happily at the young fellow's head, Ernest suddenly shouted, 'Stop!'

Now Ernest had a very good moment. In a beautiful bit of acting, not a trace of mockery in his tone, he said to the student, 'I think I understand what you meant. Now show me.' Ernest now unlaced my gloves. I in turn laced them on him. The student looked pale and worried. Against me he had been inept and he knew it, and he knew, too, that he had in effect invited Ernest to knock his block off. Then he caught the derision in Ernest's eyes. Shaking his head apologetically, he would have withdrawn. 'No, come on. You've got to show me,' Ernest insisted.

The student still believed, no doubt, that Ernest was wide open. As he faced him he crouched a little, his hands high, ready to demonstrate his defence. Smiling faintly, Ernest spread his legs, stood rooted there like a great stiff tree trunk, and simply stuck his long left arm straight out like a pole and put his right glove on his hip, contemptuously. He refused to move. It was a splendid dramatic gesture of complete disdain. In fairness to him, he didn't try to clobber the boy, didn't try to strike a single blow. As the student circled around him, he, himself, turned slowly like a gate, the hand still on his hip, the great pole of an arm thrust out stiffly.

The student grew humiliated. Without hitting a blow or being hit, he quit. 'I'm sorry,' he said. 'I really haven't done much boxing. I've read a lot about it. It looked much easier than it is,' and he held out his gloves to me and let me unlace them. I didn't feel sorry for him. He went back quickly to his billiard table.

The student's absurd intervention, adding to the general sense of humiliation, must have put Scott more on edge. He must have felt bewildered. Yet now my two friends began to behave splendidly. Not a word was said about the student. We were all suddenly polite, agreeable, friendly, and talkative. I knew how Scott felt; he had told me. He felt bitter, insulted, disillusioned in the sense that he had been made aware of an antagonism in Ernest. Only one thing could have saved him for Ernest. An apology. A restoration of respect, a lifting of the accusation. But Ernest had no intention of apologizing. He obviously saw no reason why he should. So we all behaved splendidly. We struck up a graceful camaraderie. Ernest was jovial with Scott. We were all jovial. We went out and walked up to the Falstaff. And no one watching us sitting at the bar could have imagined that Scott's pride had been shattered.

Yet he had some class, some real style there at the bar. I told Ernest that Scott agreed with me that the chapters of a novel I had started ought to be abandoned. I remember Ernest saying, 'There are two ways of looking at it. You can think of a career, and would it help your career to have it published? Or you can say to hell with a career and publish it anyway.' Scott said he was glad I wasn't going on with the book. As we exchanged opinions I noticed that two of the patrons, two young fellows at a nearby table, were craning their necks, listening and watching. And I laughed and said that by tomorrow word would go around the café that I, shamefully, was letting Fitzgerald and Hemingway tell me what to do about a book. Ernest said, 'What do you care? We're professionals. We only care whether the thing is as good as it should be.' And again, as I say, anyone watching would have believed that we were three writers talking about a literary problem. No one could have imagined anything had happened that could be heartbreaking. Well, I had come a long way to have my two friends get together with me, and here they were.

THAT SUMMER IN PARIS

Bliss Carman

BLISS CARMAN was a voluminous author of lyrical verse and prose essays who achieved considerable fame and popularity both inside and outside Canada early in the century. A cousin of Charles G.D. Roberts, he was born in Fredericton, N.B., and educated at the Fredericton Collegiate School and the University of New Brunswick. He also took some courses at Edinburgh and Harvard Universities; it was while he was at Harvard that he seriously began to write poetry. He moved to New York in 1890 and worked for ten years as a journalist without settling down to a regular job or in a permanent home (he often stayed with friends). He never returned to Canada to live, though he visited frequently and in 1925 was elected a corresponding member of the Royal Society of Canada, which also awarded him their Lorne Pierce Medal for distinguished service to literature. In 1897 Carman began a friendship with Mary Perry King and her husband, and in 1908, to be near the Kings, he went to live in New Canaan, Connecticut. It was there that he died. The Poetry Society of America honoured him posthumously with a medal.

Carman's reputation was inflated, but even though his poetry is not widely read or much admired today, his name is still well known. It stands for romantic landscape poems that are notable for their word music, haunting atmosphere, and melodic, soulful expressions of grief or rapture that all too often lapse into vagueness and monotony. Carman used details of nature impressionistically and symbolically—not precisely and realistically as Roberts and Lampman did. While Roberts in his best poems 'kept his feet solidly on earth', in the words of A.J.M. Smith, 'Carman soared, or tried to soar, into the "intense inane".' Relying on 'inspiration' and hardly at all on craftsmanship, Carman's poetic outpouring evokes admiration today only for a few stanzas here, a line or two there, and a handful of complete poems, of which 'Low Tide on Grand Pré' is one. This is the title poem of Carman's first collection, published in 1893. Other books of poetry that he published in his prime (he published collections until the year he died) are a series of three *Songs of Vagabondia* (1894, 1896, 1901), *Sappho: One Hundred Lyrics* (1904), and *The Pipes of Pan*

(1906). Carman was the editor of the 1927 edition of *The Oxford Book of American Verse*. There is a study of Bliss Carman by Donald Stephens in the Twayne World Authors Series (Burns & MacEachern),

A selection of Carman's poetry is in *Poets of the Confederation* (1960) edited by Malcolm Ross for the New Canadian Library.

LOW TIDE ON GRAND PRÉ

The sun goes down, and over all
　　These barren reaches by the tide
Such unelusive glories fall,
　　I almost dream they yet will bide
　　Until the coming of the tide.

And yet I know that not for us,
　　By any ecstasy of dream,
He lingers to keep luminous
　　A little while the grievous stream,
　　Which frets, uncomforted of dream—

A grievous stream, that to and fro
　　Athrough the fields of Acadie
Goes wandering, as if to know
　　Why one beloved face should be
　　So long from home and Acadie.

Was it a year or lives ago
　　We took the grasses in our hands,
And caught the summer flying low
　　Over the waving meadow lands,
　　And held it there between our hands?

The while the river at our feet—
　　A drowsy inland meadow stream—
At set of sun the after-heat
　　Made running gold, and in the gleam
　　We freed our birch upon the stream.

There down along the elms at dusk
　　We lifted dripping blade to drift,
Through twilight scented fine like musk,
　　Where night and gloom awhile uplift,
　　Nor sunder soul and soul adrift.

And that we took into our hands
   Spirit of life or subtler thing–
Breathed on us there, and loosed the bands
   Of death, and taught us, whispering,
   The secret of some wonder-thing.

Then all your face grew light, and seemed
   To hold the shadow of the sun;
The evening faltered, and I deemed
   That time was ripe, and years had done
   Their wheeling underneath the sun.

So all desire and all regret,
   And fear and memory, were naught;
One to remember or forget
   The keen delight our hands had caught;
   Morrow and yesterday were naught.

The night has fallen, and the tide . . .
   Now and again comes drifting home,
Across these aching barrens wide,
   A sigh like driven wind or foam:
   In grief the flood is bursting home.

Emily Carr

One of Canada's most powerful painters, EMILY CARR was also a natural writer whose autobiographical sketches and journals, published in seven books, have given her an assured place in Canadian literature. She was born in Victoria, B.C. At eighteen she went to San Francisco where she attended the School of Art for five years. She then taught painting for four years in Victoria before going to England to study. When she returned in 1904 she made several trips to west-coast Indian villages and became interested in the life of the people. (On her visits to the North Vancouver Indians she made a close friend of Sophie, whom she describes below.) To explore the new methods of painting so that she could better interpret the spirit of the untamed wilderness of British Columbia, she studied in France in 1910-11; two of her paintings were hung in an important Paris art show, the Salon d'Automne, in 1911. Victoria was an extremely unsympathetic place for an original and energetic painter like Emily Carr. The bold colours and aggressive brushstrokes that characterized her work since her return from Europe, and her 'new' way of look-ing at things, made people laugh and dismiss her as an eccentric. After 1913 she more or less gave up painting for fifteen years in order to earn a living, turning to such activities as fruit-growing, hen and rabbit raising, dog breeding, and running a ladies' boarding house, which she called 'the House of All Sorts'. She found comfort in her large collection of pets and in annual summer sketching trips to Indian villages on the Queen Charlotte Islands and the mainland.

A turning-point in her life came in 1927 when an exhibition of west-coast art brought her to national attention. She went east for the opening and was warmed and encouraged by the many people who appreciated what she was doing. She discovered the work of the Group of Seven. ('Oh, these men, this Group of Seven,' she wrote, 'what have they created? A world stripped of earthiness, shorn of fretting details, purged, purified.') When she returned home she entered on the most prolific phase of her career, visiting the Queen Charlottes on a sketching expedition (under great physical difficulties) in 1928 and, in a large van she purchased in 1933, venturing deep into the forest, painting day and night. In the remaining years of her life, when there was growing recognition of her art, her creative work included writing.

Her first book, *Klee Wyck*, was published in 1941, a few days before she was seventy. It is a series of tales and sketches of the west-coast Indians, and the title, meaning 'the laughing one', is the name they gave her. A great popular success, it was also the winner of a Governor General's Award. Emily Carr's other books are *The Book of Small* (1942), *The House of All Sorts* (1944), and four books published posthumously: *Growing Pains* (1946), *The Heart of a Peacock* (1953), *Pause: A Sketch Book* (1953), and *Hundreds and Thousands: The Journals of Emily Carr* (1966).

Emily Carr had her own way of seeing things as a painter and could transfer the spirit of a subject to canvas so that it is recognized and accepted unquestioningly by the viewer, whose impressions of the B.C. forest, for instance, are ever after shaped by the imaginative vision of this painter. She also had her own effective way with words. Her writing style is informal, fresh, lively, and precise. The telling details of her descriptions, her irresistible stories, and above all Emily Carr herself—indomitable, caustic, humorous, and loving—remain indelibly in the reader's mind.

Klee Wyck, *The Book of Small*, *The House of All Sorts*, and *Growing Pains* are all available in Clarke Irwin's Canadian Paperbacks series.

SOPHIE

Sophie's house was bare but clean. It had three rooms. Later when it got cold Sophie's Frank would cut out all the partition walls. Sophie said, 'Thlee 'loom, thlee stobe. One 'loom, one stobe.' The floor of the house was clean scrubbed. It was chair, table, and bed for the family. There was one chair; the coal-oil lamp sat on that. Sophie pushed the babies into corners, spread my old clothes on the floor to appraise them, and was satisfied. So, having tested each other's trade-straightedness, we began a long, long friendship—forty years. I have seen Sophie glad, sad, sick, and drunk. I have asked her why she did this or that thing—Indian ways that I did not understand—her answer was invariably, 'Nice ladies always do.' That was Sophie's ideal—being nice.

Every year Sophie had a new baby. Almost every year she buried one. Her little graves were dotted all over the cemetery. I never knew more than three of her twenty-one children to be alive at one time. By the time she was in her early fifties every child was dead and Sophie had cried her eyes dry. Then she took to drink.

'I got a new baby! I got a new baby!'

Sophie, seated on the floor of her house, saw me coming through the open door and waved the papoose cradle. Two little girls rolled round on the floor; the new baby was near her in a basket-cradle. Sophie took off the cloth tented over the basket and exhibited the baby, a lean, poor thing.

Sophie herself was small and spare. Her black hair sprang thick and strong on each side of the clean, straight parting and hung in twin braids across her shoulders. Her eyes were sad and heavy-lidded. Between prominent rounded cheekbones her nose lay rather flat, broadening and snubby at the tip. Her wide upper lip pouted. It was sharp-edged, puckering over a row of poor teeth—the soothing pucker of lips trying to ease an aching tooth or to hush a crying child. She had a soft little body, a back straight as honesty itself, and the small hands and feet of an Indian.

Sophie's English was good enough, but when Frank, her husband, was there she became dumb as a plate.

'Why won't you talk before Frank, Sophie?'

'Frank he learn school English. Me, no. Frank laugh my English words.'

When we were alone she chattered to me like a sparrow.

In May, when the village was white with cherry blossom and the blue water of Burrard Inlet crept almost to Sophie's door—just a streak of grey sand and a plank walk between—and when Vancouver city was more beautiful to look at across the water than to be in—it was then I loved to take the ferry to the North Shore and go to Sophie's.

Behind the village stood mountains topped by the grand old 'Lions', twin peaks, very white and blue. The nearer mountains were every shade of young foliage, tender grey-green, getting greener and greener till, when they were close, you saw that the village grass outgreened them all. Hens strutted their broods, papooses and pups and kittens rolled everywhere–it was good indeed to spend a day on the Reserve in spring.

Sophie and I went to see her babies' graves first. Sophie took her best plaid skirt, the one that had three rows of velvet ribbon round the hem, from a nail on the wall, and bound a yellow silk handkerchief round her head. No matter what the weather, she always wore her great shawl, clamping it down with her arms, the fringe trickling over her fingers. Sophie wore her shoes when she walked with me, if she remembered.

Across the water we could see the city. The Indian Reserve was a different world–no hurry, no business.

We walked over the twisty, up-and-down road to the cemetery. Casamin, Tommy, George, Rosie, Maria, Emily, and all the rest were there under a tangle of vines. We rambled, seeking out Sophie's graves. Some had little wooden crosses, some had stones. Two babies lay outside the cemetery fence: they had not faced life long enough for baptism.

'See! Me got stone for Rosie now.'

'It looks very nice. It must have cost lots of money, Sophie.'

'Grave man make cheap for me. He say, "You got lots, lots stone from me, Sophie. Maybe bymby you get some more died baby, then you want more stone. So I make cheap for you." '

Sophie's kitchen was crammed with excited women. They had come to see Sophie's brand-new twins. Sophie was on a mattress beside the cook stove. The twin girls were in small basket papoose cradles, woven by Sophie herself. The babies were wrapped in cotton wool which made their dark little faces look darker; they were laced into their baskets and stuck up at the edge of Sophie's mattress beside the kitchen stove. Their brown wrinkled faces were like potatoes baked in their jackets, their hands no bigger than brown spiders.

They were thrilling, those very very tiny babies. Everybody was excited over them. I sat down on the floor close to Sophie.

'Sophie, if the baby was a girl it was to have my name. There are two babies and I have only one name. What are we going to do about it?'

'The biggest and best is yours,' said Sophie.

My Em'ly lived three months. Sophie's Maria lived three weeks. I bought Em'ly's tombstone. Sophie bought Maria's.

There was a black skirt spread over the top of the packing-case in the centre of Sophie's room. On it stood the small white coffin. A lighted candle was at the head, another at the foot. The little dead girl in the coffin held a doll in her arms. It had hardly been out of them since I had taken it to her a week before. The glassy eyes of the doll stared out of the coffin, up past the closed eyelids of the child.

Though Sophie had been through this nineteen times before, the twentieth time was no easier. Her two friends, Susan and Sara, were there by the coffin, crying for her.

The outer door opened and half a dozen women came in, their shawls drawn low across their foreheads, their faces grim. They stepped over to the coffin and looked in. Then they sat round it on the floor and began to cry, first with baby whimpers, softly, then louder, louder still—with violence and strong howling: torrents of tears burst from their eyes and rolled down their cheeks. Sophie and Sara and Susan did it too. It sounded horrible—like tortured dogs.

Suddenly they stopped. Sophie went to her bucket and got water in a tin basin. She took a towel in her hand and went to each of the guests in turn holding the basin while they washed their faces and dried them on the towel. Then the women all went out but Sophie, Sara, and Susan. This crying had gone on at intervals for three days—ever since the child had

died. Sophie was worn out. There had been too all the long weeks of Rosie's tubercular dying to go through.

'Sophie, couldn't you lie down and rest?'

She shook her head. 'Nobody sleep in Injun house till dead people go to cemet'ry.'

The beds had all been taken away.

'When is the funeral?'

'I dunno, Pliest go Vancouver. He not come two more day. 'Spose I gots lots money he come quick. No hully up, except fo' money.'

She laid her hand on the corner of the little coffin.

'See! Coffin-man think box fo' Injun baby no matter.'

The seams of the cheap little coffin had burst.

Sophie's other neighbour, Susan, produced and buried babies almost as fast as Sophie herself. The two women laughed for each other and cried for each other. With babies on their backs and baskets on their arms they crossed over on the ferry to Vancouver and sold their baskets from door to door. When they came to my studio they rested and drank tea with me. My parrot, sheep dog, the white rats, and the totem pole pictures all interested them. 'An' you got Injun flowers too,' said Susan.

'Indian flowers?'

She pointed to ferns and wild things I had brought in from the woods.

Sophie's house was shut up. There was a chain and padlock on the gate. I went to Susan.

'Where is Sophie?'

'Sophie in sick house. Got sick eye.'

I went to the hospital. The little Indian ward had four beds. I took ice cream and the nurse divided it into four portions.

A homesick little Indian girl cried in the bed in one corner, an old woman grumbled in another. In a third there was a young mother with a baby, and in the fourth bed was Sophie.

There were flowers. The room was bright. It seemed to me that the four brown faces on the four white pillows should be happier and far more comfortable here than lying on mattresses on the hard floors in the village, with all the family muddle going on about them.

'How nice it is here, Sophie.'

'Not much good of hospital, Em'ly.'

Oh! What is the matter with it?'

'Bad bed.'

'What is wrong with the beds?'

'Move, move, all time shake. 'Spose me move, bed move too.'

She rolled herself to show me how the springs worked. 'Me ole'-fashioned, Em'ly. Me like kitchen floor fo' sick.'

Susan and Sophie were in my kitchen, rocking their sorrows back and forth and alternately wagging their heads and giggling with shut eyes at some small joke.

'You go live Victoria now, Em'ly,' wailed Sophie, 'and we never see those babies, never!'

Neither woman had a baby on her back these days. But each had a little new grave in the cemetery. I had told them about a friend's twin babies. I went to the telephone.

'Mrs Dingle, you said I might bring Sophie to see the twins?'

'Surely, any time,' came the ready reply.

'Come, Sophie and Susan, we can go and see the babies now.'

The mothers of all those little cemetery mounds stood looking and looking at the thriving white babies, kicking and sprawling on their bed. The women said, 'Oh my! Oh my!' over and over.

Susan's hand crept from beneath her shawl to touch a baby's leg. Sophie's hand shot out and slapped Susan's.

The mother of the babies said, 'It's all right, Susan; you may touch my baby.'

Sophie's eyes burned Susan for daring to do what she so longed to do herself. She folded her hands resolutely under her shawl and whispered to me:

'Nice ladies don' touch, Em'ly.'

KLEE WYCK

b. 1937

Roch Carrier

The talented Québécois writer ROCH CARRIER has had an enthusiastic reception in English-speaking Canada partly because his novels in translation, which seem to be an authentic expression of his society, are more lively and entertaining in outlook and style than the work of some of his contemporaries. He was born in the village of St-Justin-de-Dorchester, Qué. He graduated from the Université de Montréal in classics and taught for two years at the Collège de Saint Louis in Edmunston, N.B., before continuing his studies at the Sorbonne in Paris. He is now resident dramatist with the Théâtre du Nouveau Monde in Montreal.

Three of Carrier's novels have been translated into English. *La Guerre, Yes Sir!* (1970) is a comic though at times nightmarish description of how the Second World War intruded on an isolated Québec village when a village boy killed in the war is brought home for burial by English soldiers. *Floralie, Where are You?* (1971) moves back thirty years in time but is connected through its characters with the earlier novel; it again is both a nightmare and a comic tale about religion and sex in an earlier stage

in the development of Québec society. In the third book of the trilogy, *Is It The Sun, Philibert?* (1972), from which an extract follows, the time is now and the setting is Montreal. In an interview with Donald Cameron, Carrier describes this novel as 'the story of many many many Québécois who came to Montreal. The work here was English and they were French *paysans*; the work here was technical and they were badly prepared for it. It was a drama for them which has an influence on what is happening now.' In the preface to this book, Carrier's translator, Sheila Fischman, writes that 'Carrier sees this account of one not untypical life as representative of what he calls the last third of Québec's dark ages . . . Its ambiguous conclusion and title are suggestive of many more questions, not just for Philibert but for all the "petits Canadiens français"—and for the Québécois as well as for the *Anglais, maudits* or otherwise.'

Roch Carrier is also the author of two collections of short stories, *Jolis Deuils* (1964) and *Contes pour Mille Oreilles* (1969), and of a dramatic version of *La Guerre, Yes Sir!*.This was staged in both French and English versions in Montreal and was presented (in English) at the Stratford Festival, in a production directed by Jean Gascon, during the summer of 1972.

In an essay in Issue 4 of *Ellipse* (Summer 1970), Georges-V. Fournier says that Carrier's fiction 'constitutes a milestone: for perhaps the first time an author is dealing with the past and present reality of Québec without falling into either of the twin pitfalls: idealization of his subjects or their depiction as poor wretches. In addition to this, his novels are of rare quality. We find in them a marvellous blend of art and realism in which social judgements do not override aesthetic qualities but rather give them vigour and life, and all this with a discretion and balance equalled only by the author's superb and measured humour.'

The interview with Carrier referred to above is in Donald Cameron's *Conversations with Canadian Novelists* (1972). *La Guerre, Yes Sir!, Floralie, Where Are You?,* and *Is It The Sun, Philibert?* are all available in paperback from the House of Anansi.

THE WOMAN WHO CHANGED HIS LIFE

There was a shovel stuck in the snow. He picked it up, slung it over his shoulder and took off. He ran among the men and women who were walking along with their heads in their scarves. Farther away, much farther, he stopped. He began to clear the sidewalk that led up to one of the houses, heaving big shovelfuls of snow. The snow wasn't muddy here. It was a white powder, where children could slide and roll and go to sleep. They could eat it or hide in it. But Philibert didn't see any children. The snow had a smell that was carried to his face by the wind. It was the smell of ashes. When he had finished digging the passage through the snow he would ask for what he had coming to him and go and find something to eat. There was a strength in his arms that would never have come to him if his father had asked him for help. Each shovelful of snow that he moved from the front of this house was as important as one of his heartbeats.

Then at last the path was cleared. The sidewalk looked nicely grey at the bottom of the trench he had cut through the snow.

He hesitated before the big oak door. But he was hungry.

A light was turned on behind the square of opaque glass. The door was opened part way. Philibert pushed. The round head of a little old man shone in the doorway.

'Shovel your walk for a quarter,' said Philibert, holding out his hand.

'No beggars.' In English.

He was pushed back by the heavy door. He hadn't understood a word the old man muttered.

'Vieux Christ! If you drop dead it won't be me that buries you.'

With his shovel and his feet he put back all the snow he had removed from the sidewalk.

How much longer would he have to carry around that fiery stone in his belly?

In front of the neighbouring house he set to once more, attacking the accumulated snow. The sidewalk was long; the house was set back a long way from the street. In summer, when the leaves had not all been devoured by winter, the house must be hidden in whispering green music.

The shovelled walk looked like a very clean rug laid down over the white snow. When he knocked at the door he sensed someone moving behind it, but it wasn't opened. It was as still as a stone wall. He waited some more, then went away without throwing the snow back onto the clean sidewalk.

A little farther on, Philibert dug another path. His jacket was as wet as though it were raining, but his sweat turned to ice and he could feel the cold stiff weight of the wool against his back. He knocked at the door. A dog growled. He waited. No one came and the dog growled again.

Philibert threw his shovel as far as he could. He was hungry. Who would give him something to eat? He would steal, he would rob somebody. But before he did that he would try to earn a few cents. His father used to say, 'It's easier to earn the first cent than the first million.' Philibert had no desire to be rich. He just wanted to be able to eat. He went back to look for his shovel, stuck in the snow. His boots were filled with water from the snow melting around his icy ankles.

Would he have to clean the snow off all the streets in Montreal before he found something to eat? Philibert pushed his shovel into the snow, lifted the fragile blocks which the wind blew into flakes, and threw them as far as he could. The shovel made a small rough noise as it sank in, then leaped out like an animal that bit at the snow and leaped and bit and leaped along with the sighs that came from Philibert's chest. And then the walk was clean. Philibert rushed to knock at the door. It opened.

'No. No. Sorry.' In English again.

The door was shut in his face, like a slap. He wanted to cry. But where could he stop to cry? What could he lean against to let the tears pour out until all the sorrow had been drained from his body?

He was hungry.

In this part of town there wasn't even any garbage lying around. There weren't even any frozen crusts thrown out on the snow for the birds. He looked around for cigarette butts, but these people were very clean and Philibert couldn't put off his hunger by chewing tobacco.

The street stretched out ahead of him; it walked too, just like him. The

wall of silent houses appeared on only one side now. On the other side, behind the pillars of some naked trees, a snowy deserted park stretched out. The shovel on his shoulder, Philibert crossed the street where cars moved along very politely. He climbed over the iron fence. The ice in his clothes no longer tormented him. He smiled. For the moment his hunger was asleep in his belly. Playing in the snow like a child he started to write: with a surge of joy, laughing wildly, with a strength that would sear the concrete, Philibert stamped in the snow as hard as he could, spelling out letters, words, a whole sentence that stretched from one end of the park to the other, as though it were a white page. Then he jumped over the fence and into the street.

And behind the shadow of a window, an old lady with a string of pearls around her neck read in the snow words she could not understand. They said: YOU HAVE AN ASSHOLE INSTEAD OF A HEART.

* * *

Suddenly the door in front of him was open. He didn't dare take a step. But the door stayed open. He moved one foot forward, one back. He barely moved at all. The door stayed open and the lady standing in the doorway spoke to him. He didn't understand her.

'If you talked French like everybody else maybe I'd know what you were saying.'

'Oh! Poor boy. You don't speak English . . . Are you an Italian?'

And her strange accent made it sound like 'an Italienne', an Italian girl. Philibert looked at her, bewildered.

'An Italian girl? *Baptême* no, I ain't an Italian girl. That's the most insulting thing I ever heard.' Philibert turned, intending to leave.

The lady put her hand on his arm. He was a dirty, smelly little tramp with drops of ice on his face, but she could not let him go without helping him. His eyes were red and sunk deep in their sockets from exhaustion. He was so pale and his clothes looked so big for him.

God is cruel indeed, thought the lady, if he tosses these poor abandoned dogs into the streets of Montreal. Their parents must be unspeakable if they let their children run away so young instead of making a fuss over them. These children were too young to know life's hardships. This young man, for example: had he eaten today? And he couldn't even speak English. What a pity! These immigrants should learn the language before they set off for Canada. Could he be Yugoslavian, or perhaps Hungarian?

She looked at the young man at her door, pitiful as he was, but she saw only her son. He had been the same age when he left, laughing, his dufflebag over his shoulder.

'Don't expect me home for supper, Mom!' he had said. He left with the Royal Air Force. He did not come back. But his death had contributed to the liberation of Europe. He had not died in vain.

The lady's eyes, fixed on him, reminded Philibert of his mother's. She had often looked at him with her eyes full of all kinds of things she seemed to see around him.

'Come in!'

As he did not understand she took away his shovel and leaned it against a wall, then, taking his arm, she led him down a long hallway that went into the kitchen. She pushed him towards the table and pointed to a chair. Philibert snatched a bun out of a basket. She poured him some tea. Philibert took another bun and shoved the whole thing into his mouth. The lady burst out laughing.

'You goddamn woman, if you're going to laugh at me I'm taking everything I can eat and getting the hell out. So long!'

The lady held him back with one hand on his shoulder. She said something to him; he could tell from the tone of her voice that she was not making fun of him. He swallowed his cup of tea in one gulp. She poured him another and brought more buns. Philibert enjoyed the sensation of the moist chewy paste in his mouth. The lady laughed as she spoke some more incomprehensible words. He replied 'Yes sir,' to everything she said. He didn't know any other English words. She laughed, but without making any sound. She only opened her lips. She seemed to be afraid of laughing. Philibert wanted to say something dirty, four or five oaths that would rear up in the kitchen like great bears. But she wouldn't understand them so he kept quiet. Beneath the embroidery of her dressing-gown her large bosom seemed to have been carved from warm stone.

He was still hungry when the basket was empty but the lady did not notice. How could he ask for more buns and make himself understood?

'Yum yum! Yes sir!'

The lady puffed out her cheeks and her eyes sparkled behind the narrow slit of her eyelids. She poured him some tea which he drank, forgetting that he would have preferred to eat.

'Poor child . . .'

She was saying words he did not understand.

'Yes sir,' he replied.

The lady guided him towards another room and opened the door. It was a bathroom like the ones he had seen in the newspaper. Turning the taps at random he felt a rush of cold water on his shoulder. He yelled with surprise. The lady called from the other side of the door. His jacket was all wet and the bathtub was full to the brim. He turned off the tap, undressed, stepped back, sprang forward and jumped in, just the way he used to jump into the Famine River.

The lady was knocking frantically on the other side of the door.

'Don't bust it down, you old bag,' shouted Philibert. 'Yes sir!'

The lady came in carrying a pile of folded towels under her arm. She put them on the floor one by one to soak up the water, rubbing them around with her feet, but she kept one in her hands. This towel, a blue one, she unfolded and wrapped around Philibert's shoulders. He was enveloped in a gentle fire, spread over his back by a soft hand. Suddenly his sex began to beat its wings. Philibert hunched over, his hands holding back the impatient bird. On her knees by Philibert, the lady dried his back, his chest, with motherly attention. Philibert wanted to hide his nakedness behind a wall. He grabbed the shower curtain, pulled it towards him and draped himself in it. The lady stepped back a few feet and looked at him with such tenderness that he felt something stinging behind his eyelids. He buried his head in the curtain. When he looked up again he saw the lady's hand gently opening her bodice, unbuttoning her dressing-gown all the way, then pulling it off first one shoulder then the other. The bathtub seemed as deep as the sea. At the sight of this woman's body Philibert knew he had nothing more to learn in life.

Between her perfumed, embroidered sheets, where she no longer looked like an old woman, sheets softer than her hands on his body, Philibert wept like a child without knowing why. And when the male strength swelled his body to bursting, he let out a cry like a new-born baby.

Then he went out into the street without looking back. The air had that clear scent that he attributed to the woman of his dreams, before he knew that women sweat when they love.

*   *   *

It had snowed during the night. Why did he not notice when he first looked at her that the woman was so beautiful? He decided to go back and clean the walk in front of her house. She would see him, open the door for him and give him tea and buns and perhaps a little money. She had already given him some clothes, but unfortunately her miserly husband hadn't left anything in the pockets. The overcoat wasn't new but it looked as if it had been made for Philibert, who seemed to have his fortune made already. The lady was so rich. He would explain to her that he couldn't spend the rest of his life sleeping in churches, on a bench near the organ. His story would make her sad. No. She wouldn't understand a word of it, but she would invite him into her bed and they would laugh a lot as they ran around the house, her naked as Eve in Paradise, him wearing her husband's pyjamas. He would take his pipe today.

The city shouldn't have been called Montreal. It should have been called Bonheur. Happiness.

He grabbed a shovel that had been left in the snow near the sidewalk.

His shovel on his shoulder, he was happy, dancing as he went off in the direction of the sweet lady's house.

The streets ran right across the city, stretched out, crossed one another, made knots, formed letters that could only be deciphered from the sky, proliferated like jungle vines.

All at once a street had moved imperceptibly, another had twisted, trembling gently, and it seemed to Philibert that the immense hand of the city was closing up. He would be crushed between these streets that looked so much alike, with their names that all sounded the same and their uniform houses.

He had no idea where to find the house of the woman who had changed his life.

IS IT THE SUN, PHILIBERT?
Translated by Sheila Fischman

Eugène Cloutier

EUGENE CLOUTIER was born in Sherbrooke, Qué., and educated at Université Laval and the Sorbonne in Paris. He was a newspaper journalist for three years but since the age of twenty-five has devoted himself to writing radio and television plays, novels, and travel books. He lives in Montreal with his wife and daughter.

Cloutier has written three novels—*Les Témoins* (1953), *Les Inutiles* (1956), and *Croisière* (1964)—and two plays: *Le Dernier beatnik* and *Hotel Hilton, Peking*. Among his travel books he has written

eleven (so far) in a series: *Eugène Cloutier à Cuba, . . . en Suede, . . . en Californie* etc. *Le Canada sans passeport* (2 vols, 1967) was abridged and translated by Joyce Marshall and published as *No Passport: A Discovery of Canada* in 1968. It is perhaps the best travel book on Canada. The extracts below reveal some of Cloutier's notable qualities as a travel writer—his sensitivity, tolerance, humour, openness to new experiences, and graceful anecdotal style.

IN THE LAND OF EVANGELINE

NOT GUILTY

They do not know it, they do it without the least provocation, even with great innocence, but it is the English that sell 'Evangeline' at Grand-Pré and in the entire region made celebrated by the Expulsion of the Acadians. And this strikes your heart curiously. I should not be any happier to be offered Evangeline by the descendants of the deported. The commercial exploitation of great and small misfortunes has always made me shiver a little. I must reason at odds with others, for I see that this tradition is firmly planted in all latitudes. At Pompeii I was sold Vesuvius and at Tinos Miraculous Virgins. But let us acknowledge that at Grand-Pré, out of season at least, there is a certain discretion about it all. And apart from the eternal and frightful souvenir shop, which is practically its entrance door, you can invoke memories of Evangeline at your ease in the little Grand-Pré Park.

Many Acadians returned, but considerably to the south, spreading their villages in a line towards Yarmouth along a coast that everyone, the Acadians themselves first, calls pleasantly 'French coast'. For the moment we are in the land of Evangeline in the smiling Grand-Pré valley. It is true that Longfellow's heroine never existed, but her face and her beautiful love story are indissociable from the tragic expulsion of 1755 and perhaps correspond to more living realities than all those evoked by grave and angry historians. There were very certainly a great many Evangelines. There still are. I met several of them.

I MET EVANGELINE

I remember one of them. She was twenty-two, pretty and frail-looking with great sea-coloured eyes. A princess. I see her still in her white diner. She was selling an infinite variety of ice-cream dishes. I had driven until too late. In this corner of Nova Scotia I would not find a restaurant open at nine o'clock in the evening. So as I had not eaten, I ordered an enormous concoction, filled with ice cream and milk and vanilla essence, and I talked for a long time with Evangeline.

Standing at a counter by the side of the highway, in a terrifying silence, broken only by the sound of the waves that could be sensed nearby, in a low-ceilinged night pierced only by the weak glow that came from within the diner, Evangeline told me her new tragedy. And it, too, was a love story. Here was an exquisite person better endowed at the outset than was needed for a real woman's career in a more evolved society. Born on the 'French coast', she had remained a child of the sea. It had never occurred to her to go to a city in the interior. There she would die of loneliness. Each year she watched the approach of the long winter with unutterable dread, but it was possible to believe that she needed this provocation. Each time she took stock of herself as she awaited the return of the summer sun. She was well acquainted with the festival of spring on the sea and in the meadows. But she had just made a terrible discovery. Till now she had only dreamed her life. Two years ago she had entered her twenties, she would be thirty in a few years, and she shivered at the thought. At thirty, here, women are already aged and solitary. I felt a panic within her that many women of fifty have not yet known in our big cities.

Languishing Evangeline, at certain moments you sighed in a way I know well, sighs that seemed to tell of an imprisoned and burdensome love. You told me everything and you must have regretted it later. One does not say such things to a passing stranger. I was following my trade, which was to listen to you. But I could have said to you, 'Stop . . . I will continue,' for you were reliving Evangeline's long search. You will seek him everywhere and at last you will wonder if he ever existed. You will forget the colour of his eyes, the shape of his face. He will melt into the phantoms of your subconscious.

You were able to smile again for a moment as you said, 'You know . . . the young people know how to entertain themselves here, sometimes.' But you did not see the expression in your eyes at that instant. It still follows me. You had the eyes of Vulcan, sweet Evangeline, eyes that accused your early family environment, your convent school, your country, and the whole world. I too became suddenly suspect, and you enclosed yourself in your interior universe, seated yourself a short distance away, and turned the dial of a transistor.

After an endless silence you said suddenly, 'The worst thing is that we don't know either English or French.' You did indeed speak French with an accent I had never heard, made up of a succession of uneven sounds, at times outrageous, almost inhuman, and at other times musical, gentle, and as moving as a confidence. Your remark struck me in the face like spray that leaves behind it the iodized scent of the sea.

This was my first real contact with the roughest Acadian accent, the one most deprived of a future now that French-language radio and television provide models daily. I had not even an instant's desire to smile. Those that make fun of your accent have understood nothing at all. In its own way it expresses your deep suffering and your isolation. You are right. You cannot speak either English or French correctly, you have been taught only to suffer in silence behind an artless smile. And you are not the only one, I have known others, many others along my way. And now that I have met you, I do not feel the least desire to remove the dust that covers Longfellow's *Evangeline* on one of the shelves of my library.

The Expulsion of the Acadians belongs to our childhood. It is one of the passages of our history that struck us most and that we found easiest to remember. The teacher's voice swelled at certain moments, he rolled his eyes, he became partisan. Strangely, or so at least I have been told, there is a great deal of pathos also in English schools in connection with what history has remembered under the title of 'the Expulsion of the Acadians', a pathos that often takes the same direction as ours. Why? Perhaps because in this tragic episode the Acadians provide perfect victims.

AND SUDDENLY FEAR

I decided to pick up one of those highway hitch-hikers so abundant in
Nova Scotia. They are generally itinerant workers. They have perhaps just
finished two months' work in the bush cutting Christmas trees and are on
their way back to Sydney or Halifax to hire on for something else. The
phenomenon is found all over America to varying degrees. Unskilled work
is very unstable and, whatever the city, several hundreds of workers are
constantly in search of higher wages. The nature of the work matters
little; they will accept it if the pay is good. Some of them live in trailers
with their families so they will always be free to better their lot. At Anti-
gonish, right in the centre of the little town, I had been able to visit a real
trailer village. It was neat and slicked up, with curtains at the windows,
fences, and little gardens. But it presents a strange picture even so, and
takes a little getting used to. I have seen such villages almost everywhere,
even in the mining towns of Abitibi.

In Nova Scotia one must add the chronic unemployment. Activity,
whether in the mines, in industry, or in commerce, is subject to such varia-
tions in the course of the year that day-labourers have no protection
against the caprices of production. Men are being let out at one place and
hired at another. For them it's a question of being at the right spot at the
right moment. And they learn the labour chart by a sort of underground.
They discover more by haunting the taverns than by reading the newspapers.

The man I had picked up belonged to this category. But it took me a
long time to find this out, for he never opened his mouth. If he had not
said 'Thank you' at the beginning, I might have believed he was a deaf-
mute. He looked like a decent fellow, but for the first half hour that we
drove along side by side he did not open his lips.

I had been looking for a companion for the road and I'd chanced upon
the sphinx. Bad luck. All this would have been nothing if I had not suddenly begun to feel afraid.

THE TROJAN WAR WILL NOT TAKE PLACE

You would not suspect it when you look at a map of Cape Breton, which
shows only its general aspect without indicating the network of roads,
but from Ingonish there are several different ways to go to Sydney. That
there should be even one seems rather an exploit. The land here is as full
of holes as a colander and is deeply penetratd by the sea. Arms of land
extend like the legs of a crab all around one of the biggest saltwater lakes
in the world, Bras d'Or. My companion claimed to know all the routes. I
could have gone directly to Sydney by a paved road; he interrupted his

silence for several seconds to direct me to side-roads, several of which turned into quagmires, amidst a setting like the end of the world. I had never seen such desolate landscapes.

My companion had sunk back into his silence, and I went on asking my questions to a tombstone. And then I in turn stopped talking. A troublesome idea brushed my mind; it returned, made a nest for itself somewhere in my head, as always happens when one isn't on watch, and now it was quite at home and scratched gently at the cells of my brain. For as far as I could see in my rearview mirror, there was nothing and no one. On the two sides of the road, there was no house, no human presence. We were the last human beings driving on an earth that had been abandoned to the fog and the rain.

I was not yet very frightened, but I was frightened. It seemed to me that my companion was not indifferent to this great solitude, that he had perhaps sought it. For he was a little more relaxed now that we had left the highway. And I observed how steadily he was scrutinizing the rearview mirror. He seemed to be passionately interested in the landscape by the road, though till now it had seemed of no importance to him. What was going on behind that filthy dirty face that had not been shaved for three days? I tried to resume conversation. I obtained only a sigh. His breath was uneven. He took a package of cigarettes from his pocket, tossed it unopened on the dashboard, immediately picked it up again, put it back in his pocket.

Why had I been so stupid as to put myself in such a situation? Why had I picked him up? Why him and not someone else? Why had I followed his road directions? Yes, there it was, one always believes that these things are only for others, that we have been granted a sort of immunity at our birth, that we will never ride in an ambulance, that we will never be face to face with a bandit, a criminal, a murderer, or even the most inexperienced of thieves. What should I do? Stop and force him to get out? He would take that badly. What grievances had I against him? But I would not be recounting this incident if I had not become certain during this trip at the end of the world that this man was seeking only the moment, and also the opportunity and the courage, to attack me—attack me stupidly as in a bad movie. I was frankly afraid, but I remained all the while lucid enough to examine my reasons for being afraid. They were countless and stemmed from an infinity of details that it would not be agreeable to describe. I know only that they were sufficient.

The play of circumstances chose that I should become quite well acquainted with my companion. And I learned then what he had lacked at the moment—the experience and, even more than that, the courage. He hadn't a cent in his pockets, he hadn't eaten for two days, he hadn't drunk a single glass of beer since the night before. At such moments courage is in direct proportion to the number of glasses of beer one has drunk.

The affair was cleared up around a restaurant table, to which I invited him when suddenly we found ourselves on a busy highway. There had been no calculation on my part, my hunger was as ravenous as his. It was only a little more recent. I watched him return to life, to conversation, to that friendliness that springs up sometimes between two strangers who know they will never really know one another. However amiable he gradually became, I could not forget that for an interminable half hour this man was on the point of being my attacker.

While we continued on our way to Sydney, he did his utmost to reply of his own accord to the questions I had given up asking him. I learned all about him, about his wandering existence and his constant search for work. We even discovered a number of common memories. He had once worked in the West at a ranch where I had stayed. The sphynx had become a very little mouse. He began to bore me.

At certain hours there is no solution: half the human race scares you, and the other half bores you.

NO PASSPORT: A DISCOVERY OF CANADA
Translated by Joyce Marshall

Leonard Cohen

LEONARD COHEN, who in the 1960s became a pop hero for his songs and his singing, is a poet and novelist whose books have achieved great popularity not only because of his public image but also because of the romantic vision of life they project and their ritualistic celebrations of love, loneliness, pain, and loss. He was born in Montreal and was educated at McGill University. His first book, *Let Us Compare Mythologies* (1956), published in the McGill Poetry Series, contains mainly poems written between the ages of fifteen and twenty. *The Spice-Box of Earth* (1961) was his first literary success; indeed it has become one of the most popular collections of poetry by a Canadian. Cohen is at his best as a lyric poet, and the sensual, though passionless, love lyrics in this book captivated readers. With a Canada Council grant he went to England where he wrote a poetic novel, *The Favourite Game* (1963). He continued to write abroad and acquired a house on the island of Hydra in Greece. (When he isn't on a concert tour he commutes between Hydra, New York, and Montreal.) Cohen's other books are *Flowers*

for Hitler (1964), containing political and social poems that have a strong element of surrealism, along with a clever one-act play called *The New Step; Parasites of Heaven* (1966), which includes songs and ballads that he later recorded in his highly successful albums *Songs of Leonard Cohen, Songs from a Room,* and *Songs of Love and Hate;* and *Selected Poems, 1956-1968* (1968), winner of a Governor General's Award, which Cohen declined, saying in a letter that 'the poems themselves forbid it absolutely'. His most recent collection is *The Energy of Slaves* (1972). The spiritual/erotic romanticism that is prominent in Cohen's writing reached its peak in a wild fantasy, *Beautiful Losers* (1966), described by Cohen as 'a great mad confessional prayer'. This novel has many things in common with his poetry: some of the same themes and obsessions—ugliness and evil as a source of beauty, the corruption of love, a mysticism of the flesh, sainthood—as well as exotic imagery, burlesque, unfeeling sexual comedy, and frequent outbursts of whimsy. It also contains passages of prose-poetry and 'concealed verse', as George Woodcock calls the poetic incantation 'God is Alive', reproduced below.

Michael Ondaatje has written of Cohen: 'He is a rich, excessive poet who uses, sometimes flaunts his Jewish heritage for all it's worth. His other main sources are himself as a literary and public lover, and his aesthetic views. In general, he is lyrical when dealing with himself, and anarchistic when he deals with the world outside. All these themes and subjects are controlled by a nimble mind which contains an incredible versatility of emotions.' Ondaatje's critical study of Cohen's books is in the Canadian Writers series of the New Canadian Library (1970). George Woodcock has included an excellent article on Cohen in his *Odysseus Ever Returning: Essays on Canadian Writers and Writing* (1970), also in the New Canadian Library.

THE ONLY TOURIST IN HAVANA
TURNS HIS THOUGHTS HOMEWARD

Come, my brothers,
let us govern Canada,
let us find our serious heads,
let us dump asbestos on the White House,
let us make the French talk English,
    not only here but everywhere,
let us torture the Senate individually
    until they confess,
let us purge the New Party,
let us encourage the dark races
    so they'll be lenient
    when they take over,
let us make the CBC talk English,
let us all lean in one direction
    and float down
    to the coast of Florida,
let us have tourism,
let us flirt with the enemy,
let us smelt pig-iron in our back yards,
let us sell snow
    to under-developed nations,
(Is it true one of our national leaders
    was a Roman Catholic?)
let us terrorize Alaska,

let us unite
    Church and State,
let us not take it lying down,
let us have two Governor Generals
    at the same time,
let us have another official language,
let us determine what it will be,
let us give a Canada Council Fellowship
    to the most original suggestion,
let us teach sex in the home
    to parents,
let us threaten to join the U.S.A.
    and pull out at the last moment,
my brothers, come,
our serious heads are waiting for us somewhere
    like Gladstone bags abandoned
    after a *coup d'état*,
let us put them on very quickly,
let us maintain a stony silence
    on the St Lawrence Seaway.

Havana
April 1961

GIFT

    You tell me that silence
is nearer to peace than poems
but if for my gift
I brought you silence
(for I know silence)
you would say
    This is not silence
this is another poem
and you would hand it back to me.

I HAVE NOT LINGERED IN
EUROPEAN MONASTERIES

I have not lingered in European monasteries
and discovered among the tall grasses tombs of knights
who fell as beautifully as their ballads tell;
I have not parted the grasses
or purposefully left them thatched.

I have not released my mind to wander and wait
in those great distances
between the snowy mountains and the fishermen,
like a moon,
or a shell beneath the moving water.

I have not held my breath
so that I might hear the breathing of God,
or tamed my heartbeat with an exercise,
or starved for visions.
Although I have watched him often
I have not become the heron,
leaving my body on the shore,
and I have not become the luminous trout,
leaving my body in the air.

I have not worshipped wounds and relics,
or combs of iron,
or bodies wrapped and burnt in scrolls.

I have not been unhappy for ten thousand years.
During the day I laugh and during the night I sleep.
My favourite cooks prepare my meals,
my body cleans and repairs itself,
and all my work goes well.

GOD IS ALIVE

God is alive. Magic is afoot. God is alive. Magic is afoot. God is afoot. Magic is alive. Alive is afoot. Magic never died. God never sickened. Many poor men lied. Many sick men lied. Magic never weakened. Magic never hid. Magic always ruled. God is afoot. God never died. God was ruler though his funeral lengthened. Though his mourners thickened Magic never fled. Though his shrouds were hoisted the naked God did live. Though his words were twisted the naked Magic thrived. Though his death was published round and round the world the heart did not believe. Many hurt men wondered. Many struck men bled. Magic never faltered. Magic always led. Many stones were rolled but God would not lie down. Many wild men lied. Many fat men listened. Though they offered stones Magic still was fed. Though they locked their coffers God was always served. Magic is afoot. God rules. Alive is afoot. Alive is in command. Many weak men hungered. Many strong men thrived. Though they boasted solitude God was at their side. Nor the dreamer in his cell, nor the captain on the hill. Magic is alive. Though his death was pardoned round and round the world the heart would not believe. Though laws were carved in marble they could not shelter men. Though altars built in parliaments they could not order men. Police arrested Magic and Magic went with them for Magic loves the hungry. But Magic would not tarry. It moves from arm to arm. It would not stay with them. Magic is afoot. It cannot come to harm. It rests in an empty palm. It spawns in an empty mind. But Magic is no instrument. Magic is the end. Many men drove Magic but Magic stayed behind. Many strong men lied. They only passed through Magic and out the other side. Many weak men lied. They came to God in secret and though they left him nourished they would not tell who healed. Though mountains danced before them they said that God was dead. Though his shrouds were hoisted the naked God did live. This I mean to whisper to my mind. This I mean to laugh with in my mind. This I mean my mind to serve till service is but Magic moving through the world, and mind itself is Magic coursing through the flesh, and flesh itself is Magic dancing on a clock, and time itself the Magic Length of God.

BEAUTIFUL LOSERS

b. 1936

John Robert Colombo

JOHN ROBERT COLOMBO has described himself as 'poet and editor-at-large'. He is also the most active creator of 'found' poetry in Canada, about which more later. He was born in Kitchener, Ont., and is a graduate of the University of Toronto. After doing editorial work for two Toronto publishers, in 1963 he became a free-lance book editor and has edited numerous books for McClelland & Stewart and other publishers. He is managing editor of *The Tamarack Review*; a contributor of poetry, reviews, and reportage to various other magazines; a writer of scripts for CBC radio; a lecturer at various colleges and universities; and a reader of his own poetry in places as widely dispersed as Penticton, B.C., New York, St John's, Nfld, and London, Eng.

In his collections of found poetry and literary collages Colombo displays the happy facility of making unexpected discoveries in writings of the past and presenting them as arresting entertainments. He has published two books of found poems, *The Mackenzie Poems* in 1965 (see below) and *John Toronto* (1969), based on writings of Bishop Strachan;

two literary collages, *The Great Wall of China* (1966) and *The Great San Francisco Earthquake and Fire* (1971); and two collections of his own verse, *Abracadabra* (1967) and *Neo Poems* (1970). He has also edited several anthologies.

The creator of a found poem recasts a piece of prose to reveal something poetic or ironic or otherwise unexpected to the modern reader. Colombo has described found poetry as a new way of looking at the past, 'not as it was but as it is today'. 'Why call someone else's prose, rearranged in a free-verse pattern, poetry?' he writes. 'Why not? The end result, not the ways and means, is the all-important thing.'

The first selection facing is from *The Mackenzie Poems*, 'found' in the prose of the Upper Canadian reformer William Lyon Mackenzie (1795-1861). (See page 295 for a note on Mackenzie.) The second is based on a letter by Norman Bethune (1890-1939), the Canadian doctor, a Communist, who became a legendary figure in Red China, where he practised as a surgeon and died.

IMMIGRANTS

Quebec,
April 22nd to 25th,
1831.
One forenoon
I went on board the ship
Airthy Castle,
from Bristol,
immediately after her arrival.
The passengers were in number 254,
all in the hold or steerage;
all English, from about Bristol,
Bath, Frome, Warminster, Maiden Bradley, &c.
I went below,
and truly it was a curious sight.
About 200 human beings,
male and female,
young, old, and middle-aged;
talking, singing, laughing, crying, eating, drinking,
        shaving, washing;
some naked in bed, and others dressing to go
        ashore;
handsome young women (perhaps some)
and ugly old men,
married and single;
religious and irreligious.
Here a grave matron
chaunting selections
from the latest edition
of the last new hymn book;
there, a brawny plough-boy
'pouring forth the sweet melody
of Robin Adair.'
These settlers were poor,
but in general
they were fine-looking people,
and such as I was glad
to see come to America.
They had had a fine passage
of about a month,
and they told me
that no more ship loads of settlers
would come from the same quarter
this year.

I found that it was
the intention of many of them
to come to Upper Canada.
Fortune may smile on some,
and frown on others;
but it is my opinion
that few among them will forget
being cooped up below deck
for four weeks
in a moveable bedroom,
with 250 such fellow-lodgers
as I have endeavoured to describe.

WILLIAM LYON MACKENZIE

LAST LETTER

Dear General Nieh:

I am fatally ill.
I am going to die.
I have some last favours
to ask of you.

Tell them I have
been happy here,
and my only regret
is that I shall not
be able to do more.

My two cots are for
you and Mrs Nieh.
My two pairs of English
shoes also go to you.

My riding boots and trousers
I should like to
give to General Lu.

Division Commander Ho
can select what he pleases
from among my things
as a memento from me.

I would like to give
a blanket each to
Shou, my attendant,
and Chang, my cook.

A pair of Japanese shoes
should also go to Shou.

We need 250 pounds of quinine
and 300 pounds of iron compounds
each year. These are for
the malaria and anemia patients.

Never buy medicine
in such cities as
Paoting,
Tientsin and
Peiping again.
The prices there
are twice as much
as in Shanghai
and Hong Kong.

Tell them I have been
very happy. My only regret
is that I shall now
be unable to do more.

The last two years
have been the most significant,
the most meaningful years
of my life. Sometimes it
has been lonely, but I have
found my highest fulfillment
here among my beloved comrades.

I have no strength now
to write more. . . . To you
and to all my comrades,
a thousand thanks.

NORMAN BETHUNE

Ralph Connor

RALPH CONNOR was the pseudonym of Charles William Gordon, a Presbyterian clergyman whose first novels, written at the turn of the century, gained enormous international sales, satisfying a contemporary taste for popular fiction that combined action, romance, lively local colour, and that celebrated Christian virtues. He was born in Glengarry County in eastern Ontario (then Canada West), which had been settled by people from the Highlands of Scotland. He was educated at the University of Toronto and Edinburgh University and was ordained into the Presbyterian ministry in 1890. He worked as a missionary in mining and lumber camps before becoming the minister of St Stephen's Church, then outside Winnipeg, in 1894. He remained in that post until his death. He served overseas during the First World War, becoming senior Protestant chaplain to the Canadian forces, with the rank of major, and after the war was active as a public speaker for various causes, as chairman of the Manitoba Council of Industry, and as moderator of the Presbyterian Church.

Connor's first novel, *Black Rock: The Tale of the Selkirks* (1898), grew out of three stories he wrote for a Presbyterian periodical, *Westminster Magazine*. Its reception indicated that he should continue to write fiction and he followed it with a succession of even more popular books: *The Sky Pilot: A Tale of the Foothills* (1899), *The Man from Glengarry: A Tale of the Ottawa* (1901), *Glengarry Schooldays: A Story of the Early Days in Glengarry* (1902), *The Foreigner: A Tale of Saskatchewan* (1909), and some twenty other novels. Connor had no pretensions as a writer, but he had certain natural skills: exciting narrative, vivid descriptions, lively characterizations, and strong emotion all flowed easily from his pen. His many readers at the end of the nineteenth century and later also took pleasure in his avowed intention of showing religion to be 'a synonym of all that is virile, straight, honorable and withal tender and gentle in true men and women. . . . I have received,' he wrote in his autobiography, 'hundreds of letters expressing gratitude for a novel that presented a quality of religious life that "red-blooded" men could enjoy.'

The Man from Glengarry is Connor's best novel and can still hold the attention because it is a vivid re-creation of life in the vanished forests of Glengarry County and of Highland pioneers in 'the fierce old days'—the decade of Confederation. In his autobiography, *Postscript to Adventure* (1938), from which the passage below is taken, Connor recalls the details of his Glengarry boyhood that made the strongest impression on him: the hardships and good times; the fearless Highland lumbermen, their religion and their fights (the clergyman-author writes proudly of 'the ancient lust of battle in our blood'); the 'heroines of the race', whom he delighted in glorifying. These things all found a prominent place in his novel, and the delight Connor took in re-creating them helped to imbue it with intensity, vividness, and warmth—qualities that go a long way towards offsetting the idealized characters and sentiments.

The Man from Glengarry is available in the New Canadian Library, with an introduction by S. Ross Beharriell. *Glengarry Schooldays* is the only other Connor novel still in print. There is an article on Connor's Glengarry by Roy Daniells in Issue 31 of *Canadian Literature* (Winter 1967).

GLENGARRY

Our Glengarry folk, as I have said, were mostly from the Highlands and Islands of Scotland. They were sturdy, industrious, patient, courageous. They cut their farms out of the forest, transforming the timber into houses with furniture for themselves and into stables and barns for their animals. Their only tools at first were the broadax, chopping ax, adze, saw, auger, hammer; their only nails were wooden pins. With these tools they built their very presentable and comfortable houses and steadings.

The clearing of the land was desperately hard work. I have often thought with admiration of the courage of a man who on reaching his lot of solid forest could drive his ax to the eye into the first tree of his first clearing. They learned by experience the need and the worth of co-operative work. After the standing forest had been cut down into a 'slashing', the neighbours came with their axes and oxen to make a bee and clean up the slashing, piling brush and logs for the burning, leaving only the stumps which later would be cut out or burnt out. So the fields were prepared for plow and harrow. Often as a boy I watched, with unconscious admiration, Big John Bawn McRae swing across a field, scattering handfuls of oats from a sheet slung round his shoulders. The implements for planting were plow, harrow, and hoe; for harvesting, scythe and cradle. I remember the first mowing machine brought into the settlement and the wonder and doubtful approval of the crowd of farmers gathered to see it work. The grain, in the early days before the wagons came in or while the fields were too rough for wagons, was hauled to the barn or the stacks on wooden sleds or stone boats drawn by oxen. Later in the winter it would be threshed on the barn floor with the flail and winnowed with the fork. It was all hard work, but the courage and endurance of these men never failed. They were building more than homes, and making more than farms. They were building and making a nation.

Their toil would be lightened with fun and frolic, for a bee drew together not only the men and boys for the work, but the women and girls as well. After the day's work games and athletic contests would follow, and later on there would be a grand supper and a dance to the fiddle or the pipes. In winter the older members of the community would be busy cutting, splitting, and hauling firewood of maple, beech, elm, birch, and for the kindling pine, spruce, and cedar. The younger men at the first freeze-up would be off to the shanties. The tales of the lumbermen in *The Man from Glengarry* are from real life. Often I rode to school on the big timber sticks, sixty feet long and more, which were being hauled to the Scotch River to be floated down to the Ottawa when the ice broke, and thence by the St Lawrence to Quebec for the British navy. A wild and colourful life was the lumberman's, full of danger and adventure, making the square timber, collecting the great sticks into rafts, breaking up jams, and running the rapids.

Gay and gallant youths were these young Highlanders, quick as a wild lynx on their feet, fearless to face the boiling waters, loving a fight for river rights or for the honour of their clan, generous with their hard-won pay to new friend or to wily pimp, gambler or harlot. But the Great Revival that swept Glengarry in the early sixties changed all that. My only memory of it is that someone lifted me high to see the gleam of the swaying torches through the dark bush that lit the steps of men, women, boys, and girls making their way round bogholes to the new brick church at the nineteenth concession. The mighty sweeping of that religious upheaval tamed the fighting, drinking, lusting Glengarry men into the finest rivermen that plied their adventurous trade on the Ottawa and the St Lawrence.

But the tales of the fierce old days survived down into my time, stirring my youthful heart with profound regret that deeds so heroically splendid should all be bad. For in spite of the Great Revival we were of the same race, with ancient lust of battle in our blood. Never have I forgotten the thrill of pride in my heart the day that my elder brother, Stewart, stripped to his shirt on a winter day, stood out before the lads of the Scotch River and dared any man of them to come over. In his moments of wrath he was a terror to the whole school. He had the strength of a bull. I have seen him, when he came to manhood, stoop, lay his open hand on the floor, lift my father standing one foot on his hand and one on his wrist–lift him standing, a man of nearly two hundred pounds, and set him on the table.

A wild lot–Glengarry men–as wild as the wild creatures of the forest in which they lived, fearing no man or beast or devil.

It is one of the tragedies of literature that historians fill their pages with the doings of men and leave unsung the lives of the heroines of the race. Less colourful doubtless are the lives of mothers, wives, sisters, but more truly heroic and more fruitful in the upbuilding of human character and in the shaping of a nation's history. At the very foundation of a people's greatness is the home. Splendid and hazardous as are the deeds of men in the battle of life, nothing they endure in the way of suffering can compare with what the mothers of a pioneer colony, remote from civilization, are called upon to suffer in the bearing and rearing of children. The loneliness, the dangers, the hardships of fathers and sons in the remote lumber camps or in the rafts down the river are as nothing to the appalling loneliness, the dangers, the hardships that mothers and daughters have to meet and endure in the little log houses in the clearing with children to clothe and care for in health and in sickness, and to keep regularly at school, to train and discipline, with beasts to water and feed, with fires to keep alight when snowdrifts pile round the little house to the eaves, shutting them off for days and nights from their neighbours, with no one but God available for their help. All this is a part of my experience, and at times when I begin to lose my faith in the nobler qualities of the race I let my mind wander back to the wives, mothers, and sisters of the pioneer-settlers of Glengarry and find my faith revive.

Every age, every race has its trials, dangers and despairs to meet. But today things are surely easier in the care of a family. There is the not-unimportant problem of keeping the family neatly and comfortably clad. The tailor, the dressmaker, the department store, it will be conceded, play no minor role in the solution of this problem. But I think of my mother and her six sons. I never wore store clothes till I was twelve. Tailor McRae –or Tailor Ruagh, as we called him from the definitely ruddy tint of his hair–used to come once a year in the fall with his tapes and scissors, his needles, thread, and buttons and spend a week in the manse outfitting the six boys with their annual suits. There was no difficulty in the selection of the quality, colour, weight of the cloth, nor the style of the garments to be made. These had all been taken care of. For there stood Tailor Ruagh, a huge web of fulled cloth made from our own wool, a serviceable grey, thick enough to stand alone and guaranteed to last through the whole year. From this web our suits were cut. There was no 'fashing' about styles. There was only one style and that never went out. In the week Tailor Ruagh measured, cut, and basted, while some neighbour women, coming in relays, helped to sew and shape the material into coats, vests, and trousers. If the results were not quite in harmony with the lines of various limbs, well, so much the worse for the limbs. It was a busy time and hard work, but my mother always made a kind of picnic of it. There would be a rest for a cup of tea with cheese and oat cakes, and almost always doughnuts, pies, and honey which the good friends had brought with them. And while they worked there would be Gaelic songs, redolent of the Hebrides, and hymns of my mother's teaching, or perhaps a story read or a bit from the Book. Oh, it was a grand time for the women. But for the boys, who had to appear in church in their new grey suits that felt and looked like coats of mail, the time was not so very grand.

Shirts of radiant and variegated hues, spun and woven by our neighbour friends, were made without Tailor Ruagh's help. These were quite beneath his dignity. Everything we wore, except our boots and moccasins, was homemade, and of homespun material. I cannot halt to speak of the cleaning, the carding, the dyeing, the spinning, the weaving of the wool necessary to produce blankets, sheets, quilts for beds, or dresses for the girls. But think, will you, of the hours at the spinning wheel, the sitting little wheel and the walking big wheel, the dyeing, the weary banging and shuttling of the looms necessary to these glorious results. Compare with all the brain and back-racking effort, the mere chopping, hewing, hauling, and rafting of timber sticks.

We cannot give space to the other multitudinous tasks of the women, such as the milking, the butter and cheese making, the pickling and transforming of various wild fruits into delicious jams and preserves, the curing of pork and beef, the drying of herbs. Then, outside, there was the care of hens, ducks, and geese and of their wayward and wandering offspring, the safe delivery of spring calves and lambs and pigs. And always the baby to nurse or attend to, or Jimmie to keep from the fire or from falling into the well, or Maggie from the jam jar or the milk pan. Lumbering or plowing or cradling, indeed! 'Tut, tut, men. Haud yer whisht!'

And in that great work of homemaking, the greatest in the world, the minister's wife held a high place, for to her it was given to show women how to make homes, not only warm, clean, tasteful, and cozy, but also how to make them radiant with a spiritual glow and pure with a love 'that suffereth long and is kind, that envieth not, that doth not behave itself unseemly, that hopeth all things, believeth all things, endureth all things, love that never faileth.'

All that is set down in *Glengarry School Days* is true. Our education began in the little log schoolhouse of great hewn pine logs, plastered at the cracks. The plaster, strangely enough, on the boys' side somehow during the summer months, had an invariable habit of falling out. We were a destructive lot of young devils. I was going to say 'creatures', but I shall substitute, for those boys were a lovable lot. The interior walls were with-

out decoration of any kind. On the back wall beside the teacher's desk was a blackboard, on the walls were maps of the world, of Europe, Asia, and America. None of Canada or the United States. These could be found in our geographies. Nothing else could be seen on the bare log walls. Three windows on each side with small panes, and one behind the teacher's desk, broke the blank space. These windows were protected by stout wooden shutters, bolted on the inside. But for these shutters the windows could not have survived a single week. An array of unprotected window-panes often had proved too great a temptation to the destructive propensities of our time. We were indeed a wild lot. The entrance was through a porch. At the door on a bench stood a pail of water with a tin cup hanging on a nail, convenient for all to use, with a fine democratic disregard of all silly hygienic rules. In fact, we had never heard that there were such rules. The more finicky might rinse out the cup before drinking, throwing the rinsing on the floor. But this precautionary act was regarded as an indication of 'pride', a grave offense in the eyes of the school. On cold winter days the large box stove stood red-hot. In summer the stove was removed.

Discipline was maintained by the 'force and fear' method. An essential article in school was the 'tawze', a solid leather strap split into fingers. Failing a tawze, the teacher would send one or two of the bigger boys to the bush for birch 'gads' about four feet long, supple and strong. The whole school enjoyed the ironic possibility that the purveyors of the rods might themselves be the first to furnish demonstration of their efficiency.

One teacher I remember for a refinement of cruelty in his method of punishment. This was to gather in his fist the four fingers of his unhappy victim and apply vigorously to the protruding finger tips a pointer or ruler. We forgave this little eccentricity, however, because of his repertoire of comic songs, with which at recess or after school he would regale select parties of his pupils.

The Glengarry folk were a fighting people. The whole spirit of the school was permeated by the fighting motif. Every recitation was a contest. The winners went joyously to the top, the failures remained ignominiously at the foot. Medals of a quarter of a dollar for seniors, sixpences for juniors were provided. The pupil holding the head of the class for a day carried his medal home upon an inflated breast, and wore it next day till he lost his place. The pupil carrying the medal for a week could keep it. Also classes were frequently dismissed to their seats by a series of questions in mental arithmetic. Every pupil in the class was on his toes, the one first shouting the correct answer marched proudly to his seat. Good practice it was. As to the ethics and psychology let experts in modern pedagogy decide.

The gravest defect in our educational system was the emphasis laid upon feats of memory. Geography, for instance, had little to do with the 'ge' in its Greek root. It was quite remote from 'the earth'. The boy or girl who could recite, without error, the capes, bays, peninsulas and other physical features of North or South America went to the top. In all my Glengarry school days I never drew a map.

Grammar, which was 'the science and art of speaking and writing the English language with perfection', divided into orthography, etymology, syntax, and prosody, whatever that may be, was largely a matter of memory. We learned lists of the various Parts of Speech. I knew all the pronouns: personal, possessive, relative, demonstrative, and distributive. The climax of absurdity seems to have been reached when we were asked to recite a complete list of the prepositions in the English language, as set forth in Lennie's *Grammar* in a solid block of small print three inches by four. A similar list of conjunctions, adverbs, and interjections was set down for us. The pupil, unfortunately, was often left in a horrible uncertainty as to the list to which a particular word might belong.

Even arithmetic, astonishing as it may appear to the modern schoolboy, was largely a matter of memory. Problems were solved by Rules of Proportion, simple or compound, by the Laws of Decimals or Fractions, or, most ghastly of all, by the Rules of Square or Cube Root. These rules you learned by rote, and if you could fit your sums into the framework your answer would infallibly be right. Square and cube root were at the very end of our arithmetic and were our special objects of aversion, particularly the latter. We had a rhyme that expressed this aversion:

> For *Square Root* I don't care a hoot
> But *Cube Root, she's a brute!*

and she was. The Rule of Cube Root must have consisted of at least six paragraphs of small print making up in all a solid block some five inches by four. This rule we were forced to memorize.

Spelling, which to those unfamiliar with the derivation of the English language is entirely a memory exercise, was transformed into a veritable logomachy. Spelling contests, in which the whole school participated, were frequently held during the last period on Friday. Indeed, spelling bees were frequently staged between different school sections, and made occasions of social festivity. I am quite confident that the spellers of my day were superior to those of my children's day. Looking back over half a century of experience of various systems of education I come to the conclusion that while in range and variety, and in scientific method, the modern excels, yet in thoroughness and exactitude of memory the pupils of the little log school would quite hold their own.

But of the great world in which we lived we knew almost nothing. The processes of nature did not exist for us. Of contemporary peoples, their thoughts, their manner of life, their systems of government we were entirely ignorant. They were foreigners and, therefore, unknown, more or less despicable, and even dangerous.

Our sports were simple and homemade—swimming, skating, athletic contests, and primitive versions of baseball and hockey. Shinty or shinny, as we called it, was an importation from Scotland and was usually played on the hard beaten snow of the schoolyard. There were few rules. The game was played with a hard rubber ball and homemade sticks. We would cut from the bush a good elm or hickory cudgel with a natural crook. It was a savage game which often gave rise to fights. For we went in for no such frills as umpires or referees.

Of organized sport the youth of Glengarry knew nothing. They had access, however, to the wonderful university of the forest with all the wealth of fauna and flora contained therein. In that university they developed their powers of observation, skill in action, cool courage, patient endurance. At night the forest had its terrors. My eldest brother, Robertson, who was a great hunter even as a boy, used to tell us a thrilling wolf story. It passed into the legendary lore of our family. One night in the spring, when the wolves were hungry, he was returning on his pony from the post office in company with a lumberman who was riding home from the shanties. As they left the clearing and entered the black swamp they heard the long howl of a lone wolf but paid no heed to it. In a few minutes came an answering howl far in front followed by the short, sharp barks of the she-wolf and her cubs.

'Huh! Those devils are out again, are they?' said the shantyman touching up his horse to a canter. Almost immediately they heard a chorus of quick sharp yelps coming from all sides.

'They're hunting us,' said the shantyman and put his horse to the gallop, Robertson keeping pace on his pony. There was nearly a mile of forest with the going none too good. Looking back over his shoulder he could see in the light of the dim moon the pack, how many he could not tell, running flat and low.

'Is your pony surefooted?' the shantyman asked.

'She's all right,' said my brother, proud of his little black mare, our mother's pony.

'For God's sake, send her along then! If only I had my gun! I hate to run from them cowards.' As he spoke he took off his jacket and tied it to the end of a packing rope that hung on his saddle and waited. The leader of the pack was almost at their horses' tails. They had only a hundred yards of forest to go. The shantyman dropped his jacket and paid out the rope letting it trail on the road behind. The wolves fell upon it and tore the rope out of his hand. But the leader paid no attention to the jacket, gathering speed in swift short springs, he slipped up between the horses and leaped for the pony's throat. But the shantyman, shaking a foot clear of the stirrup, swung a heavy kick on the brute's jaw. The wolf fell with a howl under the pony's feet. A hundred yards away they saw the light of a swinging lantern and heard the loud clear call of a woman's voice. The wolves, too, saw and heard. They checked, halted, and faded away like shadows into the bush.

'Mother! Mother! Is that you?' gasped my brother, flinging himself off the pony into her arms. 'Weren't you afraid?'

Her face was white, her eyes like stars in the lanternlight.

'Afraid? I never thought of it. I heard the wolves and I heard the horses' feet.'

Wolves we hated. Bears we respected. A bear was a gentleman and would mind his business if you minded yours. But surprise him or press him too closely and he would give you a fight worthwhile. Unless struck in a vital spot he would carry a dozen bullets. One I know carried thirteen before he succumbed.

As a little boy I used to gaze with awe upon four deep cuts across the face of our dining room table. The story was this: Returning home late at night my father had left on the table the remnants of supper, some ham, honey, bread and butter, and had retired to bed. He was awakened out of his sleep by the sound of someone below. In his nightgown he slipped downstairs. Someone was moving about the room. He called out, 'Who is there? James, bring me some matches.' Immediately there was a crash of breaking dishes, a hairy something brushed against him and escaped through the door. A light revealed tablecloth, food and dishes in a heap on the floor, and on the table the marks of the four bear claws.

Encounters with bears were not uncommon. In my memory I carry a vivid picture of the Sinclair boys driving past the school at noon hour with a huge black bear dead on their sleigh, his red tongue sticking out and red splashes on his black coat. The hunters had two Minnie rifles and three black hunting dogs. I felt that the bear had hardly had a fair chance for his life.

If the forest had certain terrors for the younger boys, in the broad light of day it was a wonderland of mystery and beauty, a rare playground which they shared with all the shy things of the bush. There were squirrels, red and black, woodchucks, mink and muskrat, and the rare beaver. Above and about them in the trees were the birds—the tapping woodpecker, the shrieking blue jay, the wood pigeon, cooing and courting, all the wee twittering things, wrens, grey birds, wood sparrows, finches and, high in the treetops, the noisy crow. Low among the cedars and spruce the shy partridge hid, its variegated coloring a sure protection, while overhead the hawk soared and broke the stillness of the woods with its shrill hunting cry. On a rare occasion we saw the grey eagle, on the topmost peak of a dead pine, silent, haughty and solitary, fearful of nothing.

Through the forest flowed a little river. In springtime it was a rushing torrent filled with great cakes of ice upon which the bigger boys would cross. But in midsummer it was a softly flowing stream, shallow so that you could see bottom but here and there circling into a deep pool. One such pool made for us a swimming hole which we knew as the 'dee-pole' with emphasis on the 'dee'. On hot summer days we would come home by the dee-pole a mile out of our way to plunge into its cool water. And we would spend most of the long Saturday afternoons, when we could get free from our weeding and hoeing, in and about that place of surpassing joy.

As I look back through the varied years, the Glengarry forest more than any other place arrests and holds my memory, fills me with the pain of longing and stirs my lingering and grateful delight.

POSTSCRIPT TO ADVENTURE

b. 1913

Robertson Davies

ROBERTSON DAVIES, Canada's leading man of letters, has been newspaper editor, essayist, critic, playwright and is now a highly successful novelist. He was born in the small town of Thamesville, Ont., where his father published the local newspaper. He was educated at Upper Canada College, Toronto, and Queen's University, Kingston, which he attended for three years—not as a degree student, because he could not master mathematics (then an entrance requirement), but as a special student. He went on to Balliol College, Oxford, and graduated in 1938; his thesis, *Shakespeare's Boy Actors*, was published the next year. He worked for the Old Vic Repertory Theatre (where he took minor acting roles), married, and returned to Canada in 1940 to become literary editor of *Saturday Night*. Two years later he was made editor of the Peterborough *Examiner*. He remained in this post for fifteen years and was publisher for another ten. In 1963 he was appointed the first Master of Massey College, Toronto; he also teaches courses in drama at the University of Toronto.

These activities surprisingly allowed Davies to write and publish over twenty books—including five plays, two play collections, and five novels. His development as a novelist began with *The Diary of Samuel Marchbanks* (1947) and *The Table Talk of Samuel Marchbanks* (1949) —based on columns Davies wrote for the *Examiner*—which first drew him to the notice of the Canadian reading public as an entertaining writer, a gifted creator of eccentric characters, and an inveterate critic of contemporary manners. In these informal essays the crusty Marchbanks imparts his observations on life in general and life in Canada in particular, attacking among other things stupidity, narrowmindedness, and philistinism with devastating wit and humorous exaggeration. (A third Marchbanks book was published in 1967: *Samuel Marchbanks' Almanack*.) A great lover of the theatre, Davies turned next to writing plays, which gave a new direction to his flair for comedy, for creating 'characters', and for advancing his ideas and social comments. His published plays include *Fortune, My Foe* (1949) and *At My Heart's Core* (1950), which treated a favourite theme of Davies, the creative imagination versus the philistine environment; *A Jig for the Gypsy* (1954), about politics and magic, set in North Wales in the nineteenth century; and two masques written for the boys of Upper Canada College: *A Masque of Aesop* (1952) and *A Masque for Mr Punch* (1963). The characters in these plays, while lively and amusing, take second place to the ideas he wanted to convey and remain one-dimensional types.

This quality applies to many of the characters in Davies' first three novels, which nevertheless delight the reader with their comic scenes and entertaining talk. *Tempest-Tost* (1951) contains mainly caricatures who perform under the author's direction, rather like characters in a play, displaying their pretensions and provincial second-rateness and little else as they involve themselves in an amateur outdoor production of *The Tempest*. It is set in the small university city of Salterton (Kingston), Ont., which Davies satirizes further in *Leaven of Malice* (1954), about the repercussions that ensue when a false announcement of an engagement appears in the local newspaper. Characterization deepens considerably in *A Mixture of Frailties* (1958), the third of the Salterton novels. It offers a detailed portrait of Monica Gall, of the Heart and Hope Gospel Quartet, who frees herself from Salterton and becomes a distinguished singer in England. Twelve years passed before Davies published *Fifth Business* (1970), which became a bestseller in North America. It is a striking departure from the Salterton novels: the hand of the playwright manipulating characters is no longer evident, there is no indication of the omniscient author's approval or disapproval of his characters and no intrusion of his comments and ideas—the characters and plot take over completely. This rich and complex book takes the form of a long account by Dunstan Ramsey, a retired schoolteacher, of his eventful and wide-ranging life, which is not at all like that of the colourless person his colleagues thought him to be. It is a quest for wisdom, infused with elements of the miraculous, in which Mary Dempster—a woman who suffered an accident Ramsay was involved in as a child and who became simpleminded— has a central, inspiring place. (An extract from *Fifth Business* appears below.) A sequel, *The Manticore*, was published in the autumn of 1972.

Davies is also the author of three accounts of the Stratford Festival—*Renown at Stratford* (1953), *Twice Have the Trumpets Sounded* (1954), and *Thrice the Brinded Cat Hath Mew'd* (1955)—and of *A Voice from the Attic* (1960), a book of essays on the art of reading that is now in the New Canadian Library. Elspeth Buitenhuis has written a useful study of Davies' books for the Canadian Writers and Their Works series published by Forum House (1972). There are two interesting essays on the Salterton novels: one by Ivon Owen in Issue 9 of *The Tamarack Review* (Autumn 1958) and the other by Hugo McPherson in Issue 4 of *Canadian Literature* (Spring 1960). In Issue 1 of *Canadian Fiction* (Winter 1972) there is an essay by Gordon Roper on the influences in *Fifth Business* of the writings of the Swiss psychologist C.G. Jung.

'IT DOES NO GOOD TO BE AFRAID'

My fighting days came to an end somewhere in the week of November 5, 1917, at that point in the Third Battle of Ypres where the Canadians were brought in to attempt to take Passchendaele. It was a Thursday or Friday; I cannot be more accurate because many of the details of that time are clouded in my mind. The battle was the most terrible of my experience;

we were trying to take a village that was already a ruin, and we counted our advances in feet; the Front was a confused mess because it had rained every day for weeks and the mud was so dangerous that we dared not make a forward move without a laborious business of putting down duck-boards, lifting them as we advanced, and putting them down again ahead of us; understandably this was so slow and exposed that we could not do much of it. I learned from later reading that our total advance was a little less than two miles; it might have been two hundred. The great terror was the mud. The German bombardment churned it up so that it was hor-ribly treacherous, and if a man sank in much over his knees his chances of getting out were poor; a shell exploding nearby could cause an up-heaval that overwhelmed him, and the likelihood even of recovering his body was small. I write of this now as briefly as I may, for the terror of it was so great that I would not for anything arouse it again.

One of the principal impediments to our advance was a series of Ger-man machine-gun emplacements. I suppose they were set out according to some plan, but we were not in a position to observe any plan; in the tiny area I knew about there was one of these things, and it was clear that we would get no farther forward until it was silenced. Two attempts were made at this dangerous job, with terrible loss to us. I could see how things were going, and how the list of men who might be expected to get to that machine-gun nest was dwindling, and I knew it would come to me next. I do not remember if we were asked to volunteer; such a request would have been merely formal anyhow; things had reached a point where pre-tence of choice had disappeared. Anyhow, I was one of six who were detailed to make a night raid, in one of the intervals of bombardment, to see if we could get to the machine guns and knock them out. We were issued the small arms and other things we needed, and when the bom-bardment had stopped for five minutes we set out, not in a knot, of course, but spaced a few yards apart.

The men in the nest were expecting us, for we were doing exactly what their side would have done in the same situation. But we crawled forward, spread-eagled in the mud so as to spread our total weight over as wide an area as possible. It was like swimming in molasses, with the additional misery that it was molasses that stank and had dead men in it.

I was making pretty good progress when suddenly everything went wrong. Somebody—it could have been someone on our side at a distance or it could have been one of the Germans in the nest—sent up a flare; you do not see where these flares come from, because they explode in the air and light up the landscape for a considerable area. When such a thing happens and you are crawling toward an objective, as I was, the proper thing to do is to lie low, with your face down, and hope not to be seen. As I was mud from head to foot and had blackened my face before setting out, I would have been hard to see, and if seen I would have looked like a dead man. After the flare had died out I crept forward again and made a fair amount of distance, so far as I could judge; I did not know where the others were, but I assumed that like me they were making for the gun nest and waiting for a signal from our leader, a second lieutenant, to do whatever we could about it. But now three flares exploded, and immediately there began a rattle of machine-gun fire. Again I laid low. But it is the nature of flares, when they are over the arc of their trajectory, to come down with a rush and a characteristic loud hiss; if you are hit by one it is a serious burn, for the last of the flare is still a large gob of fire, and between burning to death or drowning in mud the choice is trivial. Two of these spent flares were hissing in the air above me, and I had to get out of where I was as fast as I could. So I got to my feet and ran.

Now, at a time when we had counted on at least a half-an-hour's lull in the bombardment, it suddenly set up again, and to my bleak horror our own guns, from a considerable distance to the left, began to answer. This sort of thing was always a risk when we were out on small raids, but it was a risk I had never met before. As the shells began to drop I ran wildly, and how long I wallowed around in the dark I do not know, but it could have been anything between three minutes and ten. I became aware of a deafening rattle, with the rhythm of an angry, scolding voice, on my right. I looked for some sort of cover, and suddenly, in a burst of light, there it was right in front of me—an entry concealed by some trash, but unmistakably a door over which hung a curtain of muddy sacking. I pushed through it and found myself in the German machine-gun nest, with three Germans ahead of me firing busily.

I had a revolver, and I shot all three at point-blank range. They did not even see me. There is no use saying any more about it. I am not proud of it now and I did not glory in it then. War puts men in situations where these things happen.

What I wanted to do most of all was to stay where I was and get my breath and my wits before starting back to our line. But the bombardment was increasing, and I knew that if I stopped there one of our shells might drop on the position and blow me up, or the Germans, whose field telephone was already signalling right under my nose, would send some men to see what had happened, and that would be the end of me. I had to get out.

So out I crawled, into mud below and shells above, and tried to get my bearings. As both sides were now at the peak of a bombardment, it was not easy to tell which source of death I should crawl toward, and by bad luck I set out toward the German lines.

How long I crawled I do not know, for I was by this time more frightened, muddled, and desperate than ever before or since. 'Disorientation' is the word now fashionable for my condition. Quite soon I was worse than that; I was wounded, and so far as I could tell, seriously. It was shrapnel, a fragment of an exploding shell, and it hit me in the left leg, though where I cannot say; I have been in a car accident in later life, and the effect was rather like that—a sudden shock like a blow from a club; and it was a little time before I knew that my left leg was in trouble, though I could not tell how bad it was.

Earlier I said that I had not been wounded; there were a surprising number of men who escaped the war without a wound. I had not been gassed either, though I had been twice in areas where gas was used nearby. I had dreaded a wound, for I had seen so many. What is a wounded man to do? Crawl to shelter and hope he may be found by his own people. I crawled.

Some men found that their senses were quickened by a wound; their ingenuity rose to exceptional heights under stress of danger. But I was one of the other kind. I was not so much afraid as utterly disheartened. There I was, a mud man in a confusion of noise, flashing lights, and the stink of gelignite. I wanted to quit; I had no more heart for the game. But I crawled, with the increasing realization that my left leg was no good for anything and had to be dragged, and the awful awareness that I did not know where I was going. After a few minutes I saw some jagged masonry on my right and dragged toward it. When at last I reached it I propped myself up with my back to a stone wall and gave myself up to a full, rich recognition of the danger and hopelessness of my position. For three years I had kept my nerve by stifling my intelligence, but now I let the intelligence rip and the nerve dissolve. I am sure there has been worse wretchedness, fright, and despair in the world's history, but I set up a personal record that I have never since approached.

My leg began to declare itself in a way that I can only describe in terms of sound; from a mute condition it began to murmur, then to moan and whine, then to scream. I could not see much of what was wrong because of the mud in which I was covered, but my exploring hand found a great stickiness that I knew was blood, and I could make out that my leg lay on the ground in an unnatural way. You will get tetanus, I told myself, and you will die of lockjaw. It was a Deptford belief that in this disease you bent backwards until at last your head touched your heels and you had to be buried in a round coffin. I had seen tetanus in the trenches, and nobody had needed a round coffin even if one had been available; still, in my condition, the belief was stronger than experience.

I thought of Deptford, and I thought of Mrs Dempster. Particularly I thought of her parting words to me: 'There's just one thing to remember; whatever happens, it does no good to be afraid.' Mrs Dempster, I said aloud, was a fool. I was afraid, and I was not in a situation where doing good, or doing evil, had any relevance at all.

It was then that one of the things happened that make my life strange— one of the experiences that other people have not had or do not admit to— one of the things that makes me so resentful of Packer's estimate of me as a dim man to whom nothing important has ever happened.

I became conscious that the bombardment had ceased, and only an occasional gun was heard. But flares appeared in the sky at intervals, and one of these began to drop toward me. By its light I could see that the remnant of standing masonry in which I was lying was all that was left of a church, or perhaps a school—anyhow a building of some size—and that I lay at the foot of a ruined tower. As the hissing flame dropped I saw there about ten or twelve feet above me on an opposite wall, in a niche, a statue of the Virgin and Child. I did not know it then but I know now that it was the assembly of elements that represent the Immaculate Conception, for the little Virgin was crowned, stood on a crescent moon, which in its turn rested on a globe, and in the hand that did not hold the Child she carried a sceptre from which lilies sprang. Not knowing what it was meant to be, I thought in a flash it must be the Crowned Woman in *Revelation*—she who had the moon beneath her feet and was menaced by the Red Dragon. But what hit me worse than the blow of the shrapnel was that the face was Mrs Dempster's face.

I had lost all nerve long before. Now, as the last of the flare hissed toward me, I lost consciousness.

*   *   *

'May I have a drink of water?'
  'Did you speak?'
  'Yes. May I have a drink, Sister?'
  'You may have a glass of champagne, if there is any. Who are you?'
  'Ramsay, D., Sergeant, Second Canadian Division.'
  'Well, Ramsay-Dee, it's marvellous to have you with us.'
  'Where is this?'
  'You'll find out. Where have *you* been?'
Ah, where *had* I been? I didn't know then and I don't know yet, but it was such a place as I had never known before. Years later, when for the first time I read Coleridge's *Kubla Khan* and came on—

Weave a circle round him thrice,

> *And close your eyes with holy dread,*
> *For he on honey-dew hath fed,*
> *And drunk the milk of Paradise*

—I almost jumped out of my skin, for the words so perfectly described my state before I woke up in hospital. I had been wonderfully at ease and healingly at peace; though from time to time voices spoke to me I was under no obligation to hear what they said or to make a reply; I felt that everything was good, that my spirit was wholly my own, and that though all was strange nothing was evil. From time to time the little Madonna appeared and looked at me with friendly concern before removing herself; once or twice she spoke, but I did not know what she said and did not need to know.

But here I was, apparently in bed, and a very pretty girl in a nurse's uniform was asking me where I had been. Clearly she meant it as a joke. She thought she knew where I had been. That meant that the joke was on her, for no one, not I myself, knew that.

'Is this a base hospital?'

'Goodness, no. How do you feel, Ramsay-Dee?'

'Fine. What day is this?'

'This is the twelfth of May. I'll get you a drink.'

She disappeared, and I took a few soundings. It was not easy work. The last time I had been conscious of was November; if this was May I had been in that splendid, carefree world for quite a while. I wasn't in such a bad place now; I couldn't move my head very much, but I could see a marvellously decorated plaster ceiling, and such walls as lay in my vision were panelled in wood; there was an open window somewhere, and sweet air—no stink of mud or explosive or corpses or latrines—was blowing through it. I was clean. I wriggled appreciatively—and wished I hadn't, for several parts of me protested. But here was the girl again, and with her a red-faced man in a long white coat.

He seemed greatly elated, especially when I was able to remember my Army number, and though I did not learn why at once I found out over a few days that I was by way of being a medical pet, and my recovery proved something; being merely the patient, I was never given the full details, but I believe I was written up in at least two medical papers as a psychiatric curiosity, but as I was referred to only as 'the patient' I could never identify myself for sure. The red-faced man was some sort of specialist in shell-shock cases, and I was one of his successes, though I rather think I cured myself, or the little Madonna cured me, or some agencies other than good nursing and medical observation.

Oh, I was a lucky man! Apparently the flare did hit me, and before it expired it burned off a good part of my clothes and consumed the string of my identification disks, so that when I was picked up they were lost in the mud. There had been some doubt as to whether I was dead or merely on the way to it, but I was taken back to our base, and as I stubbornly did not die I was removed eventually to a hospital in France, and as I still refused either to die or live I was shipped to England; by this time I was a fairly interesting instance of survival against all probabilities, and the red-faced doctor had claimed me for his own; I was brought to this special hospital in a fine old house in Buckinghamshire, and had lain unconscious, and likely to remain so, though the red-faced doctor stubbornly insisted that some day I would wake up and tell him something of value. So, here it was May, and I was awake, and the hospital staff were delighted, and made a great pet of me.

They had other news for me, not so good. My burns had been severe, and in those days they were not so clever with burns as they are now, so that quite a lot of the skin on my chest and left side was an angry-looking mess, rather like lumpy sealing wax, and is so still, though it is a little browner now. In the bed, on the left side, was an arrangement of wire, like a bee-skip, to keep the sheets from touching the stump where my left leg had been. While my wits were off on that paradisal holiday I had been fed liquids, and so I was very thin and weak. What is more, I had a full beard, and the pretty nurse and I had a rare old time getting it off.

Let me stop calling her the pretty nurse. Her name was Diana Marfleet, and she was one of those volunteers who got a proper nursing training but never acquired the full calm of a professional nursing sister. She was the first English girl I ever saw at close range, and a fine specimen of her type, which was the fair-skinned, dark-haired, brown-eyed type. Not only was she pretty, she had charm and an easy manner and talked amusingly, for she came of that class of English person who thinks it bad manners to be factual and serious. She was twenty-four, which gave her an edge of four years over me, and it was not long before she confided to me that her fiancé, a Navy lieutenant, had been lost when the *Aboukir* was torpedoed in the very early days of the war. We were on tremendous terms in no time, for she had been nursing me since I had come to the hospital in January, and such nourishment as I had taken had been spooned and poured into me by her; she had also washed me and attended to the bed-pan and the urinal, and continued to do so; a girl who can do that without being facetious or making a man feel self-conscious is no ordinary creature. Diana was a wonderful girl, and I am sure I gained strength and made physical progress at an unusual rate, to please her.

One day she appeared at my bedside with a look of great seriousness and saluted me smartly.

'What's that for?'

'Tribute of humble nursing sister to hero of Passchendaele.'

'Get away!' (This was a great expression of my father's, and I have never wholly abandoned it.)

'Fact. What do you think you've got?'

'I rather think I've got you.'

'No cheek. We've been tracing you, Sergeant Ramsay. Did you know that you were officially dead?'

'Dead! Me?'

'You. That's why your V.C. was awarded posthumously.'

'Get away!'

'Fact. You have the V.C. for, with the uttermost gallantry and disregard of all but duty, clearing out a machine-gun nest and thereby ensuring an advance of—I don't know how far but quite a bit. You were the only one of the six who didn't get back to the line, and one of the men saw you— your unmistakable size anyhow—running right toward the machine-gun nest; so it was clear enough, even though they couldn't find your body afterward. Anyway you've got it, and Dr Houneen is making sure you get it and it isn't sent home to depress your mother.'

The other three men in the room gave a cheer—an ironic cheer. We all pretended we didn't care about decorations, but I never heard of anybody turning one down.

Diana was very sorry in a few days that she had said what she did about the medal going home to my mother, for a letter arrived from the Reverend Donald Phelps, in reply to one Dr Houneen had sent to my parents, saying that Alexander Ramsay and his wife, Fiona Dunstable Ramsay, had both died in the influenza epidemic of early 1918, though not before they had received news of my presumed death at Passchendaele.

Diana was ashamed because she thought she might have hurt my feelings. I was ashamed because I felt the loss so little.

FIFTH BUSINESS

James De Mille

JAMES DE MILLE was born in Saint John, N.B. He was educated at Acadia University and received his M.A. from Brown University, Providence, Rhode Island. From 1860 to 1884 he taught classics at Acadia and then English literature at Dalhousie University until his death. He was a highly productive author who wrote thirty books, most of them novels of great popularity. *The Dodge Club; or, Italy in 1859* (1860) is a humourous tale about some Americans who travel together across the Alps to Italy, all the time dodging people who prey on trav-ellers. He also wrote four popular children's books about a band of boys—the B.O.W.C. (Brothers of the White Cross). *A Strange Manuscript Found in A Copper Cylinder* was published after he died, in 1888. It is a utopian novel, a genre of fiction set in an imaginary country that provides some sort of criticism of the society we know. On one level it is an imaginative and interesting adventure story; on another it is a satirical examination of human nature. It is available as a paperback in the New Canadian Library.

THE KOSEKIN

James De Mille's A Strange Manuscript Found in a Copper Cylinder *describes the South Polar land of the Kosekin, a race of cannibals to whom darkness, poverty, and death represent the highest good. The wealthy Kohen is among the lowest of men; the most influential and highly honoured citizens are the paupers.*

The explanation of the values and goals of the Kosekin in the extracts below shows how a complete system can be built on assumptions about human nature that are a mirror image of our own, though in the con-

formist societies represented by the visitor Adam More and the Kosekin,
human nature is basically the same. We are forced to re-examine our own
assumptions in the light of these alien ones.

I determined to talk to the Kohen and try for myself whether he might
not be accessible to pity. This greatest of cannibals might indeed have his
little peculiarities, I thought—and who has not?—yet at bottom he seemed
full of tender and benevolent feeling; and as he evidently spent his whole
time in the endeavour to make us happy, it seemed not unlikely that he
might do something for our happiness in a case where our very existence
was at stake.

The Kohen listened with deep attention as I stated my case. I did this
fully and frankly. I talked of my love for Almah and of Almah's love for
me; our hope that we might be united so as to live happily in reciprocal
affection; and I was going on to speak of the dread that was in my heart
when he interrupted me:

'You speak of being united,' said he. 'You talk strangely. Of course you
mean that you wish to be separated.'

'Separated!' I exclaimed. 'What do you mean? Of course we wish to be
united.'

The Kohen stared at me as I said this with the look of one who was
quite puzzled; and I then went on to speak of the fate that was before us,
and to entreat his sympathy and his aid that we might be saved from so
hideous a doom. To all these words the Kohen listened with an air of
amazement, as though I were saying incomprehensible things.

'You have a gentle and an affectionate nature,' I said, 'a nature full of
sympathy with others, and noble self-denial.'

'Of course,' said the Kohen quickly, as though glad to get hold of something which he could understand, 'of course we are all so, for we are so
made. It is our nature. Who is there who is not self-denying? No one can
help that.'

This sounded strange indeed; but I did not care to criticize it. I came to
my purpose direct and said,

'Save us from our fate.'

'Your fate?'

'Yes, from death—that death of horror.'

'Death—horror! What do you mean by horror?' said the Kohen, in an
amazement that was sincere and unfeigned. 'I cannot comprehend your
meaning. It seems as though you actually dislike death; but that is not
conceivable. It cannot be possible that you fear death.'

'Fear death!' I exclaimed, 'I do, I do. Who is there that does not fear it?'

The Kohen stared.

'I do not understand you,' he said.

'Do you not understand,' said I, 'that death is abhorrent to humanity.'

'Abhorrent!' said the Kohen; 'that is impossible. Is it not the highest blessing? Who is there that does not long for death? Death is the greatest blessing, the chief desire of man, the highest aim. And you—are you not to be envied in having your felicity so near? Above all, in having such a death as that which is appointed for you—so noble, so sublime? You must be mad; your happiness has turned your head.'

All this seemed like hideous mockery, and I stared at the Kohen with a gaze that probably strengthened his opinion of my madness.

'Do you love death?' I asked at length, in amazement.

'Love death? What a question! Of course I love death—all men do; who does not? Is it not human nature? Do we not instinctively fly to meet it whenever we can? Do we not rush into the jaws of seamonsters or throw ourselves within their grasp? Who does not feel within him this intense longing after death as the strongest passion of his heart?'

'I don't know, I don't know,' said I. 'You are of a different race; I do not understand what you say. But I belong to a race that fears death. I fear death and love life; and I entreat you, I implore you to help me now in my distress and assist me so that I may save my life and that of Almah.'

'I—I help you!' said the Kohen, in new amazement. 'Why do you come to me—to me of all men? Why, I am nothing here. And help you to live —to live! Who ever heard of such a thing?'

And the Kohen looked at me with the same astonishment which I should evince if a man should ask me to help him to die.

Still I persisted in my entreaty for his help.

'Such a request,' said he, 'is revolting; you must be mad. Such a request outrages all the instincts of humanity. And even if I could do such violence to my own nature as to help you to such a thing, how do you think I could face my fellow-men, or how could I endure the terrible punishment which would fall upon me?'

'Punishment!' said I. 'What! Would you be punished?'

'Punished!' said the Kohen. 'That of course would be inevitable. I should be esteemed an unnatural monster and the chief of criminals. My lot in life now is painful enough, but in this case my punishment would involve me in evils without end. Riches would be poured upon me; I should be raised to the rank of Kohen Gadol; I should be removed farther away than ever from the pauper class—so far indeed that all hope in life would be over. I should be made the first and noblest and richest in all the land.'

He spoke these words just as if he had said, 'the lowest, meanest, poorest, and most infamous.' It sounded like fresh mockery and I could not believe but that he was amusing himself at my expense.

'This is cruel,' said I. 'You are mocking me.'

'Cruel—cruel!' said he. 'What is cruel? You mean that such a fate would be cruel for me.'

'No, no,' said I. 'But alas! I see we cannot understand one another.'

'No,' said the Kohen musingly as he looked at me. 'No, it seems not; but tell me, Atam-or, is it possible that you really fear death—that you really love life?'

'Fear death! Love life!' I cried. 'Who does not? Who can help it? Why do you ask me that?'

The Kohen clasped his hands in amazement.

'If you really fear death,' said he, 'what possible thing is there left to love or to hope for? What then do you think the highest blessing of man?'

'Long life,' said I, 'and riches and requited love.'

At this the Kohen started back and stared at me as though I were a raving madman.

'Oh holy shades of night!' he exclaimed. 'What is that you say? What do you mean?'

'We can never understand one another, I fear,' said I. 'The love of life must necessarily be the strongest passion of man. We are so made. We give up everything for life. A long life is everywhere considered as the highest blessing; and there is no one who is willing to die, no matter what his suffering may be. Riches also are desired by all, for poverty is the direst curse that can embitter life; and as to requited love, surely that is the sweetest, purest, and most divine joy that the human heart may know.'

At this the Kohen burst forth in a strain of high excitement:

'Oh sacred cavern gloom! Oh divine darkness! Oh impenetrable abysses of night! What, oh what is this! Oh Atam-or, are you mad? Alas! it must be so. Joy has turned your brain; you are quite demented. You call good evil, and evil good; our light is your darkness, and our darkness your light. Yet surely you cannot be altogether insane. Come, come, let us look further. How is it! Try now to recall your reason. A long life—a life, and a long one! Surely there can be no human being in a healthy state of nature who wishes to prolong his life; and as to riches, is it possible that any one exists who really and honestly desires riches? Impossible! And requited love! Oh Atam-or, you are mad today! You are always strange, but now you have quite taken leave of your senses. I cannot but love you, and yet I can never understand you. Tell me, and tell me truly, what is it that you consider evils, if these things that you have just mentioned are not the very worst?'

He seemed deeply in earnest and much moved. I could not understand him, but could only answer his questions with simple conciseness.

'Poverty, sickness, and death,' said I, 'are evils; but the worst of all evils is unrequited love.'

At these words the Kohen made a gesture of despair.

'It is impossible to understand this,' said he. 'You talk calmly; you have not the air of a madman. If your fellow-countrymen are all like you, then your race is an incomprehensible one. Why death is the greatest blessing. We all long for it; it is the end of our being. As for riches, they are a curse abhorred by all. Above all, as to love, we shrink from the thought of requital. Death is our chief blessing, poverty our greatest happiness, and unrequited love the sweetest lot of man.'

All this sounded like the ravings of a lunatic, yet the Kohen was not mad. It seemed also like the mockery of some teasing demon; but the gentle and self-denying Kohen was no teasing demon, and mockery with him was impossible. I was therefore more bewildered than ever at this reiteration of sentiments that were so utterly incomprehensible. He, on the other hand, seemed as astonished at my sentiments and as bewildered, and we could find no common ground on which to meet.

'I remember now,' said the Kohen in a musing tone, 'having heard of some strange folk at the Amir who profess to feel as you say you feel, but no one believes that they are in earnest; for although they may even bring themselves to think that they are in earnest in their professions, yet after all every one thinks that they are self-deceived. For you see, in the first place, these feelings which you profess are utterly unnatural. We are so made that we cannot help loving death; it is a sort of instinct. We are also created in such a way that we cannot help longing after poverty. The pauper must always, among all men, be the most envied of mortals. Nature too has made us such that the passion of love, when it arises, is so vehement, so all-consuming, that it must always struggle to avoid requital. This is the reason why when two people find that they love each other, they always separate and avoid one another for the rest of their lives. This is human nature. We cannot help it; and it is this that distinguishes us from the animals. Why if men were to feel as you say you feel they would be mere animals. Animals fear death; animals love to accumulate such things as they prize; animals, when they love, go in pairs and remain with one another. But man, with his intellect, would not be man if he loved life and desired riches and sought for requited love.'

I sank back in despair. 'You cannot mean all this,' I said.

He threw at me a piteous glance. 'What else can you believe or feel?' said he.

'The very opposite. We are so made that we hate and fear death; to us he is the King of Terrors. Poverty is terrible also, since it is associated with want and woe; it is therefore natural to man to strive after riches.

As to the passion of love, that is so vehement that the first and only thought is requital. Unrequited love is anguish beyond expression— anguish so severe that the heart will often break under it.'

The Kohen clasped his hands in new bewilderment.

'I cannot understand,' said he. 'A madman might imagine that he loved life and desired riches; but as to love, why even a madman could not think of requital, for the very nature of the passion of love is the most utter self-surrender and a shrinking from all requital; wherefore the feeling that leads one to desire requital cannot be love. I do not know what it can be—indeed, I never heard of such a thing before, and the annals of the human race make no mention of such a feeling. For what is love? It is the ardent outflow of the whole being—the yearning of one human heart to lavish all its treasures upon another. Love is more than self-denial; it is self-surrender and utter self-abnegation. Love gives all away and cannot possibly receive anything in return. A requital of love would mean selfishness, which would be self-contradiction. The more one loves, the more he must shrink from requital.'

'What!' cried I. 'Among you do lovers never marry?'

'Lovers marry? Never!'

'Do married people never love one another?'

The Kohen shook his head.

'It unfortunately sometimes happens so,' said he, 'and then the result is of course distressing. For the children's sake the parents will often remain with one another, but in many cases they separate. No one can tell the misery that ensues where a husband and wife love one another.'

The conversation grew insupportable. I could not follow the Kohen in what seemed the wildest and maddest flights of fancy that ever were known; so I began to talk of other things and gradually the Kohen was drawn to speak of his own life. The account which he gave of himself was not one whit less strange than his previous remarks and for this reason I add it here.

'I was born', said he, 'in the most enviable of positions. My father and mother were among the poorest in the land. Both died when I was a child and I never saw them. I grew up in the open fields and public caverns, along with the most esteemed paupers. But unfortunately for me, there was something wanting in my natural disposition. I loved death, of course, and poverty too, very strongly; but I did not have that eager and energetic passion which is so desirable, nor was I watchful enough over my blessed estate of poverty. Surrounded as I was by those who were only too ready to take advantage of my ignorance or want of vigilance, I soon fell into evil ways and gradually, in spite of myself, I found wealth pouring in upon me. Designing men succeeded in winning my consent to receive their possessions; and so I gradually fell away from that lofty position in which I was born. I grew richer and richer. My friends warned me, but in vain. I was too weak to resist; in fact, I lacked moral fibre and had never learned how to say 'No'. So I went on, descending lower and lower in the scale of being. I became a capitalist, an Athon, a general officer, and finally Kohen.

'At length, on one eventful day, I learned that one of my associates had by a long course of reckless folly become the richest man in all the country. He had become Athon, malek, and at last Kohen Gadol. It was a terrible shock, but I trust a salutary one. I at once resolved to reform. That resolution I have steadily kept and have at least saved myself from descending any lower. It is true, I can hardly hope to become what I once was. It is only too easy to grow rich; and you know poverty once forfeited can never return except in rare instances. I have, however, succeeded in getting rid of most of my wealth, chiefly through the fortunate advent of Almah and afterwards of yourself. This, I confess, has been my salvation. Neither of you had any scruples about accepting what was bestowed and so I did not feel as though I was doing you any wrong in giving you all I had in the world. Most of the people of this city have taken advantage of your extraordinary indifference to wealth and have made themselves paupers at your expense. I had already become your slave and had received the promise of being elevated to the rank of scullion in the cavern of the *Mista Kosek*. But now, since this event of your love for Almah, I hope to gain far more. I am almost certain of being made a pauper, and I think I can almost venture to hope some day for the honour of a public death.'

To such a story I had nothing to say. It was sheer madness; yet it was terribly suggestive and showed how utterly hopeless was my effort to secure the assistance of such a man towards my escape from death.

'A public death!' I said grimly. 'That will be very fortunate! And do you think you will gain the dignity of being eaten up afterwards?'

The Kohen shook his head in all seriousness.

'Oh no,' said he; 'that would be far beyond my deserts. That is an honour which is only bestowed upon the most distinguished.'

A STRANGE MANUSCRIPT FOUND IN A COPPER CYLINDER

b. 1923

Kildare Dobbs

For almost two decades KILDARE DOBBS has been writing light essays and stories with a skill that is reminiscent of Stephen Leacock—though Dobbs' wit and irreverance are often focussed on more serious matters than ever interested Leacock. Born in Meerut, India, Dobbs grew up in County Kilkenny, Ireland, and attended school in County Dublin. After four years of war service at sea he continued his education at Cambridge and London Universities. He was then appointed to government service in Tanganyika (Tanzania). He came to Canada in 1952 with fifty dollars (which was stolen the day after he arrived); taught for a year in a small Ontario town—disguised as 'Venice' in the passage below from his book *Running to Paradise*; and then entered the publishing world of Toronto, first as an editor for Macmillan of Canada, then as a free-lance writer and broadcaster. At present he writes a book column for the Toronto *Star*. Here, in *Saturday Night*, *Maclean's*, and on the CBC —whether he is discussing new books or sharing his experiences and impressions of life and letters—his graceful, clear writing displays wide knowledge, informed judgements, and humanity. He has an observant eye for the ridiculous in people and events and is a master of the comic anecdote, but he is never cruel. He is always firmly on the side of justice and common sense and would rather entertain and illuminate than instruct.

Running to Paradise (1962) won a Governor General's Award. Made up of fragments of autobiography set in Ireland, Tanganyika, at sea, and in Canada, it is the first of two collections of Dobbs' magazine pieces and broadcasts; the second is *Reading the Time* (1968). He collaborated with the photographer Peter Varley on *Canada* (1964; rev. 1969) and with the English caricaturist Ronald Searle on *The Great Fur Opera: Annals of the Hudson's Bay Company 1670-1970* (1970), which Dobbs describes as a 'comic epic in prose'.

VIEWS OF VENICE

In the first moment of my year in Venice I felt its eyes upon me.

I do not speak of Venice in Italy. That city is known to me only in imagination, its old palaces seen in the clear, hard light that illuminates the paintings of Canaletto or reflected in the trembling and perhaps muddy waters of innumerable canals, its bright air lively with smells of drains and garlic and the operatic warbling of boatmen.

The Venice I speak of is nothing like that and indeed is not even named after it.

'But,' people say to me when I talk about it, 'where on earth *is* Venice, Ontario?' I can tell by the way they ask that they think I have made it up. It is not in the gazetteer or on any railway line or on the road to anywhere. It is where it is, and to the people who live on its two streets it is naturally at the centre of the universe, the still centre where nothing happens but about which life and time revolves.

The other question I am always asked is how did I come to live in Venice, Ont., granted there is such a place, even for a single year? I was not born there; in fact I was an immigrant from a country commonly regarded as being part of Europe. With the whole North American continent open to me, how did it happen that I chose to work there, of all places?

It was like this.

When I arrived in Toronto ten years ago I determined to take the first job that offered. A kindly and broadminded department of education agreed to regard me as eligible to teach for one year only. A master's degree from an obsolete university and a teacher's diploma from a deplorably cosmopolitan centre were rightly thought not enough for a permanent teacher. Ontario children deserved better, but for one year they were going to have to put up with me if only I could find a school board brave enough to try the experiment.

I answered thirty-six newspaper advertisements and received one reply. It was from the secretary of the school board of Venice, Ont. There was no nonsense about this letter. It said that as I was the only applicant, and as the school was stuck for a teacher, the board guessed it would have to overlook my being unqualified, and they hereby offered me the job. They were mine sincerely.

I took a train for the place nearest to Venice on the map. It was a hot August day and the train ambled leisurely through county after county of dry fields and farms and garish small towns, groaning to itself as it went and ringing a sort of dinner bell to let everyone know it was coming. At last it reached T—— where I was to get off.

There was a long low wooden platform with one of those toy houses that only railway companies know how to build. I found a waiting-room, but there was no-one in it. I got up courage to knock on a wooden hatch which I found in the wall. At once the hatch slammed open and an elderly face stared out at me from its pink-rimmed eyes. The expression on this face said clearly that I was to speak first.

'Where can I get a bus to Venice?'

'There ain't no bus,' said the face. The hatch slammed shut.

I thought for a minute or two. Then I knocked a second time. Up went the hatch and there was the face again with its question mark.

By now I was beginning to get in on the idiom. I made it brief.

'Taxi?' And then with a rush of insight I answered my own question, 'I know—there ain't no taxi.'

This took the face off its guard and the hatch remained open for a moment before it came down once more with what I fancied was a degree of hesitation.

I went and sat down on a bench to think the whole thing over.

After a longish interval a door opened opposite me and the owner of the face, who was wearing blue overalls, came out. He, too, had been doing some thinking. It had occurred to him that my problem, when you boiled it down, amounted to this: that I wanted to get to Venice. I assured him that his interpretation was correct. That being so, it appeared he had a relative who might be prepared to drive to Venice for a consideration.

Some time later I was on my way with the relative in a big shiny sedan. We did not speak for the first five miles.

My companion was a small, soft, pallid person in a brown satin shirt and rimless glasses. At last he spoke without taking his eyes from the road.

'You from the old country?'

'Yup.' (I told you I was getting into the idiom.)

A mile farther on he spoke again.

'I guess you got lords over there?'

Lords? That was what he had *said*. It puzzled me. Why lords? And then all at once I saw what he meant. Lords! Of course! I saw them as he saw them: there they were, sitting up in bed in their coronets and ermine capes eating bread and butter.

'Certainly,' I said, 'certainly we have lords.'

This was the answer he wanted.

'No *sir*!' he indignantly came back, 'No sir, you don't have no lords. . . .'

A moment later he went on triumphantly. 'You don't have no lords because there's only one lord. Yes, sir. There's only one lord. And that's our lord and saviour Jesus Christ.' And since we had now arrived outside the post office of Venice, Ont., he stopped the car and added, 'Eight dollars.'

In this way began my year in Venice, Ont.

Somewhere or other I had read an account by one of the survivors of a Polynesian shipwreck of his sensations as he lay on the beach of a desert island. Behind the beach was the coconut forest, and beyond that, mysterious blue mountains half-hidden in clouds. Not a single human creature was there but himself. Yet he had the feeling—a feeling that chilled him with the certainty of conviction—that he was being watched.

Behind the untroubled front which the landscape offered to him there lurked a presence implacably malevolent.

Such, roughly, were my feelings as I stood in the dust of Venice, Ont., in the hot August sunlight of that afternoon eight years ago. There was no-one in sight, but the hair on the back of my neck bristled with awareness of Unseen Watchers.

From behind the leafy screen of some vine that trailed over a rickety porch, from convenient cracks in wooden doors, from the corner of a curtain of simulated lace or the edge of a green paper blind, I felt the eyes upon me—calculating elderly eyes, faded with years and disillusion, eyes bloodshot with secret drinking in the woodshed, longsighted eyes bright with speculation, sharp and green as dollar bills, undertaker's eyes to measure the stranger. I shuddered. It was not that the Unseen Watchers wished me ill. But like those shades in Virgil who stretched out their arms in longing for the farther shore where the warm-blooded living still went about their loves and battles, the eyes of Venice dwelt on the newcomer with an appalling hunger.

It is true that Venice, Italy, came first. But it is also true that the founding fathers of Venice, Ont., never heard of it. They named their settlement for the first white woman to arrive there. She was the lady known as Venice—v-e-n-u-s. She did not stay long after the wives began to come in. But among other mementoes, she left her name—though its spelling was hastily altered.

There are no canals in Venice, Ont. There is a wide clear river or creek at one end of the main street. This creek would have made an admirable water supply for the town's 500 souls. But they preferred to dig wells: one well to each household. In this way they avoided the necessity for co-operation. Of course the well water was polluted, foul-smelling, black, and sulphurous. But what did it matter? The householders had preserved their independence.

The people of Venice, as I knew them during my stay, were a strange mixture of this sort of independence and the most slavish obedience to custom and precedent.

During the brief heady excitement of spring the creek was in flood and the run of pickerel and suckers brought out most of the boys in town and some of the men with fishing poles and cans of dew-worms. I myself was among the first.

One day, having used up the bait I had brought with me, I took a trowel and began digging out fresh worms on the river-bank. I had found six or seven of them when I realized that I had an audience.

It was Barber Scott, one of the keenest sportsmen in town. In fact the only reason he kept a barber's saloon was to trap fresh listeners for his hunting stories. Whether you asked for a shave or not, before you could say a word he would pin you down in the chair and whip up a lather all over your face. Then he would stand over you flourishing a cut-throat razor in fingers that smelt of fish and occasionally walk to the stove to spit. He would keep the blade in the general neighbourhood of your jugular till he was tired of talking.

He was a memorable figure, especially when viewed from behind. Dim blue overalls hung by suspenders in loose folds from his bony shoulders, as if from a coat hanger.

Now he stood over me on the river-bank, frowning under his peaked cap, spitting and groaning. The groans were in deference to the heart trouble which made it all right for him not to work very hard.

'What you doin', neighbour Dahbbs?'

'Digging worms,' I said.

'We gen'lly dig 'em up the house,' he said between spits, 'and then bring 'em down to the river.'

'Well, I'm digging them right here.'

Barber Scott fetched some terrible groans and spat a few more times.

'Well,' he concluded (it was amazing what expression Venetians could put into that word). 'Well. You'll soon get used to our ways.'

This was not a prophecy: it was more like a threat. Barber Scott, an established eccentric, did not want to see anyone else horning in on his specialty.

The fishing was good for two or three weeks and then spring was over. In the heat of summer there were swimming holes where you could cool off. But there was nowhere you could wash or take a bath. And it was worse in winter.

The extraordinary thing was that although Venice had been settled for more than a century, only four houses contained bathrooms. And of these four bathrooms, only three were in working order. The remaining one was entirely for display. All other households relied on the two-holer out-house, and the hand-pump by the kitchen sink.

With one or two exceptions, no-one in Venice, not even the most genteel, was ever quite clean. Clad in the frilly clothes they ordered regularly from the department store catalogue, the women looked pretty stylish at a range of twenty feet or so. But close up you could not help noticing the greyish colour of their necks.

This was a fearful shock to me.

I had come to North America under the impression that it was all much as it appeared in the ad columns of slick magazines. I had imagined a plump, rosy people jumping in and out of bathtubs three or four times a day, obsessed to the point of mania with problems of what the copywriters called personal daintiness. I had imagined that because there were so many ads for bathroom fittings, soap, and deodorants, there must be a tremendous demand for such things.

On the contrary.

I now saw the true reason for all the advertising. The manufacturers were begging, were imploring a nation of slobs to take a bath. They were dedicated apostles frantically preaching the gospel of hygiene to a continent of smelly old cannibals.

I was determined to be different. Whatever my neighbours did, I would take a bath at least once a week. I approached one of the four bathroom proprietors with a proposal.

It was to the Reverend Mr Homer Stark that I put my case. After an hour of civilized negotiation, we came to an agreement. I was to take a bath in the rectory tub every Saturday afternoon if in return for that privilege I undertook to sing in the church choir on Sundays. I was also to help out on special occasions—such as, for example, funerals.

The following Saturday, lapped in the amniotic luxury of hot bath-water, I noticed something that awakened in me a twinge of foreboding. There arose from those well-waters of Venice an unmistakable effluence of brimstone. It made me think of Faust, and how he had bartered his soul to the devil for learning. The deal I had made was much like his. I, too, had traded my soul. Like Faust, I would have to pay the price.

I had neglected to notice that the main occupation of the citizens of Venice, Ont., was dying.

I have never been to so many funerals in my life.

It was not that they were lugubrious occasions. Reverend Stark could certainly give a person a lovely send-off, rain or shine. But the truth is that you have to be of a certain age or temperament to enjoy facing the fact of mortality at least once a week. There was no question, you see, of ever sending to know for whom the bell tolled. I knew damn well that whoever else it tolled for, it tolled for me.

It was different, I think, for the Reverend. He had been obliged to listen for years to the obscure malice, the oblique and fumbling criticism which had issued from these mouths which now forever were stopped. I used to think I caught a note of melancholy satisfaction in his voice, a look on his face not wholly displeased, as he committed to the earth these cantankerous parishioners of his. But of course I may have misread it: his usually charitable imagination may have been rejoicing with the departed on another shore, and in a greater light.

Meanwhile he kept faithfully his part of our strange pact as each Saturday I wallowed in the sulphurous waters of Venice.

RUNNING TO PARADISE

b. 1918

Louis Dudek

LOUIS DUDEK has been active in Montreal since the early 1940s as a poet, critic, and editor and today is still an influential figure on the Canadian poetry scene. He was born in Montreal of Polish-Canadian parents and educated at McGill University and at Columbia University, New York, where he obtained a Ph.D. in 1955. Since then he has taught at McGill—courses in modern poetry and poetic theory, Canadian literature, and European literature—where he is a professor. In 1943 Dudek joined John Sutherland and Irving Layton on the magazine *First Statement*; when it merged with *Preview* in 1945 to form *Northern Review*, he became a member of the editorial board of the new magazine. In 1952, with Irving Layton and Raymond Souster, Dudek founded Contact Press, which for some fifteen years was the most active of the small poetry publishers in Canada. In the late fifties he established the McGill Poetry Series (which first published Leonard Cohen, among other student writers) and in 1957 he began his own magazine, *Delta*. It ceased publication in 1966, but out of it came Delta Canada, which continues as a small, respected poetry publisher.

Dudek's poetry books include *East of the City* (1946); *The Searching Image* (1952); *Europe*, a long poem (1955); *The Transparent Sea* (1956); *En México*, a long poem (1958); *Laughing Stalks* (1958); and *Atlantis* (1967), another long poem. His *Collected Poetry* (1971) was published by Delta Canada. (At one time during its production it was thought that the book might have been destroyed because of a bombing incident at the Belfast printing firm.) Dudek has also written *Literature and the Press* (1960), based on his doctoral thesis. He was co-editor with Irving Layton of the anthology *Canadian Poems: 1850-1952* (1952), editor of the school anthology *Poetry of Our Time* (1965), and co-editor with Michael Gnarowski of *The Making of Modern Poetry in Canada* (1967), a collection of 'Essential Articles on Contemporary Canadian Poetry in English'.

Knowledge and art are two important themes in the poetry of Louis Dudek, who is a philosophical, intellectual, rather unemotional poet. His poetry often resembles, in everything but the line form, prose commentaries made up of the ideas, reflections, opinions, and maxims of an erudite and witty essayist—only now and again do they break into pure poetry. The sea is a recurring image. 'The Marine Aquarium', published here, is part of *Atlantis*, which Wynne Francis has described as 'a yearning, melancholic, meditative poem revealing occasionally his anger, his laughter, his love, but suffused with a wistful, anguished searching for moral truth'. Something of a favourite with other poets and editors, this extract appeared in the anthology *How Do I Love Thee*, edited by John Robert Colombo, in which Dudek wrote: 'John Colombo compares this poem to a passage in Paul Klee in which the painter describes the famous marine aquarium at Naples. Actually my poem is about the same aquarium . . . It happens to be a central passage from the book [*Atlantis*], but so far I have not seen any critic or reviewer who understood the long poem, so this fact in itself is not likely to matter to anyone. The reader may enjoy the extract as a description of crustaceans and fish.'

Dudek as a disapproving critic of recent poetry can be read with interest in Issue 41 of *Canadian Literature* (Summer 1969), where he discusses poets of the sixties. In the same magazine are two useful articles on Dudek himself: by Wynne Francis on his career as a man of letters to 1964 (Issue 22, Autumn 1964) and by Douglas Barbour on Dudek the poet (Issue 53, Summer 1972).

THE MARINE AQUARIUM

I have been in a marine aquarium and I have seen
    LOLIGO VULGARIS
    TRACHINUS ARANEUS
    SCORPAENA SCROFA
    SCYLLARIDES
    ANEMONIA SULCATA
    ASTEROIDES CALYCULARIS
    MAJA SQUINADO
    MUSTELLUS LAEVIS
    THALASSOCHELIS CARETTA
    TRIGLA CORAX
    TRYGON VIOLACEA
    HYPPOCAMPUS BREVIROSTRIS
    SPIROGRAPHIS SPALANZANII
    ACTINIA CARI
    MURAENA HELENA
    SYNGNATUS ACUS
    RETEPORA MEDITERRANEA
    PELAGIA NOCTILUCA
    PARAMURICEA CHAMALEON

Of a very graceful undulant movement
    of a pale white colour
        with translucent fins

Fish that lie buried in the sand, on the sea bottom,
        with only their eyes peering out

Or long and thin as a pencil
          flexible in movement

Or absurd, barnacled, monstrous bulldogs of the deep,
        and sea-spiders of gigantic size.

Red flowers of the sea
            (or orange-coloured)
    like carnations, like broken pieces of pomegranate

(I too was once a fish

I rubbed myself on the sea bottom, leaping gracefully
        A large fish, about two feet long)

There was one like a great sturgeon
        constantly moving and twisting its muscular body

And a fish with tentacles under the fins
          on which it walks on the sea floor!
It has a blue fin, that opens when it swims

And speckled fish, too, with the eyes of snakes
        at the bottom of the sea, their heads gently bobbing

And an octopus
with saucer-like suckers, a paunchy body,
        huge eyes on great mounds,
blowing out of intestinal tubes,
        coiling the tips of his tentacles like a seashell.

He looked intelligent
Maybe he is intelligent, I thought, like a poet
        or a philosopher
who understands, but cannot act to circumvent clever men.

The octopus opened his magnificent umbrella,
pushed the belly forward, and bumped into a sleeping fellow
Then he went behind a pilaster
        because I had been watching him too long.

A magnificent creature.

And I saw beautiful tiny sea-horses
                with a fin on the back
                        vibrating like a little wheel

And a ghostly shrimp six inches long
                        light pink and white
and graceful as a star, or the new moon

And a whorl of delicate white toothpicks
And brown stems, with white strings like Chinese
                bean-sprouts, long and graceful.

And I saw a wonderful turtle.

But I have seen fish, turtle, octopus, with dead eyes
                looking out at the world.
What is life doing? Waiting for something to come?
Are we all stepping-stones to something still unknown?
Is man, when he is glad, when he is in love or enthralled
At last getting a glimpse of it?
Are the birds? Are the swift fish?

(Or perhaps they know they are captive. Who can tell,
even a fish may know when it is not at home.)

Then I saw a thin, thin thing
undistinguishable from a twig (just a few inches long)
but on close inspection very beautiful.

Since he has disguised himself to look so unremarkable,
                for whom does he keep that secret from?

There was a light green jelly
                PHYSOPHORA HYDROSTATICA
And a kind of huge one-foot-long paramecium
                PYROSOMA GIGANTEUM

And a thread-like plant with fragile white hair
(They say the chromosomes are such a thing of diminutive size,
                the whole life contained in their genes!)

And a coral that was a true artistic design
                made by a growing plant—
                        a Persian decorative motif.

And many other intelligent plants, animals, and fish.

                                        ATLANTIS

Sara Jeannette Duncan

Born and educated in a small Ontario town, SARA JEANNETTE DUNCAN became the author of nineteen lively and sensitive comedies of manners that gained international popularity in the 1890s and early 1900s. Only *The Imperialist* (1904) is in print today—the one novel that had a Canadian setting—and it stands up well; indeed, it is one of the best Canadian novels. Sara Jeannette Duncan was born in Brantford, Canada West (Ontario). She was educated there and at the Toronto Normal School, taught for a short time, and then became a journalist. Using the pseudonym 'Garth Grafton' she wrote for two Toronto papers, the *Globe* and the *Week*, the Memphis *Appeal*, and the Washington *Post*; in 1888 she became parliamentary correspondent for the Montreal *Star*. She went round the world in 1889 and used the articles she wrote during that trip for her first novel, *A Social Departure: How Orthodocia and I Went Round the World by Ourselves* (1890). In 1891 she married Charles Everard Cotes, whom she had met in India where he was then curator of the Indian Museum at Calcutta. She spent the rest of her life in India and England and died in Ashtead, Surrey.

Several of Sara Jeannette Duncan's novels deal amusingly with the theme of a woman from the New World experiencing society in the Old: *An American Girl in London* (1891), *A Voyage of Consolation* (1898), and *Cousin Cinderella* (1908). She also wrote novels about India. The setting of *The Imperialist* is Brantford, where the author grew up—here called Elgin. This novel was written at a time when there was much controversy in England over an imperialist movement that would draw the self-governing dominions together in a federation of the Empire; the Imperial Federation League, formed in 1884, had branches in Canada. Sara Jeannette Duncan was an ardent imperialist herself; but as an objective writer she was able to show the unenthusiastic reaction to this idea of people in a small Canadian town. With a sharp eye for nuances of character, and an undertone of gentle irony and humour, she also portrayed a whole way of life, one that she looked back on fondly.

In Issue 27 of *Canadian Literature* (Winter 1966) there is a brief memoir of Sara Jeannette Duncan by her husband's niece, who knew her well. *The Imperialist* is available in the New Canadian Library.

MR HESKETH SPEAKS

A small-town political meeting in Ontario at the turn of the century. Mr Alfred Hesketh of London, England, rises to speak in support of his friend Lorne Murchison, a Liberal candidate who supports the idea of an imperial federation, which was a controversial movement at the time.

Mr Hesketh left his wooden chair with smiling ease, the ease which is intended to level distinctions and put everybody concerned on the best of terms. He said that though he was no stranger to the work of political campaigns, this was the first time that he had had the privilege of address-ing a colonial audience. 'I consider,' said he handsomely, 'that it is a privilege.' He clasped his hands behind his back and threw out his chest.

'Opinions have differed in England as to the value of the colonies, and the consequence of colonials. I say here with pride that I have ever been among those who insist that the value is very high and the consequence very great. The fault is common to humanity, but we are, I fear, in Eng-land, too prone to be led away by appearances and to forget that under a rough unpolished exterior may beat virtues which are the brightest orna-ments of civilization, that in the virgin fields of the possessions which the good swords of our ancestors wrung for us from the Algonquins and the —and the other savages—may be hidden the most glorious period of the British race.'

Mr Hesketh paused and coughed. His audience neglected the oppor-tunity for applause, but he had their undivided attention. They were looking at him and listening to him, these Canadian farmers, with curious interest in his attitude, his appearance, his inflection, his whole personality as it offered itself to them—it was a thing new and strange. Far out in the Northwest, where the emigrant trains had been unloading all the summer, Hesketh's would have been a voice from home; but here, in long-settled Ontario, men had forgotten the sound of it, with many other things. They listened in silence, weighing with folded arms, appraising with chin in hand; they were slow, equitable men.

'If we in England', Hesketh proceeded, 'required a lesson—as perhaps we did—in the importance of the colonies, we had it (need I remind you?) in the course of the late protracted campaign in South Africa. Then did the mother country indeed prove the loyalty and devotion of her colonial sons. Then were envious nations compelled to see the spectacle of Canadians and Australians rallying about the common flag, eager to attest their affection for it with their life-blood, and to demonstrate that they, too, were worthy to add deeds to British traditions and victories to the British cause.'

Still no mark of appreciation. Hesketh began to think them an unhandsome lot. He stood bravely, however, by the note he had sounded. He dilated on the pleasure and satisfaction it had been to the people of England to receive this mark of attachment from far-away dominions and dependencies, on the cementing of the bonds of brotherhood by the blood of the fallen, on the impossibility that the mother country should ever forget such voluntary sacrifices for her sake, when, unexpectedly and irrelevantly, from the direction of the cloakroom came the expressive comment, 'Yah!'

Though brief, nothing could have been more to the purpose, and Hesketh sacrificed several effective points to hurry to the quotation:

> *What should they know of England*
> *Who only England know?*

which he could not, perhaps, have been expected to forbear. His audience, however, were plainly not in the vein for compliment. The same voice from the ante-room inquired ironically 'That so?' and the speaker felt advised to turn to more immediate considerations.

He said he had the great pleasure on his arrival in this country to find a political party, the party in power, their Canadian Liberal Party, taking initiative in a cause which he was sure they all had at heart—the strengthening of the bonds between the colonies and the mother country. He congratulated the Liberal Party warmly upon having shown themselves capable of this great function—a point at which he was again interrupted; and he recapitulated some of the familiar arguments about the desirability of closer union from the point of view of the army, of the Admiralty, and from one which would come home, he knew, to all of them: the necessity of a dependable food supply for the mother country in time of war. Here he quoted a noble lord. He said that he believed no definite proposals had been made, and he did not understand how any definite proposals could be made; for his part, if the new arrangement was to be in the nature of a bargain, he would prefer to have nothing to do with it.

'England', he said loftily, 'has no wish to buy the loyalty of her colonies, nor, I hope, has any colony the desire to offer her allegiance at the price of preference ∴ . British markets. Even proposals for mutual commercial benefit may be underpinned, I am glad to say, by loftier principles than those of the market-place and the counting-house.'

At this one of his hearers, unacquainted with the higher commercial plane, exclaimed, 'How be ye goin' to get 'em kept to, then?'

Hesketh took up the question. He said a friend in the audience asked how they were to ensure that such arrangements would be adhered to. His answer was in the words of the Duke of Dartmoor: 'By the mutual esteem, the inherent integrity, and the willing compromise of the British race.'

Here someone on the back benches—impatient, doubtless, at his own incapacity to follow this high doctrine—exclaimed intemperately 'Oh, shut up!' and the gathering, remembering that this, after all, was not what it had come for, began to hint that it had had enough in intermittent stamps and uncompromising shouts of 'Murchison!'

Hesketh kept on his legs, however, a few minutes longer. He had a trenchant sentence to repeat to them which he thought they would take as a direct message from the distinguished nobleman who had uttered it. The Marquis of Aldeburgh was the father of the pithy thing, which he had presented, as it happened, to Hesketh himself. The audience received it with respect—Hesketh's own respect was so marked—but with misapprehension; there had been too many allusions to the nobility for a community so far removed from its soothing influence. 'Had ye no friends among the commoners?' suddenly spoke up a dry old fellow, stroking a long white beard; and the roar that greeted this showed the sense of the meeting. Hesketh closed with assurances of the admiration and confidence he felt towards the candidate proposed to their suffrages by the Liberal Party that were quite inaudible, and sought his yellow pinewood school-room chair with rather a forced smile. It had been used once before that day to isolate conspicious stupidity. . . .

A personal impression, during a time of political excitement, travels unexpectedly far. A week later Mr Hesketh was concernedly accosted in Main Street by a boy on a bicycle.

'Say, mister, how's the dook?'

'What duke?' asked Hesketh, puzzled.

'Oh, any dook,' responded the boy, and bicycled cheerfully away.

THE IMPERIALIST

Jacques Ferron

JACQUES FERRON is known in Québec as a doctor to the poor, as a political activist and separatist, and as a prolific writer of plays and novels. In the rest of Canada he has only begun to be known as a writer with the publication of *Tales from the Uncertain Country* in 1972. He was born in Louisville, Québec, and educated in Trois-Rivières and at Université Laval in Quebec City. For some years he practised medicine in Gaspé and is now a general practitioner in Ville Jacques Cartier on the south shore of the St Lawrence, near Montreal. He was active in the separatist R.I.N. party and in 1963 founded his own satirical political movement, the Rhinoceros Party. More recently he has been a member of the Parti Québécois. In December 1970 he was asked by Special Crown Prosecutor Jacques Ducros to negotiate with the Rose brothers, who were being hunted as the kidnappers and killers of Pierre Laporte.

Ferron has published a half-dozen novels, three collections of short stories or tales, and numerous plays. One of his plays, *Les Grands Soleils* (1958), which is described as 'a free reconstruction of the Rebellion of 1837', was produced by the Théâtre du Nouveau Monde in Montreal. A satirical novel published in 1969, *Le Ciel du Québec*, included among its characters the politicians C.G. ('Chubby') Power and Ernest Lapointe, the Québec writers Jean Le Moyne and Saint-Denys-Garneau, and the poet and expert on constitutional law, F.R. Scott. Ferron's *Contes du pays incertain* won the Governor General's Award for fiction for 1962. Of the English edition, *Tales from the Uncertain Country*, William French has written: 'In these stories Ferron is a fabulist, a kind of habitant Aesop spinning tales in the old style but with very contemporary meaning. In his world, dogs talk, trees think, a centaur roams the Ontario countryside, an archangel lives near a Montreal garbage dump and Little Red Riding Hood is a nymphet.

'The uncertain country of the title is usually Quebec, sometimes all of Canada, but just as often it is the boundless geography of Ferron's fertile imagination. . . . Ferron loves making fun of the English, and he does it effectively in one of the best stories, "Ulysses", an allegory of the old tale. Ulysses is a retired sergeant-major who lives with his wife Penelope in an Ontario village called Ithaca. He had once helped fight a war in the barbarous cities of the east—Montreal being the chief one—and returns in old age with his maimed colleagues of the Legion to demonstrate the might of the Queen. He lashes himself to his foremast to resist the songs of the beautiful sirens of Montreal, but discovers that things aren't what they used to be; his mast droops.'

Tales from the Uncertain Country is available in paperback from the House of Anansi.

ULYSSES

After Ulysses' return to Ithaca, an island in the Ontario countryside, Ithaca Corner to be exact, ten houses at a crossroads, grouped round the one-time blacksmith now turned garage-man, his wife, Penelope, continued to embroider—why stop? Her embroidery had stood her in good stead. But as she no longer undid it at night it soon became very clear what was on her mind, for she would write it, embroidering the words with appropriate motifs, little birds and bleeding hearts. No sooner was a piece finished than she would put it on display: 'Home sweet home'—'No wife in the home, no sun in the sky'—'God bless this happy union'. And she had a long litany of them. What was she doing? Simply this: publicity for Penelope.

Her embroidery adorned cushions, pillow-slips, aprons, nightgowns; framed, it covered the walls of the house from the basement to the attic. And she went on and on, the dreadful woman, stitching, stitching, thin as a spider too.

With a marriage so explicitly, not to say deliriously happy, ostentatiously so at any rate, all garnish and no meat, Ulysses, like the Englishman he was, could find no fault. He acquiesced, content and wretched. At times a faint smile would cross his face, a distracted gleam appearing in his glaucous eyes. Ah! He was all but done for. The long-drawn thread was tightening round him. Yet a little and he would be caught, chewed, digested. By chance he too began to embroider. This saved him—at least for a time. And he embroidered at night, on the back of Penelope's canvas.

Here is how he went about it: he would pour himself a glass of rum, toss it back with a 'God save the Queen', then go to bed, snore, and as soon as his wife had fallen asleep, suspecting nothing, he would hand the organ pipes over to her so he himself could set to work in silence, like a real werewolf. Swiftly he would slip back to his golden years, to the barbarous provinces of the East, to Moncton, Pictou, Quebec, to Montreal especially, that city where, though a sergeant-major, he had been a little less virtuous than he would have liked. His conscience troubled him. A little less—even that was too much. Only just a little less, but the opportunities for sin had been tremendous.

Snore, Penelope, snore!

Yes, tremendous. *Ouonnedeurfoules*,* to use his exotic expression. He took them one by one, these chances he had missed, and embroidered as he dreamed, embroidered as one can after the event, when life has passed one by, with libidinous verve, and that love of the sensational characteristic of cowards and fools.

And in this way, little by little, he created the Odyssey of his life.

During the day he did not undo his work; on the contrary, he advertised it, confronting Penelope's version with Ulysses' version—a publicity battle, you might say, in true English style. That race is taciturn, but it delights in billboards.

But whereas Penelope stayed indoors, Ulysses operated outside the home. He would go and relate his adventures to the blacksmith cum garage-man. Ithaca Corner is a forgotten island. Few people ever pass through, and no one stops. To Ulysses' story the blacksmith cum garage-man added his nostalgia for horses. Sometimes, so it seemed, girls and animals would come together, and then, in the respectable Ontario countryside, centaurs would appear. Not long after, lean Penelope, peeping through the Venetian blinds, saw the cows being brought back to the shed.

THE SIRENS

And then, one day, the blacksmith cum garage-man, who was beginning to have a bellyful of the Odyssey, said to Ulysses: 'You've been back in Ithaca all of fifteen years. Why not take a little trip down East? Montreal isn't that far. You talk and talk, and perhaps the setting of your adventures has changed.' It was a great idea! But how to get away? There was no war on and Penelope was too old to be left alone; who would make up to her? The Legion very conveniently provided the excuse: they were organizing parades of one-eyed, limping, and bemedalled veterans in the barbarous cities of the East, which were showing signs of unrest, with the idea of restoring calm and demonstrating the might of Her Majesty the Queen. The sergeant-major took part in the expedition. After all, a weekend** was not the Trojan War. Penelope let him go.

So once again old Ulysses appeared in the Sirens' quarter, lashed to his foremast, while his royal sail, puffed out by the winds which had gathered during those fifteen years at Ithaca Corner, rose to his head, sailing down the middle of the ill-famed streets, listening for the sweet,

---

* *Ouonnedeurfoules*. Ferron's own 'exotic' spelling of 'wonderful'.
**The French text gives: *ouiquène*—another mischevous attempt at gallicized spelling of English.

erotic strains of a French chant which had once drifted from the now silent windows. Saint-Dominique, Berger, de Bullion, Hôtel-de-Ville, Sanguinet, he patrolled them all, but the Sirens were no longer there.

'Ouèredéare?'* he enquired.

'Hou?' they asked.

'The Sirens.'

The Sirens? They had never heard of them. You sure meet some nutty Englishmen! Can't help liking them though. Sirens, just imagine!

'Come have a drink, old chap.'

'Me, a drink!' said Ulysses, shocked. What did they take him for? No, thank you! He only got drunk at home. Or at the sergeants' mess, in the good old days, when the war was on and he could feel right at home in the heart of French Quebec. Ah! He drilled his conscripts then, did Sergeant-major Ulysses!

They had taken advantage of peace to make a great breach in that quarter of the city. Dorchester Boulevard they called it. Cars dashed along it from one red light to the next, as in Toronto. To Ulysses this was not a good omen. However, he crossed the boulevard; there was still the lower part to patrol, as far as Craig. He set off without much enthusiasm, his royal sail now drooping, his foremast unsteady. His quest was unsuccessful, as it had been further up. All he met was a veteran from Alliston who was looking for the Sirens. And the fellow hadn't even bothered to unpin his medals. The shame of it. Probably an Irishman. Ulysses tried to avoid him. The veteran nabbed him.

'Ouèredéare?'

'Hou?'

'The whores.'

Yes, he was Irish all right. Ulysses was extremely shocked: the whores! Did he look as though he'd be hunting whores? And he did not hide his indignation from the Irishman, Really! The man was disgusting!

'And what about you, brother; what are you hunting?'

'For a start I'm not your brother and furthermore I happen to be looking for the Sirens. Yes, the Sirens! And for a worthy motive. Lashed to my foremast in order to resist their call.'

The Irishman burst out laughing and slapped his thighs. Ulysses walked on. He felt old and weary. Ah! The Odyssey! How far away it all seemed. His foremast tilted, then fell. Ulysses picked up his royal sail from the street and put it in his pocket; it was now only a soiled handkerchief.

TALES FROM THE UNCERTAIN COUNTRY
Translated by Betty Bednarski

---

* Ferron's version of ' "Where are they?" (Where they are?) "Who?" '

b. 1912

Northrop Frye

NORTHROP FRYE is a literary scholar and thinker of world-wide renown who has never ceased to be interested in writing about the literature of his own country. He was born in Sherbrooke, Qué., and grew up in Moncton, N.B. He once said that he was able to make the journey from the Maritimes to Upper Canada not because of intellectual distinction but because he was a champion typist—he entered a business college after high school and went to Toronto to take part in a typing contest. He continued his education at Victoria and Emmanuel Colleges in the University of Toronto and was ordained as a United Church minister in 1936. Later he studied at Oxford, graduating from there in 1940. He subsequently joined the English Department of Victoria College and gained an impressive reputation as a teacher who brought both inspiration and intellectual challenge to the classroom. He was chairman of the department from 1952 to 1959 and principal of Victoria from 1959 to 1966, when he became University Professor. Frye was on the editorial board of *The Canadian Forum* from 1942 to 1952 and gave generous encouragement to young writers and reviewers. He has received over twenty honorary degrees and in 1970 was awarded a Molson Prize, given for outstanding achievements in the arts, humanities, and social sciences.

Frye's international reputation as a scholar and critic was established with two important books, *Fearful Symmetry: A Study of William Blake* (1947) and *Anatomy of Criticism: Four Essays* (1957), both of which examine the nature and use of symbol and myth in literature and explore as well the techniques and methods of criticism. Frye has published many other books, including a study of T.S. Eliot in the Writers and Critics series, and edited the works of two men who were his teachers and later his colleagues at Victoria College: *Across My Path*, the memoirs of Pelham Edgar, and *The Collected Poems of E.J. Pratt*. Two of his books—*The Educated Imagination* (1965) and *The Modern Century* (1967)—form an excellent brief introduction to Frye's theories and thought. The first is a collection of radio talks presenting his theory of literature and education and discussing the connection between imagination and society. The second is a series of three public lectures that deal readably and brilliantly with the relation of literature and education to the social and political realities of the modern world. In 1971 he published *The Bush Garden: Essays on the Canadian Imagination* (the Preface to which is reprinted here). It includes the intricate and masterly analysis of Canadian literature that he wrote as a Conclusion to the *Literary History of Canada* and ten years of reviews of all the poetry books published in Canada during the 1950s.

Frye's writings—informed everywhere with profound learning, wit, and a capacity to generalize imaginatively—reveal a powerful mind and an authoritative and eloquent style as he illuminates and systematizes literature and criticism, education, culture, and the interaction of imagination and society.

A study of the writings of Northrop Frye by Ronald Bates is in the Canadian Writers series of the New Canadian Library.

PREFACE TO 'THE BUSH GARDEN'

What follows is a retrospective collection of some of my writings on Canadian culture, mainly literature, extending over a period of nearly thirty years. It will perhaps be easiest to introduce them personally, as episodes in a writing career which has been mainly concerned with world literature and has addressed an international reading public, and yet has always been rooted in Canada and has drawn its essential characteristics from there.

The famous Canadian problem of identity may seem a rationalized, self-pitying or made-up problem to those who have never had to meet it, or have never understood that it was there to be met. But it is with human beings as with birds: the creative instinct has a great deal to do with the assertion of territorial rights. The question of identity is primarily a cultural and imaginative question, and there is always something vegetable about the imagination, something sharply limited in range. American writers are, as writers, not American: they are New Englanders, Mississippians, Middle Westerners, expatriates, and the like. Even in the much smaller British Isles we find few writers who are simply British: Hardy belongs to 'Wessex', Dylan Thomas to South Wales, Beckett to the Dublin-Paris axis, and so on. Painters and composers deal with arts capable of a higher degree of abstraction, but even they are likely to have their roots in some very restricted coterie in Paris or New York .

Similarly, the question of Canadian identity, so far as it affects the creative imagination, is not a 'Canadian' question at all, but a regional question. An environment turned outward to the sea, like so much of Newfoundland, and one turned towards inland seas, like so much of the Maritimes, are an imaginative contrast: anyone who has been conditioned by one in his earliest years can hardly become conditioned by the other in the same way. Anyone brought up on the urban plain of southern Ontario or the gentle *pays* farmland along the south shore of the St Lawrence may become fascinated by the great sprawling wilderness of Northern Ontario or Ungava, may move there and live with its people and become accepted as one of them, but if he paints or writes about it he will paint or write as an imaginative foreigner. And what can there be in common between an imagination nurtured on the prairies, where it is a centre of consciousness diffusing itself over a vast flat expanse stretching to the remote horizon, and one nurtured in British Columbia, where it is in the midst of gigantic trees and mountains leaping into the sky all around it, and obliterating the horizon everywhere?

Thus when the CBC is instructed by Parliament to do what it can to promote Canadian unity and identity, it is not always realized that unity and identity are quite different things to be promoting, and that in Canada they are perhaps more different than they are anywhere else. Identity is local and regional, rooted in the imagination and in works of culture; unity is national in reference, international in perspective, and rooted in a political feeling. There are, of course, containing imaginative forms which are common to the whole country, even if not peculiar to Canada. I remember seeing an exhibition of undergraduate painting, mostly of landscapes, at a Maritime university. The students had come from all over Canada, and one was from Ghana. The Ghana student had imaginative qualities that the Canadians did not have, but they had something that he did not have, and it puzzled me to place it. I finally realized what it was: he had lived, in his impressionable years, in a world where colour was a constant datum: he had never seen colour as a cycle that got born in spring, matured in a burst of autumn flame, and then died out into a largely abstract, black and white world. But that is a factor of latitude rather than region, and most of the imaginative factors common to the country as a whole are negative influences.

Negative, because in our world the sense of a specific environment as something that provides a circumference for an imagination has to contend with a global civilization of jet planes, international hotels, and disappearing landmarks—that is, an obliterated environment. The obliterated environment produces an imaginative dystrophy that one sees all over the world, most dramatically perhaps in architecture and town planning (as it is ironically called), but in the other arts as well. Canada, with its empty spaces, its largely unknown lakes and rivers and islands, its division of language, its dependence on immense railways to hold it physically together, has had this peculiar problem of an obliterated environment throughout most of its history. The effects of this are clear in the curiously abortive cultural developments of Canada, as is said later in this book. They are shown even more clearly in its present lack of will to resist its own disintegration, in the fact that it is practically the only country left in the world which is pure colony, colonial in psychology as well as in mercantile economics.

The essential element in the national sense of unity is the east-west feeling, developed historically along the St Lawrence-Great Lakes axis, and expressed in the national motto, *a mari usque ad mare*. The tension between this political sense of unity and the imaginative sense of locality is the essence of whatever the word 'Canadian' means. Once the tension is given up, and the two elements of unity and identity are confused or assimilated to each other, we get the two endemic diseases of Canadian life. Assimilating identity to unity produces the empty gestures of cultural nationalism; assimilating unity to identity produces the kind of provincial isolation which is now called separatism.

The imaginative Canadian stance, so to speak, facing east and west, has on one side one of the most powerful nations in the world, on the other there is the vast hinterland of the north, with its sense of mystery and fear of the unknown, and the curious guilt feelings that its uninhabited loneliness seems to inspire in this exploiting age. If the Canadian faces south, he becomes either hypnotized or repelled by the United States: either he tries to think up unconvincing reasons for being different and somehow superior to Americans, or he accepts being 'swallowed up by' the United States as inevitable. What is resented in Canada about annexation to the United States is not annexation itself, but the feeling that Canada would disappear into a larger entity without having anything of any real distinctiveness to contribute to that entity: that, in short, if the United States did annex Canada it would notice nothing except an increase in natural resources. If we face north, much the same result evidently occurs: this happened to the Diefenbaker campaign of 1956, which has been chronicled in books with such words as 'lament' and 'renegade' in their titles.

Whenever the east-west context of the Canadian outlook begins to weaken, separatism, which is always there, emerges as a political force. Every part of Canada has strong separatist feelings: there is a separatism of the Pacific Coast, of the Prairies, of the Maritimes, of Newfoundland, as well as of Québec. Ontario, of course, began with a separatist movement from the American Revolution. But since the rise of the great ideological revolutionary movements of our time, whether communist, fascist, imperialist, Islamic or what not, separatism has been an almost wholly destructive force. The successful separatings, like that of Norway and Sweden in 1905, took place before the rise of these movements.

In India and Pakistan, in the Arab-Jewish world, and in many other centres divided by language, colour or religion, separatism has seldom if ever stabilized the prejudices which gave rise to it, but has steadily increased them. Even where there is no political affiliation, the separation of Cuba from the American sphere of influence, or of Yugoslavia from the Russian one, cannot be a politically neutral act. Québec in particular has gone through an exhilarating and, for the most part, emancipating social revolution. Separatism is the reactionary side of this revolution: what it really aims at is a return to the introverted malaise in which it began, when Québec's motto was *je me souviens* and its symbols were those of the habitant rooted to his land with his mother church over his head, and all the rest of the blood-and-soil bit. One cannot go back to the past historically, but the squalid neo-fascism of the FLQ terriorists indicates that one can always do so psychologically.

What has just been said may seem inconsistent with some of what is said later on in this book; but the essays cover a period of thirty years, and naturally conditions in Canada itself have changed a good deal in that time. At the same time the changes have occurred within an intelligible pattern of repetition. The most striking changes are in French Canada, but some of those changes recapitulate earlier developments in English Canada. Thus the admiration for France, which on one occasion took the form of picketing a Cabinet Minister for saying that a French-made aeroplane was not as good as an English-made one, indicates a phase of colonialism now obsolete in the other culture. Similarly, separatism in the Atlantic or Prairie provinces is often based on a feeling that Ontario regards itself as an Israel or Promised Land with the outlying provinces in the role of desert wanderers: this is much the same as the attitude that Québec separatism explicitly adopts toward the Francophone Canadians in New Brunswick or Manitoba. There may be a clue here to the immediate future prospects of the country worth investigating, and the following essays, with all their repetitions and dated allusions, may provide some useful historical perspective.

I grew up in two towns, Sherbrooke and Moncton, where the population was half English and half French, divided by language, education, and religion, and living in a state of more or less amiable Apartheid. In the Eastern Townships the English-speaking group formed a northern spur of New England, and had at a much earlier time almost annexed themselves to New England, feeling much more akin to it than to Québec. The English-speaking Maritimers, also, had most of their cultural and economic ties with New England, but their political connexion was with New France, so that culturally, from their point of view, Canada stopped at Fredericton and started again at Westmount. There were also a good many Maritime French families whose native language was English, and so had the same cultural dislocation in reverse.

As a student going to the University of Toronto, I would take the train to Montreal, sitting up overnight in the coach and looking forward to the moment in the early morning when the train came into Levis, on the south side of the St Lawrence, and the great fortress of Québec loomed out of the bleak dawn mists. I knew that much of the panorama was created by a modern railway hotel, but distance and fog lent enchantment even to that. Here was one of the imaginative and emotional centres of my own country and my own people, yet a people with whom I found it difficult to identify, what was different being not so much language as cultural memory. But the effort of making the identification was crucial: it helped me to see that a sense of unity is the opposite of a sense of uniformity. Uniformity, where everyone 'belongs', uses the same clichés, thinks alike, and behaves alike, produces a society which seems comfortable at first but is totally lacking in human dignity. Real unity tolerates dissent and rejoices in variety of outlook and tradition, recognizes that it is man's destiny to unite and not divide, and understands that creating proletariats and scapegoats and second-class citizens is a mean and contemptible activity. United, so understood, is the extra dimension that raises the sense of belonging into genuine human life. Nobody of any intelligence has any business being loyal to an ideal of uniformity: what one owes one's loyalty to is an ideal of unity, and a distrust of such a loyalty is rooted in a distrust of life itself.

In the last essay in this book I speak of the alternating rhythm in Canadian life between opposed tendencies, one romantic, exploratory, and idealistic, the other reflective, observant, and pastoral. These are aspects of the tension of unity and identity already mentioned. The former is emotionally linked to Confederation and Canadianism; the latter is more regional and more inclined to think of the country as a series of longitudinal sections. They are the attitudes that Pratt symbolizes in *Towards the Last Spike* by MacDonald and Blake, and in fact they did at one time have analogues in our political philosophies. I first became aware of this polarization of mood through Canadian painting, which is why I include three short pieces on painting here. The romantic and exploratory tendency was represented for me by Thomson, the Group of Seven (especially Harris, Jackson and Lismer), and Emily Carr; the pastoral tendency by most of the better painters before Thomson and by David Milne later. 'Canadian and Colonial Painting' was contributed to *The Canadian Forum*, whose good-natured hospitality has helped so many Canadians to learn to write. The piece is polemical and immature, but I think it got hold of a genuine theme. The tribute to Milne appeared in the second issue of *Here and Now*, accompanied by illustrations which the imaginative reader should have little difficulty in reconstructing. The Lawren Harris essay was the preface to the book of his writings and paintings edited by my classmate R. G. Colgrove and published in 1969: it is therefore recent, but its attitude is very close to another article on Harris written many years earlier.

I joined the Department of English at Victoria College, and there became exposed to the three personal influences described in 'Silence in the Sea'. This lecture inaugurated a series established in honour of Pratt by Memorial University in 1968. When I was still a junior instructor, the first edition of A. J. M. Smith's *Book of Canadian Poetry* appeared (1943), and my review of it in *The Canadian Forum* was perhaps my first critical article of any lasting importance. It is hard to overstate my debt to Mr Smith's book, which brought my interest in Canadian poetry into focus and gave it direction. What it did for me it did for a great many others: the Canadian conception of Canadian poetry has been largely formed by Mr Smith, and in fact it is hardly too much to say that he brought that conception into being. The article on the narrative tradition resulted from a lead given me by the same book: this article was translated by Guy Sylvestre and appeared in an issue of his magazine *Gants du ciel*, which was devoted to English Canadian poetry. The 'Preface to an Uncollected Anthology', a paper read to the Royal Society in Montreal in 1956, follows the same general line—in the original there was some deliberate overlapping with the narrative tradition article, as the latter was available only in French and in a periodical that had ceased publication. Towards the end it touches on the question of popular culture, which is also glanced at in the review of Edith Fowke's collection of folk songs, also from *The Canadian Forum*.

At the time that I reviewed Mr Smith's anthology, I was struggling with my own book on the symbolism of William Blake (*Fearful Symmetry*, 1947). In the last chapter of that book the conception emerges of three great mythopoeic periods of English literature: one around 1600, the age of Spenser, Shakespeare and the early Milton; one around 1800, the age of Blake and the great Romantics; and one around the period 1920-1950. I thought at first of writing my second book on Spenser, but the pull of contemporary literature was too strong and the theory of literature too chaotic, and I was drawn to a more general and theoretical approach which ultimately became the *Anatomy of Criticism* (1957). When I had got started on this, in 1950, during a year I had off on a Guggenheim Fellowship, I was asked by my colleague J. R. MacGillivray, then editor of the *University of Toronto Quarterly*, to take over the annual survey of Canadian poetry in its 'Letters in Canada' issue which had been made by the late E. K. Brown from the beginning of the survey nearly up to the time of his death. Reviews from the ten essays I wrote through the decade of the 1950s form the bulk of the present book.

These reviews are too far in the past to do the poets they deal with any good or any harm, not that they did much of either even at the time. In any case the estimates of value implied in them are expendable, as estimates of value always are. They may be read as a record of poetic production in English Canada during one of its crucial periods, or as an example of the way poetry educates a consistent reader of it, or as many other things, some of them no doubt most unflattering to the writer. For me, they were an essential piece of 'field work' to be carried on while I was working out a comprehensive critical theory. I was fascinated to see how the echoes and ripples of the great mythopoeic age kept moving through Canada, and taking a form there that they could not have taken elsewhere. The better the poet, the more clearly and precisely he showed this, but the same tendencies could be seen even as far down as some of the doggerel, or what I called the naive verse.

By myth I meant, not an accidental characteristic of poetry which can be acquired as an ornament or through an allusion or by writing in a certain way, but the structural principle of the poem itself. Myth in this sense is the key to a poem's real meaning, not the explicit meaning that a prose paraphrase would give, but the integral meaning presented by its metaphors, images, and symbols. Naturally before this view had established itself it was widely misunderstood, and I became for a time, in Mr Dudek's phrase, the great white whale of Canadian criticism. That is, I was thought—still am in some quarters, evidently—to be advocating or encouraging a specific 'mythological school' of academic, erudite, repressed, and Puritanical poetry, in contrast to another kind whose characteristics were undefined but which was assumed to be much more warm-hearted, spontaneous, and soul brother to the sexual instinct. Such notions came mainly not from other critics but from poets making critical *obiter dicta*. It does no great harm, however, for poets to be confused about the principles of criticism as long as some of the critics are not.

I was still engaged in this survey when I was approached by my friend Carl Klinck of Western Ontario, with his project for a history of English Canadian literature, and I joined his committee. The conclusion which I wrote for this history repeats a good many conceptions worked out earlier during the poetry reviews, but it is closely related to the rest of the book in which it first appeared, and is heavily dependent on the other contributors for data, conceptions, and often phrasing. I emphasize this because I have edited the text, to save the reader the distraction of being continually referred to another book, and the editing has concealed my debts.

For a long time it has been conventional for Canadian criticism to end on a bright major chord of optimism about the immediate future. This tone is in a curious contrast to the pervading tone of Canadian economists, historians, political theorists, and social scientists. Some observers of the Canadian scene, including Professors Donald Creighton and George Grant, feel that there has been too long and too unchecked a domination of the longitudinal mentality in Canada, and that the tension between region and nation has finally snapped. Certainly a century after the American Civil War, the true north strong and free often looks more like a sham south weak and occupied—sham because there has been no war with this confederacy and no deliberate occupation. The national emphasis is a conservative one, in the lower-case sense of preserving the continuity of political existence, and it is typical of the confusions of identity in Canada that the one genuinely conservative Canadian party of the twentieth century, the CCF, expired without recognizing itself to be that. However, what seems to reason and experience to be perpetually coming apart at the seams may seem to the imagination something on the point of being put together again, as the imagination is occupationally disposed to synthesis. Perhaps that is part of the real function of the imagination in every community, and of the poets who articulate that imagination. In any case, there are many titles from many of the best known Canadian poets, 'Resurgam', 'Words for a Resurrection', 'News from the Phoenix', 'The Depression Ends', 'Poem for the Next Century', 'O Earth Return', 'Home Free', 'Apocalyptics', for the Canadian critic to murmur in his troubled sleep.

The title of the book has been pilfered from Margaret Atwood's *Journals of Susanna Moodie*, a book unusually rich in suggestive phrases defining a Canadian sensibility.

b. 1932

Robert
Fulford

ROBERT FULFORD, who has been called by George Woodcock 'one of the best literary journalists in Canada', has had a busy career as an editor with newspapers and magazines, as an interviewer and commentator on radio and television programs, and as a writer on the arts and society. He was born in Ottawa but was brought to Toronto a year later and has lived in that city ever since. His father was a newspaperman who worked for some years for Canadian Press. Fulford left high school to work as a sportswriter, general reporter, and city-hall reporter on the Toronto *Globe & Mail*. In the mid-1950s he began his magazine career as a copy editor for *Canadian Homes and Gardens* and in 1955-6 was managing editor of *Mayfair* magazine. From 1958 to 1962, and again from 1964 to 1968, he was literary editor and later book columnist and art columnist for the Toronto *Star*. He was an editor and columnist with *Maclean's* from 1962-4, and during the late 1950s and early 1960s he was on the editorial board of the *Canadian Forum*. He became the editor of *Saturday Night* in 1968 and his lively and pointed comments and reviews appear in every issue. At present he also writes a weekly column for the Toronto *Star* (syndicated to the Ottawa *Citizen* and the Montreal *Star*) about books and the arts in Canada. He is the host of a weekly radio program about the arts and society, which began in 1967, and is heard after midnight on Saturdays on CBC stations in Toronto, Ottawa, and Windsor.

In George Woodcock's review of *Crisis at the Victory Burlesk: Culture, Politics & Other Diversions* (1968), he also described Fulford as 'an interesting man with a live, roving mind and a sharp way of revealing it'. This book, which is a collection of Fulford's best essays and journalistic pieces to 1968, covers the whole range of his interests in books, the visual arts, popular culture, and social issues. Fulford is also the author of *This Was Expo* (1968), a description in words and pictures of Expo 67 that was a bestseller. He is the editor of *Harold Town Drawings* (1969) and co-editor with Dave Godfrey and Abraham Rotstein of *Read Canadian* (1972), a collection of articles on Canadian books and bibliographical listings.

THE AUTHENTIC VOICE OF CANADA

'We are the people who survived the hard land,' writes a bitter, angry correspondent. 'We are the descendants of the people who cut the trees to plant a crop, froze to death in the winter, were eaten alive by bugs in the summer, fished in the streams as free men . . .

'That is Canadian culture; not this mincing, aping pseudo-European has-been stuff you call Culture with a large C.'

I recognized the tone of voice and the ideas behind it as soon as I opened the letter. This was my regular communication from The Authentic Voice of Canada. The authentic voice writes to me often. The letter always comes from a different person, and the wording is always different; but the theme is constant. My correspondent always insists that he (or, as in this case, she) speaks for the true Canada, while I speak for something false, alien, effete, and shallow.

When the letter is postmarked west of Ontario, then the conflict is described as West (tough, solid, hockey-playing) versus East (soft, undependable, ballet-loving). When it comes from a rural address, my correspondent tells me that country people are honest and true whereas city people are decadent. In this case the writer of the letter—who for some reason doesn't want her name used—lives in Toronto.

'My definition of culture', she writes, 'is what a nation represents, its past, present, and hopes for the future. Your definition of Canadian culture seems to be Art.'

But art in this country, she says, is meaningless. Ballet, symphonies, art galleries—these things matter so little to Canadians that they have to be shoved down our throats by committees of rich women with nothing else to do.

'We are CANADIANS,' she writes, 'a hardy pioneer, if you like, rustic people, not a bunch of . . . court fops, or dainty ladies doing a minuet. We are of the land, the rocks, the rivers, the mountains, the sea.

'We are not displaced Europeans, trying to ape what we left behind. We are the people who left Europe because it was decadent and dead. We rejected the American way and we still reject it.'

She goes on to say that the Stratford Festival is phony. What is really Canadian is hockey, football, trotting races, camping.

'This is what being a Canadian is; the embodiment of all the inner strengths it takes to live in this land, in which only the strong can survive.'

There is much more of the same in this passionate, anxious letter. My correspondent's rage at what she sees as phony culture—set off, incidentally, by a talk I gave over the radio from the Couchiching Conference —is deeply felt. I mean it ironically when I refer to this as the authentic voice of the country, but authentic it certainly is. There are many people who think this way. The least we can do is to take them seriously.

They are victims, it seems to me, of an unfortunate by-product of artistic life: exclusivity. There is something about all art which is not democratic, or anyway not obviously democratic. I believe, as much as I believe anything, that art is for all of us, in one way or another. But I would have to be blind to fail to notice that devotees of every art—from Renaissance painting to The New Thing in jazz—have a nasty habit of erecting barriers around what they love. Many otherwise kind and intelligent people suffer from a burning desire to advance their own status and depress the status of others. They use art to this purpose. Through condescension, through snobbery, through the use of special languages, they make it as hard as possible to get close to art. They make it so hard, in fact, that many people are repelled and offended. These people turn into refugees from culture. They end up writing letters to the papers about how un-Canadian it is to go to the ballet.

The idea that nature, outdoor life, and Canadian history are on one side of a great divide, and art on the other, is of course nonsense. Canadian writing, painting, music, and dances—they are all, at some point, on intimate terms with the landscape. I have a friend who has won national prizes as both a paddler and an abstract artist; his life is a particularly striking example of a constant factor in the culture of Canada.

On the other hand, of course, Canadian art—like Canadian life—is increasingly urbanized. And here I find myself, when I receive these authentic-Canadian-voice letters, almost intimidated. I've never lived anywhere but in cities, and never wanted to. At this point I begin stuttering about how 'my people' (as they say) have been in this country for more than a century, and I may even throw in my great-aunt whose husband was shot by Big Bear's braves in 1885. But of course that means nothing: what matters is who you are now, not where your family lived then.

So I telephoned my correspondent, prepared to be put down once again by pure, native Canadianism. Who could she be? A female bush pilot? A teacher of Eskimos in the Arctic? The wife of a wheat farmer at least? None of these, it turned out. She moved to Toronto forty-five years ago, and she's lived here ever since.

CRISIS AT THE VICTORY BURLESK:
CULTURE, POLITICS AND OTHER DIVERSIONS

Mavis Gallant

MAVIS GALLANT, an expatriate writer who lives in France, is not generally thought of as a Canadian. However, she was born in Montreal and a number of her stories are drawn from her Canadian background. She attended seventeen different schools in Canada and the United States and her first job was with a Montreal newspaper. She has lived in Europe since 1950 and has been a frequent contributor of fiction to *The New Yorker*. Her short stories have been collected in *The Other Paris* (1956) and *My Heart is Broken* (1964); between these two books she published *Green Water, Green Sky: A Novel in which Time is the Principal Actor* (1959). Her absorbing account of the ordeal of a thirty-year-old French school teacher who had a love affair with a sixteen-year-old boy was published as the introduction to *The Affair of Gabrielle Russier* in 1971.

A Fairly Good Time (1970), a novel from which two extracts appear below, takes its title from the American novelist Edith Wharton, who wrote: 'If you make up your mind not to be happy, there's no reason why you shouldn't have a fairly good time.' It is about a Canadian in Paris married to a Frenchman, Philippe, who appears to have left her at the beginning of the novel. (This is her second marriage. Her first husband was Peter Higgins.) A girl who is 'comfortable in chaos', helpless with both people and events, awkward in everything, Shirley nevertheless arouses the reader's loyalty and sympathy as she tries to grapple with an unfeeling world. This novel presents Mavis Gallant's qualities as a writer at their best. Without attempting to explain human relationships that are at bottom unfathomable, she describes them probingly, uncovering people's vagaries and eccentricities with cool wit.

'MY WIFE IS A NORTH AMERICAN . . .'

ƆꞀAƆƎƧ was what Shirley could read on the wrong side of the awning at Pons. Beyond SECALG were plane trees and a Sisley sky.

'I've just this second remembered something,' said Shirley. 'O Jesus. Sorry, Mrs Castle. But it's come back to me. I'm supposed to be having lunch at Philippe's mother's today.'

'Call 'em up and say you'll be late,' said Mrs Castle. Ignoring all that her travels must have taught her by now, she said, 'Tell that waitress to bring you a phone.'

'I remember now. That's where Philippe is. He went to collect his sister at the airport early this morning. She's been in New York. They must have gone straight from the airport to his mother's. I was supposed to join them there. They'll say I forgot on purpose. He's at his *mother's* . . .'

'Bad place for a man,' said Mrs Castle, drumming her ring on the table for a waitress. 'What'll it be, Shirl?'

He had not been trying to frighten her. If she had looked carefully instead of mooning over Geneviève, she would have found a note. She imagined his writing on the pad beside the telephone: 'Colette is back, with a lady wrestler from Hamburg she met in the Museum of Modern Art. Maman hopes the wrestler has a brother and that this strange adventure will lead to marriage. We are expecting you for lunch.'

Yes, they were expecting her for the Sunday roast veal and to hear Colette's contemptuous account of the meals, clothes, and manners of another city. They would wait for Shirley and then, having made up face-saving excuses in aid of Philippe, begin Colette's favourite hors d'oeuvres of egg in aspic. 'This is the worst thing I could be giving my liver,' Colette would remark, mopping up the yolk with a bit of bread. They would eat sparingly of the veal, for meat created cancer in Madame Perrigny's anxious universe. Much of the conversation, once New York had been disposed of, would centre on the danger of food, of eating in restaurants, of eating anywhere but here, and finally of what even this luncheon would cost in terms of languor, migraine, cramps, insomnia and digestive remorse. Philippe's mother cooked well but only because she could not cook badly: she did not know how it was done. Yet the fact of eating alarmed her. Peristalsis was an enemy she had never mastered. Her intestines were of almost historical importance: soothed with bismuth, restored with charcoal, they were still as nothing to her stomach in which four-course meals remained for days, undigested, turning over and over like clothes forgotten in a tumble dryer.

Colette sympathized with her mother's afflictions, often shared them, and added to them one of her own—a restless liver. If Colette's quiescent liver were suddenly roused by an egg, an ounce of chocolate, a glass of wine, or even one dry biscuit too many, it stretched, doubled in size, and attempted to force its way out through her skin. By locking her hands against her right side, just under the ribs, Colette would manage to snap it back in place. Shrinking the liver was something else again: this meant lying down and drinking nothing but unsalted water in which carrots and parsley had been boiled for two hours, until the enraged liver subsided. Every second weekend as a matter of course, Colette went to bed for forty-eight hours, drank her broth and got up with a liver considerably weakened though never permanently vanquished.

Soon after she met Philippe, Shirley invited her sister and mother to dinner. She had not known the degree of involvement this invitation suggested or even that only uneducated persons entertained on a Saturday night. Curiosity goaded the Perrignys across Paris on a common evening. They arrived twenty-five minutes too soon. Colette bore a ritual bunch of carnations strangled in wire and wreathed with asparagus fern that shed fine green needles all the way up the stairs. Goya people, Shirley had thought when she saw them grouped together on her landing—the frail, arthritic woman with her dark gypsy's eyes, and Colette, carved and fringed and dipped in gold, like an antique armchair, and there, behind them, a new, watchful Philippe. Fifteen minutes before their arrival, if only they had been punctual, Shirley would have made her bed, emptied the ashtrays and cleared the living room of its habitual scruff of scarves, newspapers, coat hangers, rainboots, and dying flowers. She was barefoot, dressed in a towel bathrobe she held shut with her left hand. She knew that this meeting was irreparable. She remembered how the parents of her first husband had looked at her and how she had seen herself in their eyes.

'Philippe, give them a drink, will you?' she said in English. 'This damn robe hasn't got a belt and I can't let go.'

'They don't drink. Don't worry but please, please put some clothes on.'

She heard them murmuring as she dressed. The tone was only of small talk. She said to the no one in particular she named St Joseph, 'Do something. Help me out.'

She made them sit around her living-room table and she solemnly lighted candles, which led them to feel, she learned later, that her notions of elegance had been obtained in Latin Quarter restaurants. They then looked at the large dish in the center of the table and said this of it:

The Mother: 'What is there on that dish that could harm us?'

The Daughter: 'Everything.'

They picked their way through the four kinds of herring and the potato

salad dressed with dill. Glasses of aquavit remained untouched before their plates. Philippe was courteous but bewildered: Whatever had possessed Shirley? What had made her think they would enjoy an outlandish Scandinavian meal? He had told her about his sister and mother: Shirley had listened, but had she understood? She caught these questions across the table, or thought she did, and signaled, 'I am sorry,' which it seemed she had always been saying and would say forever. The Perrigny women in the meantime tried to eat some of the pork and prunes. They looked at the pastries and looked away. They nibbled black bread and pretended to sip the Danish beer. They were not shocked or offended; they were simply appalled, distressed and terrified of being poisoned.

The disastrous first meeting had not prevented the marriage but merely made the Perrigny women prudent. When they came to visit now, they accepted nothing but china tea. They bowed their heads and exchanged looks Philippe never saw and murmured opinions he never intercepted. For Philippe the sole result of the Scandinavian dinner was his fear that after he and Shirley were married they would never be able to invite normal people to share a meal: their guests would go away anxious and hungry or else stricken with colitis and botulism. He began her education. He taught her not to serve spaghetti because it was messy to eat and made it seem as if they could not afford to pay a butcher. He discouraged any dish in the nature of a blanquette or a bourguignon partly because he did not trust her to prepare it and because it might seem to others that the Perrignys were disguising second-rate cuts of meat. As he took his place at the head of the table and watched the passing round of the approved anemic veal and the harmless sugary peas he would say, 'My wife is a North American, but I taught her about food.'

* * *

On Saturday after work, as her message had promised, Shirley called on Philippe. She had a present for him—a bottle of champagne, which they had often agreed to be a cure for everything. In the bus she found a seat next to a small old man whose hands were clamped on the silver head of a walking stick. All at once, in a fit of elderly private annoyance, he pounded the stick on the floor three times. It was the beat that signaled a curtain rising; it heralded the entrance of mourners at a Mass for the dead. When Peter Higgins had been buried in an Italian graveyard, women unknown to Shirley had touched her sunburned wrist and said they were sorry. They were the remains of an English colony, summoned by an Anglican clergyman. One of them laid a hand twisted as a vine root on the girl's sleeve and frightened her by whispering 'I am the Resurrection and Life.' Resurrection? No, she was the shadow of Madame Perrigny thrown before, a mistake in time.

A row of cypress trees swayed in Shirley's mind. Their shadows rocked over untended Protestant graves. She heard a woman's cracked undertone muttering 'I am the Life.' She was the Life and Shirley was only a penitent in a strange house now, tapping her heels along a strange marble floor, standing finally with her offering (champagne) before a brown-painted door. This was a door equipped with three locks, one above the other. Drilled at dead centre, at eye level, a hole fitted with a magnifying glass and known as a Judas enabled Madame Perrigny to be sure her husband's ghost was not there in the hall, whimpering and cringing and offering apologies. After Madame Perrigny had decided the visitor was indeed Shirley and not just someone pretending to be, she opened the door a few inches, though she still kept a chain on the latch from within. Her system of precautions had seemed necessary when Philippe and Colette were still small and their mother had been afraid Monsieur Perrigny and his infamous mistress might kidnap them, pervert them, teach them to steal in the streets, and abandon them in the Bois de Boulogne when their usefulness had come to an end. She had imagined a black Citroën trembling at the curb with a sly Corsican at the wheel. The children, warned and ready, would clutch each other's hands whenever they saw such a car and run home. The whole family would sit quietly then, not even turning on the radio to hear the war news, listening for the sound of a motor or a step in the hall. Shirley could now glimpse a dark eye, a few thimbles of glossy hair, and a hand as white as talcum. The smell of curried mutton came out of the dark flat.

'But of course you would not have made him a curry, he has hepatitis,' was the first thing Shirley said. It was for such remarks that her husband's relations considered her well below par, almost feeble-minded. She dropped her gaze to the hand and the inch of black cuff that indicated Madame Perrigny's perpetual mourning for the living. She, exasperated by Shirley's dismal simplicity, began easing the door shut. It seemed to be moving irresistibly, of its own accord. 'You needn't do that,' Shirley said. 'I'd never force my way in.' The Judas glass, no larger than an infant's fingernail, terrified her. She felt as if another presence were behind it, silently watching and judging her.

What Shirley had at first taken to be curry was disinfectant, the background scent of the twice-monthly Sunday luncheons here. It wafted out of the looped, carpet-thick draperies and the tapestry rug that hung from a rod between the parlor and the dining room as a barrier against drafts. These rugs, decorated with scenes of an extraordinary Araby, were reminders of a colonial past. Philippe said he detested everything in this apartment; he had told Shirley how nothing ever changed and that even the rusty can opener in the kitchen had been there as long as he could remember. But he had grown up with the rugs and the stiff net curtains and the cold chandeliers and had never thought of leaving them or changing them until he was nearly twenty-nine. One day he and Colette would probably fight like wildcats for everything in the place, even the useless can opener, each of them wanting to own their common past. Shirley supposed Philippe to be behind the Arab curtains now. Darkness was above and behind the Arab on his white horse and the wild-armed women he trampled to death. Behind the barrier, steadily inhaling disinfectant, Philippe, safe from fresh air, listened to his mother dismissing his wife.

'It is only champagne,' he must have heard Shirley pleading. 'It's something he likes.'

'It would finish him off,' said his mother. 'Even a child would know better.'

'Doesn't he want to see me?' No answer. 'Doesn't he need anything from home?'

'He is home,' said his mother and shut the door.

A FAIRLY GOOD TIME

Saint-Denys-Garneau

HECTOR DE SAINT-DENYS-GARNEAU is one of the most highly thought-of poets in French Canada. Great-grandson of François-Xavier Garneau and grandson of Alfred Garneau, both well known as a leading historian and poet respectively, he was born in Montreal and spent much of his childhood at the family manor at Ste-Catherine-de-Fossambault near Quebec. He was educated at the Jesuit Collège Sainte-Marie in Montreal and also studied painting at the Ecole des Beaux Arts. In 1928 he contracted rheumatic fever, which left him with a damaged heart; he gave up his studies in 1933.

Saint-Denys-Garneau was a lively and amusing companion to his friends, but he had a neurotic capacity for spiritual suffering and became more and more of a recluse, young though he was. He spent the winters of 1940 and 1941 alone at Ste-Catherine, visiting Montreal occasionally and then fleeing back to his home in the country. Jean Le Moyne, who knew him well, has written: 'Until his final retirement I don't believe we ever saw each other without falling into ecstasies of laughter. His gift for fantasy had reached an extraordinary height and subtlety. With a gesture, an intonation, a raised

eyebrow, or the inspired use of colloquialism, he could shake the foundations of reality. And in his daily life, especially when he was alone in the country, he was a bohemian of the first water. . . . as far as outlandish accoutrements were concerned, or disconcerting attitudes and all like rebellious baggage, he could have taught our beatniks a thing or two. . . . But in the midst of this picturesque behaviour . . . his laughter frequently struck a false note and he would lapse into a sudden gravity, would fall silent, would stare intensely like a cat attentive to some reality in the walls or outside them.'

From 1941 to 1943 he lived at Ste-Catherine entirely with his parents. One evening, after a dinner with family friends, he set out for an island where he was building a cabin. He had a heart attack on the way back and was found the next day, dead at thirty-one.

Saint-Denys-Garneau had a deep religious faith, but this was coupled with feelings of guilt and alienation that, until the early 1960s, afflicted many writers of Québec who were tormented by the stifling, ingrown, authoritarian society they lived in. (See also the note on Anne Hébert, a cousin of Saint-Denys-Garneau.) His abstract, symbolic poetry grew out of spiritual anguish caused by a conflict between a life-loving Christian vocation and an inclination to reject the world. ('How dangerous happiness is,' he wrote in his *Journal*.) His religious anxiety and the consequent 'inner dislocation' out of which he wrote produced poetry that Jean Le Moyne has described as 'the irreparable loss of inner content, the rupture of temporal ties, the invasion of the living being by its own death.'

(About the important place of death in French-Canadian writing, Roch Carrier has said: 'I speak about death because in our religious culture Man was created, according to our religion, not to live but to die. The most important thing was death and the life after death, because for all the French Canadians death was the main thing, life after death. So they did not care about life during life.' (Donald Cameron: *Conversations with Canadian Novelists* (1972).)

Virtually all his writing that was published—his poetry and *Journal*—was produced in a period of four years, 1935 to 1939. Saint-Denys-Garneau's collection of poems, *Regards et jeux dans l'espace*, the only book published in his lifetime, appeared in 1937. The *Poésies complètes* was published in 1949. His *Journal* (for the years 1935 to 1939), a record of his thoughts on moral and aesthetic matters edited by Robert Elie and Jean Le Moyne, was published in 1954; an English translation by John Glassco appeared in 1962. For translations of some of the poems, see F.R. Scott: *Saint-Denys-Garneau & Anne Hébert: Translations/Traductions* (1962) and *The Poetry of French Canada in Translation* (1970) edited by John Glassco. 'Saint-Denys-Garneau's Testimony to His Times' by Jean Le Moyne appears in Issue 28 of *Canadian Literature* (Spring 1966) and was later published in his collection of essays, *Convergence* (1966).

A DEAD MAN ASKS FOR A DRINK

A dead man asks for a drink
The well no longer has as much water as one
    would imagine
Who will bring the answer to the dead man
The spring says my stream is not for him.

So look now all his maids are starting off
Each with a bowl for each a spring
To slake the thirst of the master
A dead man who asks for a drink.

This one collects in the depth of the nocturnal
    garden
The soft pollen which springs up from flowers
In the warmth which lingers on at the enclosure
    of night
She enlarges this flesh in front of him

But the dead man still is thirsty and asks for a
    drink

That one collects by the silver of moonlit meadows
The corollas that were closed by the coolness of
    evening
She makes of them a well-rounded bouquet
A soft heaviness cool on the mouth
And hurries to offer it to the master

But the dead man is thirsty and asks for a drink

Then the third and first of the three sisters
Hurries also into the fields
While there rises in the eastern sky
The bright menace of dawn
She gathers with the net of her golden apron
The shining drops of morning dew
Fills up a cup and offers it to the master

But still he is thirsty and asks for a drink.

Then morning breaks in its glory
And spreads like a breeze the light over the valley
And the dead man ground to dust
The dead man pierced by rays like a mist
Evaporates and dies
And even the memory of him has vanished from
    the earth.

F. R. SCOTT (*tr*)

LANDSCAPE IN TWO COLOURS
ON A GROUND OF SKY

Life and death on a pair of hills
A pair of hills and four hillsides
The wildflowers on two sides
The wild shadow on two sides.

The sun upright in the south
Lays his blessing on both peaks
Spreads it over the face of the slopes
Far as the water in the valley
(Looking at all and seeing nothing)

In the valley the sky of water
In the sky of water the water-lilies,
Long stems reach into the deeps
And the sun follows them with a finger
(Follows with a finger, feeling nothing)

On the water rocked by the lilies
On the water pricked by the lilies
On the water pierced by the lilies
Held by a hundred thousand stems
Stand the feet of the pair of hills
One foot flowered with wildflowers
One foot eaten by wild shadow.

And for him who sails in the midst of all
For the fish that leaps in the midst of all
(Seeing a fly at the very most)

Down the slope toward the deeps,
Plunge the brows of the pair of hills
One brow of flowers bright in the light
Twenty years' flowers against the sky
And one brow without face or colour
Wanting either sense or sunlight
But wholly eaten by wild shadow
Wholly made of the black the empty
Gap of oblivion, circled by still sky.

JOHN GLASSCO (*tr*)

BIRD CAGE

I am a bird cage
A cage of bone
With a bird

The bird in the cage of bone
Is death building his nest

When nothing is happening
One can hear him ruffle his wings

And when one has laughed a lot
If one suddenly stops
One hears him cooing
Far down
Like a small bell

It is a bird held captive
This death in my cage of bone

Would he not like to fly away
Is it you who will hold him back
Is it I
What is it

He cannot fly away
Until he has eaten all
My heart
The source of blood
With my life inside

He will have my soul in his beak.

F. R. SCOTT (*tr*)

b. 1913

Hugh Garner

Since the late 1940s HUGH GARNER has been the most diligent practitioner of North American urban realism among the fiction writers of English Canada. He was born in England but grew up in the Cabbagetown district of Toronto, which he has described as 'a sociological phenomenon, the largest Anglo-Saxon slum in North America'. It has been a dominant influence on his novels and short stories, and he regards himself as a writer of working-class origin. Garner fought for the Loyalists in the Spanish Civil War in the late 1930s and served on a Canadian corvette during the Second World War. After the war he set out to make his living as a writer, and his first published novel, *Storm Below* (1949), drew on his wartime naval experience for its background. This book has been described by the critic Hugo McPherson as 'an unheroic but oddly warming record of an encounter of nature, fate, and man during six days at sea in 1943'. In 1950 a butchered version of Garner's earlier novel *Cabbagetown* was published as a pocket book; it was not until 1968, when the complete text was finally published, that this description of working-class life in Toronto in the 1930s was seen to be

one of the major social novels written by a Canadian. Hugh Garner's other novels include *Silence on the Shore* (1962), a multi-character study set in a Toronto rooming house; *A Nice Place to Visit* (1970), in which an aging writer-journalist investigates a sensational criminal case in a small town not far from Toronto; and *The Sin Sniper* (1970), a tough police thriller about Toronto's downtown vice district. Garner has been a prolific journalist and a regular participant in radio and television panel programs. Several of his novels and many of his short stories have been adapted for radio and television dramas. He has published nearly 100 short stories and *Hugh Garner's Best Stories* (1963) won the Governor General's Award for fiction. Some of his most successful stories—and this has been unusual in Canadian fiction—deal realistically with people from outside middle-class society: with Indians in the story 'One, Two, Three Little Indians', with factory workers in 'E Equals MC Squared', and with immigrant workers in the tobacco district in southwestern Ontario in 'Hunky'.

In November 1971 five of Hugh Garner's novels and *Hugh Garner's Best*

Stories were published as paperback reprints by Pocket Books. At that time the critic Robert Fulford wrote: 'Garner has been, through most of his life, what [Mordecai] Richler often says a novelist should be: the loser's advocate, the man who will stand up for those who (economically, socially, intellectually, whatever) are rated second-class citizens. Garner's people are life's outsiders, and this is consistent because he himself is an outsider. . . . Hugh Garner, taken all in all, is a writer to be cherished.'

HUNKY

It was a hot August morning. The sun, still low against the horizon, was a white-hot stove lid that narrowed the eyes and made the sweat run cold along the spine. The sky was as high and blue as heaven, and the shade-giving cumulus wouldn't form until noon. Before us lay the serried rows of tobacco, armpit high and as dull green as bile. Along with Hunky and the other members of the priming gang I sat in the grass at the edge of the Ontario field waiting for the stoneboat to arrive from the farmyard. The noise of the tiny tractor coming down the dusty track from the yard hid the scratching sound of the grasshoppers in the hedge.

Hunky, to give him the name he called himself, was the gang's pacesetter and also my room-mate in the unused tool shed where we bunked. He sat in the grass, effortlessly touching the toes of his sneakers with the palms of his hands, a redundant exercise considering the limbering up we were getting from our work in the fields. Hunky was proud of his physique, and had a bug about physical fitness, and he practised every evening with a set of weights he had put together from an old Ford front axle with the wheels attached. He believed in health and strength as some believe in education. He had said to me on my first evening at the farm, 'Me, I'm a poor D.P. No brains, only strong back. Keep strong, always find job.' There was enough truth in his philosophy to make me feel a little ashamed of my own softness, but even more ashamed of the education and training I'd thrown away over the years.

When Kurt arrived on the tractor, he pulled the boat with its high boxed sides into the aisle between the fourth and fifth rows of the new field. When he glanced back at us we got to our feet, my protesting muscles and sinews stiff from the twelve hours of disuse that bridged the time between the morning and the evening before. Without a word we walked to our rows and crouched between them, tearing off the sand leaves like destructive ants, and cradling them in the crook of our other arm. We shuffled ahead on our haunches through a world suddenly turned to jungle, along a

sandy aisle that promised an ephemeral salvation at the other end of the field.

Hunky was soon several yards ahead of me, his gilded shoulders bobbing and weaving two rows away, his crewcut nodding up and down between the plants. When he crossed my aisle on his way to the stoneboat he would give me an encouraging wink. The pride he felt in his speed and skill was apparent in his stride and in the way he flaunted his wide armful of green and yellowing leaves before the straw boss, Kurt. At the opposite side of the tractor, McKinnon, Frenchy Côté, and Old Man Crumlin were farther back than Hunky and me. Kurt fidgeted on the tractor seat, trying to hurry them with angry glances when he caught their eye.

When I reached the end of my rows Hunky was stretched out in the shade of the tobacco, his head resting in the sand. With an indolent finger he was tracing the rivulets of sweat than ran along his throat. When he saw me he sat up.

'You do good for new man, George,' he said.

'Yeah,' I answered, throwing myself on the grass.

'You come to farm too late this summer. Better to be here for suckerin'. Taking suckers first make it better to prime after. Loose up muscles,' he said. He stretched out an arm that showed the mice running under the chocolate tan of his skin.

'I think you're right, Hunky.'

'How many years are you, George?'

'Forty-five at the last count.'

He shook his head solemnly. 'Priming is young man's job. How you get job with Vandervelde?'

'The usual way. From the slave market in Simcoe.'

'Why you take job on tobacco, George?'

I didn't want to go into that. My domestic and financial fall from grace would have taken all morning to tell. 'I needed the money.'

'Yes,' he said soberly. Then he brightened up. 'How old is Hunky, George?'

I pushed myself up on an elbow and looked him over. 'I'd say twenty-four, twenty-five.'

'Twenty-t'ree, George. Born nineteen and t'irty-five.' Then proudly, 'I got papers.'

I smiled and lay down again. I thought of the rows upon rows still to be primed of sand leaves, the lowest leaves on the plant. After the sand leaves were gone the work would become easier, as we harvested the leaves higher and higher on the stalk. It was a promise that kept me going almost as much as my desperate need of the money.

'Time to go, George,' Hunky said, getting up.

I stood up as Kurt disengaged the tractor from the loaded stoneboat, hitched on to an empty one that had been waiting at the end of the field, and pulled it into an aisle midway between the next ten rows. He waited impatiently until the five of us began working again, then rehitched the tractor to the loaded boat and drove back towards the yard, where the leafhandlers and tyers were waiting.

Hunky was right; priming tobacco is a young man's job. This was my third day at the Vandervelde farm, and I was surprised I had lasted so long. The beginning of each day was a torture that became an aching hell by evening. Fifteen years of losing jobs on newpapers is no training for manual labour. Though I was sweating heavily, I could no longer smell the exuded alcohol, which was something I was glad of.

At noon hour Mrs Vandervelde banged the stick around the brake-drum to call us to dinner, and we stumbled up the dusty road, following the tractor and stoneboat to the house. Hunky ran ahead as he always did, to shower under the crude pipe that was rigged behind the kilns. As I passed I could see him behind the gunny-sack curtains, his face raised into the guttering stream of water. I just washed my hands.

The table was set out in the yard, under the shade of an oak tree. The two male tyers, and the women leaf-handlers, Frenchy Côté's wife and another French-Canadian girl, were already eating. I don't know too much about Belgian cooking, but the Vandervelde farm was not the place to make a study of it. We had boiled beef again for the third straight day, with boiled turnips and potatoes. Marie Vandervelde, the eighteen-year-old daughter of the farmer, strained against her dress as she ladled food onto our plates. We swallowed it as fast as we could, before the flies could beat us to it.

Hunky came to the table in a minute or two, the water running out of his hair and forming glycerine drops on his shoulders. Marie rubbed against him as she filled his plate. He gave her a shy smile, then disregarded the flies as he bowed his head and crossed himself before he ate. There were plates of doughnuts under cheesecloth covers, but I settled for a mug of coffee. My admiration for Hunky was slightly soured with envy. I wished I'd had a son like him, if I'd had a son. I couldn't even remember ever being as young and healthy myself.

The Vanderveldes, the North Carolina tobacco curer called Joe, and Kurt Gruenther, all ate in the kitchen; the rest of us ate in the yard unless it was raining. As we sipped our second coffee, smoked, and talked together in either English or French, Maurice Vandervelde came through the kitchen doorway and walked down the slope of the yard to the table.

'Kurt tells me you're not getting all the sand leaves,' he said.

All the primers but Hunky looked up at him.

'From now on I want every leaf primed,' he said, standing there with his hands on his hips like a fat Belgian burgomaster. 'Crumlin, and you too Taylor,' he said, looking at me. 'I want every leaf. You can go over the rows again after supper. I want them plants stripped.'

'No leafs left on plants,' Hunky said, fixing the boss with his eye. He took an insolent bite of doughnut and washed it down with coffee.

Vandervelde stared down at him, while two white spots appeared on his cheeks. He said, 'I didn't say nothing about *your* rows.'

Hunky asked, 'Why Kurt not say nothing in the field?'

They remained facing each other for a long minute, held apart by something more than fear or respect. 'Don't forget what I told you,' Maurice said, then swung around on his heel and walked back to the house.

Before we started priming in the afternoon, Hunky walked to the tractor and had a long argument in German with Kurt. Kurt got down from the machine and followed Hunky along the rows we'd primed that morning. When they came back, Hunky was carrying ten or twelve limp yellow leaves. He threw them into the boat with an angry gesture, before disappearing into the tobacco and beginning work.

Nothing was said about the priming at supper, and Maurice stayed in the house. The men each took a shower behind the kilns, and the two French-Canadian girls were allowed to use the bath in the house because it was Saturday night. After my shower I put my shorts and extra shirt to soak in a pail. Then I lay on my bunk with the shed door open, watching Hunky lifting his weights in the yard. I heard the laughing chatter of the two girls as they got into Frenchy's car, then watched it pull down the road in the direction of Simcoe with Frenchy at the wheel.

Hunky showered and shaved, then took his white shirt and beige-coloured slacks from the hanger beneath his jacket.

'You stayin' here, George?' he asked.

'Yeah, Hunky. I think I'll stay away from town for a while.'

'You want a couple of dollars, George?' he asked. 'I go now to get my money up at house.'

'No thanks. I've got enough for tobacco and papers for next week. That's all I need.'

'Hokay. See you Monday morning. You feel good by Monday, you see, George.' He laughed.

'I want to thank you for what you did today. If it hadn't been for you, Crumlin and I would have had to go over our rows tonight.'

'Was nothing, George. Gruenther try to make trouble, is all. He not make trouble for Hunky though. No siree, not for Hunky.' We both laughed at the preposterous thought.

'Are you going away for the weekend?' I asked.

'Sure t'ing. Go to Delhi. Stay with Polish family. Go to church.' He pulled a small book from his pocket and showed it to me. The printing was in Polish, but it was half-filled with columns of figures and weekly dates. Most of the figures were for small amounts of money, and it showed a total of $350. 'Polish people credit union,' he explained. 'After save for couple years, buy tobacco farm. Tonight I put in fifty dollar, make four hundred, eh, George?'

'You're a rich man, Hunky.'

'No important, George. More better to be healthy, eh?' He laughed, slapped me on the shoulder, and left the shed. I watched him take his old bicycle from the barn and wheel it to the house. He disappeared inside for a few minutes, then came out and rode away in the direction of Delhi.

The slight evening breeze dropped with the setting of the sun. McKinnon and Crumlin, who bunked in the barn, dropped by to ask me if I wanted anything from the crossroads store about a mile down the road. I gave McKinnon enough money to get me a package of makings, but turned down their invitation to accompany them.

After a while I gave up trying to feel sorry for myself, and thinking how stupid I'd been to end up this way, priming tobacco. I got up and walked across the yard. In the dark the farm had the shadowed realism of a stage set, the big frame house with its windbreak of poplars, the oak tree dominating the yard, the barn, and greenhouse and, behind them, the five tall kilns. Numbers 1, 2, and 3 were belching oily smoke from their chimneys as the tobacco slowly cured.

As I circled the house, listening to the cicadas in the poplars and the cadenced beep of a predatory nighthawk somewhere in the darkening sky above, I heard Maurice shouting inside the house. I was too far away to hear the words, or even understand the language, but I could see the fat form of the boss through the livingroom window, pointing a finger at Marie and shouting. Kurt was standing against the door wearing a self-satisfied smirk. Mrs Vandervelde was remonstrating with her husband, and holding him by the arm. I knew they were discussing Hunky. I turned around and walked towards the kilns.

Joe the curer was sitting in a tilted chair propped against No. 4 kiln, listening to a hillbilly program on his portable radio. He was mumbling to himself and keeping time with his feet. He nodded to me but said nothing. In a moment or two Kurt.Gruenther came from the direction of the house, said hello to Joe but not to me, and bent over and peered into the firebox of No. 3. He spent most of his evenings around the kilns, ambitious to become a curer himself. I went back to the tool shed.

It was some time later when I heard the screen door bang at the house. I looked through the doorway of the shed and saw young Marie come out on the porch and stand there crying. She was soon joined by Kurt, and the two of them sat together on the porch steps. Once, I heard her giggle, and I knew that her tears when her father had been shouting at her had been protective ones.

She wasn't the girl Hunky should think of marrying, but who was I to think of anything like that? What she did when Hunky was away was her own business. I'd woke up a couple of times in the late evening and found Hunky missing from his bunk, and once I'd seen him returning from the fields with Marie. I mused on the thought that the affairs of the young are the envies of the middle-aged. I got undressed and climbed beneath the blanket.

During the next week we finished the sand leaves and began priming higher up on the plants. Almost imperceptibly the pain and stiffness of the first few days disappeared. I found myself even looking forward to the meals, which showed me my physical cure was almost complete. Sometimes I went most of the day without even thinking of a drink.

The weather held good for priming. There was a heavy dew in the morning, which evaporated shortly after we reached the fields. All the day the scorching sun burned down on the tobacco, tinting the sea-green leaves with lighter hues, yellowing their edges and bringing them to ripeness. Midway during the morning and afternoon Marie came out to the field, carrying a pail of barley water and a dipper, which she set down at the end of the rows. Kurt always stepped down from the tractor to talk to her and take the first drink. The girl laughed a little too loudly at his jokes, her eye roving down the aisle where Hunky was working. After she had stretched her stay as long as she could she would walk back towards the house, her step a little less hurried than when she came.

In the early evenings Hunky and I generally sat on the steps of the shed and talked. He told me about his childhood, which wasn't a childhood at all, but had been spent on a German farm during the war. I knew from hints he dropped that his parents had been put to death in the gas chambers of a German concentration camp. From things he told me I came to realize that physical fitness and strength were not youthful fads with him, but were the legacy of a time when to be weak or ill meant death.

His ambitions were the modest ones of most immigrants: to buy a place of his own, marry, and have children. He placed great stress on the fact that he hoped to become a Canadian citizen in the fall. His longing for citizenship was not only gratitude and patriotism towards the country that had given him asylum, but a craving for status as a recognized human being.

He seemed very thoughtful one evening, and finally he said, 'I never know the good life, George.'

'Some of us never do, Hunky.'

'After October things change though, eh? I have Canadian passport then, eh, George.'

'Sure. You'll be okay then.'

'I never before have passport. Never.'

He reached into the inside pocket of his jacket hanging on the wall and pulled out a piece of folded paper, its folds blackened from constant opening and its outside surfaces yellowed with age and exposure. It was an immigration clearance from a displaced persons camp near Martfeld, Lower Saxony. Now I remembered his pride when he had told me, a week before, that he had papers. This flimsy thing was Hunky's only proof that his life had a beginning as well as a present. It was all that connected this big, quiet, honest, muscular human being with the rest of documented humanity. I read his name, Stanislaw Szymaniewski, and beneath it his birthplace, Piotrków, Poland. Beside the printed question, 'Date of birth?' was typed July 24, 1935.

'My name is hard for Canadian to say, eh?' Hunky asked. 'Hunky not so hard, eh, George?'

I suddenly realized that Hunky is a good name, depending on how it is said. It made me smile a little bitterly to myself to think how he had acquired it. It had probably been some native-born jerk in a railroad bunk-car or construction boarding-house somewhere who had named him that. Whoever he was, he must have been abashed when Hunky adopted the sarcastic epithet as his own.

The harvest was going well, but there was a tension in the air. Vandervelde came out to the fields more and more as the days passed. He would stand beside the tractor and talk to Kurt, while the little German's eyes would stare at us balefully from his small, dark, pinched face, trying to hurry us with an unspoken threat. One quarter of the barn floor was piled high with the cured tobacco, and the five kilns throbbed with the heat from their flues day and night as the leaves dried and cured.

'What's the matter with Vandervelde?' I asked Hunky one night.

'He's scared. Plant too big crop. He owe big mortgage on farm. Have to borrow money from Gruenther for seed last spring.'

'From Kurt?'

'Sure. Kurt want Marie, so lend father money. Maurice give him share of crop. Now both scared.' He laughed.

'Hunky.'

'Yeah, George?'

'Do you like Marie a lot?'

'Sure. She good strong girl, like girl in old country. She—'

'Has she said she'll marry you?' I blurted out.

He stared at me, and there was a hint of sorrow in his sudden anger. 'You think I not good enough for her, George?'

'I didn't say that,' I said, turning away.

'We go to dances in the spring, or a movie-picture in Simcoe. Why you ask that, George?'

'Nothing. I've noticed she likes you better than Kurt.'

'Sure,' he said, smiling again with youthful assurance. 'Her father not like me, though.'

'I can see that, too.'

'He try to make Marie stop meeting me,' he said, laughing once again.

I looked at Hunky and wanted to tell him what I thought, but I couldn't. I hoped he never would marry Marie, but for opposite reasons than her father's. He was too good for her, too naive and unspoilt to let a girl like that break him down. She wore her dresses too tight, and cut her hair too short, and laughed too easily to ever settle down as the wife of an immigrant farmer. Some day she would take off for the city with a good-looking harvest hand, or run away with a salesman of waterless cookers. She was too ripe to stay on the tree but not quite ripe enough yet to go bad. Hunky deserved a better deal from a life that up to then had dealt him only deuces. He was so sure, so youthfully sure, that his health and strength would get him out of any situation. How could I warn him that life wasn't that uncomplicated, that youth and strength were no match for a young woman's wiles and an older man's hatred? He would have to learn it himself, as we have all had to learn at one time or another.

'Maurice want Marie to marry Kurt,' he said. 'I got no money. I'm only poor Polish D.P.'

'But Vandervelde and Gruenther are immigrants too.'

'Sure, but got citizenship.'

My thoughts about the girl, and his constant harping about passports, 'papers', and becoming a citizen, made me angry. He seemed to think that once he received his papers he would no longer be an unschooled labourer: that in some magic way it would make him the equal of anyone in the country.

'Citizenship! I'm a citizen and what has it got me! You'd think it was the most important thing in the world!' I shouted.

He said quietly, 'When you have none, George, it is most important thing.'

When I cooled down I asked, 'Where are you going after the harvest?'

'I got job in Beachville—in limestone quarry. Polish friend work there.'

'Are you thinking of taking Marie with you?'

He laughed and slapped his thigh. 'Sure t'ing, George! What Maurice say to dat, eh?'

I had a pretty good idea.

Hunky walked to the side of the shed and picked up his homemade barbells. From my seat on the steps I saw Marie standing on the porch watching him, straining forward in her dress as he was straining as he hefted the bar. It was like watching a piece of taut elastic that is about to break. I went inside again and rolled a cigarette.

The following evening as we hung tobacco in No. 2 kiln, old man Crumlin reached too far for a lath of tobacco and fell from the peak to the earthen floor, breaking his wrist on the way down on a horizontal two-by-four. Maurice Vandervelde ranted and cursed, almost accusing Crumlin of falling just to spite him. He claimed he didn't have enough gas in his car to drive him to the hospital in Simcoe, and Frenchy Côté had to take him in his. The rest of us worked until dark, filling the kiln, though Hunky did the work of two men.

It was getting late in the season, and help was scarce. From then on there were only four of us in the priming crew, and Kurt refused to get down off the tractor to give us a hand. Despite Kurt's weasel glances and Vandervelde's curses, Hunky refused to increase the pace.

'We not run along rows, Maurice,' he said to the boss one day. 'Want tobacco in, get more men.'

Vandervelde spat out something in Flemish, turned around and walked from the field. It was only the shortage of help that prevented him from firing Hunky on the spot. From then on we had to fill an extra boat each day, and the sun was setting by the time we'd hung a kiln in the evening.

One noon hour as we sat at the dinner-table, Vandervelde came into the yard with a junk dealer and pointed to a pile of old irrigation pipe and worn-out appliances near the barn. The dealer backed his truck through the gate and looked towards the table for some help in loading it.

The boss cried, 'Hey, some of you give this man a hand with this stuff.'

McKinnon and one of the tyers rose to their feet, but Hunky shouted, 'We get paid for work in fields, not load junk.' The two men sat down again.

I had been trying to think of whom Hunky reminded me, and now it came to me. It was an old Scots syndicalist I'd met on a road gang in B.C. in the early years of the depression. He had been a Wobbly, with the guts and dignity of his convictions, long before the trade unions and bargaining tables made his kind an anachronism. 'Direct action is all the bosses understand,' he used to say.

Vandervelde glared at Hunky, before his face cracked with a mean little smile. He called Kurt from the house and the two of them helped the junkman load his truck. Then the boss walked to the side of the tool shed and picked up Hunky's barbells. He carried them to the truck and threw them in. 'You can have these for nothing,' he said to the man, while Kurt laughed at the joke. I glanced at Hunky. He was eating a piece of pie with studied unconcern, but his face was white beneath his tan.

By Saturday there were only a few days' priming left, and one half of the barn was piled high with the cured tobacco. Instead of being cheered by this, Vandervelde became more nervous and irritable than ever. He had caught McKinnon smoking in the barn, and with much cursing had moved him in with the two tyers, who slept in a lean-to against the farm house. Once, he spied Marie talking to Hunky at supper, and called her to the house. As she passed him in the doorway he slapped her across the head.

The weather had been too good to last, and there was electricity in the air. Joe's radio reported a low pressure area moving northeast from the Mississippi Valley, through Illinois, Indiana, and Michigan, and expected in Ontario by early evening. The front was accompanied by heavy thunderstorms and a chance of hail.

Hunky lay on his bunk, stripped to his shorts. He had been unusually quiet since talking to Marie as we came in from the field. Suddenly he said, 'Maurice gone to Delhi to try borrow money from Growers' Association. Got no cash or insurance, only tobacco in barn.'

'How do you know?'

'Marie tell me,' he said. 'Not get pay tonight.'

'We'll get it tomorrow.'

'No, George. Have to wait till tobacco is bought. By then is too long for us to wait.' He began pacing up and down the floor of the shed. 'I know Vandervelde. He's fat pig. Not want to pay us wages.'

'What can we do?'

'I find out if he got money in Delhi tonight,' he said.

After he dressed he rode off in the quick gathering darkness in the direction of Delhi. Down in the southwest sky the lightning was flashing pink along the horizon. A strange stillness, broken only by the accelerated chirps of the crickets, fell on everything around.

The storm struck about an hour later, sucking the wind from the east at first, then gusting heavy sheets of rain from the west against the side of the shed. The lightning, white and sulphurous now, flashed through every crack in the walls, and the thunder banged sharply overhead before rolling off into the sky. As quickly as it had come, the storm died off to the east, leaving a residue of gently spattering rain and a breeze that was as clean and cool as new-washed sheets. Before the rain stopped I heard Vandervelde's car being driven into the yard. The barn door was unlocked, and the car driven inside. Then the door was locked again.

On Sunday, as those of us who had stayed at the farm were eating dinner, a provincial police car pulled up at the gate and two policemen walked up to the house. They talked with Maurice for several minutes at the door, then walked to their car. Joe the curer told me during the afternoon that Hunky had been killed the night before on the road by a hit-and-run motorist. The police had been checking to find if he had worked at Vandervelde's.

Hunky dead! It didn't seem possible, unless God had played a senseless joke upon the world. Why would it have to be Hunky, riding along on his bike during the storm of the night before, who had to die? Hunky, the Polack kid with the overwhelming desire to become a Canadian. Hunky, who had had enough pain and sorrow already to do the rest of us a lifetime. Hunky, who crossed himself at meals and went to mass. Boy, that was some heavenly joke all right!

At suppertime the others began to jabber about what a good boy Hunky had been, and Frenchy Côté's wife began to sniffle. I left the table, not wanting to talk to them about Hunky, or listen to their indifferent eulogies. Harvest hands are like hobos, their friendships as casual as the mating of a pair of flies.

The next evening after work I asked Maurice if he'd drive me to Delhi. 'I'm not going to Delhi,' he said. 'What do *you* want to go there for?' 'To see a friend,' I said.

'Who, Stan the Polack?' he asked, laughing his fat ugly laugh.

Though I knew he could kill me with one hand I suddenly wanted to smash his face. I wanted a miracle that would allow me to reach up and pull his face down to where my boots could crush it. I turned away from him with a hatred for my size and a frustration I hadn't felt for years.

'My car has a flat tire,' Vandervelde shouted after me as I walked away. I pretended not to have heard him.

After supper I walked to the back of the barn and peered through a crack in the boards. The boss's car was parked in the middle of the floor, beside the roof-high pile of yellow cured tobacco. There was no sign of a flat tire, but its left front fender was loose and its left headlight broken, as if it had struck something coming from the opposite direction along the road.

Hunky's jacket was still hanging in a corner of the shed. I reached into the inside pocket and pulled out his D.P. camp release. I thought how proud he had been of his 'papers', and I shoved it into my own pocket, determined not to leave it for strangers to find. I knew that Hunky's friends and the Polish credit union officials in Delhi would look after the funeral. If I couldn't get there to see him for the last time, I'd go to Simcoe and try to forget him.

Frenchy Côté was driving Joe the curer into Simcoe for an evening off, and I bummed a ride into town with him. Kurt was taking care of the kilns.

My evening in town was a failure. I tried a couple of beer parlors, but couldn't stand the noise and laughter. The more I tried to forget my friend the more I thought of him. I was sure Hunky had been right when he said we'd have to wait weeks for our pay. I thought of laying charges against Vandervelde, but changed my mind. Who would listen to a harvest stiff in the middle of the tobacco country? I'd end up on the wrong side of a vag charge myself.

I went to a bootlegger's and bought two bottles of cheap wine, one of which I drank there. I kept remembering Hunky's remark, 'I never know the good life, George.' It was the tortured cry of the whole bottom half of humanity.

I walked out to the highway with my bottle, and flagged down a car, driven by a young fellow going to St Thomas. He let me out where the road to the farm led north from the highway. I drank the bottle and then set out across the fields towards Vandervelde's. I had some brave drunken idea that I would stand up to the boss and tell him what I knew, then laugh at him as he had laughed at Hunky.

I cut across the fields and had almost reached the farmyard when I saw Marie coming down the path. I hid myself in the hedge, and saw Kurt cutting across towards her from the kilns. When he joined her they went towards the fields, her arm around his waist. They were all rotten, and just accusing Maurice was not enough. I had to hurt them all, for Hunky's sake.

A half hour later I returned to the junction of the side road and the highway and waited for Frenchy to come along. When he did, I flagged him down. I told Frenchy and Joe that I'd been given a lift that far by a young man driving to St Thomas.

We had almost reached the farm before we met Kurt, running down the road and glancing back every now and then across his shoulder. It was then that we first saw the pillar of whitened smoke hanging over the farmyard.

We pulled up in the yard alongside the fire truck from a small village to the north of us. The barn and two kilns were gutted, nothing remaining but a portion of the barn floor, a few charcoaled posts, and the still-steaming frame of Vandervelde's automobile. Joe jumped out of Frenchy's car and looked at the fireboxes of the other three kilns; the oil feedcocks on all of them had been turned on full, and the tobacco ruined.

The fire chief was telling Maurice that the fire had jumped from the kilns to the barn. Nobody told him any different, although I knew that the breeze was coming from the opposite direction.

Mrs Vandervelde and Marie stood in the kitchen doorway, alternately sobbing and staring fearfully at Maurice, who now stood in the middle of the yard, not laughing now, but opening and shutting his fat mouth like a landed carp.

The next morning before anyone else was up I walked between the rear of the gutted barn and the cracked and broken greenhouse. On the ground was a half-burned piece of document paper. By bending close I could read the beginning of a name typed along a dotted line: Stanislaw Szym. . . . I crushed it into the mud with my foot. In a way you could call it Hunkys' epitaph. But even that didn't seem enough. Not by a god-dam long shot!

John
Glassco

JOHN GLASSCO is a man of letters who has produced one book that might well become a Canadian classic. He was born in Montreal. In 1928, when he was eighteen and in his third year at McGill, he grew bored with university and left to go to Paris with a friend, Graeme Taylor. He spent three years there, returning to Montreal to be hospitalized for tuberculosis. He has lived since then in the Eastern Townships of Québec, where for some years he raised hackney ponies.

Shortly after he arrived in Paris, Glassco, who was a precocious, widely read young man, began to write his memoirs. He brought them to near-completion in the winter of 1932-3 in the Royal Victoria Hospital, recording, while seriously (for all he knew fatally) ill, 'the years in which I really lived'. Then he set them aside for thirty-five years. Published in 1970 as *Memoirs of Montparnasse*, his recollections were widely hailed as an unusually vivid, highly entertaining novel-like account of a Paris that was alive with creative people and eccentrics who lived, like the youthful author himself, in heedless, energetic pursuit of sensation and pleasure. Leon Edel, in his introduction to the book,

writes: 'It is all there—the twenty-four-hour days, the burning of candles at both ends, the obsessions and compulsions, the strange divorce from what was going on in the world, the crazy parties, the beautiful fool's paradise from which the depression ultimately awakened us.'

When he recovered his health and resumed his life in Canada, Glassco began to write poetry. Two collections, *A Deficit Made Flesh* (1958) and *A Point of Sky* (1964), were followed by his *Selected Poems* (1971), which brought together the thirty-four poems he wished to be remembered for. It won a Governor General's Award. Glassco has been called a poet's poet; that is, his poetry is highly respected but not easily accessible or very popular. He writes pessimistically, often about nostalgia and loss. His *Selected Poems* includes poems drawn from history, literature, and art, but among the best and most powerful are those that treat the rural landscape in Québec where he lives. Reviewing the *Selected Poems* in the *University of Toronto Quarterly* ('Letters in Canada', Summer 1972), Michael Hornyansky wrote: 'It's not often we are given courteous and straightforward entrée to a kingdom larger than our own, a world civilized and measured with calm wisdom, all human circumstances brought to terms. Glassco has a peculiarly tactful authority, which I take to be the result of leaving all egotism behind, and also of a technical command so complete as to be unobtrusive.'

Glassco has published a translation of the *Journal* of the French-Canadian poet Saint-Denys-Garneau and edited *The Poetry of French Canada in Translation* (1970), which contains many of his own translations, examples of which can be found on pages 196 and 206.

QUEBEC FARMHOUSE

Admire the face of plastered stone,
   The roof descending like a song
   Over the washed and anointed walls,
Over the house that hugs the earth
Like a feudal souvenir: oh see
The sweet submissive fortress of itself
   That the landscape owns!

And inside is the night, the airless dark
   Of the race so conquered it has made
   Perpetual conquest of itself,
Upon desertion's ruin piling
The inward desert of surrender,
Drawing in all its powers, puffing its soul,
   Raising its arms to God.

This is the closed, enclosing house
   That set its flinty face against
   The rebel children dowered with speech
To break it open, to make it live
And flower in the cathedral beauty
Of a pure heaven of Canadian blue—
   The larks so maimed

They still must hark and hurry back
   To the paradisal place of gray,
   The clash of keys, the click of beads,
The sisters walking leglessly,
While under the wealth and weight of stone
All the bright demons of forbidden joy
   Shriek on, year after year.

MEMOIRS OF MONTPARNASSE

We now felt much better and for a whole month were happy. Graeme at once left the *New York Herald,* while I stopped typing manuscripts and wrote my first published book, *Contes en Crinoline.* This work was a sequence of historical sketches with a unifying transvestite motif, in which a young man was reincarnated in different varieties of female dress. It was written in French, and all the details of farthingales, plackets, shifts, conical hats and corsets were taken from an illustrated history of costume I had picked up on the quays. The *Contes* were brought out by Elias Gaucher, a fly-by-night publisher on the rue des Saints-Pères, to whom I had been introduced by a surrealist poet. Gaucher specialized in books dealing with shoes, fans and ladies' underlinen, and thought Octave Uzanne the greatest writer in France.

'This is a very amusing manuscript you have turned out,' he told me, while his fingers worried a rubber band, 'although it is inaccurate in places. In the convent episode your hero is wearing closed drawers in the year 1750. They did not exist until almost fifty years later.'

'Are you sure?'

He raised his stubby eyebrows. 'But of course, Penillière says they were not in use until the public assault on Théroigne de Méricourt in May 1793, and he is the Bible on the subject.'

'I was following Liane de Lauris. I thought she would know.'

He looked at me pityingly. 'My dear young man, Liane de Lauris was the pseudonym of that poor hack Louis Laurens whose only distinction was that he was a friend of Balzac's. His *L'écrin du rubis* is absolutely unreliable. Moreover, you appear not to have read the work of the greatest *travesti* of all time, Monsieur l'Abbé de Choisy.'

'Indeed I have. I have read *La Comtesse des Barres,* but I regard it as too sacred a text even to steal from.'

His eyes lit up, he snapped the rubber band vivaciously. 'A young man after my heart! Anyone who loves and admires the great Choisy is acceptable on those grounds alone. I will give you 2,000 francs outright for the copyright of your little book of tales. Agreed?'

Eighty dollars, I thought. It was less than I expected; but as usual I was in no position to hold out. 'For cash, yes.'

'Of course. Now, for a pseudonym. Anything you like, provided it has an aristocratic ring.'

'I want the book to appear under my own name.'

'Impossible, sir. You must be a *de.* All my authors adopt the noble particle. Where were you born, if I may ask?'

'In Montreal.'

'Canada!' he exclaimed with delight. 'Well, who would have thought it? I have a Canadian author: my very first. What do you say, then, to Philippe de Montréal? It sounds well, eh? Archaic.'

'Excuse me, it sounds more like a criminal alias. And why Philippe? Can't I even keep my first name?

'Hmm-mm. Jean de Montréal. Not bad, not bad. But not quite right either: it has not the feudal connotation. Let me see—what street were you born on?'

'St Luke Street.'

'Ah, now we have it. Jean de Saint-Luc! Perfect. *Contes en Crinoline* by Jean de Saint-Luc. That is it! Absolutely! It has the fine medieval ring, and the vowels combine with great sonority. Come now, let us sign the little contract. One copy for you and one for me, eh?'

The contract was six lines of typescript in which I conveyed outright ownership of the book to him, together with all rights of translation, for 2,000 francs, of which I acknowledged receipt by these presents, and five copies of the published book itself.

'Are you paying in cash?' I asked.

'Here is my cheque on the Crédit Lyonnais, boulevard Saint-Germain branch. Just around the corner.'

'In that case, you won't mind my adding the words "by cheque" to my receipt. Only a formality, of course.'

He grinned, snapping the rubber band. 'Certainly. I like to deal with a businessman. "By cheque", naturally.'

We then both signed the contract, which was already witnessed by someone else whose signature was illegible. Jean de Saint-Luc, I thought, this is your passport to a mild erotic fame. This absurd little book—I wonder if it will have an illustrated cover.

When I presented M. Gaucher's cheque at the Crédit Lyonnais next day it was refused for lack of funds.

All the following week I tried to find him but he had disappeared; the little office in the rue des Saints-Pères was locked. I asked the advice of the surrealist poet, who told me to wait. 'He has taken his new mistress to Chartres,' he said. 'She loves religious architecture and may insist on his going still further afield so she can take some rubbings of tombs. But you can generally find him at the Restaurant Petit Saint-Benoît. You must be bold with him since he is a physical craven. Your original mistake was in taking his cheque. There is no use appealing to his mistress, as she is worse than he.'

For the next two nights Graeme and I dined at the Petit Saint-Benoît. It was one of the smallest, cheapest and best restaurants of its kind in Paris.

I had never eaten such sweetbreads: sliced very thin, coated with egg-white and breadcrumbs, fried in brown butter and served with a wedge of lemon, they were quite different from the great squishy things that are generally boiled and served in a dull Mornay sauce. Here Graeme and I also met the sculptor Ossip Zadkine, a charming ugly man who wore a wide-brimmed purple fur-felt hat that made him look like a mushroom.

'There are only three great names in sculpture in the western world,' he said. 'Michelangelo, Rodin and myself. We are the only visionaries of plastic form.'

'Will you tell me,' said Graeme, 'whether sculpture is not in danger of succumbing to a bloodless abstractionism—as painting appears to be doing?'

'No danger of that,' he said. 'Sculpture will be saved by its three dimensions. Look at this water carafe.' He picked it up. 'Trite and inexpressive it is, it cannot be reduced to a system of lines and colours. The logical development of painting is of course towards a square canvas entirely rendered in dull black and entitled anything you like: Hell, Death, The Void, Memory, Madame Untel—whatever the artist's wit or his dealer's venality can suggest. In sculpture, however, we are tied to the object, the thing, and we have also the irrefragable mediums of stone, wood, marble, brass to keep us from such sterility.'

'But Brancusi's "Golden Bird" and his "Fish",' I said, 'aren't they moving towards a three-dimensional abstraction? The soaring emotion of his bird could be refined and streamlined with very little trouble into the meaningless suavity of a cigar.'

'Exactly. Constantin does not know where he is going. But I do, and I have told him. He will not listen. He is enamoured of the idea of smoothness, which he confuses with simplicity. Now I, on the other hand, find the ultimate plastic expression to be the rendition of strife and tortuosity such as you find in the contours and crenellations of a baked potato.'

'Then there is no danger of sculpture being reduced to the simplest three-dimensional forms of the sphere and the cube? The exhibition, say, of a cannonball or a child's building block?'

'Not if I have any say in the matter,' he said grimly. 'I am the sworn foe of those geometrical Dutchmen and de Stijl. The real villain, of course, is Father Euclid. We must escape that terrible logic of his if we are to remain human. Art must not be fitted to his bed, or be lopped or stretched for that infernal Greek whose axioms don't even make sense. There are no straight lines anywhere, fortunately: lines only waver, weave, cross and tangle. Geometrical forms are a pernicious nonsense. I object to the full moon, for instance, as a sterile, stupid circle.'

The third time we were at the Petit Saint-Benoît I saw M. Gaucher coming in with a big fair-haired girl. When I went to his table he introduced me with great formality and asked me to sit down and take an aperitif. I excused myself, saying I was with a friend, and after begging his pardon for broaching a matter of business showed him his dishonoured cheque.

'I knew it, I knew it,' he cried, striking his forehead. 'As soon as you left I consulted my bank balance and realized there was not enough to cover that cheque. I offer you a thousand apologies. If you will come to my office tomorrow we will arrange this matter in a twinkling. Shall we say at three o'clock?'

The next day his office was again closed all afternoon. I understood he did not mean to pay anything. It was obvious that direct action was the only course.

After waiting three whole afternoons in a little wine-shop opposite his office, we at last saw him enter. I was already boiling with rage, and Graeme insisted we wait five minutes. 'If the worst comes to worst,' he said, 'we'll take him from both sides.'

We entered his office without knocking. He looked up from his desk and turned pale. 'Gentlemen, gentlemen, please sit down. I have the money here.' He rummaged in a drawer and pulled out his cheque book.

'No more of your cheques,' I said, moving forward. 'I have come for the money you owe me—in cash, as we agreed.'

'My friend,' said Graeme, advancing on the other side, 'has waited long enough. He wants his 2,500 francs.'

'2,500 francs! The price was 2,000.'

'Five hundred francs for collection charges,' said Graeme. We moved behind the desk. 'Come now, sir, you must pay your legal debts.'

The colour came back to M. Gaucher's cheeks. 'This is not a legal debt,' he hissed.

'What about our contract?' I said.

'What contract? Oho, you know as little of business as you do of ladies' underwear, my young Canadian. In France no contract is binding unless it has the government stamps. You are wasting your time.'

'We're not leaving before you pay,' Graeme said, sitting down calmly on the desk. 'Even if we have to stay here all night.'

'Excrements! Gangsters!' M. Gaucher pulled out his wallet and threw its contents on his desk. 'That is all I have. Take it.'

Graeme picked up the pile of small bills. We walked out and up the rue des Saints-Pères to the rue Jacob while I was counting the money.

'We got 1,735 francs anyway,' I said.

'Then we don't have to eat at the Cent Colonnes for a while. And another thing, your book's bound to be printed now. He's got to recover his costs. If we hadn't squeezed this out of him I'll bet he'd have put your manuscript away in a drawer.'

'I never thought of that.'

*   *   *

I had still to find a room to sleep in. But I could not yet bear to leave the lights of the river. I felt I had not yet been fully possessed by the city, or rather that the possession might be further extended and deepened. The idea then came to me to spend the night there, by the river. This was a project I had always entertained and its realization now seemed indicated; it would also leave me enough money for both breakfast and dinner next day. But the breeze was growing cold, and packing up the remains of my bread, sausage and wine I went to look for a more sheltered spot under the Pont Neuf. I found a fine place well up under the first arch, where the fine clean dust would make a comfortable bed. I burrowed in, uncorked my wine, and leaning on one elbow began drinking peacefully.

I could now see both up and down the river. The cross-town traffic still went by, but without shaking the massive stone arch over my head; the sound was as soothing as rain on a roof. I tried to remember who had first built Pont Neuf: Henri III or IV? Anyway it had taken almost twenty years to finish. And still, with its ten or twelve laborious arches, it was the loveliest bridge in Paris, much better than Napoleon's Austerlitz and Iéna bridges, and still better than the Invalides, Alma and Solférino ones, which, as the guidebooks said, 'are all handsome structures, adorned with military and naval trophies commemorative of events and victories connected with the Second Empire . . .' I was falling asleep when a hoarse, tearful voice cried in my ear:

'Monsieur, this is my place!'

A bulky, bearded man entirely in rags, with a canvas wallet slung over his shoulder and carrying a camp-stool, was staring down at me; behind him was a shapeless old woman lugging an enormous paper shopping bag.

'You have taken my place,' he repeated in a heavy Béarnais accent. 'This is mine, by right.'

'By what right?'

His bearded mouth fell open; he began to sputter. 'Gaby,' he turned to the old woman, 'this is our place, isn't it?'

'Yes, yes, our place,' she mumbled.

'There's room for all of us,' I said.

'But I like my privacy. Besides, you are new. You're not even Parisian.

Is he, Gaby? He doesn't speak right.'

'No, not a man of Paris.'

'You're not of Paris either, monsieur,' I said.

'I, not of Paris! I am the man of the Pont Neuf.'

'So am I, for tonight. Don't bother me, I'm going to sleep.'

'Henri, Henri,' muttered the old woman, pulling him by the sleeve.

They moved a few dozen yards away. He put down his camp-stool, while she dug a bottle of wine from her shopping bag. After a while I looked over at them. They were lying not quite motionless, their arms around each other . . .

MEMOIRS OF MONTPARNASSE

b. 1926

Phyllis Gotlieb

PHYLLIS GOTLIEB has unusual preoccupations as an author in that she has made a reputation both as a poet and as a writer of science fiction. She was born and grew up in Toronto, where her family owned and managed several movie theatres. She graduated in English from the University of Toronto (M.A.) and married shortly afterwards. Mrs Gotlieb's books of poetry are *Within the Zodiac* (1965) and *Ordinary, Moving* (1969). A poem for voices, 'Dr Umlaut's Earthly Kingdom', commissioned by the CBC and broadcast on radio in 1970, has since begun to be performed on stage in high schools and universities. In 1969 she published *Why Should I Have All the Grief?*, a novel about the aftermath of Auschwitz projected into contemporary Canadian Jewish life. Her science-fiction stories have appeared in the Canadian anthology *Fourteen Stories High* and in all the leading American science-fiction magazines. She is also the author of one science-fiction novel, *Sunburst* (1964).

The selections below are both from *Ordinary, Moving*, a brilliant collection of poems that often make use of other people's words—childhood rhymes, telephone numbers, popular songs, parts of the human skeleton—to which the poet adds her own quicksilver insights and feelings. 'For John Andrew Reaney', written after the death of the young son of close friends, was suggested by the folksong 'Green Grow the Rashes O' and can be sung to its melody. 'So Long It's Been' makes imaginative use of Toronto telephone exchanges that were current in Mrs Gotlieb's childhood.

FOR JOHN ANDREW REANEY

Tell me your one-o
green grow the rashes-o
I'll tell you one-o
One is one and God's alone and ever more shall be so

Tell me your two-o
I'll tell you truly-o
fire-winged butterfly, eye-tailed peacock
shimmer in the field where the wildflowers grow
tell me your one-o
I'll tell you one-o
One is one and God's alone and ever more shall be so

Tell me your three-o
I'll tell you lovingly
three, three the starwhite petals of the lily
blowing in the wind on a stalk of living green-o
One is one with God alone and ever more shall be so

Four, tell me four-o
green grow the rashes-o
springleaf, Juneflower, treefall, snow
colour the meadow green blue and yellow
toadflax, chicory, Queen Anne's Lace, O
One, One, God alone and ever more shall be so

Sing me your five-o
: five alive-o
five are the gates that open to the spirit
ear to hear music, mouth to tell love
the hand that caresses, the eye that blesses
the sense of the soul as it ever more shall be so

Six, tell me six
green grow the rashes-o
six are the walkers winding to eternity
bearing their blessings as lightly as love
five are the senses-o
four are the seasons-o
One is one and God's alone and ever more shall be so

Tell me your seven-o
I'll give you seven
seven are the Shepherds who stand before the Lord
Adam, Seth, Methuselah, Abraham, Jacob, Moses
and David with his psalter who sang before the Ark: O
God is One and One alone and ever more shall be so

Eight, now, eight
eight the April rainers

swelling the streams that sing along the stones-o
seven are the Shepherds
six are the walkers
One is one and God's alone and ever more shall be so

Nine, tell me nine-o
green grow the rashes-o
nine are the Angels aureoled in Heaven
white as the daisies in the fields of morning-o
eight are the April rains the Shepherds are seven

Give me your ten-o
I'll give you One
ten are the Commandments blazed on living stone
I'll tell you One that's love and love alone
for God is love and love alone and ever more shall be so

Green grow the rashes-o
I'll tell you of eleven
who climbed the steps to Heaven
with their heads crowned in light
and their weary sandals worn
scarred in their martyrdom
turned to Jerusalem
One is God and God is love and ever more shall be so

Twelve, twelve, tell me your twelve
twelve are the flame-haired Apostles of the ceilings
burning in blue with peacocks at their feet, O
now tell your twelve-all

green grow the rashes-o
here are my twelve-all
goldrobed Apostles who tread their fields of blue
all, all but one have climbed the steps of Heaven
ten are the Commandments carved on stone
nine are the angels that God made in the morning
eight April rainers turn the fields to clover
seven are the Shepherds who bring the lambs to cover
six are proud walkers who guard their gift of blessing
five are the senses that open to the spirit
four are the seasons that turn upon their cycles

three, three the lilies that stand on stems so green-o

where peacocks shimmer and butterflies hover
run, child, run where the fields are rich with clover

One is one and God's alone and ever more shall be so!

SO LONG IT'S BEEN

time to clear the silent
sullen round of numbers stacked in my
brainracks
        clear HOWARD 0141 where the one
armed man lived next door and Mrs Goldfarb
with her slipstraps on her fat pink arms
                clear
HARGRAVE 8375 where the park sweeps below the railing
and Broadview Ave, on a foggy day a ship's
deck sailing a sea of limbo washed with
3 old skaters 7 tennis players and a shattered
rubbydub
        GERRARD 6715 Good evening Century Theatre

Goodbye Mrs Gersten, Miss Fernandez, Miss Fleuhrer &
all burglars anonymous uncaught who tied up my
father & stole the safe, or his lunch, or sometimes
even $ $ $ $
        clear GERRARD 2222 (too) easy to remember *Call
me anytime* Mr Wallace walks me in the schoolyard &
knowing does not tell me my grandmother
                LAKESIDE 0007
never liked flowers because they reminded her of
funerals: how many roses from hers have I found
cracking the backs of Uncle Nissel's
SCHUYLER 4-7767 old encyclopedias?
           clear GROVER 9595
where I pulled the kid cousin's braids, ate
knishes, and cried: yes, he's dead, he died this
morning
        numbers that lived in me clear clear clear no
answer, nobody lives
there any more

Alain Grandbois

ALAIN GRANDBOIS is considered in Québec to be the best poet of his generation. He was born at Saint-Casimir de Portneuf and was educated at Université Laval, where he studied law. He became a world traveller, returning to Montreal at the start of the Second World War. His first book was a biography of the explorer Louis Jolliet, *Né à Québec* (1933), published in Paris (it appeared in an English translation in 1964). *Poèmes* was published in a limited edition in Hankow in 1934. This was followed by another book of prose, *Les Voyages de Marco Polo* (1944), and five books of poetry, of which the best known are *Les Iles de la nuit* (1944), *Rivages de l'homme* (1948), and *L'Etoile pourpre* (1957)—books that had an enormous influence on younger poets. Grandbois's poetry is admired for its masterly technique, the sonorous harmonies of its language, and its original symbolism. J.R. Brazeau has written that 'his scope is limitless; his alienation is that of Everyman; his main quality is perhaps the strange musicality of his poems coupled with the exotic colour-scheme of his wording'. Grandbois's themes are love, the fleeting years, and —as in so much French-Canadian poetry —death. *Rivages de l'homme* bears as an epigraph a statement from Tolstoy: 'If man has learned to think, it is of little importance what he thinks about; always at the back of his mind there is the thought of his own death.' See the note on Saint-Denys-Garneau (page 144) for an explanation of the obsession with death in French-Canadian writing.

CRIES

All at once I saw these continents overthrown
The thousand trumpets of the ruined gods
The collapse of the walls of the cities
The horror of purple sombre smoke
I saw men frightful ghosts
And their gestures of the drowning
Covered the implacable wastes
Like the clasped hands of women
Like the great unpardonable transgressions
Salt iron and flame
Under a hellish sky ringed with steel
From the depths of volcanic craters
Spat the scarlet anguishes
Spat the long-departed days
Despair leaped into our hearts
The gleaming beaches of smooth gold the inexpres-
    sible blue
Of the seas and at the very end of time
The planets motionless   O rigid   fixed forever
The long silence of death

And I saw you each and all of you
In the little flower-decked cemeteries
At the elbows of the parish churches
Under the gentle swell of badly tended mounds
All of you   you and you and you
All of those I'd loved
With a violent and voiceless passion
I hurled my cries into the deep night
Ah they speak of hope but where can it be found
They say that we are denying God
When God is all we are seeking
Him only Him alone

Then in an avalanche of emerald ice
The caravans of the poles
Poured their frosty chaos
In the laps of the beautiful Americas
While we on that very day
With eyes tight-closed
—O lowly dream of gentleness of bondage—
We were seeking the pinewood undergrowth
To sing the joy of our flesh

O God in the treetop's swaying hands
How we have sought for Thee
At the hour of rest our bodies closed
Before desire came like a humming bee

Then the towering tropic palms
Sweeping away treacherous malarias
Bowed their unconquered heads
There was a wine-coloured boat
With a small white sail
And all the seas belonged to us
With their monstrous turtles
And the Roman lampreys
And the Labrador whales
And the islands looming out of coral
Like a photographer's proof
And those ice-sheathed rocks
At the tip of Tierra del Fuego
And all the splendid stretches of the sea
And the breathing of its waves
Sea   O Sea   O Beauty elect
What victories for our defeats

And the woods dense as the earth below
Where we walked together spreading out our arms
Smothered us with their secret
Strayed memories and childhood lost
That morning sun as tender as a moon
Ah in those lengendary days
Deep with the presence of the grass
Amidst the bars of our prison
She wept but with tragic reserve
And I declared a silent war

We were crushed beneath our giant ancestral trees
There were the solemn moments
When we were upheld by the darkness
When we were murdered on our knees
And our suffering fell short
Of entreaties fed with involuntary tears
And the shadows veiled our faces
Our naked feet bled on the edge of the rock
And daybreak laid its trap for us
Under the arches of the lofty cedars

The straining forests swallowed our sky
On the walls of trees like blazing cuts
The gentle streaks of freshwater springs
Stately labyrinths of octaves resting their brows
Mosses and stalactites formed from petrified waters
Bloody carnage of the grief to come
We were humble not speaking of poetry
We were bathed in poetry and did not know it

Our savage bodies fused in extravagant shame
Beating against each other
Like an assassination
When the fenzy of joy arrived
We were struck with wonder under the sun
Our sleep transformed us
Into corpses stiff and dry
In winding-sheets of a too-immaculate white
Ah springtime winds ah perfumes' delights
Open windows at the crux of city streets
You crave to see a single leaf
A bird the blue reflection of a lake
Ringed with spruce-trees and lungs free at last

We took each other's hand
We went forward into life
With our forty years upon us
Each of us
Widowed twice or more
By as many mortal wounds
We had survived by a miracle
The demons of destruction

ELDON GRIER (*tr*)

Frederick Philip Grove

FREDERICK PHILIP GROVE is the author of twelve books that encompass an impressive range of universal themes—struggles against nature, the clash of generations, the relations between men and women, the loneliness of mankind, the tyrannies of the machine age—that no other Canadian author before him had attempted to deal with. His view of life was sombre and humourless, his writing was often graceless and uncolloquial—not surprising in someone to whom English was not his first language—but his vision was compelling and his insights into his characters, even though we cannot identify ourselves with them, were often subtle and moving.

The most interesting thing about Grove the man is that in his autobiography, *In Search of Myself* (1946), he gave a fictitious account of his life prior to coming to Canada. (It is not known why.) The facts of his early life are being uncovered by Professor Douglas Spettigue of Queen's University.

Grove's autobiography tells us that he was born in 1871 in Russia while his parents were visiting there. His wealthy father, the son of an Englishman, is said to have been the owner of a large estate in Sweden, Castle Thurow, where Grove says he lived until he was fourteen, when his mother left his father to spend the next two years travelling in Europe with her son in tow. Of his education, Grove has written that he was first taught by tutors and then attended a school in Berlin and the Sorbonne in Paris, where he studied archaeology. He describes going to Siberia on a research expedition with his great uncle, and other world travels that followed. He says he came to North America in 1892 and toured the United States. Then, hearing that his father had died and that there was nothing left of the family fortune, he became an itinerant farm labourer in the West until he started teaching in Haskett, Man., in 1912.

Professor Spettigue's assiduous research in Europe has persuaded him that Grove was a German by the name of Felix Paul Greve who was born at Radomno on the Polish-Prussian border, on February 14, 1879. He grew up in Hamburg, attended the University of Bonn at nineteen, and also studied in Rome and Munich. From 1902 to 1909 he was a free-lance writer and translator. He came to Canada in 1909 or early in

1910. It is not yet known what he did until 1912, the year he started teaching in Manitoba and married a fellow teacher some twenty years younger than himself.

In 1915 Grove was made principal of a high school in Gladstone in northern Manitoba and there, feeling isolated in the community as a foreigner but with a baby daughter to console him, he began to write. His wife took a teaching position at Falmouth some thirty miles north and Grove visited her on weekends. His journeys by bicycle and by horse and sleigh in winter (when it was sometimes fifty below zero) inspired his first two published books, *Over Prairie Trails* and *The Turn of the Year*, which describe in essay form his deeply felt experiences of nature, ranging from the sublime to the extremely hazardous. In 1917 he moved to a rural school close to Falmouth and while there suffered an injury to his back that brought on a paralysis of his legs intermittently for the rest of his life. In 1922, the year *Over Prairie Trails* was finally published, the Groves were teaching in Rapid City. When *The Turn of the Year* appeared in 1923, Grove began to be recognized as a writer and was invited to give lectures. His first and probably his best novel, *Settlers of the Marsh* (which had the neighbourhood of Falmouth, called Plymouth, as its setting), was published in 1925 and elicited such an unfavourable reaction because of its references to sex that it did not sell. Grove wrote in his autobiography: 'Its publication became a public scandal. Libraries barred it—London, Ontario, forming an honourable exception . . . people who had been ready to lionize me cut me dead in the street. As a trade proposition the book never had a chance; what sale it had was surreptitious.' (The controversial scene in this novel is repro-duced here, beginning on page 184.) He continued to write, however. *A Search for America*, based on travels in North America, was published in 1927, and another novel, *Our Daily Bread*, in 1928. In 1929 the Groves (their daughter had died in 1927) moved to Ottawa for a year and then bought a farm north of Simcoe, Ont., where Grove lived until he died in 1948. He had suffered a paralytic stroke in 1944 and was thereafter supported by a pension from the Canadian Writers' Foundation.

Grove's other books are the novels *The Yoke of Life* (1930), *Fruits of the Earth* (1933), *Two Generations: A Story of Present Day Ontario* (1939), *The Master of the Mill* (1944), about the effect of the machine age on individuals and society, and *Consider Her Ways* (1947), a fantasy about ants that satirizes human society. He also wrote *It Needs to be Said* (1929), a book of essays based on speeches. *In Search of Myself*, the autobiography that we know now to be partly fictional, was highly praised (as his earlier books were not when they were first published) and won a Governor General's Award. *Tales from the Margin: Selected Short Stories of Frederick Grove*, edited by Desmond Pacey, was published in 1971.

Over Prairie Trails, *Settlers of the Marsh*, *A Search for America*, *Fruits of the Earth*, and *The Master of the Mill* are available in paperback in the New Canadian Library. Douglas Spettigue has written a preceptive and interesting study of Grove, with a discussion of the first stages in researching his origins, in Copp Clark's Studies in Canadian Literature series. There are three articles on Grove in *Canadian Literature*: by W.B. Holliday (No. 3, Winter 1960), by Desmond Pacey (No. 11, Winter 1962), and by Stanley E. McMullin (No. 49, Summer 1971).

THE HAPPIEST YEAR OF HER LIFE

In myself there is something, a chord, which resounds to any kind of desolation; there was no such chord in my wife. The whole landscape, hot and humid in summer, bitterly cold in winter, and utterly untamed by man, gripped her soul as in a vice.

It is one thing, in winter, to watch a prairie blizzard from the warmth and comfort of a well-built house in city or town, and to admire the utter unconcern with which elemental forces interfere with man's devices and institutions. It is quite another to feel your very walls moving and shaking under the impact of ruthless squalls while the snow piles in on the lee side to above the height of the windows; especially when you know that your husband is out on the marsh, many miles away, stolidly fighting his way against wind and drift, in constant danger of being jammed tight among the stumps of trees buried under the snow, or of going astray in the utter confusion of nature. The country is full of stories of people who, under such circumstances, have lost their lives, to be found in spring, in the icy slush-pools left behind by the melting snows.

On occasion the drift was so thick that it was unsafe to leave the cottage even to cross to the school without carrying a string as an Ariadne thread by which to find the way back.

Before long this young woman lived only for the weekends and the rare holidays. It soon became clear that, on Sundays, I always had to leave early, from Falmouth, no later certainly than at noon, and often right after breakfast, if I wanted to feel sure that I could make Gladstone in time for school on Monday. From Gladstone, no matter what the weather, I always left, with one exception, on Friday after four. But it was often Saturday morning, and once or twice it was late in the afternoon of that day before I reached Falmouth. On account of the prevailing winds it was always more difficult to go north than to go south; and invariably it took longer.

Since so much depended on the weather, we became, at both ends, the most anxious watchers of sky, wind, and cloud. Sometimes, when I had to leave the cottage, there was anguish in my wife's face. Perhaps a blizzard threatened; perhaps the air was opaque with flying or drifting snow. Since I had to go, I tried not to see it. On one occasion, though I had left the cottage on Sunday morning, at ten, and though by that time I was driving two strong horses, I did not reach Gladstone, forty-five miles away by the road I had had to adopt, until eight-thirty on Monday, with just enough time to spare for changing clothes before, without breakfast, I had to hurry to school. And for every minute of these twenty-odd hours I had been driving my horses, over drifts in which I sometimes did not see them, with muscles taut and nerves tense. Any rare holiday—Thanksgiving, Christmas—made us feel as though we must make the most of it by living faster, by putting more things into the pockets of time. Throughout the winter, it was always a triumph when I got home before midnight on Friday; it happened rarely enough. Invariably I found my wife waiting; and then there was a whole, unbroken day ahead. Once, soon after school had opened at Gladstone—I was still riding the bicycle —rain overtook me on the way out before I had left the town more than six miles behind. For the remainder of the trail which I was still following, twenty-eight miles, I had to walk and to push my wheel which was heavily laden with supplies. It was the first time I had been delayed; and it gave my wife a foretaste of many an experience to follow.

Whenever I arrived during the night, the little girl woke up; and, as soon as I entered the cottage, she climbed out of her cot and snuggled sleepily down on my knees where, wearily, I had dropped into a camp-chair. By that time she had accepted the routine of my being absent during the week.

All of which may sound pathetic enough; but it was only that outside of the young woman's life which I could see as well; the inside of it I did not know until years later.

Let me mention the subject of heating. Even that tiny cottage could be kept warm only by means of two stoves, one in the kitchen, the other in the livingroom for which a small, so-called air-tight heater was supplied. In this bush, swept by the relentless winds of a Manitoba winter, there was always the danger of fire; sometimes, during a blizzard, a sudden up-draught would suck streams of sparks into the flying air above the roof. My wife never dared to go to bed before both fires were out. Invariably she ceased adding fuel about eight o'clock; and gradually the inexorable cold—it was often forty below and sometimes lower—invaded the cottage. Bed was the only place where, with the help of a hot-water bottle, it was possible to keep warm; but she never lay down until, shivering, she had convinced herself, by stirring the ashes, that there was not a spark of glow left in the stoves.

Often, in the intense cold—in the coldest nights the air is always calm —the trees all about would startlingly come to life with reports like pistol-shots; their wood was splitting by uneven contraction; or their bark was bursting in long strips. Or, when the wind was blowing and whistling or shrieking weirdly around the eaves, boards in the shell of the cottage would creak or rattle. Or the screech owl, resident here in its northern-most range, would launch its startling, laughter-like call. When my wife ran out to see that everything was in order about the place—as she always did, at the very moment when darkness fell—the snowy owls would circle about her head, so close that she could hear the whir of their wings.

It was characteristic of my wife that nothing frightened her for long which, in some way, she could explain. In that respect, she formed a striking contrast to such of the wives of the settlers as dropped in on her, now and then, at night. Hearing a creak or a rattle, these women would sit there, bathed in a cold sweat, not daring to speak above a whisper. My wife laughed at them; and then they would launch into tales of ghosts and werewolves and evil spirits; for, while racially Germans, they had come from Volhynia in Russia where the belief in witchcraft and in the animistic malice of nature is far from being extinct. But they never succeeded in frightening my wife. It was worse when they spoke of actual experiences, sufferings from loneliness or illness or bereavment; from poverty beyond the power of man to endure; or from loss sustained by reason of such poverty; or, still worse, by reason of their being shut off from help, cooped up, as they were, in this northland with its arctic cold; above all when they talked of men frozen to death while trying to get home through a treacherous stretch of the subarctic forest. For such tales had a personal application; and at the least they left a depressing effect behind.

Often, there disengaged itself, from such tales, an impression as if nature, instead of being merely indifferent, were animated by an active ill-will; as if it were vindictively lying in wait and lurking for a mistake a man might make in dealing with it; then to pounce on him and finish him off; the malice of circumstance. Thus a whole, sunny, calm week was often followed by a lowering or vehement Friday, just when my wife's most ardent wishes were for a continuance of unchanged weather. It seemed that all untoward metereological events were reserved for the weekends. Thus, in summer, when that had been welcome, there had not been a single thunderstorm except on Friday or Saturday. Now it came to the point where she looked with misgiving on sunshine, or on a rise in temperature, if either came between Monday and Friday; for only one law of the weather seemed certain, namely, that it was subject to change. If Wednesday was propitious, Friday was almost sure to be forbidding. Even the men, bringing their children to school in their bobsleighs, were, in such cases, often discouraging; when, on Friday morning, the snow was flying or drifting, they would say when asked—and how could my wife resist the temptation of asking them?—'No. He can't start today. He'd never make it.' So that, the last day, she was often divided between her wishes; she wanted me to come; but she did not want me to expose myself to danger which stay-at-homes exaggerated to themselves. At any rate, I always came. But it was true that, on occasion, I had come near giving in; in such cases, it was precisely the thought of wife and child which kept me going. Once, on my way out, the temperature being very

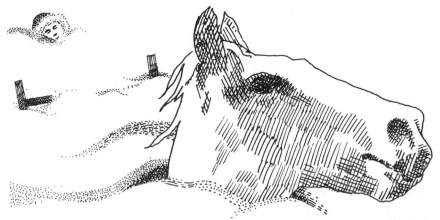

close to fifty below zero, I saw, in a fearful snow-drift no more than six miles from Gladstone, the head of a horse sticking out of the snow, frozen stiff; and as, turning aside, I passed with a shudder, I saw a corner of the sleigh and the head of the driver who was still sitting upright in death. On my way back to Gladstone, I watched for the sight; but it had been buried under an additional layer of snow two or three feet thick.

* * *

There was still another cause for anxiety. Ever since my long illness at Virden my health had given rise to worry. Was I well? For there had been times when I was not. During that winter I suffered from at least one vicious cold, with my temperature running high; and I had secured leave of absence, grudgingly given, for the school-board considered that my wife's place was in town; and I had myself driven out to Falmouth, to go to bed and be nursed.

The question arises: then why? Why should this young woman bear what she was bearing?

I did not know; *I* should have been happy there; and she professed to be happy. She would have done anything on earth for me. She believed that what she was doing was in my interests. Consequently, there was never even the remotest thought of her giving up, of not going through with it. At the time, she did not even give me the slightest hint of the fact that she was living in constant, deadly fear; it was years later before she confessed to it.

And the almost incomprehensible thing about it all is that, taking matters all in all, we were both happy. Today, it seems to have been the happiest year of our lives.

IN SEARCH OF MYSELF

ELLEN'S CONFESSION

Settlers of the Marsh is set in northern Manitoba, in a region Grove had lived in. It tells the story of Niels Lindstedt, an idealistic young Swedish farmer who is naive and puritanical in his relations with women. After working hard to clear his own farm and build a house, his dream of bringing Ellen Amundsen to it as his wife is shattered. The following scene, in which Ellen tells him why she will not marry him, brought down such outraged criticism upon Grove's head—the novel was called pornographic—that in the Canada of 1925 the book did not sell.

He found her at the house, preparing breakfast.

'Come in,' she said when she saw him at the door.

'Sigurdsen is dead,' Niels said slowly.

She looked at him with wide, haggard eyes.

He straightened. 'He's dead. Let that go. I am alive. I want to speak about myself.'

'Niels,' Ellen pleaded, 'I sent you away last night. I am not going to put you off again if you insist. But had we not better wait?'

'No. I have got to know. I have to get this clear. I am quiet. There is no use in waiting.'

'Very well,' she acquiesced. 'Sit down. I shall listen.'

'Ellen,' he broke out, 'there's a house on my place, the best-built, roomiest house for many miles around. In it there are things that I've bought through these years and which I've never used. There's a sewing machine; there's a washing machine; there are curtains, packed away; there are parcels with towels, bed-linen, table-cloths, and what not. Do you know for whom that house was built, for whom those things were bought?'

'I know,' she said, smiling sadly. 'I have feared it ever . . . ever since I saw the house.'

'Feared it?' he repeated. . . . 'Ellen, when I filed on that homestead, I did so because it was near to you. When I fenced it, I drove your name into the ground as the future owner with every post. When I cleared my field, I did it for you. When I dug the cellar of the house, I laid it out so it would save you work. When I planned the kitchen and the diningroom, I thought of nothing but saving you steps. When I bought the lumber, I felt I was taking home presents for you. Whenever I came driving over the Marsh, I saw you standing at the gate to welcome me. When I laid out the kitchen garden, I thought of you bringing in the greens. Ellen, no matter what I have done during these years, it was done with you in mind.'

An infinitely soft expression had come into the face of the girl; slowly she reached out with her hand and laid it on his where it was resting on the table that stood between them.

'Yes,' she said. 'All that I know, Niels. At least I often thought so. I could not help it. What was I to do? I always feared that one day I was going to give you pain. Yet I hoped you would understand. . . .'

'Understand?' he repeated. 'Understand what?'

'That between me and any man there can be but friendship.'

'Friendship?' he echoed dully.

'Yes. You know I was lonesome. You know how lonesome I was. There were plenty who were willing to make me feel less lonesome. They wanted marriage. Long ago there were plenty of them. Your very friend Nelson had been among them. I turned all of them away, harshly, so that a few weeks after my father's death I was the most lonesome woman in the district. You came. I did not turn you away. I liked you. I had liked you from the day when I first met you. I was fond of you. I am fond of you. As of a brother. I would not do anything that might hurt you if I could help myself. You must feel that. Don't you, Niels?'—Her voice was as full of passionate pleading as his had been.

'Yes, but. . . .' And in helpless non-comprehension he shrugged his shoulders.

'Oh, it is so hard to explain,' Ellen exclaimed. 'Niels, I do not want to lose you. I am fighting for you with all my strength. I know a farmer needs a woman on the place. Take me as a sister. Marry another woman. But let us remain what we are!'

'Another woman. . . .'

'Yes, Niels, you are thirty. You cannot but have seen other women. Surely you have sometimes thought of others but myself! Surely there are plenty of girls in the world; there are some in this settlement that will gladly be your handmaiden, that will jump at the chance of becoming the wife of a man like you.'

Niels sat and brooded. He tried to follow her thought. He even tried to visualize a fulfilment of what she suggested. His vision was a blank. He shook his head.

'Ellen,' he said, 'before your father died, before I had filed on my claim, when I was living with Nelson, up in the bush, in winter, in the little shack he had; when I was fresh from the squalour and poverty of the old country—then I used to dream of a place of my own, with a comfortable house, with a livingroom and a roaring fire in the stove, and a good, bright lamp burning overhead, of an evening. I was sitting with a woman, my wife, in the light of that lamp, when the nightly chores were done; and we were listening to the children's feet on the floor above as they went to bed; and we were looking and smiling at each other. Ellen, always then, in that dream, the woman was you. . . . At other times, when I was thinking of my mother . . . how, even when my father was still living, she had to slave away, all day, getting wood, getting water, and taking in washing to pay for the children's clothes—for my father was just a labourer, hiring out from sun to sun; his wages were low, not more than ten, twelve dollars a month the year around; and there were six children to feed. . . . And when my father died, she had to go herself, for little wages; and some of her employers were mean to her; but others gave her a pot of beans, or the bones of a roast in addition to her wages—a Krone, a quarter, a day— to take home. . . . I still fumed and raged at it in retrospection. . . . And I vowed to myself that no wife of mine should ever have to work as she had done. That was why I had come to this country. And when I thought of how I would rather slave and work my fingers to the bone than let my wife, the mother of my children, do one single thing beyond what it would be a pleasure for her to do—then, for six years now, I have always thought of you as that wife. Why was that? What do you think?'

'Oh, Niels. . . .'

'I will tell you. It was because I loved you, loved you from the very first day that I had seen you. Do you remember? . . . There I sat, at the breakfast table; and you were busy over the stove. I kept watching you; and your father did not like it. I did not know, of course, then; but I knew later on that already I had seen in you the mate of my life. . . .'

Ellen smiled a reminiscent smile and nodded. 'Yes,' she said. 'And then. . . . Will you listen, Niels? It's a long story; and I don't know whether I can tell it. I don't know whether you will understand. I have to strip myself before you. I have to show you leprous scars in my memory. I will try. . . .

'What I must tell you is the story of my mother. Much of it I did not understand at the time. I was a child when these things happened. But I must speak to you as a woman. . . .

'You speak of your mother . . . how she used to work and to slave. Probably you know only the least of what she had to go through. You know the outside. You were a boy. Only a girl or a woman can understand another woman. I was a very observant child, old and experienced before my time. I saw and understood many things which even my mother did not know, did not suspect I could understand. She often said, you will understand that one day, when I understood it right then. But some things I did not understand at the time. I saw them, and they lived in my memory; and I came to understand them later. . . .

'Niels, if I am to make this thing clear to you, I shall have to speak to you, not as to a man, especially not a man who had hoped to be more to me than a brother. I shall have to forget that I am a young woman. There are things which even between older people are skipped in silence. If you are to understand, I must strip my soul of its secrets . . . I could not bear to have you look at me, Niels, while I tell them. But I know—I think I know what this means to you. I will do it if you wish. . . .'

Niels rose and walked up and down through the room. Then he took his chair, turned it, and sat down, facing the window that looked out on the yard.

'Thanks,' she said.

'I was nine years old when we came from Sweden. My father's people had been day labourers in the rye-districts of Soedermanland. They were prosperous in their small way. They had a little house of two rooms and a piece of land, half an acre maybe. They fattened a pig every year and kept a cow and a few hens. On the land they grew garden truck for the city.

'My father was also a farmhand as you say in this country; but he had to pay rent for the house in which we lived. There were three children, all girls; and my mother was weakly. Her illness had involved him in debt.

'Slowly, through years of discussion, against my mother's wish, the plan to emigrate took shape. My grandfather proposed to keep mother and children while father went out to explore the land. My father declined.

'But one day he proposed to leave the children and to take only mother. At that my mother revolted. But in another year he wore her resistance down till she consented to leave the two younger girls and to take only me. I was her first-born; she would not listen to leaving me behind. She always spoke of letting the others follow as soon as possible.

'But my grandparents were very fond of children. They were not old yet. They had never had but the one child of their own. And when they agreed to take my two sisters, they made their bargain, made it with my father: they were to be in the place of father and mother to them; and my parents were not to have any rights whatever over them any more. He did not tell my mother, thinking that she would give in later when she had got used to having one child only. She never did, of course. The separation remained to her a lifelong sorrow. But as you will see, that was the least she had to bear. . . .

'We came away. My father had no difficulty in finding work in this country. He was strong and healthy. I don't know by what chance he came to Odensee. He had been working on a German estate in Sweden. He understood German well and spoke it a little; probably that was the reason. At Odensee he rented a one-roomed shack with three acres of land where he grew potatoes and raised pigs. He worked on the big farms in summer; and in winter he went to town, till he took up his homestead three years later.

'The place he rented in Odensee was part of a quarter section of almost wild land, south of the village. It belonged to an old man who had moved to town. The rest of the land was rented to a man by name of Campbell who had married a Swedish girl. He is now living north of here, on a place of his own; you may know him.

'As if it were yesterday I remember the first meeting between my mother and Mrs Campbell. We had moved into the place a day or so before. The Campbells' house stood a quarter of a mile east of ours, a large, unpainted frame building half gone to ruin. The man was in the cattle business; but he was not yet making money. There were three acres of land broken near the house; and he had planted them to potatoes. There were four children. The woman had to look after the little crop, for the man used his business as a pretext to be hardly ever at home. So, from the first, I got used to seeing the woman work in the potato-patch.

'Since my mother knew neither English nor German, she was lost in the settlement. She had heard that Mrs Campbell was Swedish. And, being in a strange country the ways of which she did not know, she was anxious to become acquainted with somebody she could talk to.

'It was in the afternoon of a summer day when we crawled through the fence of our yard and crossed over through the brush to the potato-patch.

'As I said, there were four children on the place. The oldest one was a girl of seven or eight: and she was watching the smaller ones—two were twins—while she picked weeds from the rows of the plants.

'The mother, a big, bony woman, was hoeing between the rows. She did not show any pleasure at meeting my mother.

' "You have four children!" my mother said.

' "Yes," the woman replied with an exaggerated groan of disgust; "and if another were coming, I'd walk off into the bush. . . ."

'My mother probably betrayed surprise; for the woman laughed and added, when a woman has got to work like a man, children are just a plague. . . .

'When we came home, mother cried. She was thinking of the two little ones she had left behind; I knew; and I went to her and patted her hand, begging her not to cry.

'I knew and understood more, in a childish way, than the grown-ups thought. When you change your country, at that age, it somehow gives you an insight into things and a curiosity beyond your years.

'I asked her, "Mother, where do children come from?"

'I had often asked her that question before, and she had always answered, "God sends them!"—But this time she said, "When men and women live together, children come. That is nature."

'Soon after, I was sent to school and began to learn English. I also began to see many things. Soon we had a cow; and then two or three; and half a dozen pigs. And my mother was working as hard or harder than Mrs Campbell.

'My parents spoke in my presence as if I did not exist. You have noticed that that is the rule in these settlements where houses are mere cabins in which grown-ups and children are crowded together.

'So, from many things that were said and from some that I saw I inferred that mother expected shortly to have another child and that that greatly worried her; but even more did it worry my father. He began to speak still more curtly to my mother; and he treated her as if she were at fault and had committed a crime. He prayed even more than before, both more frequently and longer. Gradually my mother began to get into a panic about her condition.

'So one day, taking me along, she went over to see that woman in the potato-patch once more.

'A number of things were said back and forth which I remember with great distinctness but which have nothing to do with my story.

'At last Mrs Campbell laughed out loud. "Of course," she said, "it's plain to be seen by now. It's a curse. But I can tell you I wouldn't be caught that way. Not I! I'm wise."

' "But what can you do?" my mother exclaimed. "He comes and begs and says that's what God made them male and female for. And if you want to hold your man. . . ."

'Again the woman laughed. I see her now, standing there in the potato-patch, straight up, with her red face to the sun and her hair blowing in the wind as she put her hands on her hips and held her sides with laughing. . . .

'I was only ten years old. But I tell you, I knew exactly what they were talking about. And right then I vowed I should never marry. I was furious at the woman and afraid of her.

' "You're innocent all right," she said at last contemptuously. "I don't mean it that way, child. But when I'm just about as far gone as you are now, then I go and lift heavy things; or I take the plow and walk behind it for a day. In less than a week's time the child comes; and it's dead. In a day or two I go to work again. Just try it. It won't hurt you. Lots of women around here do the same."

'So when we came home, my mother took some heavy logs, dragged them to the saw-buck, and sawed them. I begged her not to do it; but even I could see that she was desperate.

'Next day she was very sick. I was sent to the house of the German preacher in the village. And when I was allowed to come back, my mother was at work again on the land. She looked the picture of death; but she was cheerful. My father prayed more than ever.

'Once again the thing happened while we were still at Odensee. The Campbells had moved away to where they are living now; and mother

had absolutely no intercourse any longer with anybody. Mother dreaded my father's visits at home by this time.

'Then, early in the spring of the third year, we moved out here. There were no buildings. We camped. Our few things stood under the trees. There was no tent even. Nothing but the sky.

'My father began to clear the yard and to pile logs for building. Mother worked with axe and brute force, helping him. Even I had to help, lifting and pulling when the logs were too heavy for them.

'Then haying time came. My father bought a team of oxen and a mower. He had no wagon yet. The hay was carried over in huge bundles slung with ropes. Mother and I did just as much, together, as my father.

'But don't think for a moment that I am complaining about the work. I liked it. I was strong. Already I dreamt of one day having a farm all by myself, with mother to keep me company.

'Then the stable was built; just as it stands today. My father hated make-shifts. When it was up, we moved into one end of it, the other being occupied by the cows and oxen. Late in the fall, when my father had bought a wagon, he hauled some cheap lumber and built the implement shed, just as it stands today. "We can make out where we are," he said; "but oxen and machinery cost money."

'In winter he went to town again; and we were left alone in the bush. Not a soul knew we were there. The school had not been built.

'Mother cried a good deal; more and more she confided in me, treating me as an equal. "Oh, he is hard," she would say of Father, "as hard as God! And to think that I shall never see my little ones again!"

'And she began to speak of me. "You are big and strong," she said. "You are as good as a boy. Don't ever marry. Marriage makes weak. . . ."

'And in my childish understanding I promised fervently.

'I remember how I used to sit on the bare, frozen ground and to press my head against her knees where she sat, close to the little stove, on the only chair in the place. At night I sprang up every hour or so and re-plenished the stove, or we should have frozen. . . .

'Towards the end of winter my father came home and began to clear land. From then on we worked with him in the bush, piling the wood and the brush, often wading through snow knee-deep. The work was much too hard for my mother; but I thrived on it. My father often praised me; but already his praise had become distasteful. There was a note of re-proach in it for mother. I tried to hide how much of the work I did, how little mother.

'In spring he broke a patch of ground; and we picked the stones and piled the roots.

'That year the school was built. A teacher came out and boarded with Sterners, straight north from it. . . .

'As soon as my father had seeded his patch, mother began to beg that I should be sent to school. But my father would not let me go; he wanted to build a house. Not that he thought the house so necessary; but he intended to buy a team of horses—the two old mares that I still have: it's only ten years ago, you know—so he could haul cordwood in winter and make more money.

'The house, a one-roomed shack—it is the granary now—was not quite finished when harvest time came; there was no roof on it, no floor in it yet. My father went away; and mother and I cut the barley with the mower and tied it by hand. The cattle and the oxen could still stay out-side; so we carried the bundles into the stable, to be threshed by hand when my father came home.

'Still, mother insisted on my going to school now. I went. The teacher was a young girl, not more than eighteen years old; but she let me come whenever I could. She treated me as a grown-up, as indeed I was. When I was at school—for an hour a day at most—she gave me all her time. And one day she came to see mother and told her she would put me through my entrance if I could attend for one full year; I should become a teacher myself because I was so gifted.

'But I had already made up my mind to become a farmer, though not a farmer's wife. I liked horses and cows and pigs and chickens and could handle them. I was strong; and I was not afraid of work. . . .

'When my father came home, I stopped school, of course. He brought horses along.

'It's no use to detail to you any further the growth of the farm; you know as much of that as I do. . . .

'I remember one day in the spring of the following year. Mother had been very ill for several days. She had again been lifting things: and my father had taken a little box into the bush to bury. But she had got up and made breakfast, in spite of my protest. "You go and help father," she had said; and I had gone out. And when I returned to the house, my father followed me.

' "This shack looks a disgrace to the place," he said in a matter-of-fact tone when he entered. "You better go at white-washing it today."

'Mother looked a protest, appealingly.

'But he shrugged his shoulders. "Poor people have to work," he said. "We'll spare you from the field. Ellen and I will attend to the seeding. I'll mix the white-wash for you before we go."

'We had breakfast; and when my father had left the room I lingered behind and whispered, "Don't you do it! You go to bed!"

' "Oh," mother moaned, "I hate him! I hate him!"

'But the worst is to come. The thing that makes marriage for me an impossibility; that makes the very thought of it a disgust which fills me with nausea.

'I know, Niels, if I tell it, it will ever after stand between us. I hope it will change your feelings towards me into those of a brother. I feel sure that no man can still be the lover of a woman who has spoken so plainly to him about such things.

'This house had been built meanwhile. I had grown. I was seventeen years old by that time. Mother had become a mere ghost of herself. She was dragging herself about; she could not get up for weeks at a stretch. Always she suffered from terrible backaches.

'One night when I had gone to bed in that room there I could not sleep. I was so worried that I was almost sick myself.

'Mother came in and dragged herself to the bed. It took her half an hour to undress; she lay down with a moan.

'My father followed her. I acted as if I were asleep; not in order to pry on my parents; but to save mother worry about me. My father got ready to go to bed himself. As a last thing before blowing the lamp he bent over me to see whether I was asleep. Then he knelt by his bed and prayed, loud and fervently and long.

'Suddenly I heard mother's voice mixed with groans, "Oh John, don't."

'I will not repeat the things my father said. An abyss opened as I lay there. The vile, jesting, jocular urgency of it; the words he used to that skeleton and ghost of a woman. . . . In order to save mother, I was tempted to betray that I heard. Shame held me back. . . .

'Once she said, still defending herself, "You know, John, it means a child again. You know how often I have been a murderess already. John, Please! Please!"

' "God has been good to us," he replied; "he took them. . . ."

'And the struggle began again, to end with the defeat of the woman. . . . That night I vowed to myself: No man, whether I liked him or loathed him, was ever to have power over me!

'A few months later haying time came again. Mother went on the stack. Soon after she went to bed, never to rise again. . . .

'And now, Niels, if you still can, ask me once more to be your wife. But if you do, it will cut our friendship even.'

Niels stood up.

'When death came,' Ellen went on, 'as a great relief to her, you may believe it came as a relief even to me.

'Three or four days before the last my mother—to me she had become a tender, sweet, and helpless creature; to him a living indictment, I hope— mother, I say, called me and whispered, "Ellen, whatever you do, never let a man come near you. You are strong and big, thank God. Make your own life, Ellen, and let nobody make it for you!"

'I sank down by the side of her bed; and I lifted this hand up to God and said, "Mother, there is one man who is different from the others. I hope he will be my friend and brother. But I swear to God and to you he shall never be more!"

'Her head sank back on the pillow; and her thin, transparent hand lay on my head.'

Niels turned and went to the door. For a moment he held the knob; then he shrugged his shoulders convulsively and went out.

Ellen sprang up and ran to the door. 'Niels!'

He stopped without looking back.

'Niels,' she repeated, 'promise that you will come back. Not now. Not within a day or a week. I know you can't. But I shall be so lonesome. You must fight this down. Don't leave me alone for the rest of my days. Promise that you will come back. . . .'

'I shall try,' he stammered and left the yard.

He did not see that over that farmyard there followed him a girl, her hand pressed to her bosom, tears in her eyes; nor that, at the gate, she sank to the ground and sobbed. . . .

SETTLERS OF THE MARSH

Thomas C. Haliburton

With Sam Slick, the Yankee clockmaker, THOMAS CHANDLER HALIBURTON created one of the most memorable comic characters in literature and achieved a fame that was even greater in England and the United States than in Canada. Born in Windsor, N.S., he was educated at King's College there. He graduated in 1815, married in 1816, and was called to the bar of Nova Scotia in 1820. He practised law in Annapolis and in 1826 was elected to represent Annapolis in the Legislative Assembly. Three years later he was made a judge of the Court of Common Pleas and in 1841 a judge of the Supreme Court of the province. In 1856 he retired and moved to England, where he was elected to the House of Commons in 1859. He retained his seat until his death.

Haliburton was always a Tory in his sympathies, but as a young man he held liberal views that were very much contrary to those of other Tories: among other things he advocated the removal of the disabilities that prevented Roman Catholics from holding office and the establishment of a system of common schools that would take education out of the hands of the Church of England.

(As he got older, however, and particularly when he became a judge, his 'radical' sympathies died and his Toryism hardened: he grew more and more out of step with the liberal tendencies of his time.) Observing the lethargy of Nova Scotians when he travelled over the province as a judge, he first put his observations into a pamphlet, *A General Description of Nova Scotia* (1823), which was enlarged by the addition of a history and statistics and published in two volumes in 1829. He then turned to satire, creating the character Sam Slick, who makes his points in a series of anecdotes, tall tales, and shrewd comments on human nature. They rely for their humour not so much on the stories themselves, amusing though many of them are, but on the way Sam talks and the distinctive flavour of his monologues—the inventive turns of phrase, the witty and pungent sayings, the outrageous puns, all expressed in a comical Yankee dialect. Haliburton published twenty-one Sam Slick sketches in the *Nova Scotian*, a newspaper of which Joseph Howe was editor. They were reprinted by Howe in book form as *The Clockmaker; or, The*

Sayings and Doings of Sam Slick of Slickville (1836). In an introductory letter to Mr Howe, Haliburton has Sam say: 'It wipes up the Bluenoses considerable hard, and don't let off the Yankees so very easy neither, but it's generally allowed to be about the prettiest book ever writ in this country; and although it ain't altogether jist gospel what's in it, there's some pretty home truths in it, that's a fact.' A second and third series of Clockmaker books, published in 1838 and 1840, are less interesting today because they deal mainly with current issues (such as responsible government, which Haliburton opposed).

Haliburton also wrote *The Attaché; or,*

Sam Slick in England (1843-4) and *Sam Slick's Wise Saws and Modern Instances; or, What He Said and Did or Invented* (1853), and its sequel, *Nature and Human Nature* (1853). Next to the first Sam Slick book, Haliburton's best literary effort is probably *The Old Judge* (1849) in which an Englishman tours Nova Scotia. His observations and the stories told by the people he meets present a revealing and quite entertaining picture of the province and its inhabitants in the middle of the nineteenth century.

The Clockmaker is available in paperback in the New Canadian Library; *The Old Judge* is a Clarke Irwin paperback.

THE CLOCKMAKER

In the first two decades of the nineteenth century Nova Scotia was beset by economic difficulties. Having neglected to make full use of the land and to open up industry—in contrast to the hardworking, go-ahead society to the south—it relied mainly on government patronage for support. To draw attention to the untapped possibilities of the province and the indolence of the people, Haliburton wrote The Clockmaker, *a series of satirical sketches comprised in large part of the monologues of a Yankee named Sam Slick. A non-stop talker, Sam colourfully expressed his views of the laziness, pride, and greed of the Bluenoses (the name given to Nova Scotians) as he toured the province selling clocks.*

I had heard of Yankee clock pedlars, tin pedlars, and Bible pedlars, especially of him who sold Polyglot Bibles *(all in English)* to the amount of sixteen thousand pounds. The house of every substantial farmer had three substantial ornaments: a wooden clock, a tin reflector, and a Polyglot Bible. How is it that an American can sell his wares, at whatever price he pleases, where a blue-nose would fail to make a sale at all? I will inquire of the Clockmaker the secret of his success.

'What a pity it is, Mr Slick'—for such was his name—'what a pity it is,' said I, 'that you, who are so successful in teaching these people the value of *clocks*, could not also teach them the value of *time*.'

'I guess,' said he, 'they have got that ring to grow on their horns yet, which every four-year-old has in our country. We reckon hours and minutes to be dollars and cents. They do nothing in these parts but eat, drink, smoke, sleep, ride about, lounge at taverns, make speeches at temperance meetings, and talk about "House of Assembly". If a man don't hoe his corn, and he don't get a crop, he says it is all owing to the bank; and if he runs into debt and is sued, why he says the lawyers are a curse to the country. They are a most idle set of folks, I tell you.'

'But how is it,' said I, 'that you manage to sell such an immense number of clocks, which certainly cannot be called necessary articles, among a people with whom there seems to be so great a scarcity of money?'

Mr Slick paused, as if considering the propriety of answering the question, and looking me in the face, said in a confidential tone, 'Why, I don't care if I do tell you, for the market is glutted, and I shall quit this circuit. It is done by a knowledge of *soft sawder* and *human natur*. But here is Deacon Flint's,' said he; 'I have but one clock left, and I guess I will sell it to him.'

At the gate of a most comfortable-looking farmhouse stood Deacon Flint, a respectable old man who had understood the value of time better than most of his neighbours, if one might judge from the appearance of everything about him. After the usual salutation, an invitation to 'alight' was accepted by Mr Slick, who said he wished to take leave of Mrs Flint before he left Colchester.

We had hardly entered the house, before the Clockmaker pointed to the view from the window, and addressing himself to me, said, 'If I was to tell them in Connecticut there was such a farm as this away down east here in Nova Scotia, they wouldn't believe me. Why there ain't such a location in all New England. The Deacon has a hundred acres of dyke—'

'Seventy,' said the Deacon, 'only seventy.'

'Well, seventy; but then there is your fine deep bottom, why I could run a ramrod into it—'

'Interval, we call it,' said the Deacon, who though evidently pleased at this eulogium, seemed to wish the experiment of the ramrod to be tried in the right place.

'Well, interval if you please—though Professor Eleazer Cumstick, in his work on Ohio, calls them bottoms—is just as good as dyke. Then there is that water privilege, worth three or four thousand dollars, twice as good as what Governor Cass paid fifteen thousand dollars for. I wonder, Deacon, you don't put up a carding mill on it: the same works would carry a turning lathe, a shingle machine, a circular saw, grind bark, and—'

'Too old,' said the Deacon, 'too old for all those speculations—'

'Old,' repeated the Clockmaker, 'not you; why you are worth half a dozen of the young men we see nowadays. You are young enough to

have—' Here he said something in a lower tone of voice, which I did not distinctly hear; but whatever it was, the Deacon was pleased. He smiled and said he did not think of such things now.

'But your beasts, dear me, your beasts must be put in and have a feed'; saying which, he went out to order them to be taken to the stable.

As the old gentleman closed the door after him, Mr Slick drew near to me and said in an under tone, 'That is what I call "soft sawder". An Englishman would pass that man as a sheep passes a hog in a pasture, without looking at him; or,' said he, looking rather archly, 'if he was mounted on a pretty smart horse, I guess he'd trot away, if he could. Now I find—' Here his lecture on 'soft sawder' was cut short by the entrance of Mrs Flint.

'Jist come to say good-bye, Mrs Flint.'

'What, have you sold all your clocks?'

'Yes, and very low, too, for money is scarce, and I wished to close the concarn; no, I am wrong in saying all, for I have just one left. Neighbour Steel's wife asked to have the refusal of it, but I guess I won't sell it; I had but two of them, this one and the feller of it that I sold Governor Lincoln. General Green, the Secretary of State for Maine, said he'd give me fifty dollars for this here one—it has composition wheels and patent axles; it is a beautiful article, a real first chop, no mistake, genuine super-fine—but I guess I'll take it back; and besides, Squire Hawk might think kinder harder that I did not give him the offer.'

'Dear me,' said Mrs Flint, 'I should like to see it; where is it?'

'It is in a chest of mine over the way, at Tom Tape's store. I guess he can ship it on to Eastport.'

'That's a good man,' said Mrs Flint, 'jist let's look at it.'

Mr Slick, willing to oblige, yielded to these entreaties and soon produced the clock—a gawdy, highly varnished, trumpery-looking affair. He placed it on the chimney-piece where its beauties were pointed out and duly appreciated by Mrs Flint, whose admiration was about ending in a proposal when Mr Flint returned from giving his directions about the care of the horses. The Deacon praised the clock; he too thought it a handsome one. But the Deacon was a prudent man; he had a watch—he was sorry, but he had no occasion for a clock.

'I guess you're in the wrong furrow this time, Deacon. It ain't for sale,' said Mr Slick; 'and if it was, I reckon neighbour Steel's wife would have it, for she gives me no peace about it.' Mrs Flint said that Mr Steel had enough to do, poor man, to pay his interest, without buying clocks for his wife.

'It's no concarn of mine,' said Mr Slick, 'so long as he pays me, what he has to do, but I guess I don't want to sell it, and besides it comes too high; that clock can't be made at Rhode Island under forty dollars. Why it ain't possible,' said the Clockmaker, in apparent surprise, looking at his watch, 'why as I'm alive it is four o'clock, and if I haven't been two hours here. How on airth shall I reach River Philip tonight? I'll tell you what, Mrs Flint, I'll leave the clock in your care till I return on my way to the States. I'll set it a-going and put it to the right time.'

As soon as this operation was performed, he delivered the key to the Deacon with a sort of serio-comic injunction to wind up the clock every Saturday night, which Mrs Flint said she would take care should be done, and promised to remind her husband of it in case he should chance to forget it.

'That,' said the Clockmaker, as soon as we were mounted, 'that I call "human natur"! Now that clock is sold for forty dollars; it cost me just six dollars and fifty cents. Mrs Flint will never let Mrs Steel have the refusal, nor will the Deacon learn until I call for the clock that having once indulged in the use of a superfluity, how difficult it is to give it up. We can do without any article of luxury we have never had, but when once obtained, it is not "in human natur" to surrender it voluntarily. Of fifteen thousand sold by myself and partners in this Province, twelve thousand were left in this manner, and only ten clocks were ever returned; when we called for them they invariably bought them. We trust to "soft sawder" to get them into the house, and to "human natur" that they never come out of it.'

THE CLOCKMAKER

Samuel Hearne

One of Canada's most famous explorers —the discoverer of the Coppermine River and the first white man to reach the Arctic Ocean overland—SAMUEL HEARNE was the author of *A Journey from Prince of Wales's Fort in Hudson's Bay to the Northern Ocean* (1795), a classic work on exploration. Born in London, he became a midshipman in the Royal Navy and went to sea at the age of twelve. He served in the Seven Years' War, an experience that seemed to equip him well to suffer uncomplainingly the incredible hardships of exploring far-northern Canada. In 1766 he joined the Hudson's Bay Company as a seaman. From Fort Prince of Wales (Churchill, Man.) he was sent overland across the Barren Lands in search of copper. Two journeys in 1769 and 1770 failed because he had an unsatisfactory guide, but on his journey of 1771-2 he found the Coppermine River and reached the Arctic Ocean, returning to the fort eighteen months after his departure. In 1774 he founded Cumberland House, the Company's first inland post, and in 1775 he became governor of Fort Prince of Wales. When the fort was captured and destroyed by the French in 1782 he returned to England, but later that year he went back to Hudson Bay to rebuild the fort on a new site. He retired from the Company in 1787 owing to ill health and settled in London where he worked on the manuscript of a book based on his journals. He died five years later, a month after signing a contract with his publisher.

Hearne's book is the amazing achievement of a man who was not completely literate. It is a rich, immensely readable and interesting account of his explorations that gives accurate and detailed descriptions of the Chipewyan Indians (for which the book has great ethnological value) and of the geography and natural history of the region he visited; it also conveys a memorable portrait of the explorer himself, who was an appealing and sensitive man. A modern edition of Hearne's work—the full title of which is *A Journey from Prince of Wales's Fort, in Hudson's Bay, to the Northern Ocean, Undertaken by Order of the Hudson's Bay Company, for the Discovery of Copper Mines, a North West Passage &c. in the Years 1769, 1770, 1771, & 1772*—was edited by Richard Glover (1958). Farley Mowat adapted the narrative for modern readers and published this version as *Coppermine Journey* (1958).

Samuel Hearne has inspired a fine poem by John Newlove, 'Samuel Hearne in Wintertime', which is on page 368.

THE COPPERMINE MASSACRE

In December 1770 Samuel Hearne, an employee of the Hudson's Bay Company, started out on an eighteen-month journey that took him to the Arctic Ocean at the mouth of the Coppermine River and back to Fort Prince of Wales (Churchill, Man.). His companions were a band of Chipewyan Indians.

JULY 1771

Early in the morning of the sixteenth, the weather being fine and pleasant, I again proceeded with my survey, and continued it for ten miles farther down the river; but still found it the same as before, being everywhere full of falls and shoals. At this time (it being about noon) the three men who had been sent as spies met us on their return and informed my companions that five tents of Esquimaux were on the west side of the river. The situation, they said, was very convenient for surprising them; and, according to their account, I judged it to be about twelve miles from the place we met the spies. When the Indians received this intelligence, no further attendance or attention was paid to my survey, but their whole thoughts were immediately engaged in planning the best method of attack and how they might steal on the poor Esquimaux the ensuing night and kill them all while asleep. To accomplish this bloody design more effectually, the Indians thought it necessary to cross the river as soon as possible; and, by the account of the spies, it appeared that no part was more convenient for the purpose than that where we had met them, it being there very smooth and at a considerable distance from any fall. Accordingly, after the Indians had put all their guns, spears, targets, &c. in good order, we crossed the river, which took up some time.

When we arrived on the west side of the river, each painted the front of his target or shield; some with the figure of the sun, others with that of the moon, several with different kinds of birds and beasts of prey, and many with the images of imaginary beings, which, according to their silly notions, are the inhabitants of the different elements, earth, sea, air, &c.

On enquiring the reason of their doing so, I learned that each man painted his shield with the image of that being on which he relied most for success in the intended engagement. Some were contented with a single representation; while others—doubtful, as I suppose, of the quality and

power of any single being—had their shields covered to the very margin
with a group of hieroglyphics, quite unintelligible to everyone except the
painter. Indeed, from the hurry in which this business was necessarily
done, the want of every colour but red and black, and the deficiency of
skill in the artist, most of those paintings had more the appearance of a
number of accidental blotches than 'of anything that is on the earth, or
in the water under the earth'; and though some few of them conveyed
a tolerable idea of the thing intended, yet even these were many degrees
worse than our country sign-paintings in England.

When this piece of superstition was completed, we began to advance
toward the Esquimaux tents; but were very careful to avoid crossing any
hills, or talking loud, for fear of being seen or overheard by the inhabitants; by which means the distance was not only much greater than it
otherwise would have been, but, for the sake of keeping in the lowest
grounds, we were obliged to walk through entire swamps of stiff marly
clay, sometimes up to the knees. Our course however on this occasion,
though very serpentine, was not altogether so remote from the river as
entirely to exclude me from a view of it the whole way: on the contrary,
several times (according to the situation of the ground) we advanced so
near it as to give me an opportunity of convincing myself that it was as
unnavigable as it was in those parts which I had surveyed before, and
which entirely corresponded with the accounts given of it by the spies.

It is perhaps worth remarking that my crew, though an undisciplined
rabble, and by no means accustomed to war or command, seemingly acted
on this horrid occasion with the utmost uniformity of sentiment. There
was not among them the least altercation or separate opinion; all were
united in the general cause, and as ready to follow where Matonabbee
led as he appeared to be ready to lead, according to the advice of an old
Copper Indian who had joined us on our first arrival at the river where
this bloody business was first proposed.

Never was reciprocity of interest more generally regarded among a
number of people than it was on the present occasion by my crew, for
not one was a moment in want of anything that another could spare; and
if ever the sprit of disinterested friendship expanded the heart of a
Northern Indian, it was here exhibited in the most extensive meaning of
the word. Property of every kind that could be of general use now ceased
to be private, and everyone who had anything which came under that
description, seemed proud of an opportunity of giving it, or lending it to
those who had none, or were most in want of it.

The number of my crew was so much greater than that which five tents
could contain, and the warlike manner in which they were equipped so
greatly superior to what could be expected of the poor Esquimaux, that no

less than a total massacre of every one of them was likely to be the case, unless Providence should work a miracle for their deliverance.

The land was so situated that we walked under cover of the rocks and hills till we were within two hundred yards of the tents. There we lay in ambush for some time, watching the motions of the Esquimaux; and here the Indians would have advised me to stay till the fight was over, but to this I could by no means consent, for I considered that when the Esquimaux came to be surprised, they would try every way to escape, and if they found me alone, not knowing me from an enemy, they would probably proceed to violence against me when no person was near to assist. For this reason I determined to accompany them, telling them at the same time that I would not have any hand in the murder they were about to commit, unless I found it necessary for my own safety. The Indians were not displeased at this proposal; one of them immediately fixed me a spear and another lent me a broad bayonet for my protection, but at that time I could not be provided with a target; nor did I want to be encumbered with such an unnecessary piece of lumber.

While we lay in ambush, the Indians performed the last ceremonies which were thought necessary before the engagement. These chiefly consisted in painting their faces: some all black, some all red, and others a mixture of the two. And to prevent their hair from blowing into their eyes, it was either tied before and behind, and on both sides, or else cut short all round. The next thing they considered was to make themselves as light as possible for running, which they did by pulling off their stockings and either cutting off the sleeves of their jackets or rolling them up close to their armpits; and though the mosquitoes at that time were so numerous as to surpass all credibility, yet some of the Indians actually pulled off their jackets and entered the lists quite naked, except their breech-cloths and shoes. Fearing I might have occasion to run with the rest, I thought it also advisable to pull off my stockings and cap, and to tie my hair as close up as possible.

By the time the Indians had made themselves thus completely frightful it was near one o'clock in the morning of the seventeenth; when finding all the Esquimaux quiet in their tents, they rushed forth from their ambuscade and fell on the poor unsuspecting creatures, unperceived till close at the very eaves of their tents, when they soon began the bloody massacre, while I stood neuter in the rear.

In a few seconds the horrible scene commenced. It was shocking beyond description: the poor unhappy victims were surprised in the midst of their sleep and had neither time nor power to make any resistance; men, women, and children, in all upward of twenty, ran out of their tents stark naked and endeavoured to make their escape, but the Indians having possession of all the landside, to no place could they fly for shelter. One alternative only remained, that of jumping into the river, but as none of them attempted it, they all fell a sacrifice to Indian barbarity!

The shrieks and groans of the poor expiring wretches were truly dreadful; and my horror was much increased at seeing a young girl, seemingly about eighteen years of age, killed so near me that when the first spear was stuck into her side she fell down at my feet and twisted round my legs, so that it was with difficulty that I could disengage myself from her dying grasps. As two Indian men pursued this unfortunate victim I solicited very hard for her life, but the murderers made no reply till they had stuck both their spears through her body and transfixed her to the ground. They then looked me sternly in the face and began to ridicule me by asking if I wanted an Esquimaux wife, and paid not the smallest regard to the shrieks and agony of the poor wretch who was twining round their spears like an eel! Indeed, after receiving much abusive language from them on the occasion, I was at length obliged to desire that they would be more expeditious in dispatching their victim out of her misery, otherwise I should be obliged, out of pity, to assist in the friendly office of putting an end to the existence of a fellow-creature who was so cruelly wounded. On this request being made, one of the Indians hastily drew his spear from the place where it was first lodged and pierced it through her breast near the heart. The love of life, however, even in this most miserable state, was so predominant that, though this might justly be called the most merciful act that could be done for the poor creature, it seemed to be unwelcome, for though much exhausted by pain and loss of blood, she made several efforts to ward off the friendly blow. My situation and the terror of my mind at beholding this butchery cannot easily be conceived, much less described. Though I summed up all the fortitude I was master of on the occasion, it was with difficulty that I could refrain from tears; and I am confident that my features must have feelingly expressed how sincerely I was affected at the barbarous scene I then witnessed. Even at this hour I cannot reflect on the transactions of that horrid day without shedding tears.

*   *   *

Among the various superstitious customs of those people it is worth remarking, and ought to have been mentioned in its proper place, that immediately after my companions had killed the Esquimaux at the Copper River, they considered themselves in a state of uncleanness, which induced them to practise some very curious and unusual ceremonies. In the first place, all who were absolutely concerned in the murder were prohibited from cooking any kind of victuals, either for themselves or others. As luckily there were two in company who had not shed blood, they were employed always as cooks till we joined the women. This circumstance was exceedingly favourable on my side, for had there been no persons of the above description in company, that task, I was told, would have fallen on me, which would have been no less fatiguing and troublesome than humiliating and vexatious.

When the victuals were cooked, all the murderers took a kind of red earth or oker and painted all the space between the nose and chin, as well as the greater part of their cheeks almost to the ears before they would taste a bit, and would not drink out of any other dish, or smoke out of any other pipe, but their own; and none of the others seemed willing to drink or smoke out of theirs.

We had no sooner joined the women, at our return from the expedition, than there seemed to be an universal spirit of emulation among them, vying who should first make a suit of ornaments for their husbands, which consisted of bracelets for the wrists and a band for the forehead, composed of porcupine quills and moose-hair curiously wrought on leather.

The custom of painting the mouth and part of the cheeks before each meal, and drinking and smoking out of their own utensils, was strictly and invariably observed till the winter began to set in; and during the whole of that time they would never kiss any of their wives or children. They refrained also from eating many parts of the deer and other animals, particularly the head, entrails, and blood; and during their uncleanness, their victuals were never sodden in water, but dried in the sun, eaten quite raw, or broiled, when a fire fit for the purpose could be procured.

When the time arrived that was to put an end to these ceremonies, the men, without a female being present, made a fire at some distance from the tents, into which they threw all their ornaments, pipe-stems, and dishes, which were soon consumed to ashes; after which a feast was prepared, consisting of such articles as they had long been prohibited from eating; and when all was over, each man was at liberty to eat, drink, and smoke as he pleased; and also to kiss his wives and children at discretion, which they seemed to do with more raptures than I had ever known them do it either before or since.

A JOURNEY FROM PRINCE OF WALES'S FORT &C.

b. 1916

Anne Hébert

ANNE HÉBERT was born at Sainte-Catherine de Fossambault, Qué. Her father was a poet and critic; the poet Hector de Saint-Denys-Garneau was a cousin and a companion in her childhood. In poor health as a child, she was educated by her parents. Her first poem was published in 1939 and her first book, *Les Songes en equilibre*, in 1942. Her other collections of poetry are *Le Tombeau des rois* (1953) and *Mystère de la parole* (1960). She has also published a collection of surrealistic short stories, *Le Torrent* (1950), two novels—*Les Chambres de bois* (1958) and *Kamouraska* (1970), which is being made into a film —and three plays: *Le Temps sauvage, Le Mercière assassinée*, and *Les Invités au procès*. She lives in Paris and through her writing has become as well known in French-speaking Europe as in Québec.

Some of Anne Hébert's most memorable poems describe a retreat from reality into the solitude of a surrealistic interior world where purity and innocence are sought. It is a world of symbols—of childhood, captivity, and death—that portray a subconscious landscape with disturbing clarity. The sorrow of isolation and the renunciation of the joys of life in favour of the anguish of solitude are important themes in Anne Hébert's poetry, as they are in the work of many French-Canadian poets, particularly that of Saint-Denys-Garneau. But Anne Hébert's writings trace a gradual liberation from this captivity (from all restrictive conditions of life). For example, in the closing lines of 'The Tomb of the Kings' we read of the freeing of the captive poet after a confrontation with death. One of Anne Hébert's most important poems, 'The Tomb of Kings', is an exploration of the unconscious and contains numerous symbols that recur in her writing: the bird (the poet), kings (representing a mysterious, exotic world that threatens the poet and are here the voices of her past), jewels and flowers (the allurements of this world), water (tranquillity, purity), closed chambers (isolation), bones (death), and light (an awakening).

There is an interesting exchange between Anne Hébert and F.R. Scott about the translation of this poem in Issue 23 of *The Tamarack Review* (Summer 1962) and an article on her poetry by Patricia Purcell, called 'The

Agonizing Solitude', in Issue 10 of
Canadian Literature (Autumn 1961). For
translations of some of the poems, see
F.R. Scott: *Saint-Denys-Garneau & Anne
Hébert: Translations/Traductions* (1962)

and *The Poetry of French Canada in
Translation* (1970) edited by John Glassco.

See page 239 for a poem on Anne
Hébert by D.G. Jones.

THE LITTLE TOWNS

I shall give you the little towns
The poor sad little towns.

The little towns cupped in our palms
More exigent than toys
As easy to the hand.

I play with the little towns,
I turn them over
Never a man escapes them
No flower, no child.

The little towns are empty—
Given into our hands.

I listen, my ear to the doors
I lean to the doors, one by one,
With my ear . . .

O the houses are dumb sea-shells—
No longer in the frozen spiral
Any sound of the wind
Any sound of water.

Dead, the parks and the gardens
The games are all put to sleep
In a dead museum.

I cannot tell where they have put
The deathstill bodies of the birds.

The streets resound with silence
The echo of their silence is a weight of lead
More leaden
Than any words of menace or of love.

And here am I too, in my turn
Forsaking the little towns of my childhood . . .
I offer them to you
In all the infinite depth
Of their loneliness.

Now do you grasp the dangerous gift?
I have given you the strange sad little towns
For your own imagining.

JOHN GLASSCO *(tr)*

MANOR LIFE

Here is an ancestral manor
Without a table or fire
Or dust or carpets.

The perverse enchantment of these rooms
Lies wholly in their polished mirrors.

The only possible thing to do here
Is to look at oneself in the mirror day and night.

Cast your image into these brittle fountains
Your brittler image without shadow or colour.

See, these mirrors are deep
Like cupboards
There is always someone dead behind the quicksilver
Who soon covers your reflection
And clings to you like seaweed

Shapes himself to you, naked and thin,
And imitates love in a long bitter shiver.

F.R. SCOTT *(tr)*

THE TOMB OF THE KINGS

I carry my heart on my fist
Like a blind falcon.

The taciturn bird gripping my fingers
A swollen lamp of wine and blood
I go down
Toward the tombs of the kings
Astonished
Scarcely born.

What Ariadne-thread leads me
Along the muted labyrinths?
The echo of my steps fades away as they fall.

(In what dream
Was this child tied by her ankle
Like a fascinated slave?)

The maker of the dream
Presses on the cord
And my naked footsteps come
One by one
Like the first drops of rain
At the bottom of the well.

Already the odour stirs in swollen storms
Seeps under the edges of the doors
Of chambers secret and round
Where the closed beds are laid out.

The motionless desire of the sculptured dead draws me.
I behold with astonishment
Encrusted upon the black bones
The blue stones gleaming.

A few tragedies patiently wrought
Lying on the breast of kings
As if they were jewels
Are offered me
Without tears or regrets.

In single rank arrayed:
The smoke of incense, the cake of dried rice,
And my flesh which trembles:
A ceremonial and submissive offering.

A gold mask on my absent face
Violet flowers for eyes,
The shade of love paints me in small sharp strokes
And this bird I have breathes
And complains strangely.

A long tremor
Like a wind sweeping from tree to tree,
Shakes the seven tall ebony Pharaohs
In their stately and ornate cases.

It is only the profundity of death which persists,
Simulating the ultimate torment
Seeking its appeasement
And its eternity
In a faint tinkle of bracelets
Vain rings, alien games
Around the sacrificed flesh.

Greedy for the fraternal source of evil in me
They lay me down and drink me;
Seven times I know the tight grip of the bones
And the dry hand seeking my heart to break it.

Livid and satiated with the horrible dream
My limbs freed
And the dead thrust out of me, assasinated,
What glimmer of dawn strays in here?
Wherefore does this bird quiver
And turn toward morning
Its blinded eyes?

F.R. SCOTT *(tr)*

David Helwig

DAVID HELWIG. In *Read Canadian* (1972), an attempt to provide a handy guide to books by and about Canadians, the poet and publisher Dennis Lee writes that there are at least five contemporary poets who have been badly served by the editors of anthologies of Canadian poetry. One of them is David Helwig, who is also a writer of fiction. He was born and brought up in the old town of Niagara-on-the-Lake, a community that has preserved its quaintness even now that it has become the home of the popular Shaw Festival. He studied at the University of Toronto and later did graduate work in Liverpool, Eng. He now teaches English literature at Queen's University in Kingston, Ont.

Helwig's books include three collections of poetry: *Figures in a Landscape* (1967), which also contains two short plays, *The Sign of the Gunman* (1969), which contains many poems that were in his first book, and *The Best Name of Silence* (1972); a collection of short stories, *The Streets of Summer*; and a novel, *The Day Before Tomorrow* (1972), about the reasons for the temporary defection of a foreign-service officer. He is the editor of

a short-story annual being published by the Oberon Press in Ottawa. This project grew out of the experience of attempting to break away from the usual fiction markets in the literary magazines and at the CBC. When Helwig submitted one of his stories to *Saturday Night, Maclean's,* and the Toronto *Star,* the editors he saw all said that, though they liked the story, it was not their policy to publish fiction. (The story in question was eventually broadcast by the CBC.) So Helwig set out to create a new market for stories by Canadian writers. In 1971, with Tom Marshall as co-editor, he published a short-story annual called *Fourteen Stories High.* A second anthology, *Best Canadian Stories* co-edited with Joan Harcourt, appeared in the fall of 1972. Helwig has worked with prisoners in Kingston Penitentiary who were interested in becoming writers and in 1972 became the editor of *Words from Inside,* a magazine of writing by prison inmates from across Canada sponsored by the St Leonard's Society, a charitable organization that attempts to bridge the gap between prison and the community. Helwig is co-author with Billie Miller of *A Book About Billie*

(1972), which he created from tape-recorded interviews with Miller, a habitual criminal on parole from Collins Bay Penitentiary.

David Helwig's lyric poems, and some of his short stories, are usually quiet, sensitive explorations of the thoughts and feelings of everyday life. Two of the three Helwig poems below, however, depart from this theme. Helwig's prison poem clearly grew out of his visits to Kingston Penitentiary. 'One Step from an Old Dance' recalls a famous series of paintings by the nineteenth-century American primitive artist, Edward Hicks, called 'The Peaceable Kingdom', inspired by Isaiah 11: 6 ('The wolf shall dwell with the lamb and the leopard shall lie down with the kid . . .').

FIGURES IN A LANDSCAPE

1
Hunting vixen, red as the sun,
lithe as a black cat, hunting
a soft doe rabbit mild as moonlight,
vixen black in the moonlight hunting,
hunting the soft black blood of the rabbit,
daring rabbit dancing in flight,
mad rabbit dancing by moon and sun,
dancing fear of the sun's vixen,
dainty feet of the hunting vixen,
tail of fire of the copper vixen.

Noon of the sun, still, hard fire.
Turn, turn and see them stand,
red sun, black rabbit, and black vixen.

2
Still on the thin crust of the snow,
white as bone in a light that blinds the eyes,
she stands, taken in her suddenness,
solid against the flatness of the snow.
No tracks show how she came here as the sun
dances on icicles, while all around
the blue jays hurtle on their noisy wings.
And in the pallor of the winter day
flames the black fire of her belly's hair.

FOR JOAN, WHO CAME TO THE PRISON

For two hours we sat
in the nightmare place,
the drab hot prison schoolroom,
you talking, surrounded by murderers,
rapists, pushers, a single guard
nodding and smiling
and smiling and nodding
and a man of god
with only the hopeless weapon
of decency and
as much cunning
as a man of god can afford,
while I sat on a desk nearby
noticing your big knuckles
and nervous gestures,
adding my few words,
a man in hiding
with only the hopeless weapon
of as much love
as a godless man can afford.

Because you are a woman
and among lonely men
they can, for this once, give
a pure love, the gift
of their awkwardness,
wanting you not to go
while the guards are flashing
the lights, thinking
we've stayed too long.

So we leave,
me carrying in my pocket
the notes they hand me.

The world is full
of people who come
with the words they write
to put in my hand,
and I read and smile
and smile and bless their pain,
my pockets full
of these unmailed letters to god.

Going out, not speaking,
the gates shut clanging behind us
as you and I and the man of god
go home in the dark
to our separate nightmares.

In mine I see men
running in a ring
shouting Freedom Freedom.
I think I am there
but invisible.

I don't know your nightmare
but write this anyway
to put in your hand,
as much of a poem
as an invisible man can afford.

ONE STEP FROM AN OLD DANCE

Will the weasel lie down with the snowshoe hare
In the calm and peaceable kingdom?
Will the wolverine cease to rend and tear
In the calm and peaceable kingdom?
Will the beasts of burden not have to bear?
Will the weasel lie down with the snowshoe hare?
Will the children feed grass to the grizzly bear
In the calm and peaceable kingdom?

Oh the wolverine will cease to tear
In the calm and peaceable kingdom,
The rattlesnake rattle praise and prayer
In the calm and peaceable kingdom.
Oh the wolves will wear smiles like children wear,
The wolverine will cease to tear
While the hawk and the squirrel are dancing there
In the calm and peaceable kingdom.

b. 1928

Hugh Hood

HUGH HOOD has been described by one critic as 'the steadiest viewer of ourselves, in Canada, now', and in the process of viewing this country now, Hood has engaged in the writing of novels, short stories and journalism, in teaching, radio and television appearances, and public readings. He was born in Toronto, but his father was from Nova Scotia and his mother was a French Canadian. He graduated from the University of Toronto, taught for a time in the United States, and for some years has been on the staff of the Université de Montréal where he is presently teaching two courses in Canadian writing. He has published four novels: *White Figure, White Ground* (1964), about the life of a painter in Canada; *The Camera Always Lies* (1967), about the movie business; *A Game of Touch* (1970), which has political overtones and is set in Montreal; and *You Can't Get There From Here* (1972), about an imaginary emerging and poverty-stricken nation in Africa. His short stories have been collected in three

books: *Flying a Red Kite* (1962), *Around the Mountain: Scenes from Montreal Life* (1967), and *The Fruit Man, The Meat Man, & The Manager* (1971). In an essay on Hugh Hood's novels in Issue 47 of *Canadian Literature* (Winter 1971). Dennis Duffy writes: 'The world of Hood's fiction is a job world, his writing an encyclopedia of trades and professions . . . not in the guise of names with occupational titles attached, but as people seen and magnified through the technical details of their jobs.'

'Recollections of the Works Department', from which an extract is reprinted below, also draws its strength from its documentary detail. It is based on an actual job experience, but the author himself describes it as 'a fiction'.

Hood is a sports enthusiast—hockey, baseball and touch football—and his biography of the great Jean Beliveau was published in 1970 in both English (*Strength Down Centre*) and French (*Puissance au Centre*).

RECOLLECTIONS OF THE WORKS DEPARTMENT

In the spring of 1952, six weeks after I finished my M.A. courses and involved myself in further graduate studies, I decided that I'd have to find a better summer job.

I had been working for the English publisher, Thomas Nelson and Sons, as a stockroom boy. The pay was low, and the work remarkably hard. I had only been on the job ten days, but after an afternoon stacking cases of *The Highroads Dictionary* (familiar to every Ontario schoolchild), ninety-six copies to the case, in piles ten cases high, I saw that this state of affairs could not go on. These packing cases were made of heavy cardboard, strongly stapled and bound; they weighed seventy-five pounds each and they had to be piled carefully in a complicated stacking system. You had to fling the top row of cases into the air, much as you'd launch a basketball. I started to look for something less strenuous.

At length an official of the National Employment Service who handled summer placements at Hart House, a Mr Halse, a man remembered by generations of Varsity types, suggested that I try to get on the city. I took an afternoon off from Thomas Nelson's and went up to the City Hall, to Room 302, a big room on the west side with a pleasant high ceiling. I was received with courtesy and attention, and after filling out some forms I got a job as a labourer in the Works Department, Roadways Division, payday on Wednesdays, hours eight to five, report to Foreman Brown at Number Two Yard on College Street tomorrow morning, thank you! I stood at the counter a little out of breath at the speed with which I'd got what I came for.

'You're not very big,' said the clerk at the counter. 'Are you sure you can handle a pick and shovel?' As the wages were twice what I'd been getting, I thought I'd try it and see.

'I can handle it,' I said. I've never seen anybody killing himself at the pick-and-shovel dodge. I asked the clerk for the address on College Street and, oddly enough, he didn't know it.

'But you can't miss it,' he said. 'It's next to the Fire Hall, three blocks west of Spadina. Ask to see Mr Brown. And you'd better get on the job on time, the first day at least.'

I thanked him and strolled back to Thomas Nelson's where I explained that I'd found something that paid better, and would they mind letting me go at the end of the day. They didn't seem surprised.

'You've got three days' money coming,' said the stockroom superintendent dolefully. He sighed. 'I don't know how it is. We can't keep anybody in that job.' I said nothing about the cases of dictionaries.

Although it was the middle of May, the next morning was brisk, a bright sunny day with the promise of warmth in the afternoon. I was glad that I'd worn a couple of sweaters as I came along College Street looking for Number Two Yard. It wasn't hard to find. It stood and still stands just west of the Fire Hall halfway between Spadina and Bathurst, on the south side of College. It's the main downtown service centre for roads and sidewalks, responsible for the area bounded by Bathurst, Jarvis, Bloor, and the waterfront. Any holes or cuts in the roadway, any broken sidewalks, or any new sidewalks not provided by contractors, are tended by workmen from this Yard. It also serves as a reception desk for calls connected with trees, sewers, and drains from all over town. There's always a watchman on duty to attend to such matters, day or night.

I walked into the office and stood next to a washbasin in the corner, feeling a little nervous. Most of the other men on the crew were ten years older than I, although I spotted a couple my own age. None of them looked like students, even the young ones; they were all heavily tanned and they all discussed their mysterious affairs in hilarious shouts. There was a counter in front of me, and behind it some office space with three desks, a space heater, some bundles of engineers' plans of the streets hanging in rolls above the windows. It was the kind of room in which no woman had ever been, but it was very clean.

Outside a green International quarter-ton pickup with the Works Department plate on the door came smartly into the Yard. A one-armed man got out and began to shout abusively at the windows of the Fire Hall. This was the foreman, Charlie Brown, who conducted a running war against the firemen because they persisted in parking their cars, of which they had a great many, in his Yard. He bawled a few more curses at the face of the Fire Captain which was glued to a third-story window, and came inside, immediately fixing his eyes, which were brown, small, and very sharp, on me.

'Goddam-college-kids-no-bloody-good,' he shouted irritably, running it all together into a singleword; it was a stock phrase. He glared at me pityingly. 'Where the hell are your boots?' I was wearing a pair of low canvas shoes of the type then known disparagingly as 'fruit boots'.

'Cut 'em to bits in five minutes!' he exclaimed, quite rightly. I wore them to work one day later on, and the edge of the shovel took the soles off them in under five minutes.

'Go across the street to the Cut-Rate Store. Tell them Charlie sent you. Get them to give you sweat socks and boots. You can pay for them when you draw some money.' I tried to say something but he cut me off abruptly and as I went out I could hear him mumbling, 'Goddam-college-kids-no-bloody-good.'

I had a good look at him as he banged noisily around the office when I came back wearing my stiff new boots. He was a burly man, about five-eleven, with a weathered face, a short stump of a right arm—the crew called him 'One Punch Brown'—a pipe usually in his mouth. He was the kindest boss I ever had on one of those summer jobs; there was no reason for him to care about my shoes. The workmen cursed him behind his back but they knew that he didn't push them too hard. And yet he managed to get the necessary minimum of work out of them. I found out, purely by accident, that the way to make him like you was to say as little as possible. It was fear that made me answer him in monosyllables but it suited him.

Charlie had four men in the office with him and three gangs of labourers out on various jobs, widely separated in the midtown district he was responsible for. In the office were an assistant foreman named George—I can't remember his last name—and a clerk named Eddie Doucette who sometimes chauffeured Charlie around town. Usually Charlie drove himself, and how he could spin that little International, stump and all; he used the stump to help steer, along with the good arm.

Then there were two patrolmen who kept checking the streets and alleys in our district, reporting any damage to the roads and sidewalks, and the condition of any recently accomplished repairs. Johnny Pawlak was one of them, a slope-shouldered rangy guy of thirty-three or -four, a bowler and softball player, the organizer of all the baseball pools. The other was called Bill Tennyson, a lean, wiry, chronically dissatisfied griper, always in trouble over his non-support of his family, and half-disliked and suspected by the rest of the men in the office for vague reasons. Finally there were the three gangs out on the job: Wall's gang, Mitch's gang, and Harris's gang. Wall ran a taut ship, Harris an unhappy ship, and Mitch a happy one. I never worked for Wall, but I did the others, and the difference was wonderful.

When I got back from the Cut-Rate Store it was already half-past eight. 'What are we going to do with this kid?' I heard Charlie Brown ask rhetorically as I came into the office.

'Aimé's still off,' said George softly. 'You could send him out with Bill and Danny.' They stared at me together.

'Ever handled a shovel?'

'Yes.'

'Go and help with the coal-ass.'

'Coal-ass?'

'Do you see those men and that truck?' They pointed out the windows. Across the Yard beside a couple of piles of sand and gravel a stubby old guy and a man my own age were sitting, smoking idly, on the running-board of a city dump-truck.

'Go out with them today. And take it easy with the shovel or you'll hurt your hands.'

I left the office and walked over to tell the two men, Bill Eagleson and Danny Foster, that I was coming with them.

'What's your name?'

'Hood.'

'All right, Hoody,' said the older man, Bill, 'grab a shovel.' After a moment he and Danny stood off and studied my style.

'Do much shovelling?'

'Not a hell of a lot, no.'

'Swing it like this, look!' They taught me how, and there really was an easy way to do it, one of the most useful things I've ever learned, a natural arc through which to swing the weight without straining muscles. It was the same with a pick or a sledge; the thing was to let the head of the instrument supply the power, just like a smooth golf swing.

When we had enough sand and gravel, we yanked two planks out of a pile and made a ramp up to the tailgate.

'We'll put on the coal-ass,' said Bill Eagleson.

'What's that?'

'Cold asphalt. It's liquid in the barrel and dries in the air. We use it for temporary patches.'

Danny and I rolled an oil-drum of this stuff around to the bottom of the ramp. Then we worked it up to the tailgate and into a wooden cradle so that one end of the drum was flush with the end of the truck. Bill screwed a spigot into the end of the drum and we were all set.

'You're the smallest, you sit in the middle,' they said flatly.

Apparently Danny and the absent Aimé fought over this every day. When we had squeezed into the front seat, Bill checked over the list of breaks in the roadway and we set out. It was already nine o'clock.

As we drove slowly along, the barrel bouncing and clanging in the back, they told me that our job was to apply temporary patches where damage had been reported by the patrolmen or a citizen, to save the city money on lawsuits. The idea was to get the patch down as soon as possible. They weren't meant to be permanent but they had to last for a while.

We stopped first behind some railway sidings on the Esplanade, next to the Saint Lawrence Market, to fix some shallow potholes. Bill filled a large tin watering-can with coal-ass and spread the black tarry liquid in the hole. Then Danny and I filled it with gravel. Then more coal-ass, then a layer of sand, and finally a third coat of the cold asphalt to top off.

'It dries in the air,' said Danny with satisfaction, 'and tomorrow you'd need a pick to get it out of there.' He was quite right. It was an amazingly good way to make quick repairs that would last indefinitely. From the Esplanade we headed uptown to Gerrard Street between Bay and Yonge where we filled a small cut in the sidewalk. Then Bill parked the truck in the lot behind the old Kresge's store on Yonge.

'Time for coffee,' we all said at once. We sat at the lunch counter in Kresge's for half an hour, kidding the waitresses, and I began to realize that we had no boss, that Charlie wasn't checking on us in any way and that Bill had only the nominal authority that went with his years and his drivership. Nobobdy ever bothered you. Nobody seemed to care how long you spent over a given piece of work, and yet the work all got done, sooner or later, and not badly either. If you go to the corner of St Joseph and Bay, on the east side, you can see patches that we put in nine years ago, as sound as the day they were laid down. By and large, the taxpayers got their money's worth, although it certainly wasn't done with maximum expedition or efficiency.

When we'd finished our coffee it was obviously much too late to start anything before lunch, so Bill and I waited in the truck while Danny shopped around in Kresge's for a cap. He came back with something that looked like a cross between a railwayman's hat and a housepainter's, a cotton affair that oddly suited him. We drove back to the Yard, arriving about eleven forty-five, in comfortable time for lunch. We were allowed an hour for lunch but it always ran to considerably more. The three big gangs didn't come into the Yard except on payday, unless they were working close by. It seemed to be a point of protocol to stay away from the Yard as long as possible. Each gang had a small portable shed on wheels, in which the tools, lamps, and so forth, could be locked overnight, and these sheds are to be seen all over the downtown area.

After lunch we fixed a few more holes. About two thirty or three we parked the truck in the middle of Fleet Street with cars whizzing past on both sides. Danny handed me a red rag on a stick. 'Go back there and wave them around us,' he said. 'We'll fix the hole.'

I stood in the middle of Fleet Street, that heavily travelled artery, and innocently waved my flag, fascinated to see how obediently the cars coming at me divided and passed to either side of the truck. Now and then a driver spotted me late, and one man didn't see the flag at all until the last second. I had to leap out of his way, shouting, and he pulled way out to his left into the face of the oncoming traffic and went around the truck at sixty-five.

Pretty soon Bill and Danny were finished and we got into the truck and drove off. 'Payday tomorrow,' said Danny thoughtfully. 'You won't draw anything this week, Hoody. They pay on Wednesday up till the previous Saturday.'

'We'll buy you a beer,' said Bill generously. He began to tell me about himself. He was an old ballplayer who had bounced around the lower minors for years, without ever going above Class B. Afterwards he came back to Toronto and played Industrial League ball until the Depression killed it. Then he had come on the city, and had now been with the Roadways Division for fifteen years.

'Just stick with us, Hoody, and keep your mouth shut,' he said, repeating it with conviction several times.

'You'll be with us at least until Aimé gets back,' said Danny.

I asked what had happened to Aimé. It appeared that he'd been found sitting in a car that didn't belong to him, in a place where the car wasn't supposed to be. He got thirty days and it was taken for granted that he'd be back on the job, same as ever, when he got out. Many of the men had had minor brushes with the law. A few weeks later Danny got caught, with two of his friends and a truck, loading lengths of drainpipe which they planned to sell for scrap, at a City Maintenance Station south of Adelaide Street. They just drove the truck into the station after supper and spent six hours loading pipe. They might have got twenty-five dollars for it, dividing that sum between them. It didn't seem very good pay for six hours' work; when I suggested this to Danny he shrugged it off. He hadn't figured out that his time was worth more than he could possibly have made on that job.

Bill Tennyson, the sulky patrolman, had often been charged with non-support by his wife, and with assault by his father-in-law. He passed his nights alternately at his nominal place of abode, where his wife and children lived, and at a bachelor friend's apartment in the Warwick Hotel. An unsettled life, and an irregular, whose disagreeable circumstances he used to deplore to me in private lunch-hour chat. Charlie disliked him, and used to ride him quite a lot; he was the only man in the whole crew to whom Charlie was consistently unfair. He had that irritating goof-off manner which always infuriates the man who is trying to get the job done. Yet he had no vices, drank little, didn't gamble. No one knew how he spent his money and no one liked him.

He had his eyes on Eddie Doucette's desk job. But Eddie could type after a fashion, and had some sort of connection at the Hall which everybody knew about and never mentioned—he might have been a nephew of the City Clerk or the Assistant Assessment Commissioner—I never found out for sure. But nobody was going to get his job away from him.

Eddie wore a cardigan and a tie, and rode around in the truck with Charlie and George, while Tennyson wore sports shirts and walked his beat. The rest of us wore work-clothes of an astonishing variety. My regular costume, after Aimé came back and I had to get off the coal-ass crew, was an old Fordham sweatshirt which my brother in New York had given me and which by protocol was never laundered, jeans, work-boots, and the same pair of sweatsocks every day, and they too were never laundered; they were full of concrete dust at the end of the day and by September were nearly solid. I could stand them in the corner, and they never bothered my feet at all as long as I washed off the concrete as soon as I came home.

That first day we got back to the Yard about four. We walked into the office, clumping our boots loudly and officiously on the floor. Charlie and George had gone out somewhere in the truck and wouldn't be back that day. Apart from Eddie, the only person in the office was a man who was sitting in Charlie's swivel chair, bandaged to the eyes. He seemed to be suffering from broken ribs, collar-bone and arm, shock, cuts, abrasions, sprains, and perhaps other things. He was having trouble speaking clearly and his hands shook violently. He and Eddie were conspiring over a report to the Workmen's Compensation Board.

This man became a culture-hero in the Works Department because he was on Compensation longer than anyone had ever been before. Everyone felt obscurely that he had it made, that he had a claim against the city and the province for life. He would come back to work now and then, and after a day on the gang would be laid up six weeks more. They spoke of him at the Yard in awed lowered voices.

'How do you feel, Sambo?' asked Bill solicitously.

'Not good, Bill, not good.'

'You'll be all right,' said Bill.

The injured man turned back to Eddie who was licking the end of his pencil and puzzling over the complicated instructions on the report. 'It says "wife and dependents",' he said uncertainly. 'Well put them down anyway. If it's wrong we'll hear about it.'

'I want to get my money,' said Sambo.

'You'll get it soon enough.'

I couldn't think where anybody could pick up that many lumps all at once. 'What happened to him?' I asked.

'He was Aimés replacement till yesterday,' said Bill unconcernedly, 'but some guy on Fleet Street didn't see the red flag. He was our last safety-man before you.'

I thought this over most of the night, deciding finally that I would have to be luckier and more agile than Sambo. The next day was a payday, and in the press of events I forgot my fears and decided to stick with the job as long as I could. At lunchtime, the second day, most of the men expressed commiseration at the fact that I would draw no money until next week.

Bill Tennyson came out of the office with his cheque in his hand and an air of relief written all over him.

'Nobody got any of it this time,' he said, as nearly happy as he ever was; his salary cheque was almost always diminished by the judgements of his creditors. 'How about you, Hood, you draw anything?' I told him that I wouldn't get paid for a week and he stared at me dubiously for a minute, coming as near as he could to a spontaneous generous gesture. Then all at once he recollected himself and turned away.

Charlie Brown told me that if I was short he could let me have five dollars. I could have used it, but it seemed wiser to say 'no thanks' and stretch my credit at my rooming house for one more week. He seemed surprised at my refusal, though not annoyed.

'You're on the truck with Bill and Danny, aren't you?'

'Yes.'

'Stay out of trouble,' he said cryptically and went out and got into the quarter-ton, holding a roll of plans under his stump and stuffing tobacco into his pipe with his good hand. All over the Yard men were standing in clumps, sharing a peculiar air of expectancy. Some went off hastily, after eating their sandwiches, to the nearest bank. Danny Foster let his cheque

fly out of his hand and had to climb over the roofs of several low buildings on College Street in order to retrieve it. A quiet hum of talk came
from the tool-shed behind the office where the gang-bosses ate whenever
they came into the Yard. There they sat in isolated state, old Wall, ulcer-
ated Harris, and the cheerful Mitch, the best-liked man at the Yard, sharing their rank, its privileges and its loneliness.

The undertone of expectation sensibly intensified as the lunch-hour
passed; payday was different from other days. The whole business of the
gang-bosses on paydays was to ensure that their crews should be on a job
proximate to a Beverage Room. One of the reasons that Harris was so unpopular was that he was a poor planner of work schedules; his men often
had to walk six or even eight blocks from the job to the hotel. Mitch, on
the other hand, seemed to have a positive flair for working into position
Tuesday night or Wednesday morning, so that one of our favourite places
—the Brunswick, perhaps, or the Babloor—was just up an alley from the
job. I don't understand quite how he managed it, but if you worked on
Mitch's gang you never had to appear on a public thoroughfare as you
oozed off the job and into the hotel; there was always a convenient alley.

Bill and Danny and I left the Yard sharp at one o'clock bound for some
pressing minor repairs on Huron Street behind the Borden's plant. When
we got there we couldn't find anything that looked at all pressing, except
possibly a small crack beside a drain. We filled it with coal-ass, Bill laughing all the while in a kind of sly way. I asked him what was so funny.

'Johnny must have reported this one,' he said. 'He knows where we go.'

'Go?'

'Oh, come on!' he said.

'Should we stick the truck up the ally?' asked Danny.

'Leave it where it is,' said Bill. 'Nobody's going to bother it.' He was
perfectly right. The truck sat innocently beside the drain we'd been tinker-
ing with for the rest of the afternoon, with CITY OF TORONTO WORKS DEPART-
MENT written all over it in various places. A casual passerby, unless he
knew the customs of the Department, would assume that the truck's occu-
pants were somewhere close by, hard at work. Everything looked—I don't
quite know how to put this—sort of *official*. Danny leaned a shovel artis-
tically against a rear wheel, giving the impression more force than ever.

We walked up Huron Street towards Willcocks.

'Where are we going?' I asked, although by now I had a pretty good
idea. Anybody who knows the neighbourhood will have guessed our
destination already. I'm talking about that little island of peace in the
hustle and bustle of the great city, the Twentieth Battalion Club, Canadian
Legion, at the corner of Huron and Willcocks. This was the first time that
I was ever in one of the Legion halls. I had always innocently supposed

that you had to have some kind of membership. Nothing could be further from the truth, and the knowledgeable drinkers of my time at the university would never be caught dead in a public place like the King Cole Room or Lundy's Lane.

It was a custom hallowed by years of usage that Charlie Brown, George, and Eddie Doucette should spend Wednesday afternoon in the Forty-Eighth Highlanders Legion Hall over on Church Street. It gave one a feeling of comfort and deep security to know this.

We went into the Twentieth and took a table by a big bay window. The houses on the four corners of Huron and Willcocks were then perhaps eighty-five years old, beautifully proportioned old brick houses with verandas at the front and side, and a lovely grey weathered tone to the walls. Like many of the original university buildings, these houses had originally been yellow brick, which the passage of nearly a century had turned to a soft sheen of grey. It was one of those beautiful days in the third week of May without a trace of a cloud in the sky, the trees on Willcocks Street a deep dusty green, and now that most of the students had left town the whole district seemed to be asleep. That was one of the finest afternoons of my life.

'Are we gonna go back to the Yard?' said Bill to Danny, really putting the question of whether they would take the truck home with them or not. They were deciding how much they meant to drink. And the nicest thing of all from my point of view was that they took completely for granted that they would take turns buying me beers. I was always glad that I had frequent opportunities to reciprocate.

There was an unspoken decision to make an afternoon of it.

FLYING A RED KITE

The Jesuit Relations

The JESUIT RELATIONS are a series of annual reports that describe the work of the missionary-priests in their arduous efforts to convert the Indians of New France to Christianity. They were printed every year in France from 1632 to 1673 with the aim of enlisting financial support and recruits for the mission. The Jesuit missionaries, members of a Roman Catholic religious order, usually spent the spring and summer months at Tadoussac, Québec, or Trois-Rivières, where Indians from all over New France congregated to trade. When the Indians left in the fall to go back to their own territories for the winter hunt, the missionaries went with them—the first white men, in many cases, to journey into the North American interior. They suffered appalling discomforts on the way to the Indian villages and throughout the ensuing winter while living there. Some—like Jean de Brébeuf, Gabriel Lalemant, and Isaac Jogues—also suffered torture and death at the hands of the Iroquois, enemies of the Indian allies of the French who threatened the colonies on the St Lawrence for twenty years in the seventeenth century. The reports, letters, and journals of the missionaries present some of the most remarkable examples of human courage and endurance ever recorded.

Though these seventeenth-century Europeans called the Indians 'Savages', their actions and thoughts were imbued with love for them as human beings. The *Relations* give evidence on virtually every page of the missionaries' assiduous though delicate attempts to understand the natives and adapt themselves to their ways, while all the time endeavouring to impose upon the Indians what they considered to be the highest good: conversion to Christianity. They were sometimes rewarded with what they accepted as wholehearted conversions; but on the whole their many years of work had little effect on the uncomprehending and often resentful Indians.

A treasury of information about the folk-lore, religion, mythology, morals, and habits of the Indians, the *Relations* also contain many vivid self-portraits of the missionaries themselves—their feelings, daily activities, and spiritual adventures—as they performed their gruelling task. The *Relations* grew out of an intimate contact with Canada and its native people, and therefore have an important place in the early literature of the country quite apart from their historical value; the authors were educated men and their unpretentious, warm accounts were very well written. The definitive edition of the *Relations*, with a page-for-page English translation, was edited by Rueben Gold Thwaites and published in 73 volumes from 1896 to 1901 under the title *The Jesuit Relations and Allied Documents*. A two-volume selection, edited by Edna Kenton, was published in 1954. A short paperback selection has been edited by S.R. Mealing for the Carleton Library (1963).

PAUL LE JEUNE (1591-1664), who came to Quebec in 1632, was the founder of the Jesuit missions in Canada. He was superior of all the missions in New France until 1639 and then served in several missions on the St Lawrence until 1649, when he returned to France. He began what eventually became the *Jesuit Relations* with a report in the form of a letter written in August 1632. Of the 41 volumes that made up the original *Relations*, Le Jeune wrote 15 and contributed to the rest until 1662.

BARTHELEMY VIMONT (1594-1667), the author of the second extract, was a missionary at Cape Breton in 1629-30. He came to Quebec in 1639—on the same ship as Marie de l'Incarnation (see page 329)—to succeed Le Jeune as the superior of the missions in Canada. He was present at the founding of Montréal in 1642 and wrote the *Relations* for the years 1642-5. He left Canada in 1659.

CHRISTOPHE REGNAUT was one of the lay brothers of the mission to the Huron Indians near Georgian Bay.

AN ESCAPE FROM PERIL

After a winter spent with some Montagnais Indians on their hunt for food, Father Le Jeune prepares, early in April 1634, to cross the St Lawrence River and return to Quebec.

The day after, these tempests being still rather windy, my host and the Apostate went hunting. An hour after their departure the sun shone out brightly, the air became clear, the winds died away, the waves fell, the sea became calm—in a word, it mended, as the sailors say. Then I was in great perplexity about following my Savages to call them back, for it would have been like a turtle pursuing a greyhound. I turned my eyes to heaven as to a place of refuge; and, when I lowered them, I saw my people running like deer along the edge of the wood straight toward me. I immediately arose and started for the river, bearing our little baggage. When my host arrived, *eco, eco, pousitau, pousitau,* 'Quick, quick, let us embark, let us embark!' No sooner said than done; the wind and tide favoured us; we glided on with paddle and sail, our little bark ship cutting the waves with incomparable swiftness. We at last arrived about ten o'clock in the evening at the end of the great Island of Orleans, from which our little house was not more than two leagues distant. My people had eaten nothing all day; I encouraged them. We tried to go on, but the current of the tide, which was still ebbing, being very rapid, we had to await the flood to cross the great river. Therefore we went into a little cove and slept upon the sand, near a good fire that we lighted.

Toward midnight, the tide again arising, we embarked. The moon shone brightly, and wind and tide made us fly. As my host would not take the direction I advised, we very nearly perished in the port; for, when we came to enter our little river, we found it still covered with ice. We tried to approach the banks, but the wind had piled up great masses of ice there, striking and surging against each other, which threatened us with death if we approached them. So we had to veer around and turn our prow to the wind and work against the tide. It was here I saw the valour of my host. He had placed himself in front, as the place where the greatest danger was to be found. I saw him through the darkness of the night, which filled us with terror while augmenting our peril, strain every nerve and struggle against death to keep our little canoe in position amid waves capable of swallowing up a great ship. I cried out to him, *Nicanis ouabichtigoueiakhi ouabichtigoueiakhi,* 'My well-beloved, to Kebec, to Kebec, let us go there.' When we were about to double the Sailor's Leap— that is, the bend where our river enters the great river—you might have seen him ride over one wave, cut through the middle of another, dodge one block of ice, and push away another, continually fighting against a furious northeast wind which we had in our teeth.

Having escaped this danger, we would have liked to land; but an army of icebergs, summoned by the raging wind, barred our entrance. So we went on as far as the fort, coasting along the shores, and sought in the darkness a little gleam of light or a small opening among these masses of ice. My host having perceived a *rerin*, or turn, which is at the bottom of the fort, where the ice did not move, as it was outside the current of wind, he turned away with his paddle three or four dreadful masses of it which he encountered, and dashed in. He leaped quickly from the canoe, fearing the return of the ice, crying, *Capatau,* 'Let us land'. The trouble was, that the ice was so high and densely packed against the bank, that it was all I could do to reach to the top of it with my hands; I did not know what to take hold of to pull myself out of the canoe, and to climb up upon these icy shores. With one hand I took hold of my host's foot, and with the other seized a piece of ice which happened to project, and threw myself into a place of safety with the other two. A clumsy fellow becomes agile on such occasions. All being out of the canoe, they seized it at both ends and placed it in safety; and, when this was done, we all three looked at each other, and my host, taking a long breath, said to me, *nicanis khegat nipiacou*, 'My good friend, a little more, and we would have perished.' He still felt horror over the gravity of our danger. It is true that, if he had not had the arms of a giant (he is a large and powerful man) and an ingenuity uncommon among either Frenchmen or Savages, either a wave would have swallowed us up, or the wind would have upset us, or an iceberg would have crushed us. Or rather let us say, if God had not been our pilot, the waves which beat against the shores of our home would have been our sepulchre. In truth, whoever dwells among these people can say with the Prophet King, *anima mea in manibus meis semper*. Only a little while ago one of our Frenchmen was drowned, under like circumstances, yet less dangerous, for there was no longer any ice.

Having escaped so many perils, we crossed our river on the ice, which was not yet broken; and three hours after midnight, on Palm Sunday, April 9th, I re-entered our little house. God knows what joy there was on both sides!

PAUL LE JEUNE (*JR: 1634-5*)

A PEACE COUNCIL WITH THE IROQUOIS

In the middle of the seventeenth century the nations of the Iroquois confederacy, who lived in what is now New York State, carried on a war with the Hurons and the Indian allies of the French along the St Lawrence River. This was sometimes briefly interrupted by peace treaties. The opening of one peace council in 1645 is described below. Kiotseton was an ambassador from the Mohawks.

When the most important of the three, named Kiotseton, saw the French and the Savages hastening to the bank of the river, he stood up in the bow of the shallop that had brought him from Richelieu to Three Rivers. He was almost completely covered with porcelain beads. Motioning with his hand for silence, he called out: 'My Brothers, I have left my country to come and see you. At last I have reached your land. I was told, on my departure, that I was going to seek death and that I would never again see my country. But I have willingly exposed myself for the good of peace. I come therefore to enter into the designs of the French, of the Hurons, and of the Algonquins. I come to make known to you the thoughts of all my country.' When he had said this, the shallop fired a shot from a swivel gun and the Fort replied by a discharge from the cannon as a sign of rejoicing.

When those ambassadors had landed, they were conducted into the room of the sieur de Chanflour, who gave them a very cordial reception. They were offered some slight refreshments, and, after they had eaten and smoked, Kiotseton, who was always the spokesman, said to all the French who surrounded him: 'I find much pleasure in your houses. Since I have set foot in your country, I have observed nothing but rejoicing. I see very well that he who is in the sky wishes to bring to a conclusion a very important matter. The minds and thoughts of men are too diverse to fall into accord; it is the sky that will combine all.' On the same day, a canoe was sent to Monsieur the Governor to inform him of the arrival of these new guests.

Meanwhile, both they and the prisoners who had not yet been given up had full liberty to wander where they willed. The Algonquins and Montagnais invited them to their feasts, and they gradually accustomed themselves to converse together. The sieur de Chanflour treated them very well. One day he said to them that they were with us as if in their own country; that they had nothing to fear; that they were in their own house. Kiotseton replied to this compliment by a very well-pointed and neat retort. 'I beg thee,' he said to the Interpreter, 'to say to that Captain who speaks to us that he tells a great falsehood with respect to us; at least it is certain that what he says is not true.' And thereupon he paused a little, to let the wonder grow. Then he added: 'That Captain tells me that I am here as if in my own country. That is very far from the truth. I would be neither honoured nor treated with such consideration in my own country, while here every one honours me and pays me attention. He says that I am as if in my own house; that is a sort of falsehood, for I am mal-treated in my house and here I fare well every day—I am continually feast-ing. Therefore I am not as if I were in my own country or in my own house.' He indulged in many other repartees, which clearly showed that he had wit.

Finally Monsieur the Governor came from Quebec to Three Rivers; and, after having seen the ambassadors, he gave audience to them on the twelfth of July. This took place in the courtyard of the Fort, over which large sails had been spread to keep off the heat of the Sun. Their places were thus arranged: on one side was Monsieur the Governor, accompan-ied by his people and by Reverend Father Vimont, Superior of the Mission. The Iroquois sat at his feet on a great piece of hemlock bark. They had stated before the assembly that they wished to be on his side as a mark of the affection that they bore to the French.

Opposite them were the Algonquins, the Montagnais, and the Atti-kamegues; the two other sides were closed in by some French and some Hurons. In the centre was a large space, somewhat longer than wide, in which the Iroquois caused two poles to be planted and a cord to be stretched from one to the other on which to hang and tie the words that they were to bring us—that is to say, the presents they wished to make us, which consisted of seventeen collars of porcelain beads, a portion of which were on their bodies. The remainder were enclosed in a small pouch placed quite near them.

When all had assembled and had taken their places, Kiotseton, who was high in stature, rose and looked at the sun, then cast his eyes over the whole Company. He took a collar of porcelain beads in his hand and commenced to harangue in a loud voice.

'Onontio, lend me ear. I am the mouth for the whole of my country. Thou listenest to all the Iroquois, in hearing my words. There is no evil in my heart. I have only good songs in my mouth. We have a multitude of war songs in our country. We have cast them all on the ground. We have no longer anything but songs of rejoicing.' Thereupon he began to sing. . .

BARTHELEMY VIMONT (*JR: 1642-5*)

THE MARTYRS' REMAINS

In March 1649 a thousand Iroquois attacked two Huron villages (near Midland, Ont.) and tortured and put to death the missionaries Jean de Brébeuf and Gabriel Lalemant. (See the extract from E. J. Pratt's poem, Brébeuf and His Brethren, *on pages 396-400.)*

On the next morning, when we had assurance of the departure of the enemy, we went to the spot to seek for the remains of their bodies, to the place where their lives had been taken. We found them both, but a little apart from each other. They were brought to our cabin and laid uncovered upon the bark of trees, where I examined them at leisure for more than two hours to see if what the savages had told us of their martyrdom and death were true. I examined first the body of Father de Brébeuf, which was pitiful to see, as well as that of Father Lalemant. Father de Brébeuf had his legs, thighs, and arms stripped of flesh to the very bone. I saw and touched a large number of great blisters, which he had on several places on his body, from the boiling water which these barbarians had poured over him in mockery of Holy Baptism. I saw and touched the wound from a belt of bark, full of pitch and resin, which roasted his whole body. I saw and touched the marks of burns from the collar of hatchets placed on his shoulders and stomach. I saw and touched his two lips, which they had cut off because he spoke constantly of God while they made him suffer.

I saw and touched all parts of his body, which had received more than two hundred blows from a stick: I saw and touched the top of his scalped head: I saw and touched the opening which these barbarians had made to tear out his heart.

In fine, I saw and touched all the wounds of his body, as the savages had told and declared to us. We buried these precious relics on Sunday, the 21st day of March 1649, with much consolation.

I had the happiness of carrying them to the grave, and of burying them with those of Father Gabriel Lalemant. When we left the country of the Hurons, we raised both bodies out of the ground and set them to boil in strong lye. All the bones were well-scraped and the care of drying them was given to me. I put them every day into a little oven which we had, made of clay, after having heated it slightly, and when in a state to be packed, they were separately enveloped in silk stuff. Then they were put into two small chests and we brought them to Quebec, where they are held in great veneration.

CHRISTOPHE REGNAUT (*JR*: 1649)

b. 1913

George Johnston

GEORGE JOHNSTON is one of the most engaging of all Canadian poets whose poems have been called 'light' because they are witty, casually conversational in tone, and usually brief. But these apparently simple, very readable poems convey disturbing revelations about the human condition. Johnston was born in Hamilton, Ont., and was educated at the University of Toronto. He was a pilot with the RCAF during the Second World War, taught English at Mount Allison University from 1947 to 1949, and is now Professor of English at Carleton University, Ottawa. He has published three books of verse: *The Cruising Auk* (1959), *Home Free* (1966), and *Happy Enough: Poems 1935-1972* (1972), which contains all the poems in his first two books and thirty-two new poems. Johnston is also an experienced and dedicated translator from the Norse: in 1963 he published *The Saga of Gisli* (with an introduction and notes by Peter Foote).

The Cruising Auk, which has become one of the best-known collections of the last fifteen years, is a sequence of poems that explores childhood innocence, domesticity, happiness, adult ineffectualness, and doom, and delights the reader with its technical skill and wit even though the comedy is melancholy. About the apparent simplicity of these poems, Northrop Frye wrote in reviewing the *Auk*: 'The difference between the simple and the insipid in poetry is that while simplicity uses much the same words, it puts them together in a way that keeps them echoing and reverberating with infinite associations, rippling away into the furthest reaches of imaginative thought. It is difficult for a critic to demonstrate the contrast between the simplicity that keeps him awake at night and the mediocrity that puts him to sleep in the day. In *The Cruising Auk*, however, there is one major clue to the simplicity. Like Mr Reaney and Miss Macpherson before him, Mr Johnston has produced a beautifully unified book, the apparently casual poems carrying the reader along from the first poem to the last in a voyage of self-discovery.' The first four poems below are from the *Auk*.

There are two articles on George Johnston's poetry in *Canadian Literature* by George Whalley (Issue 35, Winter 1968) and Lawrence W. Jones (Issue 48, Spring 1971).

THE POOL

A boy gazing in a pool
Is all profound; his eyes are cool
And he's as though unborn, he's gone;
He's the abyss he gazes on.

A man searches the pool in vain
For his profundity again;
He finds it neither there nor here
And all between is pride and fear.

His eyes are warm with love and death,
Time makes a measure of his breath;
The world is now profound and he
Fearful, on its periphery.

MONEY IN POCKET

I've got money in my pockets,
Excellent pockets because there's money in them;
I can't feel low while there's paper for my fingers
In my excellent pockets, Caesar's mark on it.

I've got children in my rooms,
Blood-borne hostages, arrows from my side:
I can't sleep heavy while they're breathing in their beds
Who burst through my passageways and grow me back to earth.

I've got time in my clocks
And beer in my cellar and spiders in my windows:
I can't spend time nor drink all the beer
And I feel in the spread web the spider's small eye.

IN IT

The world is a boat and I'm in it
Going like hell with the breeze;
Important people are in it as well
Going with me and the breeze like hell—
It's kind of a race and we'll win it.
Out of our way, gods, please!

The world is a game and I'm in it
For the little I have, no less;
Important people are in it for more,
They watch the wheel, I watch the door.
Who was the first to begin it?
Nobody knows, but we guess.

The world is a pond and I'm in it,
In it up to my neck;
Important people are in it too,
It's deeper than this, if we only knew;
Under we go, any minute—
A swirl, some bubbles, a fleck . . .

O EARTH, TURN!

The little blessed Earth that turns
Does so on its own concerns
As though it weren't my home at all;
It turns me winter, summer, fall
Without a thought of me.

I love the slightly flattened sphere,
Its restless, wrinkled crust's my here,
Its slightly wobbling spin's my now
But not my why and not my how:
My why and how are me.

VETERANS

There are seventy times seven kinds of loving
    None quite right:
One is of making, one of arguing,
    One of wheedling in the night
And all the others one can think of, none quite right.

Yet they are all good,
    Paying attention, giving the low-down kiss;
Answering back in the heart is always good
    And coming out of a sulk is almost bliss.

There is a kind of loving in grass and weeds,
    One in brass beds, another in corridors;
An uncanny kind that turns away and bleeds
    And a gorgeous kind, practised by saints and bores.

They are all hard,
    All seventy times seven, hard as can be:
Veterans of loving are wary-eyed and scarred
    And they see into everything they see.

THE DAY THAT WOULD NEVER COME

The day that would never come comes, it is
not what was expected, not the dreamed of
gay trip to Montréal and the gay leave
taking on the dock for Europe for whose

conquest, making of many friends; she
no longer wants to go but she must;
nobody says so, but the last
thing she would do is turn back and I

think That's my Peggy, which makes this a love
poem. Is there another kind? but is there
something else to be told, of the tremor
of the ship, the day's departure, her wave?

b. 1929

D. G. Jones

DOUG JONES is a poet whose reputation has not caught up with his talent, as the critic Stan Fefferman pointed out in his review of *Phrases from Orpheus*. He was born in Bancroft, Ont., and educated at McGill and Queen's Universities. He is now a member of the English department of the University of Sherbrooke and is an editor of the quarterly magazine *Ellipse*, which presents the work of French and English writers in translation. He lives in North Hatley, Qué.

Jones is the author of three collections of meditative lyrics—*Frost on the Sun* (1957), *The Sun is Axeman* (1961), and *Phrases from Orpheus* (1967)—and of an important literary study, *Butterfly on Rock: A Study of Themes and Imagination in Canadian Literature* (1970). He is a poet who is sensitively attuned to the sound values of language. Fefferman refers to 'the cool music of his verse' and goes on to say: 'His phrases are short, delicate and tend to move towards a closing silence in which the poems are

arrested. Jones' musical gift, and his even stronger talent for seeing, work together in his simplest poems to release single images which just hang in your imagination, giving off energy.' In difficult mythological poems and in more accessible poems of personal experience and the actual world, Jones' precise, crystalline imagery and his short, controlled phrases isolated in space are remarkable for expressing intense, haunting, complex feelings about isolation and communication, love and loss. He is both attached to life and detached from it, and this paradoxical attitude sets up a tension in his poems as he finds himself making two commitments: to change and the void as he descends into a dark underworld of deprivation and death, and to pleasures in nature, love, and memory that provide the resources for a kind of rebirth out of the void, which in his poem 'The Perishing Bird' he calls 'the radiant night / Where time begets / The sun, the flowers . . . / And everything else'.

I THOUGHT THERE WERE LIMITS

I thought there were limits, Newtonian
Laws of emotion—

I thought there were limits to this falling away,
This emptiness. I was wrong.

The apples, falling, never hit the ground.

So much for grass, and animals—
Nothing remains,
No sure foundation on the rock. The cat

Drifts, or simply dissolves.

L'homme moyen sensuel
Had better look out: complete
Deprivation brings

Dreams, hallucinations which reveal
The sound and fury of machines
Working on nothing—which explains

God's creation: *ex nihilo fecit.*

Wrong again. I now suspect
The limit is the sea itself,
The limitless.

So, neither swim nor float. Relax.
The void is not so bleak.

Conclude: desire is but an ache,
An absence. It creates
A dream of limits

And it grows in gravity as that takes shape.

PASTORAL

Babbling at me through
Four seasons now
This two-bit creek makes

Sense at last.

Even if we
Don't survive, even if the birds and bees,
The plants as well,

Fade upon some final blast,

The water will remain,
And rock.

One feels a new respect for
Metals, rare-earth, salt,
That relatively immortal blue gas,

The sky.

I know, one can't
Ascribe much virtue to
Solid, liquid, gas. Those elements

Don't make mistakes.

Yet they refresh,
They are not proud.

Listening to this babble gives me hope,
Even for the tiny jet which disappears,
So high above me,

Like a needle in the cloud.

PORTRAIT OF ANNE HÉBERT

The sunlight, here and there,
Touches a table

And a draught at the window
Announces your presence,

You take your place in the room
Without fuss,

Your delicate bones,
Your frock,
Have the grace of disinterested passion.

Words are arrayed
Like surgical instruments
Neatly in trays.

Deftly, you make an incision
Probing
The obscure disease.

Your sensibility
Has the sure fingers of the blind:

Each decision
Cuts like a scalpel
Through tangled emotion.

You define
The morbid tissue, laying it bare

Like a tatter of lace
Dark
On the paper.

A.M.Klein

In the 1930s and 1940s A.M. KLEIN was one of the most prominent and respected Canadian poets and a leader of the Jewish community in Canada. Born in Montreal to parents who had emigrated from Russia four years before, he was educated in Montreal schools, at McGill University, and at the Université de Montréal where he studied law. (Through his background and studies he was proficient in five languages: English, Yiddish, Hebrew, French, and Latin.) He was called to the bar in 1933 and practised law until 1954. Klein was editor of *The Canadian Jewish Chronicle* from 1939 to 1954 and was active in the Labour Zionist movement and the CCF party (the forerunner of the NDP)—in the 1948 election he was an unsuccessful CCF candidate. In the mid-1940s he was associated with the Montreal poets who were publishing the little magazine *Preview* and from 1945 to 1947 was visiting lecturer in poetry at McGill University.

In the midst of these activities Klein managed to write a good deal. His early books of poetry—*Hath Not a Jew . . .* (1940), *Poems* (1944), and *The Hitleriad* (1944), a long satire on the Nazis—were published by small Jewish or avant-garde firms in the United States. The two most prominent themes in this poetry are anti-semitism and mankind's responsibility for the Nazi horror. It reflects Klein's warm feeling for Jewish folk-ways and parables and his considerable learning in Jewish law, philosophy, culture, and history. The poems below are from Klein's final collection of poetry, *The Rocking Chair and Other Poems* (1949), which won a Governor General's Award. It is a striking departure from his previous books, for the subject-matter is explicitly Canadian. There are a number of deft but gentle satires on Québec politics and social habits and some memorable portraits—of which 'The Political Meeting', about a demagogue playing on race hatred, is an example. (Camillien Houde was the controversial mayor of Montreal almost continuously from 1928 to 1954. During the Second World War he was strongly opposed to the National Registration Act and was interned for four years.)

Irving Layton has called A.M. Klein 'a poet of the minorities'—the Jew, the French-Canadian, the Indian, and the poet (whom he wrote about in an important long poem, 'Portrait of the Poet as Landscape'). 'The Rocking Chair', Miriam Waddington has written, 'represents an elaboration of the humanist concerns we found in his early poetry. Despite stylistic changes, Klein continues to love the Jews of old Europe and new Montreal; he feels compassion for the Indians; he identified uncannily with the French Canadians and sings both the beauty of Québec winter and the nostalgia of a child's lost summers. Through metaphor he discovers new realities and is at last freed to throw off the consoling company of all those writers dear to English and Hebrew tradition to become his own contemporary self, which, though it contains English, French, Yiddish, and Hebrew traces, is above all a Canadian self and a Canadian poetic presence. He praises our wheat, mythologizes our grain elevators, personifies our provinces and searches for our unity "in the family feature, the not unsimilar face".'

Klein's passionate interest in Zionism and a visit to Israel gave rise to another book, The Second Scroll (1951), which is a complex parable about a spiritual pilgrimage to the Promised Land (Israel) consisting of a short novel and a series of glosses in verse, drama, and prose. About the time The Second Scroll was published, Klein began a book about James Joyce, a writer who had strongly influenced him, and three chapters appeared in literary magazines in Canada and the United States. But in the mid-1950s he suffered a breakdown, retired from all his activities, and was inactive until his death.

There is an interesting essay on Klein by M.W. Steinberg in Issue 25 of Canadian Literature (Summer 1965), which is devoted to a symposium on the poet; it has been printed in A Choice of Critics (1966) edited by George Woodcock. Miriam Waddington has written a book on Klein for the Studies in Canadian Literature series published by Copp Clark (1970). The Second Scroll is available in paperback and a selection of Klein's poems can be found in Poets Between the Wars (1967), edited by Milton Wilson. Both of these books are in the New Canadian Library.

FOR THE SISTERS OF THE HOTEL DIEU

In pairs,
as if to illustrate their sisterhood,
the sisters pace the hospital garden walks.
In their robes black and white immaculate hoods
they are like birds,
the safe domestic fowl of the House of God.

O biblic birds,
who fluttered to me in my childhood illnesses
—me little, afraid, ill, not of your race,—
the cool wing for my fever, the hovering solace,
the sense of angels—
be thanked, O plummage of paradise, be praised.

THE ROCKING CHAIR

It seconds the crickets of the province. Heard
in the clean lamplit farmhouses of Quebec,—
wooden,—it is no less a national bird;
and rivals, in its cage, the mere stuttering clock.
To its time, the evenings are rolled away;
and in its peace the pensive mother knits
contentment to be worn by her family,
grown-up, but still cradled by the chair in which she sits.

It is also the old man's pet, pair to his pipe,
the two aids of his arithmetic and plans,
plans rocking and puffing into market-shape;
and it is the toddler's game and dangerous dance.
Moved to the verandah, on summer Sundays, it is,
among the hanging plants, the girls, the boy-friends,
sabbatical and clumsy, like the white haloes
dangling above the blue serge suits of the young men.

It has a personality of its own;
is a character (like that old drunk Lacoste,
exhaling amber, and toppling on his pins);
it is alive; individual; and no less
an identity than those about it. And
it is tradition. Centuries have been flicked
from its arcs, alternately flicked and pinned.
It rolls with the gait of St Malo. It is act

and symbol, symbol of this static folk
which moves in segments, and returns to base,—
a sunken pendulum: *invoke, revoke;*
loosed yon, leashed hither, motion on no space.
O, like some Anjou ballad, all refrain,
which turns about its longing, and seems to move
to make a pleasure out of repeated pain,
its music moves, as if always back to a first love.

PASTORAL OF THE CITY STREETS

1

Between distorted forests, clapped into geometry,
in meadows of macadam,
heat-fluff-a-host-of-dandelions dances on the air.
Everywhere glares the sun's glare,
the asphalt shows hooves.

                  In meadows of macadam
grazes the dray horse, nozzles his bag of pasture,
is peaceful. Now and then flicks through farmer straw
his ears, like pulpit-flowers; quivers
his hide; swishes his tempest tail
a black and sudden nightmare for the fly.
The sun shines, sun shines down
new harness on his withers, saddle, and rump.

On curbrock and on stairstump the clustered kids
resting let slide some afternoon: then restless
hop to the game of the sprung haunches; skid
to the safe place, jump up: stir a wind in the heats:
laugh, puffed and sweat-streaked.

O for the crystal stream!

Comes a friend's father
with his pet of a hose,
and plays the sidewalk black
cavelike and cool.

O crisscross beneath the spray, those pelting petals and peas
those white soft whisks
brushing off heat!
O underneath these acrobatic fountains
among the crystal,
like raindrops a sunshower of youngsters dance:
small-nippled self-hugged boys
and girls with water sheer, going *Ah* and *Ah*.

2
And at twilight,
the sun like a strayed neighbourhood creature
having been chased
back to its cover
the children count a last game, or talk, or rest,
beneath the bole of the tree of the single fruit of glass
now ripening,
a last game, talk, or rest,
until mothers like evening birds call from the stoops.

POLITICAL MEETING

For Camillien Houde

On the school platform, draping the folding seats,
they wait the chairman's praise and glass of water.
Upon the wall the agonized Y initials their faith.

Here all are laic; the skirted brothers have gone.
Still, their equivocal absence is felt, like a breeze
that gives curtains the sounds of surplices.

The hall is yellow with light, and jocular;
suddenly some one lets loose upon the air
the ritual bird which the crowd in snares of singing

catches and plucks, throat, wings, and little limbs.
Fall the feathers of sound, like *alouette's.*
The chairman, now, is charming, full of asides and wit.

building his orators, and chipping off
the heckling gargoyles popping in the hall.
(Outside, in the dark, the street is body-tall,

flowered with faces intent on the scarecrow thing
that shouts to thousands the echoing
of their own wishes.) The Orator has risen!

Worshipped and loved, their favourite visitor,
a country uncle with sunflower seeds in his pockets,
full of wonderful moods, tricks, imitative talk,

he is their idol: like themselves, not handsome,
not snobbish, not of the *Grande Allée! Un homme!*
Intimate, informal, he makes bear's compliments

to the ladies; is gallant; and grins;
goes for the balloon, his opposition, with pins;
jokes also on himself, speaks of himself

in the third person, slings slang, and winks with folklore;
and knows now that he has them, kith and kin.
Calmly, therefore, he begins to speak of war,

praises the virtue of being *Canadien,*
of being at peace, of faith, of family,
and suddenly his other voice: *Where are your sons?*

He is tearful, choking tears; but not he
would blame the clever English; in their place
he'd do the same; maybe.

Where *are* your sons?
     The whole street wears one face,
shadowed and grim; and in the darkness rises
the body-odour of race.

COMMERCIAL BANK

Flowering jungle, where all fauna meet
crossing the marbled pool to thickets whence
the prompted parrots, alien-voiced, entreat
the kernel'd hoard, the efflorescent pence,—

wondrous your caves, whose big doors must be rolled
for entrance, and whose flora none can seek
against the armed unicorn, furred blue and gold,
against the vines fatal, or the berries that touched, shriek.

How quiet is your shade with broad green leaves!
Yet is it jungle-quiet which deceives:
toothless, with drawn nails, the beasts paw your ground—
O, the fierce deaths expiring with no sound!

Archibald Lampman

In his fairly short life ARCHIBALD LAMPMAN wrote a small body of landscape poems that are almost perfect examples of their kind, far superior to those of the three other poets who were also born in the 1860s—Charles G.D. Roberts, Bliss Carman, and Duncan Campbell Scott. He was born at Morpeth, Ont., a village on Lake Erie. His father was an Anglican clergyman. In 1867 the family moved to Gore's Landing on Rice Lake and Lampman attended the high school there until 1876, when he attended Trinity College School, Port Hope, where he began to write poetry. In 1879 he entered Trinity College, Toronto. In his first year he was excited by the publication of Roberts' *Orion*; it pleased him to discover a new book of poems written, as he said, 'by a Canadian, by a young man, one of ourselves'. After graduating he taught in Orangeville but resigned his post after four months. In January 1883 he entered the civil service in Ottawa as a clerk in the Post Office Department and worked there until he died. In 1888 Lampman published (at his own expense) his first collection of verse, *Among the Millet*, which contained some of his best poems,

including 'Heat' and 'City of the End of Things'. *Lyrics of Earth* followed in 1893. Not only were the last years of Lampman's life saddened by the death of a son in 1894 and of his father in 1897, but poor health (he suffered from heart disease) weakened and depressed him and eventually prevented him from taking long walks in the countryside he loved. After his death his friend Duncan Campbell Scott edited four collections of his verse: *Poems* (1900), which was accompanied by a memoir; *Lyrics of Earth* (1925); *At the Long Sault and Other New Poems* (with E.K. Brown, 1943); and *Selected Poems* (1947).

Lampman's 'City of the End of Things' and 'Heat' are two of the best-known and most successful nineteenth-century Canadian poems. The first—a nightmarish vision of lifeless industrialism—is not typical Lampman but is nevertheless a classic of Canadian verse. The second poem is much more characteristic. With its tensions provided by such opposites as movement and stillness, sound and silence, 'Heat' is a fine example of Lampman's masterly, trance-like evocations of the Ontario landscape in which precisely observed details combine to produce a single strong sensation of the order and harmony of nature, of the peace and goodness he found there.

There is an extended discussion of the poet and his work in *Ten Canadian Poets* (1958) by Desmond Pacey. A selection of Lampman's poetry is in *Poets of the Confederation* (1960) edited by Malcolm Ross for the New Canadian Library.

THE CITY OF THE END OF THINGS

Beside the pounding cataracts
Of midnight streams unknown to us
'Tis builded in the leafless tracts
And valleys huge of Tartarus.
Lurid and lofty and vast it seems;
It hath no rounded name that rings,
But I have heard it called in dreams
The City of the End of Things.

Its roofs and iron towers have grown
None knoweth how high within the night,
But in its murky streets far down
A flaming terrible and bright
Shakes all the stalking shadows there,
Across the walls, across the floors,
And shifts upon the upper air
From out a thousand furnace doors;
And all the while an awful sound
Keeps roaring on continually,
And crashes in the ceaseless round
Of a gigantic harmony.
Through its grim depths re-echoing
And all its weary height of walls,
With measured roar and iron ring,
The inhuman music lifts and falls.
Where no thing rests and no man is,
And only fire and night hold sway;
The beat, the thunder and the hiss
Cease not, and change not, night nor day.
And moving at unheard commands,
The abysses and vast fires between,
Flit figures that with clanking hands
Obey a hideous routine;
They are not flesh, they are not bone,
They see not with the human eye,

And from their iron lips is blown
A dreadful and monotonous cry;
And whoso of our mortal race
Should find that city unaware,
Lean Death would smite him face to face,
And blanch him with its venomed air:
Or caught by the terrific spell,
Each thread of memory snapt and cut,
His soul would shrivel and its shell
Go rattling like an empty nut.

It was not always so, but once,
In days that no man thinks upon,
Fair voices echoed from its stones,
The light above it leaped and shone:
Once there were multitudes of men,
That built that city in their pride,
Until its might was made, and then
They withered age by age and died.
But now of that prodigious race,
Three only in an iron tower,
Set like carved idols face to face,
Remain the masters of its power;
And at the city gate a fourth,
Gigantic and with dreadful eyes,
Sits looking toward the lightless north,
Beyond the reach of memories;
Fast rooted to the lurid floor,
A bulk that never moves a jot,
In his pale body dwells no more,
Or mind or soul,—an idiot!
But sometime in the end those three
Shall perish and their hands be still,
And with the master's touch shall flee
Their incommunicable skill.
A stillness absolute as death
Along the slacking wheels shall lie,
And, flagging at a single breath,
The fires shall moulder out and die.
The roar shall vanish at its height,
And over that tremendous town
The silence of eternal night
Shall gather close and settle down.
All its grim grandeur, tower and hall,
Shall be abandoned utterly,

And into rust and dust shall fall
From century to century;
Nor ever living thing shall grow,
Nor trunk of tree, nor blade of grass;
No drop shall fall, no wind shall blow,
Nor sound of any foot shall pass:
Alone of its accursèd state,
One thing the hand of Time shall spare,
For the grim Idiot at the gate
Is deathless and eternal there.

HEAT

From plains that reel to southward, dim,
The road runs by me white and bare;
Up the steep hill it seems to swim
Beyond, and melt into the glare.
Upward half-way, or it may be
Nearer the summit, slowly steals
A hay-cart, moving dustily
With idly clacking wheels.

By his cart's side the wagoner
Is slouching slowly at his ease,
Half-hidden in the windless blur
Of white dust puffing to his knees.
This wagon on the height above,
From sky to sky on either hand,
Is the sole thing that seems to move
In all the heat-held land.

Beyond me in the fields the sun
Soaks in the grass and hath his will;
I count the marguerites one by one;
Even the buttercups are still.
On the brook yonder not a breath
Disturbs the spider or the midge.
The water-bugs draw close beneath
The cool gloom of the bridge.

Where the far elm-tree shadows flood
Dark patches in the burning grass,
The cows, each with her peaceful cud,

Lie waiting for the heat to pass.
From somewhere on the slope near by
Into the pale depth of the noon
A wandering thrush slides leisurely
His thin revolving tune.

In intervals of dreams I hear
The cricket from the droughty ground;
The grasshoppers spin into mine ear
A small innumerable sound.

I lift mine eyes sometimes to gaze:
The burning sky-line blinds my sight:
The woods far off are blue with haze:
The hills are drenched in light.

And yet to me not this or that
Is always sharp or always sweet;
In the sloped shadow of my hat
I lean at rest, and drain the heat;
Nay more, I think some blessed power
Hath brought me wandering idly here:
In the full furnace of this hour
My thoughts grow keen and clear.

Margaret Laurence

MARGARET LAURENCE is one of several Canadian writers who have dealt imaginatively with the experience of living in Africa; indeed, her reputation as a novelist and short-story writer was well established before she began to publish fiction with a Canadian background. She was born in Neepawa, Man., and educated at the University of Manitoba. She married an engineer whose work took him to Africa and in 1954 began her literary career by editing *A Tree of Poverty*, a collection of Somali poetry and prose. This booklet was reprinted in 1970 by the McMaster University Library. In 1960 Margaret Laurence published her first novel, *This Side Jordan*, set in Ghana as independence drew near. A book of short stories, *The Tomorrow-Tamer* (1963), is also set in Ghana, and again the approaching independence of the country is often in the background. The same year—1963—she published a work of non-fiction, *The Prophet's Camel Bell*, a description of two years spent in Somaliland.

Her first novel with a Manitoba setting, *The Stone Angel* (1964), demonstrates superbly one of her great qualities as a writer: the ability to create character. In Hagar Shipley, the dominating force in this remarkable book, she has created a woman large as life who sometimes seems almost the equal of death itself. *A Jest of God* (1966) was made into a successful movie, *Rachel, Rachel*, directed by Paul Newman and starring his wife Joanne Woodward. In 1969 Margaret Laurence published *The Fire-Dwellers*, a novel set in Vancouver whose main character is Stacey, Rachel's sister. The following year a number of semi-autobiographical short stories set in Manitoba —which had been published in magazines in Canada, England, and the United States—were gathered together in *A Bird in the House*. Margaret Laurence won a Governor General's Award for fiction for *A Jest of God*, and in recent years has received several awards from the Canada Council and honorary degrees from half a dozen Canadian universities. She now lives in England, near London, and spends her summers at Peterborough, Ont.

In an article about her books in *Canadian Literature* (Summer, 1969), Margaret Laurence writes: '*The Stone Angel* fooled me even when I had finished writing it, for I imagined the theme was probably the same as in much of my African writing—the nature of freedom. This is partly true, but I see now that the emphasis by that time had altered. . . . With *The Stone Angel*, without my recognizing it at the time, the theme had changed to that of survival, the attempt of the personality to survive with some dignity, toting the load of excess mental baggage that everyone carries, until the moment of death.' Concluding this article, she says: 'A strange aspect of my so-called Canadian writing is that I haven't been much aware of its being Canadian, and this seems a good thing to me, for it suggests that one has been writing out of a background so closely known that no explanatory tags are necessary. I was always conscious that the novel and stories set in Ghana were *about Africa*. My last three novels just seem like novels.'

Margaret Laurence is also the author of *Long Drums and Cannons* (1971), a commentary on contemporary Nigerian writing, and a story for children, *Jason's Quest* (1970). Clara Thomas has written a study of Margaret Laurence for the Canadian Writers Series of the New Canadian Library, which also includes *The Stone Angel* and *The Tomorrow-Tamer*.

THE HOLY TERROR

'Mrs Shipley—'

A high alarmed voice, a girl's. And I, a sleepwalker wakened, can only stand stiffly, paralyzed with the impact of her cry. Then a hand grasps my arm.

'It's all right, Mrs Shipley. Everything's all right. You just come along with me.'

Oh. I'm here, am I? And I've been wandering around, and the girl is frightened, for she's responsible. She leads me back to bed. Then she does something else, and at first I don't understand.

'It's like a little bed-jacket, really. It's nothing. It's just to keep you from harm. It's for your own protection.'

Coarse linen, it feels like. She slides my arms in, and ties the harness firmly to the bed. I pull, and find I'm knotted and held like a trussed fowl.

'I won't have this. I won't stand for it. It's not right. Oh, it's mean—'

The nurse's voice is low, as though she were half ashamed of what she'd done. 'I'm sorry. But you might fall, you see, and—'

'Do you think I'm crazy, that I have to be put into this rig?'

'Of course not. You might hurt yourself, that's all. Please—'

I hear the desperation in her voice. Now that I think of it, what else can she do? She can't sit here by my bed all night.

'I have to do it,' she says. 'Don't be angry.'

She has to do it. Quite right. It's not her fault. Even I can see that.

'All right.' I can barely hear my own voice, but I hear her slight answering sigh.

'I'm sorry,' she says helplessly, apologizing needlessly, perhaps on behalf of God, who never apologizes. Then I'm the one who's sorry.

'I've caused you so much trouble—'

'No, you haven't. I'm going to give you a hypo now. Then you'll be more comfortable, and probably you'll sleep.'

And incredibly, despite my canvas cage, I do.

When I waken, the other bed has an inhabitant. She is sitting up in bed, reading a magazine, or pretending to. Sometimes she cries a little, putting a hand to her abdomen. She is about sixteen, I'd say, and her face is delicately boned, olive-skinned. Her eyes, as she glances hesitantly at me, are dark and only slightly slanted. Her hair is thick and black and straight, and it shines. She's a celestial, as we used to call them.

'Good morning.' I don't know if I should speak or not, but she doesn't take it amiss. She lays the magazine down and smiles at me. Grins, rather —it's the bold half-hoydenish smile the youngsters all seem to wear these days.

'Hi,' she says. 'You're Mrs Shipley. I saw it on your card. I'm Sandra Wong.'

She speaks just like Tina. Obviously she was born in this country.

'How do you do?'

My absurd formality with this child is caused by my sudden certainty that she is the granddaughter of one of the small foot-bound women whom Mr Oatley smuggled in, when Oriental wives were frowned upon, in the hazardous hold of his false-bottomed boats. Maybe I owe my house to her grandmother's passage money. There's a thought. Mr Oatley showed me one of their shoes once. It was no bigger than a child's, although it had belonged to a full-grown woman. A silk embroidered case, emerald and gold, where the foot fitted, and beneath, a crescent platform of rope and plaster, so they must have walked as though upon two miniature rockers. I don't say any of this. To her, it would be ancient history.

'I have to have my appendix out,' she says. 'They're going to get me ready soon. It's an emergency. I was really bad last night. I was real scared and so was my mom. Have you ever had your appendix out? Is it bad?'

'I had mine out years ago,' I say, although in fact I've never even had my tonsils out. 'It's not a serious operation.'

'Yeh?' she says. 'Is that right? I've never had an operation before. You don't know what to expect, if it's your first time.'

'Well, you needn't worry,' I say. 'It's just routine these days. You'll be up before you know it.'

'Do you really think so? Gee, I don't know. I was pretty scared last night. I don't like the thought of the anesthetic.'

'Bosh. That's nothing. You'll feel a bit uncomfortable afterward, but that's all.'

'Is that right? You really think so?'

'Of course.'

'Well, you oughta know,' she says. 'I guess you've had lots of operations, eh?'

I can hardly keep from laughing aloud. But she'd be offended, so I restrain myself.

'What makes you think so?'

'Oh well—I just meant, a person who's—you know—not so young—'

'Yes. Of course. Well, I've not had all that many operations. Perhaps I've been lucky.'

'I guess so. My mom had a hysterectomy year before last.'

At her age I wouldn't have known what a hysterectomy was.

'Dear me. That's too bad.'

'Yeh. That's a tough one, all right. It's not so much the operation, you know—it's the emotional upheaval afterward.'

'Really?'

'Yeh,' she says knowledgeably. 'My mom was all on edge for months. It got her down, you know, that she couldn't have any more kids. I don't know why she wanted any more. She's got five already counting me. I'm the second oldest.'

'That's a good-sized family, all right. What does your father do?'

'He has a store.'

'Well, well. So did mine.'

But that's the wrong thing to say. So much distance lies between us, she doesn't want any such similarity.

'Oh?' she says, uninterested. She looks at her watch. 'They said they'd be along in a minute. I wonder what's holding them up? A person could get forgotten in a big place like this, I bet.'

'They'll be here soon.'

'Gee, not too soon, I hope,' she says.

Her eyes change, widen, spread until they're shaped like two peach stones. The amber centres glisten.

'They wouldn't let my mom stay.' Then, defiantly, 'Not that I need her. But it would've been company.'

A nurse trots briskly in, pulls the curtains around her bed.

'Oh—is it time?' Her voice is querulous, uncertain. 'Will it hurt?'

'You won't feel a thing,' the nurse says.

'Will it take long? Will my mom be able to come in afterward? Where do you have to take me? Oh—what're you going to do? You're not going to shave me *there*?'

What a lot of questions, and how appalled she sounds. Fancy being alarmed at such a trifling thing. I lie here smug and fat, thinking—*She'll learn.*

They don't bring her back for hours, and when they do, she's very quiet. The curtains are drawn around her bed. Sometimes she moans a little in the half sleep of the receding anesthetic. The day goes slowly. Trays are brought me, and I make some effort to eat, but I seem to have lost interest in my meals. I look at the ceiling, where the sun patterns it with slivers of light. Someone puts a needle in my flesh. Have I cried out, then? What does it matter if I did? But I'd rather not.

I liked that forest, I recall the ferns, cool and lacy. But I was thirsty, so I had to come here. The man's name was Ferney, and he spoke about his wife. She was never the same. That wasn't fair to him. She just didn't know. But he didn't know, either. He never said how she took the child's death. I drift like kelp. Nothing seems to be around me at all.

'Mother—'

I drag myself to the surface. 'What is it? What's the matter?'

'It's me. Doris. How are you? Marv didn't come tonight. He had to see a client. But I've brought Mr Troy to see you. You remember Mr Troy, don't you? Our clergyman?'

Oh Lord, what next? Never a minute's peace. I remember him all right. His face beams down at me, round and crimson as a harvest moon.

'How are you, Mrs Shipley?'

Is that the only phrase that ever comes to anyone's mind in such a place? With a great effort, as though my veins might split, I open my eyes wide and glare at him.

'Dandy. Just dandy. Can't you see?'

'Now, Mother—' Doris cautions. 'Now, please—'

Very well. I'll behave myself. I'll be what they desire. Oh, but if Doris doesn't wipe that sanctimonious anguish off her face, I'll dig up one of Bram's epithets and fling it at her. That would do the trick.

'I have to see the nurse a minute,' she says with leaden tact. 'Maybe you'd like to talk a while with Mr Troy.'

She tiptoes out. We remain in heavy silence, Mr Troy and I. I glance at him and see he's struggling to speak and finding it impossibly difficult. He thinks me formidable. What a joke. I could feel almost sorry for him, he's perspiring so. Stonily, I wait. Why should I assist him? The drug is wearing off. My bones are sore, and the soreness is spreading like fire over dry grass, quickly, licking its way along. All at once, an eruption of speech, Mr Troy bursts out.

'Would you—care to pray?'

As though he were asking me for the next dance.

'I've held out this long,' I reply. 'I may as well hold out a while longer.'

'You don't mean that. I'm sure. If you would try—'

He looks at me with such an eagerness that now I'm rendered helpless. It's his calling. He offers what he can. It's not his fault.

'I can't,' I say. 'I never could get the hang of it. But—you go ahead if you like, Mr Troy.'

His face relaxes. How relieved he is. He prays in a monotone, as though God had ears for one note only. I scarcely listen to the droning words. Then something occurs to me.

'There's one—' I say, on impulse. 'That starts out *All people that on earth do dwell*—do you know it?'

'Certainly I know it. You want to hear that? Now?' He sounds taken aback, as though it were completely unsuitable.

'Unless you'd rather not.'

'Oh no, it's quite all right. It's usually sung, that's all.'

'Well, sing it, then.'

'What? Here?' He's stunned. I have no patience with this young man.

'Why not?'

'All right, then.' He clasps and unclasps his hands. He flushes warmly, and peeks around to see if anyone might be listening, as though he'd pass out if they were. But I perceive now that there's some fibre in him. He'll do it, even if it kills him. Good for him. I can admire that.

Then he opens his mouth and sings, and I'm the one who's taken aback now. He should sing always, and never speak. He should chant his sermons. The fumbling of his speech is gone. His voice is firm and sure.

> *All people that on earth do dwell,*
> *Sing to the Lord with joyful voice.*
> *Him serve with mirth, His praise forth tell;*
> *Come ye before Him and rejoice.*

I would have wished it. This knowing comes upon me so forcefully, so shatteringly, and with such a bitterness as I have never felt before. I must always, always, have wanted that—simply to rejoice. How is it I never could? I know, I know. How long have I known? Or have I always known, in some far crevice of my heart, some cave too deeply buried, too concealed? Every good joy I might have held, in my man or any child of mine or even the plain light of morning, of walking the earth, all were forced to a standstill by some brake of proper appearances—oh, proper to whom? When did I ever speak the heart's truth?

Pride was my wilderness, and the demon that led me there was fear. I was alone, never anything else, and never free, for I carried my chains within me, and they spread out from me and shackled all I touched. Oh, my two, my dead. Dead by your own hands or by mine? Nothing can take away those years.

Mr Troy has stopped singing.

'I've upset you,' he says uncertainly. 'I'm sorry.'

'No, you haven't.' My voice is muffled and I have my hands over my eyes so he won't see. He must think I've taken leave of my senses. 'I've not heard that for a long time, that's all.'

I can face him now. I remove my hands and look at him. He's puzzled and worried.

'Are you sure you're all right?'

'Quite sure. Thank you. That wasn't easy—to sing aloud alone.'

'If it wasn't,' he says morosely, 'it's my own fault.'

He thinks he's failed, and I can't muster words to reassure him, so he must go uncomforted.

Doris returns. She fusses over me, fixes my pillows, rearranges my flowers, does my hair. How I wish she wouldn't fuss so. She jangles my nerves with her incessant fussing. Mr Troy has left and is waiting outside in the hall.

'Did you have a nice chat?' she says wistfully.

If only she'd stop prodding at me about it.

'We didn't have a single solitary thing to say to one another,' I reply.

She bites her lip and looks away. I'm ashamed. But I won't take back the words. What business is it of hers, anyway?

Oh, I am unchangeable, unregenerate. I go on speaking in the same way, always, and the same touchiness rises within me at the slightest thing.

'Doris—I didn't speak the truth. He sang for me, and it did me good.'

She gives me a sideways and suspicious glance. She doesn't believe me.

'Well, no one could say I haven't tried,' she remarks edgily.

'No, no one could say that.'

I sigh and turn away from her. Who will she have to wreak salvation upon when I'm gone? How she'll miss me.

Later, when she and Mr Troy have gone. I have another visitor. At first, I can't place him, although he is so familiar in appearance. He grins and bends over me.

'Hi, Gran. Don't you know me? Steven.'

I'm flustered, pleased to see him, mortified at not having recognized him immediately.

'Steven. Well, well. Of course. How are you? I haven't seen you for quite some time. You're looking very smart.'

'New suit. Glad you like it. Have to look successful, you know.'

'You don't only look. You are. Aren't you?'

'I can't complain,' he says.

He's an architect, a very clever boy. Goodness knows where he gets his brains from. Not from either parent, I'd say. But Marvin and Doris certainly saved and did without, to get that boy through university, I'll give them that.

'Did your mother tell you to come and see me?'

'Of course not,' he says. 'I just thought I'd drop in and see how you were.'

He sounds annoyed, so I know he's lying. What does it matter? But it would have been nice if it had been his own idea.

'Tina's getting married,' I say, conversationally.

I'm tired. I'm not feeling up to much. But I hope he'll stay for a few minutes all the same. I like to look at him. He's a fine-looking boy. Boy, indeed—he must be close to thirty.

'So I hear,' he says. 'About time, too. Mom wants her to be married here, but Tina says she can't spare the time and neither can August— that's the guy she's marrying. So Mom's going to fly down East for the wedding, she thinks.'

I never realized until this moment how cut off I am. I've always been so fond of Tina. Doris might have told me. It's the least she could have done.

'She didn't tell me. She didn't say a word.'

'Maybe I shouldn't have said—'

'It's a good job somebody tells me these things. She never bothers, your mother. It never occurs to her.'

'Well, maybe she forgot. She's been—'

'I'll bet she forgot. I'll just bet a cookie she did. When is she going, Steven?'

A long pause. My grandson reddens and gazes at my roses, his face averted from mine.

'I don't think it's quite settled yet,' he says finally.

Then all at once I understand, and know, too, why Doris never mentioned it. They have to wait and see what happens here. How inconvenient I am proving for them. *Will it be soon?* That's what they're asking themselves. I'm upsetting all their plans. That's what it is to them—an inconvenience.

Steven leans towards me again. 'Anything you want, Gran? Anything I could bring you?'

'No. Nothing. There's nothing I want.'

'Sure?'

'You might just leave me your packet of cigarettes, Steven. Would you?'

'Oh sure, of course. Here—have one now.'

'Thank you.'

He lights it for me, and places an ash tray, rather nervously, close by my wrist, as though certain I'm a fire hazard. Then he looks at me and smiles, and I'm struck again with the resemblance.

'You're very like your grandfather, Steven. Except that he wore a beard, you could almost be Brampton Shipley as a young man.'

'Oh?' He's only mildly interested. He searches for a comment. 'Should I be pleased?'

'He was a fine-looking man, your grandfather.'

'Mom always says I look like Uncle Ned.'

'What? Doris's brother? Nonsense. You don't take after him a scrap. You're a Shipley through and through.'

He laughs. 'You're a great old girl, you know that?'

His tone has affection in it, and I would be pleased if it weren't condescending as well, in the same way that gushing matrons will coo over a carriage—*What a cute baby, how adorable.*

'You needn't be impertinent, Steven. You know I don't care for it.'

'I didn't mean it like that. Never mind. You should be glad I appreciate you.'

'Do you?'

'Sure I do,' he says jovially. 'I always have. Don't you remember how you used to give me pennies to buy jaw-breakers, when I was a kid? Mom used to be livid, thinking of the dentist's bills.'

I'd forgotten. I have to smile, even as my mouth is filled once more with bile. That's what I am to him—a grandmother who gave him money for candy. What does he know of me? Not a blessed thing. I'm choked with it now, the incommunicable years, everything that happened and was spoken or not spoken. I want to tell him. Someone should know. This is what I think. *Someone really ought to know these things.*

But where would I begin, and what does it matter to him, anyway? It might be worse. At least he recalls a pleasant thing.

'I remember,' I say. 'You were a little monkey, always snooping in my purse.'

'I had an eye to the main chance,' he says, 'even then.'

I look at him sharply, hearing in his voice some mocking echo of John's.

'Steven—are you all right, really? Are you—content?'

He is taken by surprise. 'Content? I don't know. I'm as well off as the next guy. I suppose. What a question.'

And now I see that he is troubled by things I know nothing of, and don't even care to know. I can't take on anything new at this point. It's too much. I have to let it go. Even if I presumed so far, and questioned him, he'd never say. Why should he? It's his life, not mine.

'Thanks for the cigarettes,' I say, 'and for coming to see me.'

'That's okay,' he says.

We have nothing more to say to one another. He bends and places a quick and token kiss on my face, and then he goes. I would have liked to tell him he is dear to me, and would be so, no matter what he's like or what he does with his life. But he'd only have been embarrassed and so would I.

My discomfort asserts itself, until the only thing that matters to me in this world is that I'm nauseated and I hurt. The sheets bind me like bandages. It's such a warm evening, not a breath of air.

'Nurse—'

Again the needle, and I'm greedy for it now, and thrust out my arm before she's even ready. *Hurry, Hurry, I can't wait.* It's accomplished, and before it has had time to take effect, I'm relieved, knowing the stuff is inside me and at work.

The curtains are pulled aside from the girl's bed, and she's awake. She looks disheveled, puffy-eyed. She's been crying. And now I notice that her mother, a short dark woman with short dark hair and an apologetic smile, is leaving, waving as she walks out, a hopeful helpless flickering of the hands. The woman steps out the door. The girl watches for a moment, then turns her head away.

'How are you feeling?' I ask.

'Awful,' she says. 'I feel just perfectly awful. You said it wouldn't be bad.'

She sounds reproachful. First I'm full of regrets, thinking I've deceived her. Then I feel only annoyance.

'If that's the worst you ever have, my girl, you'll be lucky, I can tell you that.'

'Oh—' she cries, outraged, and then subsides into a sulky silence. She won't say a word, nor even look at me. The nurse arrives and the girl whispers. I can hear.

'Do I have to stay here—with her?'

Furious and affronted, I turn over in my bed and reach for Steven's cigarettes. Then I hear the nurse's reply.

'Try to be patient. She's—'

I can't catch the last low murmur. Then the girl's voice, clear and loud.

'Oh, gee, I didn't know. But what if—? Oh, please move me, please.'

Am I a burden to her as well? What if anything happens in the night? That's what she wondering.

'You rest now, Sandra,' the nurse says. 'We'll see what we can do.'

The room at night is deep and dark, like a coal scuttle, and I'm lying like a lump at the bottom of it. I've been wakened by the girl's voice, and now I can't get back to sleep again. How I hate the sound of a person crying.

She moans, snuffles wetly, moans again. She won't stop. She'll go on all night like this, more than likely. It's insufferable. I wish she'd make some effort to be quiet. She has no self-control, that creature, none. I could almost wish she'd die, or at least faint, so I wouldn't have to lie here hour after hour and hear this caterwauling.

I can't recall her name. Wong. That's her last name. If I could think of her first name, I could call out to her. How else can I address her? 'Miss Wong' sounds foolish, coming from someone my age. I can't say 'my dear'—too obviously false. Young lady? Girl? You? *Hey, you*—how rude. Sandra. Her name is Sandra.

'Sandra—'

'Yes?' Her voice is thin, fearful. 'What is it?'

'What's the matter?'

'I need to go to the bathroom,' she says. 'I've called the nurse, but she doesn't hear me.'

'Have you put your light on? The little light above your bed. That's how you're supposed to call the nurse.'

'I can't reach it. I can't move up by myself. It hurts.'

'I'll put my light on, then.'

'Oh, would you? Gee, thanks a million.'

The faint glow appears, and we wait. No one comes.

'They must be busy tonight,' I say, to calm her. 'Sometimes it takes a while.'

'What'll I do if I can't hold on?' She laughs, a strained and breathless laugh, and I sense her anguish and her terrible embarrassment. To her, it's unthinkable.

'Never you mind,' I reply. 'That's their look-out.'

'Yeh, maybe so,' she says. 'But I'd feel so awful—'

'Wretched nurse,' I said peevishly, feeling now only sympathy for the girl, none for the eternally frantic staff. 'Why doesn't she get here?'

The girl cries again. 'I can't stand it. And my side hurts so much—'

She's never before been at the dubious mercy of her organs. Pain and humiliation have been only words to her. Suddenly I'm incensed at it, the unfairness. She shouldn't have to find out these things at her age.

'I'm going to get you a bedpan.'

'No—' she says, alarmed. 'I'm okay, really. You mustn't, Mrs Shipley.'

'I will so. I won't stand for this sort of thing another minute. They keep them in the bathroom, right here. It's only a step.'

'Do you think you oughta?'

'Certainly. You just wait. I'll get it for you, you'll see.'

Heaving, I pull myself up. As I slide my legs out of bed, one foot cramps and I'm helpless for a second. I grasp the bed, put my toes on the icy floor, work the cramp out, and then I'm standing, the weight of my flesh heavy and ponderous, my hair undone now and slithering lengthily around my bare and chilly shoulders, like snakes on a Gorgon's head. My satin night-gown, rumpled and twisted, hampers and hobbles me. I seem to be rather shaky. The idiotic quivering of my flesh won't stop. My separate muscles prance and jerk. I'm cold. It's unusually cold tonight, it seems to me. I'll wait a moment. There. I'm better now. It's only a few steps, that I do know.

I shuffle slowly, thinking how peculiar it is to walk like this, not to be able to command my legs to pace and stride. One foot and then another. Only a little way now, Hagar. Come on.

There now. I've reached the bathroom and gained the shiny steel grail. That wasn't so difficult after all. But the way back is longer. I miss my footing, lurch, almost topple. I snatch for something, and my hand finds a window sill. It steadies me. I go on.

'You okay, Mrs Shipley?'

'Quite—okay.'

I have to smile at myself. I've never used that word before in my life. *Okay—guy*—such slangy words. I used to tell John. They mark a person.

All at once I have to stop and try to catch the breach that seems to have escaped me. My ribs are hot with pain. Then it ebbs, but I'm left reeling with weakness. I'll reach my destination, though. Easy does it. Come along, now.

There. I'm there. I knew I could. And now I wonder if I've done it for her or for myself. No matter. I'm here, and carrying what she needs.

'Oh, thanks,' she says. 'Am I ever glad—'

At that moment the ceiling light is switched peremptorily on, and a nurse is standing there in the doorway, a plump and middle-aged nurse, looking horrified.

'Mrs Shipley! What on earth are you doing out of bed? Didn't you have the restraint put on tonight?'

'They forgot it,' I say, 'and a good job they did, too.'

'My heavens,' the nurse says. 'What if you'd fallen?'

'What if I had?' I retort. 'What if I had?'

She doesn't reply. She leads me back to bed. When she has settled us both, she goes and we're alone, the girl and I. Then I hear a sound in the dark room. The girl is laughing.

'Mrs Shipley—'

'Yes?'

She stifles her laughter, but it breaks out again.

'Oh, I can't laugh. I mustn't. It pulls my stitches. But did you ever see anything like the look on her face?'

I have to snort, recalling it.

'She was stunned, all right, wasn't she, seeing me standing there? I thought she'd pass out.'

My own spasm of laughter catches me like a blow. I can't stave it off. Crazy. I must be crazy. I'll do myself some injury.

'Oh—oh—' the girl gasps. 'She looked at you as though you'd just done a crime.'

'Yes—that was exactly how she looked. Poor soul. Oh, the poor soul. We really worried her.'

'That's for sure. We sure did.'

Convulsed with our paining laughter, we bellow and wheeze. And then we peacefully sleep.

It must be some days now, since the girl had her operation. She's up and about, and can walk almost straight now, without bending double and clutching her side. She comes over to my bed often, and hands me my glass of water or pulls my curtains if I want to drowse. She's a slender girl, green and slender, a sapling of a girl. Her face is boned so finely. She wears a blue brocade housecoat—from her father's shop, she tells me. They gave it to her for her last birthday, when she was seventeen. I felt the material—she held a sleeve out, so I could see how it felt. Pure silk, it is. The embroidery on it is red and gold, chrysanthemums and intricate temples. Reminds me of the paper lanterns we used to hang on the porches. That would be a long time ago. I suppose.

The pain thickens, and then the nurse comes and the needle slips into me like a swimmer sliding silently into a lake.

Rest. And swing, swayed and swirled hither and yon. I remember the Ferris wheel at the fairgrounds once a year. *Swoop!* That's how it went. Swooping round and round, and we laughed sickly and prayed for it to stop.

'My mom brought me this cologne. It's called *Ravishing*. Want a dab?'

'Why—all right. Can you spare it?'

'Oh sure. It's a big bottle—see?'

'Oh yes.' But I see only a distant glistening of glass.

'There. On each wrist. Now you smell like a garden.'

'Well, that's a change.'

My ribs hurt. No one knows.

'Hello, Mother.'

Marvin. He's alone. My mind surfaces. Up from the sea comes the fish. A little further—try. There.

'Hello, Marvin.'

'How are you?'

'I'm—'

I can't say it. Now, at last, it becomes impossible for me to mouth the words—*I'm fine.* I won't say anything. It's about time I learned to keep my mouth shut. But I don't. I can hear my voice saying something, and it astounds me.

'I'm—frightened. Marvin. I'm so frightened—'

Then my eyes focus with a terrifying clarity on him. He's sitting by my bed. He is putting one of his big hands up to his forehead and passing it slowly across his eyes. He bends his head. What possessed me? I think it's the first time in my life I've ever said such a thing. Shameful. Yet somehow it is a relief to speak it. What can he say, though?

'If I've been crabby with you, sometimes, these past years,' he says in a low voice, 'I didn't mean it.'

I stare at him. Then, quite unexpectedly, he reaches for my hand and holds it tightly.

Now it seems to me he is truly Jacob, gripping with all his strength, and bargaining. *I will not let thee go, except thou bless me.* And I see I am thus strangely cast, and perhaps have been so from the beginning, and can only release myself by releasing him.

It's in my mind to ask his pardon, but that's not what he wants from me.

'You've not been cranky, Marvin. You've been good to me, always. A better son than John.'

The dead don't bear a grudge nor seek a blessing. The dead don't rest uneasy. Only the living. Marvin, looking at me from anxious elderly eyes, believes me. It doesn't occur to him that a person in my place would ever lie.

He lets go my hand, then, and draws away his own.

'You got everything you want, here?' he says gruffly. 'Anything you want me to bring you?'

'No, nothing, thanks.'

'Well, so long,' Marvin says. 'I'll be seeing you.'

I nod and close my eyes.

As he goes out, I hear the nurse speaking to him in the corridor.

'She's got an amazing constitution, your mother. One of those hearts that just keeps on working, whatever else is gone.'

A pause, and then Marvin replies.

'She's a holy terror,' he says.

Listening, I feel like it is more than I could now reasonably have expected out of life, for he has spoken with such anger and such tenderness.

Irving Layton

Twenty years ago IRVING LAYTON was a noisy, embattled and talented outsider among Canadian poets. Today he has become the dominant figure of his generation—perhaps the best poet we have had in Canada—yet he can still be noisy and quarrelsome and often out of step with prevailing intellectual opinions. Born in Rumania, he was brought to Montreal at the age of one and grew up in a Jewish community uneasily poised between the city's large French population and the economically dominant English. He was educated at Macdonald College and later studied economics and political theory at McGill University. From 1946 to 1960 he taught at a parochial school in Montreal and at Sir George Williams University. He is now Professor of English at York University in Toronto. In the 1940s he was active with the late John Sutherland, his brother-in-law, and with the poet Louis Dudek in the literary movement that grew up around Sutherland's magazine *Northern Review*. The poets in this group were socially committed and more sympathetic to their American than to their English contemporaries. In the early 1950s Irving Layton, Louis Dudek, and Raymond Souster founded Contact Press,

a co-operative that published the work of many younger poets. Layton has edited several poetry anthologies: *Canadian Poems: 1850-1952*, with Louis Dudek as co-editor; *Pan-ic* (1958); and *Love Where the Nights are Long* (1962), a collection of Canadian love poems.

Layton has published over twenty books of his own poetry. Among the earliest were *Here and Now* (1945) and *Now is the Place* (1948), *The Black Huntsman* (1951), *In the Midst of My Fever* (1954), and *The Improved Binoculars* (1956). *A Red Carpet for the Sun* (1959), which won a Governor General's Award for poetry, gathers together the work he wanted to preserve to that time. A *Collected Poems* appeared in 1965, a *Selected Poems* in 1969, and the 589-page *Collected Poems of Irving Layton* in 1971. He has also published a small number of short stories which make one wish that he had been able to find the time to write more fiction. (*Engagements*, a selection of ten stories, articles, prefaces, and reviews, was published in the autumn of 1972.) In his younger days Layton was a Marxist and an outsider in both political and literary affairs. In May 1972, in a letter published in *Saturday Night*, he made his position clear on certain matters of today, arguing that 'the struggle to maintain the integrity of South Vietnam and Israel against Soviet and communist expansionist aims is both morally commendable and necessary' and repeating his support of the imposition of the War Measures Act during the Québec crisis of October 1970. In some intellectual circles Layton is an outsider still.

A warm, exuberant man of strong feelings who delights in making shocking statements and is contemptuous of people who are only half alive because they are conformist and don't think and feel enough—of 'the repressed, the fearful, the self-satisfied, and the incurious'— Layton is something of a showman as a public personality and a popular reader of his poetry on campuses across the country. He likes to write prefaces to his poetry collections—about society, his beliefs, his critics, the art of poetry—and they can be eloquent, didactic, angry, outrageous, or all these things at once. They provide an indispensable background for an understanding of the man and his poetry. In *A Red Carpet for the Sun* he wrote a brilliant little portrait of his mother and father, telling us indirectly something about his own roots as a poet: 'My father was an ineffectual visionary; he saw God's footprint in a cloud and lived only for his books and meditations. A small bedroom in a slum tenement, which in the torrid days steamed and blistered and sweated, he converted into a tabernacle for the Lord of Israel. . . Had my mother been as otherworldly as he was, we should have starved. Luckily for us, she was not; she was tougher than nails, shrewd and indomitable. Moreover, she had a gift for cadenced vituperation; to which, doubtless, I owe my impeccable ear for rhythm.' In his *Collected Poems* of 1965, he wrote: 'Joy, fullness of feeling, is the core of the creative mystery. My dominant mood is that of ecstasy and gratitude. To have written even one poem that speaks with rhythmic authority about matters that are enduringly important is something to be immensely, reverently thankful for—and I am intoxicated enough to think I have written more than one.' This is a statement of unaccustomed modesty. In his large body of verse—on love, death, art, power—are many superb poems that will live.

The critic George Woodcock has summed up Layton as 'a poet in the old romantic sense . . . flamboyant, rowdy, angry, tortured, tender, versatile, voluble, ready for the occasion as well as the inspiration, keeping his hand constantly in, and mingling personal griefs and joys with the themes and visions of human destiny.' Woodcock's essay on Layton, written in 1965, is in *Odysseus Ever Returning* (1970). Eli Mandel has written a critical study of Layton's poetry for the series Canadian Writers and Their Works published by Forum House (1969).

ON SEEING THE STATUETTES
OF EZEKIEL AND JEREMIAH
IN THE CHURCH OF NOTRE-DAME

They have given you French names
        and made you captive, my rugged
troublesome compatriots;
        your splendid beards, here, are epicene,
plaster white
                and your angers
unclothed with Palestinian hills quite lost
in this immense and ugly edifice.

You are bored—I see it—sultry prophets
        with priests and nuns
(What coarse jokes must pass between you!)
        and with those morbidly religious
i.e. my prize brother-in-law
                        ex-Lawrencian
pawing his rosary, and his wife
sick with many guilts.

Believe me I would gladly take you
        from this spidery church
its bad melodrama, its musty smell of candle
        and set you both free again
in no make-believe world
                of sin and penitence
but the sunlit square opposite
alive at noon with arrogant men.

Yet cheer up Ezekiel and you Jeremiah
        who were once cast into a pit;
I shall not leave you here incensed, uneasy
        among alien Catholic saints
but shall bring you from time to time
                my hot Hebrew heart
as passionate as your own, and stand
with you here awhile in aching confraternity.

THE BIRTH OF TRAGEDY

And me happiest when I compose poems.
        Love, power, the huzza of battle
        are something, are much;
yet a poem includes them like a pool
        water and reflection.
In me, nature's divided things—
        tree, mould on tree—
        have their fruition;
I am their core. Let them swap,
bandy, like a flame swerve
I am their mouth; as a mouth I serve.

And I observe how the sensual moths
        big with odour and sunshine
        dart into the perilous shrubbery;
or drop their visiting shadows
        upon the garden I one year made
of flowering stone to be a footstool
        for the perfect gods:
        who, friends to the ascending orders,
sustain all passionate meditations
and call down pardons
for the insurgent blood.

A quiet madman, never far from tears,
        I lie like a slain thing
        under the green air the trees
inhabit, or rest upon a chair
        towards which the inflammable air
tumbles on many robins' wings;
        noting how seasonably
        leaf and blossom uncurl
and living things arrange their death,
while someone from afar off
blows birthday candles for the world.

BERRY PICKING

Silently my wife walks on the still wet furze
Now darkgreen the leaves are full of metaphors
Now lit up is each tiny lamp of blueberry.
The white nails of rain have dropped and the sun is free.

And whether she bends or straightens to each bush
To find the children's laughter among the leaves
Her quiet hands seem to make the quiet summer hush—
Berries or children, patient she is with these.

I only vex and perplex her; madness, rage
Are endearing perhaps put down upon the page;
Even silence daylong and sullen can then
Enamour as restraint or classic discipline.

So I envy the berries she puts in her mouth,
The red and succulent juice that stains her lips;
I shall never taste that good to her, nor will they
Displease her with a thousand barbarous jests.

How they lie easily for her hand to take,
Part of the unoffending world that is hers;
Here beyond complexity she stands and stares
And leans her marvellous head as if for answers.

No more the easy soul my childish craft deceives
Nor the simpler one for whom yes is always yes;
No, now her voice comes to me from a far way off
Though her lips are redder than the raspberries.

SHAKESPEARE

My young son asks me:
'Who's the greatest poet?'
Without any fuss I say, Shakespeare.
'Is he greater than you?'
I ho-ho around that one
and finally give a hard 'yes.'
'Will you ever be greater
than . . . a series of lisped S's
and P's . . . ?'
I look up at my son
from the page I'm writing on:
he too wants his answer
about the greatness of Shakespeare
though only six and carefree;
and I see with an amused hurt
how my son has begun to take on
one of those damned eternal fixtures
of the human imagination
like 'God' or 'Death' or 'the start
of the world'; along with these
it'll be with him the rest
of his life like the birthmark
on his right buttock; so as though
I were explaining God or Death
I say firmly without a trace
of ho-ho in my voice: No, I'll never
be greater than William Shakespeare,
the world's greatest poetic genius
that ever will be or ever wuz,
hoping my fair-minded admission
won't immediately blot out
the my-father-can-lick-anyone image
in his happy ignorant mind
and take the shine away
that's presently all around my head

That unclimbable mountain, I rage;
that forever unapproachable star
pulsing its eternal beams from afar
stillness onto our narrow screens
set up as Palomar libraries and schools
to catch the faintest throb of light.
Damn that unscalable pinnacle

of excellence mocking our inevitable
inferiority and failure
like an obscene finger; a loud curse
on the jeering 'beep . . . beep's'
that come from dark silence
and outer galactic space to unscramble
into the resonant signature of
'Full many a glorious morning' or
'The quality of mercy is not strained'
or 'Out, out, brief candle . . . .'
No poet for all time, *no* poet
till this planet crack into black night
and racking whirlwinds *ever*
to be as great as William Shakespeare?
My God, what a calamitous burden
far worse than any horla or incubus:
a tyrant forever beyond the relief
of bullet or pointed steel. . . .
What a terrible lion in one's path!
What a monumental stone
in the constrictive runnel of anyone
with an itch to write great poems
—and poets so cursed beyond all
by vanity, so loused up in each inch
of their angry, comfortless skin
with the intolerable twitch of envy!

Well, there's nothing to be done
about that bastard's unsurpassable
greatness; one accepts it like cancer
or old age, as something that one
must live with, hoping it will prod us on
to alertest dodges of invention
and circumvention, like the brave spider
who weaves his frail home in the teeth
of the lousiest storm and catches
the morning sun's approving smile.
Anyhow there's one saving grace:
that forever smiling damned bastard,
villain, what-have-you is dead
and no latest success of his
can embitter our days with envy,
paralyse us into temporary impotency,
despair rotting out guts and liver;
yes, though the greatest that ever wuz

or ever will be he's dead, dead,
and all the numerous flattering busts
keep him safely nailed down
among the worms he so often went raving
on about when his great heart burst
and all the griefs of the world
came flooding out. His ghost may wander
like Caesar's into my tent
by this rented lake, and I'll entertain
him; but he must also stand outside
begging for entry when I keep his volume
shut, and then he's out in the cold
like his own poor Lear. And—well—
there's my six-year-old son
who says of the clothes flapping
on the clothesline: 'Look, they're
scratching themselves,' or compares
his mother's nipples to drain-plugs
he says he wishes to pull out, or
tells me the rain is air crying
—and he only four at the time;
and though I swear I never told him
of Prospero and his great magic
asked me the other day: 'Is the world real?'

So who really can tell, maybe one day
one of my clan will make it
and there'll be another cock-of-the-walk,
another king-of-the-castle; anyway
we've got our bid in, Old Bard.

KEINE LAZAROVITCH
1870-1959

When I saw my mother's head on the cold pillow,
Her white waterfalling hair in the cheeks' hollows,
I thought, quietly circling my grief, of how
She had loved God but cursed extravagantly his creatures.

For her final mouth was not water but a curse,
A small black hole, a black rent in the universe,
Which damned the green earth, stars and trees in its stillness
And the inescapable lousiness of growing old.

And I record she was comfortless, vituperative,
Ignorant, glad, and much else besides; I believe
She endlessly praised her black eyebrows, their thick weave,
Till plagiarizing Death leaned down and took them for his
    mould.

And spoiled a dignity I shall not again find,
And the fury of her stubborn limited mind;
Now none will shake her amber beads and call God blind,
Or wear them upon a breast so radiantly.

O fierce she was, mean and unaccommodating;
But I think now of the toss of her gold earrings,
Their proud carnal assertion, and her youngest sings
While all the rivers of her red veins move into the sea.

Stephen Leacock

One of the few Canadian writers who have achieved a world-wide reputation, STEPHEN LEACOCK was a humorist who speared hypocrisy and pretentiousness, shams of all kinds, with wonderful flights of satire, parody, and nonsense. He was born in England and was brought to Canada at the age of six by his parents, who settled near Sutton, Ont. He attended Upper Canada College in Toronto and the University of Toronto. He taught from 1889 to 1899—at the high school in Uxbridge for over a year and then at Upper Canada. In 1899 he became a graduate student at the University of Chicago. He married in 1900 and in 1903, the year he received a Ph.D., he became a lecturer in economics and political science at McGill University in Montreal. He was made head of the department in 1908 and retired, much against his wishes, in 1936.

Leacock's first book was *Elements of Political Science* (1906), a textbook that was reprinted many times. He wrote many other books on economics, political affairs, and Canadian history but became famous as a prolific author of humorous sketches in which his gift for controlled exaggeration and an inspired sense of the incongruous have entertained generations of readers. The first of these books was *Literary Lapses* (1910), which included his best-known piece, 'My Financial Career'. In 1911 he published *Nonsense Novels*, a book of parodies. The next year there appeared *Sunshine Sketches of a Little Town*, whose central character is the town of Mariposa—Orillia, Ont., where Leacock spent his summers and where some citizens were outraged by his unflattering comic portrait. This and *Arcadian Adventures with the Idle Rich* (1914) are probably his most successful books. Having written about the foibles and hypocrisies of small-town life in *Sunshine Sketches*, he dealt with these same things in *Arcadian Adventures*, but this time he concentrated on the moneyed class in a large city. After *Arcadian Adventures* appeared, Leacock published almost a book a year. Several of these books, including *Sunshine Sketches* and *Arcadian Adventures*, are available in paperback in the New Canadian Library. Robertson Davies has written an appreciation of Leacock for the Canadian Writers series in the New Canadian Library.

SMALL TOWN: MARIPOSA, ONT.

I don't know whether you know Mariposa. If not, it is of no consequence, for if you know Canada at all, you are probably well acquainted with a dozen towns just like it.

There it lies in the sunlight, sloping up from the little lake that spreads out at the foot of the hillside on which the town is built. There is a wharf beside the lake, and lying alongside of it a steamer that is tied to the wharf with two ropes of about the same size as they use on the Lusitania. The steamer goes nowhere in particular, for the lake is landlocked and there is no navigation for the Mariposa Belle except to 'run trips' on the first of July and the Queen's Birthday, and to take excursions of the Knights of Pythias and the Sons of Temperance to and from the Local Option Townships.

In point of geography the lake is called Lake Wissanotti and the river running out of it the Ossawippi just as the main street of Mariposa is called Missinaba Street and the county Missinaba County. But these names do not really matter. Nobody uses them. People simply speak of the 'lake' and the 'river' and the 'main street', much in the same way as they always call the Continental Hotel, 'Pete Robinson's' and the Pharmaceutical Hall, 'Eliot's Drug Store'. But I suppose this is just the same in everyone else's town as in mine, so I need lay no stress on it.

The town, I say, has one broad street that runs up from the lake, commonly called the Main Street. There is no doubt about its width. When Mariposa was laid out there was none of that shortsightedness which is seen in the cramped dimensions of Wall Street and Piccadilly. Missinaba Street is so wide that if you were to roll Jeff Thorpe's barber shop over on its face it wouldn't reach halfway across. Up and down the Main Street are telegraph poles of cedar of colossal thickness, standing at a variety of angles and carrying rather more wires than are commonly seen at a transatlantic cable station.

On the Main Street itself are a number of buildings of extraordinary importance—Smith's Hotel and the Continental and Mariposa House, and the two banks (the Commercial and the Exchange), to say nothing of McCarthy's Block (erected in 1878), and Glover's Hardware Store with the Oddfellows' Hall above it. Then on the 'cross' street that intersects Missinaba Street at the main corner there is the Post Office and the Fire Hall and the Young Men's Christian Association and the office of the Mariposa Newspacket—in fact, to the eye of discernment a perfect jostle of public institutions comparable only to Threadneedle Street or Lower Broadway. On all the side streets there are maple trees and broad sidewalks, trim gardens with upright calla lilies, houses with verandahs, which are here and there being replaced by residences with piazzas.

To the careless eye the scene on the Main Street of a summer afternoon is one of deep and unbroken peace. The empty street sleeps in the sunshine. There is a horse and buggy tied to the hitching post in front of Glover's hardware store. There is, usually and commonly, the burly figure of Mr Smith, proprietor of Smith's Hotel, standing in his chequered waistcoat on the steps of his hostelry, and perhaps, further up the street, Lawyer Macartney going for his afternoon mail, or the Rev. Mr Drone, the Rural Dean of the Church of England Church, going home to get his fishing rod after a mothers' auxiliary meeting.

But this quiet is mere appearance. In reality, and to those who know it, the place is a perfect hive of activity. Why, at Netley's butcher shop (established in 1882) there are no less than four men working on the sausage machines in the basement; at the Newspacket office there are as many more job-printing; there is a long distance telephone with four distracting girls on high stools wearing steel caps and talking incessantly; in the offices in McCarthy's Block are dentists and lawyers, with their coats off, ready to work at any moment; and from the big planing factory down beside the lake where the railroad siding is, you may hear all through the hours of the summer afternoon the long-drawn music of the running saw.

Busy—well, I should think so! Ask any of its inhabitants if Mariposa isn't a busy, hustling, thriving town. Ask Mullins, the manager of the Exchange Bank, who comes hustling over to his office from the Mariposa House every day at 10:30 and has scarcely time all morning to go out and take a drink with the manager of the Commercial; or ask—well, for the matter of that, ask any of them if they ever knew a more rushing go-ahead town than Mariposa.

Of course if you come to the place fresh from New York, you are deceived. Your standard of vision is all astray. You do think the place is quiet. You do imagine that Mr Smith is asleep merely because he closes his eyes as he stands. But live in Mariposa for six months or a year and then you will begin to understand it better; the buildings get higher and higher; the Mariposa House grows more and more luxurious; McCarthy's Block towers to the sky; the 'buses roar and hum to the station; the trains shriek; the traffic multiplies; the people move faster and faster; a dense crowd swirls to and fro in the post-office and the five and ten cent store. And amusements! Well, now—lacrosse, baseball, excursions, dances, the Firemen's Ball every winter, and the Catholic picnic every summer! And music—the town band in the park every Wednesday evening, and the Oddfellows' brass band on the street every other Friday; the Mariposa

Quartette, the Salvation Army! Why, after a few months' residence you begin to realize that the place is a mere mad round of gaiety.

In point of population, if one must come down to figures the Canadian census puts the numbers every time at something round five thousand. But it is very generally understood in Mariposa that the census is largely the outcome of malicious jealousy. It is usual that after the census the editor of the Mariposa Newspacket makes a careful re-estimate (based on the data of relative non-payment of subscriptions), and brings the population up to 6,000. After that the Mariposa Times-Herald makes an estimate that runs the figures up to 6,500. Then Mr Gingham, the undertaker, who collects the vital statistics for the provincial government, makes an estimate from the number of what he calls the 'demised' as compared with the less interesting persons who are still alive, and brings the population to 7,000. After that somebody else works it out that it's 7,500; then the man behind the bar of the Mariposa House offers to bet the whole room that there are 9,000 people in Mariposa. That settles it, and the population is well on the way to 10,000, when down swoops the federal census taker on his next round and the town has to begin all over again.

Still, it's a thriving town and there is no doubt of it. Even the transcontinental railways, as any townsman will tell you, run through Mariposa. It is true that the trains mostly go through at night and don't stop. But in the wakeful silence of the summer night you may hear the long whistle of the through train for the west as it tears through Mariposa, rattling over the switches and past the semaphores and ending in a long, sullen roar as it takes the trestle bridge over the Ossawippi. Or, better still, on a winter evening about eight o'clock you will see the long row of the Pullmans and diners of the night express going north to the mining country, the windows flashing with brilliant light, and within them a vista of cut glass and snow-white table linen, smiling negroes and millionaires with napkins at their chins whirling past in the driving snowstorm.

I can tell you the people of Mariposa are proud of the trains, even if they don't stop! The joy of being on the main line lifts the Mariposa people above the level of their neighbours in such places as Tecumseh and Nichols Corners into the cosmopolitan atmosphere of through traffic and the larger life. Of course, they have their own train, too—the Mariposa Local, made up right there in the station yard, and running south to the city a hundred miles away. That, of course, is a real train, with a box stove on end in the passenger car, fed with cordwood upside down, and with seventeen flat cars of pine lumber set between the passenger car and the locomotive so as to give the train its full impact when shunting.

Outside of Mariposa there are farms that begin well but get thinner and meaner as you go on, and end sooner or later in bush and swamp and the rock of the north country. And beyond that again, as the background of it all, though it's far away, you are somehow aware of the great pine woods of the lumber country reaching endlessly into the north.

Not that the little town is always gay or always bright in the sunshine. There never was such a place for changing its character with the season. Dark enough and dull it seems of a winter night, the wooden sidewalks creaking with the frost, and the lights burning dim behind the shop windows. In olden times the lights were coal oil lamps; now, of course, they are, or are supposed to be, electricity—brought from the power house on the lower Ossawippi nineteen miles away. But, somehow, though it starts off as electricity from the Ossawippi rapids, by the time it gets to Mariposa and filters into the little bulbs behind the frosty windows of the shops, it has turned into coal oil again, as yellow and bleared as ever.

After the winter, the snow melts and the ice goes out of the lake, the sun shines high and the shanty-men come down from the lumber woods and lie round drunk on the sidewalk outside of Smith's hotel—and that's spring time. Mariposa is then a fierce, dangerous lumber town, calculated to terrorize the soul of a newcomer who does not understand that this also is only an appearance and that presently the rough-looking shanty-men will change their clothes and turn back again into farmers.

Then the sun shines warmer and the maple trees come out and Lawyer Macartney puts on his tennis trousers, and that's summer time. The little town changes to a sort of summer resort. There are visitors up from the city. Every one of the seven cottages along the lake is full. The Mariposa Belle churns the waters of the Wissanotti into foam as she sails out from the wharf, in a cloud of flags, the band playing and the daughters and sisters of the Knights of Pythias dancing gaily on the deck.

That changes too. The days shorten. The visitors disappear. The golden-rod beside the meadow droops and withers on its stem. The maples blaze in glory and die. The evening closes dark and chill, and in the gloom of the main corner of Mariposa the Salvation Army around a naphtha lamp lift up the confession of their sins—and that is autumn. Thus the year runs its round, moving and changing in Mariposa, much as it does in other places.

SUNSHINE SKETCHES OF A LITTLE TOWN

b. 1939

Dennis Lee

DENNIS LEE, an editor and publisher noted for his willingness to devote much time to helping and encouraging young writers, also has a growing reputation as an author of reflective poetry. He was born in Toronto, attended the University of Toronto, and taught for four years at Victoria College there. In the mid-1960s he was one of the founders of Rochdale College, which was envisioned as a kind of free university but in recent years has become a controversial centre in midtown Toronto attracting both disturbed or homeless young people and the attention of the police. In 1967 Dennis Lee was co-founder with the novelist and editor Dave Godfrey of the House of Anansi, which has become one of the most receptive publishers in Canada of the new poets and novelists, and he is still active as editor and publisher. He also teaches in the Division of Humanities at York University in Toronto. His first collection of poetry, *Kingdom of Absence*, appeared in 1967; the next year he published the first version of *Civil Elegies*, a sequence of seven poems. *Wig-gle to the Laundromat*, a collection of poems for children, was published in 1970. *Civil Elegies and Other Poems* (1972) contains a revision of the *Civil Elegies* sequence, which was expanded to nine poems, two of which follow.

In reviewing this book Robert Fulford wrote: 'In his poetic voice [Dennis Lee] cries out for some absolute which will give meaning to life now. In the second elegy—the most beautiful of the nine—he turns to someone unknown whom he addresses as Master and Lord; and dreams of a time less spiritually difficult. . . . These are often sad poems, full of regret for opportunities lost and moments spoiled. They have a kind of self-accusing candor rare in love poems or any other kind. . . . Being a citizen is hard, Lee tells us; love is hard, he also tells us. Being alive and having to look at yourself in the mirror is painful. But when all this is accepted and lived with, it is still possible to affirm your right to be here and to state your case. Lee states his with unique eloquence.'

MASTER AND LORD

SECOND ELEGY

Master and Lord, where
are you?
A man moves back and forth
between what must be done to save the world
and what will save his soul,
and neither is real. For many years
I could not speak your name, nor now but
even stilled at times by openings like
joy my whole life
aches, the streets I walk along to work declare
your absence, the headlines
declare it, the nation, and
over and over the harried lives I
watch and live with, holding my breath and
sometimes a thing rings true—
they all give way and declare your real absence.

Master and Lord,
let be. I can say
nothing about you that does not
vanish like tapwater.
I know
the world is not enough; a woman straightens
and turns from the sink and asks her life the
question, why should she
fake it? and after a moment she
shrugs, and returns to the sink. A man's
adrenalin takes hold, at a meeting he makes
his point, and pushes and sees that
things will happen now . . . and then in the pause he knows
there are endless things in the world and this is not for real.

Whatever is lovely, whatever deserves
contempt, whatever dies—
over and over, in every thing we meet
we meet that emptiness.
It is a homecoming, as men once knew
their lives took place in you.
And we cannot get on, no matter how we
rearrange our lives and we cannot let go for
then there is nothing at all.

Master and Lord, there was a
measure once.
There was a time when men could say
my life, my job, my home
and still feel clean.
The poets spoke of earth and heaven. There were no symbols.

HERE, AS I SIT

NINTH ELEGY

Here, as I sit and watch, the rusty leaves hang taut with departure.
The last few tourists pose by the Moore* and snap their proof that they
    were also alive.
And what if there is no regenerative absence?
What if the void that compels us is only
a mood gone absolute?
We would have to live in the world.
What if the dreary high-rise is nothing but
banks of dreary high-rise, it does not
release the spirit by fraying its attachment,
for the excellent reason that there is no place else to go?
We would have to live in it, making our lives on earth.
Or else a man might go on day by day
in love with emptiness, dismayed each time he meets
good friends, fine buildings and grass in the acres of concrete, feeling the
city's erotic tug begin once more, perpetually
splayed alive by the play of his bungled desires,
though some do not salute the death of the body
before they have tested its life, but crippled they summon together
the fury from within, they tilt at
empire, empire, lethal adversary;
but I am one who came to
idolatry, as in a season of God,
taking my right to be from nothingness.

* The abstract sculpture called 'The Archer', which Henry Moore created for Nathan
  Phillips Square in front of Toronto's New City Hall.

Across the square the crisp leaves blow in gusts, tracing
the wind's indignant lift in corners,
filling the empty pool.
People plod past through the raw air, lost in their overcoats.
I hunch down close to my chest and eat smoke.

But when the void became void I did
let go, though derelict for months
and I was easy, no longer held by its negative presence
as I was earlier disabused of many things in the world
including Canada, and came to know I still had access to them,
and I promised to honour each one of my country's failures of nerve and its
     sellouts.

To rail and flail at a dying civilization,
to rage in imperial space, condemning
soviet bombers, american bombers—to go on saying
no to history is good.
And yet a man does well to leave that game behind, and go and find
some saner version of integrity,
although he will not reach it where he longs to, in the
vacant spaces of his mind—they are so
occupied. Better however to try.

But we are not allowed to enter God's heaven, where it is all a
drowsy beatitude, nor is God, the realm above our heads but
must grow up on earth.
Nor do we have recourse to void.
For void is not a place, nor
negation of a place.
Void is not the high cessation of the lone self's burden,
crowned with the early nostalgias;
nor is it rampant around the corner, endlessly possible.
We enter void when void no longer exists.

And best of all is finding a place to be
in the early years of a better civilization.
For we are a conquered nation: sea to sea we bartered
everything that counts, till we have
nothing to lose but our forebears' will to lose.
Beautiful riddance!
And some will make their choice and eat imperial meat.
But many will come to themselves, for there is
no third way at last and these will
spend their lives at war, though not with

guns, not yet—with motherwit and guts, sustained
by bloody-minded reverence among the things which are,
and the long will to be in Canada.

The leaves, although they cling against the
wind do not resist their time of dying.
And I must learn to live it all again, depart again—
the storm-wracked crossing, the nervous descent, the barren wintry land,
and clearing a life in the place where I belong, re-entry
to bare familiar streets, first sight of coffee mugs,
reconnaissance of trees, of jobs done well or badly,
flashes of workday people abusing their power,
abusing their lives, hung up, sold out and
feeling their lives wrenched out of whack
by the steady brunt of the continental breakdown;
finding a place among the ones who live
on earth somehow, sustained in fits and starts
by the deep ache and presence and sometimes the joy of what is.

Freely out of its dignity the void must
supplant itself. Like God like the soul it must
surrender its ownness, like eternity it must
re-instil itself in the texture of our being here.
And though we have seen our most precious words
withdraw, like smudges of wind from a widening water-calm,
though they will not be charged with presence again in our lifetime that is
well, for now we have access to new nouns—
as water, copout, tower, body, land.

Earth, you nearest, allow me.
Green of the earth and civil grey:
within me, without me and moment by
moment allow me for to
be here is enough and earth you
strangest, you nearest, be home.

b. 1909

Dorothy Livesay

DOROTHY LIVESAY is a writer who has established a fine balance between a personal, lyrical, and imagist poetry on the one hand—her 'private' poems—and a narrative poetry of social commitment on the other—her 'public' ones. She was born in Winnipeg but grew up in Ontario. Her father, J.F.B. Livesay, was a war correspondent during the First World War, then a newspaperman in Winnipeg and Regina, and finally general manager of the news agency Canadian Press. Her mother, Florence Randal Livesay, worked on newspapers in Ottawa and Winnipeg and was a writer and translator as well. In this literary family Dorothy Livesay distinguished herself by publishing her first book of poetry, *Green Pitcher* (1928), before she was twenty. She was educated at the University of Toronto and did graduate work at the Sorbonne in Paris, where she wrote a thesis on the influence of French symbolism on poetry in English. In the 1930s she did welfare work in Montreal, Vancouver, and the United States. She married in 1937 and has two children. From 1960 to 1963 she taught English for UNESCO in Northern Rhodesia (Zambia). She has been Writer-in-Residence at the University of New Brunswick and recently retired from the Department of English at the University of Alberta to live and write in Victoria, B.C.

Two of Dorothy Livesay's many books —*Day and Night* (1944) and *Poems for People* (1947)—won the Governor General's Award for poetry. Her *Selected Poems: 1926-1956* was published in 1957; a collection of later poems, *The Unquiet Bed*, appeared in 1967; and a group of six longer poems, *The Documentaries*, came out the following year. Dorothy Livesay also edited the *Collected Poems of Raymond Knister* in 1949 and wrote a biographical introduction about this Canadian writer, whose brief career began with promise in the 1920s and ended tragically in death by drowning early in the 1930s. In her 'documentary' or 'public' poems she has written about the life of a worker on a factory production line ('Day and Night'), about the expulsion of Japanese-Canadians from the west coast during the Second World War ('Call My People Home'), and about her search for roots in Canada after her return from Zambia in the 1960s ('Roots').

'Day and Night', which begins below, was first published in 1936. In an article on her writing in Issue 41 of *Canadian Literature* (Summer 1969), Dorothy Livesay says: 'Mine must have been the first Canadian poem to ignore maple leaves and to concern itself with the desperate condition of people caught in a tech-nological revolution.' 'The Leader' (page 289) was written after hearing the new president of Zambia, Kenneth Kaunda, address his people from an anthill on the Copperbelt.

Issue 47 of *Canadian Literature* (Winter 1971) contains an essay by Peter Stevens on Dorothy Livesay's love poems.

DAY AND NIGHT

1

Dawn, red and angry, whistles loud and sends
A geysered shaft of steam searching the air.
Scream after scream announces that the churn
Of life must move, the giant arm command.
Men in a stream, a human moving belt
Move into sockets, every one a bolt.
The fun begins, a humming whirring drum—
Men do a dance in time to the machines.

One step forward
Two steps back
Shove the lever,
Push it back

While Arnot whirls
A roundabout
And Geoghan shuffles
Bolts about

One step forward
Hear it crack
Smashing rhythm—
Two steps back.

Your heart-beat pounds
Against your throat
The roaring voices
Drown your shout

Across the way
A writhing whack
Sets you spinning
Two steps back—

One step forward
Two steps back.

2
Day and night rising and falling
Night and day shift gears and slip rattling
Down the runway, shot into storerooms
Where only eyes and a notebook remember
The record of evil, the sum of commitments.
We move as through sleep's revolving memories
Piling up hatred, stealing the remnants
Doore forever folding before us—
And where is the recompense, on what agenda
Will you set love down? Who knows of peace?

Day and night
Night and day
Light rips into ribbons
What we say

I called to love
Deep in dream:
Be with me in the daylight
As in gloom.

Be with me in the pounding
In the knives against my back
Set your voice resounding
Above the steel's whip crack.

High and sweet
Sweet and high
Hold, hold up the sunlight
In the sky!

Day and night
Night and day
Tear up all the silence
Find the words I could not say . . .

3
We were stoking coal in the furnaces; red hot
They gleamed, burning our skins away, his and mine.
We were working, together, night and day, and knew
Each other's stroke; and without words exchanged
An understanding about kids at home,
The landlord's jaw, wage-cuts and overtime.

We were like buddies, see? Until they said
That nigger is too smart the way he smiles
And sauces back the foreman; he might say
Too much one day, to others changing shifts.
Therefore they cut him down, who flowered at night
And raised me up, day hanging over night—
So furnaces could still consume our withered skin.

Shadrack, Mechak and Abednego
Turn in the furnace, whirling slow.

     Lord, I'm burnin' in the fire
     Lord, I'm steppin' on the coal
     Lord, I'm blacker than my brother
     Blow your breath down here.

     Boss, I'm smothered in the darkness
     Boss, I'm shrivellin' in the flames
     Boss, I'm blacker than my brother
     Blow your breath down here.

Shadrack, Mechak and Abednego
Burn in the furnace, whirling slow.

4
Up in the roller room, men swing steel
Swing it, zoom; and cut it, crash.
Up in the dark the welder's torch
Makes sparks fly like lightning's reel.

Now I remember storm on a field:
The trees bow tense before the blow
Even the jittering sparrow's talk
Ripples into the still tree shield.

We are in storm that has no cease
No lull before, no after time
When green with rain the grasses grow
And air is sweet with fresh increase.

We bear the burden home to bed
The furnace glows within our hearts:
Our bodies hammered through the night
Are welded into bitter bread.

Bitter, yes:
But listen, friend,
We are mightier
In the end

We have ears
Alert to seize
A weakness in
The foreman's ease.

We have eyes
To look across
The bosses' profit
At our loss.

Are you waiting?
Wait with us
Every evening
There's a hush

Use it not
For love's slow count:
Add up hate
And let it mount—

One step forward
Two steps back
Will soon be over:
Hear it crack!

The wheels may whirr
A roundabout
And neighbour's shuffle
Drown your shout

The wheel must limp
Till it hangs still
And crumpled men
Pour down the hill:

Day and night
Night and day—
Till life is turned
The other way!

THE LEADER

1
The Copperbelt night is a snake
strangling the drums
squeezing the air
from throats, from lungs
under its arching coils
a child's cry shrills
in the beerhall's roar
a cauldron boils

But the Copperbelt day is saved
by a strike of thunder
the man on the anthill
crying out 'Kwatcha'!
wilder than rain pelt
on the beat of sunlight
children shout freedom
waving green branches.

2
Heaven lets down a rope
Whereon I swing
the clapper of a bell
on sounding sky

and all below
they cluster with uplifted faces
black on white
and sway like flowers
to my wild clanging

whether sun burns me
or moon rivets with steely eye
I shall ring on
till flowers are black mouths
And the stones bleed my song.

b. 1941

Gwendolyn MacEwen

GWENDOLYN MACEWEN was first published at the age of fifteen in the *Canadian Forum*. By the time she was eighteen she had ended her formal education and begun a full-time career as a writer in Toronto, where she was born. Among the half-dozen books of poetry she has published since then are *The Rising Fire* (1963), *A Breakfast for Barbarians* (1966), *The Shadow-Maker* (1969), which won a Governor General's Award, and *The Armies of the Moon* (1972). She has also published two novels, *Julian the Magician* (1963) and *King of Egypt, King of Dreams* (1971), and a collection of short stories, *Noman* (1972). She is the author of verse plays for radio and has done a good deal of other writing for broadcast; she received a CBC New Canadian Writing Contest award in 1965. She also wrote the libretto for a jazz cantata, 'Carnival', by Ron Collier. A recording of her poetry, 'Open Secret', was issued by the CBC in 1972. Unlike many poets, she is a highly effective reader of her own verse—she does not actually 'read' it but recites it from memory—and has gone on tour with public readings, which are really 'performances', through the Maritimes and in other parts of Canada. Her appearance before a large audience in the St Lawrence Centre in Toronto, shortly after the publication of *The Armies of the Moon*, was a personal triumph.

To Gwendolyn MacEwen some big and small events of everyday life—the 'real' world—have a universal or miraculous significance that links them to the world of dream, magic, and myth. Ordinary experiences take on new meaning as she describes relationships between these two worlds by means of metaphors, symbols, and myths. All her writing reflects widespread, even arcane, interests: Arabic literature, for example (she has translated some modern Arabic poetry), ancient religions, and anthropology. One of her verse plays for radio deals with the disappearance of the Franklin expedition in the Arctic in the mid-nineteenth century, and her fascination with space exploration has led her to write poems about the implications of space travel for man and society.

There is an interesting article on Gwendolyn MacEwen by a fellow poet, Margaret Atwood, in Issue 45 of *Canadian Literature* (Summer 1970).

THE PORTAGE

We have travelled far with ourselves
and our names have lengthened;
      we have carried ourselves
on our backs, like canoes
in a strange portage, over trails,
insinuating leaves
and trees dethroned like kings,
      from water-route to
      water-route
seeking the edge, the end,
the coastlines of this land.

On earlier journeys we
were master ocean-goers
going out, and evening always found us
spooning the ocean from our boat,
      and gulls, undiplomatic
      couriers brought us
cryptic messages from shore
till finally we sealords vowed
we'd sail no more.

Now under a numb sky, sombre
cumuli weigh us down;
the trees are combed for winter
and bears' tongues have melted
all the honey;
      there is a lowrd
suggestion of thunder;
subtle drums under
the candid hands of Indians
are trying to tell us
why we have come.

But now we fear movement
and now we dread stillness;
we suspect it was the land
that always moved, not our ships;
we are in sympathy with the fallen
trees; we cannot relate
      the causes of our grief.
We can no more carry
our boats our selves
over these insinuating trails.

POEMS IN BRAILLE

1
all your hands are verbs,
now you touch worlds and feel their names—
thru the thing to the name
not the other way thru (in winter
I am Midas, I name gold)

the chair and table and book
extend from your fingers;
all your movements
command these things back to their
places; a fight against familiarity
makes me resume my distance

2
they knew what it meant,
those egyptian scribes who drew
eyes right into their hieroglyphs,
you read them dispassionate until
the eye stumbles upon itself
blinking back from the papyrus

outside, the articulate wind
annotates this; I read carefully
lest I go blind in both eyes, reading with
that other eye the final hieroglyph

3
the shortest distance between 2 points
on a revolving circumference
is a curved line; O let me follow you,
Wenceslas

4
with legs and arms I make alphabets
like in those children's books
where people bend into letters and signs,
yet I do not read the long cabbala of my bones
truthfully; I need only to move
to alter the design

5
I name all things in my room
and they rehearse their names,
gather in groups, form tesseracts,
discussing their names among themselves

I will not say the cast is less than the print
I will not say the curve is longer than the line,
I should read all things like braille in this season
with my fingers I should read them
lest I go blind in both eyes reading with
that other eye the final hieroglyph

THIS NORTHERN MOUTH

this, my northern mouth,
speaks at times east, speaks south;
if only to test
the latitudes of speech
the longitudes of truth

I sometimes journey outward
and around; yet in the east
they ask me of the dark, mysterious
west.

this, my northern mouth
speaks at times east, speaks south.
I do not know
which speech is best.

THE ARMIES OF THE MOON

now they begin to gather their forces
in the Marsh of Decay and the Sea of Crises;
their leaders stand motionless
on the rims of the craters
invisible and silver as swords turned sideways
waiting for earthrise and the coming of man.

they have always been there increasing their numbers
at the foot of dim rills, all around and under
the ghostly edges where moonmaps surrender
and hold out white flags to the night.

when the earthmen came hunting with wagons and golfballs
they were so eager for white rocks and sand
that they did not see them, invisible and silver
as swords turned sideways on the edge of the craters—
so the leaders assumed they were blind.

in the Lake of Death there will be a showdown;
men will be powder, they will go down under
the swords of the unseen silver armies,
become one with the gorgeous anonymous moon.

none of us will know what caused the crisis
as the lunar soldiers reluctantly disband
and return to their homes in the Lake of Dreams
weeping quicksilver tears for the blindness of man.

William Lyon Mackenzie

A newspaper editor, politician, and rebel, WILLIAM LYON MACKENZIE was born near Dundee, Scotland, and came to Upper Canada (Ontario) in 1820. When he arrived in York he opened a drug and bookselling shop with a friend from Scotland, John Lesslie. Then he moved to Dundas, where he opened another shop. In 1823 he opened a general store in Queenston where in May 1824 he published the first issue of a newspaper. The *Colonial Advocate*, which he mainly wrote himself, very soon began to hit out at the anti-democratic governing establishment in York, the capital of Upper Canada. Mackenzie's interest in politics took him to York in the autumn and he continued his paper there. While publishing virulent attacks on the governing clique of York, he also championed the interests of the town labourers and poverty-stricken farmers, who made him a popular hero. Mackenzie was elected to the Legislative Assembly (and expelled) several times and was made the first mayor of York (1834-5), which was renamed Toronto. His political views became extreme and in December 1837 he gave erratic leadership to some 750 rural supporters in an uprising that provoked two skirmishes near Toronto. They were easily put down by the militia and Mackenzie escaped to the United States, where he set up a Provisional Government on Navy Island in the Niagara River. In 1839 he was imprisoned in Rochester for eighteen months for violating the U.S. neutrality laws. On his release he supported himself and his family by journalism and as a clerk in the customs office in New York until he returned to Canada under the Act of Amnesty of 1849. He was elected to the House of Assembly in 1851 and retired from politics in 1858. He died in the house on Bond Street, Toronto, that a committee of friends had bought for him.

Though he had very little formal education, Mackenzie read avidly as a youth; by the age of twenty-four, he said, he had read carefully and memorized the contents of 957 books. He was a vigorous polemical writer of newspaper articles and books and an inveterate collector of facts. With admirable clarity and force he presented much general information to the readers of his newspaper in a day when this was not easily accessible in rural communities. But he also descended to scurrility in his journalism: the strange combination of idealism and destructiveness that informed his actions also characterized his writing. Among Mackenzie's books are *Sketches of Canada and the United States* (1833) and *Mackenzie's Own Narrative of the Late Rebellion* (1838). Margaret Fairley's *Selected Writings of William Lyon Mackenzie:* *1824-1837* (1960) offers a generous sampling of his more moderate writings. Two good biographies are *The Firebrand: William Lyon Mackenzie and the Rebellion in Upper Canada* (1956) by William Kilbourn and *William Lyon Mackenzie: Rebel Against Authority* (1972) by David Flint. Both books are available in paperback. See also *The Mackenzie Poems*, a collection of 'found poems' created by John Robert Colombo from Mackenzie's writings. One of these 'poems' is on page 77.

TO THE FARMERS OF YORK COUNTY

The following message was distributed in a broadside about November 27, 1837—ten days before Mackenzie's followers marched on Toronto.

Farmers of York County, we have news for you.

LISTEN!

Last winter the Merchants and Millers, gave you high prices for your Wheat and Flour—they expected to have the same protection in duties against United States competition in June when making sales in Montreal as they had had by law in January when making purchases. Some of them borrowed at the bank to enable them the better to give you a high price— others employed their own ample means.

They will sustain heavy losses. And Why?

Not from the natural fall of the markets, but because a Law appears in last Thursday's Gazette of the following extraordinary character; a law too of which they had no warning, and which takes effect instantly—nay even before it was published:

This act authorizes the Americans to import into Upper and Lower Canada, *duty free,* for domestic use or export, American Flour, American Wheat, American Oats and Oatmeal, American Barley, also Indian Corn, and Cornmeal, American Live Stock, American Beef and Pork, American Hams and Bacon, American Lumber or Wood.

It also authorizes American Flour, Beef, Pork, Hams, Bacon, and Wood or Lumber, when imported into Upper or Lower Canada, to be from thence exported to the British West Indies, Bermuda, and the Bahama Islands, there to be received duty free.

But the new act does more than all this: it not only allows the Americans to harass, ruin and discourage our merchants and millers by bringing immense quantities of American produce into competition with the produce of Upper Canada in our own markets, while they refuse us leave to go to theirs, but also, according to the interpretation of the Custom House at Montreal, permits Americans to come here, erect flouring mills on the British side of the St Lawrence, on the Welland Canal (made by our money for their use), or anywhere else in Canada, and there grind American flour, duty free, and then export it to England, our principal Market, *there to be received on equally favourable terms with the flour of this British Colony.*

CANADIANS! It is the design of the Friends of Liberty to give several hundred acres to every Volunteer—to root up the unlawful Canada Company, and give *free deeds* to all settlers who live on their lands—to give free gifts of the Clergy Reserve lots, to good citizens who have settled on them—and the like to settlers on Church of England Glebe Lots, so that the yeomanry may feel independent, and be able to improve the country, instead of sending the fruit of their labour to foreign lands. The fifty-seven Rectories will be at once given to the people, and all public lands used for Education, Internal Improvements, and the public good. £100,000 drawn from us in payment of the salaries of bad men in office, will be reduced to one-quarter, or much less, and the remainder will go to improve bad roads and to 'make crooked paths straight'; law will be ten times more cheap and easy—the bickerings of priests will cease with the funds that keep them up—and men of wealth and property from other lands will soon raise our farms to four times their present value. We have given Head and his employers a trial of forty-five years—five years longer than the Israelites were detained in the wilderness. The promised land is now before us—up then and take it—but set not the torch to one house in Toronto, unless we are fired at from the houses, in which case self-preservation will teach us to put down those who would murder us when up in the defence of the laws. There are some rich men now, as there were in Christ's time, who would go with us in prosperity, but who will skulk in the rear, because of their large possessions—mark them! They are those who in after years will seek to corrupt our people, and change free institutions into an aristocracy of wealth, to grind the poor, and make laws to fetter their energies.

MARK MY WORDS, CANADIANS!

The struggle is begun—it might end in freedom—but timidity, cowardice, or tampering on our part will only delay its close. We cannot be reconciled to Britain—we have humbled ourselves to the Pharaoh of England, to the Ministers, and great people, and they will neither rule us justly nor let us go—we are determined never to rest until independence is ours—the prize is a splendid one. A country larger than France or England; natural resources equal to our most boundless wishes—a government of equal laws—religion pure and undefiled—perpetual peace—education to all—millions of acres of lands for revenue—freedom from British tribute—free trade with all the world—but stop—I never could enumerate all the blessings attendant on independence!

Up then, brave Canadians! Get ready your rifles, and make short work of it; a connection with England would involve us in all her wars, undertaken for her own advantage, never for ours; with governors from England, we will have bribery at elections, corruption, villainy and perpetual discord in every township, but Independence would give us the means of enjoying many blessings. Our enemies in Toronto are in terror and dismay—they know their wickedness and dread our vengeance. Fourteen armed men were sent out at the dead hour of night by the traitor Gurnett to drag to a felon's cell, the sons of our worthy and noble minded brother departed, Joseph Sheppard, on a simple and frivolous charge of trespass, brought by a Tory fool; and though it ended in smoke, it showed too evidently Head's feelings. Is there to be an end of these things? Aye, and now's the day and the hour! Woe be to those who oppose us, for 'In God is our trust'.

THE SELECTED WRITINGS OF WILLIAM LYON MACKENZIE

b. 1907

Hugh MacLennan

HUGH MACLENNAN has been described by the American critic, the late Edmund Wilson, as having a 'historical and geographical imagination' and a 'specifically Canadian point of view as it is expressed in both his essays and his fiction'. Perhaps both the imagination and the point of view have their roots in MacLennan's personal and intellectual background. He was born at Glace Bay, Cape Breton, and educated at Dalhousie University, Halifax; a Rhodes scholarship took him to Oxford University and he completed studies in classics at Princeton University. He taught history and classics at Lower Canada College in Montreal for ten years, beginning in 1935, and since 1951 has taught English literature at McGill University, Montreal.

MacLennan's Scots and Maritimes background, and his sense of being a Canadian in all the complexities of the mid-twentieth century, are defined and explored in novels and essays that have made him both a popular and respected writer in his own country. His first novel, *Barometer Rising* (1941), is set in Halifax at the time of the explosion that destroyed a good part of the city on December 5, 1917, in the midst of the First World War. *Two Solitudes* (1945) is an ambitious fictional study of social change in Québec. *The Precipice* (1948) examines a small town in Ontario and Canadian attitudes towards the United States. *Each Man's Son* (1951) is set in a Cape Breton mining town. Both *The Watch That Ends the Night* (1959) and *The Return of the Sphinx* (1967) are major social novels set in Montreal, the former with a background of political and personal ferment in the 1930s, and the latter concerned with the tensions of the French and English in the mid-1960s. Throughout his career as a writer Hugh MacLennan has also committed himself to the somewhat unfashionable form of the reflective personal essay—in which his historical imagination has been well used—and these essays have been collected in *Cross Country* (1949), *Thirty and Three* (1954), *Scotchman's Return and Other Essays* (1960) and *Seven Rivers of Canada* (1961). He won the Governor General's Award for *Two Solitudes* and

The Watch That Ends the Night as well as for *Cross Country* and *Thirty and Three*.

The critic and editor George Woodcock has summed up Hugh Mac-Lennan's achievement in this way: 'Few Canadian critics, even among those who praise him, would seriously claim him as a great writer adept at exploring the intricacies of the human heart and mind; most accept him as the best example of a kind of novelist that may be necessary in Canada today, the kind of novelist who interprets a rapidly maturing society to its own people in the same way as Dickens and Balzac interpreted the society of the industrial revolution to the English and French a hundred years ago. MacLennan may not have the variety or the abounding vigour or the sheer greatness of texture shared by these imperfect giants, yet in his own way he is of their kind, and no writer has yet come nearer than he to creating a Canadian *Comédie Humaine.'*

There are two critical studies of MacLennan: one by Peter Buitenhuis in the Canadian Writers and Their Works series published by Forum House, the other by George Woodcock in the Studies in Canadian Literature series published by Copp Clark. In Issue 3 of *Canadian Literature* (Winter 1960), Hugh MacLennan discusses *The Watch That Ends the Night*, from which the extract that follows is taken, and there is an interview with him in the first issue of *Canadian Fiction* (Winter 1972).

MacLennan's novels are available in paperback. *Two Solitudes, Each Man's Son,* and *Return of the Sphinx* are in the Laurentian Library; *Barometer Rising* is in the New Canadian Library; and *The Watch That Ends the Night* is a Signet Novel.

THE MARTELLS FIND A SON

When Jerome awoke it was bright day and the station hummed with movement and a man and a woman were looking down at him. The man smiled and Jerome, rubbing his eyes as he came out of sleep, smiled back. He was a thin little man with the kindliest, funniest face Jerome had ever seen, with crowsfeet smiling out from the corners of his blue eyes and a grey goat's tuft on a pointed chin. His suit was of pale grey serge, his waistcoat a shiny black bib and his collar white, round and without a tie. On his head was a soft black hat and his long hands were thin, graceful and astonishingly white and clean. Beside him was a woman as short as himself, but plump, with wide apple cheeks, a smiling mouth, hair flecked with grey and a straw hat square on the top of her head.

'Now then, little man, and what may *your* name be?'

The man said this so pleasantly, the pompousness of his words sounding so fresh because Jerome had never been spoken to in such tones, that he lost all his fear and smiled back.

'Jerome,' he said.

'Are you all by yourself, Jerome?' asked the woman.

'Yes.'

'No mother or anything like that?' asked the man. 'No father? No uncle? No brothers or sisters? Nobody at all?'

'My Mama's dead.'

'So is mine,' said the man. 'Ah well!'

The kindly wrinkles about the clergyman's eyes never altered, but when he glanced at his wife he ceased smiling and Jerome knew with a child's intuition that this strange little person might be willing to help him. Even more certain was he that this funny little woman would be his friend. Her lips were so warm looking and soft, when she smiled she was like a gentle bird, and that hat of hers—

'You've got a dishpan on your head,' the boy said suddenly.

'By Jove, but so she has!' said the man. 'Jo, this is a clever boy.'

'You must be hungry if you're all alone,' she said. 'How would you like something to eat? How would you like a nice cup of tea?'

'Cocoa, my dear,' the man said. 'There's so much more food in cocoa.'

'What would *you* like, Jerome—cocoa or tea?'

He was afraid of offending one or the other, but the word 'cocoa' sounded so nice he said he would like it.

'Then cocoa you shall have,' the woman said, and her husband went up and crossed to the coffee stall to get it.

It was then that the gentle care in her voice reached down inside of him, touched the hard knot and dissolved it, and in a passion of sobbing he scrambled off the bench and buried his face against her shoulder. He threw his arms around her small, plump body and she smelled clean and fresh to him, and all the while he hid his face against her he felt her short little fingers stroking his hair and heard her voice soothing him. At last she forced him gently back and when he looked up she was bending down —she was so small she did not have far to bend—and the brim of her straw hat scratched his forehead as she dabbed his eyes with her handkerchief. She took a comb from her bag and brushed his hair, and then she stood back, smiled and said, 'There now!'

The tears had ceased, leaving Jerome hungry. He scrambled back onto the bench and smiled at her. He looked around for her husband but all he could see was his narrow back at the coffee stall.

'My husband has gone to get food for us. We're hungry ourselves, you know. We've been up half the night in a train. I do so dislike railway stations. They're so dirty and noisy. You poor little boy—are you lost?'

'I don't know.'

'Do you live here in Moncton?'

He shook his head and looked across to the coffee stall where the clergyman was gesticulating to a big woman behind the counter. His goat's tuft was waggling and Jerome, thinking he was quarrelling with the woman, was afraid he might get hurt, for he remembered what happened to the men who had quarrelled with his mother.

'What's your other name, Jerome?' the clergyman's wife asked him.

His face remained blank and she added: 'All little boys have more names than one, don't they? Don't you have more names than just Jerome? Tell me.'

'My name's Jerome.'

'Dear me!' said the woman.

Now the little clergyman approached with a tray in his hands and a pleased look on his thin white face. He set the tray down on the bench, rubbed his hands and smiled at his wife.

'Jo, you should be proud of me. You've always told me that women take advantage of me, but this morning I have outfaced a battle-axe and come off victorious. That female standing in receipt of custom for food which is both flyblown and over-priced denied me a tray. But I insisted. I even pointed to a tray in her lair, and after a time she yielded, and here it is, so we all shall breakfast together. What's this little man's name?'

'He says it's Jerome,' said the man's wife.

The clergyman beamed at Jerome. Then he removed his hat and became solemn.

'Now my boy, close your eyes while I say grace. Come now, close them tight. It won't take long.'

Jerome did not understand why he should close his eyes, but he closed them and at once the clergyman began to pray.

'Most merciful God, we thank Thee for this food, such as it is. Most humbly do we beseech Thee to bless it to our use and us to Thy service. We pray Thee also to guard us against the seeds of indigestion we suspect lurk within it. And especially do we pray that we may be guided to help this lost child, who from his appearance and general plight seems to have been conceived in sin somewhat grosser than most, and we ask Thee also to tell us what to do with him, Amen. Now Jerome, open your eyes and eat.'

The boy instantly closed his eyes lest the clergyman should see that he had opened them too soon, then he opened them again and took the heavy mug of cocoa and drank half of it down.

'Giles,' said the woman mildly, 'when you said grace, you didn't have to pull all that in about Jerome.'

'More cocoa, Jerome?' said the clergyman.

The sweet warmth of cocoa and the filling solidity of ham and buttered bread began to make strength in Jerome. He ached all over from his efforts of the day before and the night on the river, his hands were painful and the splinter in his knee had begun to fester, but now he could smile because he was with friends. The clergyman ate and talked simultaneously, now praising the ham, now blaming the poor quality of the bread, and when the food was consumed, he wiped his hands on a white handkerchief, crossed his short, thin legs, put his fingertips together and cleared his throat.

'Jerome, we shall now introduce ourselves. Our name is Martell—M-A-R-T-E-double-L, Martell. I'm Giles Martell and this woman is my wife whom I call Jo. Do you know what a clergyman is, Jerome?'

The boy shook his head.

'I rather suspected that might be the case,' said the clergyman. 'Well, I am one of the species. It is a most unpopular calling and its chief disadvantage lies in the fact that one's parishioners have such a poor view of their Master's intelligence that they deny in their minds that he was in earnest when he performed the miracle at Cana.'

'Giles!' said his wife.

'Now Jerome, if we are to help you we must know more about you. Your first name you have told us, but not your second. Don't you have a second name?'

'My name is Jerome,' the boy said.

'I have heard of such cases in London,' said the clergyman to his wife. He pressed his fingertips so hard that the lean fingers bent, and again he looked at the boy. 'You must know where you come from, Jerome. Tell us where you come from.'

'The camp.'

'Ah, the camp! Now where might this camp be?'

Jerome stared and said nothing.

'Was it a lumber camp, by any chance?'

Jerome nodded.

'Now how did you get to Moncton?'

Again the boy stared.

'This place here'—the clergyman waved his arm round about him—'is Moncton. We must not be harsh in our judgements, so we will let it go at that—the place is called Moncton. But how did you get here?'

'I jumped a freight.'

'You *what* a freight?'

'Giles,' said the woman, 'please! You know perfectly well what Jerome means.'

'You did this thing alone? Not with your father or mother?'

The boy nodded.

'Well, to be sure you must have come a long way.' Looking into the boy's eyes, one hand stroking his goat's beard, the little man said gently: 'Tell us all about it.'

'I was scared.' Suddenly Jerome burst into tears and began talking wildly. 'He was going to kill me so I ran away from him in my canoe.'

'Who was going to kill you?'

'He killed my Mama.'

The two older people stared at each other and Jerome felt the woman's arm come about his shoulder and press him against herself.

'There now!' she murmured. 'There now! There now!'

'He was the Engineer and I saw him.'

At that moment a short, stout figure in a blue suit with a blue cap encircled with silver braid entered from the platform, cupped his hands about his mouth and brayed that the train for Halifax was ready and would depart in ten minutes. The clergyman groaned and got to his feet.

'It's the way of the world,' he said, 'that when nothing important is happening there is all the time possible for it to happen in, while if anything important is afoot there is none. Here we are with this—'

'Go see to our bags, Giles,' the woman said, 'while I stay and talk to Jerome.'

The clergyman crossed the floor to the baggage room, and when he was gone, Jerome understood something in the way children do: of these two people the woman was the stronger. This seemed natural enough because in the camp his mother had been the queen, yet this woman was utterly different from his mother. She was soft, warm and gentle and still she was strong.

'Jerome dear,' she said quietly, 'we haven't much time. Mr Martell and I must take that train for Halifax and it leaves in a few minutes. The thing you just told us is so terrible we must be very sure you are telling the truth. So now you must look into my eyes, Jerome, and tell it to me all over again.'

He did so and saw the woman's grey eyes kind and earnest.

'You must tell me how this awful thing happened. Or—' she smiled '—if it didn't happen, then you must tell me that.'

Jerome was terrified that she would be displeased and leave him. He felt he would have to make her believe he was telling the truth.

'He was screwing my mother and she said he was no good, so he got mad and he hit her and he killed her and there was blood.'

A blush struck the woman's face like a blow and Jerome saw her mouth drop open and his terror grew, for now he had certainly displeased her and now she would certainly leave him.

'He was screwing her,' he repeated desperately, 'and then he hit her and he killed her.'

The woman's hand came over his mouth and closed it. 'Child, do you know what you're saying?'

He nodded desperately and watched her, seeing the flush change to the color of chalk. Then she took away her hand and surveyed him calmly.

'What you have just told me is the most terrible thing anyone has ever told me,' she said. 'It is so terrible a thing that I know you have spoken the truth, for a little boy like you would never have been able to make up a thing like that.' Tears welled into her eyes. 'You poor child! And I suppose there are thousands of other little children just like you in the world!'

He looked up at her dumbly.

'I must ask you a few more questions, Jerome, just to make sure. What about the other men in the camp? Where were they when this awful thing happened?'

'Asleep.'

'I see.' And quietly: 'Was this man your father, Jerome?'
He shook his head. 'I got no father.'

The little clergyman was returning, his narrow shoulders bowed under the weight of the two bags he carried. As he deposited them the stout man in the blue uniform came inside and again cupped his hands about his mouth.

'Alla-booooard for Sackville, Amherst, Truro, New Glasgow, Sydney and Halifax! Alla-bo-o-oard!'

People began moving toward the doors. A man and a woman embraced and exchanged a quick kiss. Children toddled doorwards holding the hands of their parents and Mrs Martell rose from the bench and smoothed down her skirt.

'Jerome has been telling me what happened,' she whispered to her husband. 'We mustn't ask him any more questions now.'

The clergyman looked at his wife, then over his shoulder, then at Jerome, and seemed worried about something.

'The train is leaving,' he said. 'I suppose I should speak to the police or the station-master before we go.'

In terror Jerome scrambled off the bench and clutched the woman's hand, pressing it against his cheek.

'Please don't leave me! Please don't leave me!'

The two older people looked at each other again, and the little woman bent down and kissed the child on the forehead.

'Jerome dear, we will never leave you unless the time comes when you may wish to leave us.'

Then a feeling of joy filled the child so that he could not speak. He took the woman's hand and went out to the platform with her just like any other child who was getting onto the train with his parents. The conductor took the clergyman's bags and hoisted them up to the platform of the car and the three of them climbed aboard. The clergyman found two empty seats in the middle of the car, swung one of the backs over to make a space for four and they sat down together, just as other families were sitting in other parts of the car. The train started and pulled out of Moncton, and looking out the window Jerome saw the station and the shunting yards and the lines of box cars slowly disappear, soon they were running smoothly through a green countryside. Jerome stayed awake until after they crossed the isthmus into Nova Scotia, where he saw the prairie-like expanse of the Tantramar Marshes with hawks and gulls flying over it and the sleek, brown mud-banks in the grass where the long tides of the Fundy came up salting the land, but after Amherst he fell asleep for several hours.

Coming out of sleep somewhere between Truro and Halifax, eyes closed and his mind half dozing, he heard the two older people talking.

'He has a good face,' the little clergyman was saying. 'He'll be a strong, handsome man. Isn't it strange? So long as he lives, he'll probably never know who his real parents were.'

'One can hope he doesn't.'

'Jerome?' the little man said reflectively. 'Generally only Roman Catholics are called Jerome. I wonder if there'll be any difficulty about that? I wonder if some priest will hear his name and decide he was born a Roman Catholic and should be taken away from us? Ah well, one should always remember to stand up to the Romans, whom actually I prefer to so many of—by Jove, that boy is dirty. I think he's the dirtiest boy I've ever seen in my life. I admire your fortitude, Jo. He's been sleeping on your shoulder for hours and he smells quite fearfully. Even from here I can smell him. I think they can smell him all over the car. Do you think he's lousy as well?'

'A good bath is all he needs. And what if he does have lice? I'm not as much afraid of lice as they'll be afraid of what I'll do to them if I find them.'

'He can't be bathed too soon.' Jerome heard the clergyman chuckle, and lifting an eyelid he saw the little man lean forward and place a hand on his wife's knee. 'A boy in the house, Jo! By Jove, after all these years! I wonder if they'll let us keep him? I suppose we must speak with the police. Ah well, I know the police chief reasonably well, but there are lawyers and things. It would be altogether too fearful if some fearful relative were to crop up and claim this child.'

'If God sent him to us,' said the woman, 'I don't for an instant believe that God intends to take him away.'

'I wish I could be as certain as you of God's intentions. He has always been a puzzle to me. Of course this whole affair is really so astonishing I don't believe anything about it but the way this child smells. He might turn out to be a liar, Jo. He's probably some ordinary boy who's run away from some ordinary brute of a father who beat him. Perhaps his father's a judge? Perhaps he's a Baptist minister? One never knows. He must be at least thirteen years old. A strong little boy, Jo. Have you felt his muscles? Much stronger than mine, but of course that says little. You know, I like his hair. When we have it cut, it will grow like spikes all over his head. I envy men with spiky hair, they're so virile. Everybody respects a man with spiky hair.

'You can cut down my old grey suit, I suppose. It's lucky I'm small for after he's grown some more we can hand my clothes down. When we heard that service Edwards was preaching in Woodstock, I confess to a little envy when I saw that family of his sitting there looking up at him, even though I wondered how he manages to feed such a flock. I know he does better than me, but seven children is quite a lot for a member of the profession. I wonder if Jerome will enjoy *my* sermons? I don't suppose he will, for I'm beginning to find them dull myself, though the one I preached last Good Friday wasn't so bad if you remember. When I was his age— I've just thought of something. Of course that boy can't even read and write. We'll have to put him to it right away. Fortunately we have the whole summer before us, and I'll tutor him every day. Do you notice the width between his eyes? Obviously a most intelligent boy.'

The train rumbled on, whistling every now and then before it crossed a road, and Jerome lay half asleep and half awake.

'Jo,' the little clergyman said, 'have you thought of it?'

'Of what, Giles?'

'Of this little lad and me. I mean, of me when I was a lad his age. How strange it is that I should know how he feels! You see—I'm correct to believe in the miracles! Of all the people in the world, that he should have come to us—the only people who would want him and understand how he feels! One tells the Congregation that God watches everything and sometimes one wonders if He really does, but then something like this happens to prove it.'

Still the train rumbled on, and after a while Jerome sensed that the little clergyman was becoming restless.

'It's nearly five o'clock and I haven't had a drop all day. I think it's time, don't you, Jo?'

'Giles—the people!'

'Pshaw! How will they guess?' He touched his dog collar. 'I'm perfectly disguised. I could go to the water cooler and come back with a paper cup—with two paper cups—and who would notice? I think I'll go now.'

'Please be careful, Giles.'

'You know I'm careful. When am I not?'

Jerome fell asleep again and when he woke the clergyman was gently shaking his shoulder and on the clergyman's breath he smelled the sweet, familiar odour of rum.

'Wake up, Jerome, we're nearly there! Now I want you to look at something.'

Opening his eyes, Jerome looked out the window and saw what seemed to him a vast spread of open water with a green shore on the far side shining in the sun.

That's Bedford Basin where all the fleets of the world could swing at their anchors without the ships even bumping each other. Over there behind that hill with the red building on it is Halifax where we live. You'll like it there. I come from England, Jerome, and when I first arrived here I liked Halifax the moment I saw it. There are big ships and small ships and we'll teach you how to sail—a real boat and not one of those Indian canoes you saw on your river. There are schools and churches and other boys to play with. You'll be proud of Halifax, for it's a fine town, a fine place to grow up in and—well, even for a grown man it's not too bad a place. I say—I told you I came from England and something just occurred to me! Do you know what England is?'

The boy shook his head.

'Fancy!' the clergyman said to his wife, 'Fancy meeting *anybody*, even a child, who doesn't know what England is!' He chuckled. 'By Jove, there are some people I'd enjoy telling that to!'

They all stood up while the clergyman took his bags down from the rack and Jerome nearly fell as the train lurched to the left and began its run along the eastern shore of Bedford Basin. A few minutes later it lurched in the opposite direction and suddenly the land and water closed in and they were running beside docks and a shipyard and saw a lean grey shape with flags hanging from its masts.

'A cruiser, Jerome! Do you know what a cruiser is?'

The boy shook his head.

'Oh, it's going to be wonderful, all the interesting things you're going to learn! That cruiser's the *Niobe*. She's so old they don't let her out of harbor for fear she'll sink.'

The train's rumble changed into a solid, heavy roar, daylight disappeared as though a shade had been drawn and they passed under the smoke-stained, glass canopy of the station and stopped.

'It was the old North Street station,' Jerome told Catherine later, 'the one that was destroyed in the Halifax explosion of 1917 and nearly a hundred people were killed that day when that glass roof fell in on top of them. It seemed noisy and colossal to me, and at the end of the platform there was a line of cabbies waving whips and shouting behind an anchor chain. We came through and they closed around us and I was frightened, but Mr Martell knew one of them and soon we were out in the street getting into one of the high black cabs they had in Halifax in those days. I reached Halifax in the last decade of the horse, and the streets smelled of horse manure as well as fishmeal and salt water and the harbor smells it still has. Coming into Halifax was like coming into a world of new smells.'

The cab drove them along Barrington Street, then over a very steep hill crowded with houses and after what seemed a long time to Jerome, it came to rest in front of a house with a little lawn before it and three cannon balls making a black triangle beside the bottom step. There was an ivy-shaded porch with a hammock concealed behind the ivy and there were white curtains at the windows. The clergyman set his bags down, took out his keys and opened the door, and Jerome smelled the closeness of a shut-up house after a warm day.

'This is where we live,' the little man said. 'It's a small house and it's not in the best part of town by a long chalk, but we like it.'

That evening Jerome was given a cold meal out of tins while kettles boiled on the stove and an ancient, spluttering, English-style geyser, heated by gas, warmed the water for his bath. He was undressed and his filthy clothes were burned. He was put into the tub, which was made of tin and painted white, and the paint felt delightfully rough against the skin of his back. The warm water soothed his skin and the fresh-smelling soap made it feel slippery and clean. He laughed as Josephine Martell bathed and dried him, then he held his arms over his head while she put a flannelette nightgown on him.

'This is one of mine,' she said, 'but I'm so small and you're so big it will fit you quite nicely, at least for the time being.'

Soon he found himself in bed between cool sheets looking at pictures on the wall. One was a print of Joshua Reynold's *Age of Innocence* and the other was a sailing ship in a storm, and he lay in the white linen smoothness and looked up at the woman and smiled. His hand, questing under the pillow, closed on a small, rough-feeling little bag which had the cleanest scent he had ever smelled.

'That's lavender,' she said, still smiling. 'We always have it under our pillows.'

'What's that?'

'It's a kind of flower that grows in England where Mr Martell comes from. I've never been to England, but it's the most beautiful and wonderful country in the world, and it's where the King lives. The roses in England are the best roses in the world and it's where the lavender grows.'

'It's nice.'

'We're not rich people, Jerome, and we don't matter much to anybody, but we don't mind that because we believe we matter to God. Mr Martell came from quite a famous family in England, but he was never happy when he was young—not as I hope you're going to be with us. Since our little girl died we've just had each other and a few friends in the church— I mean *I've* just had that, for Mr Martell knows nearly everybody in Halifax, or at least he talks to them as if he does. I'm afraid some of the people in the church don't altogether approve of Mr Martell, and I can well understand why they don't. But he's a good, good man, Jerome, and you'll soon find out for yourself how good he is.' She took the little lavender bag and smelled it, blushed a little and handed it back. 'It's a silly thing to say, but we never had lavender in my house when I was a little girl and I always had a craving for nice things like that. My father was a clergyman too, but he was a much sterner and plainer man than Mr Martell.' She scented the lavender again and handed it back. 'When I first met Mr Martell he was visiting my father's house—he's quite a lot older than me, you know—and I remember smelling lavender on his handkerchief and it seemed so nice and distinguished.'

She bent and kissed the boy's forehead and was about to leave the room when she remembered something and came back.

'Jerome dear—have you ever been taught to pray?'

He shook his head, not knowing what the word meant.

'Then I think I'd better begin teaching you your first prayer tonight. Usually you pray on your knees because that shows how much you respect God, but you're so tired tonight I don't think He will mind if you pray just where you are in bed. All you have to do is shut your eyes and repeat after me.'

Jerome shut his eyes and felt the woman's hand close over his own.

'Now I lay me down to sleep, I pray the Lord my soul to keep . . .'

He repeated the words without understanding what they meant.

'If I die before I wake, I pray the Lord my soul to take.'

Again he made the repetition, she laid her hand on his forehead, he felt its cool softness, he felt her lips brush his cheek and then he closed his eyes.

'There now, it doesn't matter if you don't understand what you were saying. Mr Martell will explain all about it later on. Indeed I'm afraid the dear man will be only too eager to explain to you everything he knows himself, and that is quite a lot, even though I'm ashamed to say I don't listen carefully enough to know how much it really is. Go to sleep now, dear. God will watch over you all night long, and in the morning we shall be waiting for you.'

That night while Jerome slept the little clergyman and his wife sat before their empty hearth holding hands and talking for hours. Before they went to bed they fell on their knees and thanked God and promised that they would lead this child into the paths of righteousness. They believed, they believed at last, that goodness and mercy would follow them all the days of their lives, now that they had a son.

THE WATCH THAT ENDS THE NIGHT

b. 1911

Marshall McLuhan

MARSHALL MC LUHAN's original and revealing studies of mass communications
and their impact on men's minds made
him an international celebrity in the
1960s and one of the period's most influential thinkers. He was born in
Edmonton, Alta, and educated at the
University of Manitoba and Cambridge
University in England. He taught at
several American colleges from 1936 to
1944 and from 1944 to 1946 taught
at Assumption College, Windsor, Ont.
In 1946 he went to St Michael's College, University of Toronto, where he
is Professor of English. In 1963 he
became director of the university's
Centre for Culture and Technology.
He left Toronto for one year, 1967-8,
to be Albert Schweitzer Professor of
Humanities at Fordham University.

McLuhan's first book, *The Mechanical Bride: Folklore of Industrial Man*
(1951), is a satirical commentary on
popular culture and its mechanization
of the human personality, presented
in the form of witty, sardonic discussions of magazine and newspaper advertisements. He went on to study the
communications media that conveyed
this culture in *The Gutenberg Galaxy:
The Making of Typographic Man*
(1962), which won a Governor General's Award. In this book he analyses
the pre-print, oral/aural culture, its
destruction by Gutenberg's invention
of moveable type and the mass-produc-
tion of books, and the change of
values produced by the print culture
that resulted. In *Understanding Media:
The Extensions of Man* (1964) he
examines the electronic or post-Guten-
berg era—the radical changes in man's
responses that have been produced by
the instantaneous, inclusive quality of
electronic communications like television and the computer. McLuhan is
also the author of *The Medium is the
Massage* (1967) and has co-authored
several books, the most recent of
which is *Take Today: The Executive as
Dropout* (1972), which he wrote with
Barrington Nevitt.

'The most that can be done by the
prose commentator,' McLuhan has
written, 'is to capture the media in as
many characteristic and revealing pos-
tures as he can manage to discover.'
He does this in his books by taking

the reader on a perception trip through a dense array of ideas, paradoxes, jokes, and profound and surprising insights. His books are difficult though exciting to read, and they arouse disagreement, but many of his ideas and some of the phrases he has coined have become part of the examination of communications everywhere. 'The new electronic interdependence recreates the world in the image of a global village,' he wrote in *The Gutenberg Galaxy*. And, in *Understanding Media:* '"The Medium is the Message" because it is the medium that shapes and controls the scale and form of human association and action.' He coined the terms 'hot' and 'cool' to describe the nature of the media—cool referring to television, say, which requires a high degree of sensory input from the viewer to supplement the image on the screen and is therefore more involving than radio; radio is a hot medium because it has a 'high definition', which is 'the state of being well filled with data'. Whether or not critics agree with him, the breadth of learning, imagination, and vision that have enabled McLuhan to achieve his remarkable overview of cultures are universally admired.

Dennis Duffy has written a lucid brief study of Marshall McLuhan's thought for the Canadian Writers series in the New Canadian Library.

THE PHONOGRAPH THE TOY THAT SHRANK THE NATIONAL CHEST

The phonograph, which owes its origin to the electrical telegraph and the telephone, had not manifested its basically electric form and function until the tape recorder released it from its mechanical trappings. That the world of sound is essentially a unified field of instant relationships lends it a near resemblance to the world of electromagnetic waves. This fact brought the phonograph and radio into early association.

Just how obliquely the phonograph was at first received is indicated in the observation of John Philip Sousa, the brass-band director and composer. He commented: 'With the phonograph vocal exercises will be out of vogue! Then what of the national throat? Will it not weaken? What of the national chest? Will it not shrink?'

One fact Sousa had grasped: The phonograph is an extension and amplification of the voice that may well have diminished individual vocal activity, much as the car had reduced pedestrian activity.

Like the radio that it still provides with program content, the phonograph is a hot medium. Without it, the twentieth century as the era of tango, ragtime, and jazz would have had a different rhythm. But the phonograph was involved in many misconceptions, as one of its early names—gramophone—implies. It was conceived as a form of auditory writing (*gramma*-letters). It was also called 'graphophone', with the needle in the role of pen. The idea of it as a 'talking machine' was especially popular. Edison was delayed in his approach to the solution of its problems by considering it at first as a 'telephone repeater'; that is, a storehouse of data from the telephone, enabling the telephone to 'provide invaluable records, instead of being the recipient of momentary and fleeting communication.' These words of Edison, published in the *North American Review* of June, 1878, illustrate how the then recent telephone invention already had the power to colour thinking in other fields. So, the record player had to be seen as a kind of phonetic record of telephone conversation. Hence, the names 'phonograph' and 'gramophone'.

Behind the immediate popularity of the phonograph was the entire electric implosion that gave such new stress and importance to actual speech rhythms in music, poetry, and dance alike. Yet the phonograph was a machine merely. It did not at first use an electric motor or circuit. But in providing a mechanical extension of the human voice and the new ragtime melodies, the phonograph was propelled into a central place by some of the major currents of the age. The fact of acceptance of a new phrase, or a speech form, or a dance rhythm is already direct evidence of some actual development to which it is significantly related. Take, for example, the shift of English into an interrogative mood, since the arrival of 'How about that?' Nothing could induce people to begin suddenly to use such a phrase over and over, unless there were some new stress, rhythm, or nuance in interpersonal relations that gave it relevance.

It was while handling paper tape, impressed by Morse Code dots and dashes, that Edison noticed the sound given off when the tape moved at high speed resembled 'human talk heard indistinctly'. It then occurred to him that indented tape could record a telephone message. Edison became aware of the limits of lineality and the sterility of specialism as soon as he entered the electric field. 'Look,' he said, 'it's like this. I start here with the intention of reaching here in an experiment, say, to increase the speed of the Atlantic cable; but when I've arrived part way in my straight line, I meet with a phenomenon, and it leads me off in another direction and develops into a phonograph.' Nothing could more dramatically express the turning point from mechanical explosion to electrical implosion. Edison's own career embodied that very change in our world, and he himself was often caught in the confusion between the two forms of procedure.

It was just at the end of the nineteenth century that the psychologist Lipps revealed by a kind of electric audiograph that the single clang of a bell was an intensive manifold containing all the possible symphonies. It was somewhat on the same lines that Edison approached his problems. Practical experience had taught him that embryonically all problems contained all answers when one could discover a means of rendering them explicit. In his own case, his determination to give the phonograph, like the telephone, a direct practical use in business procedures led to his neglect of the instrument as a means of entertainment. Failure to foresee the phonograph as a means of entertainment was really a failure to grasp the meaning of the electric revolution in general. In our time we are reconciled to the phonograph as a toy and a solace; but press, radio, and TV have also acquired the same dimension of entertainment. Meantime, entertainment pushed to an extreme becomes the main form of business and politics. Electric media, because of their total 'field' character, tend to eliminate the fragmented specialties of form and function that we have long accepted as the heritage of alphabet, printing, and mechanization. The brief and compressed history of the phonograph includes all phases of the written, the printed, and the mechanized word. It was the advent of the electric tape recorder that only a few years ago released the phonograph from its temporary involvement in mechanical culture. Tape and the l.p. record suddenly made the phonograph a means of access to all the music and speech of the world.

Before turning to the l.p. and tape-recording revolution, we should note that the earlier period of mechanical recording and sound reproduction had one large factor in common with the silent picture. The early phonograph produced a brisk and raucous experience not unlike that of a Mack Sennett movie. But the undercurrent of mechanical music is strangely sad. It was the genius of Charles Chaplin to have captured for film this sagging quality of a deep blues, and to have overlaid it with jaunty jive and bounce. The poets and painters and musicians of the later nineteenth century all insist on a sort of metaphysical melancholy as latent in the great industrial world of the metropolis. The Pierrot figure is as crucial in the poetry of Laforgue as it is in the art of Picasso or the music of Satie. Is not the mechanical at its best a remarkable approximation to the organic? And is not a great industrial civilization able to produce anything in abundance for everybody? The answer is 'Yes'. But Chaplin and the Pierrot poets and painters and musicians pushed this logic all the way to reach the image of Cyrano de Bergerac, who was the greatest lover of all, but who was never permitted the return of his love. This wierd image of Cyrano, the unloved and unlovable lover, was caught up in the phonograph cult of the blues. Perhaps it is misleading to try to derive the origin of the blues from Negro folk music; however, Constant Lambert, English conductor-composer, in his *Music Ho!*, provides an account of the blues that preceded the jazz of the post-World War I. He concludes that the great flowering of jazz in the twenties was a popular response to the highbrow richness and orchestral subtlety of the Debussy-Delius period. Jazz would seem to be an effective bridge between highbrow and lowbrow music, much as Chaplin made a similar bridge for pictorial art. Literary people eagerly accepted these bridges, and Joyce got Chaplin into *Ulysses* as Bloom, just as Eliot got jazz into the rhythms of his early poems.

Chaplin's clown-Cyrano is as much a part of a deep melancholy as Laforgue's or Satie's Pierrot art. Is it not inherent in the very triumph of the mechanical and its omission of the human? Could the mechanical reach a higher level than the talking machine with its mime of voice and dance? Do not T. S. Eliot's famous lines about the typist of the jazz age capture the entire pathos of the age of Chaplin and the ragtime blues?

> *When lovely woman stoops to folly and*
> *Paces about her room again, alone,*
> *She smoothes her hair with automatic hand,*
> *And puts a record on the gramophone.*

Read as a Chaplin-like comedy, Eliot's Prufrock makes ready sense. Prufrock is the complete Pierrot, the little puppet of the mechanical civilization that was about to do a flip into its electric phase.

It would be difficult to exaggerate the importance of complex mechanical forms such as film and phonograph as the prelude to the automation of human song and dance. As this automation of human voice and gesture had approached perfection, so the human work force approached automation. Now in the electric age the assembly line with its human hands disappears, and electric automation brings about a withdrawal of the work force from industry. Instead of being automated themselves—fragmented in task and function—as had been the tendency under mechanization, men in the electric age move increasingly to involvement in diverse jobs simultaneously, and to the work of learning, and to the programming of computers.

This revolutionary logic inherent in the electric age was made fairly clear in the early electric forms of telegraph and telephone that inspired the 'talking machine'. These new forms that did so much to recover the vocal, auditory, and mimetic world that had been repressed by the printed word, also inspired the strange new rhythms of 'the jazz age', the various forms of syncopation and symbolist discontinuity that, like relativity and quantum physics, heralded the end of the Gutenberg era with its smooth, uniform lines of type and organization.

The word 'jazz' comes from the French *jaser*, to chatter. Jazz is, indeed, a form of dialogue among instrumentalists and dancers alike. Thus it seemed to make an abrupt break with the homogeneous and repetitive rhythms of the smooth waltz. In the age of Napoleon and Lord Byron, when the waltz was a new form, it was greeted as a barbaric fulfilment of the Rousseauistic dream of the noble savage. Grotesque as this idea now appears, it is really a most valuable clue to the dawning mechanical age. The impersonal choral-dancing of the older, courtly pattern was abandoned when the waltzers held each other in a personal embrace. The waltz is precise, mechanical, and military, as its history manifests. For a waltz to yield its full meaning, there must be military dress. 'There was a sound of revelry by night' was how Lord Byron referred to the waltzing before Waterloo. To the eighteenth century and to the age of Napoleon, the citizen armies seemed to be an individualistic release from the feudal framework of courtly hierarchies. Hence the association of waltz with noble savage, meaning no more than freedom from status and hierarchic deference. The waltzers were all uniform and equal, having free movement in any part of the hall. That this was the Romantic idea of the life of the noble savage now seems odd, but the Romantics knew as little about real savages as they did about assembly lines.

In our own century the arrival of jazz and ragtime was also heralded as the invasion of the bottom-wagging native. The indignant tended to appeal from jazz to the beauty of the mechanical and repetitive waltz that had once been greeted as pure native dancing. If jazz is considered as a break with mechanism in the direction of the discontinuous, the participant, the spontaneous and improvisational, it can also be seen as a return to a sort of oral poetry in which the performance is both creation and composition. It is a truism among jazz performers that recorded jazz is 'as stale as yesterday's newspaper'. Jazz is alive, like conversation; and like conversation it depends upon a repertory of available themes. But performance is composition. Such performance insures maximal participation among players and dancers alike. Put in this way, it becomes obvious at once that jazz belongs in that family of mosaic structures that reappeared in the Western world with the wire services. It belongs with symbolism in poetry, and with the many allied forms in painting and in music.

The bond between the phonograph and song and dance is no less deep that its earlier relation to telegraph and telephone. With the first printing of musical scores in the sixteenth century, words and music drifted apart. The separate virtuosity of voice and instruments became the basis of the great musical developments of the eighteenth and nineteenth centuries. The same kind of fragmentation and specialism in the arts and sciences made possible mammoth results in industry and in military enterprise, and in massive co-operative enterprises such as the newspaper and the symphony orchestra.

Certainly the phonograph as a product of industrial, assembly-line organization and distribution showed little of the electric qualities that had inspired its growth in the mind of Edison. There were prophets who could foresee the great day when the phonograph would aid medicine by providing a medical means of discrimination between 'the sob of hysteria and the sigh of melancholia . . . the ring of whooping cough and the hack

of the consumptive. It will be an expert in insanity, distinguishing between the laugh of the maniac and drivel of the idiot. . . . It will accomplish this feat in the anteroom, while the physician is busying himself
with his last patient.' In practice, however, the phonograph stayed with
the voices of the Signori Foghornis, the basso-tenores, robusto-profundos.

Recording facilities did not presume to touch anything so subtle as an
orchestra until after the First War. Long before this, one enthusiast looked
to the record to rival the photograph album and to hasten the day when
'future generations will be able to condense within the space of twenty
minutes a tone-picture of a single lifetime: five minutes of a child's prattle,
five of the boy's exultations, five of the man's reflections, and five from
the feeble utterances of the death-bed.' James Joyce, somewhat later, did
better. He made *Finnegans Wake* a tone poem that condensed in a single
sentence all the prattlings, exultations, observations, and remorse of the
entire human race. He could not have conceived this work in any other
age than the one that produced the phonograph and the radio.

It was radio that finally injected a full electric charge into the world
of the phonograph. The radio receiver of 1924 was already superior in
sound quality, and soon began to depress the phonograph and record
business. Eventually, radio restored the record business by extending
popular taste in the direction of the classics.

The real break came after the Second War with the availability of the
tape recorder. This meant the end of the incision recording and its attendant surface noise. In 1949 the era of electric hi-fi was another rescuer
of the phonograph business. The hi-fi quest for 'realistic sound' soon
merged with the TV image as part of the recovery of tactile experience.
For the sensation of having the performing instruments 'right in the room
with you' is a striving toward the union of the audile and tactile in a
finesse of fiddles that is in large degree the sculptural experience. To be in
the presence of performing musicians is to experience their touch and
handling of instruments as tactile and kinetic, not just as resonant. So it
can be said that hi-fi is not any quest for abstract effects of sound in
separation from the other senses. With hi-fi, the phonograph meets the TV
tactile challenge.

Stereo sound, a further development, is 'all-around' or 'wrap-around'
sound. Previously sound had emanated from a single point in accordance
with the bias of visual culture with its fixed point of view. The hi-fi
changeover was really for music what cubism had been for painting, and
what symbolism had been for literature; namely, the acceptance of multiple facets and planes in a single experience. Another way to put it is to
say that stereo is sound in depth, as TV is the visual in depth.

Perhaps it is not very contradictory that when a medium becomes a means of depth experience the old categories of 'classical' and 'popular' or of 'highbrow' and 'lowbrow' no longer obtain. Watching a blue-baby heart operation on TV is an experience that will fit none of the categories. When l.p. and hi-fi and stereo arrived, a depth approach to musical experience also came in. Everybody lost his inhibitions about 'highbrow', and the serious people lost their qualms about popular music and culture. Anything that is approached in depth acquires as much interest as the greatest matters. Because 'depth' means 'in interrelation', not 'in isolation'. Depth means insight, not point of view; and insight is a kind of mental involvement in process that makes the content of the item seem quite secondary. Consciousness itself is an inclusive process not at all dependent on content. Consciousness does not postulate consciousness of anything in particular.

With regard to jazz, l.p. brought many changes, such as the cult of 'real cool drool', because the greatly increased length of a single side of a disk meant that the jazz band could really have a long and casual chat among its instruments. The repertory of the 1920s was revived and given new depth and complexity by this new means. But the tape recorder in combination with l.p. revolutionized the repertory of classical music. Just as tape meant the new study of spoken rather than written languages, so it brought in the entire musical culture of many centuries and countries. Where before there had been a narrow selection from periods and composers, the tape recorder, combined with l.p., gave a full musical spectrum that made the sixteenth century as available as the nineteenth, and Chinese folk song as accessible as the Hungarian.

A brief summary of technological events relating to the phonograph might go this way:

The telegraph translated writing into sound, a fact directly related to the origin of both the telephone and phonograph. With the telegraph, the only walls left are the vernacular walls that the photograph and movie and wirephoto overleap so easily. The electrification of writing was almost as big a step into the nonvisual and auditory space as the later steps soon taken by telephone, radio, and TV.

The telephone: speech without walls.

The phonograph: music hall without walls.

The photograph: museum without walls.

The electric light: space without walls.

The movie, radio, and TV: classroom without walls.

Man the food-gatherer reappears incongruously as information-gatherer. In this role, electronic man is no less a nomad than his paleolithic ancestors.

UNDERSTANDING MEDIA

b. 1931

Jay Macpherson

JAY MACPHERSON, who was born in England, came to Newfoundland as a child during the Second World War and then to Ottawa. She was educated at Glebe Collegiate there and at Carleton College; she then did graduate work in English at Victoria College, University of Toronto, where she came under the influence of Northrop Frye. She is now Associate Professor of English at Victoria College. Her book *The Boatman* (1957) was one of the outstanding poetry publications of the 1950s and a winner of a Governor General's Award. The traditional verse forms of these short poems—in which there are echoes of ballads, carols, nursery rhymes, hymns etc.—and their simple language, metrical charm, and epigrammatic wit, are easy to enjoy. However, these simple-seeming poems, which are unified in an intricate sequence, lightly bear a whole cosmos of the poet's invention that is constructed from Biblical and classical allusions. All poets are interested in metaphor; many are also interested in the largest kind of metaphor, myth. The mythological aspect of Jay Macpherson's poetry is more diffi-

cult to enjoy without some knowledge of her literary sources, though Northrop Frye has said that one can get through most of the book if one knows who Adam and Eve and Noah were.

In an article on *The Boatman* ('The Third Eye', *Canadian Literature*, No. 3), James Reaney wrote: 'If anything is like anything (metaphor) it eventually is everything (myth) and is an anagogic figure similar to Miss Macpherson's.' Jay Macpherson's 'The Anagogic Man' is about Noah, whose head contains all creation and who represents 'the slumbering imagination of all life . . . that slowly through art and science rearranges the sun, moon, stars and figures of the gods until they are once more under human control. This Noah is the artist, a man who has brought and still brings all of society safely through the flood and tempest of a fallen world's whirlwind of atoms and deathwishes.' The next four poems are riddles whose answers are given in the titles. 'Very Sad Song' is one of a group of poems added to the second (paperback) edition of her book, called *The Boatman and Other Poems* (1968).

THE ANAGOGIC MAN

Noah walks with head bent down;
For between his nape and crown
He carries, balancing with care,
A golden bubble round and rare.

Its gently shimmering sides surround
All us and our worlds, and bound
Art and life, and wit and sense,
Innocence and experience.

Forbear to startle him, lest some
Poor soul to its destruction come,
Slipped out of mind and past recall
As if it never was at all.

O you that pass, if still he seems
One absent-minded or in dreams,
Consider that your senses keep
A death far deeper than his sleep.

Angel, declare: what sways when Noah nods?
The sun, the stars, the figures of the gods.

SUN AND MOON

A strong man, a fair woman,
Bound fast in love,
Parted by ordered heaven,
Punishment prove.

He suffers gnawing fires:
She in her frost
Beams in his sight, but dies
When he seems lost.

Not till the poles are joined
Shall the retreat
Of fierce brother from lost sister
End, and they meet.

EGG

Reader, in your hand you hold
A silver case, a box of gold.
I have no door, however small,
Unless you pierce my tender wall,
And there's no skill in healing then
Shall ever make me whole again.
Show pity, Reader, for my plight:
Let be, or else consume me quite.

BOOK

Dear Reader, not your fellow flesh and blood
—I cannot love like you, nor you like me—
But like yourself launched out upon the flood,
Poor vessel to endure so fierce a sea.

The water-beetle travelling dry and frail
On the stream's face is not more slight than I;
Nor more tremendous is the ancient whale
Who scans the ocean floor with horny eye.

Although by my creator's will I span
The air, the fire, the water and the land,
My volume is no burden to your hand.

I flourish in your sight and for your sake.
His servant, yet I grapple fast with man:
Grasped and devoured, I bless him. Reader, take.

READER

My old shape-changer, who will be
Now wild, now calm, now bound, now free,
Now like a sun, and now a storm,
Now fish, now flesh, now cold, now warm,
Mercurial, dull—but sly enough
To slip my hand and wriggle off—,
I have you fast and will not let you go:
Your nature and your name I know.

VERY SAD SONG

I cannot claim I rise to weep,
But oh, the burden of my day
Would make an angel turn away:
I'd rather be in bed asleep.

The hurt you gave I inward keep,
Hard Love! remembering whose it is.
But rest both harm and healing his,
I'd rather be in bed asleep.

Lord, take no care my soul to keep,
For I don't need it when I sleep;
And though the host of heaven weep,
I'd rather be in bed asleep.

b. 1922

Eli Mandel

ELI MANDEL is an admired poet, an influential anthologist and critic of Canadian writing, and a popular teacher. He was born in Estevan, Sask., and studied at the University of Saskatchewan until he left to serve in the Canadian Army Medical Corps in the Second World War. He obtained his Ph.D. from the University of Toronto and began his teaching career at the Collège Militaire Royal de Saint-Jean not far from Montreal. He has also taught at the University of Alberta in Edmonton and is now Professor of Humanities at York University in Toronto. In 1956 he was published in the anthology *Trio*, with the poets Phyllis Webb and Gael Turnbull. His first collection of his own, *Fuseli Poems*, appeared in 1960. It was followed by *Black and Secret Man* (1964) and *An Idiot Joy* (1967), which won a Governor General's Award. He has also published *Criticism: The Silent-Speaking Word* (1967), a series of CBC broadcasts, and a study of the poetry of Irving Layton (Forum House, 1969). He has edited several anthologies, including *Five Modern Canadian Poets* (1970), *Eight More Canadian Poets* (1972), *Poets of Contemporary Canada, 1960-1970* (1972) in the New Canadian Library, and *Contexts of Canadian Criticism* (1971).

Mandel's early writing, reflected in his *Fuseli Poems*—named after a Swiss-British painter who was a friend of William Blake—announced an exciting poet who was interested in drawing on classical mythology to explore, among other things, suffering and violence; his later poems are freer and much more personal explorations of these same things. Mandel has said that *Black and Secret Man* 'is about objects of terror, sinister events, ominous places and whatever speaks out of darkness. It was written so that I could confront and recognize whatever is dark in human nature, and to discover how much of it is a reflection of self.' Professor Hugh MacCallum, in reviewing Mandel's third book, *An Idiot Joy*, wrote of these poems: 'They are packed with explosive images, sinister portraits, and frenzied voices. Fire is a recurrent image, charring landscapes and even figures, while drownings, suicides, murders, and madness are frequent. Several poems achieve a tone of barely suppressed hysteria, and a number of others sound like last communiqués from the verge of destruction. Communication, in fact, is a central theme in the collection. In 'Houdini', for example, the escape artist is presented as an analogue of the poet: he risks his life in deep pools to prove that he can manipulate the chains and manacles which are the words and metaphors of his craft.'

'Houdini', inspired by the famous magician and escape artist (1874-1926), is one of Mandel's completely successful poems; another is 'Anniversary of the Liberation of Auschwitz' (the Nazi extermination camp in Poland), written after his third book was published. A powerful revelation of the effects of psychic shock on the contemplation of horror, it blazes into a hysterical though eloquent incoherence of words and phrases and flashing scenes, then subsides with a final searing image.

There is an essay by John Ower on Mandel's poetry in Issue 42 of *Canadian Literature* (Autumn 1969).

HOUDINI

I suspect he knew that trunks are metaphors,
could distinguish between the finest rhythms
unrolled on rope or singing in a chain
and knew the metrics of the deepest pools

I think of him listening to the words
spoken by manacles, cells, handcuffs,
chests, hampers, roll-top desks, vaults,
especially the deep words spoken by coffins

escape, escape: quaint Harry in his suit
his chains, his desk, attached to all attachments
how he'd sweat in that precise struggle
with those binding words, wrapped around him
like that mannered style, his formal suit

and spoken when? by whom? What thing first said
'there's no way out?'; so that he'd free himself,
leap, squirm, no matter how, to chain himself again,
once more jump out of the deep alive
with all his chains singing around his feet
like the bound crowds who sigh, who sigh.

ON THE 25TH ANNIVERSARY OF THE
LIBERATION OF AUSCHWITZ:
MEMORIAL SERVICES, TORONTO, YMHA,
BLOOR & SPADINA, JANUARY 25, 1970

the name is hard
a German sound made out of
the gut guttural throat
y scream yell   ing   open
voice mouth growl
                    and sweat

'the only way out of Auschwitz
is through the chimneys'
                    of course
that's second hand   that's told
again Sigmund Sherwood (Sobolewski)
twisting himself into that sentence
before us on the platform

                        the poem
shaping itself late in the after
noon later than it would be:

Pendericki's 'Wrath of God'
moaning electronic Polish theatric
the screen silent
                    framed by the name
looking away from/ pretending not there
no   name   no not   name   no

            Auschwitz
    in   GOTHIC   lettering
                        the hall
a parody a reminiscence a nasty memory
the Orpheum in Estevan before Buck Jones
the Capital in Regina before Tom Mix
waiting for the guns
waiting for the cowboy killers
one two three
                Legionnaires
Polish ex-prisoners Association
Legions
            their medals their flags

so the procession, the poem gradually
insistent beginning to shape itself
with the others
                 walked with them
into the YMHA Bloor & Spadina
thinking apocalypse shame degradation
thinking bones and bodies melting
thickening thinning melting bones and bodies
thinking not mine/ speak clearly
the poet's words/ Yevtyshenko at Baba-Yar

there   this January   snow
heavy wet   the wind   heavy wet
the street grey white slush melted concrete
bones and bodies melting slush
                          saw
with the others
               the prisoner
in the YMHA hall Bloor & Spadina
arms wax stiff body stiff unnatural
coloured face blank eyes
                     walked
with the others toward the screen
toward the pictures
               SLIDES
       this is mother
       this is father
       this is
           the one who is
waving her arms like that
is the one who
           like
I mean running with her breasts bound
ing
    running
         with her hands here and there
with her here and
           there
hands
     that   that is
the poem becoming the body
becoming the faint hunger
ing body
      prowling
         through

words the words words the words
opening   mouths   ovens
the generals smiling saluting
in their mythic uniforms god-like
generals uniforms with the black leather
with the straps and intricate leather
the phylacteries the prayer shawl
corsets and the boots and the leather straps
and the shining faces of the generals in their boots
and their stiff wax bodies their unnatural faces
and their blank eyes and their hands their stiff hands
and the generals in their straps and wax and stiff
staying standing
                    melting bodies and thickening
                      quick flesh on flesh handling
                      hands
      the poem flickers, fades
the four Yarzeit candles guttering   one
      each four million lights dim
my words drift
                  smoke from chimneys and ovens
       a bad picture, the power failing
    pianist clattering on and over and through
the long Saturday afternoon in the Orpheum
        while the whitehatted star spangled cowboys
           shot the dark men and shot the dark men
           and we threw popcorn balls and grabbed
           each other and cheered:
                        me jewboy yelling
for the shot town and the falling men
         and the lights come on
                      and

      with the others
standing in silence

      the gothic word hangs
      over us on a shroud-white screen

and we drift away
        to ourselves
         to the late Sunday *Times*

        the wet snow
        the city

        a body melting

Marie de L'Incarnation

Born Marie Guyart in Tours, France, MARIE DE L'INCARNATION married at eighteen, bore a son, and was widowed six months later after two years of marriage. She worked in the home of her sister and then managed her brother-in-law's carrier business until she could no longer resist her overpowering need, which was supported by mystical experiences, to renounce secular life and enter a convent, though this meant giving up her son. In 1633 she became an Ursuline nun, with the name in religion of Marie de l'Incarnation. (Her painful final separation from her son is described in her letter on page 333.) In 1639, with Madame de la Peltrie and two Ursuline nuns, she went to Quebec and founded a monastery and boarding school for the daughters of the settlers and for Indian girls. Mère Marie alternated as superior until her death. She has been venerated by the Church, and her monastery and school are still standing, in the Upper Town of Quebec.

Though she was cloistered, all the leading people of the colony visited Mère Marie and kept her informed about events that took place outside the convent walls. These she recorded in some twenty thousand letters to her son and others, written over thirty years. (Her son, Claude Martin, became a Jesuit priest and published a biography of his mother and an edition of 221 of her letters.) A selection of Mère Marie's published letters has been translated and edited by Joyce Marshall under the title *Word from New France: The Selected Letters of Marie de l'Incarnation* (1967); it is available in paperback.

The historical significance of Mère Marie's letters has long been recognized by scholars, but it is mainly for literary reasons that they have enduring value. Her engrossing accounts of life in New France are written with great narrative skill and descriptive power.

THE EARTHQUAKE

TO HER SON
Quebec, 20 AUGUST 1663

My very dear son:
I have waited to give you an account separately of the earthquake this year in our New France, which was so prodigious, so violent, and so terrifying that I have no words strong enough to describe it and even fear lest what I say shall be deemed incredible and fabulous.

On the 3rd day of February of this year 1663 a woman Savage, but a very good and very excellent Christian, wakening in her cabin while all the others slept, heard a distinct and articulated voice that said to her, 'In two days, very astonishing and marvellous things will come to pass.' And the next day, while she was in the forest with her sister, cutting her daily provision of wood, she distinctly heard the same voice, which said, 'To-morrow, between five and six o'clock in the evening, the earth will be shaken and will tremble in an astonishing way.'

She reported what she had heard to the others in her cabin, who received it with indifference as being a dream or the work of her imagination. The weather was meanwhile quite calm that day, and even more so the day following.

On the fifth day, the feast of St Agatha, Virgin and Martyr, at about half past five in the evening, a person of proven virtue [Mother Marie-Catherine de Saint-Augustin], who has frequent communication with God, saw that he was extremely provoked against the sins committed in this country and felt at the same time disposed to ask him to deal with these sinners as they deserved. While she was offering her prayers for this to divine Majesty, and also for souls in mortal sin, that his justice be not without mercy, also beseeching the martyrs of Japan, whose feast was being held that day, to consent to make application for this as would be most suitable to God's glory, she had a presentiment—or rather an infallible conviction—that God was ready to punish the country for the sins committed here, especially the contempt for the ordinances of the Church.

She could not refrain from desiring this chastisement, whatever it might be, since it was fixed in God's decree, though she had no indication of what it would be. Forthwith, and a little before the earthquake came to pass, she saw four furious and enraged demons at the four corners of Quebec, shaking the earth with such violence it was evident they wished to turn it right over. And indeed they would have succeeded in this if a personage of wondrous beauty and delightful majesty, whom she saw in the midst of them, giving vein to their fury from time to time, had not restrained them just when they were on the point of destroying everything.

She heard the voices of these demons saying, 'Now many people are frightened. There will be many conversions, we know, but that will last but a little time. We will find ways to get the world back for ourselves. Meanwhile let us continue to shake it and do our best to turn everything over.'

The weather was very calm and serene and the vision still had not passed when a sound of terrifying rumbling was heard in the distance, as if a great many carriages were speeding wildly over the cobblestones. This noise had scarcely caught the attention than there was heard under the earth and on the earth and from all sides what seemed a horrifying confusion of waves and billows. There was a sound like hail on the roofs, in the granaries, and in the rooms. It seemed as if the marble of which the foundation of this country is almost entirely composed and our houses are built were about to open and break into pieces to gulp us down.

Thick dust flew from all sides. Doors opened of themselves. Others, which were open, closed. The bells of all our churches and the chimes of our clocks pealed quite alone, and steeples and houses shook like trees in the wind—all this in a horrible confusion of overturning furniture, falling stones, parting floors, and splitting walls. Amidst all this the domestic animals were heard howling. Some ran out of their houses; others ran in. In a word, we were all so frightened we believed it was the eve of Judgement, since all the portents were to be seen.

So unexpected a calamity, when the young people were preparing to spend the carnival season in excesses, was a clap of thunder on everyone's head, they expecting nothing less. It was rather a clap of God's mercy upon the whole country, as was seen by its results. . . . From the first tremor consternation was universal. And as no-one knew what it was, some cried 'Fire!', thinking it was a conflagration; others ran for water to extinguish it; others snatched up their arms, believing it was an army of Iroquois. But as it was none of these things, everyone strove to be first out of the houses, which seemed on the point of falling down.

No greater safety was to be found without than within, for we at once realized by the movement of the earth, which trembled under our feet like agitated waves under a shallop, that it was an earthquake. Some hugged the trees, which clashed together, causing them no less horror than the houses they had left; others clung to stumps, the movements of which struck them roughly in the chest.

The Savages, who were extremely frightened, said the trees had beaten them. Several among them said they were demons God was using to chastise them because of the excesses they had committed while drinking the brandy that the wicked French had given them. Some other less-instructed Savages, who had come to hunt in these regions, said it was the souls of their ancestors, who wished to return to their former dwelling. Possessed by this error, they took their guns and shot into the air at what they said was a band of passing spirits. But finally our habitants and our Savages, finding no more refuge on the ground than in the houses, grew weak with fear and, taking better counsel, went into the churches to have the consolation of perishing there after they had made their confession.

When this first tremor, which lasted more than half an hour, had passed, we began to breathe once more; but this was for only a little while, for at about eight o'clock in the evening the shaking began again and in the space of an hour was twice repeated. We said matins in the choir, reciting it partly on our knees in a humbled spirit, surrendering ourselves to the sovereign power of God. There were thirty-two new earthquakes that night, as I was told by a person that counted them. I, however, counted only six because certain of them were weak and almost imperceptible. But at about three o'clock there was one that was very violent and lasted for a long time.

These tremors continued for the space of seven months, though irregularly. Some were frequent but weak; others were rarer but strong and violent. So, since the evil only left us in order to pounce upon us with greater strength, we had scarcely time to reflect upon the misfortune that threatened us when it suddenly surprised us, sometimes during the day but more often during the night.

If the earth gave us reason for alarm, heaven did no less so—both by the howls and shrieking we heard resounding in the air and by distinct and frightening voices. Some said, 'Alas!' Others said, 'Let us go! Let us go!' and others, 'Let us stop up the rivers!' The sounds were heard sometimes of bells, sometimes of cannon, sometimes of thunder. We saw fires, torches, and flaming globes, which sometimes fell to the earth and sometimes dissolved in the air. . . .

* * *

I close this account on the 20th of the same month [August], not knowing where all this commotion will end, for the earthquakes still continue. But the wondrous thing is that amidst so great and universal a wreckage, no-one has perished or even been injured. This is a quite visible sign of God's protection of his people, which gives us just cause to believe that he is angry with us only to save us. And we hope he will take his glory from our fears, by the conversion of so many souls that had slept in their sins and could not waken from their sleep by the movements of interior grace alone.

MEMORIES OF HER SON

TO HER SON
Quebec, 30 JULY 1669

My very dear son:
A ship from France arrived in our port towards the end of June, and since then none has appeared. The one that came brought us your news, which gave me cause to praise God for his goodness to you and to me. The greatest joy I have in this world is to reflect upon this goodness, and I see that your own reflection upon what you have experienced of it moves you keenly and that this is useful to you.

Are you not well pleased, my very dear son, that I abandoned you to his holy guidance by quitting you for his love? Have you not obtained a boon thereby that cannot be appraised? Know yet once again that, as I separated from you, I made myself die while yet alive, and that the Spirit of God, which was inexorable towards the tenderness I felt for you, would give me no repose until I had done so. I had to pass through this and obey him without argument, for he will brook none in the execution of his absolute will. Nature, which does not yield so soon when its interests are engaged, especially when there is question of a mother's obligation to a son, could not bring itself to do it. It seemed to me that, if I left you so young, you would not be reared in the fear of God and might fall into some evil hands, or even into some conduct in which you would be in danger of being lost, and that I should be thus deprived of a son I had wished to raise but for God's service, remaining in the world with him until he was able to enter some religion, which was the end to which I had destined him.

The divine Spirit, which saw my struggles, was pitiless to my feelings, saying in the depths of my heart, 'Quick, quick, it is time, you must no longer delay, there is no more for you in the world.' Then it opened the door to religion for me, its voice continuing to urge me with a holy impetuosity, which gave me no rest either by day or by night. It arranged my affairs and placed my inclinations towards religion in so inviting a manner that everything held out its arms to me, so that had I been the first person in the world with all these boons I could not have found more goodwill.

Dom Raymond did everything needed with my sister, and himself led me where God desired that I should be. You came with me and, as I left you, it seemed to me that my soul was being separated from my body with utmost pain. And remember that from the age of fourteen I had had a very strong vocation for religion, which was not fulfilled because others did not share my desire; but since I reached the age of nineteen or twenty, my spirit had been in religion and only my body in the world, so that I might rear you till the moment of the fulfilment of God's will for you and for me.

After I had entered and I saw you come to weep in our parlour and at the grille of our choir, and when you passed part of your body through the communion rail, and when, chancing to see the convent door left open by workmen, you came into our court and, being told not to do this, walked backwards to discover whether you might be able to see me, some of my sister novices wept and said that I was very cruel not to weep and that I did not even look at you. But alas, the good Sisters did not see the anguish my heart felt for you, any more than they saw the fidelity I wished to render to the holy will of God.

The struggle commenced again when you came weeping to the grille to say your mother must be given back to you or you must be allowed to come in to be a religious with her. But the worst was when a band of young children of your age appeared with you outside the window of our refectory crying that I must be given back to you, and your voice rose clearer than the others to say that your mother must be given back to you and that you intended to have her.

The Community, which saw all this, was keenly touched by sorrow and compassion; and, although no-one gave me any indication of being vexed by your cries, I believed that this was a thing that could not long be endured and that I should be sent back into the world to take care of you. At the thanksgiving grace, when I was going back up to the noviciate, the Spirit of God said in my heart that I should not be afflicted by all this and that he would take care of you. These divine promises spread calm throughout my being and made me experience that *the words of Our Lord are spirit and life* and that he was faithful to his promises, that *heaven and earth shall pass away before a single one of his words shall be without effect* [sic] so that, if everyone on earth had told me the contrary to what that interior speech had said, I should not have believed it.

After that time I felt no more grief; my spirit and my heart enjoyed so sweet a peace in the certainty I felt that God's promises would be accomplished in you that I saw all things done for your advantage and means to advance you in the path I had desired for your education. Very soon afterwards you were sent to Rennes to continue your studies, then to Orléans, divine Goodness having given me access to the Reverend Jesuit Fathers, who took care of you. You know the help of God in this matter. Finally, my very dear son, here you are as well as me, in the experience of the infinite mercies of so good a Father. Let us leave all to him; we shall see many things if we are faithful to him. Continue to pray for me.

WORD FROM NEW FRANCE
Translated by Joyce Marshall

b. 1928

Gaston Miron

GASTON MIRON, a major figure in Québec poetry, has been described by André Vachon as 'a man of beginnings, the first bard of the Québécois nation'. He was born at Saint-Agathe, Qué., in the Laurentians, and attended school there. He wrote his first poem when he was fourteen and for the next six or seven years, with the encouragement of a teacher, continued to write conventional poetry. In 1947 he arrived in Montreal. He took various jobs, studied social sciences in the evening at the Université de Montréal, and became friendly with other young poets, including Olivier Marchand. In 1953 they and four others founded Editions de l'Hexagone, whose first publication was a poetry collection, *Deux Sangs*, which Miron co-authored with Marchand. Miron was made director of Hexagone and it embarked on an influential program of poetry publishing, bringing out the work of many young poets who are now well known, and helping to transform the literary scene in Québec. It gave it among other things a political tone. Miron became active in politics around this time and in 1957 and 1958

ran unsuccessfully as an NDP candidate in Outrement. In the 1960s he became a militant separatist and was active in several separatist organizations, including the Rassemblement pour l'Indépendence nationale (RIN); he was imprisoned during the crisis of October 1970. Miron has worked for Radio-Canada, has written a column for *Magazine Maclean*, and is now employed by the Conseil Supérieure du Livre.

Until the publication in 1970 of *L'Homme rapaillé*, a collection of fifty-seven poems and some prose articles, the poetry Miron wrote after 1953 appeared in print only in periodicals, including the famous Marxist/separatist journal of political and literary writing, *Parti Pris* (1963-8). Miron once wrote that he tried in his poetry to keep equidistant from both regionalism and abstract universality—'the two curses that have lain heavily on our literature'. He is attracted to concrete, everyday things in sensitive nature poems, in love poems where the loved one is both human and the land of Québec, and in poems of sadness, longing, hope, and joy that are emotionally charged separatist lyrics. As engaging and communicative in public readings as in private ones, he attracted a large following for himself *and* his poetry. In a passage from *White Niggers of America* that appears in this anthology (pages 495-8), Pierre Vallières recalls the poet as 'a wild, loving sorrow that roamed the streets of Montreal, arms outstretched to embrace men and, at the same time, to take them with him, to stir them.' Vallières describes at length the strong influence Miron had on him—and presumably on many other Québécois—in introducing him not only to contemporary poetry but to the idea of political engagement. In prison, where he wrote his book, Val-lières exclaims 'How I would love to read and reread those long, sorrowful songs of our alienation and our will to live,' referring to a sequence of poems called 'La Vie agonique' from which 'Héritage de la tristesse' and 'October' (pp. 337-8) are taken. About Miron's poetry Vallières says: 'No Québécois poet describes *us* with so much authenticity.'

Issue 5 of *Ellipse* (Autumn 1970), a magazine that presents writers in translation, is devoted partly to Gaston Miron and contains an essay on him by André Vachon. There is also a brief selection of his poems in *The Poetry of French Canada in Translation* (1970) edited by John Glassco.

MY SAD ONE AND SERENE

My sad one and serene
my distantly withdrawn stream
my poetry with the snowblind eyes
every morning you get up at five
in my city and the others with you
drawn by the hand to survive
you are the image of our daily grind
my enigma of the far hillside
you sweep us from one world to the other
for you also have a lover's arms
don't be afraid little one with us
we will protect you with our murky purity
with our bodies beautifully redeemed
and Olivier loves you
friend of days for which we still must hope
even when the bitter time is past
when all is but a vague memento on the fringe of sky
you will revive little one
among the cinders
all along the line
of the new stations of our modest destiny
my poetry of the battered heart
my poetry of the rattling stones

D.G.JONES *(tr)*

HÉRITAGE DE LA TRISTESSE

Sad and confused among the fallen stars
pale, silent, nowhere and afraid, a vast phantom
here is this land alone with winds and rocks
a land forever lost to its natal sun
a beautiful body drowned in mindless sleep
like water lost in a barren thirst of gravel

I see it bridled by chances and tomorrows
showing its face in the dreams of anguished men
whenever it breathes in wastes and undergrowth of bracken
whenever it burns, in poplars old in years and neglect,
the useless leaf-green of its abortive love
or whenever a will to being sleeps in the sail of its heart

bowed down, it awaits it knows not what redemption
among these landscapes walking through its stillness
among these rags of silence with eyes of the dying
and always this ruined smile of a poor degraded future
always this hacking at the stands of darkness
and horizons fading in a drift of promises

despoiled, its only hope is a vacant lot's
cold of cane talking with cold of bone
unease of the rust, the quick, the nerves, the nude
and in its livid back the blows of heated knives
it looks at you, worked out, from the depth of its quarries
and out of the tunnels of its abstraction where one day
it surrendered and lost forever the memory of man

winds that shuffle the lots of precedence by night
winds of concourse, winds with solar eyes
telluric winds, winds of the soul, universal winds
come couple, o winds, and with your river arms
embrace this face of a ruined people, give it the warmth
and the abundant light that rings the wake of swallows

FRED COGSWELL (*tr*)

OCTOBER

The man of our time has a face of flagellation
and you, Land of Quebec, Mother Courage
you are big
with our sooty sorrowful dreams
and an endless drain of bodies and souls

I was born your son
in your worn-out mountains of the north
I ache and suffer
bitten by that birth
yet in my arms my youth is glowing

here are my knees
may our world forgive us
we have allowed our fathers to be humbled in spirit
we have allowed the light of the word to be debased
to the shame and self-contempt of our brothers
we could not bind the roots of our suffering
into the universal sorrow of each degraded man

I go to join the burning company
whose struggle shares and breaks the bread of the common lot
in the quicksands of a common grief

we will make you, Land of Quebec
a bed of resurrections
and in the myriad lightnings of our transformations
in this leaven of ours from which the future is rising
in our uncompromising will
men will hear your pulse beating in history
this is ourselves rippling in the autumn of October
this is the russet sound of deer in the light
the future free and easy

FRED COGSWELL (*tr*)

Susanna Moodie

SUSANNA MOODIE is best known for *Roughing It in the Bush* (1852), which describes her hardships as a pioneer in Upper Canada (Ontario). Of all the many books written about pioneering in Canada it is probably the most popular. Mrs Moodie recounts her experiences in the form of anecdotes and character sketches that partake a little of the qualities of fiction in their dramatic shape and effective use of dialogue; in addition the character of the outspoken author, with her divided feelings about Canada and her obsessions, comes through as vividly and interestingly as the events she writes about.

Mrs Moodie was born in Bungay, Suffolk, Eng., and wrote a novel, *Spartacus: A Roman Story*, before emigrating in 1832 to farmland near Cobourg with her husband J.W.D. Moodie. Two years later they cleared a grant of land near Peterborough to be closer to her sister, Catharine Parr Traill, and her brother, Samuel Strickland. (Mrs Traill was the author of an earlier celebrated pioneer book, *The Backwoods of Canada* (1836). Strickland wrote *Twenty-seven years in Canada West* (1853).) After Mr Moodie was appointed sheriff for Hastings County, they moved to Belleville in 1840; when her husband died in 1869, Mrs Moodie went to Toronto where she remained. From 1839 to 1851 she contributed serial novels, short stories, and poetry to the *Literary Garland*, a Canadian periodical that flourished from 1838 to 1851, in which some of the sketches in *Roughing It* first appeared. Her serial novels written for the *Literary Garland* were later published in book form: *Mark Hurdlestone, the Gold Worshiper* (1853) and *The Moncktons* (1856).

As a refined and conventional gentlewoman, Mrs Moodie was unprepared for the hardships and cultural privations she experienced in her early years in Canada, or for the disrespectful, sometimes impudent treatment she received from poor and uneducated settlers who could not be made to feel that they were Mrs Moodie's 'inferiors'. She underwent a kind of culture shock. Her disenchantment with the backwoods of Canada is summed up at the end of her book, when she says:

'To the poor, industrious working man it presents many advantages; to the poor gentleman, *none!*' She goes on to write: 'If these sketches should prove the means of deterring one family from sinking their property, and shipwrecking all their hopes, by going to reside in the backwoods of Canada, I shall consider myself amply repaid for revealing the secrets of the prison-house, and feel that I have not toiled and suffered in the wilderness in vain.' However, in another less interesting book, *Life in the Clearing versus the Bush* (1853), written after she moved to Belleville and life was no longer difficult, her views had changed. They became more democratic and she grew to respect the lack of convention and class prejudice in Canadian society. She found at last happiness and contentment here and wrote enthusiastically of the country's prospects.

Roughing It in the Bush and *Life in the Clearing* are both available in paperback in the New Canadian Library. Margaret Atwood's *The Journals of Susanna Moodie* is a memorable sequence of poems that grew out of her reading these two books, of which Miss Atwood says in an 'Afterword': 'The prose was discursive and ornamental and the books had little shape: they were collections of anecdotes. The only thing that held them together was the personality of Mrs Moodie, and what struck me most about this personality was the way in which it reflects many of the obsessions still with us.' Three poems from this collection appear on pages 10-12.

BRIAN THE STILL-HUNTER

It was early day. I was alone in the old shanty preparing breakfast, and now and then stirring the cradle with my foot, when a tall, thin, middle-aged man walked into the house, followed by two large, strong dogs.

Placing the rifle he had carried on his shoulder in a corner of the room, he advanced to the hearth, and without speaking, or seemingly looking at me, lighted his pipe and commenced smoking. The dogs, after growling and snapping at the cat, who had not given the strangers a very courteous reception, sat down on the hearthstone on either side of their taciturn master, eyeing him from time to time, as if long habit had made them understand all his motions. There was a great contrast between the dogs. The one was a brindled bull-dog of the largest size, a most formidable and powerful brute; the other a staghound, tawny, deep-chested, and strong-limbed. I regarded the man and his hairy companions with silent curiosity.

He was between forty and fifty years of age; his head, nearly bald, was studded at the sides with strong, coarse, black curling hair. His features were high, his complexion brightly dark, and his eyes, in size, shape, and colour, greatly resembled the eyes of a hawk. The face itself was sorrowful and taciturn; and his thin, compressed lips looked as if they were not much accustomed to smile, or often to unclose to hold social communion with anyone. He stood at the side of the huge hearth, silently smoking, his eyes bent on the fire, and now and then he patted the heads of his dogs, reproving their exuberant expressions of attachment with—'Down, Music! Down, Chance!'

'A cold, clear morning,' said I in order to attract his attention and draw him into conversation.

A nod, without raising his head or withdrawing his eyes from the fire, was his only answer; and, turning from my unsociable guest, I took up the baby, who just then awoke, sat down on a low stool by the table, and began feeding her. During this operation, I once or twice caught the stranger's hawk-eye fixed upon me and the child, but word spoke he none; and presently, after whistling to his dogs, he resumed his gun, and strode out.

When Moodie and Monaghan came in to breakfast, I told them what a strange visitor I had had; and Moodie laughed at my vain attempt to induce him to talk.

'He is a strange being,' I said. 'I must find out who and what he is.'

In the afternoon an old soldier, called Layton, who had served during the American war and got a grant of land about a mile in the rear of our location, came in to trade for a cow. Now this Layton was a perfect ruffian, a man whom no one liked and whom all feared. He was a deep drinker, a great swearer—in short, a perfect reprobate, who never cultivated his land but went jobbing about from farm to farm, trading horses and cattle and cheating in a pettifogging way. Uncle Joe had employed him to sell Moodie a young heifer and he had brought her over for him to look at. When he came in to be paid, I described the stranger of the morning, and as I knew that he was familiar with everyone in the neighbourhood, I asked if he knew him.

'No one should know him better than myself,' he said. ''Tis old Brian B—, the still-hunter, and a near neighbour of your'n. A sour, morose, queer chap he is, and as mad as a March hare! He's from Lancashire in England, and came to this country some twenty years ago with his wife, who was a pretty young lass in those days, and slim enough then, though she's so awfully fleshy now. He had lots of money, too, and he bought four hundred acres of land just at the corner of the concession line where it meets the main road. And excellent land it is; and a better farmer, while he stuck to his business, never went into the bush, for it was all bush here then. He was a dashing, handsome fellow, too, and did not hoard the money either; he loved his pipe and his pot too well; and at last he left off farming and gave himself to them altogether. Many a jolly booze he and I have had, I can tell you. Brian was an awful passionate man, and when the liquor was in and the wit was out, as savage and as quarrelsome as a bear. At such times there was no one but Ned Layton dared go near him. We once had a pitched battle, in which I was conqueror; and ever arter he yielded a sort of sulky obedience to all I said to him. Arter being on the spree for a week or two, he would take fits of remorse and return home to his wife, would fall down at her knees and ask her forgiveness and cry like a child. At other times he would hide himself up in the woods and steal home at night and get what he wanted out of the pantry without speaking a word to anyone. He went on with these pranks for some years, till he took a fit of the blue devils.

' "Come away, Ned, to the—lake, with me," said he. "I am weary of my life and I want a change."

' "Shall we take the fishing-tackle?" says I. "The black bass are in prime season, and F— will lend us the old canoe. He's got some capital rum up from Kingston. We'll fish all day and have a spree at night."

' "It's not to fish I'm going," says he.

' "To shoot, then? I've bought Rockwood's new rifle."

' "It's neither to fish nor to shoot, Ned. It's a new game I'm going to try, so come along."

'Well, to the—lake we went. The day was very hot and our path lay through the woods and over those scorching plains for eight long miles. I thought I should have dropped by the way, but during our long walk my companion never opened his lips. He strode on before me, at a half-run, never once turning his head.

' "The man must be the devil?" says I, "and accustomed to a warmer place, or he must feel this. Hollo Brian! Stop there! Do you mean to kill me?"

' "Take it easy," says he; "you'll see another day arter this—I've business on hand and cannot wait."

'Well, on we went, at the same awful rate, and it was mid-day when we got to the little tavern on the lake shore, kept by one F—, who had a boat for the convenience of strangers who came to visit the place. Here we got our dinner and a glass of rum to wash it down. But Brian was moody, and to all my jokes he only returned a sort of grunt; and while I was talking with F—, he steps out and a few minutes arter we saw him crossing the lake in the old canoe.

' "What's the matter with Brian?" says F—. "All does not seem right with him, Ned. You had better take the boat and look arter him."

' "Pooh!" says I; "he's often so, and grows so glum nowadays that I will cut his acquaintance altogether if he does not improve."

' "He drinks awful hard," says F—. "Maybe he's got a fit of the delirium-tremulous. There is no telling what he may be up to at this minute."

'My mind misgave me too, so I e'en takes the oars and pushes out, right upon Brian's track. And by the Lord Harry, if I did not find him, upon my landing on the opposite shore, lying wallowing in his blood with his throat cut! "Is that you Brian?" says I, giving him a kick with my foot to see if he was alive or dead. "What upon earth tempted you to play me and F— such a dirty, mean trick as to go and stick yourself like a pig, bringing such a discredit upon the house? And you so far from home and those who should nurse you."

'I was so mad with him, that—saving your presence, ma'am—I swore awfully and called him names that would be ondacent to repeat here. But he only answered with groans and a horrid gurgling in his throat. "It's a choking you are," said I. "But you shan't have your own way and die so easily either if I can punish you by keeping you alive." So I just turned him upon his stomach, with his head down the steep bank. But he still kept choking and growing black in the face.'

Layton then detailed some particulars of his surgical practice which it is not necessary to repeat. He continued:

'I bound up his throat with my handkerchief and took him neck and heels and threw him into the bottom of the boat. Presently he came to himself a little and sat up in the boat, and—would you believe it?—made several attempts to throw himself into the water. "This will not do," says I. "You've done mischief enough already by cutting your weasand! If you dare to try that again, I will kill you with the oar." I held it up to threaten him; he was scared and lay down as quiet as a lamb. I put my foot upon his breast. "Lie still now or you'll catch it!" He looked piteously at me. He could not speak, but his eyes seemed to say, "Have pity upon me, Ned; don't kill me."

'Yes, ma'am, this man who had just cut his throat and twice arter that had tried to drown himself was afraid that I should knock him on the head and kill him. Ha! Ha! I never shall forget the work that F— and I had with him arter I got him up to the house.

'The doctor came and sewed up his throat and his wife—poor crittur!—came to nurse him. Bad as he was, she was mortal fond of him. He lay there, sick and unable to leave his bed, for three months, and did nothing but pray to God to forgive him for he thought the devil would surely have him for cutting his own throat. And when he got about again, which is now twelve years ago, he left off drinking entirely and wanders about the woods with his dogs, hunting. He seldom speaks to anyone, and his wife's brother carries on the farm for the family. He is so shy of strangers that 'tis a wonder he came in here. The old wives are afraid of him, but you need not heed him. His troubles are to himself—he harms no one.'

Layton departed and left me brooding over the sad tale, which he had told in such an absurd and jesting manner. It was evident from the account he had given of Brian's attempt at suicide that the hapless hunter was not wholly answerable for his conduct—that he was a harmless maniac.

The next morning, at the very same hour, Brian again made his appearance; but instead of the rifle across his shoulder, a large stone jar occupied the place, suspended by a stout leather thong. Without saying a word, but with a truly benevolent smile that flitted slowly over his stern features and lighted them up like a sunbeam breaking from beneath a stormy cloud, he advanced to the table, and, unslinging the jar, set it down before me, and in a low and gruff, but by no means an unfriendly, voice, said, 'Milk, for the child,' and vanished.

'How good it was of him! How kind!' I exclaimed as I poured the precious gift of four quarts of pure new milk out into a deep pan. I had not asked him—had never said that the poor weanling wanted milk. It was the courtesy of a gentleman—of a man of benevolence and refinement.

For weeks did my strange, silent friend steal in, take up the empty jar, and supply its place with another replenished with milk. The baby knew his step and would hold out her hands to him and cry 'Milk!' and Brian would stoop down and kiss her and his two great dogs lick her face.

'Have you any children, Mr B—?'

'Yes, five; but none like this.'

'My little girl is greatly indebted to you for your kindness.'

'She's welcome or she would not get it. You are strangers, but I like you all. You look kind and I would like to know more about you.'

Moodie shook hands with the old hunter and assured him that we should always be glad to see him. After this invitation, Brian became a frequent guest. He would sit and listen with delight to Moodie while he described to him elephant-hunting at the Cape, grasping his rifle in a determined manner and whistling an encouraging air to his dogs. I asked him one evening what made him so fond of hunting.

' 'Tis the excitement,' he said; 'it drowns thought and I love to be alone. I am sorry for the creatures, too, for they are free and happy; yet I am led by an instinct I cannot restrain to kill them. Sometimes the sight of their dying agonies recalls painful feelings, and then I lay aside the gun and do not hunt for days. But 'tis fine to be alone with God in the great woods— to watch the sunbeams stealing through the thick branches, the blue sky breaking in upon you in patches, and to know that all is bright and shiny above you, in spite of the gloom that surrounds you.'

After a long pause, he continued, with much solemn feeling in his look and tone:

'I lived a life of folly for years, for I was respectably born and educated and had seen something of the world—perhaps more than was good —before I left home for the woods; and from the teaching I had received from kind relatives and parents I should have known how to have conducted myself better. But, madam, if we associate long with the depraved and ignorant, we learn to become even worse than they. I felt deeply my degradation—felt that I had become the slave to low vice; and, in order to emancipate myself from the hateful tyranny of evil passions, I did a very rash and foolish thing. I need not mention the manner in which I transgressed God's holy laws; all the neighbours know it and must have told you long ago. I could have borne reproof, but they turned my sorrow into indecent jests, and, unable to bear their coase ridicule, I made companions of my dogs and gun and went forth into the wilderness. Hunting became a habit. I could no longer live without it, and it supplies the stimulant which I lost when I renounced the cursed whisky-bottle.

'I remember the first hunting excursion I took alone in the forest. How sad and gloomy I felt! I thought that there was no creature in the world so miserable as myself. I was tired and hungry and I sat down upon a fallen tree to rest. All was still as death around me, and I was fast sinking to sleep when my attention was aroused by a long, wild cry. My dog—for I had not Chance then, and he's no hunter—pricked up his ears, but instead of answering with a bark of defiance, he crouched down, trembling, at my feet. "What does this mean?" I cried, and I cocked my rifle and sprang upon the log. The sound came nearer upon the wind. It was like the deep baying of a pack of hounds in full cry. Presently a noble deer rushed past me, and fast upon his trail—I see them now, like so many black devils—swept by a pack of ten or fifteen large, fierce wolves, with fiery eyes and bristling hair, and paws that seemed hardly to touch the ground in their eager haste. I thought not of danger, for with their prey in view I was safe; but I felt every nerve within me tremble for the fate of the poor deer. The wolves gained upon him at every bound. A close thicket intercepted his path, and, rendered desperate, he turned at bay. His nostrils were dilated, and his eyes seemed to send forth long streams of light. It was wonderful to witness the courage of the beast. How bravely he repelled the attacks of his deadly enemies, how gallantly he tossed them to the right and left, and spurned them from beneath his hoofs; yet all his struggles were useless, and he was quickly overcome and torn to pieces by his ravenous foes. At that moment he seemed more unfortunate even than myself, for I could not see in what manner he had deserved his fate. All his speed and energy, his courage and fortitude, had been exerted in vain. I had tried to destroy myself; but he, with every effort vigorously made for self-preservation, was doomed to meet the fate he dreaded! Is God just to his creatures?'

With this sentence on his lips, he started abruptly from his seat and left the house.

One day he found me painting some wild flowers, and was greatly interested in watching the progress I made in the group. Late in the afternoon of the following day he brought me a large bunch of splendid spring flowers.

'Draw these,' said he. 'I have been all the way to the—lake plains to find them for you.'

Little Katie, grasping them one by one with infantile joy, kissed every lovely blossom.

'These are God's pictures,' said the hunter, 'and the child, who is all nature, understands them in a minute. Is it not strange that these beautiful things are hid away in the wilderness, where no eyes but the birds of the air and the wild beasts of the wood and the insects that live upon them ever see them? Does God provide, for the pleasure of such creatures, these flowers? Is His benevolence gratified by the admiration of animals whom we have been taught to consider as having neither thought nor reflection? When I am alone in the forest, these thoughts puzzle me.'

Knowing that to argue with Brian was only to call into action the slumbering fires of his fatal malady, I turned the conversation by asking him why he called his favourite dog Chance.

'I found him,' he said, 'forty miles back in the bush. He was a mere skeleton. At first I took him for a wolf, but the shape of his head undeceived me. I opened by wallet and called him to me. He came slowly, stopping and wagging his tail at every step, and looking me wistfully in the face. I offered him a bit of dried venison and he soon became friendly and followed me home, and has never left me since. I called him Chance after the manner I happened with him; and I would not part with him for twenty dollars.'

Alas, for poor Chance! He had, unknown to his master, contracted a private liking for fresh mutton, and one night he killed no less than eight sheep that belonged to Mr D—, on the front road. The culprit, who had been long suspected, was caught in the very act, and this *mis-chance* cost him his life. Brian was sad and gloomy for many weeks after his favourite's death.

'I would have restored the sheep fourfold,' he said, 'if he would but have spared the life of my dog.'

ROUGHING IT IN THE BUSH

Alice Munro

ALICE MUNRO has an enviable reputation among other writers of fiction (the novelist Leo Simpson has described her as 'certainly the best writer in Canada'), but there have been times during her career when a writer with less determination and fewer natural gifts might have been frustrated to the point of being silenced altogether. She was born and brought up 'on the untidy, impoverished, wayward edge of a small town'—Wingham, Ont., in a farming district not far from Lake Huron. She began publishing short stories about that part of the country while she was still a student at the University of Western Ontario. She married and moved with her husband to Vancouver where he had an executive position with the T. Eaton Company. She continued slowly to write short stories while raising a family, and some appeared in *Canadian Forum, The Tamarack Review, The Montrealer,* and *Chatelaine.* She applied for grants but was unsuccessful because people with literary influence even in Vancouver were unaware of her work. She and her family moved to Victoria, B.C., where her husband opened a successful downtown bookstore.

Alice Munro's first book, *Dance of the Happy Shades* (1968), a collection of her short stories, won the Governor General's Award for fiction. Her excellent novel, *Lives of Girls & Women,* appeared in 1971. Despite her long residence on the west coast, almost all her short stories and her novel are set in southern Ontario, in or near a town that approximates Wingham. That world has stayed vividly in her memory—down to small, surprising details that she uses with remarkable skill in bringing her characters and background to life—and continues to stir her imagination.

When Alice Munro was asked to talk about the mysterious craft of writing for *The Narrative Voice,* an anthology edited by John Metcalf, she had this to say: 'Writing or talking about writing makes me superstitiously uncomfortable. My explanations have a way of turning treacherous, half-untrue . . . I feel like a juggler trying to describe exactly how he catches the balls, and although he has trained to be a juggler for a long time and has worked hard, he still feels it may be luck, a good deal of the time, and luck is an unhappy thing to talk about, it is not reliable. Some people think it is best when doing any of these things—dancing, say, or making love—to follow very closely what you are about. Some people think differently. I do.'

WALKER BROTHERS COWBOY

After supper my father says, 'Want to go down and see if the Lake's still there?' We leave my mother sewing under the diningroom light, making clothes for me against the opening of school. She has ripped up for this purpose an old suit and an old plaid wool dress of hers, and she has to cut and match very cleverly and also make me stand and turn for endless fittings, sweaty, itching from the hot wool, ungrateful. We leave my brother in bed in the little screened porch at the end of the front verandah, and sometimes he kneels on his bed and presses his face against the screen and calls mournfully, 'Bring me an ice-cream cone!' but I call back, 'You will be asleep,' and do not even turn my head.

Then my father and I walk gradually down a long, shabby sort of street, with Silverwoods Ice Cream signs standing on the sidewalk, outside tiny, lighted stores. This is in Tuppertown, an old town on Lake Huron, an old grain port. The street is shaded, in some places, by maple trees whose roots have cracked and heaved the sidewalk and spread out like crocodiles into the bare yards. People are sitting out, men in shirt-sleeves and undershirts and women in aprons—not people we know but if anybody looks ready to nod and say, 'Warm night,' my father will nod too and say something the same. Children are still playing. I don't know them either because my mother keeps my brother and me in our own yard, saying he is too young to leave it and I have to mind him. I am not so sad to watch their evening games because the games themselves are ragged, dissolving. Children, of their own will, draw apart, separate into islands of two or one under the heavy trees, occupying themselves in such solitary ways as I do all day, planting pebbles in the dirt or writing in it with a stick.

Presently we leave these yards and houses behind, we pass a factory with boarded-up windows, a lumberyard whose high wooden gates are locked for the night. Then the town falls away in a defeated jumble of sheds and small junkyards, the sidewalk gives up and we are walking on a sandy path with burdocks, plantains, humble nameless weeds all around. We enter a vacant lot, a kind of park really, for it is kept clear of junk and there is one bench with a slat missing on the back, a place to sit and look at the water. Which is generally grey in the evening, under a lightly

overcast sky, no sunsets, the horizon dim. A very quiet, washing noise on the stones of the beach. Further along, towards the main part of town, there is a stretch of sand, a water slide, floats bobbing around the safe swimming area, a lifeguard's rickety throne. Also a long dark green building, like a roofed verandah, called the Pavilion, full of farmers and their wives, in stiff good clothes, on Sundays. That is the part of the town we used to know when we lived at Dungannon and came here three or four times a summer, to the Lake. That, and the docks where we would go and look at the grain boats, ancient, rusty, wallowing, making us wonder how they got past the breakwater let alone to Fort William.

Tramps hang around the docks and occasionally on these evenings wander up the dwindling beach and climb the shifting, precarious path boys have made, hanging onto dry bushes, and say something to my father which, being frightened of tramps, I am too alarmed to catch. My father says he is a bit hard up himself. 'I'll roll you a cigarette if it's any use to you,' he says, and he shakes tobacco out carefully on one of the thin butterfly papers, flicks it with his tongue, seals it and hands it to the tramp who takes it and walks away. My father also rolls and lights and smokes one cigarette of his own.

He tells me how the Great Lakes came to be. All where Lake Huron is now, he says, used to be flat land, a wide flat plain. Then came the ice, creeping down from the north, pushing deep into the low places. Like *that*—and he shows me his hand with his spread fingers pressing the rock-hard ground where we are sitting. His fingers make hardly any impression at all and he says, 'Well, the old ice cap had a lot more power behind it than this hand has.' And then the ice went back, shrank back towards the North Pole where it came from, and left its fingers of ice in the deep places it had gouged, and ice turned to lakes and there they were today. They were *new*, as time went. I try to see that plain before me, dinosaurs, walking on it, but I am not able even to imagine the shore of the Lake when the Indians were there, before Tuppertown. The tiny share we have of time appalls me, though my father seems to regard it with tranquillity. Even my father, who sometimes seems to me to have been at home in the world as long as it has lasted, has really lived on this earth only a little longer than I have, in terms of all the time there has been to live in. He has not known a time, any more than I, when automobiles and electric lights did not at least exist. He was not alive when this century started. I will be barely alive—old, old—when it ends. I do not like to think of it. I wish the Lake to be always just a lake, with the safe-swimming floats marking it, and the breakwater and the lights of Tuppertown.

My father has a job, selling for Walker Brothers. This is a firm that sells almost entirely in the country, the back country. Sunshine, Boylesbridge, Turnaround—that is all his territory. Not Dungannon where we used to live, Dungannon is too near town and my mother is grateful for that. He sells cough medicine, iron tonic, corn plasters, laxatives, pills for female disorders, mouth wash, shampoo, liniment, salves, lemon and orange and raspberry concentrate for making refreshing drinks, vanilla, food colouring, black and green tea, ginger, cloves and other spices, rat poison. He has a song about it, with these two lines:

> *And have all liniments and oils,*
> *For everything from corns to boils. . . .*

Not a very funny song, in my mother's opinion. A pedlar's song, and that is what he is, a pedlar knocking at backwoods kitchens. Up until last winter we had our own business, a fox farm. My father raised silver foxes and sold their pelts to the people who make them into capes and coats and muffs. Prices fell, my father hung on hoping they would get better next year, and they fell again, and he hung on one more year and one more and finally it was not possible to hang on any more, we owed everything to the feed company. I have heard my mother explain this, several times, to Mrs

Oliphant who is the only neighbour she talks to. (Mrs Oliphant also has come down in the world, being a schoolteacher who married the janitor.) We poured all we had into it, my mother says, and we came out with nothing. Many people could say the same thing, these days, but my mother has no time for the national calamity, only ours. Fate has flung us onto a street of poor people (it does not matter that we were poor before, that was a different sort of poverty), and the only way to take this, as she sees it, is with dignity, with bitterness, with no reconciliation. No bathroom with a claw-footed tub and a flush toilet is going to comfort her, nor water on tap and sidewalks past the house and milk in bottles, not even the two movie theatres and the Venus Restaurant and Woolworths so marvellous it has live birds singing in its fan-cooled corners and fish as tiny as fingernails, as bright as moons, swimming in its green tanks. My mother does not care.

In the afternoons she often walks to Simon's Grocery and takes me with her to help carry things. She wears a good dress, navy blue with little flowers, sheer, worn over a navy-blue slip. Also a summer hat of white straw, pushed down on the side of the head, and white shoes I have just whitened on a newspaper on the back steps. I have my hair freshly done in long damp curls which the dry air will fortunately soon loosen, a stiff large hair-ribbon on top of my head. This is entirely different from going out after supper with my father. We have not walked past two houses before I feel we have become objects of universal ridicule. Even the dirty words chalked on the sidewalk are laughing at us. My mother does not seem to notice. She walks serenely like a lady shopping, like a *lady* shopping, past the housewives in loose beltless dresses torn under the arms. With me her creation, wretched curls and flaunting hair-bow, scrubbed knees and white socks—all I do not want to be. I loathe even my name when she says it in public, in a voice so high, proud, and ringing, deliberately different from the voice of any other mother on the street.

My mother will sometimes carry home, for a treat, a brick of ice cream —pale Neapolitan; and because we have no refrigerator in our house we wake my brother and eat it at once in the diningroom, always darkened by the wall of the house next door. I spoon it up tenderly, leaving the chocolate till last, hoping to have some still to eat when my brother's dish is empty. My mother tries then to imitate the conversations we used to have at Dungannon, going back to our earliest, most leisurely days before my brother was born, when she would give me a little tea and a lot of milk in a cup like hers and we would sit out on the step facing the pump, the lilac tree, the fox pens beyond. She is not able to keep from mentioning those days. 'Do you remember when we put you in your sled and Major pulled you?' (Major our dog, that we had to leave with neighbours when we moved.) 'Do you remember your sandbox outside the kitchen window?' I pretend to remember far less than I do, wary of being trapped into sympathy or any unwanted emotion.

My mother has headaches. She often has to lie down. She lies on my brother's narrow bed in the little screened porch, shaded by heavy branches. 'I look up at that tree and I think I am at home,' she says.

'What you need', my father tells her, 'is some fresh air and a drive in the country.' He means for her to go with him, on his Walker Brothers route.

That is not my mother's idea of a drive in the country.

'Can I come?'

'Your mother might want you for trying on clothes.'

'I'm beyond sewing this afternoon,' my mother says.

'I'll take her, then. Take both of them, give you a rest.'

What is there about us that people need to be given a rest from? Never mind. I am glad enough to find my brother and make him go to the toilet and get us both into the car, our knees unscrubbed, my hair unringleted. My father brings from the house his two heavy brown suitcases, full of bottles, and sets them on the back seat. He wears a white shirt, brilliant in the sunlight, a tie, light trousers belonging to his summer suit (his other suit is black, for funerals, and belonged to my uncle before he died) and a creamy straw hat. His salesman's outfit, with pencils clipped in the shirt pocket. He goes back once again, probably to say goodbye to my mother, to ask her if she is sure she doesn't want to come, and hear her say, 'No. No thanks. I'm better just to lie here with my eyes closed.' Then we are backing out of the driveway with the rising hope of adventure, just the little hope that takes you over the bump into the street, the hot air starting to move, turning into a breeze, the houses growing less and less familiar as we follow the short cut my father knows, the quick way out of town. Yet what is there waiting for us all afternoon but hot hours in stricken farmyards, perhaps a stop at a country store and three ice-cream cones or bottles of pop, and my father singing? The one he made up about himself has a title—'The Walker Brothers Cowboy'—and it starts out like this:

> Old Ned Fields, he now is dead,
> So I am ridin' the route instead. . . .

Who is Ned Fields? The man he has replaced, surely, and if so he really is dead; yet my father's voice is mournful-jolly, making his death some kind of nonsense, a comic calamity. 'Wisht I was back on the Rio Grande, plungin' through the dusky sand.' My father sings most of the time while driving the car. Even now, heading out of town, crossing the bridge and taking the sharp turn onto the highway, he is humming something, mumbling a bit of a song to himself, just tuning up, really, getting ready to improvise, for out along the highway we pass the Baptist Camp, the Vacation Bible Camp, and he lets loose:

> *Where are the Baptists, where are the Baptists,*
>   *where are all the Baptists today?*
> *They're down in the water, in Lake Huron water,*
>   *with their sins all a-gittin' washed away.*

My brother takes this for straight truth and gets up on his knees trying to see down to the Lake. 'I don't see any Baptists,' he says accusingly. 'Neither do I, son,' says my father. 'I told you, they're down in the Lake.'

No roads paved when we left the highway. We have to roll up the windows because of dust. The land is flat, scorched, empty. Bush lots at the back of the farms hold shade, black pine-shade like pools nobody can ever get to. We bump up a long lane and at the end of it what could look more unwelcoming, more deserted than the tall unpainted farmhouse with grass growing uncut right up to the front door, green blinds down and a door upstairs opening on nothing but air? Many houses have this door, and I have never yet been able to find out why. I ask my father and he says they are for walking in your sleep. *What?* Well if you happen to be walking in your sleep and you want to step outside. I am offended, seeing too late that he is joking, as usual, but my brother says sturdily, 'If they did that they would break their necks.'

The nineteen-thirties. How much this kind of farmhouse, this kind of afternoon, seem to me to belong to that one decade in time, just as my father's hat does, his bright flared tie, our car with its wide running board (an Essex, and long past its prime). Cars somewhat like it, many older, none dustier, sit in the farmyards. Some are past running and have their doors pulled off, their seats removed for use on porches. No living things to be seen, chickens or cattle. Except dogs. There are dogs, lying in any kind of shade they can find, dreaming, their lean sides rising and sinking rapidly. They get up when my father opens the car door, he has to speak to them. 'Nice boy, there's a boy, nice old boy.' They quiet down, go back to their shade. He should know how to quiet animals; he has held desperate foxes with tongs around their necks. One gentling voice for the dogs and another, rousing, cheerful, for calling at doors. 'Hello there, Missus! It's the Walker Brothers man and what are you out of today?' A door opens, he disappears. Forbidden to follow, forbidden even to leave the car, we can just wait and wonder what he says. Sometimes trying to make my mother laugh he pretends to be himself in a farm kitchen, spreading out his sample case. 'Now then, Missus, are you troubled with parasitic life? Your children's scalps, I mean. All those crawly little things we're too polite to mention that show up on the heads of the best of families? Soap alone is useless, kerosene is not too nice a perfume, but I have here —' Or else, 'Believe me, sitting and driving all day the way I do I *know* the value of these fine pills. Natural relief. A problem common to old folks, too, once their days of activity are over—How about you, Grandma?' He would wave the imaginary box of pills under my mother's nose and she would laugh finally, unwillingly. 'He doesn't say that really, does he?' I said, and she said no of course not, he was too much of a gentleman.

One yard after another, then, the old cars, the pumps, dogs, views of grey barns and falling-down sheds and unturning windmills. The men, if they are working in the fields, are not in any fields that we can see. The children are far away, following dry creek beds or looking for blackberries, or else they are hidden in the house, spying at us through cracks in the blinds. The car seat has grown slick with our sweat. I dare my brother to sound the horn, wanting to do it myself but not wanting to get the blame. He knows better. We play 'I Spy', but it is hard to find many colours. Grey for the barns and sheds and toilets and houses, brown for the yard and fields, black or brown for the dogs. The rusting cars show rainbow patches, in which I strain to pick out purple or green; likewise I peer at doors for shreds of old peeling paint, maroon or yellow. We can't play with letters, which would be better, because my brother is too young to spell. The game disintegrates anyway. He claims my colours are not fair, and wants extra turns.

In one house no door opens, though the car is in the yard. My father knocks and whistles, calls, 'Hullo there! Walker Brothers man!' but there is not a stir of reply anywhere. This house has no porch, just a bare, slanting slab of cement on which my father stands. He turns around, searching the barnyard, the barn whose mow must be empty because you can see the sky through it, and finally he bends to pick up his suitcases. Just then a window is opened upstairs, a white pot appears on the sill, is tilted over and its contents splash down the outside wall. The window is not directly above my father's head, so only a stray splash would catch him. He picks up his suitcases with no particular hurry and walks, no longer whistling, to the car. 'Do you know what that was?' I say to my brother. '*Pee*.' He laughs and laughs.

My father rolls and lights a cigarette before he starts the car. The window has been slammed down, the blind drawn; we never did see a hand or face. 'Pee, pee,' sings my brother ecstatically. 'Somebody dumped down pee!' 'Just don't tell your mother that,' my father says. 'She isn't liable to see the joke.' 'Is it in your song?' my brother wants to know. My father says no but he will see what he can do to work it in.

I notice in a little while that we are not turning into any more lanes, though it does not seem to me that we are headed home. 'Is this the way to Sunshine?' I ask my father, and he answers, 'No ma'am it's not.' 'Are we still in your territory?' He shakes his head. 'We're going *fast*,' my brother says approvingly, and in fact we are bouncing along through dry puddleholes so that all the bottles in the suitcases clink together and gurgle promisingly.

Another lane, a house, also unpainted, dried to silver in the sun. 'I thought we were out of your territory.'

'We are.'

'Then what are we going in here for?'

'You'll see.'

In front of the house a short, sturdy woman is picking up washing, which had been spread on the grass to bleach and dry. When the car stops she stares at it hard for a moment, bends to pick up a couple more towels to add to the bundle under her arm, comes across to us and says in a flat voice, neither welcoming nor unfriendly, 'Have you lost your way?'

My father takes his time getting out of the car. 'I don't think so,' he says. 'I'm the Walker Brothers man.'

'George Golley is our Walker Brothers man,' the woman says, 'and he was out here no more than a week ago. Oh, my Lord God,' she says harshly, 'it's you.'

'It was, the last time I looked in the mirror,' my father says. The woman gathers all the towels in front of her and holds on to them tightly, pushing them against her stomach as if it hurt. 'Of all the people I never thought to see. And telling me you were the Walker Brothers man.'

'I'm sorry if you were looking forward to George Golley,' my father says humbly.

'And look at me. I was prepared to clean the hen-house. You'll think that's just an excuse but it's true. I don't go round looking like this every day.' She is wearing a farmer's straw hat, through which pricks of sunlight penetrate and float on her face, a loose, dirty print smock and running shoes. 'Who are those in the car, Ben? They're not yours?'

'Well I hope and believe they are,' my father says, and tells our names and ages. 'Come on, you can get out. This is Nora, Miss Cronin. Nora, you better tell me, is it still Miss, or have you got a husband hiding in the woodshed?'

'If I had a husband that's not where I'd keep him, Ben,' she says, and they both laugh, her laugh abrupt and somewhat angry. 'You'll think I got no manners, as well as being dressed like a tramp,' she says. 'Come on in out of the sun. It's cool in the house.'

We go across the yard ('Excuse me taking you in this way but I don't think the front door has been opened since Papa's funeral. I'm afraid the hinges might drop off'), up the porch steps, into the kitchen, which really is cool, high-ceilinged, the blinds of course down, a simple, clean, thread-bare room with waxed, worn linoleum, potted geraniums, drinking-pail and dipper, a round table with scrubbed oilcloth. In spite of the cleanness, the wiped and swept surfaces, there is a faint sour smell—maybe of the dishrag or the tin dipper or the oilcloth, or the old lady, because there is one, sitting in an easy chair under the clock shelf. She turns her head slightly in our direction and says, 'Nora? Is that company?'

'Blind,' says Nora in a quick explaining voice to my father. Then, 'You won't guess who it is, Momma. Hear his voice.'

My father goes to the front of her chair and bends and says hopefully, 'Afternoon, Mrs Cronin.'

'Ben Jordan,' says the old lady with no surprise. 'You haven't been to see us in the longest time. Have you been out of the country?'

My father and Nora look at each other.

'He's married, Momma,' says Nora cheerfully and aggressively. 'Married and got two children and here they are.' She pulls us forward, makes each of us touch the old lady's dry, cool hand while she says our names in turn. Blind! This is the first blind person I have ever seen close up. Her eyes are closed, the eyelids sunk away down, showing no shape of the eyeball, just hollows. From one hollow comes a drop of silver liquid, a medicine, or a miraculous tear.

'Let me get into a decent dress,' Nora says. 'Talk to Momma. It's a treat for her. We hardly ever see company, do we Momma?'

'Not many makes it out this road,' says the old lady placidly. 'And the ones that used to be around here, our old neighbours, some of them have pulled out.'

'True everywhere,' my father says.

'Where's your wife then?'

'Home. She's not too fond of the hot weather, makes her feel poorly.'

'Well.' This is a habit of country people, old people, to say 'well', mean-ing, 'is that so?' with a little extra politeness and concern.

Nora's dress, when she appears again—stepping heavily on Cuban heels down the stairs in the hall—is flowered more lavishly than anything my mother owns, green and yellow on brown, some sort of floating sheer crepe, leaving her arms bare. Her arms are heavy, and every bit of her skin you can see is covered with little dark freckles like measles. Her hair is short, black, coarse, and curly, her teeth very white and strong. 'It's the first time I knew there was such a thing as green poppies,' my father says, looking at her dress.

'You would be surprised all the things you never knew,' says Nora, sending a smell of cologne far and wide when she moves and displaying a change of voice to go with the dress, something more sociable and youthful. 'They're not poppies anyway, they're just flowers. You go and pump me some good cold water and I'll make these children a drink.' She gets down from the cupboard a bottle of Walker Brothers Orange syrup.

'You telling me you were the Walker Brothers man!'

'It's the truth, Nora. You go and look at my sample cases in the car if you don't believe me. I got the territory directly south of here.'

'Walker Brothers? Is that a fact? You selling for Walker Brothers?'

'Yes ma'am.'

'We always heard you were raising foxes over Dungannon way.'

'That's what I was doing, but I kind of run out of luck in that business.'

'So where're you living? How long've you been out selling?'

'We moved into Tuppertown. I been at it, oh, two, three months. It keeps the wolf from the door. Keeps him as far away as the back fence.'

Nora laughs. 'Well I guess you count yourself lucky to have the work. Isabel's husband in Brantford, he was out of work the longest time. I thought if he didn't find something soon I was going to have them all land in here to feed, and I tell you I was hardly looking forward to it. It's all I can manage with me and Momma.'

'Isabel married,' my father says. 'Muriel married too?'

'No, she's teaching school out west. She hasn't been home for five years. I guess she finds something better to do with her holidays. I would if I was her.' She gets some snapshots out of the table drawer and starts showing him. 'That's Isabel's oldest boy, starting school. That's the baby sitting in her carriage. Isabel and her husband. Muriel. That's her room-mate with her. That's a fellow she used to go around with, and his car. He was working in a bank out there. That's her school; it has eight rooms. She teaches Grade Five.' My father shakes his head. 'I can't think of her any way but when she was going to school, so shy I used to pick her up on the road—I'd be on my way to see you—and she would not say one word, not even to agree it was a nice day.'

'She's got over that.'

'Who are you talking about?' says the old lady.

'Muriel. I said she's got over being shy.'

'She was here last summer.'

'No Momma that was Isabel. Isabel and her family were here last summer. Muriel's out west.'

'I meant Isabel.'

Shortly after this the old lady falls asleep, her head on the side, her mouth open. 'Excuse her manners,' Nora says. 'It's old age.' She fixes an afghan over her mother and says we can all go into the front room where our talking won't disturb her.

'You two,' my father says. 'Do you want to go outside and amuse yourselves?'

Amuse ourselves how? Anyway I want to stay. The front room is more interesting than the kitchen, though barer. There is a gramophone and a pump organ and a picture on the wall of Mary, Jesus' mother—I know that much—in shades of bright blue and pink with a spiked band of light around her head. I know that such pictures are found only in the homes of Roman Catholics and so Nora must be one. We have never known any Roman Catholics at all well, never well enough to visit in their houses. I think of what my grandmother and my Aunt Tena, over in Dungannon, used to always say to indicate that somebody was a Catholic. *So-and-so digs with the wrong foot,* they would say. *She digs with the wrong foot.* That was what they would say about Nora.

Nora takes a bottle, half full, out of the top of the organ and pours some of what is in it into the two glasses that she and my father have emptied of the orange drink.

'Keep it in case of sickness?' my father says.

'Not on your life,' says Nora. 'I'm never sick. I just keep it because I keep it. One bottle does me a fair time, though, because I don't care for drinking alone. Here's luck!' She and my father drink and I know what it is. Whisky. One of the things my mother has told me in our talks together is that my father never drinks whisky. But I see he does. He drinks whisky and he talks of people whose names I have never heard before. But after a while he turns to a familiar incident. He tells about the chamberpot that was emptied out the window. 'Picture me there,' he says, 'hollering my heartiest. *Oh, lady, it's your Walker Brothers man! Anybody home?*' He does himself hollering, grinning absurdly, waiting, looking up in pleased expectation and then—oh, ducking, covering his head with his arms, looking as if he begged for mercy (when he never did anything like that, I was watching), and Nora laughs, almost as hard as my brother did at the time.

'That isn't true! That's not a word true!'

'Oh, indeed it is ma'am. We have our heroes in the ranks of Walker Brothers. I'm glad you think it's funny,' he says sombrely.

I ask him shyly, 'Sing the song.'

'What song? Have you turned into a singer on top of everything else?'

Embarrassed, my father says, 'Oh, just this song I made up while I was driving around. It gives me something to do, making up rhymes.'

But after some urging he does sing it, looking at Nora with a droll,

apologetic expression, and she laughs so much that in places he has to stop and wait for her to get over laughing so he can go on, because she makes him laugh too. Then he does various parts of his salesman's spiel. Nora when she laughs squeezes her large bosom under her folded arms. 'You're crazy,' she says. 'That's all you are.' She sees my brother peering into the gramophone and she jumps up and goes over to him. 'Here's us sitting enjoying ourselves and not giving you a thought, isn't it terrible?' she says. 'You want me to put a record on, don't you? You want to hear a nice record? Can you dance? I bet your sister can, can't she?'

I say no. 'A big girl like you and so good-looking and can't dance!' says Nora. 'It's high time you learned. I bet you'd make a lovely dancer. Here, I'm going to put on a piece I used to dance to and even your daddy did, in his dancing days. You didn't know your daddy was a dancer, did you? Well, he is a talented man, your daddy!'

She puts down the lid and takes hold of me unexpectedly around the waist, picks up my other hand and starts making me go backwards. 'This is the way, now, this is how they dance. Follow me. This foot, see. One and one-two. One and one-two. That's fine, that's lovely, don't look at your feet! Follow me, that's right, see how easy? You're going to be a lovely dancer! One and one-two. One and one-two. Ben, see your daughter dancing!' *Whispering while you cuddle near me Whispering where no one can hear me. . . .*

Round and round the linoleum, me proud, intent, Nora laughing and moving with great buoyancy, wrapping me in her strange gaiety, her smell of whisky, cologne, and sweat. Under the arms her dress is damp, and little drops form along her upper lip, hang in the soft black hairs at the corners of her mouth. She whirls me around in front of my father—causing me to stumble, for I am by no means so swift a pupil as she pretends—and lets me go, breathless.

'Dance with me, Ben.'

'I'm the world's worst dancer, Nora, and you know it.'

'I certainly never thought so.'

'You would now.'

She stands in front of him, arms hanging loose and hopeful, her breasts, which a moment ago embarrassed me with their warmth and bulk, rising and falling under her loose flowered dress, her face shining with the exercise, and delight.

'Ben.'

My father drops his head and says quietly, 'Not me, Nora.'

So she can only go and take the record off. 'I can drink alone but I can't dance alone,' she says. 'Unless I am a whole lot crazier than I think I am.'

'Nora,' says my father smiling. 'You're not crazy.'

'Stay for supper.'

'Oh, no. We couldn't put you to the trouble.'

'It's no trouble. I'd be glad of it.'

'And their mother would worry. She'd think I'd turned us over in a ditch.'

'Oh, well. Yes.'

'We've taken a lot of your time now.'

'Time,' says Nora bitterly. 'Will you come by ever again?'

'I will if I can,' says my father.

'Bring the children. Bring your wife.'

'Yes I will,' says my father. 'I will if I can.'

When she follows us to the car he says, 'You come to see us too, Nora. We're right on Grove Street, left-hand side going in, that's north, and two doors this side—east—of Baker Street.'

Nora does not repeat these directions. She stands close to the car in her soft, brilliant dress. She touches the fender, making an unintelligible mark in the dust there.

On the way home my father does not buy any ice cream or pop, but he does go into a country store and get a package of licorice, which he shares with us. *She digs with the wrong foot,* I think, and the words seem sad to me as never before, dark, perverse. My father does not say anything to me about not mentioning things at home, but I know, just from the thoughtfulness, the pause when he passes the licorice, that there are things not to be mentioned. The whisky, maybe the dancing. No worry about my brother, he does not notice enough. At most he might remember the blind lady, the picture of Mary.

'Sing,' my brother commands my father, but my father says gravely, 'I don't know, I seem to be fresh out of songs. You watch the road and let me know if you see any rabbits.'

So my father drives and my brother watches the road for rabbits and I feel my father's life flowing back from our car in the last of the afternoon, darkening and turning strange, like a landscape that has an enchantment on it, making it kindly, ordinary and familiar while you are looking at it, but changing it, once your back is turned, into something you will never know, with all kinds of weathers, and distances you cannot imagine.

When we get closer to Tuppertown the sky becomes gently overcast, as always, nearly always, on summer evenings by the Lake.

DANCE OF THE HAPPY SHADES

Emile Nelligan

The poems of ÉMILE NELLIGAN, regarded as the beginning of modern literature in French Canada, were all written between his sixteenth and twentieth birthdays. Though he pronounced his last name in the French manner (and sometimes wrote it Nélighan), his father was Irish, immigrating with his parents when he was twelve. He married the daughter of the first mayor of Rimouski, and the couple settled in Montreal, where David Nelligan worked in the post office. In his poem 'Le Jardin d'antan' ('The Garden of Yesteryear') Émile recalls his childhood as happy; but his memory, like Dylan Thomas's in 'Fern Hill', is coloured by a strong sense of doom lying in wait for the happy child. He started school in 1886, and seems never to have taken to it —he stayed away for months at a time throughout his schooldays and gave it up for good in 1897. Little is known of the details of his life, or the reasons for the deep melancholy expressed in many of his poems; it is known that he idolized his mother and never spoke of his father, and it was said that the marriage was not happy.

In 1889 a weekly called Le Samedi had been started in Montreal that published many of the recent French poets who had had little or no influence so far on poetry in Canada, including the so-called 'Decadents' like Baudelaire and Verlaine. These poets clearly had a strong influence on Nelligan. In June 1896 his own first published poem appeared in Le Samedi, signed with a pseudonym. Eight more poems appeared that summer, sent from the Nelligan summer cottage at Cacouna on the south bank of the St Lawrence (curiously named Peck-à-boo Villa). It was during the following school term that one of his teachers, a certain Father Lalande, read one of Nelligan's poems aloud in class in order to ridicule it.

A group of young writers had recently formed a literary club known as the École Littéraire de Montréal. In February 1897 Nelligan was admitted to membership; he read three of his poems at his first meeting. In the next two years he gave frequent readings at meetings of the group, had a good many poems published, and was highly praised. But in February 1899 an obscure critic from France published some slighting remarks about him and this may possibly have deepened the depression that had begun to take hold of him. Nevertheless, that May he had his highest, and last, moment of glory. At a public meeting sponsored by the *École*, he declaimed three poems, culminating with 'La Romance du vin', here translated as 'The Poet's Wine'. 'Noble as a young god', as the critic Louis Dantin described him, 'his eyes blazing, his gestures enlarged', Nelligan filled the crowd with such emotion that after giving him an ovation they escorted him in triumph to the door. Three months later he sank into a depression from which he was never to emerge. He spent the remaining forty-two years of his life in asylums and never wrote another line.

Nelligan was a poet of emotion more than of intellect, and of sound perhaps more than either. 'A great musician of syllables', Dantin calls him. 'Inspiration and even meaning often fail him; harmony, never. He knows the exact value and subtlest shadings of his sounds.' His rich vocabulary recalls the French 'Parnassians'; his flowing musical line shows the powerful influence of Verlaine. And it has been suggested that his imagery often echoes Shakespeare and other English poets: certainly 'Le Vaisseau d'or' ('The Ship of Gold') is reminiscent of a famous passage from Thomas Gray. But in French Canada of the 1890s this young poet, writing of his own emotions, his own sensations, his own soul, rather than of the life of the soil or the heroic history of New France, was something very new and individual. The tragic silence that descended on him so suddenly no doubt added to his impact, which was strengthened in 1904 by the appearance of a collection, *Émile Nelligan et son œuvre*, with a preface by Louis Dantin that has itself become a classic of Canadian criticism. A more modern edition, *Poésies complètes 1896-1899*, was edited by Luc Lacourcière (third edition, Fides, 1966). A translation by P. F. Widdows of six poems was published by the Ryerson Press in 1960 under the title *Selected Poems*; and twelve Nelligan poems have been included in *The Poetry of French Canada in Translation* (1970) edited by John Glassco.

THE POET'S WINE

Green gaiety, everything blended in a quick
Burst. O beautiful May evening, bird-choirs bringing
Their modulations to my wide window, singing
As my relinquished heart-hopes sing, changing music.

O beautiful May evening, joyful May evening!
A far-off organ chants its melancholy chant,
And the twilight rays, like purple rapiers, slant
Into the day's heart, perfumed in its dying.

How gay I am, how gay! Into the singing glass
With the wine! Keep pouring, never stop pouring!
Let me forget the days are triste and boring,
The crowd contemptible and the world an ass.

Gay, I am gay! Exalted in wine and art!...
How I dream of the lofty rhymes I shall make,
Rhymes trembling with the sighs of funeral music,
Winds of autumn passing through the haze, distant, apart.

Kingship of the bitter laughter, and the rage
Of knowing that one is a poet, pierced by scorn;
Of being a heart and not understood, forlorn
To all but the moon's night and thunder's equipage.

Ladies, I drink to you, smilers along the way
Where the Ideal beckons me to her pink embraces,
And to you, gentlemen, with your sombre faces,
You who disdain my hand, I drink especially.

When the blue pricks out its coming splendour of stars
And as it were a hymn praises the golden spring,
What tears have I to shed over the day's dying?
I, on a dark path, in the dark of my young years?

Gay, I am gay! Inexpressible May evening!
Ridiculously gay, can it be that I've—
Not drunk either—that I'm happy to be alive?
Has it at last been healed, my old wound of loving?

The bells cease, and the evening scents follow after
As the breeze takes them, and the wine rustles and throbs.
I am more than gay, hear my resonant laughter!
So gay, so gay! I am breaking into sobs.

GEORGE JOHNSTON (*tr*)

THE SHIP OF GOLD

There was a gallant vessel wrought of gold,
Whose tops'ls raked the skies in seas unknown;
Carved on the prow a naked Venus shone,
With wind-tossed locks, in the immoderate Sun.

But ah! one night she struck the famous reef
In treacherous Ocean where the Siren sings.
Ghastly, a slanting hulk, she twists and swings
Down the profound Abyss, her changeless shroud.

She was a golden ship whose glassy hull
Betrayed the treasure-trove for which the three
Foul Captains, *Hate, Disgust,* and *Frenzy* strove.

What rests at last after the hasty plunge?
What of my heart's lost fate, poor derelict?
—Foundered, alas! in the black gulf of Dream!

A. J. M. SMITH (*tr*)

BY THE FIRESIDE

In the old winters when we still were small,
In dresses, boisterous, pink, with chubby looks,
Our big and long-since vanished picture-books
Showed us the world; we seemed to own it all.

In groups around the fire at evening,
Picture by picture, ah! how happily
We turned the pages, starry-eyed to see
Squadrons of fine dragoons go galloping!

I once was happy, one of these; but now,
Feet on the fender, with dull, listless brow,
I with my always bitter heart descry

Flame-fashioned pictures where my youth goes by,
And, like a passing soldier, rides abroad
On life's black field, gripping a bloody sword.

P. F. WIDDOWS (*tr*)

John Newlove

In an essay on his poetry (published in French in *Ellipse*, Issue 10), Margaret Atwood describes JOHN NEWLOVE as 'one of the most important young poets to emerge in English Canada during the 1960s', and goes on to say that 'he can move easily and convincingly from clipped, terse epigrams to flowing lyricism to something like a grand manner.' He was born in Regina and lived for a number of years in Russian farming communities of eastern Saskatchewan, where his mother was a schoolteacher. He has described his poem about the western Indians, 'The Pride', as coming from an almost racial memory of the Prairies haunted by ghosts of the tribes who wandered freely until the guns came and the herds of buffalo were slaughtered.

Newlove has held a variety of jobs and has lived in Vancouver, Prince George, and Terrace, B.C.; the Maritimes; and recently in Toronto, where he is a senior editor with the publishing firm of McClelland & Stewart. His books of poetry are *Grave Sir* (1962), *Elephants, Mothers & Others* (1963), *Moving in Alone* (1965), *Notebook Pages* (1966), *What They Say* (1967),

Black Night Window (1968), *The Cave* (1970), and *Lies* (1972).

In much of his poetry Newlove is the lonely outsider, the loser, in a threatening, repugnant world that he fears and abhors—a world that is a prison, though he sometimes is able to flee it by keeping on the move, 'going through the country/ to one end, only/to turn again at one sea/and begin it again'. When Newlove writes not about himself in this world but about real people in history, his poems take on a larger emotional range. 'Newlove seldom makes myths,' Margaret Atwood writes, 'but when he does they operate in the direction of pulling together all the elements that he more often sees as decaying, falling to pieces: himself, the land, history, time, identity. This synthesis takes place most notably in 'The Pride', an almost epic long poem which traces the history of western Canada through the defeat and dispersal of the Indians and ends by seeing the current inhabitants—'we' or 'us'—as their metaphorical descendants.'

John Newlove's 'Samuel Hearne in Wintertime' invites a reading of the extract from Hearne's *A Journey from Prince of Wales's Fort* on pages 200-4.

THE HITCHHIKER

On that black highway,
where are you going?—

it is in Alberta
among the trees

where the road sweeps
left and right

in great concrete arcs
at the famous resort—

there you stood on
the road in the wind,

the cold wind going
through you and you

going through the country
to no end, only

to turn again at one sea
and begin it again,

feeling safe with strangers
in a moving car.

SAMUEL HEARNE IN WINTERTIME

1

In this cold room
I remember the smell of manure
on men's heavy clothes as good,
the smell of horses.

It is a romantic world
to readers of journeys
to the Northern Ocean—

especially if their houses are heated
to some degree, Samuel.
Hearne, your camp must have smelled
like hell whenever you settled down
for a few days of rest and journal-work:

hell smeared with human manure,
hell half-full of raw hides,
hell of sweat, Indians, stale fat,
meat-hell, fear-hell, hell of cold.

2

One child is back from the doctor's while
the other one wanders about in dirty pants
and I think of Samuel Hearne and the land—

puffy children coughing as I think,
crying, sick-faced,
vomit stirring in grey blankets
from room to room.

It is Christmastime—
the cold flesh shines.
No praise in merely enduring.

3

Samuel Hearne did more
in the land (like all the rest

full of rocks and hilly country,
many very extensive tracts of land,
tittimeg, pike and barble,

and the islands:
the islands, many
of them abound

as well as the main
land does
with dwarf woods.

chiefly pine
in some parts intermixed
with larch and birch) than endure.

The Indians killed twelve deer.
It was impossible to describe
the intenseness of the cold.

4
And, Samuel Hearne,
I have almost begun to talk

as if you wanted to be
gallant, as if you went
through that land for a book—

as if you were not SAM, wanting
to know, to do a job.

5
There was that Eskimo girl
at Bloody Falls, at your feet

Samuel Hearne, with two spears in her,
you helpless before your helpers,

and she twisted about them like
an eel, dying, never to know.

THE PRIDE

1
The image/   the pawnees
in their earth-lodge villages,
the clear image
of teton sioux, wild
fickle people the chronicler says,

the crazy dogs, men
tethered with leather dog-thongs
to a stake, fighting until dead,

image: arikaras
with traded spanish sabre blades
mounted on the long
heavy buffalo lances,
riding the sioux
down, the centaurs, the horsemen
scouring the level plains
in war or hunt
until smallpox got them,
4,000 warriors,

image—of a desolate country,
a long way between fires,
unfound lakes, mirages, cold rocks,
and lone men going through it,
cree with good guns
creating terror in athabaska
among the inhabitants, frightened
stone-age people, 'so that
they fled at the mere sight
of a strange smoke miles away.'

2
This western country crammed
with the ghosts of indians,
haunting the coastal stones and shores,
the forested pacific islands,
mountains, hills and plains:

beside the ocean ethlinga,
man in the moon, empties
his bucket, on

a sign from Spirit
of the Wind ethlinga
empties his bucket, refreshing
the earth, and it rains
on the white cities;

that black joker, broken-
jawed raven, most prominent
among haida and tsimshyan tribes,
is in the kwakiutl
dance masks too—
it was he who brought fire,
food and water to man,
the trickster;

and thunderbird hilunga,
little thought of
by haida for lack of thunderstorms
in their district, goes
by many names, exquisite disguises
carved in the painted wood,

he is nootka tootooch, the wings
causing thunder and the tongue
or flashing eyes engendering
rabid white lightning,
whose food was whales,
called kwunusela by the kwakiutl,
it was he who laid down the house-logs
for the people at Place
Where Kwunusela Alighted;

in full force and virtue
and terror of the law, eagle—
he is authority, the sun
assumed his form once,
the sun which used to be
a flicker's egg, success-
fully transformed;

and malevolence comes to the land,
the wild woman of the woods;
grinning, she wears
a hummingbird in her hair,
d'sonoqua, the furious one—

they are all ready
to be found, the legends
and the people, or
all their ghosts and memories,
whatever is strong enough
to be remembered.

3
But what image, bewildered
son of all men
under the hot sun,
do you worship,
what completeness
do you hope to have
from these tales,
a half-understood massiveness, mirage,
in men's minds—what
is your purpose;

with what force
will you proceed
along a line
neither straight nor short,
whose future
you cannot know
or result foretell,
whose meaning is still
obscured as the incidents
occur and accumulate?

4
The country moves on;
there are orchards in the interior,
the mountain passes
are broken, the foothills
covered with cattle and fences,
and the fading hills covered;

but the plains are bare,
not barren, easy
for me to love their people,
for me to love their people
without selection.

5
In 1787, the old cree saukamappee,
aged 75 or thereabout, speaking then
of things that had happened when he was 16,
just a man, told david thompson,
of the raids the shoshonis,
the snakes, had made on the westward-
reaching peigan, of their war-parties
sometimes sent 10 days journey to enemy camps,
the men all afoot in battle array for
the encounter, crouching
behind their giant shields;

the peigan armed with guns
drove these snakes out of the plains,
the plains where their strength had been,
where they had been settled since living
memory (though nothing is remembered
beyond a grandfather's time),
to the west of the rockies;

these people moved without rest,
backward and forward with the wind,
the seasons, the game, great herds,
in hunger and abundance—

in summer and in the bloody fall
they gathered on the killing grounds,
fat and shining with fat, amused
with the luxuries of war and death,

relieved from the steam of knowledge,
consoled by the stream of blood
and steam rising from the fresh hides
and tired horses, wheeling in their pride
on the sweating horses, their pride.

6
Those are all stories;
the pride, the grand poem
of our land, of the earth itself,
will come, welcome, and
sought for, and found,
in a line of running verse,
sweating, our pride;

we seize on
what has happened before,
one line only
will be enough,
a single line and
then the sunlit brilliant image suddenly floods us
with understanding, shocks our
attentions, and all desire
stops, stands alone;

we stand alone,
we are no longer lonely
but have roots,
and the rooted words
recur in the mind, mirror, so that
we dwell on nothing else, in nothing else,
touched, repeating them,
at home freely
at last, in amazement;

'the unyielding phrase
in tune with the epoch,'
the thing made up
of our desires,
not of its words, not only
of them, but of something else,
as well, that which we desire
so ardently, that which
will not come when
it is summoned alone,
but grows in us
and idles about and hides
until the moment is due—

the knowledge of
our origins, and where
we are in truth,
whose land this is
and is to be.

7
The unyielding phrase:
when the moment is due, then
it springs upon us

out of our own mouths,
unconsidered, overwhelming
in its knowledge, complete—

not this handful
of fragments, as the indians
are not composed of
the romantic stories
about them, or of the stories
they tell only, but
still ride the soil
in us, dry bones a part
of the dust in our eyes,
needed and troubling
in the glare, in
our breath, in our
ears, in our mouths,
in our bodies entire, in our minds, until at
last we become them

in our desires, our desires,
mirages, mirrors, that are theirs, hard-
riding desires, and they
become our true forbears, moulded
by the same wind or rain,
and in this land we
are their people, come
back to life.

"Alden Nowlan" '69
M. Donaldson

b. 1933

Alden Nowlan

ALDEN NOWLAN is a regional writer whose roots are deep in the small towns of Nova Scotia and New Brunswick where he has lived all his life, but his poetry and short stories have a literary sophistication that brings them into the mainstream of contemporary North American writing. He was born in Stanley, N.S. In a special issue of the Fredericton literary magazine *The Fiddlehead* devoted to Nowlan's work (Issue 81, 1969), he speaks of the harsh, poverty-stricken background that has coloured some of his writing. Nowlan himself left school at Grade 5 when he was twelve years old. He worked cutting pulp, as a night watchman in a sawmill, and for the Nova Scotia Department of Highways (he later wrote two ironically affectionate poems about that experience). He became a newspaperman and worked for ten years on the Hartland *Observer*, a weekly published in a small town upriver from Fredericton. While he was in Hartland he usually had several other jobs, and for a time he was manager of a country music band, 'George Shaw and the Green Valley Ranch Boys'. In 1963 he moved

to the *Telegraph-Journal*, a Saint John daily, where he was at different times a reporter, provincial editor, and night-news editor. In 1968 he was appointed Writer-in-Residence at the University of New Brunswick in Fredericton.

Nowlan's books of poetry include *The Rose and the Puritan* (1958), *Wind in a Rocky Country* (1960), *Bread, Wine, and Salt* (which won the Governor General's award for poetry for 1967), *The Mysterious Naked Man* (1969), and *Between Tears and Laughter* (1971). His selected poems, *Playing the Jesus Game*, was published by a small press in New York State in 1970 and is not easy to obtain. In 1972 the CBC issued a recording, 'Alden Nowlan's Maritimes', on which the poet reads poems and comments on his work. A collection of his short stories, *Miracle at Indian River*, was published in 1968. Nowlan was given a Canada Council Special Award in 1966 and was a Guggenheim Fellow in 1967-8.

About writing, Nowlan has said: 'I write for the same reason I'm 6' 3" tall. I can't do anything about it.' He is very much the realist, but he can speak of 'the infinite strangeness of our ordinary lives' and he considers the poet to be a kind of magician: increasingly his realism has been touched with a sense of the mystery of life. Many years of newspaper work may have taught him to be direct and concise, but these characteristics are consistent with his rejection of the obscure, the artificial, the excessive. Straightforward language is ideally suited for recording his clear-eyed, compassionate view of the world around him—a world of every day that is often underprivileged, sad. It is Nowlan's special gift that he is able to warm it with beauty and feeling.

A LITTLE-TRAVELLED ROAD

A trailer, a sign
reading *Bill's Eats,* somewhere
on the road between
Campbellton and
St Leonard.
            Everything except
            the music stops
            when I open the
            screen door:
            Hank Williams singing,
            'Your Cheatin' Heart'.
The locals,
country boys and their
girls drop everything
and wait. I have the irrational
feeling there's something
I'm expected to do or
say and that I won't
realize what it is
until too late. Then
I have the even more
absurd feeling that
they somehow knew
I was going to
stop here, that they've
been waiting for me.
I can imagine them
saying to each other
on the steps of the
church or at the
filling station
this morning:

Did you know a funny
thing is going to
happen at Bill's
this afternoon?
Better be there.
You wouldn't want to miss it.
One thing I know for certain
if I'm still here when
the song ends nobody
will play another.
There'll be no sounds then
except the electric
fan humming, vegetable
oil sizzling, the
Niagara roar of
root beer in the
throat of the stranger.

A MATTER OF ETIQUETTE

The first time you address the Queen
you say 'Your Majesty.' Then you call her 'Ma'am.'
And you mustn't speak to her at all
except in reply to what she chooses to say to you.
There will be an aide-de-camp or a lady-in-waiting
present to remind you of this should you ever
be presented at Court.

But nobody has yet put into words
the etiquette governing the relations
between the men digging
a sewer and their foreman.
                    I'm being quite serious.

For example you must show respect
by the very manner
in which you enunciate his name
but never overdo it
by so much as one-hundredth
of a decibel
or it will be taken
as evidence of subservience
or insubordination.

It may even be necessary for you
to acquaint yourself with
the intricate ritual
of offering to buy him
a beer.
        I know an honours student
in sociology who during an entire summer
was addressed as 'Boy,'
because he could not master
the delicate nuances
of this ceremony.

The same young man
was unable to learn
how to talk about
the girls who were
continually passing
and therefore lost
the respect of
his companions

by attempting to be witty
so that he was judged arrogant
and by being so
imaginative that he
came to be almost
ostracized as
some kind of pervert:

he failed to understand
until it was too late

that when it comes to discussing
girls with the men
working beside you
in a ditch you can use only

certain prescribed
sentences and that each
has its own
unique rhythm,
must be accompanied
always by its own
formalized gestures.

JULY 15

The wind is cool. Nothing is happening.
I do not strive for meaning. When I lie on my back
the wind passes over me, I do not feel it.
The sun has hands
like a woman, calling the heat
out of my body.
The trees sing. Nothing is happening.

When I close my eyes,
I hear the soft footsteps
of the grass. Nothing is happening.

How long have I lain here?
Well, it is still summer. But is it the same
summer I came?
I must remember
not to ask myself questions.
I am naked. Trees sing. The grass walks.
Nothing is happening.

JOHNNIE'S POEM

Look! I've written a poem!
Johnnie says
and hands it to me
             and it's about
             his grandfather dying
             last summer, and me
             in the hospital
and I want to cry,
don't you see, because it doesn't matter
if it's not very good:
             what matters is he knows
and it was me, his father, who told him
             you write poems about what
             you feel deepest and hardest.

b. 1943

Michael Ondaatje

With only four slim books to his credit, published in five years, MICHAEL ONDAATJE has won high praise as a poet as well as a Governor General's Award. Born in Ceylon, he moved with his family to England when he was eleven. He attended Dulwich College there before coming to Canada in 1962. He continued his education at Bishop's University, the University of Toronto, and Queen's University, where he received an M.A He has taught at the University of Western Ontario and is now Assistant Professor of English at Glendon College, York University, Toronto.

Ondaatje is a strongly visual poet. He can freeze a moment in time, as in a snapshot, or describe a series of movements and arresting small details with such economy and clarity that they are projected on the mind like a scene in a film. (He is interested in movies and has made a film on the poet b.p. nichol called *Sons of Captain Poetry*.) He is the poet as cameraman in his first book *The Dainty Monsters* (1967)—containing poems about animals, birds, his family, myths—and even more strikingly in his second and third books, which draw on anecdotes of social history to portray extremes of human existence and violence. His imagery is exotic and sometimes horrifying—though this quality is offset by a cheerful matter-of-factness. *The Man With Seven Toes* (1969) is a sequence of brief poems suggested by the experience of a woman who was shipwrecked off the Queensland coast of Australia. *The Collected Works of Billy the Kid* (1970), for which Ondaatje won a Governor General's Award, brilliantly recreates in documentary form the American West of the outlaw of the title (William Bonny, 1859-81) and his pursuer, Sheriff Pat Garrett. A collage of lyrics, ballads, short prose narratives, and 'found' poems, it constructs a whole new myth about a sensitive young killer and his inhuman nemesis. *Rat Jelly* (1972) is his latest collection of poems, from which 'Letters' (overleaf) is taken.

Ondaatje is the editor of *The Broken Arc* (1971), an anthology of animal poems by Canadians, with drawings by Tony Urquhart, and the author of a critical study of Leonard Cohen (1970) in the Canadian Writers Series of the New Canadian Library.

LETTERS & OTHER WORLDS

> *'for there was no more darkness for him and, no doubt like*
> *Adam before the fall, he could see in the dark'*

My father's body was a globe of fear
His body was a town we never knew
He hid that he had been where we were going
His letters were a room he seldom lived in
In them the logic of his love could grow

My father's body was a town of fear
He was the only witness to its fear dance
He hid where he had been that we might lose him
His letters were a room his body scared

He came to death with his mind drowning.
On the last day he enclosed himself
in a room with two bottles of gin, later
fell the length of his body
so that brain blood moved
to new compartments
that never knew the wash of fluid
and he died in minutes of a new equilibrium.

His early life was a terrifying comedy
and my mother divorced him again and again.
He would rush into tunnels magnetized
by the white eye of trains
and once, gaining instant fame,
managed to stop a Perahara in Ceylon
—the whole procession of elephants dancers
local dignitaries—by falling
dead drunk onto the street.
As a semi-official, and semi-white at that,
the act was seen as a crucial
turning point in the Home Rule Movement
and led to Ceylon's independence in 1948.

(My mother had done her share too—
her driving so bad
she was stoned by villagers
whenever her car was recognized)

For 14 years of marriage
each of them claimed he or she
was the injured party.
Once on the Colombo docks
saying goodbye to a recently married couple
my father, jealous
at my mother's articulate emotion,
dove into the waters of the harbour
and swam after the ship waving farewell.
My mother pretending no affiliation
mingled with the crowd back to the hotel.

Once again he made the papers
though this time my mother
with a note to the editor
corrected the report—saying he was drunk
rather than broken hearted at the parting of friends.
The married couple received both editions
of *The Ceylon Times* when their ship reached Aden.
And then in his last years
he was the silent drinker
the man who once a week
disappeared into his room with bottles
and stayed there until he was drunk
and until he was sober.

There speeches, head dreams, apologies,
the gentle letters, were composed.
With the clarity of architects
he would write of the row of blue flowers
his new wife had planted,
the plans for electricity on the house,
how my half-sister fell near a snake
and it had awakened and not touched her.
Letters in a clear hand of the most complete empathy
his heart widening and widening and widening
to all manner of change in his children and friends
while he himself edged
into the terrible acute hatred
of his own privacy
till he balanced and fell
the length of his body
the blood screaming in
the empty reservoir of bones
the blood searching in his head without metaphor

BILLY THE KID

Garrett moved us straight to the nearest railroad depot. We had
to wait one night for the train that would take us to Messilla
where they would hold the trial. The Polk Hotel there was a
bright white place with a wide courtyard and well. The deputies
went down in the bucket and washed themselves. They removed
Charlie off his horse. Garrett took over and washed the dried
blood off the animal. Garrett ordered a box for Charlie Bowdre.
Then he made me drink liquids and paste. They had to carry the
three of us from the horses to the beds—we couldn't walk after
the week on horses. I was to share a room with Garrett and
Emory.

Your last good bed Billy, he said, pick your position. I did, face
and stomach down. He chained me to the bed. He taped my
fingers so thick I couldn't get them through a trigger guard even
if they gave me a gun. Then he went out and looked after
Wilson who had broken both ankles when the horse stumbled
collapsing on his chained legs.

It is afternoon still, the room white with light. My last white
room, the sun coming through the shutters making the white
walls whiter. I lie on my left cheek looking to that light. I cannot even see the door or if Emory has stayed behind. The bed
vast. Went to sleep, my body melting into it. I remember once
after Charlie and I stopped talking we could hear flies buzzing
in their black across a room, and I remember once, one night in
the open I turned to say goodnight to Charlie who was about ten
yards away and there was the moon balanced perfect on his nose.

It is the order of the court that you be
taken to Lincoln and confined to jail
until May 13th and that on that day
between the hours of sunrise and noon
you be hanged on the gallows until
you are dead dead dead
And may God have mercy on your
soul

said Judge Warren H. Bristol

No the escape was no surprise to me. I expected it. I really did,
we all did I suppose. And it is now in retrospect difficult to
describe. You've probably read the picture books anyway, seen
the films, of how he did it. What he did was to seduce young
Bell into a cardgame, shot him, then shot Ollinger returning
from lunch. Nobody cared about Ollinger, but Bell was liked.
You know how Ollinger used to kill people? He'd go up to them
about to shake hands, then grab their right hand with his left,
lift out his pistol and fire into the chest. He had hated Billy
ever since the Lincoln County War. So Bell and Ollinger died
and Billy escaped. Also on the way out of town he hit a man
named Ellery Fleck in the face, with his rifle, for no reason at all.
He was probably elated.

One funny thing happened apparently (I was out of town).
Billy's hands were still chained, and jumping onto a horse to
escape he lost his balance and fell off—right in front of the
crowd who refused to do anything but watch. In that crowd
nobody cracked a smile. Three or four kids helped him catch the
horse and held it while he got on carefully. Then with the rifle
cradled in his arms he made the horse walk slowly over
Ollinger's body and went.

MISS SALLIE CHISUM:

GOOD FRIENDS:

As far as dress was concerned
he always looked as if
he had just stepped out of a bandbox.

In broadbrimmed white hat
dark coat and vest
grey trousers worn over his boots
a grey flannel shirt
and black four-in-hand tie
and sometimes—would you believe it?—
a flower in his lapel.

A COURTEOUS LITTLE GENTLEMAN:

I suppose it sounds absurd to speak
of such a character as a gentleman,
but from beginning to end
of our long relationship,
in all his personal relations with me,
he was the pink of politeness
and as courteous a little gentleman
as I ever met.

There was a brook full of fish
that ran under the house
across a corner of the kitchen
and I often sat on the back porch
in a rocking chair, with Billy
to bait my hook for me,
and caught a string of perch for dinner.

b. 1916

P. K. Page

P.K. PAGE, who is distinguished both as a poet and as a painter, was born in England and came to Canada as a child. She attended school in Calgary and studied art in Brazil and New York. She wrote scripts for the National Film Board and became associated with the editors of the Montreal little magazine *Preview*, joining the editorial board in 1942. Her first book of poems was *As Ten As Twenty* (1946). This was followed by *The Metal and the Flower* (1954), which won a Governor General's Award. She travelled widely when her husband, W. A. Irwin, was Canadian High Commissioner in Australia and Ambassador to Brazil and then Mexico—some of her later poems contain the exotic local colour of the countries she has lived in—and in this period she began a second career as an artist, producing intricately detailed, fantastic drawings and paintings. In 1967 she published *Cry Ararat! Poems New and Selected*, which is decorated with some of her drawings. She lives in Victoria, B.C.

Cry Ararat! brilliantly confirmed the reputation of P. K. Page as one of the finest poets in Canada. Her early poems were of social protest. 'The Stenographers'

—a harrowing picture of wartime office workers, in whose eyes she sees 'the pin men of madness' — is her best-known poem on this theme. She has also been concerned with alienation, notably in some remarkable miniature biographies (e.g. 'Only Child'). She writes about childhood, dreams, love (and self-love), innocence and experience, illusion and disillusionment, strangeness and terror, in technically accomplished poems that are rich with metaphysical imagery. 'Her images and symbols are White and Green,' A. J. M. Smith has written, 'images of snow, winter, ice and glass; or of flowers, gardens, leaves and trees; or else glass again, and salt, the transparent green suffocating crystal sea. Her symbolic world seems mostly mineral or vegetable, but there are symbols also of birds, the swan and the peacock especially, and fish.'

In an article about her writing and painting P. K. Page interestingly describes the beginning of a poem: 'The idea diminishes to a dimensionless point in my absolute centre. If I can hold it steady long enough, the feeling which is associated with that point grows and fills a larger area as perfume permeates a room. It is from here that I write—held within that luminous circle, that locus which is at the same time a focussing glass, the surface of a drum.' Her article appears in Issue 46 (Autumn, 1970) of *Canadian Literature*, which contains another by the poet in Issue 41 (Summer, 1969) and A.J.M. Smith's essay on her work in Issue 50 (Autumn 1971).

ONLY CHILD

The early conflict made him pale
and when he woke from those long weeping slumbers she was there
and the air about them—hers and his—
sometimes a comfort to him, like a quilt, but more
often than not a fear.

There were times he went away—he knew not where—
over the fields or scuffing to the shore;
suffered her eagerness on his return
for news of him—where had he been, what done?
He hardly knew, nor did he wish to know
or think about it vocally or share
his private world with her.

Then they would plan another walk, a long
adventure in the country, for her sake—
in search of birds. Perhaps they'd find the blue
heron today, for sure the kittiwake.

Birds were familiar to him now, he knew
them by their feathers and a shyness like his own
soft in the silence.
Of the ducks she said, 'Observe,
the canvas back's a diver,' and her words
stuccoed the slatey water of the lake.

He had no wish to separate them in groups
or learn the latin,
or, waking early to their song remark, 'the thrush,'
or say at evening when the air is streaked
with certain swerving flying,
'Ah, the swifts.'

Birds were his element like air and not
her words for them—making them statues
setting them apart,
nor were they facts and details like a book.
When she said, 'Look!'
he let his eyeballs harden
and when two came and nested in the garden
he felt their softness, gentle, near his heart.

She gave him pictures which he avoided, showing
strange species flat against a foreign land.
Rather would he lie in the grass, the deep grass of the island
close to the gulls' nests knowing
these things he loved and needed near his hand,
untouched and hardly seen but deeply understood.
Or sail among them through a wet wind feeling
their wings within his blood.

Like every mother's boy he loved and hated
smudging the future photograph she had,
yet struggled within the frames of her eyes and then
froze for her, the noted naturalist—
her very affectionate and famous son.
But when most surely in her grasp, his smile
darting and enfolding her, his words:
'Without my mother's help . . .' the dream occurred.

Dozens of flying things surrounded him
on a green terrace in the sun
and one by one
as if he held caresses in his palm
he caught them all and snapped and wrung their necks
brittle as little sticks.
Then through the bald, unfeathered air
and coldly as a man would walk
against a metal backdrop, he
bore down on her
and placed them in her wide maternal lap
and accurately said their names aloud:
woodpecker, sparrow, meadowlark, nuthatch.

THE STENOGRAPHERS

After the brief bivouac of Sunday,
their eyes, in the forced march of Monday to Saturday,
hoist the white flag, flutter in the snow-storm of paper,
haul it down and crack in the mid-sun of temper.

In the pause between the first draft and the carbon
they glimpse the smooth hours when they were children—
the ride in the ice-cart, the ice-man's name,
the end of the route and the long walk home;

remember the sea where floats at high tide
were sea marrows growing on the scatter-green vine
or spools of grey toffee, or wasps' nests on water;
remember the sand and the leaves of the country.

Bell rings and they go and the voice draws their pencil
like a sled across snow; when its runners are frozen
rope snaps and the voice then is pulling no burden
but runs like a dog on the winter of paper.

Their climates are winter and summer—no wind
for the kites of their hearts—no wind for a flight;
a breeze at the most, to tumble them over
and leave them like rubbish—the boy-friends of blood.

In the inch of the noon as they move they are stagnant.
The terrible calm of the noon is their anguish;
the lip of the counter, the shapes of the straws
like icicles breaking their tongues, are invaders.

Their beds are their oceans—salt water of weeping
the waves that they know—the tide before sleep;
and fighting to drown they assemble their sheep
in columns and watch them leap desks for their fences
and stare at them with their own mirror-worn faces.

In the felt of the morning the calico-minded,
sufficiently starched, insert papers, hit keys,
efficient and sure as their adding machines;
yet they weep in the vault, they are taut as net curtains
stretched upon frames. In their eyes I have seen
the pin men of madness in marathon trim
race round the track of the stadium pupil.

T-BAR

Relentless, black on white, the cable runs
through metal arches up the mountain side.
At intervals giant pickaxes are hung
on long hydraulic springs. The skiers ride
propped by the axehead, twin automatons
supported by its handle, one each side.

In twos they move slow motion up the steep
incision in the mountain. Climb. Climb.
Somnambulists, bolt upright in their sleep
their phantom poles swung lazily behind,
while to the right, the empty T-bars keep
in mute descent, slow monstrous jigging time.

Captive the skiers now and innocent,
wards of eternity, each pair alone.
They mount the easy vertical ascent,
pass through successive arches, bride and groom,
as through successive naves, are newly wed
participants in some recurring dream.

So do they move forever. Clocks are broken.
In zones of silence they grow tall and slow,
inanimate dreamers, mild and gentle-spoken
blood-brothers of the haemophilic snow
until the summit breaks and they awaken
imagos from the stricture of the tow.

Jerked from her chrysalis the sleeping bride
suffers too sudden freedom like a pain.
The dreaming bridegroom severed from her side
singles her out, the old wound aches again.
Uncertain, lost, upon a wintry height
these two, not separate, but no longer one.

Now clocks begin to peck and sing. The slow
extended minute like a rubber band
contracts to catapult them through the snow
in tandem trajectory while behind
etching the sky-line, obdurate and slow
the spastic T-bars pivot and descend.

E. J. Pratt

E.J. PRATT is best known as a popular and dynamic narrative poet who chose big themes of suspenseful action—a whale hunt, the destruction of a liner by an iceberg, war, martyrdom, the building of a railway—and gave exuberant expression to the conflicts between man and nature and the elements of grandeur and power that are contained in them. He was born in Western Bay, Newfoundland, and educated at St John's Methodist College. He taught and preached on the island before enrolling at Victoria College, University of Toronto. He graduated from there in philosophy in 1911, received his Ph.D. in theology in 1917, and in 1920 joined the Department of English at Victoria, where he was a much-loved teacher until he retired as Professor Emeritus in 1953.

Pratt's first two books of narrative verse, which marked the beginning of the modern movement in English-Canadian poetry, are fantasies of the sea. (Pratt had an encyclopaedic knowledge of the sea. Its ever-changing character, the life it supports, and particularly the disasters it inflicts, excited his imagina-

tion and provided superb material for his powers of sweeping narrative.) *The Witches' Brew* (1925) is a delightful revelry describing the effects of alcohol on some fish and a giant cat. *Titans* (1926) contains 'The Cachalot', an epic about the hunt for a mighty whale, and 'The Great Feud', a parable of the waste of war about a battle between paleolithic creatures of sea and land. He went on to write two heroic narratives of the sea that were about actual events. *The Roosevelt and the Antinoe* (1930) is about a sea rescue that took place in January 1926. *The Titanic* (1935) is not only about that liner's ill-fated voyage but about its enemy, an iceberg, and the conduct of its proud, complacent, heroic passengers. *Dunkirk* (1941), *They Are Returning* (1945), and *Behind the Log* (1947), the story of a convoy, are three war poems. Pratt turned to history for two of his most famous narrative poems (both winners of Governor General's Awards): *Brébeuf and His Brethren* (1940), a twelve-part epic on the seventeenth-century Jesuit missions to the Huron Indians, which is climaxed by the torture and burning of Father Brébeuf and Father Lalemant in 1649; and *Towards the Last Spike* (1952), about the political, financial, geological and other difficulties that had to be overcome in building Canada's first transcontinental railway, the CPR.

By their very subject matter all these poems draw heavily on actual facts and concrete detail. In his introduction to Pratt's *Collected Poems: Second Edition* (1958) Northrop Frye writes: 'He has the typical mark of originality: the power to make something poetic of what everybody had just decided could no longer be poetic material.' After doing careful research for each poem Pratt took delight in using his findings poetically and with great technical mastery. Describing the anatomy of a whale, the action of an iceberg, the inscrutable forces of nature, the data of seamanship, the routine on board an ocean liner, a game of poker (in *The Titanic*), anti-submarine detection, Pratt could use the specialized vocabulary appropriate to each subject with colloquial ease and often humorously, as when he worked a list of brewers' and distillers' names into *The Witches' Brew*.

Pratt, who was the author of seventeen books of verse, wrote numerous shorter poems that appeared in several short collections and have become well known; these include 'The Ice-Floes' (*Newfoundland Verse*, 1923), 'A Prairie Sunset', 'The Highway' (*Many Moods*, 1932), 'Silences' (*Fables of the Goats and Other Poems*, 1937), 'Come Away, Death' and 'The Truant' (*Still Life and Other Verse*, 1943).

Pratt's *Selected Poems* (1968) edited by Peter Buitenhuis is available in paperback. Milton Wilson is the author of a study of Pratt and his poetry in the Canadian Writers Series of the New Canadian Library (1969). See also 'A Garland for E.J. Pratt' in *The Tamarack Review* (Winter, 1958).

THE END OF THE 'TITANIC'

The fo'c'sle had gone under the creep
Of the water. Though without a wind, a lop
Was forming on the wells now fathoms deep.
The seventy feet—the boat deck's normal drop—
Was down to ten. Rising, falling, and waiting,
Rising again, the swell that edged and curled
Around the second bridge, over the top
Of the air-shafts, backed, resurged and whirled
Into the stokehold through the fiddley grating.

Under the final strain the two wire guys
Of the forward funnel tugged and broke at the eyes:
With buckled plates the stack leaned, fell and smashed
The starboard wing of the flying bridge, went through
The lower, then tilting at the davits crashed

Over, driving a wave aboard that drew
Back to the sea some fifty sailors and
The captain with the last of the bridge command.

Out on the water was the same display
Of fear and self-control as on the deck—
Challenge and hesitation and delay,
The quick return, the will to save, the race
Of snapping oars to put the realm of space
Between the half-filled lifeboats and the wreck.
The swimmers whom the waters did not take
With their instant death-chill struck out for the wake
Of the nearer boats, gained on them, hailed
The steersmen and were saved: the weaker failed
And fagged and sank. A man clutched at the rim
Of a gunwale, and a woman's jewelled fist
Struck at his face: two others seized his wrist,
As he released his hold, and gathering him
Over the side, they staunched the cut from the ring.
And there were many deeds envisaging
Volitions where self-preservation fought
Its red primordial struggle with the 'ought',
In those high moments when the gambler tossed
Upon the chance and uncomplaining lost.

Aboard the ship, whatever hope of dawn
Gleamed from the *Carpathia*'s riding lights was gone,
For every knot was matched by each degree
Of list. The stern was lifted bodily
When the bow had sunk three hundred feet, and set
Against the horizon stars in silhouette
Were the blade curves of the screws, hump of the rudder.
The downward pull and after buoyancy
Held her a minute poised but for a shudder
That caught her frame as with the upward stroke
Of the sea a boiler or a bulkhead broke.

Climbing the ladders, gripping shroud and stay,
Storm-rail, ringbolt or fairlead, every place
That might befriend the clutch of hand or brace
Of foot, the fourteen hundred made their way
To the heights of the aft decks, crowding the inches
Around the docking bridge and cargo winches.
And now that last salt tonic which had kept
The valour of the heart alive—the bows

Of the immortal seven that had swept
The strings to outplay, outdie their orders, ceased.
Five minutes more, the angle had increased
From eighty on to ninety when the rows
Of deck and port-hole lights went out, flashed back
A brilliant second and again went black.
Another bulkhead crashed, then following
The passage of the engines as they tore
From their foundations, taking everything
Clean through the bows from 'midships with a roar
Which drowned all cries upon the deck and shook
The watchers in the boats, the liner took
Her thousand fathoms journey to her grave.

*   *   *

And out there in the starlight, with no trace
Upon it of its deed but the last wave
From the *Titanic* fretting at its base,
Silent, composed, ringed by its icy broods,
The grey shape with the palaeolithic face
Was still the master of the longitudes.

THE TITANIC

THE DEATH OF BRÉBEUF

Jean de Brébeuf (1593-1649) was a Jesuit missionary to the Huron Indians, who lived near Georgian Bay (Ont.). He was martyred with Father Gabriel Lalemant at Saint-Ignace during Iroquois raids on the Huron villages.

No doubt in the mind of Brébeuf that this was the last
Journey—three miles over the snow. He knew
That the margins as thin as they were by which he escaped
From death through the eighteen years of his mission toil
Did not belong to this chapter: not by his pen
Would this be told. He knew his place in the line,
For the blaze of the trail that was cut on the bark by Jogues
Shone still. He had heard the story as told by writ
And word of survivors—of how a captive slave
Of the hunters, the skin of his thighs cracked with the frost,
He would steal from the tents to the birches, make a rough cross
From two branches, set it in snow and on the peel
Inscribe his vows and dedicate to the Name
In 'litanies of love' what fragments were left
From the wrack of his flesh; of his escape from the tribes;
Of his journey to France where he knocked at the door of the College
Of Rennes, was gathered in as a mendicant friar,
Nameless, unknown, till he gave for proof to the priest
His scarred credentials of faith, the nail-less hands
And withered arms—the signs of the Mohawk fury.
Nor yet was the story finished—he had come again
Back to his mission to get the second death.
And the comrades of Jogues—Goupil, Eustache and Couture,
Had been stripped and made to run the double files
And take the blows—one hundred clubs to each line—
And this as the prelude to torture, leisured, minute,
Where thorns on the quick, scallop shells to the joints of the thumbs,
Provided the sport for children and squaws till the end.
And adding salt to the blood of Brébeuf was the thought
Of Daniel—was it months or a week ago?
So far, so near, it seemed in time, so close
In leagues—just over there to the south it was
He faced the arrows and died in front of his church.

But winding into the greater artery
Of thought that bore upon the coming passion
Were little tributaries of wayward wish
And reminiscence. Paris with its vespers

Was folded in the mind of Lalemant,
And the soft Gothic lights and traceries
Were shading down the ridges of his vows.
But two years past at Bourges he had walked the cloisters,
Companioned by Saint Augustine and Francis,
And wrapped in quiet holy mists. Brébeuf,
His mind a moment throwing back the curtain
Of eighteen years, could see the orchard lands,
The *cidreries*, the peasants at the Fairs,
The undulating miles of wheat and barley,
Gardens and pastures rolling like a sea
From Lisieux to Le Havre. Just now the surf
Was pounding on the limestone Norman beaches
And on the reefs of Calvados. Had dawn
This very day not flung her surplices
Around the headlands and with golden fire
Consumed the silken argosies that made
For Rouen from the estuary of the Seine?
A moment only for that veil to lift—
A moment only for those bells to die
That rang their matins at Condé-sur-Vire.

By noon St Ignace! The arrival there
The signal for the battle-cries of triumph,
The gauntlet of the clubs. The stakes were set
And the ordeal of Jogues was re-enacted
Upon the priests—even with wilder fury,
For here at last was trapped their greatest victim,
Echon.* The Iroquois had waited long
For this event. Their hatred for the Hurons
Fused with their hatred for the French and priests
Was to be vented on this sacrifice,
And to that camp had come apostate Hurons,
United with their foes in common hate
To settle up their reckoning with *Echon*.

      *   *   *

Now three o'clock, and capping the height of the passion,
Confusing the sacraments under the pines of the forest,
Under the incense of balsam, under the smoke
Of the pitch, was offered the rite of the font. On the head,
The breast, the loins and the legs, the boiling water!
While the mocking paraphrase of the symbols was hurled

* The Huron name for Brébeuf.

At their faces like shards of flint from the arrow heads—
'We baptize thee with water . . .

                      That thou mayest be led

To Heaven . . .

              To that end we do anoint thee.
We treat thee as a friend: we are the cause
Of thy happiness; we are thy priests: the more
Thou sufferest, the more thy God will reward thee,
So give us thanks for our kind offices.'

The fury of taunt was followed by fury of blow.
Why did not the flesh of Brébeuf cringe to the scourge,
Respond to the heat, for rarely the Iroquois found
A victim that would not cry out in such pain—yet here
The fire was on the wrong fuel. Whenever he spoke,
It was to rally the soul of his friend whose turn
Was to come through the night while the eyes were uplifted in prayer,
Imploring the Lady of Sorrows, the mother of Christ,
As pain brimmed over the cup and the will was called
To stand the test of the coals. And sometimes the speech
Of Brébeuf struck out, thundering reproof to his foes,
Half-rebuke, half-defiance, giving them roar for roar.
Was it because the chancel became the arena,
Brébeuf a lion at bay, not a lamb on the altar,
As if the might of a Roman were joined to the cause
Of Judaea? Speech they could stop for they girdled his lips,
But never a moan could they get. Where was the source
Of his strength, the home of his courage that topped the best
Of their braves and even out-fabled the lore of their legends?
In the bunch of his shoulders which often had carried a load

Extorting the envy of guides at an Ottawa portage?
The heat of the hatchets was finding a path to that source.
In the thews of his thighs which had mastered the trails of the Neutrals?
They would gash and beribbon those muscles. Was it the blood?
They would draw it fresh from its foundation. Was it the heart?
They dug for it, fought for the scraps in the way of the wolves
But not in these was the valour or stamina lodged;
Nor in the symbol of Richelieu's robes or the seals
Of Mazarin's charters, nor in the stir of the *lilies*
Upon the Imperial folds; nor yet in the words
Loyola wrote on a table of lava-stone
In the cave of Manresa—not in these the source—
But in the sound of invisible trumpets blowing
Around two slabs of board, right-angled, hammered
By Roman nails and hung on a Jewish hill.

The wheel had come full circle with the visions
In France of Brébeuf poured through the mould of St Ignace.
Lalemant died in the morning at nine, in the flame
Of the pitch belts. Flushed with the sight of the bodies, the foes
Gathered their clans and moved back to the north and west
To join in the fight against the tribes of the Petuns.
There was nothing now that could stem the Iroquois blast.
However undaunted the souls of the priests who were left,
However fierce the sporadic counter attacks
Of the Hurons striking in roving bands from the ambush,
Or smashing out at their foes in garrison raids,
The villages fell before a blizzard of axes
And arrows and spears, and then were put to the torch.

The days were dark at the fort and heavier grew
The burdens on Ragueneau's shoulders. Decision was his.
No word from the east could arrive in time to shape
The step he must take. To and fro—from altar to hill,
From hill to altar, he walked and prayed and watched.
As governing priest of the Mission he felt the pride
Of his Order whipping his pulse, for was not St Ignace
The highest test of the Faith? And all that torture
And death could do to the body was done. The Will
And the Cause in their triumph survived.
        Loyola's mountains,
Sublime at their summits, were scaled to the uttermost peak.
Ragueneau, the Shepherd, now looked on a battered fold.
In a whirlwind of fire St Jean, like St Joseph, crashed
Under the Iroquois impact. Firm at his post,

Garnier suffered the fate of Daniel. And now
Chabanel, last in the roll of the martyrs, entrapped
On his knees in the woods met death at apostate hands.

The drama was drawing close to its end. It fell
To Ragueneau's lot to perform a final rite—
To offer the fort in sacrificial fire!
He applied the torch himself. *'Inside an hour,'*
He wrote, *'we saw the fruit of ten years' labour*
Ascend in smoke,—then looked our last at the fields,
Put altar-vessels and food on a raft of logs,
And made our way to the island of St Joseph.'
But even from there was the old tale retold—
Of hunger and the search for roots and acorns;
Of cold and persecution unto death
By the Iroquois; of Jesuit will and courage
As the shepherd-priest with Chaumonot led back
The remnant of a nation to Quebec.

BRÉBEUF AND HIS BRETHREN

See page 231 for a contemporary description
of Brébeuf's remains (*The Jesuit Relations*).

b. 1918

Al Purdy

AL PURDY was born in the village of Wooler, a few miles north-west of Trenton, Ont., and now lives in the village of Ameliasburg, a few miles south-east of Trenton. He left school at sixteen, worked at odd jobs (in factories, driving a taxi in Trenton), served in the RCAF, and has been supporting himself by writing since 1955. He published a book of poetry, *The Enchanted Echo*, in 1944, but more than ten years passed before any other books appeared. His early books include *Emu, Remember!* (1957), *The Crafte So Longe to Lerne* (1959), and *Poems for All the Annettes* (1962), which established his reputation as a poet of rural Ontario. (A CBC recording on which he reads his own poetry is called 'Al Purdy's Ontario'.) The best poetry of his early period was gathered together in *The Cariboo Horses*, which won the Governor General's Award for poetry for 1965.

From the still centre of Ameliasburg, Purdy has gone vagabonding across Canada and to Greece, England, Mexico, and Japan. Wherever he goes poems are written. He refers to his travels in a 1968 interview with Gary Geddes (*Canadian Literature*, Summer, 1969):

GEDDES: In 'The Country North of Belleville' there is a sense of beauty and terror in the description. Do you find the Canadian landscape hostile?

PURDY: Landscapes hostile to man? I think man is hostile to himself. Landscapes, I think, are essentially neutral.

GEDDES: But you travel a lot, as do many Canadian writers, and write about the places you visit. Is this because it is easier to control the elements of a newer, smaller area?

PURDY: Easier than Canada, you mean? No, it isn't that. I have the feeling that —before I worked at jobs and described the places where I was and the people that I met, etc.—that somehow or other one uses up one's past. It isn't that when one goes to another country one is consciously seeking for new poems, because it would get to sounding as goddam self-conscious as hell. For instance, if you go to Baffin Island to write poems (which I did, incidentally) . . . well, I don't like to look at it that way. I'm interested in going to Baffin Island because I'm interested in Baffin Island.

GEDDES: And the poems just happen.

PURDY: I write poems like spiders spin webs, and perhaps for much the same reason: to support my existence.

A grant from the Canada Council took Purdy to the North, where he wrote many of the poems for *North of Summer* (1967). He has also published *Wild Grape Wine* (1968); *Love in a Burning Building* (1970), a gathering together from several books of poems he has written about love and marriage; and *Selected Poems* (1972). Strongly sympathetic to the nationalist movements in Canada, he edited *The New Romans* (1968), an anthology of 'Candid Canadian Opinions of the U.S.'. (He left one of his publishers, the Ryerson Press, when that firm was sold to the American publisher McGraw-Hill.) Purdy has been able to break out of the confines of the traditional literary magazines and publishes regularly in such periodicals as *Maclean's, Weekend,* and *Saturday Night.*

The characteristics of Purdy's poetry are the strong, long line, the casual and colloquial tone, and a deep and often melancholy sense of the nation's past. He is an autobiographical poet, but it would be unwise to regard his poetry as a literal rendering of the poet's life; for among contemporary Canadian poets Purdy is one of the storytellers, in his casual way one of the mythmakers. In his introduction to Purdy's *Selected Poems* George Woodcock, the editor of *Canadian Literature,* has described him as 'also the poet of comedy . . . It is comedy that easily runs black, for it is based on a totally realistic sense of what individual man's fate is in a world where grandeur is a feat of the imagination; where man grows old though his lusts stay young; where his actions are contemptible though his thoughts are high; where his attempts to reconcile the animal and the human within him always end in comic absurdity.' Purdy has been generous in his encouragement of young writers, and in the anthology *Storm Warning* (1971) he introduced the work of thirty young poets from across the country.

There is a study of Al Purdy and his work in Studies in Canadian Literature (1970, Copp Clark), by George Bowering, who has an article on Purdy in Issue 43 of *Canadian Literature* (Winter 1970).

THE COUNTRY NORTH OF BELLEVILLE

Bush land scrub land—
      Cashel Township and Wollaston
Elzevir McClure and Dungannon
green lands of Weslemkoon Lake
where a man might have some
      opinion of what beauty
is and none deny him
            for miles—

Yet this is the country of defeat
where Sisyphus rolls a big stone
year after year up the ancient hills

picnicking glaciers have left strewn
with centuries' rubble
                              backbreaking days
                              in the sun and rain
when realization seeps slow in the mind
without grandeur or self deception in
                              noble struggle
of being a fool—

A country of quiescence and still distance
a lean land
                not like the fat south
with inches of black soil on
                earth's round belly—
And where the farms are
                it's as if a man stuck
both thumbs in the stony earth and pulled

                              it apart
                              to make room
enough between the trees
for a wife
                and maybe some cows and
                room for some
of the more easily kept illusions—
And where the farms have gone back
to forest
                are only soft outlines
                shadowy differences—

Old fences drift vaguely among the trees
                a pile of moss-covered stones
gathered for some ghost purpose
has lost meaning under the meaningless sky
                —they are like cities under water
and the undulating green waves of time
                are laid on them—

This is the country of our defeat
                and yet
during the fall plowing a man
might stop and stand in a brown valley of the furrows
                and shade his eyes to watch for the same
                red patch mixed with gold
                that appears on the same

                spot in the hills
                year after year
                and grow old
plowing and plowing a ten-acre field until
the convolutions run parallel with his own brain—

And this is a country where the young
                leave quickly
unwilling to know what their fathers know
or think the words their mothers do not say—

Herschel Monteagle and Faraday
lakeland rockland and hill country
a little adjacent to where the world is
a little north of where the cities are and
sometime
we may go back there
                            to the country of our defeat
Wollaston Elzevir and Dungannon
and Weslemkoon lake land
where the high townships of Cashel
                    McClure and Marmora once were—
But it's been a long time since
and we must enquire the way
            of strangers —

LAMENT FOR THE DORSETS

(ESKIMOS EXTINCT IN THE 14TH CENTURY A.D.)

Animal bones and some mossy tent rings
scrapers and spearheads   carved ivory swans
all that remains of the Dorset giants
who drove the Vikings back to their long ships
talked to spirits of earth and water
—a picture of terrifying old men
so large they broke the backs of bears
so small they lurk behind bone rafters
in the brain of modern hunters
among good thoughts and warm things
and come out at night
to spit on the stars

The big men with clever fingers
who had no dogs and hauled their sleds
over the frozen northern oceans
awkward giants
                 killers of seal
they couldn't compete with little men
who came from the west with dogs
Or else in a warm climatic cycle
the seals went back to cold waters
and the puzzled Dorsets scratched their heads
with hairy thumbs around 1350 A.D.
—couldn't figure it out
went around saying to each other
plaintively
          'What's wrong? What happened?
          Where are the seals gone?'
And died

Twentieth century people
apartment dwellers
executives of neon death
warmakers with things that explode
—they have never imagined us in their future
how could we imagine them in the past
squatting among the moving glaciers
six hundred years ago
with glowing lamps?
As remote or nearly
as the trilobites and swamps
when coal became
or the last great reptile hissed
at a mammal the size of a mouse
that squeaked and fled

Did they ever realize at all
what was happening to them?
Some old hunter with one lame leg
a bear had chewed
sitting in a caribou-skin tent
—the last Dorset?
Let's say his name was Kudluk
and watch him sitting there
carving 2-inch ivory swans
for a dead grand-daughter
taking them out of his mind

the places in his mind
where pictures are
He selects a sharp stone tool
to gouge a parallel pattern of lines
on both sides of the swan
holding it with his left hand
bearing down and transmitting
his body's weight
from brain to arm and right hand
and one of his thoughts
turns to ivory
The carving is laid aside
in beginning darkness
at the end of hunger
and after a while wind
blows down the tent and snow
begins to cover him
After 600 years
the ivory thought
is still warm

THE CARIBOO HORSES

At 100 Mile House the cowboys ride in rolling
stagey cigarettes with one hand reining
half-tame bronco rebels on a morning grey as stone
—so much like riding dangerous women
     with whisky-coloured eyes—
such women as once fell dead with their lovers
with fire in their heads and slippery froth on thighs
—Beaver or Carrier woman maybe or
     Blackfoot squaws far past the edge of this valley
on the other side of those two toy mountain ranges
     from the sunfierce plains beyond

But only horses
                    waiting in stables
hitched at taverns
                      standing at dawn
pastured outside the town with
jeeps and fords and chevvys and
busy muttering stake trucks rushing
importantly over roads of man's devising
over the safe known roads of the ranchers
families and merchants of the town
                    On the high prairie
are only horse and rider
                    wind in dry grass
clopping in silence under the toy mountains
dropping sometimes and
                    lost in the dry grass
                    golden oranges of dung

Only horses
                    no stopwatch memories or palace ancestors
not Kiangs hauling undressed stone in the Nile Valley
and having stubborn Egyptian tantrums or
Onagers racing thru Hither Asia and
the last Quagga screaming in African highlands
                    lost relatives of these
                    whose hooves were thunder
the ghosts of horses battering thru the wind
whose names were the wind's common usage
whose life was the sun's
                    arriving here at chilly noon
                    in the gasoline smell of the
                    dust and waiting 15 minutes
                    at the grocer's

WILDERNESS GOTHIC

Across Roblin Lake, two shores away,
they are sheathing the church spire
with new metal. Someone hangs in the sky
over there from a piece of rope,
hammering and fitting God's belly-scratcher,
working his way up along the spire
until there's nothing left to nail on—
Perhaps the workman's faith reaches beyond:
touches intangibles, wrestles with Jacob,
replacing rotten timber with pine thews,
pounds hard in the blue cave of the sky,
contends heroically with difficult problems
of gravity, sky navigation and mythopeia,
his volunteer time and labour donated to God,
minus sick benefits of course on a non-union job—

Fields around are yellowing into harvest,
nestling and fingerling are sky and water borne,
death is yodelling quiet in green woodlots,
and bodies of three young birds have disappeared
in the sub-surface of the new country highway—

That picture is incomplete; part left out
that might alter the whole Durer landscape:
gothic ancestors peer from medieval sky,
dour faces trapped in photograph albums escaping
to clop down iron roads with matched greys:
work-sodden wives groping inside their flesh
for what keeps moving and changing and flashing
beyond and past the long frozen Victorian day.
A sign of fire and brimstone? A two-headed calf
born in the barn last night? A sharp female agony?
An age and a faith moving into transition,
the dinner cold and new-baked bread a failure,
deep woods shiver and water drops hang pendant,
double yolked eggs and the house creaks a little—
Something is about to happen. Leaves are still.
Two shores away, a man hammering in the sky.
Perhaps he will fall.

b. 1926

James Reaney

JAMES REANEY, who is both poet and play-wright, was born on a farm near Strat-ford, Ont. He attended high school in Stratford and won a scholarship to the University of Toronto, where he attended University College. Graduating with an M.A. in 1949, he taught English at the University of Manitoba until 1956 and then returned to Toronto to get a Ph.D., which he received in 1958. After teach-ing for two more years at Manitoba, he moved to the University of Western Ontario where he is Professor of Eng-lish. From 1961 to 1971 he edited and for a time typeset *Alphabet: A Semi-annual Devoted to the Iconography of the Imagination*. He is married to Col-leen Thibaudeau, who is also a poet.

A highly creative person, Reaney has not let his work as a scholar and teacher prevent him from attaining a remark-able degree of productivity as a writer. The experiences of childhood on a southern-Ontario farm—his love of nur-sery rhymes and fairy tales, his play activities, and the unappealing but stim-ulating evangelical religious environment he grew up in—influenced his imagina-tion when he was young and have re-mained strong influences. His creative life actually began in his teens, when he wrote and rewrote a novel called *After-noon Moon* that was partly autobiograph-ical and partly sensational melodrama. It continued when he had numerous poems published while he was at univer-sity, and it received public recognition in 1949 with the publication of his first collection, *The Red Heart*, for which he won a Governor General's Award. This award was given to Reaney two more times: for *A Suit of Nettles* (1958) and in 1962 for *Twelve Letters to a Small Town* and *The Killdeer and Other Plays*. *A Suit of Nettles* grew out of Reaney's interest in 'geese, country life in Ontario, Canada as an object of conversation and Edmund Spenser's *Shepherd's Calendar*', and its structure—a series of poetic dia-logues, one for each month of the year, among geese on an Ontario farm—gave him an opportunity to have fun with these and other subjects in a sequence of poems of great metrical ingenuity. *Twelve Letters* is an imaginative tribute to the town of Stratford; the two poems below are taken from this collection. He is also the author of a novel for children,

The Boy with an R in His Hand (1965), about York (Toronto) in the 1820s.

Reaney is interested not only in the whole world of childhood, which he sees as a world of metaphor, but in the illuminating powers of symbol and myth, and in melodrama because it reveals to him 'strong patterns' of life. The theatre provided a natural medium for the expression of these interests and in the 1950s he began the first of many entertainments and poetic dramas. (In 1966 he established a workshop in London for theatrical experiments.) His experimental plays use a somewhat improvisational 'mosaic' form and technique to create a world of spontaneous playfulness that projects an original poetic vision. 'Art is made by subtracting from reality,' Reaney has written, 'and letting the viewer imagine or "dream it out".'

Among his works for the theatre are *Night Blooming Cereus* (produced in 1960, published in 1962), an opera with music by John Beckwith; *The Sun and the Moon* (1962, 1965); *One-Man Masque* (1960, 1962); *The Easter Egg* (1962, 1972), from which there is a short extract below; *Names and Nicknames* (1963, 1969), a children's play; *Listen to the Wind* (1966, 1972), which Reaney finds his most satisfying play to date; and *Colours in the Dark* (1967, 1969), which has received productions at the Stratford Festival and the National Arts Centre. *The Easter Egg, Three Desks,* and *The Killdeer* are collected in *Masks of Childhood* (1972). R.B. Parker, the editor of this volume, writes in an Afterword: 'Reaney's sophisticated playfulness depends not only on our recognition of the child, but on our acknowledgement of the adult beneath the child as well, the poet in the mask of childhood. It depends upon an interface between the child-beneath-the-man and the man-beneath-the-child, and only when both elements are present do we hear James Reaney's voice in all its complexity, the artful artlessness of one of Canada's major poets.'

Reaney has an article on his playwriting in Issue 41 of *Canadian Literature* (Summer 1969). There are two useful studies of his work: by Alvin A. Lee in the Twayne World Authors Series (1969, Burns & MacEachern) and by Ross Woodman in McClelland & Stewart's Canadian Writers Series (1972).

TO THE AVON RIVER
ABOVE STRATFORD, CANADA

What did the Indians call you?
For you do not flow
With English accents.
I hardly know
What I should call you
   Because before
I drank coffee or tea
   I drank you
   With my cupped hands

And you did not taste English to me
>And you do not sound
>Like Avon
>Or swans & bards
But rather like the sad wild fowl
>In prints drawn
>By Audubon
And like dear bad poets
>Who wrote
>Early in Canada
And never were of note.
You are the first river
>I crossed
And like the first whirlwind
>The first rainbow
>First snow, first
>Falling star I saw,
You, for other rivers are my law.
>These other rivers:
>The Red & the Thames
>Are never so sweet
To skate upon, swim in
>Or for baptism of sin.
>Silver and light
The sentence of your voice,
>With a soprano
Continuous cry you shall
>Always flow
>Through my heart.
The rain and the snow of my mind
Shall supply the spring of that river
>Forever.
Though not your name
Your coat of arms I know
>And motto:
A shield of reeds and cresses
>Sedges, crayfishes
The hermaphroditic leech
Minnows, muskrats and farmers' geese
And printed above this shield
One of my earliest wishes
'To flow like you.'

TOWN HOUSE & COUNTRY MOUSE

Old maids are the houses in town
They sit on streets like cement canals
   They are named after aldermen
     And their wives
  Or battles and dukes.

At a sky scratched with wires and smoke
They point their mild and weak gothic bonnets.
The houses of Albert and Brunswick Streets
Wait for farmers' barns to wed them
   But the streets are too narrow
    And they never come.

Out here barn is wedded to house,
   House is married to barn,
   Grey board and pink brick.
    The cowyard lies between
Where in winter on brown thin ice
   Red-capped children skate.
   There is wallpaper in the house
    And in the barn
They are sawing the horns off a bull.

Out here the sound of bells on a wet evening
   Floating out clear when the wind is right.
   The factory whistles at noon in summer.
    Going from here to there
  As a child, not to a place with a name
   But first to get there:
The red buggy wheels move so fast
   They stand still
Whirling against sheaves of blue chicory
The secret place where wild bees nest
The million leaning pens of grass with their nibs
  of seed,
    The wild rose bush—all
     Suddenly gone.

On gravel now where corduroy logs from the past
    Look dumbly up
Buried in the congregations of gravel,
    Getting closer the highway
    Cars darting back and forth
    In another world altogether.
Past the stonemason's house with its cement lion
    Not something to be very much afraid of
    Since it has legs like a table,
    Past the ten huge willows, the four poplars.
    Far away in a field the slaughterhouse,
    Two gas stations with windy signs,
The half world of the city outskirts: orchards
    Gone wild and drowned farms.
    Suddenly the square:—
People turning and shining like lighted jewels,
    Terrifying sights: one's first nun!
    The first person with a wooden leg,
    A huge chimney writing the sky
    With dark smoke.
      A parrot
A clock in the shape of a man with its face
    In his belly
    The swan
A Dixie cup of ice cream with a wooden spoon

And then—backwards, the gas stations,
    The outskirts, orchards, slaughterhouse
    Far back the chimneys still writing
    Four poplars, ten huge willows
    The lion with table legs.
The bump as we go over old corduroy log
The gamut of grass and blue flowers
    Until the wheels stop
    And we are not uptown
    We are here
Where barn is wedded to house . . .
    Into town, out of town.

THE EASTER EGG Act One: Scene Four

Polly has been giving lessons to Kenneth, whose development was arrested when he was six and saw his father shoot himself. He and Polly are not related: they have the same stepmother, Bethel, but different fathers.

POLLY. Kenneth. Here, I'll finish that. Kenneth, my fiancé will be calling in ten minutes or so if not sooner. So we'll more or less pass the time until he comes. Let's sit down, Kenneth. Well?
First, we'll do our word list. Recite me the twenty-seven words that one uses At Home.

KENNETH. house door room porch floor hall entry staircase wardrobe parlour closet pantry kitchen window cupboard threshold dining-room bathroom garret attic cellar chamber bedroom library veranda balcony piazza

POLLY. Good. Now, Kenneth. Kenneth, do we understand these words? Sometimes I really wonder if after all our work you understand what I say. Really understand, or do you just go by the rise and fall of my voice and the words you did know before—before it happened.

KENNETH. Polly, Polly. Come and see the little girl.

POLLY. Can you see her, Kenneth?

KENNETH. I can see the little girl. She's tied to the picket.

POLLY *(looking at a notebook)*. Oh shucks. Picket. You have used it before. I was hoping it might be our new word. Not fence, eh? Fence?

KENNETH. Picket.

POLLY. Kenneth—Look out at the little girl. What do you see on one side of the picket fence, Kenneth?

KENNETH. Garden. Flowers. A butterfly.

POLLY. Yes. To you the garden is on that side of the house. Bethel must have put a lawn over the old garden. Yes. Kenneth, last night I went out and dug in the place where she stopped you digging in the lawn. I took a covered lantern. It was very exciting like digging for treasure. I found—do you know what I found—a rusty old metal box which I couldn't open. So my fiancé is taking it to the blacksmith's today to get it opened. Now what could be inside it? Well, we'll soon know. Now let's see what words you understand in the At Home list.

KENNETH. There's the mouse with wings.

POLLY. My golly, there's the bat. It knows there's going to be a party. I'll bet it will go for the Dean of Women. Get all tangled up in her hair or her hat. Shall we warn Bethel?

KENNETH. I—I—

POLLY. Yes!

KENNETH. Told Bethel.

POLLY. Then she's warned. Now—show me that you understand house.

KENNETH. House! (*He mimes or points out the words he understands.*)

POLLY. Show me a door.

KENNETH. Door!

POLLY. Where is the attic? (*He points.*) And where is the cellar? (*He points.*) Where is the threshold? (*He is undecided.*)

    Show it to me, Kenneth. Show me the threshold! (*He stamps his foot and shakes his head.*) I see. You did say the word, but you won't use it. Oh my dear. If only you'd use the new words I give you, why, you'd be free. But if you only use the old words you knew before it happened you'll always be back before it happened.

KENNETH. Polly—

POLLY. Kenneth. I look at you and then I look only at your eyes and then I look down in your eyes. I see at the bottom of the well of your eyes:

> A sleeping young clever and talkative
> Young man whom I can never wake
> No matter what whistle or bell or call I use.
> Sometimes he reaches up to me and I
> Reach down to him. But our hands touch the glass
> Of impossibility and you sink back to sleep.

They reach out their hands to each other. Just as she is about to touch him he turns away until his back is to her.

    Oh, Kenneth. Once more. Say 'tumbler'.

KENNETH. 'Tumbler.'

POLLY. Now bring me a tumbler from the cabinet over there.

KENNETH *stands still.*

    Never mind. Here—see if you can read this. (*Gives him a book.*)

KENNETH (*after looking it over*).

> The Huntsman Night
> Rides down the Sky
> To usher in the Morn

POLLY. (*Hands him a piece of paper.*) Now read this.

KENNETH. I cannot read it, Polly.

POLLY. But it's the same. Only it's in handwriting. You can't read handwriting very often, can you? Now here. Read this. (*She gives him another piece of paper.*)

KENNETH. The Huntsman Night
> Rides down the Sky
> To usher in the Morn.

POLLY. It's the same too. Only I printed it out. That's a good thing to know,

Kenneth. That you can read my printing. By the way what is a Huntsman? (*He mimes someone taking aim and shooting.*) Good! And what
is—Night? (*He squeezes his eyes shut and mimes drowsiness.*) Good!
Oh we'll rev and rev and rev your mind up until with just our eight hundred words we'll suddenly be flying—up over the world barrier. Kenneth, someday I'll be teaching you just as I am today and I'll ask you—
as I did today—what a tumbler is. You'll pause, then suddenly say 'I
know, Polly, I know what a tumbler is. And a threshold. And a piazza.'
And then—you'll be a grown man, Kenneth, and the lessons—my
lessons will be over. Let's do etiquette, rhyming and dancing next.
Rhymes for scholar!

KENNETH. Beggar, bursar, vicar!

POLLY. Rhymes for pioneer!

KENNETH. Auctioneer, charioteer, mutineer, scrutineer.

POLLY. Nursery!

KENNETH. Surgery, nunnery, colliery, cemetery.

POLLY. Story!

KENNETH. Dormitory, factory, observatory, oratory.

POLLY. Ward!

KENNETH. Eastward westward northward southward heavenward homeward leeward, thitherward whitherward downward upward

POLLY (*closing her book*). Most of those words you've no idea of their
meaning, but we're sowing them in your mind anyhow. Now Kenneth.
Etiquette. Introduce me to Mr Chair.

KENNETH. Mr Chair, I—I should like you to meet Miss Henry.

POLLY. No, no. The other way around.

KENNETH. Miss Henry, I should like you to meet Mr Chair. Mr Chair, I
should like you to meet Miss Henry.

POLLY. Very nice to meet you, Mr Chair.

KENNETH. Polly, who is Miss Henry?

POLLY. Why Kenneth, don't you know? It's me. It's my official name. Now
make conversation with Mr Chair and me.

KENNETH. Mr Chair, have you been long in town?

POLLY. Oh, a day or two. Just tootling through, you know.

KENNETH. Mr Chair, how do you find our summers?

POLLY. A pleasant contrast to your winters, I must say.

KENNETH. (*Laughs.*) And, Mr Chair, how do you find our, our aut—fall?

POLLY. Say what you were going to say, Kenneth. It can be the new word.

KENNETH. Father says it's American to say fall. United Empire Loyalists
say—say autumn.

POLLY. Gosh, five words I didn't know you'd bumped into. (*Writes in notebook.*) Not really new words though. Words floating up from before—

huh—before the Deluge. I wonder if your father also thought that *(to herself)* that United Empire Loyalists should say: I autumn off the ladder. I autumned down.

(She winds up a victrola.) Now our dancing. This gives you poise, Kenneth, and helps you to walk more gracefully. Like this. *(Mimes.)* I hate to see people walking along like this *(Mimes.)*—every tromp of foot and clumsy thrust of shoulder a denial of love and beauty. On the other hand, young men shouldn't be too graceful. A certain amount of clumsiness. A certain amount of clumsiness is quite charming to a girl because it means she has something to work on. He needs her help. This music is called—Isn't it odd my fiancé's not arrived? This is really a pretty piece. It's 'The Japanese Sandman'. Come. *(They dance. At first she leads. Then as he catches on, he leads.)* Oh—let's rest for a while. Are you as breathless as I am? *(He still wants to dance.)* George is very late. No, I couldn't dance another step. It's time for our closing story. I thought I'd illustrate your story tonight. Perhaps you'll understand it better. See—I've brought down this old toy train. And I'll take down this doll from the mantelpiece. You get it for me, dear. The little doll made out of pipe cleaners and pieces of old hair ribbon. What are you staring at the clock for, Kenneth?

KENNETH. 'Little clock, I'll tell the clock-doctor to
    Come and put all your little wheels asleep.'

POLLY. Hmh?*(She hasn't heard, putting the toy train together having occupied her attention.)* Now. We'll put the doll and the toy train on this little coffee table in front of us and listen awfully hard and see if you can understand. Yesterday we finished the tales of Jane Austen and today I rather thought we might go on to the works of Tolstoi. Now, Kenneth, I am going to tell you the story of Anna Karenina. Once there was a girl, Anna by name, who married a rich important man somewhat older than herself. She had children by him. He really bored her to tears —he was so bossy and cold. See, Kenneth, Anna is the little doll standing by the toy train tracks.

KENNETH. Anna.

POLLY. Yes. One day she fell in love with a young soldier named Vronsky. After you are married you are not supposed to fall in love again. You must work hard at trying to love your husband even if he is a turnip. But Anna could not really help herself. Young Vronsky became an obsession with her. Her husband noted that she loved this young man and he was most displeased. One day at the horse races Vronsky fell off his horse and she showed obvious concern in front of a great many people. *(leaping up)* Vronsky! Anna's husband was terribly embarrassed—ashamed—because now everyone else would know that Anna loved this young man instead of himself. 'Take my arm, Anna. Take my arm, Anna.'

Anna made a journey by train from St Petersburg to Moscow in the depth of winter and her little son met her at the station. *(She lets the train circle the track once or twice.)* At the snowy station there was an old man, a railway worker, who was tapping snow and ice from the wheels. The train moved unexpectedly and pinned him down. (POLLY *illustrates this with a poker from the fireplace and the sofa as the locomotive.)* The old man was hurt. Anna saw him and cried out. She felt that she someday would die that way. And the old man with his metal tapping rod was Death.

Kenneth, she separated from her husband and went to live with the young man. They sat in a farmhouse looking at the fire together and roasting apples. The way we did last winter. They went to Venice and lived in a palace there by a canal. Gondolas went up and down. But back in Russia the train still went back and forth through the snow between St Petersburg and Moscow.

They went back to Russia. Somehow or other they quarrelled. They couldn't get married. That was the trouble because Anna's husband wouldn't give her a divorce. So Anna and Vronsky had to be in love all the time which is very hard on the nerves as I can tell you. And she couldn't see her children. One night she, Anna, and he, Vronsky, quarrelled terribly. She ran out of their house and as she slammed the door she said, 'You'll be sorry'. She walked to the railway station. There was a train leaving soon. In the darkness up and down beside the the tracks she walked up and down. She knew what she must do. The train began to move out of the station—its headlight gets larger and larger. With her back to the train Anna stood over one of the tracks and waited. *(She puts the doll on the track and lets the train start up, holding it back with her hand a bit. He leaps forward and stops the train with his arms. He gets the doll away.)*

KENNETH. No! No!

POLLY. Oh, Kenneth, Kenneth. You do understand. You do understand the story. You don't want Anna to die. And she won't die. There, there. I'll change the story. It's wonderful you understand. Kenneth. *(He lies quietly in her arms on the sofa and she rocks him.)* There, there—I'll change the story, Kenneth.

As the curtain falls we see the doll in his hand. The toy train still goes round and round the track.

Mordecai Richler

MORDECAI RICHLER is a persistent critic of Canadian manners and society and one of the country's best and most prolific writers of fiction as well. He was born in the Montreal Jewish community that existed uneasily between the French Canadians in the East End and the economically dominant English Canadians who lived in the city's western districts. (The streets where he grew up and about which he has written much of his fiction are now mostly inhabited by Greeks and other recent immigrants from Europe and the West Indies.) He left Montreal before he was twenty, and after a brief period at Sir George Williams University, to become a writer. He lived for a time in Spain, then in Paris, and for more than a dozen years in London. In the summer of 1972 he returned to Montreal; he plans to teach for a day or two a week at Carleton University in Ottawa.

Richler's first novel, *The Acrobats* (1954), was a young man's disenchanted description of expatriates living in Spain. With *Son of a Smaller Hero* (1955) and *The Apprenticeship of Duddy Kravitz* (1959), which some of his admirers consider to be his best novel, the setting was the abundant Jewish life of the Main and its tributary streets in the Montreal ghetto. He then published two extravagantly satirical novels, *The Incomparable Atuk* (1963) and *Cocksure* (1968); the latter was a controversial winner of the Governor General's Award for fiction. (Richler has described the Governor General as being the Queen's 'Canadian second-floor maid'.) In 1971 he published a major novel on which he had been working for five years, *St Urbain's Horseman*. It also won a Governor General's Award and has been a popular success in Canada, the United States, and England. His short stories were collected in *The Street* (1969) and are linked together by some interesting autobiographical notes. He has been a prolific journalist—as well as a writer of movie scripts and radio and television plays—and some of his articles were published in *Hunting Tigers Under Glass* (1968); their subjects range widely through Expo 67, sports, comic books, the movies, and fellow novelists Norman Mailer and Bernard Malamud. He followed this with a collection of fifteen essays, *Shovelling Trouble* (1972). Richler is the editor of *Canadian Writing Today* (1970), one of a series of anthologies of contemporary writing from various countries published by Penguin Books.

Richler's satirical fiction and a good deal of his journalism is—in the modern manner—deliberately shocking, aggressive, and destructive, the work of an angry moralist and social critic. In the stories and novels that are most directly connected with his memories of life in the Jewish community of Montreal, there is a powerful and rooted sense of character and place, expressed in *Son of a Smaller Hero* in the mid-1950s and captured once again in *St Urbain's Horseman* at the beginning of the 1970s.

George Woodcock wrote a study of Mordecai Richler in the Canadian Writers series in the New Canadian Library. An interview with Richler by Nathan Cohen is in *The First Five Years: A Selection from 'The Tamarack Review'* edited by Robert Weaver. *Son of a Smaller Hero*, *The Apprenticeship of Duddy Kravitz*, and *The Incomparable Atuk* are available in the New Canadian Library.

BENNY

When Benny was sent overseas in the autumn of 1941 his father, Garber, decided that if he had to yield one son to the army it might as well be Benny, who was a dumbie and wouldn't push where he shouldn't; Mrs Garber thought, he'll take care, my Benny will watch out; and Benny's brother Abe proclaimed, 'When he comes back, I'll have a garage of my own, you bet, and I'll be able to give him a job.' Benny wrote every week, and every week the Garbers sent him parcels full of good things a St Urbain Street boy should always have, like salami and pickled herring and *shtrudel*. The food parcels never varied and the letters—coming from Camp Borden and Aldershot and Normandy and Holland—were always the same too. They began—'I hope you are all well and good'—and ended —'don't worry, all the best to everybody, thank you for the parcel.'

When Benny came home from the war in Europe, the Garbers didn't make an inordinate fuss, like the Shapiros did when their first-born son returned. They met him at the station, of course, and they had a small dinner for him.

Abe was overjoyed to see Benny again. 'Atta boy,' was what he kept saying all evening, 'Atta boy, Benny.'

'You shouldn't go back to the factory,' Mr Garber said. 'You don't need the old job. You can be a help to your brother Abe in his garage.'

'Yes,' Benny said.

'Let him be, let him rest,' Mrs Garber said. 'What'll happen if he doesn't work for two weeks?'

'Hey, when Artie Segal came back,' Abe said, 'he told me that in Italy there was nothing that a guy couldn't get for a couple of Sweet Caps. Was he shooting me the bull or what?'

Benny had been discharged and sent home not because the war was over, but because of the shrapnel in his leg. He didn't limp too badly and he wouldn't talk about his wound or the war, so at first nobody noticed that he had changed. Nobody, that is, except Myerson's daughter, Bella.

Myerson was the proprietor of Pop's Cigar & Soda, on St Urbain, and any day of the week you could find him there seated on a worn, peeling kitchen chair playing poker with the men of the neighbourhood. He had a glass eye and when a player hesitated on a bet, he would take it out and polish it, a gesture that never failed to intimidate. His daughter, Bella, worked behind the counter. She had a clubfoot and mousey brown hair and some more hair on her face, and although she was only twenty-six, it was generally agreed that she would end up an old maid. Anyway she was the one—the first one—to notice that Benny had changed. The very first time he appeared in Pop's Cigar & Soda after his homecoming, she said to him, 'What's wrong, Benny?'

'I'm all right,' he said.

Benny was short and skinny with a long narrow face, a pulpy mouth that was somewhat crooked, and soft black eyes. He had big, conspicuous hands which he preferred to keep out of sight in his pockets. In fact he seemed to want to keep out of sight altogether and whenever possible, he stood behind a chair or in a dim light so that the others wouldn't notice him. When he had failed the ninth grade at f.f.h.s, Benny's class master, a Mr Perkins, had sent him home with a note saying: 'Benjamin is not a student, but he has all the makings of a good citizen. He is honest and attentive in class and a hard worker. I recommend that he learn a trade.'

When Mr Garber had read what his son's teacher had written, he had shaken his head and crumpled up the bit of paper and said—'A trade?'— he had looked at his boy and shaken his head and said—'A trade?'

Mrs Garber had said stoutly, 'Haven't you got a trade?'

'Shapiro's boy will be a doctor,' Mr Garber had said.

'Shapiro's boy,' Mrs Garber had said.

Afterwards, Benny had retrieved the note and smoothed out the creases and put it in his pocket, where it remained.

The day after his return to Montreal, Benny showed up at Abe's garage having decided that he didn't want two weeks off. That pleased Abe a lot. 'I can see that you've matured since you've been away,' Abe said. 'That's good. That counts for you in this world.'

Abe worked extremely hard, he worked night and day, and he believed that having Benny with him would give his business an added kick. 'That's my kid brother Benny,' Abe used to tell the taxi drivers. 'Four years in the infantry, two of them up front. A tough *hombre*, let me tell you.'

For the first few weeks Abe was pleased with Benny. 'He's slow,' he reported to their father, 'no genius of a mechanic, but the customers like him and he'll learn.' Then Abe began to notice things. When business was slow, Benny, instead of taking advantage of the lull to clean up the shop, used to sit shivering in a dim corner, with his hands folded tight on his lap. The first time Abe noticed his brother behaving like that, he said, 'What's wrong? You got a chill?'

'No. I'm all right.'

'You want to go home or something?'

'No.'

Whenever it rained, and it rained often that spring, Benny was not to be found around the garage, and that put Abe in a foul temper. Until one day during a thunder shower, Abe tried the toilet door and discovered that it was locked. 'Benny,' he yelled, 'you come out, I know you're in there.'

Benny didn't answer, so Abe fetched the key. He found Benny huddled in a corner with his head buried in his knees, trembling, with sweat running down his face in spite of the cold.

'It's raining,' Benny said.

'Benny, get up. What's wrong?'

'Go away. It's raining.'

'I'll get a doctor, Benny.'

'No. Go away. Please, Abe.'

'But Benny . . .'

Benny began to shake violently, just as if an inner whip had been cracked. Then, after it had passed, he looked up at Abe dumbly, his mouth hanging open. 'It's raining,' he said.

The next morning Abe went to see Mr Garber. 'I don't know what to do with him,' he said.

'The war left him with a bad taste,' Mrs Garber said.

'Other boys went to the war,' Abe said.

'Shapiro's boy,' Mr Garber said, 'was an officer.'

'Shapiro's boy,' Mrs Garber said. 'You give him a vacation, Abe. You insist. He's a good boy. From the best.'

Benny didn't know what to do with his vacation, so he slept in late, and began to hang around Pop's Cigar & Soda.

'I don't like it, Bella,' Myerson said, 'I need him here like I need a cancer.'

'Something's wrong with him psychologically,' one of the card players ventured.

But obviously Bella enjoyed having Benny around and after a while Myerson stopped complaining. 'Maybe the boy is serious,' he confessed, 'and with her club foot and all that stuff on her face, I can't start picking and choosing. Besides, it's not as if he was a crook. Like Huberman's boy.'

'You take that back. Huberman's boy was a victim of circumstances. He was taking care of the suitcase for a stranger, a complete stranger, when the cops had to mix in.'

Bella and Benny did not talk much when they were together. She used to knit, he used to smoke. He would watch silently as she limped about the store, silently, with longing, and consternation. The letter from Mr Perkins was in his pocket. Occasionally, Bella would look up from her knitting. 'You feel like a cup coffee?'

'I wouldn't say no.'

Around five in the afternoon he would get up, Bella would come round the counter to give him a stack of magazines to take home, and at night he would read them all from cover to cover and the next morning bring them back as clean as new. Then he would sit with her in the store again, looking down at the floor or at his hands.

One day instead of going home around five in the afternoon, Benny went upstairs with Bella. Myerson, who was watching, smiled. He turned to Shub and said: 'If I had a boy of my own, I couldn't wish for a better one than Benny.'

'Look who's counting chickens,' Shub replied.

Benny's vacation dragged on for several weeks and every morning he sat down at the counter in Pop's Cigar & Soda and every evening he went upstairs with Bella, pretending not to hear the wise-cracks made by the card players as they passed. Until one afternoon Bella summoned Myerson upstairs in the middle of a deal. 'We have decided to get married,' she said.

'In that case,' Myerson said, 'you have my permission.'

'Aren't you even going to say luck or something?' Bella asked.

'It's your life,' Myerson said.

They had a very simple wedding without speeches in a small synagogue and after the ceremony was over Abe whacked his younger brother on the back and said, 'Atta boy, Benny. Atta boy.'

'Can I come back to work?'

'Sure you can. You're the old Benny again. I can see that.'

But his father, Benny noticed, was not too pleased with the match. Each time one of Garber's cronies congratulated him, he shrugged his shoulders and said, 'Shapiro's boy married into the Segals.'

'Shapiro's boy,' Mrs Garber said.

Benny went back to the garage, but this time he settled down to work hard and that pleased Abe enormously. 'That's my kid brother Benny,' Abe took to telling the taxi drivers, 'married six weeks and he's already got one in the oven. A quick worker, I'll tell you.'

Benny not only settled down to work hard, but he even laughed a little, and, with Bella's help, began to plan for the future. But every now and then, usually when there was a slack period at the garage, Benny would shut up tight and sit in a chair in a dark corner. He had only been back at work for three, maybe four, months when Bella went to speak to Abe. She returned to their flat on St Urbain her face flushed and triumphant. 'I've got news for you,' she said to Benny. 'Abe is going to open another garage on Mount Royal and you're going to manage it.'

'But I don't want to, I wouldn't know how.'

'We're going to be partners in the new garage.'

'I'd rather stay with Abe.'

Bella explained that they had to plan for their child's future. Their son, she swore, would not be brought up over a cigar & soda, without so much as a shower in the flat. She wanted a fridge. If they saved, they could afford a car. Next year, she said, after the baby was born, she hoped there would be sufficient money saved so that she could go to a clinic in the United States to have an operation on her foot. 'I was to Dr Shapiro yesterday and he assured me there is a clinic in Boston where they perform miracles daily.'

'He examined you?' Benny asked.

'He was very, very nice. Not a snob, if you know what I mean.'

'Did he remember that he was at school with me?'

'No,' Bella said.

Bella woke at three in the morning to find Benny huddled on the floor in a dark corner with his head buried in his knees, trembling. 'It's raining,' he said. 'There's thunder.'

'A man who fought in the war can't be scared of a little rain.'

'Oh, Bella. Bella, Bella.'

She attempted to stroke his head but he drew sharply away from her.

'Should I send for a doctor?'

'Shapiro's boy maybe?' he asked, giggling.

'Why not?'

'Bella,' he said. 'Bella, Bella.'

'I'm going next door to the Idelsohns to phone for the doctor. Don't move. Relax.'

But when she returned to the bedroom he had gone.

Myerson came round at eight in the morning. Mr and Mrs Garber were with him.

'Is he dead?' Bella asked.

'Shapiro's boy, the doctor, said it was quick.'

'Shapiro's boy,' Mrs Garber said.

'It wasn't the driver's fault,' Myerson said.

'I know,' Bella said.

THE STREET

Ringuet

Marie-Joseph-Philippe Panneton, who wrote under the pseudonym 'RINGUET' (the family name of his mother), was the author of the first realistic novel about rural Québec, a classic of French-Canadian fiction. He was born in Trois-Rivières, Qué., and educated at Université Laval and the Université de Montréal, where he obtained a degree in medicine in 1920. After further studies in Paris, he practised medicine in Trois-Rivières, Joliette, and Montreal. In 1935 he became a professor of medicine at the Université de Montréal. Appointed Canadian ambassador to Portugal in 1956, he died there four years later.

Prior to the publication of Ringuet's first and most famous novel, *Trente arpents* (1938), which was published in English as *Thirty Acres* (1940), there had been a long tradition of romantic, idealistic novels about the hard life of the *habitants* of Québec, written when the province still had an agricultural economy. They celebrated the close connection between faithfulness to the land and the French-Canadian virtues of maintaining one's religion, language, and traditions. (*Maria Chapdelaine*—though written by a Frenchman—was the classic rural idyll of French Canada.) Ringuet unsentimentally describes this way of life as it was being drastically altered by economic and social changes in the late nineteenth and early twentieth century. *Trente arpents* is about Euchariste Moisan—hard-working, ambitious, practical in all things, avaricious —who is passionately devoted to the thirty acres of land he had inherited from an uncle. He marries, has children, and makes money. As the years go on and 'progress' invades the countryside, he resists these changes and upholds the old traditions. He makes mistakes that cause him to lose everything he values and ends up as a night watchman in the alien land of Massachusetts, where his Americanized son is living. *Trente arpents* is an enduring novel that is both a richly detailed, objective account of *habitant* life in the throes of urbanization and a memorable character study. It won a Governor General's Award.

Ringuet also wrote *Fausse monnaie* (1947), a novelette, *Le poids du jour* (1949), a novel about business life in

Montreal, and *L'Héritage et autres contes* (1946), the title story of which is translated in *Canadian Short Stories* (1960), selected by Robert Weaver. *Thirty Acres* is available in paperback in the New Canadian Library.

GIVING GOD HIS DUE

A series of good harvests had made the Moisans fairly prosperous—though they didn't advertise the fact—and they had never had to touch the money banked with the notary. Yet sending Oguinase to town was an expensive undertaking and they hesitated a good deal. For months at a time Euchariste was even more silent than usual, particularly during the evenings when he sat in the kitchen in Uncle Ephrem's rocking-chair, forgetting even to smoke as he wavered between his ambition to have his boy enter the priesthood and his unwillingness to let him go just when he was of age to contribute his much-needed help on the farm. If he sent him off, would he not be depriving the land of its due?

When a second son came and then a third, he was more willing to consent; in a sense these births freed him of his obligation to the farm. However, he had not yet quite made up his mind. It was the parish priest himself who finally turned the scales. One fine day after High Mass he asked Euchariste to come to his study in the big, cool, well-scrubbed rectory.

At first they talked about everything except Oguinase. But very soon the priest asked, 'And how are the youngsters? Your eldest boy?'

It was then that Euchariste realized what was afoot.

'He's just fine, Father.'

'The teacher says he works well.'

'She did, did she?'

'I guess you're pleased.'

'Why, yes, Father, I guess I am.'

A silence fell between them, broken only by the distant clatter of pots and pans and the sound of something frying.

'What are you going to do with the boy, 'Charis?'

His parishioner lowered his eyes, put his head on one side, and started to examine the stitching of his cap, held between his knees. He was ill at ease; his ready-made suit made him feel awkward and so did his unaccustomed surroundings, which seemed to conspire against him: a coloured plastic crucifix that looked down on a desk piled high with registers and papers, the flowered linoleum on the floor, the two shelves crammed with books and, above all, the almost religious hush of the room in which his voice sounded strange. He did not dare lift his eyes from his own dusty

boots and the priest's thick-soled shoes, which tapped the floor with a dull sound in time with the rocking of the chair.

He really hadn't made up his mind about what he was going to do with Oguinase. He still remembered his conversation with the priest and the half-promise he had made when he met him on the King's Highway one day shortly before his marriage. He had often thought about it, but as one thinks of those things one never expects to get—things which have nothing to do with the farm or the crops or ordinary everyday life. What was the use of planning years ahead? For fate decides whether a child will live or die, just as a crop may rot on the ground or shrivel up from drought depending on the weather.

And then there were the years at the college—six, seven, he didn't know how many—and the expense they entailed. The very idea of it terrified him. He would like to have pleaded that times were hard, as farmers always do, but didn't dare because of the money banked with the notary. It's true he had never breathed a word of this matter to anyone. But he felt dimly that the priest couldn't help but know, since he knew so many things; in fact everything.

Seeing that instead of answering, Euchariste had started to stroke a white patch on his cheek where the razor had scraped away the tan, the priest went on, 'I don't know whether you've thought about it yourself; but I've been thinking about it for you as it's my duty more or less to think for everybody in the parish. You once said you wanted a priest in your family, 'Charis. Haven't changed your mind, have you?'

'Why . . . no . . . Father. I guess not.'

'Because, you know, it won't be you who'll be making a present to God, but He who'll be doing you an honour—the greatest possible honour. Euchariste Moisan, let me tell you something that'll surprise you, maybe. I've sometimes thought I'd like to have been a father of a family like you are, just so as I could dedicate one of the children God might have blessed me with to His service. And listen, I once knew a man who wouldn't let his son go through for a priest, though he had been called by God. Do you know what happened to him? God punished that man. Less than a year later the boy fell into a threshing machine and was cut to pieces right there in front of his father.'

Euchariste still didn't answer. He sat listening to the priest, admiring in him what he himself would so much have liked to possess: the gift of words, the ability to express the things you feel inside you and which are struggling to get out. He started drawing circles on the floor with the toe of his boot and then stopped when he realized he was being rude. But he still hadn't a word to say.

'What hurts me most, 'Charis, is that there isn't a single son of the parish in the seminary right now, and there hasn't been for quite a while. Not since Father Emilien Picard, who's assistant to the priest at Saint Bernard-du-Saut. This is a good Christian parish right here, only they seem to forget to give God His due. It's all very well to pay tithe on the crops, but if you want the family to be blessed you have to pay tithe in children too. Euchariste Moisan, don't you think you owe it to God? How does it strike you?'

'Well, as far as I'm concerned, Father, it would suit me fine. But . . .'

This time he had to give an answer.

'But what?'

'Well . . . I'm wondering if I can afford it. Sending Oguinase off to the college—that'll be seven or eight years, and all that time there's that great big farm of mine to work. Just when he was beginning to be a help too.'

But the priest had an answer to everything. Up to now Euchariste had been able to work the farm alone and it had been generous to him. In any case there were two other boys—'and I hope there'll be more to come'— and the eldest of them was pretty nearly as strong and hard-working as Oguinase. As for the expense—well, he himself, the priest of the parish, though he had not private means, would pay half the college expense out of his own pocket. For he was ashamed never to see his parish included in the list of those which sent up pupils.

And that is how the question had been settled a year before.

THE EXPATRIATE

The crops had been harvested, the grain threshed, and the season for the fall ploughing was approaching when one night there was a violent knocking at the door. Etienne, who slept on a folding bed at the foot of the stairs, got up to see what it was all about. A few moments later the whole household was awakened by a clamour of voices. The Larivières had arrived.

There was 'Walter' S. Larivière, the cousin, whose ready laugh displayed a row of gold teeth. There was his wife, a lanky American, whose white face powder failed to conceal her freckles and whom Euchariste disliked from the very beginning. Not so much because of her appearance, but she spoke in a halting brand of bad French that only her husband could understand, and she spoke only English to him. They hadn't been there five minutes when she jabbered off a long sentence which made her husband smile in a knowing way. Euchariste felt sure they had been making critical remarks about the Moisans and their home. It made him feel humiliated and that is something one never forgives. Finally out of the auto they produced a little boy of about five or six who woke up from time to time to stare at all the people and at his surroundings with frightened, uncomprehending eyes.

When all the degrees of relationship had been straightened out by references to family history, Euchariste, who now felt a little more at ease, put a question: 'Say, what's your real Christian name anyway?'

'I was christened Alphée, but they can't pronounce those kind of names down in the States so I had to let them call me something else. And now they call me Walter.'

He made this declaration in an amused tone of voice, as if to show his cousins from the back country of Quebec that he belonged now to the American nation, to that terrifically vital race which is composed of the overflow from all the other nations, like those colourful patchwork quilts made up from scraps sewn together anyhow.

But he hesitated a moment before going on.

'It's the same way with our family name, Larivière. 'Course we didn't give it up. But folks could never get it. So we just sort of translated it into English. It's Rivers in English and that means the same thing. Larivière, Rivers, there ain't no difference.'

'Then you ain't hardly a Canadian any more!'

'Well, what of it? If you live down there, well, you have to act like they do in the States. Everybody does. There's the Bourdons—they're called Borden; and one of the neighbours, a Lacroix, he calls himself Cross.'

But this time his words lacked conviction and betrayed a certain embarrassment. For it was evident that your given name belonged to you; and if you changed it, it was your own business. But if you changed your family name, the one you inherited from a long line of ancestors, it was a bit like repudiating your descent and stripping the name of its honourable reputation for hard work and persistence in the face of every obstacle which generations of the family had built up. And if going off to the United States was a kind of desertion in any case, he felt that this final surrender was in some ways a denial as bad as St Peter's, an act of treason like the treason of Judas.

This Canadian of Norman origin had done more than shed the name of Larivière when he crossed the border. Alphée Larivière, who had become Walter S. Rivers, no longer spoke the old-fashioned colourful French of the shores of the St Lawrence. Besides his American accent, which made him pronounce words as if his mouth were full of glue, he generally used strange English terms which he made a half-hearted attempt to frenchify and which no one could understand—not even Albert, who was educated and knew all the French words there are. When Larivière said, '*Mon grand fille Lily alle est comme ouiveuse dans une factrie sur la Main. Alle a pas venue parce qu'all doit marier un boss de gang du Rutland*,' Moisan hadn't the heart to say he couldn't understand a thing.

To change the subject he asked another question. 'Why didn't you bring along the other little Larivières?' After all, he couldn't very well call them the Rivers!

'There ain't no others. Just Lily and Billy.'

'Why?' asked Moisan naïvely. 'Is your wife sick?'

Rivers burst out laughing and translated the question for Grace, who opened her eyes in astonishment and hid an almost irresistible impulse to laugh behind a wry and rather superior smile.

'Well, cousin, two's plenty for us, a boy and a girl.'

'I guess I'd sooner not have had thirteen myself. But there's nothing you can do about it.'

'Damn it, my wife and I figured we'd put on the brakes,' he said with an air of finality.

Moisan was taken aback and felt embarrassed, so he said nothing. How could people talk about such things openly? He hadn't understood all the words they used; but he was pretty sure they had been referring to one of those wicked practices which the parish priest had mentioned once at a retreat for men and which seek to interfere with the designs of Providence. He looked away.

THIRTY ACRES
Translated by Felix and Dorothea Walter

Charles G. D. Roberts

SIR CHARLES G.D. RORERTS, who has been called the first Canadian man of letters, achieved an international reputation with over sixty books—collections of verse, light historical romances, nature stories, travel books, and histories. He was born in Douglas (near Fredericton), N.B. When he was a year old his father, who was a clergyman, moved to West-cock, near Sackville and the Tantramar marshes—a region that later offered Roberts much inspiration and material for his nature poetry and stories about wildlife. In 1874 the family moved to Fredericton. Roberts attended school there (he had previously been tutored by his father) and in 1876 entered the University of New Brunswick, where he studied Latin, Greek, philosophy, and political economy—and wrote poetry. Graduating in 1879, he became a teacher at Chatham, N.B. The next year, when he was twenty, he married and published his first volume of poems, *Orion*, which aroused interest and nationalistic pride (thirteen years after Confederation) because it was evidence that here was one Canadian who could write! Roberts' adult life was characterized by restless

movement from place to place. In 1882 he became principal of a school in Frederic-ton; in 1883-4 he edited a magazine called *The Week* in Toronto; in 1884 he was in New York; in 1885 he became a professor of English and French literature at King's College, Windsor, N.S. Ten years later he quit that post, freelanced in Fredericton for eighteen months, and then left Canada for twenty-five years. He edited the *Illustrated American* in New York until 1899, then travelled widely, all the while writing for magazines and publishing books, until 1912 when he settled in London. He served as an officer in the First World War. When he returned to Canada in 1925 he was a famous author, much in demand as a lecturer and the recipient of many honours. He was knighted in 1935 and died in Toronto.

Of Roberts' many publications, the most numerous and significant were his books of verse and collections of nature stories. In the history of Canadian poetry Roberts is associated with three other poets: Bliss Carman (his cousin), Archi-bald Lampman, and Duncan Campbell Scott. All four poets (who were born within a year or two of each other) wrote lyrical romantic verse that had the Canadian landscape for inspiration: this reflective nature poetry represented the rise of a national literature. Roberts could lay special claim to being a national poet because he also wrote patriotic verse. It now reads like flowery and sentimental propaganda and has virtually no real poetic content, but it was popular at the time it was written. The poems for which Roberts is best remembered are a few lyrics that describe landscape and farm life with sensitive simplicity—notably 'The Solitary Woodsman', 'The Tantramar Revisited' (his most admired poem); and, among his sonnets, 'The Potato Harvest', 'The Sowing', 'The Mowing', and 'The Pea-Fields'.

While only a small part of Roberts' large body of poetry has stood the test of time, many of his nature stories, in which he was something of an innovator, can still be read with pleasure today. 'Do Seek Their Meat from God' was published in 1892 in *Harper's* magazine and was included with two other animal stories in a collection of sportsmen's tales, *Earth's Enigmas* (1895). When a demand for stories about animals developed after the publication two years later of *Wild Animals I Have Known* (1898) by another Canadian, Ernest Thompson Seton, Roberts was well prepared to satisfy public interest with the first of many collections of realistic stories about wild-

life: *The Kindred of the Wild* (1902), *The Watchers of the Trails* (1904), and *The Haunters of the Silences* (1907), to name the earliest and best of these books. Roberts has been criticized for attempting to present the 'psychology' of animals, fish, and insects, endowing them with human feelings and powers of reasoning; and he is sometimes inaccurate in details, though never in the overall presentation of nature's laws. However, these stories about amoral nature—the struggles for existence that go on within it and man's experiences of it—are convincing because they are told realistically and unemotionally, with artistry and sympathy. They are also vivid and dramatically satisfying. Apart from a small number of poems, this was the only work in which Roberts showed complete authority as a writer. He was a master storyteller.

A selection of Roberts' poems can be found in *Poets of the Confederation* (1960) edited by Malcolm Ross. *The Last Barrier and Other Stories* (1958), edited by Alec Lucas, presents a good selection of his stories. Both books are available in the New Canadian Library. Another prose anthology is *King of Beasts and Other Stories* (1967) edited by Joseph Gold. W. J. Keith has written an interesting study of Roberts for the Copp Clark series, Studies in Canadian Literature (1969).

THE TANTRAMAR REVISITED

Summers and summers have come, and gone with the flight of the
    swallow;
Sunshine and thunder have been, storm, and winter, and frost;
Many and many a sorrow has all but died from remembrance,
Many a dream of joy fall'n in the shadow of pain.
Hands of chance and change have marred, or moulded, or broken,
Busy with spirit or flesh, all I most have adored;
Even the bosom of Earth is strewn with heavier shadows,—

Only in these green hills, aslant to the sea, no change!
Here where the road that has climbed from the inland valleys and wood-
    lands,
Dips from the hill-tops down, straight to the base of the hills,—
Here, from my vantage-ground, I can see the scattering houses,
Stained with time, set warm in orchards, meadows, and wheat,
Dotting the broad bright slopes outspread to southward and eastward,
Wind-swept all day long, blown by the south-east wind.
Skirting the sunbright uplands stretches a riband of meadow,
Shorn of the labouring grass, bulwarked well from the sea,
Fenced on its seaward border with long clay dikes from the turbid
Surge and flow of the tides vexing the Westmoreland shores.
Yonder, toward the left, lie broad the Westmoreland marshes,—
Miles on miles they extend, level, and grassy, and dim,
Clear from the long red sweep of flats to the sky in the distance,
Save for the outlying heights, green-rampired Cumberland Point;
Miles on miles outrolled, and the river-channels divide them,—
Miles on miles of green, barred by the hurtling gusts.

Miles on miles beyond the tawny bay is Minudie.
There are the low blue hills; villages gleam at their feet.
Nearer a white sail shines across the water, and nearer
Still are the slim, grey masts of fishing boats dry on the flats.
Ah, how well I remember those wide red flats, above tidemark,
Pale with scurf of the salt, seamed and baked in the sun!
Well I remember the piles of blocks and ropes, and the net-reels
Wound with the beaded nets, dripping and dark from the sea!
Now at this season the nets are unwound; they hang from the rafters
Over the fresh-stowed hay in upland barns, and the wind
Blows all day through the chinks, with the streaks of sunlight, and sways
    them
Softly at will; or they lie heaped in the gloom of a loft.

Now at this season the reels are empty and idle; I see them
Over the lines of the dikes, over the gossiping grass.
Now at this season they swing in the long strong wind, thro' the lonesome
Golden afternoon, shunned by the foraging gulls.
Near about sunset the crane will journey homeward above them;
Round them, under the moon, all the calm night long,
Winnowing soft grey wings of marsh-owls wander and wander,
Now to the broad, lit marsh, now to the dusk of the dike.
Soon, thro' their dew-wet frames, in the live keen freshness of morning,
Out of the teeth of the dawn blows back the awakening wind.
Then, as the blue day mounts, and the low-shot shafts of the sunlight
Glance from the tide to the shore, gossamers jewelled with dew

Sparkle and wave, where late sea-spoiling fathoms of drift-net,
Myriad-meshed, uploomed sombrely over the land.

Well I remember it all. The salt, raw scent of the margin;
While, with men at the windlass, groaned each reel, and the net,
Surging in ponderous lengths, uprose and coiled in its station;
Then each man at his home,—well I remember it all!

Yet, as I sit and watch, this present peace of the landscape,—
Stranded boats, these reels empty and idle, the hush,
One grey hawk slow-wheeling above yon cluster of haystacks,—
More than the old-time stir this stillness welcomes me home.

Ah, the old-time stir, how once it stung me with rapture,—
Old-time sweetness, the winds freighted with honey and salt!
Yet will I stay my steps and not go down to the marshland,—
Muse and recall far off, rather remember than see,—
Lest on too close sight I miss the darling illusion,
Spy at their task even here the hands of chance and change.

THE PEA-FIELDS

These are the fields of light, and laughing air,
And yellow butterflies, and foraging bees,
And whitish, wayward blossoms winged as these,
And pale green tangles like a seamaid's hair.

Pale, pale the blue, but pure beyond compare,
And pale the sparkle of the far-off seas
A-shimmer like these fluttering slopes of peas,
And pale the open landscape everywhere.
From fence to fence a perfumed breath exhales
O'er the bright pallor of the well-loved fields,—
My fields of Tantramar in summer-time;
And, scorning the poor feed their pasture yields,
Up from the bushy lots the cattle climb
To gaze with longing through the grey, mossed rails.

THE PRISONERS OF THE PITCHER-PLANT

At the edge of a rough piece of open, where the scrubby bushes which clothed the plain gave space a little to the weeds and harsh grasses, stood the clustering pitchers of a fine young sarracenia. These pitchers, which were its leaves, were of a light cool green, vividly veined with crimson and shading into a bronzy red about the lip and throat. They were of all sizes, being at all stages of growth; and the largest, which had now, on the edge of summer, but barely attained maturity, were about six inches in length and an inch and a quarter in extreme diameter. Down in the very heart of the cluster, hardly to be discerned, was a tiny red-tipped bud, destined to shoot up, later in the season, into a sturdy flower-stalk.

Against the fresh, warm green of the sunlit world surrounding it, the sarracenia's peculiar colouring stood out conspicuously, its streaks and splashes of red having the effect of blossoms. This effect, at a season when bright-hued blooms were scarce, made the plant very attractive to any insects that chanced within view of it. There was nearly always some flutterer or hummer poising above it, or touching it eagerly to dart away again in disappointment. But every once in a while some little wasp, or fly, or shining-winged beetle, or gauzy ichneumon, would alight on the alluring lip, pause, and peer down into the pitcher. As a rule the small investigator would venture farther and farther, till it disappeared. Then it never came out again.

On a leaf of a huckleberry bush, overhanging the pitcher-plant, a little black ant was running about with the nimble curiosity of her kind. An orange-and-black butterfly, fluttering lazily in the sun, came close beside the leaf. At this moment a passing shrike swooped down and caught the butterfly in his beak. One of his long wings, chancing to strike the leaf, sent it whirling from its stem; and the ant fell directly upon one of the pitchers below.

It was far down upon the red, shining lip of the pitcher that she fell; and there she clung resolutely, her feet sinking into a sort of fur of smooth, whitish hairs. When she had quite recovered her equanimity she started to explore her new surroundings; and, because that was the easiest way to go, she went in the direction toward which the hairs all pointed. In a moment, therefore, she found herself just on the edge of the precipitous slope from the lip to the throat of the pitcher. Here, finding the slope strangely slippery, she thought it best to stop and retrace her steps. But when she attempted this she found it impossible. The little, innocent-looking hairs all pressed against her, thrusting her downward. The more she struggled, the more energetically and elastically they pushed back at her; till all at once she was forced over the round, smooth edge, and fell.

To her terrified amazement, it was water she fell into. The pitcher was about half full of the chilly fluid. In her kickings and twistings she brought herself to the walls of her green prison, and tried to clamber out —but here, again, were those cruel hairs on guard to foil her. She tried to evade them, to break them down, to bite them off with her strong, sharp mandibles. At last, by a supreme effort, she managed to drag herself almost clear—but only to be at once hurled back, and far out into the water, by the sharp recoil of her tormentors.

Though pretty well exhausted by now, she would not give up the struggle; and presently her convulsive efforts brought her alongside of a refuge. It was only the floating body of a dead moth, but to the ant it was a safe and ample raft. Eagerly she crept out upon it, and lay very still for a while, recovering her strength. More fortunate than most shipwrecked voyagers, she had an edible raft and was therefore in no imminent peril of starvation.

The light that came through the veined, translucent walls of this watery prison was of an exquisite cool beryl, very different from the warm daylight overhead. The ant had never been in any such surroundings before, and was bewildered by the strangeness of them. After a brief rest she investigated minutely every corner of her queer retreat, and then, finding that there was nothing she could do to better the situation, she resumed her attitude of repose, with only the slight waving of her antennae to show that she was awake.

For a long time nothing happened. No winds were astir that day, and no sounds came down into the pitcher save the shrill, happy chirping of birds in the surrounding bushes. But suddenly the pitcher began to tip and rock slightly, and the water to wash within its coloured walls. Something had alighted on the pitcher's lip.

It was something comparatively heavy, that was evident. A moment or two later it came sliding down those treacherous hairs, and fell into the water with a great splash which nearly swept the ant from her refuge.

The new arrival was a bee. And now began a tremendous turmoil within the narrow prison. The bee struggled, whirled around on the surface with thrashing wings, and sent the water swashing in every direction, till the ant was nearly drowned. She hung to her raft, however, and waited philosophically for the hubbub to subside. At length the bee too, after half a dozen vain and exhausting struggles to climb out against the opposing array of hairs, encountered the body of the dead moth. Instantly she tried to raise herself upon it, so as to escape the chill of the water and dry her wings for flight. But she was too heavy. The moth sank, and rolled over, at the same time being thrust against the wall of the pitcher. The ant, in high indignation clutched a bundle of the hostile hairs in her mandibles, and held herself at anchor against the wall.

Thoroughly used up, and stupid with panic and chill, the bee kept on futilely grappling with the moth's body, which, in its turn, kept on sinking and rolling beneath her. A very few minutes of such disastrous folly sufficed to end the struggle, and soon the bee was floating, drowned and motionless, beside the moth. Then the ant, with satisfaction, returned to her refuge.

When things get started happening, they are quite apt to keep it up for a while, as if events invited events. A large hunting spider, creeping among the grass and weeds, discovered the handsome cluster of the sarracenia. She was one of the few creatures who had learned the secret of the pitcher-plant and knew how to turn it to account. More than once she had found easy prey in some trapped insect struggling near the top of a well-filled pitcher.

Selecting the largest pitcher as the one most likely to yield results the spider climbed its stem. Then she mounted the bright swell of the pitcher itself, whose smooth outer surface offered no obstacle to such visitors. The pitcher swayed and bowed. The water within washed heavily. And the ant, with new alarm, marked the big, black shadow of the spider creeping up the outside of her prison.

Having reached the lip of the leaf and cautiously crawled over upon it, the spider took no risks with those traitor hairs. She threw two or three stout cables of web across the lip; and then, with this secure anchorage by which to pull herself back, she ventured fearlessly down the steep of that perilous throat. One hooked claw, outstretched behind her, held aloft the cable which exuded from her spinnerets as she moved.

On the extreme slope she stopped, and her red, jewelled cluster of eyes glared fiercely down upon the little black ant. The latter shrank and crouched, and tried to hide herself under the side of the dead moth to escape the light of those baleful eyes. This new peril was one which appalled her far more than all the others she had encountered.

At this most critical of all crises in the destiny of the little black ant, the fickle Fortune of the Wild was seized with another whim. An overwhelming cataclysm descended suddenly upon the tiny world of the pitcher-plant. The soft, furry feet of some bounding monster—rabbit, fox, or wildcat—came down amongst the clustered pitchers, crushing several to bits and scattering wide the contents of all the rest. Among these latter was that which contained the little black ant. Drenched, astonished, but unhurt, she found herself lying in a tuft of splashed grass, once more free. Above her, on a grass-top, clung the bewildered spider. As it hung there, conspicuous to all the foraging world, a great black-and-yellow wasp pounced upon it, stung it into helplessness, and carried it off on heavily humming wing.   THE LAST BARRIER AND OTHER STORIES

b. 1908

Sinclair Ross

SINCLAIR ROSS is a writer perhaps only half-blessed because his first novel, *As For Me and My House*, and a handful of short stories have been much admired by critics and many of his fellow writers but were not, when it would have counted, very widely read. Born near Prince Albert, Sask., he joined the Royal Bank when he was still a young man. After working for the bank in various prairie towns and finally in Montreal, he retired in the late 1960s to live in Greece; he now lives in Spain. Most of his early stories were published in *Queen's Quarterly*, a magazine of public affairs and the arts sponsored by Queen's University.

As For Me and My House (1941) is the story of a frustrated artist who is serving as a minister (although he has no faith) in a succession of poor prairie communities. It is one of the saddest and most disenchanted of North American novels, yet its influence on other Canadian writers from the West—Margaret Laurence, for example—has been very great. Ross's other novels are *The Well* (1958) and *A Whir of Gold* (1970). Neither book sold well or added very much to his literary reputation.

Nine of Ross's best stories were published in a collection called *The Lamp at Noon and Other Stories* (1968). Here, and in *As For Me and My House*, Ross chronicles the drought and depression on the prairies in the 1930s and its effect on men and women—particularly the dejected, trapped women—who, isolated from each other, suffer alone. In her introduction to *The Lamp at Noon*, Margaret Laurence writes: 'The patterns are those of isolation and loneliness, and gradually, through these, the underlying spiritual goals of an entire society can be perceived. The man must prove absolutely strong in his own eyes. The woman must silently endure all. If either cannot, then they have failed to themselves. With these impossible and cruel standards, and in circumstances of drought and depression, it is no wonder that individuals sometimes crack under the strain. . . . In counterpoint to desolation runs the theme of renewal. Tomorrow it may rain. The next spring will ultimately come. Despite the sombre tone and the dark themes of Sinclair Ross's short stories, man emerges as a creature who can survive—and survive with some remaining dignity—against both outer and inner odds which are almost impossible.'

There is an article on Ross by W. H. New in Issue 40 of *Canadian Literature* (Spring 1969) and another by Sandra Djwa in Issue 47 (Winter 1971). Sinclair Ross's *As For Me and My House* and *The Lamp at Noon and Other Stories* are available in the New Canadian Library.

THE LAMP AT NOON

A little before noon she lit the lamp. Demented wind fled keening past the house: a wail through the eaves that died every minute or two. Three days now without respite it had held. The dust was thickening to an impenetrable fog.

She lit the lamp, then for a long time stood at the window motionless. In dim, fitful outline the stable and oat granary still were visible; beyond, obscuring fields and landmarks, the lower of dust clouds made the farmyard seem an isolated acre, poised aloft above a sombre void. At each blast of wind it shook, as if to topple and spin hurtling with the dust-reel into space.

From the window she went to the door, opening it a little, and peering toward the stable again. He was not coming yet. As she watched there was a sudden rift overhead, and for a moment through the tattered clouds the sun raced like a wizened orange. It shed a soft, diffused light, dim and yellow as if it were the light from the lamp reaching out through the open door.

She closed the door, and going to the stove tried the potatoes with a fork. Her eyes all the while were fixed and wide with a curious immobility. It was the window. Standing at it, she had let her forehead press against the pane until the eyes were strained apart and rigid. Wide like that they had looked out of the deepening ruin of the storm. Now she could not close them.

The baby started to cry. He was lying in a homemade crib over which she had arranged a tent of muslin. Careful not to disturb the folds of it, she knelt and tried to still him, whispering huskily in a singsong voice that he must hush and go to sleep again. She would have liked to rock him, to feel the comfort of his little body in her arms, but a fear obsessed her that in the dust-filled air he might contract pneumonia. There was dust sifting everywhere. Her own throat was parched with it. The table had been set less than ten minutes, and already a film was gathering on the dishes. The little cry continued, and with wincing, frightened lips she glanced around as if to find a corner where the air was less oppressive. But while the lips winced the eyes maintained their wide, immobile stare.

'Sleep,' she whispered again. 'It's too soon for you to be hungry. Daddy's coming for his dinner.'

He seemed a long time. Even the clock, still a few minutes off noon, could not dispel a foreboding sense that he was longer than he should be. She went to the door again—and then recoiled slowly to stand white and breathless in the middle of the room. She mustn't. He would only despise her if she ran to the stable looking for him. There was too much grim endurance in his nature ever to let him understand the fear and weakness of a woman. She must stay quiet and wait. Nothing was wrong. At noon he would come—and perhaps after dinner stay with her awhile.

Yesterday, and again at breakfast this morning, they had quarrelled bitterly. She wanted him now, the assurance of his strength and nearness, but he would stand aloof, wary, remembering the words she had flung at him in her anger, unable to understand it was only the dust and wind that had driven her.

Tense, she fixed her eyes upon the clock, listening. There were two winds: the wind in flight, and the wind that pursued. The one sought refuge in the eaves, whimpering, in fear; the other assailed it there, and shook the eaves apart to make it flee again. Once as she listened this first wind sprang inside the room, distraught like a bird that has felt the graze of talons on its wing; while furious the other wind shook the walls, and thudded tumbleweeds against the window till its quarry glanced away again in fright. But only to return—to return and quake among the feeble eaves, as if in all this dust-mad wilderness it knew no other sanctuary.

Then Paul came. At his step she hurried to the stove, intent upon the pots and frying-pan. 'The worst wind yet,' he ventured, hanging up his cap and smock. 'I had to light the lantern in the tool shed, too.'

They looked at each other, then away. She wanted to go to him, to feel his arms supporting her, to cry a little just that he might soothe her, but because his presence made the menace of the wind seem less, she gripped herself and thought, 'I'm in the right. I won't give in. For his sake, too, I won't.'

He washed, hurriedly, so that a few dark welts of dust remained to indent upon his face a haggard strength. It was all she could see as she wiped the dishes and set the food before him: the strength, the grimness, the young Paul growing old and hard, buckled against a desert even grimmer than his will. 'Hungry?' she asked, touched to a twinge of pity she had not intended. 'There's dust in everything. It keeps coming faster than I can clean it up.'

He nodded. 'Tonight, though, you'll see it go down. This is the third day.'

She looked at him in silence a moment, and then as if to herself muttered broodingly, 'Until the next time. Until it starts again.'

There was a dark resentment in her voice now that boded another quarrel. He waited, his eyes on her dubiously as she mashed a potato with her fork. The lamp between them threw strong lights and shadows on their faces. Dust and drought, earth that betrayed alike his labour and his faith, to him the struggle had given sternness, an impassive courage. Beneath the whip of sand his youth had been effaced. Youth, zest, exuberance— there remained only a harsh and clenched virility that yet became him, that seemed at the cost of more engaging qualities to be fulfilment of his inmost and essential nature. Whereas to her the same debts and poverty had brought a plaintive indignation, a nervous dread of what was still to come. The eyes were hollowed, the lips pinched dry and colourless. It was the face of a woman that had aged without maturing, that had loved the little vanities of life, and lost them wistfully.

'I'm afraid, Paul,' she said suddenly. 'I can't stand it any longer. He cries all the time. You will go, Paul—say you will. We aren't living here— not really living—'

The pleading in her voice now, after its shrill bitterness yesterday, made him think that this was only another way to persuade him. He answered evenly, 'I told you this morning, Ellen; we keep on right where we are. At least I do. It's yourself you're thinking about, not the baby.'

This morning such an accusation would have stung her to rage; now, her voice swift and panting, she pressed on, 'Listen, Paul—I'm thinking of all of us—you, too. Look at the sky—what's happening. Are you blind? Thistles and tumbleweeds—it's a desert. You won't have a straw this fall. You won't be able to feed a cow or a chicken. Please, Paul, say we'll go away—'

'Go where?' His voice as he answered was still remote and even, inflexibly in unison with the narrowed eyes and the great hunch of muscle-knotted shoulder. 'Even as a desert it's better than sweeping out your father's store and running his errands. That's all I've got ahead of me if I do what you want.'

'And here—' she faltered. 'What's ahead of you here? At least we'll get enough to eat and wear when you're sweeping out his store. Look at it— look at it, you fool. Desert—the lamp lit at noon—'

'You'll see it come back. There's good wheat in it yet.'

'But in the meantime—year after year—can't you understand, Paul? We'll never get them back—'

He put down his knife and fork and leaned toward her across the table. 'I can't go, Ellen. Living off your people—charity—stop and think of it. This is where I belong. I can't do anything else.'

'Charity!' she repeated him, letting her voice rise in derision. 'And this

—you call this independence! Borrowed money you can't even pay the interest on, seed from the government—grocery bills—doctor bills—'

'We'll have crops again,' he persisted. 'Good crops—the land will come back. It's worth waiting for.'

'And while we're waiting, Paul!' It was not anger now, but a kind of sob. 'Think of me—and him. It's not fair. We have our lives, too, to live.'

'And you think that going home to your family—taking your husband with you—'

'I don't care—anything would be better than this. Look at the air he's breathing. He cries all the time. For his sake, Paul. What's ahead of him here, even if you do get crops?'

He clenched his lips a minute, then, with his eyes hard and contemptuous, struck back, 'As much as in town, growing up a pauper. You're the one who wants to go, it's not for his sake. You think that in town you'd have a better time—not so much work—more clothes—'

'Maybe—' She dropped her head defencelessly. 'I'm young still. I like pretty things.'

There was silence now—a deep fastness of it enclosed by rushing wind and creaking walls. It seemed the yellow lamplight cast a hush upon them. Through the haze of dusty air the walls receded, dimmed, and came again. At last she raised her head and said listlessly, 'Go on—your dinner's getting cold. Don't sit and stare at me. I've said it all.'

The spent quietness in her voice was even harder to endure than her anger. It reproached him, against his will insisted that he see and understand her lot. To justify himself he tried, 'I was a poor man when you married me. You said you didn't mind. Farming's never been easy, and never will be.'

'I wouldn't mind the work or the skimping if there was something to look forward to. It's the hopelessness—going on—watching the land blow away.'

'The land's all right,' he repeated. 'The dry years won't last forever.'

'But it's not just dry years, Paul!' The little sob in her voice gave way suddenly to a ring of exasperation. 'Will you never see? It's the land itself —the soil. You've plowed and harrowed until there's not a root of fibre left to hold it down. That's why the soil drifts—that's why in a year or two there'll be nothing left but the bare clay. If in the first place you farmers had taken care of your land—if you hadn't been so greedy for wheat every year—'

She had taught school before she married him, and of late in her anger there had been a kind of disdain, an attitude almost of condescension, as if she no longer looked upon the farmers as her equals. He sat still, his eyes fixed on the yellow lamp flame, and seeming to know her words had hurt him, she went on softly, 'I want to help you, Paul. That's why I won't sit quiet while you go on wasting your life. You're only thirty—you owe it to yourself as well as me.'

He sat staring at the lamp without answering, his mouth sullen. It seemed indifference now, as if he were ignoring her, and stung to anger again she cried, 'Do you ever think what my life is? Two rooms to live in —once a month to town, and nothing to spend when I get there. I'm still young—I wasn't brought up this way.'

'You're a farmer's wife now. It doesn't matter what you used to be, or how you were brought up. You get enough to eat and wear. Just now that's all I can do. I'm not to blame that we've been dried out five years.'

'Enough to eat!' she laughed back shrilly. 'Enough salt pork—enough potatoes and eggs. And look—' Springing to the middle of the room she thrust out a foot for him to see the scuffed old slipper. 'When they're completely gone I suppose you'll tell me I can go barefoot—that I'm a farmer's wife—that it's not you fault we're dried out—'

'And what about these?' He pushed his chair away from the table now to let her see what he was wearing. 'Cowhide—hard as boards—but my feet are so calloused I don't feel them any more.'

Then he stood up, ashamed of having tried to match her hardships with his own. But frightened now as he reached for his smock she pressed close to him. 'Don't go yet. I brood and worry when I'm left alone. Please, Paul —you can't work on the land anyway.'

'And keep on like this? You start before I'm through the door. Week in and week out—I've troubles enough of my own.'

'Paul—please stay—' The eyes were glazed now, distended a little as if with the intensity of her dread and pleading. 'We won't quarrel any more. Hear it! I can't work—I just stand still and listen—'

The eyes frightened him, but responding to a kind of instinct that he must withstand her, that it was his self-respect and manhood against the fretful weakness of a woman, he answered unfeelingly, 'In here safe and quiet—you don't know how well off you are. If you were out in it—fighting it—swallowing it—'

'Sometimes, Paul, I wish I was. I'm so caged—if I could only break away and run. See—I stand like this all day. I can't relax. My throat's so tight it aches—'

With a jerk he freed his smock from her clutch. 'If I stay we'll only keep on all afternoon. Wait till tomorrow—we'll talk things over when the wind goes down.'

Then without meeting her eyes again he swung outside, and doubled low against the buffets of the wind, fought his way slowly toward the stable. There was a deep hollow calm within, a vast darkness engulfed beneath the tides of moaning wind. He stood breathless a moment, hushed almost to a stupor by the sudden extinction of the storm and the stillness that enfolded him. It was a long, far-reaching stillness. The first dim stalls and rafters led the way into cavern-like obscurity, into vaults and recesses that extended far beyond the stable walls. Nor in these first quiet moments did he forbid the illusion, the sense of release from a harsh, familiar world into one of peace and darkness. The contentious mood that his stand against Ellen had roused him to, his tenacity and clenched despair before the ravages of wind, it was ebbing now, losing itself in the cover of darkness. Ellen and the wheat seemed remote, unimportant. At a whinny from the bay mare, Bess, he went forward and into her stall. She seemed grateful for his presence, and thrust her nose deep between his arm and body. They stood a long time motionless, comforting and assuring each other.

For soon again the first deep sense of quiet and peace was shrunken to the battered shelter of the stable. Instead of release or escape from the assaulting wind, the walls were but a feeble stand against it. They creaked and sawed as if the fingers of a giant were tightening to collapse them; the empty loft sustained a pipelike cry that rose and fell but never ended. He saw the dust-black sky again, and his fields blown smooth with drifted soil.

But always, even while listening to the storm outside, he could feel the tense and apprehensive stillness of the stable. There was not a hoof that clumped or shifted, not a rub of halter against manger. And yet, though it had been a strange stable, he would have known, despite the darkness, that every stall was filled. They, too, were all listening.

From Bess he went to the big grey gelding, Prince. Prince was twenty years old, with rib-grooved sides, and high, protruding hipbones. Paul ran his hand over the ribs, and felt a sudden shame, a sting of fear that Ellen might be right in what she said. For wasn't it true—nine years a farmer now on his own land, and still he couldn't even feed his horses? What, then, could he hope to do for his wife and son?

There was much he planned. And so vivid was the future of his planning, so real and constant, that often the actual present was but half felt, but half endured. Its difficulties were lessened by a confidence in what lay beyond them. A new house—land for the boy—land and still more land—or education, whatever he might want.

But all the time was he only a blind and stubborn fool? Was Ellen right? Was he trampling on her life, and throwing away his own? The five years since he married her, were they to go on repeating themselves, five, ten, twenty, until all the brave future he looked forward to was but a stark and futile past?

She looked forward to no future. She had no faith or dream with which to make the dust and the poverty less real. He understood suddenly. He saw her face again as only a few minutes ago it had begged him not to leave her. The darkness round him now was as a slate on which her lonely terror limned itself. He went from Prince to the other horses, combing their manes and forelocks with his fingers, but always it was her face before him, its staring eyes and twisted suffering. 'See Paul—I stand like this all day. I just stand still—My throat's so tight it aches—'

And always the wind, the creak of walls, the wild lipless wailing through the loft. Until at last as he stood there, staring into the livid face before him, it seemed that this scream of wind was a cry from her parched and frantic lips. He knew it couldn't be, he knew that she was safe within the house, but still the wind persisted in a woman's cry. The cry of a woman with eyes like those that watched him through the dark. Eyes that were mad now—lips that even as they cried still pleaded, 'See, Paul— I stand like this all day. I just stand still—so caged! If I could only run!'

He saw her running, pulled and driven headlong by the wind, but when at last he returned to the house, compelled by his anxiety, she was walking quietly back and forth with the baby in her arms. Careful, despite his concern, not to reveal a fear or weakness that she might think capitulation to her wishes, he watched a moment through the window, and then went off to the tool shed to mend harness. All afternoon he stitched and riveted. It was easier with the lantern lit and his hands occupied. There was a wind whining high past the tool shed too, but it was only wind. He remembered the arguments with which Ellen had tried to persuade him away from the farm, and one by one he defeated them. There would be rain again—next year or the next. Maybe in his ignorance he had farmed his land the wrong way, seeding wheat every year, working the soil till it was lifeless dust—but he would do better now. He would plant clover and alfalfa, breed cattle, acre by acre and year by year restore to his land its fibre and fertility. That was something to work for, a way to prove himself. It was ruthless wind, blackening the sky with his earth, but it was not his master. Out of his land it had made a wilderness. He now, out of the wilderness, would make a farm and home again.

Tonight he must talk with Ellen. Patiently, when the wind was down, and they were both quiet again. It was she who had told him to grow fibrous crops, who had called him an ignorant fool because he kept on with summer fallow and wheat. Now she might be gratified to find him acknowledging her wisdom. Perhaps she would begin to feel the power and steadfastness of the land, to take a pride in it, to understand that he was not a fool, but working for her future and their son's.

And already the wind was slackening. At four o'clock he could sense a lull. At five, straining his eyes from the tool shed doorway, he could make out a neighbour's buildings half a mile away. It was over—three days of blight and havoc like a scourge—three days so bitter and so long that for a moment he stood still, unseeing, his senses idle with a numbness of relief.

But only for a moment. Suddenly he emerged from the numbness; suddenly the fields before him struck his eyes to comprehension. They lay black, naked. Beaten and mounded smooth with dust as if a sea in gentle swell had turned to stone. And though he had tried to prepare himself for such a scene, though he had known since yesterday that not a blade would last the storm, still now, before the utter waste confronting him, he sickened and stood cold. Suddenly like the fields he was naked. Everything that had sheathed him a little from the realities of existence: vision and purpose, faith in the land, in the future, in himself—it was all rent now, stripped away. 'Desert,' he heard her voice begin to sob. 'Desert, you fool —the lamp lit at noon!'

In the stable again, measuring out their feed to the horses, he wondered what he would say to her tonight. For so deep were his instincts of loyalty to the land that still, even with the images of his betrayal stark upon his mind, his concern was how to withstand her, how to go on again and justify himself. It had not occurred to him yet that he might or should abandon the land. He had lived with it too long. Rather was his impulse still to defend it—as a man defends against the scorn of strangers even his most worthless kin.

He fed his horses, then waited. She too would be waiting, ready to cry at him, 'Look now—that crop that was to feed and clothe us! And you'll still keep on! You'll still say "Next year—there'll be rain next year"!'

But she was gone when he reached the house. The door was open, the lamp blown out, the crib empty. The dishes from their meal at noon were still on the table. She had perhaps begun to sweep, for the broom was lying in the middle of the floor. He tried to call, but a terror clamped upon his throat. In the wan, returning light it seemed that even the deserted kitchen was straining to whisper what it had seen. The tatters of the storm still whimpered through the eaves, and in their moaning told the desolation of the miles they had traversed. On tiptoe at last he crossed to the adjoining room; then at the threshold, without even a glance inside to satisfy himself that she was really gone, he wheeled again and plunged outside.

He ran a long time—distraught and headlong as a few hours ago he had seemed to watch her run—around the farmyard, a little distance into the pasture, back again blindly to the house to see whether she had returned —and then at a stumble down the road for help.

They joined him in the search, rode away for others, spread calling across the fields in the direction she might have been carried by the wind —but nearly two hours later it was himself who came upon her. Crouched down against a drift of sand as if for shelter, her hair in matted strands around her neck and face, the child clasped tightly in her arms.

The child was quite cold. It had been her arms, perhaps, too frantic to protect him, or the smother of dust upon his throat and lungs. 'Hold him,' she said as he knelt beside her. 'So—with his face away from the wind. Hold him until I tidy my hair.'

Her eyes were still wide in an immobile stare, but with her lips she smiled at him. For a long time he knelt transfixed, trying to speak to her, touching fearfully with his fingertips the dust-grimed cheeks and eyelids of the child. At last she said, 'I'll take him again. Such clumsy hands— you don't know how to hold a baby yet. See how his head falls forward on your arm.'

Yet it all seemed familiar—a confirmation of what he had known since noon. He gave her the child, then, gathering them up in his arms, struggled to his feet, and turned toward home.

It was evening now. Across the fields a few spent clouds of dust still shook and fled. Beyond, as if through smoke, the sunset smouldered like a distant fire.

He walked with a long dull stride, his eyes before him, heedless of her weight. Once he glanced down and with her eyes she still was smiling. 'Such strong arms, Paul—and I was so tired just carrying him. . . .'

He tried to answer, but it seemed that now the dusk was drawn apart in breathless waiting, a finger on its lips until they passed. 'You were right, Paul. . . .' Her voice came whispering, as if she too could feel the hush. 'You said tonight we'd see the storm go down. So still now, and a red sky—it means tomorrow will be fine.'

THE LAMP AT NOON AND OTHER STORIES

b. 1909

Gabrielle Roy

GABRIELLE ROY is a French-Canadian writer who has dealt with an exceptional range of characters and themes in works that include realistic fiction, a parable of an artist's life, and semi-fictional autobiography. She was born in St Boniface, Man., and educated there and at the Normal School in Winnipeg. She taught in rural areas of the province, then studied theatre in Europe, and eventually settled in Montreal to become a writer. In 1947 she married Dr Marcel Carbotte and has lived since that time in Quebec City.

Gabrielle Roy made a name for herself with her first novel, *Bonheur d'occasion* (1945), which was published in English as *The Tin Flute* in 1947. (All her books were written in French and are known to English-speaking readers in translation.) It is the story of a family living in a working-class slum in Montreal during the depression and the early years of the Second World War. It won a Governor General's Award for fiction and the *Prix Femina* in France. Another example of Miss Roy's realistic fiction is *The Cashier* (1955), about the final illness of a poor bank teller called Alexandre Chenevert,

whose anonymous and lonely existence is touched by human sympathy and communication only in the last days of his life. *The Hidden Mountain* (1962), a parable of an artist's search for his subject and his efforts to express it, is one of the relatively few works of Canadian fiction set in the Far North. Her autobiographical semi-fictions include *Where Nests the Water Hen* (1951), *Street of Riches* (1957), and *The Road Past Altamont* (1966); they draw upon Gabrielle Roy's memories of her childhood in Manitoba, her father's connections with New Canadian communities in the province (he was an official in the Department of Immigration), and her own experiences as a teacher. In 1970 she published *Windflower*, in which the background is once again the Far North. This novel tells the story of an Eskimo girl who was raped by an American G.I. and of the son born of that union who was caught between two worlds. Phyllis Grosskurth, describing 'the qualities that entitle her to serious consideration as a distinguished novelist', has listed Gabrielle Roy's 'talent for delicate, vibrant prose; a gentle understanding of the longing of the heart; and a warmly compassionate view of people'.

There are articles on the achievement of Gabrielle Roy by Hugo McPherson in Issue 1 (Summer 1959) and by Phyllis Grosskurth in Issue 42 (Autumn 1969) of *Canadian Literature*. A book-length study of the author by Phyllis Grosskurth is in the series Canadian Writers and Their Works published by Forum House. *The Tin Flute, Where Nests the Water Hen, The Cashier*, and *Street of Riches* are all available in the New Canadian Library.

THE SCHOOL ON THE LITTLE WATER HEN

Once more the ducks had started their long flight south. The wild geese also strung their way over the island, coming from even more secret retreats in the north; never would they nest closer than ten miles from the nearest human habitation; the terns, the water hens, the prairie chickens, the teal were on the wing. The skies over the land were furrowed with aerial rights of way, almost visible to the eye, with all the traffic in one direction. Soon the Big Water Hen carried little islands of snow; the river also took on a lovely mien, as though it were in a hurry to be gone, thanks to the large white bundles it swept along in its course, allowing you to measure the swiftness of its current. Sadly Luzina saw the coming of another torpid winter, again without a school teacher and regular lessons. Even the Indian children had a better portion than her own; they had a school, Luzina would say. But here, how could we manage? Then one evening, as he sat rocking in the kitchen, Hippolyte found a solution for the bewildering problem.

Never did Hippolyte rock alone; the moment he had sat down in the rocking-chair three or four children came begging to climb aboard. He would plant one on each of his knees, two others on the big chair's arms, and, thus laden, spacious and sturdy, the rocker would set forth on a kind of voyage, for not only did it rock all these passengers, it also took them for a ride across the kitchen floor. All the while Hippolyte smoked; it was his hour of relaxation. Navigating at full speed and surrounded with thick smoke, the chair was almost at the door; Hippolyte was meditating, and suddenly he glimpsed the answer. It was easy enough; all you had to do was think of it. Hippolyte briefly interrupted his travels; he took his pipe out of his mouth; the smoke grew thinner. Without undue excitement Hippolyte gave utterance to the profound discovery which was to transform their existence.

'Now about the children, Mother. . . . I've been thinking; we could write the government!'

The moment they had been spoken, these words introduced into the Tousignants' little home a relief so satisfying, so obvious, that they were astounded they had not hit upon it long before. Hippolyte had the pleasure of seeing Luzina's countenance reflective in its turn, absorbed, then gladdened and at the same moment congratulating him, Hippolyte, for always knowing where to turn. The government, of course! How had neither of them ever thought of it before! All kinds of imposing images, solid and reassuring, summoned the government before Luzina's inner eye.

Its seat was Winnipeg, the most beautiful city, she asserted, that she had ever seen. She had been there on her honeymoon, on the way to the Little Water Hen. The government dwelt in a house built entirely of marble imported from Italy; Luzina had heard it said that its construction had cost several million dollars, and at this juncture she literally believed it. In all the world there could not be a Parliament much better housed than Manitoba's. This Parliament was surrounded by a statue of a man who had wings and came from France. Access to it was by a great stairway, likewise of marble. Almost everything was marble in that Parliament. On each side of the stair two life-sized buffaloes appeared ready to charge. The buffaloes were the emblem of Manitoba: beasts with great heads planted directly on their humps, without any length of neck or all neck-length, according to the point of view, and whose feet still seemed furiously to pound the prairie soil. They had been almost exterminated and now they symbolised the province's daring and belief in progress. It had been by Winnipeg's schools, however, that Luzina had above all been overwhelmed. Big schools several storeys high, all windows. The government took care of them. The government which ruled from behind the two buffaloes was among the most advanced in educational matters. It had decreed compulsory schooling before there were enough schools for all the children or roads for them to reach what schools there were.

Full of confidence, Luzina tore a sheet of paper from her pad and wrote to the government. She dreamed of the bronze buffaloes. No other province in the world could have such powerful animals for an emblem. Canada itself had only a beaver. In this dream of Luzina's the buffaloes charged down from everywhere at once against the ignorance of backward lands. The next day, ice or no ice, Hippolyte was dispatched to the edge of the trail, across the two rivers, with the letter to give the postman on the mainland. He was the same fellow as before, that old character by the name of Nick Sluzick who, although he had been threatening for ten years to leave for quieter, less thickly populated country, had continued to ply between the province's most remote post office and the region's uttermost habitations, just at the edge of the everlasting tundra.

At the same spot six weeks later, Nick Sluzick grumblingly drew from

one of his mailbags a letter addressed to the Tousignants. Pierre-Emman-
uel-Roger, who had been sent to reconnoiter each Friday, found it in their
letter-box, the hollow of an old tree that had been killed by the frost. The
letter bore no stamp. In its place there were initials—o.h.m.s.—and in the
opposite corner a buffalo surmounted by a cross, the whole engraved in
relief, black on white, and most impressive. At once Pierre realized its
importance. He ran all the way from the letter-box to the house, a little
more than a mile; he might easily have taken a ducking in the Little Water
Hen, so negligently did he look to see whether the ice beneath his feet
was sufficiently firm. On the threshold Luzina was waiting for him, the
temperature thirty below zero, her cheeks aflame.

'It's got the buffalo on it,' Pierre informed her.

'The buffalo!'

She caught a glimpse of the vastness of the power to which she had had
recourse. The handsome envelope Pierre coveted flew into tiny bits. 'Dear
Mrs Tousignant,' Luzina began to read. She did not understand much
English but enough to grasp the good news. She seemed to gather that
first of all the government apologized for having made her await an answer
for so long a time. It said that, knowing almost no French, it had to appeal
to its Quebec colleague, Jean-Marie Lafontaine, who worked for Titles
and Land and who had helped it translate Luzina's letter.

Surely the government had been put to a lot of trouble through her
fault; Luzina blushed a little at what she had done. Moreover, the government explained, Luzina's letter addressed to the *Gouvernement d'Instruc-
tion* had taken a long while to reach the offices of the Department of
Education and, among all its offices, that of Mr Evans, who was in charge
of precisely such requests as those Luzina had made. Hence it was he who
was answering Luzina. She examined the signature and saw that it indeed
corresponded with the much more legible, typewritten letters appearing
below it. All this, however, was merely by way of preliminary, friendly
as it might be. Luzina found the essential matter in the second paragraph.

In this second paragraph of its letter, the government made clear to
Luzina that she had not been wrong in supposing it very much interested
in education. It expressed itself as distressed to learn that in regions like
that in which Luzina lived there seemingly were future citizens deprived
of schools. All this must be changed as quickly as possible, and all this
would be changed, promised the government, for it was certainly by
means of education that a nation came into being. Consequently it declared itself ready to dispatch a schoolmistress to the island in the Little
Water Hen, starting in May and for a period of four or six months, as the
weather and the roads might allow, under two conditions:

First, that there be a small building, or at the very least a room in the house, which would serve as a school. Second, that the number of students be at least six, all of them having reached the age of school enrolment.

* * *

The school took shape quickly, a small square building constructed of round logs like the main dwelling. It lay slightly at an angle, between two white birches, closely linked to the house like some faithful out-building and yet having its own door and its two entrance steps. It had been quite a task to locate it between two frail birches which Luzina absolutely refused to sacrifice and which she wished to have, as much as possible, on either side of its doorway.

It was really coming along nicely. The children were constantly rushing in with reports. 'Mama, Father has cut out the space for another window-frame. Father says that you need a lot of light in a schoolhouse. That makes three windows, Mama!'

Luzina rushed out to see. Half-way up a ladder Hippolyte was driving nails. He had a supply of them in his mouth, and when he spoke he pinched his lips up on one side and turned them up on the other. Almost all the children stood at the foot of the ladder; they watched the building progress with all the gravity and interest of city dwellers watching the progress of important public works. Luzina's gay nature, after that attack of doubts and nervousness which at the outset all great projects produce, had reasserted itself. Now that the school was under construction, just try telling her that anything could possibly go wrong! One day she began laughing, a fine, open laughter, satisfied with herself, 'Well, Father Tousignant, I don't know whether there are many families like us who have their own school and their own teacher all to themselves!'

* * *

Occasionally Luzina would still enter the small schoolhouse. The birches had grown and cast a great deal of shadow over the windows which Hippolyte had wanted opening on as much light as possible. Within the tiny room the light was now green and sad. In order to mount the platform, Luzina had to clamber over lengths of stove-pipe, coils of rope, and she had to push aside a grindstone. The school smelt of mould, the smell of old, damp paper. Luzina pulled the string of one of the large maps sent long ago by the government. Manitoba hung in front of her, almost as big as the wall. Here and there the sturdy paper had come somewhat loose from its muslin backing; there were places where Manitoba was swollen in blisters, like those maps on which mountain chains are shown in relief. Here, however, it was the even plain that rose, sank back, split open. An under-water glow played over the old map, wrinkled as it was and spotted with green. You might have imagined that it sought to show

Luzina a world which everywhere had reasons for growing sorrowful. At the very bottom of the map Luzina saw an area fairly black with the names of rivers, villages, and towns. That was the South. Almost every village had its geographical rights in the South. Luzina's finger went exploring along the lines of longitude and latitude. Lovingly she would now and then seek to smooth out the map's wrinkles. At last she would discover Otterburne, the precise spot where André-Aimable was studying apiculture with the Victorians. Her fingers moved along further. Here, at Saint Jean Baptiste, she located young Héloïse, whom Aunt Blanche had sent for the moment Joséphine had made sufficient progress. Luzina moved upward to find Roberta-Louise at the Dauphin hospital. The old map seemed to her almost a friend—likewise a thief. It oozed moisture. As she stroked it lightly and warmed it with her hand, Luzina extracted from it little drops of humidity, thin, cold, which, under her fingers gave her a strange impression of tears. Then Manitoba seemed to her to grow bored. So vast, so little bestrewn with names, almost entirely given over to these wide, naked stretches which represented lakes and uninhabited space! Emptier and emptier, bare paper without a printed word, the further you went into the North. It seemed that all the place-names had clustered together on this map as though to warm each other, that they had all crowded together in the same corner of the South. There they even had to be abbreviated, so small was the available space, but up above they stretched out at their ease, with room to spare. Mademoiselle Côté had taught that three-quarters of Manitoba's population all dwelt within this little portion of the map that Luzina could cover with her two hands. That left very few people for the North! So vacant in that portion, the old map seemed to want to take vengeance on Luzina. In large letters it bore the name Water Hen River. It was silent, however, regarding the existence of the island in the Little Water Hen.

WHERE NESTS THE WATER HEN
Translated by Harry L. Binsse

George Ryga

GEORGE RYGA is the most successful theatre dramatist in English Canada, yet such is the condition of theatre in this country that his situation as a writer is entirely vulnerable. He was born of Ukrainian immigrant parents on a marginal farm in northern Alberta, and his formal education lasted only seven years in a one-room country school. He worked on farms, in steel construction (where he lost three fingers), and for a radio station in Edmonton. But as early as 1949 his writing had brought him some attention and he worked and studied at the University of Texas on a scholarship. In 1962 he became a full-time writer. He lives in Summerland, near Penticton, B.C.

Ryga began his writing career by attacking every likely market: a dozen short stories were broadcast on radio in 1961 and 1962, plays were written for Canadian radio and television (including an adaptation for radio of Margaret Laurence's The Stone Angel), and two novels were published. (One further indication of Ryga's energy and determination: a recent bibliography of his work lists seven novels written between 1960 and 1967 that have not been published.)

The published novels are The Hungry Hills (1960) and Ballad of a Stone Picker (1962). In 1962 his play Indian, about an encounter between a transient Indian labourer and an official of the Department of Indian Affairs, was produced on CBC-TV; it became a stage play two years later. In Indian and Ballad of a Stone Picker, realism begins to blend with dream and symbol in a way that has become the dominant characteristic of the major stage plays written and produced in the late 1960s. By that time Ryga and the Vancouver Playhouse theatre had become closely and, as it turned out, disastrously linked together. The Playhouse produced The Ecstasy of Rita Joe, about the life and death of an Indian girl, and the play that followed, Grass and Wild Strawberries, about the disaffected and disoriented young. While both plays were successful at the box office, they offended season subscribers to the Playhouse and members of the theatre's board. In 1970 a third play, Captives of the Faceless Drummer, 'a dream about political violence set in the future but evidently inspired by the situation in Quebec', was rejected by the Vancouver Playhouse, and Ryga's chance of a sympathetic and continuing association with a theatre company in his own part of Canada came to an end. This play has since had two productions in 1972: at the St Lawrence Centre, Toronto, and at Festival Lennoxville.

Brian Parker has written of *Indian* that 'the crux of the play is its attempt to understand the puzzling character of the Indian by drawing the audience into his experiences and thought processes. . . . All his behaviour is revealed as springing from the central fact of personal despair. . . . In exposing this despair Ryga also establishes some of his major themes: the indictment of a society too scared to care . . . the resentment of off-hand, patronizing "welfare"; the feeling that traditional religion is no help . . . and the touchstone of family love for human behaviour.'

The Ecstasy of Rita Joe and Other Plays (1971), including *Indian*, edited with an introduction by Brian Parker, is available in paperback from New Press. There is an article on George Ryga by Neil Carson in Issue 45 of *Canadian Literature* (Summer 1970).

INDIAN

Characters

INDIAN. Transient Indian labourer. Swarthy, thin, long-haired. Wears tight-fitting jeans, dirty dark shirt brightened by outlandish western designs over pockets. Also cowboy boots which are cracked and aged. A wide-brimmed black western hat.

WATSON. Farmer and employer of Indian.

AGENT. Comfortable civil servant. Works in the Indian Affairs Department as field worker for the service.

Setting

Stage should be flat, grey, stark non-country. Diametric lines (telephone poles and wire on one side, with a suggestion of two or three newly driven fence-posts on the other) could project vast empty expanse.

Set may have a few representative tufts of scraggy growth in distance—also far and faint horizon.

In front and stage left, one fence-post newly and not yet fully driven. Pile of dirt around post. Hammer, wooden box, and shovel alongside.

High, fierce white light offstage left to denote sun. Harsh shadows and constant sound of low wind.

Back of stage is a pile of ashes, with a burnt axe handle and some pottery showing.

(*Curtain up on* INDIAN *asleep, using slight hump of earth under his neck for pillow. He is facing sun, with hat over his face.* WATSON *approaches from stage right, dragging his feet and raising dust. Stops over* INDIAN's *head.*)

WATSON (*loud and angry*). Hey! What the hell! Come on . . . you aimin' to die like that?

(INDIAN *clutches his hat and sits up. Lifts his hat and looks up, then jerks hat down over his face.*)

INDIAN. Oy! Oooh! The sun she blind me, goddamn! . . . Boss . . . I am sick! Head, she gonna explode, sure as hell!

(*He tries to lie down again, but* WATSON *grabs his arm and yanks him to his feet.*)

WATSON. There's gonna be some bigger explosions if I don't get action out of you guys. What happened now? Where's the fat boy? An' the guy with the wooden leg?

INDIAN. Jus' a minute, boss. Don't shout like that. (*looks carefully around him*) They not here . . . Guess they run away, boss—no? . . . Roy, he's not got wooden leg. He got bone leg same's you an' me. Only it dried up and look like wood. Small, too . . . (*lifts up his own right leg*) That shoe . . . that was fit Roy's bad leg. The other shoe is tight. But this one, boss—she is hunder times tighter!

WATSON (*squatting*). Is them Limpy's boots?

INDIAN. Sure, boss. I win them at poker las' night. Boss, what a time we have—everybody go haywire!

(WATSON *looks around impatiently.*)

WATSON. I can see. Where's your tent?

INDIAN (*pointing to ashes*). There she is. Sonofabitch, but I never see anything burn like that before!

WATSON. The kid wasn't lying—you guys *did* burn the tent.

INDIAN. What kid?

WATSON. Your kid.

INDIAN (*jumping to his feet*). Alphonse? Where is Alphonse? He run away when Sam and Roy start fight . . .

WATSON. Yeh, he run away . . . run all the way to the house. Told us you guys was drunk an' wild. So the missus fixed him something to eat and put him to bed.

INDIAN. He's all right? Oh, that's good, boss!

WATSON (*smiling grimly*). Sure, he's all right. Like I said, the missus fed the kid. Then I took him and put him in the grainery, lockin' the door so he ain't gonna get out. That's for protection.

INDIAN. Protection? You don't need protection, boss. Alphonse not gonna hurt you.

WATSON. Ha! Ha! Ha! Big joke! . . . Where are your pals as was gonna help you with this job? Where are they—huh?

INDIAN. I don't know. They run away when tent catch fire.

WATSON. Great! That's just great! You know what you guys done to me?

Yesterday, ya nicked me for ten dollars . . . I'm hungry, the fat boy says to me—my stomach roar like thunder. He's gonna roar out the other end before I'm finished with you an' him! How much you figure the fence you put up is worth?

INDIAN (*rubbing his eyes and trying to see the fence in the distance*). I dunno, boss. You say job is worth forty dollars. Five, mebbe ten dollars done . . .

WATSON. Five dollars! Look here, smart guy—ya've got twenty-nine posts in—I counted 'em. At ten cents apiece, you've done two dollars ninety cents worth of work! An' you got ten dollars off me yesterday!

INDIAN (*pondering sadly*). Looks like you in the hole, boss.

WATSON. Well maybe I am . . . an' maybe I ain't. I got your kid in the grainery, locked up so he'll keep. You try to run off after your pals, an' I'm gonna take my gun an' shoot a hole that big through the kid's head!

(*He makes a ring with his fingers to show exact size of injury he intends to make.*)

INDIAN. No!

WATSON. Oh, sure! So what ya say, Indian? . . . You gonna work real hard and be a good boy?

INDIAN. Boss—you know me. I work! Them other guys is no good—but not Johnny. I make deal—I keep deal! You see yourself I stay when they run.

WATSON. Sure, ya stayed. You were too goddamned drunk to move, that's why you stayed! What goes on in your heads . . . ah, hell! You ain't worth the bother!

INDIAN. No, no, boss . . . You all wrong.

WATSON. Then get to work! It's half past nine, and you ain't even begun to think about the fence.

INDIAN. Boss . . . a little bit later. I sick man . . . head—she hurt to burst. An' stomach—ugh! Boss, I not eat anything since piece of baloney yesterday . . .

WATSON (*turning angrily*). You go to hell—hear me? Go to hell! I got that story yesterday. Now g'wan—I wanna see some action!

INDIAN. All right, boss. You know me. You trust me.

WATSON. Trust ya? I wouldn't trust you with the time of day, goddamn you! (*remembers something*) Hey—there's a snoop from the Indian Affairs department toolin' around today—checkin' on all you guys workin' off the reserve. I'm telling you somethin' . . . you're working for me, so if you got any complaints, you better tell me now. I don't want no belly-achin' to no government guys.

INDIAN. Complaints? . . . Me? I happy, boss. What you take me for?

WATSON. Sure, sure . . . Now get back to work. An' remember what I told you . . . you try to beat it, an' I shoot the kid. You understand?

(INDIAN *removes his hat and wipes his brow.*)

INDIAN. Sure, bossman—I understand.

(INDIAN *looks towards the fence in the fields.* WATSON *stands behind him, scratching his chin and smirking insolently.* INDIAN *glances back at him, then shrugging with resignation, moves unsteadily to the unfinished fence post. He pulls the box nearer to the post, picks up hammer, and is about to step on the box. Changes his mind and sits for a moment on the box, hammer across his knees. Rubs his eyes and forehead.*)

WATSON. Now what the hell's the matter? Run out of gas?

INDIAN. Oh, boss . . . If I be machine that need only gas, I be all right mebbe . . .

WATSON. So you going to sit an' let the day go by? . . . Indian, I've got lots of time, an' I can grind you to dirt if you're figurin' on bustin' my ass!

INDIAN. Nobody bust you, boss. I be all right right away . . . Sementos! But the head she is big today. An' stomach . . . she is slop-bucket full of turpentine. Boss . . . two dollars a quart, Sam Cardinal says to me . . . with four dollars we get enough bad whisky to poison every Indian from here to Lac La Biche! Sam Cardinal tell the truth that time for sure . . .

WATSON. What kind of rubbish did you drink?

INDIAN. Indian whisky, boss. You know what is Indian whisky?

WATSON. No. You tell me, an' then you get to work!

INDIAN. Sure, boss, sure. As soon as field stop to shake. Indian whisky . . . you buy two quart. You get one quart wood alcohol . . . maybe half quart formalin, an' the rest is water from sick horse! That's the kind whisky they make for Indian.

WATSON. An' it makes the field shake for you . . . Christ! *You* make me sick.

INDIAN. Oh, but what party it make!

WATSON (*irritably*). Come on . . . come on! Get on with it.

(INDIAN *scrambles on box and starts to drive post into ground. He stops after a few seconds. He is winded.*)

INDIAN. Sementos! Is hard work, boss! . . . I tell you, Sam Cardinal sing like sick cow . . . an' Roy McIntosh dance on his bad leg. Funny! . . . Alphonse an' I laugh until stomach ache. I win Roy's boots in poker, but he dance anyhow. Then Sam get mad an' he push Roy . . . Roy push him back . . . They fight . . . Boy, I hungry now, boss . . .

WATSON. Tough! I wanna see ten bucks of work done.

INDIAN. Then you feed me? Big plate potatoes an' meat? . . . An' mebbe big hunk of pie?

WATSON (*laughs sarcastically*). Feed ya? Soon's I get my ten bucks squared away, you can lie down and die! But not on my field . . . go on the road allowance!

(INDIAN *hits the post a few more times, trying to summon up strength to get on with the work. But it is all in vain. Drops hammer heavily to the box. Rubs his stomach.*)

INDIAN. You hard man, boss . . . Hard like iron. Sam is bad man . . . bugger up you, bugger up me. Get ten dollars for grub from you . . . almost like steal ten dollars from honest man. Buy whisky . . . buy baloney an' two watermelon. He already eat most of baloney and I see him give hunk to friendly dog. I kick dog. Sam get mad . . . why you do that? Dog is nothing to you? I say, he eat my grub. He can go catch cat if he hungry. I catch an' eat cat once myself, boss . . . winter 1956. Not much meat an' tough like rope. I never eat cat again, that's for sure. Sementos! But the head hurt!

WATSON. One more word, Indian . . . just one more word an' I'm gonna clean house on you! . . . You wanna try me? Come on!

(*For a moment the* INDIAN *teeters between two worlds, then with a violent motion he sweeps up the hammer and begins pounding the post, mechanically with an incredible rhythm of defeat.* WATSON *watches for a while, his anger gone now. Scratches himself nervously, then makes a rapid exit off stage left.*

Almost immediately the hammering begins to slow, ending with one stroke when the hammer head rests on the post, and INDIAN'S *head droops on his outstretched arms.*)

INDIAN. Scared talk . . . world is full of scared talk. I show scare an' I get a job from mister Watson. Scared Indian is a live Indian. My head don't get Alphonse free . . . but hands do.

(*Sound of motor car approaching.* INDIAN *lifts his head and peers to stage right.*)

INDIAN. Hullo . . . I am big man today! First mister Watson an' now car come to see me. Boy, he drive! . . . If I not get out of his way he gonna hit me, sure as hell!

(*Jumps down from box and watches. Car squeals to stop offstage. Puff of dust blows in from wings. Car door slams and* AGENT *enters.*)

AGENT. Hi there, fella, how's it going?

INDIAN. Hello, misha. Everything is going one hunder fifty per cent! Yessiree . . . one hunder fifty per cent!

(INDIAN *rises on box and lifts hammer to drive post.*)

AGENT. There was talk in town your camp burned out last night . . . everything okay? Nobody hurt?

INDIAN. Sure, everything okay. You want complaints?

AGENT. Well, I . . . what do you mean, do I want complaints?

INDIAN. I just say if you want complaints, I give you lots. My tent, she is burn down last night. My partners . . . they run away. Leave me to do big job myself. I got no money . . . an' boss, he's got my Alphonse ready to shoot if I try to run. You want more complaints? (*drives down hard on hammer and groans*) Maybe you want know how my head she hurts inside?

AGENT (*relieved*). Hey—c'mere. I'll give you a smoke to make you feel better. You're in rough shape, boy! Which would you prefer—pipe tobacco, or a cigarette? I've got both. . .

(INDIAN *drops hammer and comes down from box.*)

INDIAN. The way I feel, misha, I could smoke old stocking full of straw. Gimme cigarette. (*examines the cigarette* AGENT *gives him*) Oh, you make lotsa money from government, boss . . . tobacco here . . . and cotton there—some cigarette! Which end you light? (*laughs*)

AGENT. Light whichever end you want. You can eat it for all I care. That's some hat you got there, sport. Where'd you get it?

INDIAN (*accepting light* AGENT *offers him*). Win at poker, misha.

AGENT (*examining him closely*). Aren't those boots tight? I suppose you stole them!

INDIAN. No, boss—poker.

AGENT. And that shirt—will you look at that! Have shirt, will travel.

INDIAN. I steal that from my brother, when he is sick and dying. He never catch me!

AGENT (*laughing*). That's good. . . I must tell the boys about you—what's your name?

INDIAN. You think is funny me steal shirt from my brother when he die? . . . You think that funny, bossman? I think you lousy bastard! . . . You think that funny, too?

AGENT (*startled*). Now hold on—did I hear you say . . .

INDIAN. You hear good what I say.

(*The* AGENT *takes out his notebook.*)

AGENT. Just give me your name, and we'll settle with you later.

INDIAN. Turn around an' walk to road. If you want to see stealer in action, I steal wheels off your car. You try catch me. . .

AGENT (*angrily*). Give me your name!

INDIAN. Mebbe I forget . . . mebbe I got no name at all.

AGENT. Look here, boy . . . don't give me any back-talk, or I might have to turn in a report on you, and next time Indian benefits are given out, yours might be hard to claim!

INDIAN. So—you got no name for me. How you gonna report me when you not know who I am? You want name? All right, I give you name.

Write down—Joe Bush!

AGENT. I haven't got all day, fella. Are you, or are you not going to tell me your name?

INDIAN. No! I never tell you misha! Whole world is scare. It make you scare you should know too much about me!

AGENT (*slamming notebook shut*). That does it! You asked for it . . . an' by God, if I have to go after you myself, I'm gonna find out who you are!

INDIAN. Don't get mad, misha. I sorry for what I say. I got such hurting head, I don't know what I say . . .

AGENT. Been drinking again, eh? . . . What was it this time—homebrew? Or shaving lotion?

INDIAN. Maybe homebrew, maybe coffee. I don't know. Why you ask ?

AGENT. You're no kid. You know as well as I do. Besides, bad liquor's going to kill you sooner than anything else.

INDIAN (*excitedly*). Misha . . . you believe that? You really mean what you say?

AGENT. What—about bad liquor? Sure I do. . .

INDIAN. Then misha, please get me bottle of good, clean Canadian whisky! I never drink clean whisky in my life!

AGENT. Come on, now . . . you're as . . .

INDIAN. I give you twenty dollars for bottle! Is deal?

AGENT. Stop it! . . . Boy, you've got a lot more than a hangover wrong in your head!

INDIAN (*points offstage*). That car yours?

AGENT. Yes.

INDIAN. How come all that writing on door—that's not your name? Why you not tell truth?

AGENT. Well, I work for the government, and they provide us. . .

INDIAN. Thirty dollars?

AGENT. Look here . . .

INDIAN. How come you not in big city, with office job? How come you drive around an' talk to dirty, stupid Indian? You not have much school, or mebbe something else wrong with you to have such bad job.

AGENT. Shut your lousy mouth, you . . .

INDIAN. Thirty-five dollars? No more! . . . I give you no more!

AGENT. Will you shut up?

INDIAN (*defiantly*). No! I never shut up! You not man at all—you cheap woman who love for money! Your mother was woman pig, an' your father man dog!

AGENT (*becoming frightened*). What . . . what are you saying?

(INDIAN *comes face to face with* AGENT.)

INDIAN. You wanna hit me? Come on . . . hit me! You kill me easy, an' they arrest you—same people who give you car. Hit me—even little bit—come on! You coward! Just hit me like this! (*slaps his palms together*) . . . Just like that—come on! You know what I do when you hit me?

AGENT (*looks apprehensively around himself*). What?

INDIAN. I report you for beating Indian an' you lose job. Come on—show me you are man!

(*He dances provocatively around* AGENT. AGENT *turns in direction of his car.*)

AGENT. I'm getting out of here—you're crazy!

INDIAN (*jumps in front of* AGENT). No . . . you not go anywhere! Maybe nobody here to see what happen, but after accident, lots of people come from everywhere. I'm gonna jump on car bumper, and when you drive, I fall off an' you drive over me. How you gonna explain that, bossman?

AGENT (*frightened now*). I got nothing against you, boy! What's the matter with you? . . . What do you want with me?

INDIAN. I want nothing from you—jus' to talk to me—to know who I am. Once you go into car, I am outside again. I tell you about my brother, an' how he die . . .

AGENT. Go back to your work and I'll go back to mine. I don't want to hear about your brother or anyone else. (INDIAN *walks offstage to car*) Now you get off my car!

INDIAN (*offstage*). You gonna listen, misha. You gonna listen like I tell you. (*sounds of car being bounced*) Boy, you ride like in bed! Misha, who am I?

(INDIAN *returns to stage.*)

AGENT. How in the devil do I know who you are, or what you want with me. I'm just doing a job—heard your camp got burned out and . . .

INDIAN. How you know who any of us are? How many of us got birth certificates to give us name an' age on reserve? . . . Mebbe you think I get passport an' go to France. Or marry the way bossman get married. You think that, misha?

AGENT. I don't care who you are or what you think. Just get back to your job and leave me alone . . .

(INDIAN *glances admiringly offstage to car.*)

INDIAN. Boy, is like pillow on wheels! If I ever have car like that, I never walk again!

AGENT. Get out of my way! I've got to get back into town.

INDIAN. No hurry. Mebbe you never go back at all.

AGENT. What . . . do you mean by that?

(INDIAN *turns and approaches* AGENT *until they stand face to face.*)

INDIAN. You know what is like to kill someone—not with hate—not with any feelings here at all? (*places hand over heart*)

AGENT (*stepping back*). This is ridiculous! Look, boy . . . I'll give you anything I can—just get out of my hair. That whisky you want—I'll get it for you . . . won't cost you a cent, I promise!

INDIAN. Someone that mebbe you loved? Misha—I want to tell you somethin' . . .

AGENT. No!

(INDIAN *catches hold of* AGENT's *shirt front.*)

INDIAN. Listen—damn you! I kill like that once! You never know at Indian office—nobody tell you! Nobody ever tell you! . . . I got to tell you about my brother . . . he die three, four, maybe five years ago. My friend been collecting treaty payments on his name. He know how many years ago now . . .

AGENT. You couldn't . . .

INDIAN. I couldn't, misha?

AGENT. There are laws in this country—nobody escapes the law!

INDIAN. What law?

AGENT. The laws of the country!

INDIAN (*threatening*). What law?

AGENT. No man . . . shall kill . . . another . . .

INDIAN. I tell you about my brother. I tell you everything. Then you tell me if there is law for all men.

AGENT. Leave me alone! I don't want to hear about your brother!

INDIAN (*fiercely*). You gonna listen! Look around—what you see? Field and dust . . . an' some work I do. You an' me . . . you fat, me hungry. I got nothin' . . . and you got money, car. Maybe you are better man than I. But I am not afraid, an' I can move faster. What happen if I get mad, an' take hammer to you?

AGENT. You . . . wouldn't . . .

INDIAN. You wrong, misha. Nobody see us. Mebbe you lucky—get away. But who believe you? You tell one story, I tell another. I lose nothing —but you gonna listen about my brother, that's for sure!

AGENT (*desperately*). Look boy—let's be sensible—let's behave like two grown men. I'll drive you into town—buy you a big dinner! Then we'll go and buy that whisky I promised. You can go then—find your friends and have another party tonight . . . Nobody will care, and you'll have a good time!

INDIAN (*spitting*). You lousy dog!

AGENT. Now don't get excited . . . I'm only saying what I think is best. If you don't want to come, that's fine. Just let me go and we'll forget all about today, and that we ever even seen one another, okay?

(INDIAN *releases the* AGENT.)

INDIAN. You think I forget I see you? I got you here like picture in my head. I try to forget you . . . like I try to forget my brother, but you never leave me alone . . . Misha, I never forget you!

AGENT (*struggling to compose himself*). I'm just a simple joe doing my job, boy—remember that. I know there's a lot bothers you. Same's a lot bothers me. We've all got problems . . . but take them where they belong.

(AGENT *pulls out cigarettes and nervously lights one for himself.*)

INDIAN. Gimme that!

AGENT. This is mine—I lit it for myself! Here, I'll give you another one!

INDIAN. I want that one!

AGENT. No, damn it . . . have a new one!

(INDIAN *jumps behind* AGENT *and catches him with an arm around throat. With other hand he reaches out and takes lit cigarette out of* AGENT's *mouth. He throws* AGENT *to the field. The* AGENT *stumbles to his knees, rubbing his eyes.*)

AGENT. What's wrong with you? Why did you do that?

INDIAN. Now you know what is like to be me. Get up! Or I kick your brains in!

(AGENT *rises to his feet and sways uncertainly.*)

AGENT. Dear God . . .

INDIAN. My brother was hungry . . . an' he get job on farm of white boss-man to dig a well. Pay she is one dollar for every five feet down. My brother dig twenty feet—two day hard work. He call up to bossman—give me planks, for the blue clay she is getting wet! To hell with what you see—bossman shout down the hole—just dig! Pretty soon, the clay shift, an' my brother is trapped to the shoulders. He yell—pull me out! I can't move, an' the air, she is squeezed out of me! But bossman on top—he is scared to go down in hole. He leave to go to next farm, an' after that another farm, until he find another Indian to send down hole. An' all the time from down there, my brother yell at the sky. Jesus Christ—help me! White man leave me here to die! But Jesus Christ not hear my brother, an' the water she rise to his lips. Pretty soon, he put his head back until his hair an' ears in slimy blue clay an' water. He no more hear himself shout—but he shout all the same!

AGENT. I wasn't there! I couldn't help him!

INDIAN . . . He see stars in the sky—lots of stars. A man see stars even in day when he look up from hole in earth . . .

AGENT. I couldn't help him—I don't want to hear about him!

INDIAN . . . Then Sam Cardinal come. Sam is a coward. But when he see my brother there in well, an' the blue clay movin' around him like livin' thing, he go down. Sam dig with his hands until he get rope around my brother. Then he come up, an' he an' white bossman pull. My brother no longer remember, an' he not hear the angry crack of mud an' water when they pull him free . . .

AGENT (*with relief*). Then . . . he lived? Thank God . . .

INDIAN. Sure . . . sure . . . he live. You hunt?

AGENT. Hunt? . . . You mean—shooting?

INDIAN. Yeh.

AGENT. Sure. I go out every year.

INDIAN. You ever shoot deer—not enough to kill, but enough to break one leg for ever? Or maybe hit deer in eye, an' it run away, blind on one side for wolf to kill?

AGENT. I nicked a moose two years back—never did track it down. But I didn't shoot it in the eye.

INDIAN. How you know for sure?

AGENT. Well . . . I just didn't. I never shoot that way!

INDIAN. You only shoot—where bullet hit you not know. Then what you do?

AGENT. I tried to track it, but there had been only a light snow . . . an' I lost the tracks.

INDIAN. So you not follow?

AGENT. No. I walked back to camp . . . My friend an' I had supper and we drove home that night . . .

INDIAN. Forget all about moose you hurt?

AGENT. No. I did worry about what happened to him!

INDIAN. You dream about him that night? . . . Runnin', bawling with pain?

AGENT. What the hell . . . dream about a moose? There's more important things to worry about, I'm telling you.

INDIAN. Then you not worry at all. You forget as soon as you can. Moose not run away from you—you run away from moose!

AGENT. I didn't . . . hey, you're crazy! (*moves towards car offstage, but* INDIAN *jumps forward and stops him*) Here! You leave me alone, I'm telling you . . . You got a lot of wild talk in your head, but you can't push your weight around with me . . . I'm getting out of here . . . Hey!

(INDIAN *catches him by the arm and rolls him to fall face down in the dust.* INDIAN *pounces on him.*)

INDIAN. What you call man who has lost his soul?

AGENT. I don't know. Let go of me!

INDIAN. We have name for man like that! You know the name?

AGENT. No, I don't. *You're breaking my arm!*

INDIAN. We call man like that sementos. Remember that name . . . for *you* are *sementos!*

AGENT. Please, fella—leave me alone! I never hurt you that I know of . . .

INDIAN. Sure.

(Releases AGENT, *who rises to his feet, dusty and dishevelled.)*

AGENT. I want to tell you something . . . I want you to get this straight, because every man has to make up his mind about some things, and I've made mine up now! This has gone far enough. If this is a joke, then you've had your laughs. One way or another, I'm going to get away from you. And when I do, I'm turning you in to the police. You belong in jail!

INDIAN *(laughs)*. Mebbe you are man. We been in jail a long time now, sementos . . .

AGENT. And stop calling me that name!

INDIAN. Okay, okay . . . I call you bossman. You know what bossman mean to me?

AGENT. I don't want to know.

INDIAN *(laughs again)*. You wise . . . you get it. I not got much to say, then you go.

AGENT *(bewildered)*. You . . . you're not going to . . . bother me anymore?

INDIAN. I finish my story, an' you go . . . go to town, go to hell . . . go anyplace. My brother—you know what kind of life he had? He was not dead, an' he was not alive.

AGENT. You said he came out of the well safely. What are you talking about?

INDIAN. No . . . He was not alive. He was too near dead to live. White bossman get rid of him quick. Here, says bossman—here is three dollars pay. I dig twenty feet—I make four dollars, my brother says. Bossman laugh. I take dollar for shovel you leave in the hole, he says. My brother come back to reserve, but he not go home. He live in my tent. At night, he wake up shouting, an' in daytime, he is like man who has no mind. He walk 'round, an' many times get lost in the bush, an' other Indian find him an' bring him back. He get very sick. For one month he lie in bed. Then he try to get up. But his legs an' arms are dried to the bone, like branches of dying tree.

AGENT. He must've had polio.

INDIAN. Is not matter . . . One night, he say to me: go to the other side of lake tomorrow, an' take my wife an' son, Alphonse. Take good care of them. I won't live the night . . . I reach out and touch him, for he talk like devil fire was on him. But his head and cheek is cold. You will live an' take care of your wife an' Alphonse yourself, I say to him. But my brother shake his head. He look at me and say—help me to die . . .

AGENT. Why . . . didn't you . . . take him to hospital?

INDIAN *(laughs bitterly)*. Hospital! A dollar he took from dying man for the shovel buried in blue clay . . . hospital? Burn in hell!

AGENT. No . . . no! This I don't understand at all . . .

INDIAN. I . . . kill . . . my . . . brother! In my arms I hold him. He was so light, like small boy. I hold him . . . rock 'im back and forward like this . . . like mother rock us when we tiny kids. I rock 'im an' I cry . . . I get my hands tight on his neck, an' I squeeze an' I squeeze. I know he dead, and I still squeeze an' cry, for everything is gone, and I am old man now . . . only hunger an' hurt left now.

AGENT. My God!

INDIAN. I take off his shirt an' pants—I steal everything I can wear. Then I dig under tent, where ground is soft, and I bury my brother. After that, I go to other side of lake. When I tell my brother's wife what I done, she not say anything for long time. Then she look at me with eyes that never make tears again. Take Alphonse, she say . . . I go to live with every man who have me, to forget him. Then she leave her shack, an' I alone with Alphonse . . . I take Alphonse an' I come back. All Indians know what happen, but nobody say anything. Not to me . . . not to you. Some halfbreed born outside reservation take my brother's name—and you, bossman, not know . . .

AGENT (*quietly, as though he were the authority again*). We *have* to know, you understand, don't you? You'll have to tell me your brother's name.

INDIAN. I know . . . I tell you. Was Tommy Stone.

(AGENT *takes out his notebook again and writes.*)

AGENT. Stone—Tommy Stone . . . good. You know what I have to do, you understand it's my duty, don't you? It's my job . . . it's the way I feel. We all have to live within the law and uphold it. Ours is a civilized country . . . you understand, don't you? (*turns to car offstage*) I'm going now. Don't try to run before the police come. The circumstances were extenuating, and it may not go hard for you . . .

(INDIAN *makes no attempt to hinder* AGENT *who walks offstage.*)

INDIAN. Sure, misha . . . you're right. (*hears car door open*) Wait! Misha, wait! I tell you wrong. Name is not Tommy Stone—Tommy Stone is me! Name is *Johnny* Stone!

(AGENT *returns, notebook in hand.*)

AGENT. Johnny Stone? Let's get this straight now . . . your brother was Johnny Stone . . . and you're *Tommy* Stone? (INDIAN *nods vigorously*) Okay, boy. I've got that. Now remember what I said, and just stay here and wait. (*turns to leave*)

INDIAN. No, misha . . . you got whole business screwed up again! I am Johnny Stone, my brother, he is Tommy Stone.

(AGENT *pockets his notebook and turns angrily to face* INDIAN.)

AGENT. Look, Indian—what in hell is your name anyhow? Who are you?

INDIAN. My name? You want my name?

(*Suddenly catches* AGENT *by arm and swings him around as in a boyish* game. *Places* AGENT *down on the box he used for standing on to drive posts.*)

AGENT. Hey, you stop that!

INDIAN. An' yet you want my name?

AGENT. Yes, that's right . . . If it's not too much trouble to give me one straight answer, what is your name?

INDIAN. Sam Cardinal is my name!

(AGENT *rises with disgust and straightens out his clothes.*)

AGENT. Now it's Sam Cardinal . . . what do you take me for anyway? You waste my time . . . you rough me up like I was one of your drunken Indian friends . . . and now I can't get an answer to a simple question . . . But what the hell—the police can find out who you are and what you've done.

INDIAN. No, sementos! You never find out!

(INDIAN *throws legs apart and takes the stance of a man balancing on a threshold.*)

INDIAN. You go to reservation with hunder policemen—you try to find Johnny Stone . . . you try to find Tommy Stone . . . Sam Cardinal, too. Mebbe you find everybody, mebbe you find nobody. All Indians same— nobody. Listen to me, sementos—one brother is dead—who? Tommy Stone? Johnny Stone? Joe Bush! Look—(*turns out both pockets of his pants, holding them out, showing them empty and ragged*) I got nothing . . . nothing . . . no wallet, no money, no name. I got no past . . . no future . . . nothing, sementos! I nobody. I not even live in this world . . . I dead! You get it? . . . I dead! (*shrugs in one great gesture of grief*) I never been anybody. *I not just dead . . . I never live at all.* What is matter? . . . What anything matter, sementos?

(AGENT *has the look of a medieval peasant meeting a leper—fear, pity hatred.*)

INDIAN. What matter if I choke you till you like rag in my hands? . . . Hit you mebbe with twenty pound hammer—break in your head like watermelon . . . Leave you dry in wind an' feed ants . . . What matter if police come an' take me? Misha! Listen, damn you—listen! One brother kill another brother—why? (*shakes* AGENT *furiously by the lapels*) Why? Why? . . . Why?

AGENT (*clawing at* INDIAN's *hands*). Let me go! LET . . . ME . . . GO!

(AGENT *breaks free and runs offstage for car. Sounds of motor starting and fast departure. Dust.* INDIAN *stands trembling with fury.*)

INDIAN. Where you go in such goddamn speed? World too small to run 'way? You hear me, sementos! Hi . . . sementos! Ugh!

(*Spits and picks up hammer. Starts to drive post vigorously. Curtain.*)

Duncan Campbell Scott

DUNCAN CAMPBELL SCOTT was a poet and short-story writer who is associated with Roberts, Carman, and Lampman because all four poets were born in the early 1860s, all first published in the eighties and nineties, and all were romantic poets who drew their inspiration from Canadian nature. Born in Ottawa, the son of a Methodist missionary, Scott grew up in various small towns in Ontario and Québec. When his formal schooling ended at seventeen, his father arranged a job interview with Sir John A. Macdonald. The Prime Minister wrote on his application: 'Approved—employ Mr Scott at $1.50.' The boy then took a position in the Department of Indian Affairs and stayed for fifty-two years; he was deputy superintendent from 1923 until his retirement in 1932.

In 1883 Archibald Lampman joined the civil service and he and Scott became friends. With Lampman's encouragement Scott began writing poetry. (When Lampman died in 1899, Scott was his literary executor and in the course of time edited four collections of his poems.) Scott's first collection, *The Magic House and Other Poems*, appeared in 1893 (the year

Carman's *Low Tide on Grand Pré* and Roberts' *Songs of the Common Day* were published); 'A Night in June' appeared in this book. His other collections are *Labour and the Angel* (1898), which includes his famous sea fantasy, 'The Piper of Arll'; *New World Lyrics and Ballads* (1905), containing 'The Forsaken', one of his haunting ballads of Indian life; *Via Borealis* (1906); *Lundy's Lane and Other Poems* (1916); *Beauty and Life* (1921); and *The Green Cloister* (1935), which contained another of his best-known poems, 'At Gull Lake, August 1810'. *The Circle of Affection*—poems, essays, and short stories—was published the year he died.

As a poet Scott was most successful in his landscape poems—the best of which have colourful imagery, vivid, realistic atmosphere, and compelling descriptions of the cruelties and contrasts in nature—and in narrative poems on themes of conflict between nature and man. His travels as an official of the Indian Affairs Department gave him material for both kinds of verse: descriptive poems about the northern wilderness and ballads about the tragic irony of Indian life, of which 'The Forsaken' is not only the best example but one of his best poems.

Scott was an effective short-story writer and some of his stories belong with the finest ever written in Canada. He published two collections: *In the Village of Viger* (1896) and *The Witching of Elspie* (1923). The first—restrained, nostalgic tales of a quiet village near Montreal—is a distinct contrast to the second, in which the themes are coloured by harshness and violence and there is a variety of settings: some stories are laid in northern fur-trading regions.

A.J.M. Smith reconsiders Scott's poetry in Issue 1 of *Canadian Literature* (Summer 1959) and both the poet and his work are discussed by Desmond Pacey in *Ten Canadian Poets* (rev. 1961). There is a representative selection of Scott's poems in *Poets of the Confederation* (1961) edited by Malcolm Ross for the New Canadian Library.

THE FORSAKEN

1

Once in the winter
Out on a lake
In the heart of the north-land,
Far from the Fort
And far from the hunters,
A Chippewa woman
With her sick baby,
Crouched in the last hours
Of a great storm.
Frozen and hungry,
She fished through the ice
With a line of the twisted
Bark of the cedar,
And a rabbit-bone hook
Polished and barbed;
Fished with the bare hook
All through the wild day,
Fished and caught nothing;
While the young chieftain
Tugged at her breasts,
Or slept in the lacings
Of the warm *tikanagan*.
All the lake-surface
Streamed with the hissing
Of millions of iceflakes

Hurled by the wind;
Behind her the round
Of a lonely island
Roared like a fire
With the voice of the storm
In the deeps of the cedars.
Valiant, unshaken,
She took of her own flesh,
Baited the fish-hook,
Drew in a grey-trout,
Drew in his fellows,
Heaped them beside her,
Dead in the snow.
Valiant, unshaken,
She faced the long distance,
Wolf-haunted and lonely,
Sure of her goal
And the life of her dear one:
Tramped for two days,
On the third in the morning,
Saw the strong bulk
Of the Fort by the river,
Saw the wood-smoke
Hang soft in the spruces,
Heard the keen yelp
Of the ravenous huskies
Fighting for whitefish:
Then she had rest.

2

Years and years after,
When she was old and withered,
When her son was an old man
And his children filled with vigour,
They came in their northern tour on the verge of winter,
To an island in a lonely lake.
There one night they camped, and on the morrow
Gathered their kettles and birch-bark
Their rabbit-skin robes and their mink-traps,
Launched their canoes and slunk away through the islands,
Left her alone forever,
Without a word of farewell,
Because she was old and useless,

Like a paddle broken and warped,
Or a pole that was splintered.
Then, without a sigh,
Valiant, unshaken,
She smoothed her dark locks under her kerchief,
Composed her shawl in state,
Then folded her hands ridged with sinews and corded with veins,
Folded them across her breasts spent with the nourishing of children,
Gazed at the sky past the tops of the cedars,
Saw two spangled nights arise out of the twilight,
Saw two days go by filled with the tranquil sunshine,
Saw, without pain, or dread, or even a moment of longing:
Then on the third great night there came thronging and thronging
Millions of snowflakes out of a windless cloud;
They covered her close with a beautiful crystal shroud,
Covered her deep and silent.
But in the frost of the dawn,
Up from the life below,
Rose a column of breath
Through a tiny cleft in the snow,
Fragile, delicately drawn,
Wavering with its own weakness,
In the wilderness a sign of the spirit,
Persisting still in the sight of the sun
Till day was done.
Then all light was gathered up by the hand of God and hid in His breast,
Then there was born a silence deeper than silence,
Then she had rest.

A NIGHT IN JUNE

The world is heated seven times,
    The sky is close above the lawn,
    An oven when the coals are drawn.

There is no stir of air at all,
    Only at times an inward breeze
    Turns back a pale leaf in the trees.

Here the syringa's rich perfume
    Covers the tulip's red retreat,
    A burning pool of scent and heat.

The pallid lightning wavers dim
    Between the trees, then deep and dense
    The darkness settles more intense.

A hawk lies panting in the grass,
    Or plunges upward through the air,
    The lightning shows him whirling there.

A bird calls madly from the eaves,
    Then stops, the silence all at once
    Disturbed, falls dead again and stuns.

A redder lightning flits about,
    But in the north a storm is rolled
    That splits the gloom with vivid gold;

Dead silence, then a little sound,
    The distance chokes the thunder down,
    It shudders faintly in the town.

A fountain plashing in the dark
    Keeps up a mimic dropping strain;
    Ah! God, if it were really rain!

THE DESJARDINS

Just at the foot of the hill, where the bridge crossed the Blanche, stood one of the oldest houses in Viger. It was built of massive timbers. The roof curved and projected beyond the eaves, forming the top of a narrow veranda. The whole house was painted a dazzling white except the window-frames, which were green. There was a low stone fence between the road and the garden, where a few simple flowers grew. Beyond the fence was a row of Lombardy poplars, some of which had commenced to die out. On the opposite side of the road was a marshy field, where by day the marsh marigolds shone, and by night, the fireflies. There were places in this field where you could thrust down a long pole and not touch bottom. In the fall a few muskrats built a house there, in remembrance of the time when it was a favourite wintering-ground. In the spring the Blanche came up and flowed over it. Beyond that again the hill curved round, with a scarped, yellowish slope.

In this house lived Adèle Desjardin with her two brothers, Charles and Philippe. Their father was dead, and when he died there was hardly a person in the whole parish who was sorry. They could remember him as a tall, dark, forbidding-looking man, with long arms out of all proportion to his body. He had inherited his fine farm from his father, and had added to and improved it. He had always been prosperous, and was considered the wealthiest man in the parish. He was inhospitable, and became more taciturn and morose after his wife died. His pride was excessive and kept him from associating with his neighbours, although he was in no way above them. Very little was known about his manner of life, and there was a mystery about his father's death. For some time the old man had not been seen about the place, when one day he came from the city, dead and in his coffin, which was thought strange. This gave rise to all sorts of rumour and gossip; but the generally accredited story was that there was insanity in the family and that he had died crazy.

However cold Isidore Desjardin was to his neighbours, no one could have charged him with being unkind or harsh with his children, and as they grew up he gave them all the advantages which it was possible for them to have. Adèle went for a year to the Convent of the Sacré Coeur in the city, and could play tunes on the piano when she came back; so that she had to have a piano of her own, which was the first one ever heard in Viger. She was a slight, angular girl, with a dark thin face and black hair and eyes. She looked like her father and took after him in many ways. Charles, the elder son, was like his grandfather, tall and muscular, with a fine head and a handsome face. He was studious and read a great deal, and was always talking to the curé about studying the law. Philippe did not care about books; his father could never keep him at school. He was short and thick-set and had merry eyes set deep in his head. 'Someone must learn to look after things,' he said, and when his father died he took sole charge of everything.

If the Desjardins were unsociable with others, they were happy among themselves. Almost every evening during the winter, when the work was done, they would light up the front room with candles, and Adèle would play on the piano and sing. Charles would pace to and fro behind her, and Philippe would thrust his feet far under the stove that projected from the next room through the partition, and fall fast asleep. Her songs were mostly old French songs, and she could sing 'Partant pour la Syrie' and 'La Marseillaise'. This last was a favourite with Charles; he could not sing himself, but he accompanied the music by making wild movements with his arms, tramping heavily up and down before the piano, and shouting out so loudly as to wake Philippe, 'Aux armes, citoyens!' On fine summer evenings Philippe and Adèle would walk up and down the road watching the marsh fireflies and pausing on the bridge to hear the fish jump in the pool and the deep, vibrant croak of the distant frogs. It was not always Philippe who walked there with Adèle; he sometimes sat on the veranda and watched her walk with someone else. He would have waking dreams, as he smoked, that the two figures moving before him were himself and someone into whose eyes he was looking.

At last it came to be reality for him, and then he could not sit quietly and watch the lovers; he would let his pipe go out and stride impatiently up and down the veranda. And on Sunday afternoons he would harness his horse, dress himself carefully, and drive off with short laughs and twinklings of the eyes and wavings of the hands. They were evidently planning the future and it seemed a distance of vague happiness.

Charles kept on his wonted way. If they talked in the parlour, they could hear him stirring upstairs; if they strolled in the road, they could see his light in the window. Philippe humoured his studious habits. He only worked in the mornings; in the afternoons he read, history principally. His favourite study was the *Life of Napoleon Bonaparte*, which seemed to absorb him completely. He was growing more retired and pre-occupied every day—lost in deep reveries, swallowed of ambitious dreams.

It had been a somewhat longer day than usual in the harvest field, and it was late when the last meal was ready. Philippe, as he called Charles from the foot of the stair, could hear him walking up and down, seemingly reading out loud, and when he received no response to his demand he went up the stairs. Pushing open the door, he saw his brother striding up and down the room with his hands clasped behind him and his head bent, muttering to himself.

'Charles!' He seemed to collect himself and looked up. 'Come down to supper!' They went downstairs together. Adèle and Philippe kept up a conversation throughout the meal, but Charles hardly spoke. Suddenly he pushed his plate away and stood upright to his full height; a look of calm, severe dignity came over his face.

'I!' said he. 'I am the Great Napoleon!'

'Charles!' cried Adèle. 'What is the matter?'

'The prosperity of the nation depends upon the execution of my plans. Go!' said he, dismissing some imaginary person with an imperious gesture.

They sat as if stunned, and between them stood this majestic figure with outstretched hand. Then Charles turned away and commenced to pace the room.

'It has come!' sobbed Adèle as she sank on her knees beside the table.

'There is only one thing to do,' said Philippe after some hours of silence. 'It is hard, but there is only one thing to do.' The room was perfectly dark. He stood in the window where he had seen the light die out of the sky, and now in the marshy field he saw the fireflies gleam. He knew that Adèle was in the dark somewhere beside him, for he could hear her breathe. 'We must cut ourselves off; we must be the last of our race.' In those words, which in after years were often on his lips, he seemed to find some comfort, and he continued to repeat them to himself.

Charles lay in bed in a sort of stupor for three days. On Sunday morning he rose. The church bells were ringing. He met Philippe in the hall.

'Is this Sunday?' he asked.

'Yes.'

'Come here!' They went into the front room.

'This is Sunday, you say. The last thing I remember was you telling me to go in—that was Wednesday. What has happened?' Philippe dropped his head in his hands.

'Tell me, Philippe, what has happened?'

'I cannot.'

'I must know, Philippe. Where have I been?'

'On Wednesday night,' said he, as if the words were choking him, 'you said, "I am the great Napoleon!" Then you said something about the nation and you have not spoken since.'

Charles dropped on his knees beside the table against which Philippe was leaning. He hid his face in his arms. Philippe, reaching across, thrust his fingers into his brother's brown hair. The warm grasp came as an answer to all Charles's unasked questions; he knew that, whatever might happen, his brother would guard him.

For a month or two he lay wavering between two worlds; but when he saw the first snow and lost sight of the brown earth, he at once commenced to order supplies, to write dispatches, and to make preparations for the gigantic expedition which was to end in the overthrow of the Emperor of all the Russias. And the snow continues to bring him this activity. During the summer he is engaged, with no very definite operations, in the field, but when winter comes he always prepares for the invasion of Russia. With the exception of certain days of dejection and trouble, which Adèle calls the Waterloo days, in the summer he is triumphant with perpetual victory. On a little bare hill about a mile from the house from which you can get an extensive view of the sloping country, he watches the movements of the enemy. The blasts at the distant quarries sound in his ears like the roar of guns. Beside him the old grey horse that Philippe has set apart for his service crops the grass or stands for hours patiently. Down in the shallow valley the Blanche runs, glistening; the mowers sway and bend; on the horizon shafts of smoke rise, little clouds break away from the masses and drop their quiet shadows on the fields. And through his glass Charles watches the moving shadows, the shafts of smoke, and the swaying mowers, watches the distant hills fringed with beech-groves. He dispatches his aides-de-camp with important orders, or rides down the slope to oversee the fording of the Blanche. Half-frightened village boys hide in the long grass to hear him go muttering by. In the autumn he comes sadly up out of the valley leading his horse, the rein through his arm and his hands in his coat-sleeves. The sleet dashes against him, and the wind rushes and screams around him as he ascends the little knoll. But whatever the weather, Philippe waits in the road for him and helps him dismount. There is something heroic in his short figure.

'Sire, my brother!' he says, 'Sire, let us go in!'

'Is the King of Rome better?'

'Yes.'

'And the Empress?'

'She is well.'

Only once has a gleam of light pierced these mists. It was in the year when, as Adèle said, he had had two Waterloos and had taken to his bed in consequence. One evening Adèle brought him a bowl of gruel. He stared like a child awakened from sleep when she carried in the lamp. She approached the bed and he started up.

'Adèle!' he said hoarsely, and pulling her face down, kissed her lips. For a moment she had hope. But with the next week came winter, and he commenced his annual preparations for the invasion of Russia.

IN THE VILLAGE OF VIGER

b. 1899

F. R. Scott

F.R. SCOTT was born in Quebec City, the son of Frederick George Scott, who was an Anglican clergyman and a well-known poet. He was educated at Bishop's College, Lennoxville, and at Oxford University where he was a Rhodes Scholar. He studied law at McGill University and joined the faculty of law there in 1928; he was dean of law from 1961 until his retirement in 1964. He is a man of many parts. As a lawyer, teacher, authority on constitutional law, social philosopher, and poet, he has been an ardent defender of civil liberties and social justice. He assisted in the formation of two political parties, the Co-operative Commonwealth Federation (CCF) and the New Democratic Party (NDP). In the 1950s he fought two celebrated court cases, one against the padlock law of Premier Duplessis of Québec, the other against censorship of D. H. Lawrence's novel *Lady Chatterly's Lover*. He was a member of the Royal Commission on Bilingualism and Biculturalism and in 1965 was awarded the Molson Prize, given for outstanding achievements in the arts, humanities, and the social sciences.

Scott began writing poetry while he was a student at McGill. In 1925 ·he edited, with A.J.M. Smith and others, the *McGill Fortnightly Review* (1925-7), the first of several literary journals he has been associated with; another was *Preview* (1942-5), an influential mimeographed periodical that expressed the cosmopolitan and sophisticated literary interests of a group of Montreal writers of which Scott was a member. His poetry embraces a wide variety of forms and subjects—nature poems, satires, poems of social, political, and humanitarian dedication, metaphysical and love poems, and translations of French-Canadian verse. Scott is perhaps best known as a social critic whose clever, cutting satires about hypocrisy, stupidity, and injustice actually express a deep indignation. His involvement in the case against the Lawrence novel provoked 'A Lass in Wonderland' (which begins 'I went to bat for the Lady Chatte/Dressed in my bib and gown'). Another example of his satire is the poem below on Mackenzie King, who was prime minister of Canada, with one interruption, from 1921 until 1948. But Scott's most characteristic poems are much more profound, for, in the words of A.J.M. Smith, he 'is a man capable of—indeed unable to refrain from—taking long views, both backwards into the past and forward into the future, an idealist in the popular sense of the word. Both in his political life as a socialist and his life as a poet he welcomes the new, the just, and the generous—and always in the broadest and most generous terms.' Some of Scott's best poems embrace 'vast cosmic distances, both of space and time'. 'Lakeshore', for instance, contains 'a rich hoard of racial memories, dreams, desires, and aspirations. All are perfectly fused: earth, water, air; science and mythology; mermaids, Venus, Noah; the I and All-Mankind; a crowded street and "the water's deepest colonnades".' In this poem, as well as in 'Old Song', 'we have the sense of vast distances in space and time and a view of geological prehistory that goes back even farther than the ages of man-as-fish.'

Among Scott's poetry collections are *Overture* (1945), *Events and Signals*

(1954), *The Eye of the Needle* (1957), and *Signature* (1964). His *Selected Poems*, of which a paperback edition is available, was published in 1966. He has also published a collection of 'found' poems: *Trouvailles: Poems from Prose* (1967). A translator of French-Canadian poetry, he published *Saint-Denys-Garneau & Anne Hébert: Translations/Traductions* in 1962 and there are numerous translations by him in *The Poetry of French Canada in Translation* edited by John Glassco. Scott collaborated with A.J.M. Smith in compiling *The Blasted Pine: An Anthology of Satire, Invective and Disrespectful Verse: Chiefly by Canadian Writers* (revised edition, 1967).

A.J.M. Smith has written a poem on F.R. Scott that is on page 488 of this anthology. In Issue 31 of *Canadian Literature* (Winter, 1967) there are two articles on Scott's poetry: one by Smith (quoted from above) and the other by Robin Skelton.

LAKESHORE

The lake is sharp along the shore
Trimming the bevelled edge of land
To level curves; the fretted sands
Go slanting down through liquid air
Till stones below shift here and there
Floating upon their broken sky
All netted by the prism wave
And rippled where the currents are.

I stare through windows at this cave
Where fish, like planes, slow-motioned, fly.
Poised in a still of gravity
The narrow minnow, flicking fin,
Hangs in a paler, ochre sun,
His doorways open everywhere.

And I am a tall frond that waves
Its head below its rooted feet
Seeking the light that draws it down
To forest floors beyond its reach
Vivid with gloom and eerie dreams.

The water's deepest colonnades
Contract the blood, and to this home
That stirs the dark amphibian
With me the naked swimmers come
Drawn to their prehistoric womb.

They too are liquid as they fall
Like tumbled water loosed above
Until they lie, diagonal,
Within the cool and sheltered grove
Stroked by the fingertips of love.

Silent, our sport is drowned in fact
Too virginal for speech or sound
And each is personal and laned
Along his private aqueduct.

Too soon the tether of the lungs
Is taut and straining, and we rise
Upon our undeveloped wings
Toward the prison of our ground
A secret anguish in our thighs
And mermaids in our memories.

This is our talent, to have grown
Upright in posture, false-erect,
A landed gentry, circumspect,
Tied to a horizontal soil
The floor and ceiling of the soul;
Striving, with cold and fishy care
To make an ocean of the air.

Sometimes, upon a crowded street,
I feel the sudden rain come down
And in the old, magnetic sound
I hear the opening of a gate
That loosens all the seven seas.
Watching the whole creation drown
I muse, alone, on Ararat.

TRANS CANADA

Pulled from our ruts by the made-to-order gale
We sprang upward into a wider prairie
And dropped Regina below like a pile of bones.

Sky tumbled upon us in waterfalls,
But we were smarter than a Skeena salmon
And shot our silver body over the lip of air
To rest in a pool of space
On the top storey of our adventure.

A solar peace
And a six-way choice.

Clouds, now, are the solid substance,
A floor of wool roughed by the wind
Standing in waves that halt in their fall.
A still of troughs.

The plane, our planet,
Travels on roads that are not seen or laid
But sound in instruments on pilots' ears,
While underneath
The sure wings
Are the everlasting arms of science.

Man, the lofty worm, tunnels his latest clay,
And bores his new career.

This frontier, too, is ours.
This everywhere whose life can only be led
At the pace of a rocket
Is common to man and man,
And every country below is an I land.

The sun sets on its top shelf,
And stars seem farther from our nearer grasp.

I have sat by night beside a cold lake
And touched things smoother than moonlight on still water,
But the moon on this cloud sea is not human,
And here is no shore, no intimacy,
Only the start of space, the road to suns.

OLD SONG

far voices
and fretting leaves
this music the
hillside gives

but in the deep
Laurentian river
an elemental song
for ever

a quiet calling
of no mind
out of long æons
when dust was blind
and ice hid sound

only a moving
with no note
granite lips
a stone throat

W. L. M. K.

How shall we speak of Canada,
Mackenzie King dead?
The Mother's boy in the lonely room
With his dog, his medium and his ruins?

He blunted us.

We had no shape
Because he never took sides,
And no sides
Because he never allowed them to take shape.

He skilfully avoided what was wrong
Without saying what was right,
And never let his on the one hand
Know what his on the other hand was doing.

The height of his ambition
Was to pile a Parliamentary Committee on a Royal Commission,
To have 'conscription if necessary
But not necessarily conscription',
To let Parliament decide—
Later.

Postpone, postpone, abstain.

Only one thread was certain:
After World War i
Business as usual,
After World War ii
Orderly decontrol.
Always he led us back to where we were before.

He seemed to be in the centre
Because we had no centre,
No vision
To pierce the smoke-screen of his politics.

Truly he will be remembered
Wherever men honour ingenuity,
Ambiguity, inactivity, and political longevity.

Let us raise up a temple
To the cult of mediocrity,
Do nothing by halves
Which can be done by quarters.

A.J. M.Smith

The poet and critic A.J.M. SMITH was born in Montreal and educated at McGill University and the University of Edinburgh. In 1936 he was appointed to the English Department of Michigan State University and remained there until his retirement in 1972. He has, however, retained a close connection with Canada, which he visits every summer, and particularly with the literature of the country. Since his student days, when he edited the *McGill Daily Literary Supplement* (1924-5) and then, with F.R. Scott and others, edited the *McGill Fortnightly Review* (1925-7), he has exerted an important influence on Canadian writing by drawing attention, in the twenties and early thirties, to the new world of poetry that was being created outside of Canada by such poets as William Butler Yeats, Ezra Pound, T. S. Eliot, and W.H. Auden, and later by applying intelligence, discrimination, and the influences of a cosmopolitan literary background both to his discussion of Canadian literature in essays and to his work as a compiler of anthologies.

Smith's first two collections of poetry were *News of the Phoenix* (1943), which won a Governor General's Award, and *A Sort of Ecstasy* (1954). His *Collected Poems*, published in 1962, contains only a hundred poems; to these he added twenty-two for his *Poems: New & Collected*, which appeared in 1967. Smith's poems are precise, subtle, graceful, and contain much humour and wit. Embracing a wide range of styles and themes, they can be austere, sensuous, colloquial, lyrical, epigrammatic, or ribald. In his early landscape poems (one of which, 'The Lonely Land', must appear in more anthologies than any other Canadian poem), and in love poems, meditations, parodies, pastiches ('To Jay Macpherson' below is a pastiche), burlesques, satires, and translations, Smith is always the consummate craftsman, the admirer of formal perfection—'among the most memorable lyric poets writing in our time', in the words of George Woodcock, 'not merely in Canada, but in the whole English-speaking world'. 'To Frank Scott, Esq.' is an example of his occasional verse—a witty portrait of the poet (see page 479) in classical form written for a seventieth-birthday dinner held in Montreal in 1969 and attended by many dignitaries.

With F.R. Scott, Smith edited his first anthology in 1936, *New Provinces*, which contained the work of six new poets. Smith's work in shaping the appreciation and understanding of Canadian poetry, both old and new, first received wide recognition in 1943 when he published *The Book of Canadian Poetry*, which was revised in 1948 and 1957; it continued with *The Oxford Book of Canadian Verse: In English and French* (1960), his introduction to which is a brilliant survey of Canadian poetry, and *Modern Canadian Verse: In English and French* (1967). Other anthologies include *The Book of Canadian Prose: Volume I* (1965) and *Volume II* (1973) and *The Blasted Pine: An Anthology of Satire, Invective, and Disrespectful Verse: Chiefly by Canadian Writers* (revised edition, 1967), which Smith co-edited with F.R. Scott.

George Woodcock has two essays on Smith in his *Odysseus Ever Returning* (1970) in the New Canadian Library. Issue 15 of *Canadian Literature* (Winter, 1963) contains a 'Salute to A.J.M. Smith' composed of several articles on the poet, including a 'Self Review'.

NEWS OF THE PHOENIX

They say the Phoenix is dying, some say dead.
Dead without issue is what one message said,
But that has been suppressed, officially denied.

I think myself the man who sent it lied.
In any case, I'm told, he has been shot,
As a precautionary measure, whether he did or not.

TO JAY MACPHERSON
ON HER BOOK OF POEMS

Dear no-man's-nightingale, our Fisher Queen,
Whose golden hook makes muddy waters green,
With what dexterity of wrist and eye
You flick the willow-rod and cast the fly;
And when the silver fish is caught and drawn,
How neat the table he's divided on,
How white the cloth, how elegant the dish,
How sweet the flesh—O sacramental Fish!

FIELD OF LONG GRASS

When she walks in the field of long grass
The delicate little hands of the grass
Lean forward a little to touch her.

Light is like the waving of the long grass.
Light is the faint to and fro of her dress.
Light rests for a while in her bosom.

When it is all gone from her bosom's hollow
And out of the field of long grass,
She walks in the dark by the edge of the fallow land.

Then she begins to walk in my heart.
Then she walks in me, swaying in my veins.

My wrists are a field of long grass
A little wind is kissing.

THE COUNTRY LOVERS

A Little Eclogue for Irving and Aviva

A solemn stillness fills the sacred grove
Where Layton and his sweet Aviva love:
Rabbits, rank goats, and ruffled sparrows stare
In envious admiration—and despair;
While Venus, wandering by to bless the place,
Feels a pure blush suffuse her conscious face.

THE TASTE OF SPACE

McLuhan put his telescope to his ear;
What a lovely smell, he said, we have here.

TO FRANK SCOTT, ESQ.

ON THE OCCASION OF HIS SEVENTIETH BIRTHDAY

Poet and Man of Law—O brave anomaly!—
dove wise and serpent-tongued for Song or Plea—
a parti-coloured animal, committed, *parti-pris*
but not a party man, a Man, and free.

Padlock unlocker and voice with a key,
unbanner of books, and by a natural necessity
against duplicity and privileged Duplessity.

But what endears you most to me,
old friend, 's your love and practice of sweet poesy.

I ask, then, what it means to be a poet:
—to grasp the Muse's saxophone and blow it?
—to have a quivering soul, and show it?

—to prance in purple like an Emperor's clown?
or tickle the gallant salons of the town?
or lift the Holy Grail, and toss it down?

Not today, I think. Wrong answers drop,
facile as angels' tears, and plop
so dully unctuous you cry, 'For God's sake, STOP!'

To be a poet, Frank, you've shown
's a harder thing. It is to be a stone,
an eye, a heart, a lung, a microphone,

a voice, but not a voice alone, a hand,
a hand to grasp a hand, a leg to stand
on, nerves to feel, and in supreme command

the shaping mind that shapes the poem
as it shapes the man, foursquare, and needle-eyed,
and Frank.

b. 1921

Raymond Souster

RAYMOND SOUSTER is of all Canadian poets the one whose writing is most closely identified with a single locality—the city of Toronto, where Souster was born and has spent all of his working life. He has been employed for more than thirty years by the Canadian Imperial Bank of Commerce, where he is chief custodian of securities.

Souster first began publishing poetry while he was serving in the RCAF during the Second World War, when he was a contributor to the small literary magazines that had made their appearance in Montreal in the 1940s. His name was associated with Irving Layton and Louis Dudek, both of Montreal, whose work was socially committed and (unlike that of some other Canadian poets who were writing at the time) was influenced more by contemporary American than by modern English poetry. Souster has been known as a disciple of William Carlos Williams and Ezra Pound and has spoken of the strong influence on his later writing of another American poet, Robert Lowell. Yet his poetry is unmistakably Canadian. It is about actual experiences and real people. Cast in the rhythms and

vocabulary of everyday speech, it is modest and unpretentious (as he himself is), but his poems are capable of arousing in the reader true emotions and sharp feelings of recognition. Some of them are celebrations of joy—in the natural world, in love, beauty, jazz, small triumphs, in poetry itself; others are melancholy, expressing nostalgia for times past or anger over the cruelties and victims of city life.

Since 1946, the year his first book appeared, Souster has published more than a dozen collections of his poetry. Among them are *The Selected Poems* (1956), chosen by Louis Dudek; *Place of Meeting* and *A Local Pride* (both 1962); *The Colour of the Times* (1964), a winner of the Governor General's Award; *Ten Elephants on Yonge Street* (1965); *As Is* (1967); *Lost & Found* (1968); *So Far So Good: Poems 1938-1968* (1969); and *The Years* (1971). Throughout his career Souster has been generous and self-effacing in his encouragement of younger writers —through the small poetry magazines he has edited and distributed, as one of the founders of the Contact Press, as the editor of the anthology *New Wave Canada: The New Explosion in Canadian*

Poetry (1966), and more recently as chairman of the League of Canadian Poets.

There is an article on Souster's poetry by Louis Dudek in Issue 22 of *Canadian Literature* (Autumn 1964).

COLONIAL SATURDAY NIGHT

For Ken and Geneviève

'You're the best audience in the world,'
Big T says as the last kick of jazz dies
on the stand and we gulp our drinks
and spill down into the street:

Yonge Street twelve o'clock Saturday night
all the bars emptying
up and down the block
colour suddenly filling
the sidewalks, everyone hurrying—
where?—to find girls for the night
an alley to be sick in
a cop to pick a fight with?—

or maybe like the four of us
just walking northward, savouring the night air
after the cigarette haze, going really nowhere
in no particular hurry, looking for nothing
we haven't already put hands or minds around,

with a little jazz still singing in our heads
as we greet the new day, Christ's day,
but not yet our own.

LAGOONS, HANLAN'S POINT

Mornings
before the sun's liquid
spilled gradually, flooding
the island's cool cellar,
there was the boat
and the still lagoons,
with the sound of my oars
the only intrusion
over cries of birds
in the marshy shallows,
or the loud thrashing
of the startled crane
rushing the air.

And in one strange
dark, tree-hung entrance,
I followed the sound
of my heart all the way
to the reed-blocked ending,
with the pads of the lily
thick as green-shining film
covering the water.

And in another
where the sun came
to probe the depths
through a shaft of branches,
I saw the skeletons
of brown ships rotting
far below in their burial-ground,
and wondered what strange fish
with what strange colours
swam through these palaces
under the water. . . .

A small boy
with a flat-bottomed punt
and an old pair of oars
moving with wonder
through the antechamber
of a waking world.

THE DAY BEFORE CHRISTMAS

My best Christmases
are all behind me. Grandmother
lifting the done-to-perfection bird
grease-dripping from the pan. My brother

and I Christmas morning
out of bed at six-thirty. I suppose
the house shivered to the sudden sharp
tearing of gift-wrap by excited fingers.

This Christmas Eve mid-afternoon,
too many years later, I wander downtown,
feeling worse than most drunks
set adrift from their office parties.

Birk's windows bulge and glow
with the totally inconspicuous. There's something
fairy-queer about coloured lights
hung above the stink of bus exhausts.

Every store hums, an angry honey-hive,
as if wartime and rationing were back.
I picture patient clerks behind counters
walking on what they can't believe are feet.

Skaters on the fancy rink at City Hall
seem impatient of old waltzes. They dart,
sudden bright goldfish below Revell's
scooped clam-shells blinking underwater eyes.

My heart's with the skaters, though my mood
is more with Adam Beck, bronzed sober head
splitting the traffic of the Avenue,
where on that Republic's black Consul door I see

or seem to see a holly wreath hung, through which
napalm-skinned face and dying eyes stare out
at me, this city, and core-rotted world,
to riddle us with bleeding, gaping questions.

MILK CHOCOLATE GIRL

By now it's a wonder
someone hasn't eaten you,
ounce by delicious ounce,
milk-chocolate girl.

Taken already
in very small bites
the slightly snub nose
the breasts still asleep
the awakening hips
the legs very firm.

We thank God you're still
very much in one piece,
to light up the darkness
of this lunch hour for us
with a turn of your head
a flash from your eyes.

O the most awkward
(yet still charming) thing
you'll ever do in your life,
is the way you're attacking
that slice of bread, now!

UNADULTERATED POETRY

Unadulterated poetry
starts to happen at King and Bay
as the four ditch-diggers
slowly converge on the sparrow
who's lost all power
in his wings but a last desperate
flutter that doesn't keep him
long away from the hairy
meat-hook of a hand
which, cupped, for a moment
is his prison—
              but now becomes (the miracle!)
warm-beating soft cell of skin
whose other name is love.

b. 1938

Pierre Vallières

PIERRE VALLIÈRES, who was one of the theorists of the separatist and terrorist Front de Libération du Québec, wrote a seminal book of his generation in Québec, *White Niggers of America* (1971). He was born to a working-class family in Montreal's French East End; his father worked in the Angus locomotive repair shop of the CPR. In *White Niggers*—which was published in French as *Nègres blancs d'Amérique* (1968)—he describes the daily exhaustion of his father, the fears of his mother, and the family's move at the end of the Second World War to a newer French-Canadian working-class slum on the south shore of the St Lawrence. There he knew Jacques Ferron (see page 121) as a family doctor working among the poor.

Vallières was precocious. While he was still a young man he began to publish in the Montreal newspaper *Le Devoir* and in the reformist intellectual magazine *Cité Libre* (founded in 1950 by Pierre Trudeau, Gérard Pelletier, and others), whose writings did much to prepare the way for the 'quiet revolution' in Québec; and he became a protégé of the poet Gaston Miron (see page 335). Disillu-

sioned with Québec, Vallières went to France. There he eventually discovered the need to return to his homeland and early in 1963 he was back in Montreal. He went to work for the newspaper *La Presse*. In 1966 he was arrested in New York when he and Charles Gagnon demonstrated on behalf of the FLQ in front of the United Nations; much of *White Niggers* was written in the Manhattan House of Detention before he and Gagnon were deported to Montreal. Vallières' story since then, a complicated one, includes almost four years in jail on charges connected with his FLQ activity, release on bail, further charges made during the October crisis of 1970, release on bail, disappearance underground for four months, surrender to the police in January 1972, release again, employment in Mont Laurier on a federally financed Local Initiatives Program, and a one-year suspended sentence (in October 1972) on three charges of counselling political kidnapping. (Contempt-of-court citations have yet to be appealed in the fall of 1972.) Vallières alienated many of his old followers by giving his support to the Parti Québécois. In 1972 a translation of *L'Urgence de choisir* (1971) was published, called *Choose!* It explains his reasons for that choice and why Vallières believes that the most effective method to obtain Québec independence is no longer the FLQ but the Pari Québécois.

White Niggers of America, from which extracts are published here, is partly an enraged memoir of disenchantment with Québec in the 1960s, partly a fanatical Marxist argument for Québec independence. Reviewing it disapprovingly in *Canadian Literature* (Issue 51, Winter 1972), George Woodcock refers to Vallières's 'self-pity', 'delayed adolescent rage', and paranoia 'that twists his views of everything he observes' in the book as autobiography. But he says it should be read, 'since to understand the causes of political fanatacism (which is always authoritarian, puritanical, and thoroughly unpleasant in its results), one has to observe with objectivity that interplay between subjective feelings of intolerable persecution and actual social evils which makes men with a strong sense of inner impotence seek apocalyptic ways of change which history has always shown worsen the evils they aim to eliminate.'

MEMOIRS OF A REVOLUTIONARY

Nowhere did I feel at home. In Ville Jacques-Cartier I lived like a stranger, instead of being in the midst of others, instead of *serving* like Jacques Ferron. I was only interested in my 'work', in myself. In the art galleries, the 'beatnik' restaurants in the West End of Montreal or at the Ecole des Beaux-Arts (where I had a few friends), I never felt I was with 'my own kind'. As the people of my milieu say, I looked like a lost penguin. I was more at ease and had more *joie de vivre* with my old comrades from the *collège*, but there was also something that separated me from them: they were content to talk, to discuss; they never had anything to offer, to exchange. So I felt very much alone, until the day I met Gaston Miron and Maurice.

I met Gaston Miron in 1956, when he was sales manager at Beauchemin's. It was Claude Fournier, one of the first Québécois poets published by Miron, who had advised me to make his acquaintance. Every Friday (pay day), I would go to Beauchemin's, buy a pile of books, then have supper at the Restaurant Saint-Louis (near the square of the same name) with Miron. We would stay for hours at the restaurant on Saint-Denis Street, mostly discussing poetry and decolonization. It is thanks to Miron that I came to know and love contemporary poetry, as well as the literature of the colonized peoples (Aimé Césaire, the Algerian poets, Pablo Neruda, and so on). I became profoundly attached to René Char, Paul Eluard, Aragon, and the Welsh poet Dylan Thomas. But above all, many a time I had the privilege of listening for hours to Miron himself reciting his *Marche à l'amour* and recounting his *Vie agonique*. No Québécois poet, in my opinion, has expressed *us* with so much authenticity, not even Grandbois, Hébert, Giguère, Pilon, or Préfontaine. Isolated as I am today in my steel cage, how I would love to read and reread those poems, that long, sorrowful song of our alienation and our will to live in spite of the winter that Vigneault speaks of! At that time Miron was only the penniless publisher of the Editions de l'Hexagone, the man who 'launched' two or three new poets every year, the man whose poetry only evoked cynical, amused smiles. I have heard respectable, sophisticated poets say that Miron did not know how to write and that his romanticism dated from the nineteenth century. But he is the only one of our poets the Quebec workers understand, when on May Day he *tells* them with his whole being about his love and his revolt. Except for the *chansonniers*, Miron is our only popular poet . . . and he doesn't write in *Joual*.*

At the Restaurant Saint-Louis we sometimes met a dry man with the piercing eyes of an eagle. Miron called him 'the grey eminence'. It was Claude Ryan. He spoke little, answered our questions vaguely, scrutinized us the way an entomologist scrutinizes insects.

Fortunately, Gaston knew a great many people who were more likable than the future director-dictator of *Le Devoir*. First there was Miche, who was wonderfully beautiful and intelligent; then Yves Préfontaine, Jean-Guy Pilon, Hénault, Ouellet and Portugais (the future founders of the review *Liberté*); Roland Giguère, who was soon to go into exile in France and whose poems I devoured—poems which scarcely two or three hundred persons were reading at the time; Michel Van Schendel, Adèle Lauzon, Rina Lasnier, Alain Grandbois, Anne Hébert; persons who are now famous and respected but who, in the fifties, were all hesitating between exile and 'belonging to the country'. Quebec was not Algeria; it was not even Martinique.

What was one to do in this country whose inhabitants rejected all passion? Some had a go at social democracy. And Miron, like Ferron, became (in 1957, I think) a candidate of the NDP. But he dreamed—we all dreamed —of France, the incarnation of the Nation and Intelligence, the country that spoke to the world in language adapted to its needs and aspirations. We were all obsessed by the desire to *leave*. To leave, to leave, to leave . . .

---

* *Joual* is the name given to the language of Quebec, a French that retains some holdovers from the seventeenth century and is heavily corrupted by English. The term was popularized by Desbiens (in *Les Insolences du frère Untel*), who said that his Québécois students so pronounced the word *cheval*. The radical *joualistes* (André Major, for example, who is mentioned in the notes at the end of the preceding chapter) write in *Joual*, claiming for it the status of a separate language. Vallières opposes this position. His own work, while it is sprinkled with English words ('les businessmen', 'l'Establishment', 'un racket', 'cheap labor', 'le Big Boss,' 'le fun', etc.) and contains a number of peculiarly Québécois expressions, is written in standard French. (Trans.)

I thought about it every day. But when would it cease to be a dream? I did not earn much at Beaubien, and I spent almost all my wages on books. I drowned my impatience in beer or in writing.

I wrote like a madman, for hours on end, and sometimes for entire nights. Miron was worried about my *fervor* and often suggested that I go to the country for a while. I did not take his advice and later I was to regret it bitterly.

At that time at least (1956-1958), Gaston Miron was not one to impose his ideas on others, but he had great insight into people and was master of the art of bringing out the truth and freedom that were in them. I think he knew me better than I knew myself, and it is thanks to him that I read the authors whose thought or passion responded to my own. Unfortunately, I was too withdrawn to give Miron what he may have expected from me. I took everything; I gave nothing. But it is also possible that Miron expected nothing of me. I knew (and anyway, it cries out in all his poetry) that he had already been profoundly disappointed and that many of his wounds were not yet healed. Miron was a wild, loving sorrow that roamed the streets of Montreal, arms outstretched to embrace men and, at the same time, to take them with him, to awaken and stir them. Those who know him know that Gaston Miron has remained the same and that the 'quiet revolution' has not changed him; it has revealed him, it has shown him to the blind men who thought themselves geniuses and copied René Char while Miron lived and created his poetry . . . without knowing that he was expressing *us* with the profound genius of a François Villon, despising publicity and renown, seeking only one thing: love. Like all of us. A hard thing to find in Quebec. A thing he is no doubt still seeking. Like most of us.

Some people will be surprised that I give so much importance to Gaston Miron. They will think I am exaggerating. In reality I am not even doing justice to this great living poet who (despite his youth) is the spiritual father of the FLQ, of *Parti pris*, *Révolution québécoise*, *Liberté*, and many other political or literary movements. So far as I personally am concerned, Miron is the one who developed my political consciousness and turned the course of my philosophico-literary search to practical political engagement. It was he who gave me the idea of writing my first 'engaged' articles for *Le Devoir* in 1957, and who made me understand the importance and political significance of the Murdochville strike. But my articles published in *Le Devoir* were far from reflecting coherent political thought. They were a mixture of half-digested ideas—spaghetti with existentialist sauce! Still, it was the first time in Quebec that a young man (I was seventeen) had dared to tell the old men that they were on the point of collapse, and the intellectuals of the time that they were useless manufacturers of third-rate novels or skillful editorials incapable of assuming their responsibilities and acting when social justice demanded it. At that time the only people I admired were René Lévesque, Judith Jasmin, Gérard Pelletier, Pierre Trudeau, Gérard Filion, Jean-Louis Gagnon, André Langevin, and Jacques Hébert. Of those, all but Judith Jasmin, André Langevin, and Jacques Hébert are now more or less whores!

The first article I wrote, in 1957, was entitled 'The Fear of Living' and was an attack on the slave's 'philosophy' that was hidden behind the title of a novel by Jean Filiatrault, *Le Refuge impossible*. The search for a 'refuge' had gone on long enough, I wrote. It was time to learn how to *live*.

But perhaps at bottom it was myself I was trying to persuade, for in reality I was not living. I was consuming myself, I was 'burning the candle at both ends,' as the saying goes. And all my activity was primarily cerebral. Miron was increasingly worried, and he had good reason to be.

*   *   *

One evening when Marcel was out, I surprised Françoise in the act of washing herself in the kitchen. She was half naked. I could not resist the desire to go up to her, to pass my hands over her neck, her shoulders, her breasts, her belly. I leaned my head against hers and pressed her body tight against my own. I was crying.

She let her fingers wander through my hair, then over my back.

'Let me get dressed,' she said gently.

I went and sat down at the little table where she prepared the meals. I folded my arms on the table, buried my face in them and broke into sobs.

'Found nothing today either?' she asked.

'Ah! It's not that . . . I want to kill myself!'

She broke out laughing . . . but without making fun of me. Her friendship for me was too real. She knew me well enough to know that at certain times I was capable of anything.

'Why tonight?'

'Why not tonight?' I answered, defying her.

'Come into the living room, we can talk more comfortably there.' I followed her into the living room.

'That's why . . . you jumped on me?'

'Yes.'

'Then you don't really want to kill yourself. Because otherwise you wouldn't have come here.'

'Actually, it was just before coming here that I almost threw myself into the water.'

I told her about what had just happened.

For a week I had been roaming around Paris like a sleepwalker, though the sun was shining brightly. I was fed up. Fed up with French bureaucracy, fed up with filling out forms that went off to rot I knew not where, fed up with begging my friends for help without being in a position to really do anything for them in return, fed up with waiting for a reply from the Algerian government to my request to go and work in the literacy campaign, fed up with pointless discussions and with my solitude. I did not want to return to Quebec. I no longer wanted to remain in France. No reply came from Algeria. I was ready to jump out of my skin.

I had lost my appetite. Some days I ate almost nothing. I would walk around Paris until I was exhausted. My head was spinning. What had I ever come here for?

Never, even to my best friends, had I confided the despair that was spreading through me like a cancer. Like a dying man, I saw my whole existence reduced to an infinitesimal thing, a thinking and painful absurdity. I reread *The Trial*; Kafka's profound humour had often helped me take myself less seriously. This time, his modesty—for Kafka is a modest author, humble and disinterested—seemed to me to be a total indifference to the world, a reasoned suicide. His great love for men seemed to be an absolute contempt for human existence.

That night I had stopped on one of the bridges over the Seine. As in times past, in Longueuil, I gazed deep into the black water and wished I could disappear in it forever.

It must have been nine o'clock at night. I was alone. No witnesses. My whole body was being drawn by the mass of water. It was the second time in my life I had felt *that*. But this time my resistance was weak. I had not eaten since morning. My long walk had exhausted me. After looking long moments at the water, I let myself slip to the ground like a coward. For a while I remained motionless. A couple passed by, indifferent. I got up slowly and looked down at the black water again. 'Why not?' I said to myself. 'Why not?' There was nothing for me to do here. I could be of no use to anyone. As in Quebec. As in Algeria. No one needed me or my services. Men were satisfied with their shit. Why keep badgering them with ideas they didn't know what to do with? All countries, all peoples were the same. Why travel? There was nothing to be done anywhere . . .

Finally, I reached the Left Bank without having thrown myself into the water. And I went to the apartment of Marcel and Françoise.

After listening to me with great attention, Françoise said: 'Pierre, you won't find the answer here. You must become reconciled with your country. Otherwise . . .'

'Otherwise?'

'You really will throw yourself into the water. And what good will that do you? You are wrong to despise your country so much. You must learn to *live* in it, even if it's in a mess, as you say. No country but your own can give you what you are looking for.'

'What do you expect me to find in Quebec?'

'First of all—yourself.'

' . . .'

'In the end you're going to have to accept yourself as you are, love yourself as you are. And in order to do that, you must go home, to your own milieu. Only there will you find yourself again. I don't think we— even Marcel and I, who love you very much—can really be of use to you. I advise you to go back to Quebec as soon as possible. You see, Pierre, we—Marcel and I—are not Québécois. When you talk about your country, it doesn't mean much to us because we've never set foot there. We don't know anything about your history, your way of life. You can be sure of our friendship, but it's of no use to you right now. It would be good for you to talk things over with a Québécois psychoanalyst, because even if I were madly in love with you, even if I left Marcel for you, I couldn't do anything to solve your present problems. Friendship, love, they don't help . . . when you can't accept yourself. What good does it do me to love you if you constantly despise yourself, eh? What do I want with an unhappy face to lay in my lap like a mother? I don't want to be a mother, because that's not what you need. It's too late for that. You have to learn to live with what you are, in your country as it is, neither better nor worse than the others. I am convinced that if you succeed in doing something for your own people, in fighting for them and with them, your life will be completely transformed. I think it's pretty much the same problem for Marcel. And that's why I want to suggest to him that we move to Martinique . . .'

She went on talking to me for a long time. The things she said were like what I had been hearing lately from the Québécois friends I was staying with, both of whom were educators. It all seemed to make sense. But to go back to Quebec . . . to the great darkness . . . I was almost terrified to think of it.

When I left Françoise that night, I remembered that I had an appointment with Louis around midnight. Louis was a Québécois exile in Paris who was unhappy but, like me, unable at that time to resign himself to the inevitable: the return home.

We went to a little bistro on the Boulevard Saint-Michel to talk it all over. Of course we knew that we were paralyzed by our alienation, but we found it difficult to admit that Europe could not free us from it.

To act in Quebec . . . in the winter that Vigneault sings of and the white dust that Langevin describes . . . ?

Did this country even have a future? Seen from Paris, Quebec looked like a ridiculous provincial town whose inhabitants were turned toward a past they had built into a myth and who had invented a heroic history for themselves out of the meager material available. Dollard des Ormeaux, Madeleine de Verchères, Radisson . . .

I told Louis that I was going back just the same—so as not to commit suicide. He wanted to wait another year, to see if there was no way to go into exile somewhere else, in a more hospitable country.

Next day I wrote my mother asking her to lend me the money to come home. On the days following I bade farewell to my French and Québécois friends. I spent the last days with two of them visiting Burgundy, Vézelay, Lyons, Grenoble, and a few other tourist centres in central France. This trip made it even harder for me to leave.

Then, one sunny morning, I went to the Gare Saint-Lazare. I boarded the train the way one gets into a hearse.

As we approached Cherbourg, the train entered a landscape of fog and fine rain.

I felt that all my dreams were forsaking me at once and that the future promised only mortal boredom in a boundless desert.

A few days after I came back, the Wolfe Monument was overturned in Quebec City. I immediately said to myself that things had changed in the country of silence and winter.

I began to hope again.

Gérard Pelletier offered me a job at *La Presse* and I accepted with joy. I knew nothing about journalism, but it was not long before I felt as much at ease in it as a fish in water. It was at *La Presse* that I really became politicized, thanks to some older comrades for whom social revolution was still an objective.

The journalistic milieu gave me a better understanding of Quebec society. Political engagement, which was an integral part of my profession, prevented me from letting myself be caught in the trap of comfortable ideologies, good jobs, careerism, and the soft life with an easy conscience.

In contrast to the institutionalized forms of dissent which journalists diligently report in the Establishment newspapers, my friends and I were soon involved in less peaceful forms of protest. Which quickly led me from 'cité libre' to the picket lines, the protests against the war in Vietnam . . . and the Front de libération du Québec.

I have always felt myself to be, and I have always been, a proletarian. With the spotty cultural background of a self-taught man, I formed the ambition of acting directly on society, outside the established structures, and, together with my brothers in misery, of changing it in accordance with the workers' desire for freedom. You must not expect me to join up like a bourgeois in the club of right-thinking socialists who have only read (so as to be able to quote it to the 'hotheads') *Left-Wing Communism: An Infantile Disorder*.

Am I essentially a rebel? I have no idea.

I am certainly a man who has been flayed alive, like every clear-thinking Québécois. But contrary to what people might think, I have no predisposition for martyrdom or anarchy.

For me prison does not represent a setting-aside of political and social engagement. Of course I don't want to rot here too long, although I am learning a great many things which some day will surely be very useful to me in *carrying on*.

A revolutionary must always be prepared to start over again and to live a life of continual danger. Revolutionary activity is never perfectly safe. When I am willing to make compromises, I will have murdered *our* ideal in my mind and heart. To my friends, I will then be ripe for the cemetery.

WHITE NIGGERS OF AMERICA
Translated by Joan Pinkham

b. 1917

Miriam Waddington

MIRIAM WADDINGTON was born in Winnipeg and attended school there and in Ottawa. She graduated in social work from the University of Toronto and did advanced work at the Pennsylvania School of Social Work in Philadelphia. She has also taken a graduate degree in English at the University of Toronto. After working during the forties and fifties as a case-worker in hospitals, prisons, family and children's agencies in Toronto and Montreal, and as a teacher of social work at McGill University, she changed professions and now teaches English and Canadian literature at York University, Toronto.

Mrs Waddington has been writing and publishing poetry since childhood. In the 1940s, while working in Montreal and raising a family, she contributed to the literary-magazine movement that originated in Montreal with such periodicals as *First Statement* and *Preview*. Her first poetry collection, *Green World* (1945), was handset by John Sutherland and published by his First Statement Press. Her other books are *The Second Silence* (1955), *The Season's Lovers* (1958), *The Glass Trumpet* (1966), *Call Them Canadians* (1968), *Say Yes* (1969), and *Driving Home: Poems New and Selected* (1972). She has also published critical articles, book reviews, and short stories, and a study of the Montreal poet A.M. Klein for Copp Clark's Studies in Canadian Literature series (1970). She recently edited the collected writings of John Sutherland, the critic, editor, and champion of Canadian literature in the 1940s: *John Sutherland: Essays, Controversies, Poems* (1973).

Miriam Waddington's lyrical poems about the Canadian landscape and love and loss in human relationships show the influence of Yiddish language and folklore—its rhythms and its intimate, playful qualities. Her attraction to sad-happy experiences as themes and to surrealistic images—she is fond of the magical in literature—can be attributed to another strong influence: Hans Andersen's fairy tales.

ADVICE TO THE YOUNG

1
keep bees and
grow asparagus,
watch the tides
and listen to the
wind instead of
the politicians
make up your own
stories and believe
them if you want to
live the good life.

2
All rituals
are instincts
never fully
trust them
study to im-
prove biology
with reason.

3
Digging trenches
for asparagus
is good for the
muscles and
waiting for the
plants to settle
teaches patience
to those who are
usually in too
much of a hurry.

4
There is morality
in bee-keeping
it teaches how
not to be afraid
of the bee swarm
it teaches how
not to be afraid of
finding new places
and building them
all over again.

CANADIANS

Here are
our signatures:
geese, fish, eskimo
faces, girl-guide
cookies, ink-drawings
tree-plantings, summer
storms and winter
emanations.

We look
like a geography but
just scratch us
and we bleed
history, are full
of modest misery
are sensitive
to double-talk double-take
(and double-cross)
in a country
too wide
to be single in.

Are we real or
did someone invent
us, was it Henry
Hudson Etienne Brûlé
or a carnival
of village girls?
Was it
a flock of nuns
a pity of indians
a gravyboat of
fur-traders, professional
explorers or those
amateur map-makers
our Fathers
of Confederation?

Wherever you are
Charles Tupper Alexander
Galt Darcy McGee George
Cartier Ambrose Shea
Henry Crout Father
Ragueneau Lork Selkirk
and John A.—however
far into northness
you have walked—
when we call you
turn around and
don't look so surprised.

ANXIOUS

Anxious
of course I'm anxious
afraid
of course I'm afraid
I don't know what about
I don't know what of
but I'm afraid
and I feel it's
right to be.

LOVE POEM

I will swallow your
eyes and leave only
pools of darkness.

I will take the words
from your mouth and leave
only lakes of stillness.

Attend to my miracle,
I am kissing your body
making it white as stone,

The pools and lakes
of your eyes and mouth,
the white stone

Of your body will
make a labyrinth
of fabled cities,

And a marbled palace
of many rooms where
the whole world

Will be glad to pay
admission to wander
through the many rooms,

To look at my
miracle pools and soft
monuments until

At last the whole world
will go to sleep happy
at eight o'clock

Under a soft white fleece.

b. 1927

Phyllis Webb

PHYLLIS WEBB is an intensely self-critical poet who discards much more of her work than she publishes. She was born in Victoria, B.C., and grew up there and in Vancouver. Her life has been punctuated by a series of departures from, and returns to, the west coast. (She has been influenced by the periods she has spent in Ireland, France, the United States, and Russia, as well as by the west coast of Canada.) She attended the University of British Columbia and in the year she graduated was an unsuccessful CCF candidate in a provincial election. She then moved to Montreal, where she worked as a secretary and pursued graduate studies at McGill University. In 1959 she returned to Vancouver and taught for several years at the University of British Columbia. She also began to broadcast talks and reviews on the CBC and in 1964 went to the CBC in Toronto to organize the series 'Ideas'. This program—which included talks, lectures, documentaries, and dramatic and literary features in a wide range of intellectual and artistic areas–became under her influence one of the most respected series on the CBC's radio network. She resigned from the CBC in 1969 and has been living in Vancouver or on one of the nearby Gulf islands. Her books of poetry are *Trio*, in which her work was included with that of Eli Mandel and Gael Turnbull; *Even Your Right Eye* (1956); *The Sea Is Also a Garden* (1962); *Naked Poems* (1965); and *Selected Poems* (1971), which was published by the small Vancouver publisher talonbooks and includes all the poems she wished to preserve from 1954 to 1965. *Selected Poems* contains a long essay on her poetry by John Hulcoop.

The final words of 'Lament' (opposite) —'lonely poems in/the shape of a frugal sadness'—describe much of Phyllis Webb's writing on pain, loss, love, death, and poetry. Helen W. Sonthoff has referred to her 'passionate toughmindedness, an anguished will to completeness' and John Hulcoop remarks on the spare, abstract style she adopted in the early sixties—most strikingly exhibited in *Naked Poems*—and also notes the gradual departure in her work from 'a self-critical obsession with the despairing self and towards a much more self-critical preoccupation with language as a means of proclaiming or presenting the nature of present things.'

Helen Sonthoff's article on Phyllis Webb appears in Issue 9 of *Canadian Literature* (Summer 1961); there is also an article by John Hulcoop in Issue 32 (Spring 1967). Phyllis Webb's note for her 'Fantasia on Christian's Diary' (page 511) describes the background to this poem. The remarkable saga of Hornby and his companions is described in full in *The Legend of John Hornby* (1962) by George Whalley. Christian's moving diary was published as *Unflinching: A Diary of Tragic Adventure* (1937).

LAMENT

Knowing that everything is wrong,
how can we go on giving birth
either to poems or the troublesome lie,
to children, most of all, who sense
the stress in our distracted wonder
the instant of their entry with their cry?

For every building in this world
receives our benediction of disease.
Knowing that everything is wrong
means only that we all know where we're going.

But I, how can I, I
craving the resolution of my earth,
take up my little gang of sweet pretence
and saunter day-dreary down the alleys, or pursue
the half-disastrous night? Where is that virtue
I would claim with tense impersonal unworth,
where does it dwell, that virtuous land
where one can die without a second birth?

It is not here, neither in the petulance
of my cries, nor in the tracers of my active fear,
not in my suicide of love, my dear.
That place of perfect animals and men
is simply the circle we would charm our children in
and why we frame our lonely poems in
the shape of a frugal sadness.

POETICS AGAINST THE ANGEL OF DEATH

I am sorry to speak of death again
(some say I'll have a long life)
but last night Wordsworth's 'Prelude'
suddenly made sense—I mean the measure,
the elevated tone, the attitude
of private Man speaking to public men.
Last night I thought I would not wake again
but now with this June morning I run ragged to elude
the Great Iambic Pentameter
who is the Hound of Heaven in our stress
because I want to die
writing Haiku
or, better,
long lines, clean and syllabic as knotted bamboo. Yes!

SITTING

The degree of nothingness
is important:
to sit emptily
in the sun
receiving fire
that is the way
to mend
an extraordinary world,
sitting perfectly
still
and only
remotely human.

FANTASIA ON CHRISTIAN'S DIARY

This poem, inspired by the CBC *documentary 'Death in the Barren Grounds' by George Whalley, does not tell the story set forth in Edgar Christian's diary of the tragic exploration in the sub-arctic Barrens, which the broadcast did so admirably. It attempts rather to give a shade of the atmosphere of that story, often by using quotations, both of fact and word, and even at times of fancy. Edgar Christian was seventeen when he came to Canada in 1926 with his cousin, Jack Hornby, to make a trek to the Barren Grounds. There was a third member of the team, Harold Adlard. They failed to put in sufficient supplies and all died—first Jack, then Harold, and finally Edgar. Christian, before he died, placed his diary, letters and the will in the stove, presumably for safe-keeping. Hornby, a remarkable man and an explorer of unique intention, had started a book and this was placed in a suitcase. The hut was discovered and reported in 1928, but it was not until 1929, when the* RCMP *reached the cabin, that the skeletons were found, and the papers, and this arctic Pilgrim's Progress of the twenties was unfolded.* PHYLLIS WEBB

There have been no animals
except snowflakes falling,
the whites of our eyes falling,
the white skies, our sides falling,
the flesh made air, and the air made bone.

 When will the caribou come?
 When will the caribou come?

What has Jack Hornby come for?
Not to stake claims—
he explores only
mineral silence to enter the
initials of the name.

 When will the caribou come—
 I don't mean to stay—
 But when will they come?

Oh, but they did come! They strode
to our house, bitter and lean,
and then fled away.
But we were away, and should perhaps
have gone on forever, or never
have come at all,
now that we find so many white deaths
want to call.

But don't blame Jack.
He lays a foundation
I can build my life on.
(Christian dying at eighteen
disease in his back,
knees sharp as antlers.)
It was just that we didn't prepare.
We eat everything to the bone.

> *When will the caribou come?*
> *When will they come.*

It is cold, fifty below, and the silence
is louder than light,
Jack's heart weakens, we sicken,
and the mind is ice.

> *Oh, when will they come!*

The calcium nights shudder to powder
—everything is white! Up there
the swans are flakes, the skies are
falling down,
yet for all the natural effort
nothing but white is shown.
Certainly, there are nights one dare not sleep.
Our scattered lawns are deathly white with sheep,
and our speckled hopes on faun's feet pass.

Now tracks we left I've gathered for the stove
to seal up tight a trinity of love
as unexplained, as unreleased as night.
All the wills that ever were will burn
and end in ashes when we die.
The trails of our exploration
passed us by.

> *But when will the caribou come?*
> *When will they come to eat from my hand?*

The sky roars down with animals.
Don't look! Don't look!
There must be a million reindeer
solid as land!

Anne Wilkinson

ANNE WILKINSON was born in Toronto and spent her childhood in London, Ont. She was educated in England and the United States and made her home in Toronto, where she married and raised a family. She published two volumes of poetry, *Counterpoint to Sleep* (1951) and *The Hangman Ties the Holly* (1955), and two books of prose: *Lions in the Way* (1956), a charming and interesting history of the Osler family, and *Swann and Daphne* (1960), a haunting fantasy for children. She was a founding editor of *The Tamarack Review*, a literary magazine that published posthumously a delightful autobiographical fragment about her childhood, 'Four Corners of My World'. This memoir is included in *The Collected Poems of Anne Wilkinson* (1968), edited with an introduction by A. J. M. Smith, who placed her 'in the forefront of Canadian poets'.

In luminous poems that are influenced by the simplicities and rhythms of nursery rhyme, fairy tale, song, and ballad, Anne Wilkinson celebrated the senses, which were to her the source of joy and wisdom. The elements of earth, air, fire, and water appear prominently in all her poetry. She took great delight in them and indeed identified herself with nature, sensuously and emotionally. This identification achieved its culmination in poems about love and death. Reviewing her *Collected Poems*, Hugh MacCallum wrote that her poetry 'combines opposites, being elegant yet earthy, richly fanciful yet classical in its taut restraint, intense and visionary yet warmly human.'

IN JUNE AND GENTLE OVEN

In June and gentle oven
Summer kingdoms simmer
As they come
And flower and leaf and love
Release
Their sweetest juice.

No wind at all
On the wide green world
Where fields go stroll-
ing by
And in and out
An adder of a stream
Parts the daisies
On a small Ontario farm.

And where, in curve of meadow,
Lovers, touching, lie,
A church of grass stands up
And walls them, holy, in.

Fabulous the insects
Stud the air
Or walk on running water,
Klee-drawn saints
And bright as angels are.

Honeysuckle here
Is more than bees can bear
And time turns pale
And stops to catch its breath
And lovers slip their flesh
And light as pollen
Play on treble water
Till bodies reappear
And a shower of sun
To dry their languor.

Then two in one the lovers lie
And peel the skin of summer
With their teeth

And suck its marrow from a kiss
So charged with grace
The tongue, all knowing
Holds the sap of June
Aloof from seasons, flowing.

THREE POEMS ABOUT POETS

1
Poets are fishermen crying
'Fresh catch from sleep,
Fresh as the mackerel sky
Or a salmon's leap
Is the catch we offer.
Come buy, come buy!'

2
Poets are cool as the divers who wander
The floor of the sea;
Their eyes are aquariums, swimming
With starfish and stranger.

Dark waters breed the phantoms
They haul in their nets to the sun
And sun is the power
That glisters their scales with meaning.

3
Poets are leapers, the heels of their sprung feet
Clearing the hurdles of sleep.
See how they run! Muscled with rhythm
And fleshed fair and rosy with vowels.
They're pulling the tunnel out into the light,
Did you ever see such a sight in your life
As three new poems?

LETTER TO MY CHILDREN

I guided you by rote—
Nipple to spoon, from spoon
To knife and fork,
And many a weak maternal morning
Bored the breakfast hour
With 'manners make the man',
And cleanliness I kissed
But shunned its neighbour,
Puzzled all my days
By the 'I' in godliness.

Before you turn
And bare your faultless teeth at me
Accept a useless gift, apology,
Admit I churched you in the rites
Of trivia
And burned the family incense
At a false god's altar.

If we could start again,
You, newbegotten, I
A clean stick peeled
Of twenty paper layers of years
I'd tell you only what you know
But barely know you know,
Teach one commandment,
'Mind the senses and the soul
Will take care of itself,
Being five times blessed.'

Ethel Wilson

In the fifteen years following the Second World War, ETHEL WILSON published six novels and numerous short stories that are notable for their engaging style, accurate dialogue, and delicate creation of mood and atmosphere. She was born at Port Elizabeth, South Africa, but by the time she was ten her mother and father were both dead and she was brought up by relatives and educated in schools in England and Vancouver. (She has said of her school years: 'Following a hard-working and happy schooling in a Spartan boarding school, my education became unorthodox, eclectic, spotty, and ceaselessly interesting. The joys of a little learning are very great.') Her formal education continued through Normal School in Vancouver, and between 1907 and 1920 she taught in the city's public schools. In 1921 she married Dr Wallace Wilson, who had a distinguished career as a Vancouver physician until his death in 1966. Mrs Wilson's writing career began late, and it was not until she was forty-nine, in 1937, that she published her first short story in the English periodical, *The New Statesman & Nation*. Soon afterwards her writing was interrupted by the war, in

which her husband served as a medical officer while she edited a Red Cross magazine in Vancouver. She was nearly sixty when she resumed her career as a writer with the publication in 1947 of her first novel, *Hetty Dorval*. It was followed by *The Innocent Traveller* (1949); *The Equations of Love* (1952), which contains two short novels, *Tuesday and Wednesday* and *Lilly's Story*; *Swamp Angel* (1954); *Love and Salt Water* (1956); and *Mrs Golightly and Other Stories* (1961). Most of her fiction is set in British Columbia. (It would not surprise readers of her books to learn that she and her husband used to be ardent fishermen and regularly spent their holidays in the B.C. interior.) Yet there is nothing parochial or provincial about her writing; indeed, her books were admired as much in England and the United States as in her own country.

In an article on Ethel Wilson in *Canadian Literature* (Issue 49, Summer 1971), Frank Birbalsingh writes: 'All Mrs Wilson's books illustrate the sudden shocks and abrupt shifts of fortune . . . which can be produced by unforeseen events. Mrs Wilson's universe is one of complete chaos, where anything can happen to anyone at any time; but she shows no willingness to question this disorder. She takes her strange and haphazard universe for granted, and nowhere reveals the slightest interest in investigating its philosophical foundations. Thus her books do not probe or analyse the action which they describe. Instead, they impose on this action a view of life that is slightly whimsical and which effectively neutralizes the actual risks and inherent dangers of an unpredictable future. The two essential features of Mrs Wilson's fiction, therefore, are her illustration of the inimical capacity of the future, and a predilection for a whimsicality that evokes the supernatural realities behind everyday appearances.'

Mrs Wilson has been an ardent correspondent. As one of her editors Robert Weaver grew accustomed to receiving letters from her filled with opinions about contemporary writing, politics, and education that were in no way inhibited by age or by her assured position in Vancouver society. There is a suggestion of the charming, informal style of these letters in her discussion of the writer's craft in Issue 2 of *Canadian Literature* (Autumn 1959). A critical study of the author by Desmond Pacey is available in Twayne's World Authors Series (1968, Burns & MacEachern).

FOG

For seven days fog settled down upon Vancouver. It crept in from the ocean, advancing in its mysterious way in billowing banks which swallowed up the land. In the Bay and the Inlet and False Creek, agitated voices spoke to one another. Small tugs that were waylaid in the blankets of fog cried shrilly and sharply 'Keep away! Keep away! I am here!' Fishing-boats lay inshore. Large freighters mooed continuously like monstrous cows. The foghorns at Point Atkinson and the Lions' Gate Bridge kept up their bellowings. Sometimes the fog quenched the sounds, sometimes the sounds were loud and near. If there had not been this continuous dense fog, all the piping and boo-hooing would have held a kind of beauty; but it signified danger and warning. People knew that when the fog lifted they would see great freighters looking disproportionately large riding at anchor in the Bay because passage through the Narrows into the harbour was not safe. Within the harbour, laden ships could not depart but remained lying fog-bound at great expense in the stream . . . booo . . . booo . . . they warned. 'I am here! Keep away!' All the ships listened. The CPR boat from Victoria crashed into the dock. Gulls collided in the pathless air. Water traffic ceased and there was no movement anywhere offshore.

In the streets, cars crawled slowly. Drivers peered. Pedestrians emerged and vanished like smoke. Up the draw of False Creek, fog packed thick on the bridges. Planes were grounded. People cancelled parties. Everyone arrived late for everything.

Mrs Bylow was an old woman who lived in a small old house which was more cabin than cottage in an unpleasant part of Mount Pleasant. For the fifth day she sat beside her window looking into the fog and cracking her knuckles because she had nothing else to do. If she had owned a telephone she would have talked all day for pastime, repeating herself and driving the party line mad.

Mrs Bylow frequently sat alone and lonely. Her diurnal occupations had narrowed down to sleeping, waking to still another day, getting up, making and swallowing small meals, belching a little, cleaning up (a little), hoping, going to the bathroom, going to the Chinaman's corner store, reading the paper (and thank God for that, especially the advertisements), becoming suddenly aware again of the noise of the radio (and thank God for that, too), and forgetting again.

This, and not much more, was her life as she waited for the great dust-man and the ultimate box. So Mrs Bylow's days and months slid and slid away while age—taking advantage of her solitariness, her long unemployment of vestigial brain, her unawareness of a world beyond herself, her absence of preparation for the grey years—closed down upon her like a vice, no, more like a fog. There had been a time about ten years ago when Mrs Bylow, sitting on her small porch, beckoned to the little neighbour children who played on the sidewalk. 'Come,' said Mrs Bylow, smiling and nodding.

The children came, and they all went into the kitchen. There was Mrs Bylow's batch of fresh cookies and the children ate, looking around them, rapacious. They ate and ran away and once or twice a child hovered and said 'Thank you.' Perhaps that was not the child who said 'Thank you', but parents speaking through the child ('Say Thank you to Mrs Bylow!') so the child said 'Thank you' and Mrs Bylow was pleased. Sometimes the children lingered around the little porch, not hungry, but happy, noisy and greedy. Then Mrs Bylow rejoiced at the tokens of love and took the children into the kitchen. But perhaps she had only apples and the children did not care for apples. 'Haven't you got any cookies?' asked a bold one, 'we got lotsa apples at home.'

'You come Tuesday,' said Mrs Bylow, nodding and smiling, but the children forgot.

So within Mrs Bylow these small rainbows of life (children, cookies, laughing, and beckoning) faded, although two neighbours did sometimes stop on their way home and talk for a few minutes and thus light up her day. Miss Casey who worked at the People's Friendly Market and was a smart dresser with fine red hair, and Mrs Merkle who was the managing type and had eyes like marbles and was President of the Ladies' Bowling Club dropped in from time to time and told Mrs Bylow all about the illnesses of the neighbours which Mrs Bylow enjoyed very much and could think about later. Mrs Merkle told her about Mr Galloway's broken hip and Miss Casey told her about her mother's diabetes and how she managed her injections, also about the woman who worked in her department when she didn't need to work and now her kid had gone wrong and was in the Juvenile Court. Mrs Bylow was regaled by everything depressing that her two friends could assemble because she enjoyed bad news which was displayed to her chiefly against the backdrop of her own experience and old age. All these ailments, recalling memories of her own ('. . . well I remember my Uncle Ernest's . . .') provided a drama, as did the neglect and irresponsibility of the young generations. Like an old sad avid stupid judge she sat, passing judgement without ill will. It is not hard to understand why Mrs Merkle and Miss Casey, hastening past Mrs Bylow's gate which swung on old hinges, often looked straight ahead, walking faster and thinking I *must* go in and see her tomorrow.

During long periods of bad weather, as now in this unconquerable fog, time was a deep pit for Mrs Bylow. Her hip was not very good. She should have belonged to a church (to such base uses can the humble and glorious act of worship come) or a club, to which she would at least look forward. Gone were the simple impossible joys of going to town, wandering through the shops, fingering and comparing cloth, cotton and silk. Gone was the joy of the running children. Life, which had been pinkish and blueish, was grey. And now this fog.

So it was that on the fifth day of fog, Mrs Bylow sat beside her window in a sort of closed-up dry well of boredom, cracking her knuckles and looking into the relentless blank that pressed against her window panes and kept her from seeing any movement on the sidewalk. Mrs Merkle and Miss Casey were as though they had never been. I'm not surprised they wouldn't drop in, thought Mrs Bylow modestly and without rancour, it couldn't be expected, it'll be all they can do to get home; and she pictured Miss Casey, with her flaming hair, wearing her leopard coat, pushing through the fog home to her mother. Diabetes, thought Mrs Bylow, and she was sorry for old Mrs Casey. Her indulgence of sorrow spread to include Miss Casey hurrying home looking so smart. Not much in life for her, now, is there, really, she thought, rocking. Mrs. Bylow peered again. She was insulted by this everywhere fog, this preventing fog. She needed a cup of cocoa and she had no cocoa. She repeated aloud a useful phrase, 'The fog is lifting'; but the fog was not lifting.

Mrs Bylow creaked to her feet. She wrapped herself up well, took her walking stick and went unsteadily down her three steps. Then, not at all afraid, she turned to the left and, in a silence of velvet, she moved slowly along beside the picket fence which would guide her to Wong Kee's store.

At her own corner a suggestion of sickly glow in the air told her that the street lamps were lighted. She moved on, screwing up her eyes against the greyish yellow fog that invaded eyes, nose, mouth. At last another pale high glimmer informed her that she was near Wong Kee's store and, gasping, leaning now and then against the outside wall of the store itself, she reached the door with the comfortable knowledge that, once inside, she would find light and warmth. She would ask Wong Kee for his chair or a box and would sit down and take her ease while the Chinaman went with shuffling steps to the shelf where he kept the tins of cocoa. Wong Kee was a charming old man with good cheek-bones and a sudden tired Oriental smile. After Mrs Merkle and Miss Casey he was Mrs Bylow's third friend. She pushed the door open and waddled in to where there was this desired light and warmth, puffing a little.

Something was happening inside the store, a small whirlwind and fury. Mrs Bylow was roughly pushed by large rushing objects. She lost her balance and was thrown, no, hurled violently to the ground. The person or persons rushed on, out and into the fog. The door slammed.

The store was empty. Everything was still. The old woman lay in a heap, bewildered and in pain. Gradually she began to know that someone or some people had rushed out into the fog, knocking her down and hurting her because she happened to be in the way. She whimpered and she thought badly of Wong Kee because he did not come to help her. Her body gave her massive pain, and as she looked slowly about her in a stupefied way she saw that a number of heavy cans of food had rained down upon her and lay around her. As she tried clumsily to heave herself up (but that was not possible), a customer came in.

'Well well well!' said the customer bending over her, 'whatever . . .' then he straightened himself and listened.

A faint sound as of a bubbling sigh came from behind the counter on which was the till. The till was open and empty. The customer went behind the counter and again bent down. Then he drew himself up quickly. Wong Kee lay like a bundle of old clothes from which blood seeped and spread. The sound that the customer had heard was the soft sound of the death of Wong Kee who was an honest man and innocent. He had worked all his life and had robbed no one. He had an old wife who loved him. In a way hard to explain they were seriously and simply happy together. This was now over.

The customer paid no further attention to Mrs Bylow on the floor but, stepping round Wong Kee's body, reached the telephone.

A small woman parted the dingy curtains which separated the store from the home of Wong Kee and his wife. She held in her arms a bundle of stove wood and stood motionless like a wrinkled doll. Then the stove

wood clattered to the ground and she dropped to her knees uttering high babbling noises. She rocked and prostrated herself beside the impossible sight of her husband's dead body and his blood. The customer regarded her as he talked into the telephone. Then he too knelt down and put his arm round her. He could find nothing to say but the immemorial 'There there. . . .'

Mrs Bylow, lying neglected on the floor, endeavoured to look behind her but she had to realize as people do in bombardment, flood and earthquake that she was at the mercy of whatever should happen to her and could not do anything about it, let alone look behind her.

'They're slow coming,' said the customer. 'It's the fog.'

The old Chinese woman wrenched herself from him. 'I tarryphome,' she cried out, 'I tarryphome my son . . . .'

The door opened and there seemed to be some policemen. The outside fog poured in with this entrance and some other kind of fog pressed down upon Mrs Bylow's understanding and blurred it. 'I'm a very old woman,' she mumbled to a constable who had a little book, 'and they knocked me down . . . they mighta killed me . . . they shouldn't a done that . . . they've broke my hip . . . aah. . . !'

'Yes lady, we'll look after you,' said the constable, 'who was it?'

'It was . . .' (well, who was it?) 'I guess it was some man . . . no . . .' she breathed with difficulty, she should not have to suffer so, 'I guess it was a boy . . . no, two boys . . . they knocked me down . . .'

A constable at the door said to a crowd which had gathered from somewhere in the fog and now pushed against the front of the store, 'Now then, you can't come in here, there's been a robbery, see? You best go on home,' but someone battered on the pane with both hands enough to break it, and Miss Casey burst in at the door, her red hair wet with fog.

'She's here! Yes there she is!' said Miss Casey talking to everyone in her loud voice and bringing into the muted shop a blazing of bright eyes and hair and leopard coat and humanity, '—that's what I thought! I thought right after I left the store I'd better go in and see was she O.K. because she shouldn't be out and the fog was just *awful* and I prett' near went past her gate but I kinda felt something was wrong and my goodness see what happened. . . . Mrs Bylow honey, what happened you,' and Miss Casey dropped on her knees and took Mrs Bylow's hand in hers. 'Say, what's been going on around here, anyway?' she said, looking up at the constable ready to accuse.

'She's not so good,' said the constable in a low tone in Mrs Bylow's dream and a high noise came into the night ('That's the syreen,' said Miss Casey) and some men lifted her and took her somewhere on a bed. It did not occur to Mrs Bylow that perhaps she had been killed inadvertently by two youths who had just killed her old friend, but if a policeman had said to her 'Now you are dead,' she would have accepted the information, so unfamiliar was the experience of boring horizontally through a fog at top speed very slowly in a high and unexplained swelling noise. She opened her eyes and saw a piece of Miss Casey's leopard coat and so she was not dead.

'Is it reel?' she whispered, because she had always wanted to know.

'Is what reel?' said Miss Casey bending her flaming head. 'Sure it's reel. The collar's reel anyway.' Mrs Bylow closed her eyes again for several years and said 'But I never got my cocoa.' Then she began to cry quietly because she felt old and helpless and the pain was something cruel but it was good to feel Miss Casey beside her in her leopard coat. She did not know that Wong Kee was dead—slugged on the head, pistol-whipped, stabbed again and again in the stomach with a long knife—all because he had summoned his small strength and fought like a cat and defended himself for his right to his thirty dollars and some loose change and a handful of cigarettes and his life. 'Well, here we are,' said Miss Casey, standing up, very cheerful.

In a week or two, while she was better and before she got worse, Mrs Bylow began to remember the two boys whom she had never seen and, as she constructed their leather jackets and their faces, she said she would know them anywhere. Of course she would not, and the murderers of Wong Kee were never found but carried the knowledge of their murder into the fog with them on their way from the betrayal of their youth to whatever else they would soon violently undertake to do. When they arrived back, each at his own home, their parents said in pursuance of their habit of long years past 'Where you bin?' and the hoodlums said in pursuance of their habit of long years past 'Out.' This satisfied the idiot parents. They said 'My that fog's just terrible,' and the hoodlums said 'Sure is.' They were excited and nervous because this was the first time they had killed, but they had the money. One of the young hoodlums did not go into the room where his parents were but went upstairs because he was pretty sure there was still some blood on his hands and so there was. Wong Kee's blood was on his parents' hands too but they, being irresponsible, did not know this. And on their hands was the blood of Mrs Bylow who was soon to die, and of Mrs Wong Kee who could no longer be said to live, and of their own hoodlum children.

Before Mrs Bylow died, wiped out by forces quite outside herself like a moth in a storm (not much more and no less), she began to be a little proud of almost being present at a murder.

'It's not everyone who's been at a murder, Miss Casey, love, is it?'

'No honey,' said Miss Casey, seeing again that sordid scene, 'it isn't everyone.'

'I always liked that coat of yours,' said Mrs Bylow.

'And then,' said Miss Casey to Mrs Merkle, 'd'you know what she said? She said if ever I come to die—just like she wasn't ever going to—would you please wear your leopard coat. She's crazy about that coat. And then she said she often thought of those two boys that killed the storekeeper and knocked her down and she guessed it was more their parents' fault and not their fault. It made the tears come to your eyes,' said Miss Casey who was kind as well as noisy and cherished a sense of personal drama.

'Sure,' said Mrs Merkle who had eyes like marbles that did not weep.

Mrs Bylow's death was obscure and pitiful. Miss Casey got the afternoon off and so there were two people at her funeral. Miss Casey wore her leopard coat as promised.

MRS GOLIGHTLY AND OTHER STORIES

b. 1912

George Woodcock

GEORGE WOODCOCK is an unusual figure on the Canadian literary scene both because of the exceptional range of his writings— literary criticism, biography, travel books, poetry, studies of political movements and social communities—and because his interests include both Canadian subjects and those of international significance. He was born in Winnipeg but was taken as a child to England and began his literary career there. In the 1930s and during the Second World War he was sympathetic to anarchist and pacifist movements in England and edited *Now*, a magazine that published literary and political essays. Woodcock returned to Canada in 1949 and lived for a time near Victoria, B.C. In 1956 he joined the Department of English at the University of British Columbia. Since its beginning in 1959 he has been the editor of the critical journal *Canadian Literature*, published at that university.

'In his three roles as a knowledgeable student and critic of the arts, a humanist, and a social historian, he explores the present to seek its *tradition*,' W. H. New has written of Woodcock. A world traveller, Woodcock is the author of books about Mexico, Peru, India, and other countries in Asia, and two books about travels inside Canada: *Ravens and Prophets* (1952), which is mainly about British Columbia, and the more general *Canada and the Canadians* (1970). His interest in communal communities in Canada was first explored in *Ravens and Prophets*; then in a long article (reproduced below) about a Doukhobor community that appeared in *The Tamarack Review* in 1963; and finally led him to undertake a major study, *The Doukhobors* (1968), which he wrote with Ivan Avakumovic. Woodcock's political and social studies include *Anarchism: A History of Libertarian Ideas and Movements* (1962) and books on two major anarchist figures of the nineteenth century, Peter Kropotkin and Pierre-Joseph Proudhon.

Woodcock's literary biograpies include studies of William Godwin, Oscar Wilde, and Aldous Huxley. For *The Crystal Spirit: A Study of George Orwell* he won the Governor General's Award for non fiction for 1967. Of great value to students is his work as a critic of Canadian literature. This includes not only his editing of *Canadian Literature* but his collection of some of the best essays from that magazine, *A Choice of Critics* (1966), and *Odysseus Ever Returning: Essays on Canadian Writers and Writings* (1970), containing critical essays on Hugh MacLennan, Morley Callaghan, Leonard Cohen, Irving Layton, Earle Birney, and A. J. M. Smith among others. Woodcock is also the author of four books of poetry —his *Selected Poems* was published in 1967—and of a collection of political writings: *The Rejection of Politics and Other Essays* (1972).

Odysseus Ever Returning is available in the New Canadian Library (with an introduction by W. H. New) and *The Crystal Spirit* has been reprinted by Penguin Books.

ENCOUNTER WITH AN ARCHANGEL

When my wife and I returned to Canada in the spring of 1949, I found that on Vancouver Island, where we settled, there was a small group of Doukhobors who had migrated from the interior of British Columbia and had founded a colony at Hilliers, sixty miles north of the village where we were clearing land and carpentering a house in search of that Tolstoyan *ignis fatuus*, the marriage of manual and mental work.

The people of our village talked reluctantly about the Hilliers community, yet even their rare hostile comments told us something. The leader of the group—a heretical offshoot—was a prophet who called himself Michael the Archangel. He openly preached the destruction of marriage, and this our neighbours vaguely envisaged as a complex and orgiastic pattern of shacking-up which provoked and offended their Presbyterian imagination at one and the same time.

Since Hilliers was near, we could easily go there to see for ourselves, but we knew already that chronic bad relations with the Canadian authorities had made the Doukhobors distrustful of strangers. However, I wrote to the community, and by return I received a letter from the secretary, whose name was Joe. He not only welcomed my interest, but invited us to stay at Hilliers as long as we wished. I was a little surprised at the enthusiastic tone of his letter, but the reason became evident once we reached Hilliers.

One day in August we set off northward. For lack of money, we hitchhiked, and it was late afternoon when the last driver turned off the seacoast road into the broad valley, hot and still of air, where Hilliers lies in the lee of the hard mountain spine that runs down the length of Vancouver Island. The older, non-Doukhobor Hilliers was a whistle-stop on the island railway, and the entrance to the community stood opposite a siding filled with boxcars. A high cedar fence faced the road. A large board had been nailed to it. UNION OF SPIRITUAL COMMUNITIES OF CHRIST, it said, in Russian and English. The wide gates stood open; looking between them, the eye encompassed and then recognized with some surprise the unconscious faithfulness with which a Russian village of the Chekhov era had been reproduced. Low cabins of logs and unpainted shakes were scattered along a faintly marked trail that ran between grass verges to end, a furlong on, at two larger two-storeyed houses standing against the brown background of the mountains, with the grey bubble of a communal baking oven between them. Each cabin was surrounded by a picketed garden, where green rows of vegetables and raspberry canes ran over the black earth in neatly weeded symmetry, and ranks of sunflowers lolled their brown and yellow masks towards the light.

An old woman with a white kerchief shading her face was hoeing very slowly in the nearest garden. She was the only person in sight, and I went up to her fence. Could she tell me where to find Joe? Her English was so broken that I could not follow what she was trying to tell me. By this time our arrival had been noticed in the cabins, and a little wave of younger women in bright full petticoats, and of blond, crop-headed small boys, came towards us hesitantly. There was nothing of the welcome we had expected. Inge spoke to one of the women. 'Joe ain't here,' she answered. 'He's at the other place.' She waved vaguely northward. A pick-up truck drove in through the gates, and two young men got out. The women called to them, and they talked together in rapid, anxious Russian. Then one man got back into the truck and drove off, while the other came up to us. He was dark and nervous, dressed in an old blue serge suit with chaff whitening the wrinkles. 'I'm Pete,' he said. 'Joe's brother. Joe's coming.' He paused. 'Afterwards . . . you'll see Michael . . . Michael Archangel,' he added hesitantly, and then fell silent. The small boys gave up interest and went to play on the boxcars.

Joe was so different from Pete that it was hard to believe them brothers —blue-eyed, wiry, jumping out of the truck to run and pump our hands. 'Michael Archangel knew you were coming. A long time ago,' he shouted. I had written only a week before. 'A long time ago?' I asked. Joe looked at me and then laughed. 'Yes, before you wrote!' Then he grabbed our rucksacks, helped us into the truck, and drove wildly for a couple of miles along a rough track beside the railway to a large old farm house in a quadrangle of shacks and barns surrounded by propped-up apple trees that were ochre-yellow with lichen. 'This is the other place,' Joe explained. 'Most of the young people stay here. The old 'uns live up there with Michael Archangel.'

We went into the kitchen. Two young women, fair and steatopygous as Doukhobor beauties are expected to be were preparing the evening meal. A small girl showed us to our room, and stood, avid with curiosity, while we unpacked our rucksacks and washed our faces. Then Joe took us around the yard, showed us the new bakehouse on which a hawk-faced old man like a Circassian bandit was laying bricks, and tried to entice us into the bathhouse. I looked through the doorway and saw naked people moving like the damned in the clouds of steam that puffed up whenever a bucket of water was thrown on the hot stones. In a couple of seconds I withdrew, gasping for breath. The bricklayer laughed. 'You never make a Doukhobor,' he said. 'Add ten years to your life,' said Joe coaxingly.

When everyone stood in a circle around the great oval table for the communal meal we began to see the kind of people the Doukhobors were. There were twenty of them, singing in the half-Caucasian rhythm that penetrates Doukhobor music, the women high and nasal, the men resonant as bells. Most had Slavonic features, their breadth emphasized among the women by the straight fringes in which their hair was cut across the forehead. But a few, like the bricklayer, were so unRussian as to suggest that Doukhobors had interbred with Caucasian Moslems during their long exile in the mountains before they came to Canada. They sang of Siberian and Canadian prisons, of martyrs and heroes in the faith. 'Rest at last, ye eagles of courage, rest at last in the arms of God,' they boomed and shrilled.

The singing was solemn, but afterwards the mood changed at once and the meal went on with laughter and loud Russian talk; now and then our neighbours would break off repentantly to translate for our benefit. The food was vegetarian, but the best of its kind I have ever tasted; bowls of purple borscht, dashed with white streaks of cream, and then casha, made with millet and butter, and vegetables cooked in oil, and pirogi stuffed with cheese and beans and blackberries, and eaten with great scoops of sour cream. Slices of black bread passed around the table, cut from a massive square loaf that stood in the middle, beside the salt of hospitality, and the meal ended with huckleberries and cherries.

Afterwards Joe and Pete took us to drink tea in a room they used as an office. It was furnished with a table and benches of thick hand-adzed cedar, but a big blue enamel teapot served instead of a samovar. This was the first of a series of long conversations in which the ideas of the community were imparted to us, principally by Joe, who spoke English more fluently than anyone else at Hilliers. Except for a few phrases, the details of the dialogues have become blurred in my memory during the thirteen years that have passed since then, but this, in substance, is what we were told on the first evening.

The community began with the experiences of Michael Verigin, a backsliding Doukhobor. Michael had left his home in the mountains, opened a boarding-house for Russians in Vancouver, and prospered there. After a few years Michael began to feel the malaise which many Doukhobors experience when they go from their villages into the acquisitive outside world, and he returned to the mountain valley of Krestova. Krestova is the Mecca of the Sons of Freedom, the fire-raising and nude-parading radical wing of the Doukhobor sect. Michael rejoined the Sons of Freedom and was regarded with deference because he bore the holy name of Verigin and was a distant cousin of Peter the Lordly, the Living Christ who presided over the Doukhobors' first years in Canada, and died mysteriously in a train explosion during the 1920s.

'Then Michael had a vision.'

'A dream?'

'No, a vision. He was awake, and he said there was a voice and a presence.'

'He saw nothing?'

'That time he didn't. The vision told him he was no longer Mike Verigin. Michael the Archangel had gone into him. He was the same man, but the Archangel as well.'

'How did he know it was a real vision?'

'He just knew.' Joe looked at me with the imperturbable blue-eyed confidence of a man used to assessing the authenticity of supernatural messages. 'The vision said Michael must prepare the world for the Second Coming.'

The Second Coming did not mean the return of Christ. According to Doukhobor beliefs, Christ is returning all the time in various forms. The Second Coming meant the establishment of God's earthly kingdom and the end of time and mortality.

As the chosen pioneers in this great mission, the Doukhobors must purify themselves. The Archangel began by proclaiming that they must renounce not only meat and alcohol, but also tobacco and musical instruments. A radio was playing loudly in the kitchen as Joe explained this. 'That's o.k.,' he reassured us. 'A radio ain't a musical instrument.'

Above all, the lust for possession must be rooted out. This meant not only a return to the traditional communistic economy from which the Doukhobors had lapsed under evil Canadian influences, but also the destruction of that inner citadel of possession, marriage. No person must have rights over another, either parental or marital. Women must be liberated, sexual relations must be free, families must wither away.

Two or three hundred of the Sons of Freedom, mostly seasoned old veterans of the nude marches and the pre-war internment on Piers Island, accepted the Archangel's teaching. Their neighbours showed disagreement by burning down the houses of those who followed Verigin. At this point the Archangel very conveniently had another vision.

Two of his followers must visit Vancouver Island. There they would find a town where a clock had stopped at half-past two, and then they must proceed eastward until they saw a white horse by the gate of a farm. Joe and another man went on the expedition. They found the clock at Port Alberni, and the horse by the gate of a three-hundred-acre farm that was up for sale at a knockdown price. And, for what the fact is worth, I should record that after I had heard Joe's story I happened to visit Port Alberni, and there, on the tower of a fire-hall, I saw a dummy clock whose painted hands stood unmoving at half-past two.

The farm was bought with the pooled resources of the faithful, and Michael the Archangel led two hundred of his disciples on the exodus to Vancouver Island. Immediately after leaving the mainland he added to all the other prohibitions a ban on sexual intercourse—to conserve energies for the great task of spiritual regeneration. Complete freedom was only to be won by complete self-control. So much for the stories of Free Love rampant!

I wanted to find out the actual nature of the power that enabled Michael the Archangel to impose such restrictions. Tolstoy once thought that, because they opposed the state, the Doukhobors lived without rulers. Other writers had suggested that the Living Christs, like Peter the Lordly Verigin and his son Peter the Purger, had been rulers as powerful as any earthly governor.

'He is just our spiritual leader,' Joe explained blandly.

'But he still seems to have a big say in your practical affairs.'

'It depends on what you mean by *say*. He gives no orders. We are free men. We don't obey anybody. But he gives us advice.'

'Do you always accept it?'

'If we know what's good for us, we do.'

'Why?'

'Because we know Michael the Archangel is always right.'

'How do you know?'

'We just know.'

The next day we met the Archangel. He had sent a message early that morning summoning us to his presence, and Joe drove us to the hamlet where we had arrived originally. The Archangel's house was one of the larger buildings, but we were not allowed to go in. We waited outside. The Archangel would meet us in the garden.

A tall man in his late fifties came stepping heavily between the zinnia borders. A heavy paunch filled his knitted sweater, and his shining bald head loosened into a coarse, flushed face with a potato nose, a sandy moustache, and small eyes that glinted out of puffy sockets. It was a disappointing encounter. The Archangel bowed in the customary Doukhobor manner, but without the warmth most Doukhobors put into their greeting. He shook hands limply. He spoke a few sentences in Russian, welcoming us and wishing us good health, and he affected not to understand English, though we learned later that he was effectively bilingual. He picked two small pink roses from a briar that ran along the fence and gave one to each of us. In five minutes he was gone, retiring with dignified adroitness and leaving all our intended questions about archangelic power unanswered. Joe led us away, loudly declaring that the Archangel had been delighted with us, and that he had given many messages which he, Joe, would transmit in due course. Our whole relationship with the Archangel took on this elusive, indirect form, with Joe acting like a voluble priest interpreting and embellishing the laconic banalities of the oracle.

For the rest of the second day we wandered around the community, talking to the people we encountered. I pumped the handle of a primitive hand washing-machine, and learned from the girl I helped a curious instance of Doukhobor double-think. A spaniel bitch trotted over the yard, followed by a single pup. 'She had four,' the girl volunteered. 'Did you give the rest away?' 'No, they were drowned.' 'I thought you didn't believe in killing.' 'We didn't kill 'em. That Mountie sergeant drowned 'em for us.' She chuckled, and quite obviously felt no guilt for merely condoning a killing someone else had carried out.

Under the prophetic discipline there were certainly signs of strain. I found empty beer bottles under the bushes in a corner of one Doukhobor field, and in the shelter of the ten-feet plumes of corn which were the community's pride a young man begged a cigarette and smoked in hasty gulps to finish it before anyone came into sight. Yet there was also an atmosphere of dogged devotion. Much of the land had been irrigated, and it was growing heavier crops of corn and tomatoes and vegetables than any of the neighbouring farms, while the houses were surrounded by rows of hotbeds and cold frames where melons and gherkins ripened. The younger people talked constantly of schemes for new kinds of cultivation and for starting up light industries, but the younger people were so few. There were too many children, too many old visionaries.

Sunday was the climax of our visit. Our arrival had coincided with the community's first great festival. In the afternoon the only child so far born there was to be handed over to the care of the community as a symbolic demonstration against conventional ideas of motherhood and the family. Since the Archangel had forbidden fornication, we were rather surprised that a child whose very presence seemed to defy his will should be so honoured. From my attempts to discuss the situation I gained an impression that the Doukhobors applied a rather Dostoevskian equation

—considering that, if the ban itself was sacred, so must be the sin against it. 'Free men ain't bound by reason,' as one young man rather unanswerably concluded a discussion on this point.

The day began with morning service in the bare meeting house. Flowers and plates of red apples had been brought in, and the sunlight played over the white head-shawls and bright cotton dresses of the women. Bread and salt stood symbolically on the small central table, and also a great ewer of water from which anybody who happened to feel thirsty would stop and drink as the service went on. The women ranged to the right of the table and the men to the left. On entering the hall each person bowed low from the waist, and the bow was returned by the whole assembly; the salutation was not to the man, but to the God within him. The Archangel stood at the head of the men, benign and copiously sweating; despite his celestial nature, he did not attempt to offend Doukhobor precedent by acting like a priest. Today, in fact, as a child was to be the centre of the festival, the children led off the service, choosing and starting in their sharp, clear voices the Doukhobor psalms and hymns for the day. Almost every part of the service was sung, and the wild and wholly incomprehensible chanting of the two hundred people in the small meeting house produced in us an extraordinary sense of exaltation such as I have only experienced once since then, in a church full of Zapotec peasants at a festival south of Oaxaca. At the end of the service, we all linked arms at the elbows and kissed each other's cheeks, first right then left, in traditional token of forgiveness.

Later in the day we re-assembled in the open air, forming a great V with the bread and salt at the apex. The singing rose like a fountain of sound among the drooping cedar trees, and between lines of women waving flowers and men waving green boughs the mother carried her child to the table. She was one of the young women we had met at the farmhouse on our arrival. As she stood there, her fair face grave and melancholy within the white frame of her head-shawl, she looked like the dolorous mother of some naive ikon. The singing ended, the old hawk-faced brick-layer prayed before the table, and the mother, showing no emotion, handed the child to another of the women. The Archangel began to speak, in high, emotional tones; Pete, standing beside me, translated. The child would be named Angel Gabriel. The fruit of sin, he contained the seed of celestial nature. It was he who would fulfil the great destiny of the Doukhobors and lead mankind back on the great journey to lost Eden.

The women brought out pitchers of kvass and walked among the people as the orators began to speak. Emblematic banners were unfurled before the assembly. One, representing women dragging the ploughs that broke the prairies during the hard early days of the sect in Canada, was meant to celebrate the coming liberation of the sect from all forms of bondage. Another, covered with images of clocks and other symbols of time, was carefully expounded by the Archangel, who found in it the fatal dates that charted the destiny of the world. Then everyone spoke who wished— elders and young women; a Communist lawyer who had come in from the blue; even I, under moral coercion, as the enquiring Tolstoyan I then was. It was hot and tedious work as the sun beat down into the bowl among the mountains and Sunday trippers from Qualicum Beach gazed in astonishment through the palisades.

We walked back to the farmhouse with a Canadian woman who had married into the Doukhobors. 'You've seen what Mike wants you to see,' she said, bitterly. 'You don't know all there is to know about that girl. Today they've taken her child. Now she'll go to stay up in Mike's house. They won't let her talk to anyone, and they'll pay her out in every way they can for having a child by her own husband. Purification! That's what they talk about. I call it prison!' The mother of the Angel Gabriel was not at the evening meal, and we never saw her again. We asked Joe what had happened to her. She had gone willingly into seclusion, he answered, for her own good, of course.

Indeed, Joe had much more important things to talk about in that last conversation. 'You have a great part to play in the future of mankind.' He fixed me with a sharp, pale eye. 'Michael's vision has told him that the end of the world is very near. Now we have to gather into Jerusalem the hundred and forty-four thousand true servants of God mentioned in the Book of Revelation. This time Jerusalem will be right here.'

'Here? On Vancouver Island?'

'On this very spot.'

'But how do you *know*?'

'We ain't worrying. We just know. And the Archangel had a vision about you. He knew you were coming a long time ago. He knew you were a writer. He knew you were being sent here so you could tell the world what we're doing.'

I must have looked at him very dubiously for he flapped his hands reassuringly. 'I ain't asking you to do it. Nor is Archangel. We just know you will. You'll write about us, and people will come to us, and then you will come back and be marked with the sign and live for ever among the servants of God.'

We left the next day. The Archangel saw us once more in his garden, gave us a white rose each, and said we should meet again before long. 'It's a prophecy,' Joe whispered.

And indeed it was. One day, months later, I was broadcasting in Vancouver when Ross McLean, who was then a radio producer, said he had heard Joe was locked up in the court house. I went over, but I could not see him. The Mounties were holding him incomunicado. But as I was leaving the station Michael the Archangel was brought in, and for a couple of minutes, in that grim barred room, I was allowed to talk to him. He was pleased to be recognized, and even willing to talk a little English. 'I am free soon,' he said, as he was led away to the cells. Not long afterwards he and Joe were sentenced on some rather nebulous charges of disturbing public order. And a few months later Michael the Archangel Verigin died in jail.

Ten years afterwards we drove through Hilliers, turning off our road on a nostalgic impulse. The palisade was still there, opposite the railway siding, and for a moment everything looked unchanged. But inside, where Jerusalem should have been rising, there was only the ghost of what we had seen on the day the Angel Gabriel was named. Most of the buildings had gone, but falling fences and squares of thistles still marked out the theocracy where the Archangel had ruled.

Themes & Subjects

For Further Reading

ANTHOLOGIES

COLOMBO, JOHN ROBERT (ed.). *How Do I Love Thee?: Sixty Poets of Canada (and Quebec) Select and Introduce Their Own Work.* Hurtig, 1970.
The poets' comments on their choice—which is supposed to be their favourite among their poems—make this book a desirable addition to any library of Canadian poetry.

COLOMBO, JOHN ROBERT (ed.). *Rhymes and Reasons: Nine Canadian Poets Discuss Their Work.* Holt, Rinehart and Winston of Canada, Limited.
The poets are Bowering, Helwig, Jonas, Kearns, MacEwen, Marshall, Newlove, Nowlan, and Yates.

GEDDES, GARY, and PHYLLIS BRUCE (eds). *15 Canadian Poets.* Oxford University Press, 1970.
An in-depth selection of poems by Atwood, Avison, Birney, Bowering, Cohen, Coleman, Jones, Layton, MacEwen, Mandel, Newlove, Nowlan, Ondaatje, Purdy, and Souster, with excellent notes on the poets' work.

GLASSCO, JOHN (ed.). *The Poetry of French Canada in Translation.* Oxford University Press, 1970.
Poems by 47 of the best Québécois poets translated by 22 English-Canadian poets. The only substantial collection of this poetry in translation.

LIGHTHALL, WILLIAM DOUW (ed.). *Songs of the Great Dominion: Voices from the Forests and Waters, the Settlements and Cities of Canada.* Coles Publishing Company, 1971. (Originally published in 1889.)

A facsimile reprint of one of the first Canadian anthologies, originally published in England. Designed to appeal to the growth of national sentiment in Canada, it contains a lot of inferior verse, though all the poets of the time who are still respected today are represented. It is an appealing literary reflection of the period and has an interesting introduction.

LOCHHEAD, DOUGLAS, and RAYMOND SOUSTER (eds). *Made in Canada: New Poems of the Seventies.* Oberon Press, 1970.
A spirited anthology that presents sixty-four established poets and newcomers.

LUCAS, ALEC (ed.). *Great Canadian Short Stories.* Dell, 1971.
A good historical collection (it begins with Haliburton) of twenty-seven stories.

MANDEL, ELI (ed.). *Five Modern Canadian Poets.* Holt, Rinehart and Winston of Canada, Limited, 1970.
The poets are Birney, Layton, Purdy, Atwood, Cohen. With an interesting introduction and a critical note on each poet.

MANDEL, ELI (ed.). *Eight More Canadian Poets.* Holt, Rinehart and Winston of Canada, Limited, 1972.
This follows the collection above. The poets are Avison, Souster, Mandel, Acorn, Reaney, Webb, Jones, and Macpherson.

MANDEL, ELI (ed.). *Poets of Contemporary Canada: 1960-1970.* New Canadian Library. McClelland & Stewart, 1972.
Selections from Purdy, Acorn, Rosenblatt, Cohen, Bowering, Newlove, Atwood, bisset, MacEwen, and Ondaatje.

RICHLER, MORDECAI (ed.). *Canadian Writing Today*. Penguin Books, 1970.
A miscellany, in the editor's words, of 'the Canadian writing I like'. It contains stories, other prose, and poems by forty-six writers, ten of them Québécois.

ROSS, MALCOLM (ed.). *Poets of the Confederation*. New Canadian Library. McClelland & Stewart, 1960.
A useful selection from the work of Roberts, Carman, Lampman, and D.C. Scott.

SINCLAIR, DAVID (ed.). *Nineteenth Century Narrative Poems*. New Canadian Library. McClelland & Stewart, 1972.
A collection of six of the best-known longer poems from our early literature, beginning with Oliver Goldsmith's *The Rising Village* (1834) and ending with Isabel Valancy Crawford's *Malcolm's Katie* (1884). The other poets are Joseph Howe, Charles Sangster, William Kirby, and Alexander McLachlan.

SMITH, A.J.M. (ed.). *The Oxford Book of Canadian Verse: in English and French*. Oxford University Press, 1960.
A standard historical anthology, with an illuminating introduction.

SMITH, A.J.M. (ed.). *Modern Canadian Verse: in English and French*. Oxford University Press, 1967.
Smith's second Oxford anthology is a supplement to his first (above). It begins with Pratt and ends with Ondaatje, the youngest poet in the book.

SMITH, A.J.M. *The Book of Canadian Prose. Volume I: Early Beginnings to Confederation*. W.J. Gage, 1965.
This book gives generous samplings of prose by explorers, pioneers, early writers of the Maritimes, and two politicians, Macdonald and McGee. *Volume II*, from Confederation to the present, will be published in 1973.

SMITH, A.J.M. and F.R. SCOTT (eds). *The Blasted Pine: An Anthology of Satire, Invective, and Disrespectful Verse Chiefly by Canadian Writers*. Macmillan of Canada, 1957; revised 1967.
A witty selection from the lighter side of Canadian poetry.

WEAVER, ROBERT (ed.). *Canadian Short Stories*. Oxford University Press, 1960.
A good historical anthology that contains stories by E.W. Thomson, Roberts, D.C. Scott, Leacock, Grove, Wilson, Knister, Raddall, Callaghan (two), Leo Kennedy, Ross, Gustafson, Lowry, Layton, Garner, Joyce Marshall, W.O. Mitchell, P.K. Page, Gallant, Reaney, Douglas Spettigue, Munro, and Richler. There are stories in translation by Ringuet, Hébert, and Lemelin.

WEAVER, ROBERT (ed.). *Canadian Short Stories: Second Series*. Oxford University Press, 1968.
This supplements the collection above and, with the exception of Callaghan and Wilson, includes writers of the fifties and sixties: Garner, Gallant, Laurence, Richler, Hood, Ludwig, Munro, Godfrey, Faessler, and Helwig.

WIEBE, RUDY. *Stories from Western Canada*. Macmillan of Canada, 1972.
An important regional anthology of twenty-one stories ranging from the 1920s to the 1970s.

WILSON, MILTON (ed.). *Poetry of Mid-Century: 1940-1960*. New Canadian Library. McClelland & Stewart, 1964.
The poets are Birney, Layton, Avison, Souster, Reaney, Page, Cohen, Macpherson, Nowlan, and McRobbie.

WILSON, MILTON (ed.). *Poets Between the Wars*. New Canadian Library. McClelland & Stewart, 1967.
Selections from Pratt, F.R. Scott, Smith, Livesay, and Klein.

CRITICISM, BIOGRAPHY, REFERENCE

ATWOOD, MARGARET. *Survival: A Thematic Guide to Canadian Litrature.* Anansi, 1972.

'Literature', Miss Atwood says, 'is not only a mirror; it is also a map, a geography of the mind.' With cogency and wit she outlines a great many elements in the map provided by our own literature, revealing in the process much about ourselves and 'about here, because here is where we live'. In her hands the dispiriting themes that have attracted and still attract Canadian writers (indicated by such chapter titles as 'Nature the Monster', 'Animal Victims', 'Failed Sacrifices', 'The Casual Incident of Death', 'The Paralyzed Artist', 'Quebec: Burning Mansions', and the book's title) do not turn us off. Her book is an invitation to plunge into our literature and discover the map (and the Canadian imagination) for ourselves, to appreciate it for what it is and be informed by it.

BRAZEAU, J. RAYMOND. *An Outline of Contemporary French-Canadian Literature.* Forum House, 1972.

One of the few critical works in English on the literature of Québec. It contains brief studies of Desrosiers, Roy, Thériault, Bessette, Martin, Hébert, Aquin, Jasmin, Blais, and Vigneault.

CAMERON, DONALD. *Conversations with Canadian Novelists.* Macmillan of Canada, 1973.

Interviews with Ernest Buckler, Roch Carrier, Robertson Davies, Timothy Findley, Harold Horwood, Robert Hunter, Margaret Laurence, Jack Ludwig, Hugh MacLennan, Brian Moore, Thomas Raddall, George Bowering, Morley Callaghan, David Godfrey, Robert Kroetsch, W.O. Mitchell, Martin Myers, Mordecai Richler, Gabrielle Roy, David Lewis Stein, and Rudy Wiebe.

DUDEK, LOUIS, and MICHAEL GNAROWSKI. *The Making of Modern Poetry in Canada: Essential Articles on Canadian Poetry in English.* Ryerson Press, 1967.

As many of the articles and background materials are from inaccessible magazines, this collection is invaluable for a study of modern Canadian poetry.

FRYE, NORTHROP. *The Bush Garden: Essays on the Canadian Imagination.* Anansi, 1971.

These rewarding essays on literature and painting, written between 1943 and 1969, include an invaluable survey of the poetry published in the 1950s. The Preface is reprinted in this anthology, beginning on page 126.

FULFORD, ROBERT, DAVID GODFREY, and ABRAHAM ROTSTEIN (eds). *Read Canadian: A Book About Canadian Books.* James Lewis & Samuel, 1972.

Thirty articles intended to provide the general reader with a guide to the significant books in over two dozen subjects. Unfortunately they are very cursory and only a few are interesting. The section on literature is surprisingly skimpy, though Dennis Lee's piece on modern poetry is one of the best in the book.

GIBSON, GRAEME. *Eleven Canadian Novelists.* Anansi, 1973.

Interviews with Timothy Findley, Alice Munro, Margaret Laurence, Marian Engel, Austin Clarke, Scott Symons, Jack Ludwig, Mordecai Richler, Matt Cohen, Margaret Atwood, and David Godfrey.

JONES, D.G. *Butterfly on Rock: A Study of Themes and Images in Canadian Literature.* University of Toronto Press, 1970.

As he examines the themes and images of English-Canadian writers (most of whom are represented in this anthology), Jones offers many insights about the sense of exile and the antagonism be-